Cross–Disciplinary Models and Applications of Database Management:

Advancing Approaches

Keng Siau
University of Nebraska – Lincoln, USA

Managing Director:	Lindsay Johnston
Senior Editorial Director:	Heather Probst
Book Production Manager:	Sean Woznicki
Development Manager:	Joel Gamon
Development Editor:	Michael Killian
Acquisitions Editor:	Erika Gallagher
Typesetter:	Lisandro Gonzalez
Cover Design:	Nick Newcomer, Lisandro Gonzalez

Published in the United States of America by
Information Science Reference (an imprint of IGI Global)
701 E. Chocolate Avenue
Hershey PA 17033
Tel: 717-533-8845
Fax: 717-533-8661
E-mail: cust@igi-global.com
Web site: http://www.igi-global.com

Library of Congress Cataloging-in-Publication Data

Cross-disciplinary models and applications of database management : advancing approaches / Keng Siau, editor.
    p. cm.
 Includes bibliographical references and index.
 Summary: "This book is an updated look at the latest tools and technology within the burgeoning field of database management, covering issues of database languages, models, and systems change"--Provided by publisher.
 ISBN 978-1-61350-471-0 (hardcover) -- ISBN 978-1-61350-472-7 (ebook) -- ISBN 978-1-61350-473-4 (print & perpetual access) 1. Database management. I. Siau, Keng, 1964-
 QA76.9.D3C795 2012
 005.74--dc23
                           2011049597

British Cataloguing in Publication Data
A Cataloguing in Publication record for this book is available from the British Library.

All work contributed to this book is new, previously-unpublished material. The views expressed in this book are those of the authors, but not necessarily of the publisher.

Balasubramaniam Ramesh, *Georgia State University, USA*
Chino Rao, *University of Texas-San Antonio, USA*
Jan Recker, *Queensland University of Technology, Australia*
Jacquelyn M. Rees, *Purdue University, USA*
Fiona Rohde, *University of Queensland, Australia*
Colette Rolland, *University of PARIS-1 Pantheon/Sorbonne, France*
John R. Rose, *University of South Carolina, USA*
Michael Rosemann, *Queensland University of Technology, Australia*
Matti Rossi, *Helsinki School of Economics, Finland*
Marcus A. Rothenberger, *University of Nevada-Las Vegas, USA*
Shazia W. Sadiq, *University of Queensland, USA*
Rathindra Sarathy, *Oklahoma State University, USA*
Christoph Schlueter-Langdon, *University of Southern California, USA*
Ming-Chien Shan, *Hewlett-Packard Laboratories, USA*
Graeme Shanks, *Monash University, Australia*
Hong Sheng, *University of Missouri-Rolla, USA*
Peretz Shoval, *Ben-Gurion University of Negev, Israel*
Choon Ling Sia, *City University of Hong Kong, Hong Kong*
Riyaz Sikora, *University of Texas at Arlington, USA*
Israel Spiegler, *Tel Aviv University, Israel*
Jan Stage, *Aalborg University, Denmark*
Jan Stallaert, *University of Connecticut, USA*
Diane Strong, *Worcester Polytechnic University, USA*
Vijayan Sugumaran, *Oakland University, USA*
Sherry Xiaoyun Sun, *City University of Hong Kong, Hong Kong*
Anjana Susarla, *University of Washington, USA*
Ah-Hwee Tan, *Nanyang Technological University, Singapore*
Chuan-Hoo Tan, *City University of Hong Kong, Hong Kong*
Kian Lee Tan, *National University of Singapore, Singapore*
Swee Lin Sharon Tan, *National University of Singapore, Singapore*
Xin Tan, *Fairleigh Dickinson University, USA*
Yong Tan, *University of Washington, USA*
David Tegarden, *Virginia Tech, USA*
Yuhong Tian, *Washington University, USA*
Heikki Topi, *Bentley College, USA*
Arvind K. Tripathi, *University of Washington, USA*
Dan Turk, *Colorado State University, USA*
Ramesh Venkataraman, *Indiana University, USA*
Wenli Wang, *Touro University International, USA*
Xiaoyang "Sean" Wang, *University of Vermont, USA*
Chih-Ping Wei, *National Sun Yat-Sen University, Taiwan*
John D. Wells, *Washington State University, USA*
Mu Xia, *Santa Clara University, USA*
Weidong Xia, *Florida International University, USA*

Table of Contents

Detailed Table of Contents

Chapter 1

Palash Bera, Texas A&M International University, USA
Anna Krasnoperova, Bootlegger, Canada
Yair Wand, University of British Columbia, Canada

Conceptual models are used to support understanding of and communication about application domains in information systems development. Such models are created using modeling grammars (usually employing graphic representation). To be effective, a grammar should support precise representation of domain concepts and their relationships. Ontology languages such as OWL emerged to define terminologies to support information sharing on the Web. These languages have features that enable representation of semantic relationships among domain concepts and of domain rules, not readily possible with extant conceptual modeling techniques. However, the emphasis in ontology languages has been on formalization and being computer-readable, not on how they can be used to convey domain semantics. Hence, it is unclear how they can be used as conceptual modeling grammars. We suggest using philosophically based ontological principles to guide the use of OWL as a conceptual modeling grammar. The paper presents specific guidelines for creating conceptual models in OWL and demonstrates, via example, the application of the guidelines to creating representations of domain phenomena. To test the effectiveness of the guidelines we conducted an empirical study comparing how well diagrams created with the guidelines support domain understanding in comparison to diagrams created without the guidelines. The results indicate that diagrams created with the guidelines led to better domain understanding of participants.

Chapter 2

Galia Shlezinger, Technion-Israel Institute of Technology, Israel
Iris Reinhartz-Berger, University of Haifa, Israel
Dov Dori, Technion-Israel Institute of Technology, Israel

Design patterns provide reusable solutions for recurring design problems. They constitute an important tool for improving software quality. However, correct usage of design patterns depends to a large extent on the designer. Design patterns often include models that describe the suggested solutions, while other aspects of the patterns are neglected or described informally only in text. Furthermore, design pattern solutions are usually described in an object-oriented fashion that is too close to the implementation, masking the essence of and motivation behind a particular design pattern. We suggest an approach to modeling the different aspects of design patterns and semi-automatically utilizing these models to improve software design. Evaluating our approach on commonly used design patterns and a case study of an automatic application for composing, taking, checking, and grading analysis and design exams, we found that the suggested approach successfully locates the main design problems modeled by the selected design patterns.

Chapter 3

In this article, we address the problem of delayed query processing raised by tree-based index structures in wireless broadcast environments, which increases the access time of mobile clients. We propose a novel distributed index structure and a clustering strategy for streaming XML data that enables energy and latency-efficient broadcasting of XML data. We first define the DIX node structure to implement a fully distributed index structure which contains the tag name, attributes, and text content of an element, as well as its corresponding indices. By exploiting the index information in the DIX node stream, a mobile client can access the stream with shorter latency. We also suggest a method of clustering DIX nodes in the stream, which can further enhance the performance of query processing in the mobile clients. Through extensive experiments, we demonstrate that our approach is effective for wireless broadcasting of XML data and outperforms the previous methods.

Chapter 4

Information systems development (ISD) is a complex process involving interconnected resources, stake holders, and outcomes. Understanding factors contributing to ISD success has attracted keen interest from both researchers and practitioners, and many research studies have been published in this area. However, most studies focus on one or two factors affecting ISD success. A holistic view of factors impacting ISD success is missing. This paper synthesizes past research on the topic and proposes a unified model on ISD success through a systematic and comprehensive literature review. The unified model highlights that ISD is a complex and interactive process involving individual, team, and organization factors, as well as ISD methodology. These factors impact the ISD process as well as its success.

How classes of things and properties in general should be represented in conceptual models is a funda-mental issue. For example, proponents of object-role modelling argue that no distinction should be made between the two constructs, whereas proponents of entity-relationship modelling argue the distinction is important but provide ambiguous guidelines about how the distinction should be made. In this paper, the authors use ontological theory and cognition theory to provide guidelines about how classification should be represented in conceptual models. The authors experimented to test whether clearly distinguishing between classes of things and properties in general enabled users of conceptual models to better understand a domain. They describe a cognitive processing study that examined whether clearly distinguishing between classes of things and properties in general impacts the cognitive behaviours of the users. The results support the use of ontologically sound representations of classes of things and properties in conceptual modelling.

Chapter 6

To facilitate product selection and purchase decisions on e-commerce Web sites, the presentation of product information is very important. In this research, the authors study how disposition styles influence users' search patterns in product comparison services of e-commerce Web sites. The results show that people use relatively more feature paths and less product paths in vertical disposition style than horizontal disposition style. The findings also indicate that there are relatively more feature paths and less product paths in the first half than second half of the information search paths. This is consistent with Gensch's two-stage choice model which suggests that people use attribute processing to derive a consideration set before they apply alternative processing to arrive at a final choice in product comparison services.

Chapter 7

Virtual worlds (e.g., Second Life), where users interact and form relationships with other users' virtual identities represented by avatars (i.e., human-avatar relationships), are increasingly influential in today's businesses and society. Nevertheless, the sustainability and impact of virtual worlds depend largely on the closeness of human-avatar relationships. This study investigates the antecedents of the closeness of such relationships. The authors conceptualize human-avatar relationship closeness as composed of interaction frequency, activity diversity, and relational influence. They identify its antecedents (perceived needs fulfillment, relationship irreplaceableness, and resource investment) by extending Rusbult's investment model of interpersonal relationship commitment to the domain of human-computer interaction. The authors test the hypotheses through an online survey of Second Life users and find that (1) resource investment is positively associated with all three human-avatar relationship closeness dimensions; (2) needs fulfillment is positively associated with interaction frequency and relational influence; and (3) relationship irreplaceableness is positively associated with relational influence.

Massively Multiplayer Online Game (MMOG) dependency has been widely studied but research results suggest inconclusive antecedent causes. This study proposes and empirically tests three predictive models of MMOG dependency using a survey of online gaming participants. It finds multimedia realism for social interaction serves as an original antecedent factor affecting other mediating factors to cause MMOG dependency. These mediating factors derive from Uses and Gratifications theory and include: (1) participation in a virtual community, (2) diversion from everyday life, and (3) a pleasant aesthetic experience. Of these, participation in a virtual community has a strong positive relationship with MMOG dependency, and aesthetics has a modest negative relationship. Moderator analyses suggest neither gender nor "frequency of game playing" are significant but experience playing online games is a significant moderating factor of MMOG dependency.

Chapter 9

Pnina Soffer, University of Haifa, Israel

Maya Kaner, Ort Braude College, Israel

Yair Wand, University of British Columbia, Canada

A common way to represent organizational domains is the use of business process models. A Workflow-net (WF-net) is an application of Petri Nets (with additional rules) that model business process behavior. However, the use of WF-nets to model business processes has some shortcomings. In particular, no rules exist beyond the general constraints of WF-nets to guide the mapping of an actual process into a net. Syntactically correct WF-nets may provide meaningful models of how organizations conduct their business processes. Moreover, the processes represented by these nets may not be feasible to execute or reach their business goals when executed. In this paper, the authors propose a set of rules for mapping the domain in which a process operates into a WF-net, which they derived by attaching ontological semantics to WF-nets. The rules guide the construction of WF-nets, which are meaningful in that their nodes and transitions are directly related to the modeled (business) domains. Furthermore, the proposed semantics imposes on the process models constraints that guide the development of valid process models, namely, models that assure that the process can accomplish its goal when executed.

Chapter 10

Yuan An, Drexel University, USA

Xiaohua Hu, Drexel University, USA

Il-Yeol Song, Drexel University, USA

This paper describes a round-trip engineering approach for incrementally maintaining mappings between conceptual models and relational schemas. When either schema or conceptual model evolves to accommodate new information needs, the existing mapping must be maintained accordingly to continuously provide valid services. In this paper, the authors examine the mappings specifying "consistent" relationships between models. First, they define the consistency of a conceptual-relational mapping through "semantically compatible" instances. Next, the authors analyze the knowledge encoded in the standard database design process and develop round-trip algorithms for incrementally maintaining the consistency of conceptual-relational mappings under evolution. Finally, they conduct a set of comprehensive experiments. The results show that the proposed solution is efficient and provides significant benefits in comparison to the mapping reconstructing approach.

Chapter 11

Fiona Fui-Hoon Nah, University of Nebraska-Lincoln, USA

Brenda Eschenbrenner, University of Nebraska-Lincoln, USA

David DeWester, University of Nebraska-Lincoln, USA

So Ra Park, University of Nebraska-Lincoln, USA

This research is a partial test of Park et al.'s (2008) model to assess the impact of flow and brand equity in 3D virtual worlds. It draws on flow theory as its main theoretical foundation to understand and empirically assess the impact of flow on brand equity and behavioral intention in 3D virtual worlds. The findings suggest that the balance of skills and challenges in 3D virtual worlds influences users' flow experience, which in turn influences brand equity. Brand equity then increases behavioral intention. The authors also found that the impact of flow on behavioral intention in 3D virtual worlds is indirect because the relationship between them is mediated by brand equity. This research highlights the importance of balancing the challenges posed by 3D virtual world branding sites with the users' skills to maximize their flow experience and brand equity to increase the behavioral intention associated with the brand.

Chapter 12

Yurong Yao, Suffolk University, USA

Denis M. Lee, Suffolk University, USA

Yang W. Lee, Northeastern University, USA

The Application Service Provision (ASP) model offers a new form of IS/IT resource management option for which the vendor remotely provides the usage of applications over a network. Currently, the ASP industry appears to be more vendor-driven. But without a good understanding of how the ASP offerings might appeal to prospective customers, the industry might not survive. This study investigates empirically the intention to adopt an ASP service from the customers' perspective, using survey data collected from a national sample of IS/IT executives. Based on the Transaction Cost Theory (Williamson, 1979, 1985) and service capability, a causal model is developed to examine the effects of perceived cost savings and service capability, as well as their antecedent factors, on the intention to adopt an ASP service. The results show a dominant effect of cost savings consideration on ASP adoption intention.

Chapter 13

Keng Siau, University of Nebraska-Lincoln, USA

Fiona Fui-Hoon Nah, University of Nebraska-Lincoln, USA

Brian E. Mennecke, Iowa State University, USA

Shu Z. Schiller, Wright State University, USA

One of the most successful and useful implementations of 3D virtual worlds is in the area of education and training. This paper discusses the use of virtual worlds in education and describes an innovative 3D visualization design project using one of the most popular virtual worlds, Second Life. This ongoing project is a partnership between IBM and three universities in the United States: the University of Nebraska-Lincoln, Iowa State University, and Wright State University. More than 400 MBA students have participated in this project by completing a creative design project that involves co-creation and collaboration in Second Life. The MBA students from the three universities worked in pairs to create designs to represent concepts related to IBM Power Systems, a family of IBM servers. The paper discusses observations and reflections on the 3D visualization design project. The paper concludes with a discussion of future research directions in applying virtual worlds in education.

Much of the prior work in business process modeling is activity-centric. Recently, an information-centric approach has emerged, where a business process is modeled as the interacting lifecycles of business entities. The benefits of this approach are documented in a number of case studies. In this paper, the authors formalize the information-centric approach and derive the relationships between the two approaches. The authors formally define the notion of a business entity, provide an algorithm to transform an activity-centric model into an information-centric process model, and demonstrate the equivalence between these two models. Further, they show the value of transforming from the activity-centric paradigm to the information-centric paradigm in business process componentization and Service-Oriented Architecture design and also provide an empirical evaluation.

This paper proposes a cooperative query answering approach that relaxes query conditions to provide approximate answers by utilizing similarity relationships between data values. The proposed fuzzy abstraction hierarchy (FAH) represents a similarity relationship based on the integrated notion of data abstraction and fuzzy relations. Based on FAH, the authors develop query relaxation operators like query generalization, approximation, and specialization of a value. Compared with existing approaches, FAH supports more effective information retrieval by processing various kinds of cooperative queries through elaborate relaxation control and providing ranked query results according to fitness scores. Moreover, FAH reduces maintenance cost by decreasing the number of similarity relationships to be managed.

The appropriate deployment of web service operations at the service provider site plays a critical role in the efficient provision of services to clients. In this paper, the authors assume that a service provider has several servers over which web service operations can be deployed. Given a workflow of web services and the topology of the servers, the most efficient mapping of operations to servers must then be discovered. Efficiency is measured in terms of two cost functions that concern the execution time of the workflow and the fairness of the load distribution among the servers. The authors study different topologies for the workflow structure and the server connectivity and propose a suite of greedy algorithms for each combination.

Identifying matching attributes across heterogeneous data sources is a critical and time-consuming step in integrating the data sources. In this paper, the author proposes a method for matching the most frequently encountered types of attributes across overlapping heterogeneous data sources. The author uses mutual information as a unified measure of dependence on various types of attributes. An example is used to demonstrate the utility of the proposed method, which is useful in developing practical attribute matching tools.

This paper examines privacy protection in a statistical database from the perspective of an intruder using learning theory to discover private information. With the rapid development of information technology, massive data collection is relatively easier and cheaper than ever before. The challenge is how to provide database users with reliable and useful data while protecting the privacy of the confidential information. This paper discusses how to prevent disclosing the identity of unique records in a statistical database. The authors' research extends previous work and shows how much protection is necessary to prevent an adversary from discovering confidential data with high probability at small error.

Preface

Database and database technologies are at the heart of many business information systems. New techniques and tools are continuously being introduced. This volume, "Cross-Disciplinary Models and Applications of Database Management: Advancing Approaches," presents eighteen excellent chapters of exemplary research in the areas of database theory, systems design, systems building, virtual environments, ontologies, and others. Many disciplines are converging, and many disciplines can benefit from theories, models, and research results from other disciplines. Cross fertilization of ideas from different disciplines will help to produce innovative research and create new disciplines. This book consists of many examples of convergence of ideas from various disciplines.

The following presents a brief synopsis of each chapter.

Chapter 1, "*Using Ontology Languages for Conceptual Modeling*," discusses the benefits of using ontology languages for conceptual modeling. Conceptual models are used to facilitate communication about application domains in Information Systems development. Conceptual models are created using modeling grammars to represent domain concepts and their relationships. Ontology languages have features that enable the representation of semantic relationships among domain concepts and of domain rules.

Chapter 2, "*Modeling Design Patterns for Semi-Automatic Reuse in System Design*," discusses reusable solutions for recurring design problems. It presents an approach to modeling different aspects of design patterns, and semi-automatically utilizing these models to improve software design.

Chapter 3, "*Energy and Latency Efficient Access of Wireless XML Stream*," addresses the problem of delayed query processing raised by tree-based index structures in wireless broadcast environments, which increases the access time of mobile clients. It proposes a novel distributed index structure and a clustering strategy for streaming XML data that enables energy and latency-efficient broadcasting of XML data.

Chapter 4, "*Toward a Unified Model of Information Systems Development Success*," presents a model that depicts the factors contributing to Information Systems development (ISD) success. Information Systems development (ISD) is a complex process with interconnected resources, stakeholders, and outcomes. The chapter synthesizes past research on the topic and proposes a unified model on ISD success through a systematic and comprehensive literature review. The unified model highlights that ISD is a complex and interactive process involving individual, team, and organization factors.

Chapter 5, "*Representing Classes of Things and Properties in General in Conceptual Modeling: An Empirical Evaluation*," argues that how classes of things and properties in general should be represented in conceptual models is a fundamental issue. In this chapter, the authors use ontological theory and cognition theory to provide guidelines on how classification should be represented in conceptual models and describes a cognitive processing study that examined whether a clear distinction between classes of things and properties in general impacts the cognitive behaviors of users.

Chapter 6, "*Information Search Patterns in E-Commerce Product Comparison Services,*" studies the effect of the presentation of product information to facilitate product selection and purchase decisions in e-commerce. This chapter further discusses how disposition styles influence users' search patterns in product comparison services of e-commerce Web sites. Gensch's two-stage choice model suggests that people use attribute processing to derive a consideration set before people apply alternative processing to arrive at a final choice in product comparison services. The results of this study are consistent with the Gensch's two-stage choice model.

Chapter 7, "*Antecedents of the Closeness of Human-Avatar Relationships in a Virtual World,*" presents an interesting study in the area of Virtual World. The idea of Virtual Worlds where users interact and form relationship with other users' virtual identities represented by avatars, is increasingly important in today's businesses and society. This chapter investigates the antecedents of the closeness of such relationships and also conceptualizes the closeness of human-avatar relationship as composed of interaction frequency, activity diversity, and relational influence.

Chapter 8, "*Antecedents of Online Game Dependency: The Implications of Multimedia Realism and Uses and Gratifications Theory,*" proposes and empirically tests three predictive models of Massively Multiple Online Game (MMOG) dependency by surveying online gaming participants. This chapter focuses on multimedia realism for social interaction that serves as an original antecedent factor affecting other mediating factors to cause MMOG dependency.

Chapter 9, "*Assigning Ontological Meaning to Workflow Nets,*" presents a Workflow-net (WF-net), which is an application of Petri Nets (with additional rules), that models business process behavior. The chapter proposes a set of rules for mapping the domain in which a process operates into a WF-net, derived by attaching ontological semantics to WF-nets. These rules guide the construction of WF-nets, which are meaningful because their nodes and transitions are directly related to the modeled (business) domains.

Chapter 10, "*Maintaining Mappings between Conceptual Models and Relational Schemas,*" describes a round-trip engineering approach for incrementally maintaining mappings between conceptual models and relational schemas. It examines the mapping specifying "consistent" relationships between models by defining the consistency of a conceptual-relational mapping, analyzing the knowledge encoded in the standard database design process, and developing round-trip algorithms for incrementally maintaining the consistency of conceptual-relational mappings under evolution.

Chapter 11, "*Impact of Flow and Brand Equity in 3D Virtual Worlds,*" draws on flow theory as its main theoretical foundation to understand and empirically assess the impact of flow on brand equity and behavioral intention in 3D virtual worlds. It suggests that the balance of skills and challenges in 3D virtual worlds influences users' flow experience, which in turn influences brand equity. This chapter further highlights the importance of balancing the challenges posed by 3D virtual world branding sites with the users' skills to maximize their flow experience and brand equity to increase their behavioral intention associated with the brand.

Chapter 12, "*Cost and Service Capability Considerations on the Intention to Adopt Application Service Provision Services,*" introduces the Application Service Provision (ASP) model that offers a new form of IS/IT resource management option for which the vendor remotely provides the usage of applications over a network. The authors used survey data collected from a national sample of IS/IT executives to investigate empirically the intention to adopt an ASP service from the customers' perspective.

Chapter 13, "*Co-Creation and Collaboration in a Virtual World: A 3D Visualization Design Project in Second Life,*" discusses the use of virtual worlds in education and describes an innovative 3D visualization design project using one of the most popular virtual worlds, Second Life. The chapter also discusses observations and reflections on the 3D visualization design project and concludes with a discussion of future research directions in applying virtual worlds in education.

Chapter 14, "*Transforming Activity-Centric Business Process Models into Information-Centric Models for SOA Solutions,*" formalizes the information-centric approach and derives the relationships between the two approaches. This chapter further defines the notion of a business entity, provides an algorithm to transform an activity-centric model into an information-centric process model, and demonstrates the equivalence between these two models.

Chapter 15, "*An Integrated Query Relaxation Approach Adopting Data Abstraction and Fuzzy Relation,*" proposes a cooperative query approach that relaxes query conditions to provide approximate answers by utilizing similarity relationships between data values. It introduces the fuzzy abstraction hierarchy (FAH) that represents a similarity relationship based on the integrated notion of data abstraction and fuzzy relations. FAH supports more effective information retrieval by processing various kinds of cooperative queries and reduces maintenance cost by decreasing the number of similarity relationships.

Chapter 16, "*Accelerating Web Service Workflow Execution via Intelligent Allocation of Services to Servers,*" studies the Web service operations at the service provider site with the assumption that a service provider has several servers over which Web service operations can be deployed. The authors explore different topologies for the workflow structure and the server connectivity, and propose a suite of greedy algorithms for each combination.

Chapter 17, "*Matching Attributes Across Overlapping Heterogeneous Data Sources Using Mutual Information,*" proposes a method for matching the most frequently encountered types of attributes across overlapping heterogeneous data sources. Mutual information is used as a unified measure of dependence on various types of attributes.

Chapter 18, "*Disclosure Control of Confidential Data by Applying PAC Learning Theory,*" examines privacy protection in a statistical database from the perspective of an intruder using learning theory to discover private information. The chapter discusses how to prevent disclosing the identity of unique records in a statistical database and shows how much protection is necessary to prevent an adversary from discovering confidential data with high probability at small error.

Chapter 1
Using Ontology Languages for Conceptual Modeling

Palash Bera
Texas A&M International University, USA

Anna Krasnoperova
Bootlegger, Canada

Yair Wand
University of British Columbia, Canada

ABSTRACT

Conceptual models are used to support understanding of and communication about application domains in information systems development. Such models are created using modeling grammars (usually employing graphic representation). To be effective, a grammar should support precise representation of domain concepts and their relationships. Ontology languages such as OWL emerged to define terminologies to support information sharing on the Web. These languages have features that enable representation of semantic relationships among domain concepts and of domain rules, not readily possible with extant conceptual modeling techniques. However, the emphasis in ontology languages has been on formalization and being computer-readable, not on how they can be used to convey domain semantics. Hence, it is unclear how they can be used as conceptual modeling grammars. We suggest using philosophically based ontological principles to guide the use of OWL as a conceptual modeling grammar. The paper presents specific guidelines for creating conceptual models in OWL and demonstrates, via example, the application of the guidelines to creating representations of domain phenomena. To test the effectiveness of the guidelines we conducted an empirical study comparing how well diagrams created with the guidelines support domain understanding in comparison to diagrams created without the guidelines. The results indicate that diagrams created with the guidelines led to better domain understanding of participants.

DOI: 10.4018/978-1-61350-471-0.ch001

1. INTRODUCTION

An *Information Systems (IS) or formalized ontology* is an "explicit specification of a conceptualization," where a conceptualization is an "abstract, simplified view of the world" (Gruber, 1993). IS ontologies, also termed *computational ontologies*, have been introduced to support communication, information sharing, and reuse of IS components (Uschold & Gruninger, 1996). In the Semantic Web context, IS ontologies are used to represent semantics of web sources. Manola and Miller (2004) proposed the Resource Description Framework (RDF), an infrastructure to enable the encoding, exchange, and reuse of structured metadata on the Web. Using RDF as a framework, ontology languages such as OWL (*Web Ontology Language*) have been proposed for creating formal ontologies to serve as descriptions of terminologies used in web documents (McGuinness, Smith, & Welty, 2004).

While IS ontologies can be used to represent terminologies of domains of interest, they are intended for computational purposes, not for domain representation. In this paper we address the use of an ontology language to create representations of business domains. Such representations are termed Conceptual Models (Mylopoulos, 1992; Wand & Weber, 2002). Smith (2001) has observed that a philosophical ontology establishes truth about reality, while an IS ontology is a software artefact designed with specific uses and computational environments in mind. Accordingly, we adopt a philosophical ontology to suggest guidelines for using OWL in conceptual modeling.

Below, Section 2 discusses OWL and difficulties that may arise when using it for conceptual modeling. Section 3 introduces the ontological model we use to assign semantics to OWL constructs. Sections 4 and 5 provide specific suggestions on using OWL in conceptual modeling. Section 6 describes an empirical study to test the suggestions. Section 7 is the conclusion.

2. BACKGROUND

Conceptual modeling is the activity of formally describing some aspects of the physical and social world around us for purposes of understanding and communication (Mylopoulos, 1992). The more common uses of conceptual models in the IS field are to: (1) facilitate communications between users and analysts, (2) support the analysts' understanding of the domain, (3) serve as the basis for design and implementation of IS, and (4) record design rationales (Kung & Solvberg, 1986). While conceptual models provide input for design, they do not represent the IS artefact. In particular, conceptual models are different than semantic data models. In particular, conceptual models are created for studying a business, while semantic data models are created for designing a database.

While an IS ontology defines a set of concepts, a conceptual model uses concepts to represent a specific domain. Conceptual models are created using modeling grammars comprising constructs for representing domain phenomena, and rules for combining these constructs (Shanks *et al.*, 2003). There are at least two reasons why it might be advantageous to use an ontology language as a conceptual modeling grammar. First, using a formalized ontology language can provide for including the semantics of domain concepts as part of the conceptual model. Second, ontology language statements are intended to be processed by software applications and can be subject to automated reasoning. Hence, conceptual models represented in ontology languages can be subject to automated processing, in particular to verification beyond what graphical representation affords.

However, ontology language constructs do not have the domain semantics required from conceptual models. We propose that since philosophical theories of ontology can represent domain phenomena (Shanks *et al.*, 2003; Wand & Weber, 2002), such theories can guide the use of ontology languages for conceptual modeling.

2.1 OWL

OWL (McGuinness *et al.*, 2004) has been created by the W3C (World Wide Web Consortium) ontology working group to enable publishing and sharing of IS ontologies on the web. OWL is currently considered one of the key semantic web technologies that provide a framework for data sharing and reuse on the Web (Gomez-Perez, Fernandez-Lopez, & Corcho, 2004). OWL constructs are classes, individuals, properties of classes and individuals, and assertions about these properties. Further, OWL allows reasoning about classes and individuals (based on its formal semantics). OWL is divided into three layers of increasing level of expressiveness: OWL Lite, OWL Description Logic (DL) and OWL Full (McGuinness *et al.*, 2004). In this paper we refer to OWL DL unless specified otherwise. The key OWL concepts are summarized in Table 1. A brief description of OWL is provided in Appendix A.

The following are some features of interest of OWL. First, a *property restriction* is a condition of properties of individuals. OWL has two types of property restrictions: value constraints and cardinality constraints for repetitive properties. Second, a *class axiom* is a condition which is part of a class definition and states a necessary and/or sufficient condition of class membership. A class axiom can refer to properties of individuals or to relationships among classes (e.g. union). Third, *anonymous classes* are unnamed classes created using property restrictions.

2.2 Advantages of Using OWL for Conceptual Modeling

Several modeling languages have been used, or proposed for use for conceptual modeling. In particular, the entity-relationship (ER) model, especially in its extended form (EER), is widely used to describe the semantics of data (Davies *et al.*, 2006). As well, the Unified Modeling Language (UML) provides many modeling constructs, and its possible use for conceptual modeling has been explored (Evermann and Wand, 2005). Like OWL, both grammars provide strong support for class modeling. However, OWL possesses some unique features not available in EER model and in UML. The most important of these features are listed in Table 2.

OWL enables the representation of classes and their properties similar to UML class diagrams and EER diagrams. However, its features can be used to model additional domain information and provides capabilities not available in conceptual modeling techniques. In particular: (1) a much richer set of ways to create classes (e.g. forming a class that is considered useful even before identifying its full properties), (2) the ability to express a much richer set of relationships among classes, (3) the use of property restrictions and class axioms to explicitly convey domain (business) rules, (4) arranging properties in related classes, thus enabling inclusion of domain semantics (in the form of relationships among properties), and (5) OWL statements can be subject to reasoning.

Table 1. Concepts of OWL (adapted from McGuinness et al., 2004)

Concepts	Description
Class	A class is a name and a collection of properties that describe a set of individuals. Individuals belong to one or more classes and inherit properties of these classes. The set of individuals that are members of a class is called the *extension* of the class.
Individuals	An individual exists in the "universe of things" and can be declared without being associated with a class.
Properties	Properties assert general facts about members of classes and specific facts about individuals. Properties are distinguished according to whether they relate individuals to individuals (*object properties*) or individuals to datatypes (*datatype properties*). Properties can be specified in several ways such as being transitive, symmetrical, inverse of, and functional.

Table 2. Some differences between OWL and UML

OWL Feature	Description
Implementable	OWL ontologies are machine-readable and can be processed by software applications
Expressiveness	1. OWL provides several mechanisms to define classes, in particular, by class axioms and by assigning individuals to classes 2. Anonymous classes can be defined 3. Classes can be declared as being equivalent 4. Various logical relationships among classes can be defined (e.g. disjoint, intersection, and union) 5. An instance can be assigned to a class explicitly or by properties, and can belong to multiple unrelated classes
Independence of constructs	A class can exist independent of any instances or properties Properties can exist independent of classes
Reasoning	OWL allows inferences and automated reasoning support

Therefore, OWL models can be made to comply with general modeling rules and can be checked for correct representation of specific domain rules.

2.3 Possible Difficulties in Representing Real-World Concepts in OWL

OWL is intended to define terminologies including inter-relationships among terms. Users of OWL are allowed substantial freedom and flexibility (within the OWL syntax rules) in how they apply it. OWL constructs—individuals, properties, and classes—can be defined independently of each other. The flexibility afforded by OWL exceeds that of the EER and UML where, for example, the definition of a relationship requires that the entity types exist and attributes can only be attached to classes or entity types, or to their associations. In OWL, no clear rules exist for using OWL constructs to properly represent a terminology or the semantics of a modeled domain. Several technical papers (e.g. Horridge *et al.*, 2004; McGuinness *et al.*, 2004) present guidance for developing ontologies in OWL. However, these are mostly suggestions on how to construct terminologies in OWL, not on how to use its constructs to convey domain semantics.

We claim that, for several reasons, the flexibility of using OWL constructs and the lack of

modeling guidelines and constraints may become a drawback if the purpose is to use OWL for conceptual modeling. First, because no clear rules exist to map from domain information to OWL constructs, the same phenomenon might be represented in different ways. A domain fact may be represented as an individual, a property or a class. Different modelers might represent the same domain phenomena differently. Moreover, a given model might not provide sufficient cues to determine the original intention of the modeler. Thus, interpretation of domain facts represented in OWL may be difficult. Second, models might require significant changes when more domain knowledge is acquired. The problem might affect applications depending on the information contained in the ontology. Third, some general phenomena in the domain may be difficult to represent, leading to incomplete representations.

To solve the possible problems of modeling and interpretation we propose to guide the use of OWL constructs in conceptual modeling by rules taken from a philosophical ontology.

3. USING PHILOSOPHICAL ONTOLOGY

In recent years IS researchers have realized that the theory and practice of IS can benefit from the application of ontological theories (Milton, 2000; Weber, 2003) In philosophy, Ontology is the branch of philosophy that deals with the order and structure of reality in the broadest sense possible (Angeles, 1981). As well, various efforts have been made to develop specific ontologies to support IS development.

3.1 Ontologies and Information Systems Analysis

The possible roles of philosophical and computational ontologies in the IS development context have been recognized in the literature. Sharman, Kishore, and Ramesh (2004) distinguish between three main themes relating ontologies and IS development. First, *ontologies of information systems* provide sets of concepts to reason about IS and their (organizational) environments. Examples are the FRISCO framework (Falkenberg *et al.*, 1998) and Sysperanto (Alter, 2005). Such ontologies are intended to support system development, in particular, systems analysis and requirements engineering. Second, *ontologies for information systems* deal with grammars for various aspects of system development. Sharman *et al.* include in this type of ontologies conceptual modeling grammars (such as the ER model, Dataflow diagrams, and the UML). A third theme involves the use of philosophical ontologies to evaluate, compare, and develop modeling grammars. A general approach for ontological evaluation of modeling grammars has been proposed under the concept of ontological expressiveness (Wand and Weber, 1993). Examples for grammar evaluation work include the analysis of data modeling languages using Chisholm's ontology (Milton & Kazmierczak, 2004), the evaluation of NIAM using Bunge's ontology (Weber & Zhang, 1996), and evaluation of different modeling approaches employed in ARIS (Scheer, 1999) using Bunge's ontology (Green & Rosemann, 2000). Some more examples are mentioned in the next sub-section.

Finally, the application of philosophical ontologies to modeling grammars includes the assignment of semantics to modeling grammar constructs and the development of rules for the application of such grammars. Such analysis has been applied to the UML (Evermann & Wand, 2005, 2009; Guizzardi, Herre, & Wagne, 2002), to the ER model (Wand, Storey, & Weber, 1999), and to MibML (Zhang, Kishore, & Ramesh, 2007).

The present work belongs in the category of assigning ontological semantics to an existing grammar. While previous such work analyzed grammars used in conceptual modeling and in systems design, this work applies a philosophical ontology OWL, which is an ontology definition language. As discussed above (Section 2), this makes the unique characteristic of OWL available in the conceptual modeling context.

3.2 Bunge's Ontology

We use concepts from Bunge's ontological work (1977) to prescribe guidelines for representing domain semantics in OWL. Bunge's ontology has been adapted and extended for IS (Wand *et al.*, 1995; Wand & Weber, 1990a, 1993, 1997). As mentioned in the previous sub-section, it has been applied to the analysis of various modeling grammars. Several predictions that resulted from such analysis have been empirically examined and corroborated (Burton-Jones & Meso, 2006; Gemino & Wand, 2005; Shanks *et al.*, 2008). Bunge's ontology has been used to distinguish between instance, class, and properties (Parsons & Wand, 1997). Such distinction is important when modeling real-world concepts. Below, we briefly present Bunge's ontological view.

Bunge's ontology (1977) includes a set of high-level constructs and relationships. In Bunge's ontology the world is made of things which possess *properties*. Properties must be attached to things. Bunge distinguishes substantial things (which exist spatio-temporally) from *conceptual things* (such as sets and propositions). A property can

Table 3. Concepts of Bunge's ontology (Wand & Weber, 1993)

Concept	Description
Thing	The world is made of things. A distinction is made between substantial things (e.g. a book) and conceptual things (e.g. a mathematical set). A domain in the world can be described by substantial things and the linkages between them.
Properties	Things possess properties. A property can be *intrinsic*, or *mutual* if it is meaningful only in the context of two or more things. For example, height is an intrinsic property of a person and salary is a mutual property between a person and a company.
Attribute	Properties are modeled (by humans) via *attributes* which are characteristics of things as viewed by humans.
Functional Schema	A set of attribute functions used to model a set of things with similar properties.
State	The set of values of the attribute functions at a given time.
Interaction	The ability of things to affect the states traversed by other things. Interactions are manifested via the mutual properties of the interacting things.
Laws	A law is a restriction on the possible values of attributes and reflects relationships among properties.
Class and kind	A class is a set of things that possess a common property. A kind is a set of things possessing more than one common property.

be *intrinsic* to a thing or *mutual* to several things. Properties of conceptual entities are called *attributes*. People conceive of things in terms of *models* (which are conceptual things) comprising sets of attribute functions (usually over time). Attributes are characteristics assigned to things by humans and can represent actual properties. *Classes* and *kinds* are defined in terms of properties. A class is a set of things possessing a common property and a kind is set of things possessing a set of common properties. The concepts of Bunge's ontology relevant to this work are described in Table 3.

Finally, we note that other ontological approaches that have been used in the IS context (Chisholm, 1996; Sowa, 2000) recognize *things* or *entities*, their *properties* or *attributes*, and *classes* of things or entities.

4. GUIDELINES FOR MODELING INSTANCES, CLASSES, AND PROPERTIES IN OWL

In this section we propose *mapping rules* between ontological concepts and OWL constructs. We employ the concepts from Bunge's ontology as listed in Table 3. Since we model domains as perceived by humans, we do not distinguish

between properties and their representations as attributes. As well, for simplicity, we will use the word "class" to mean "class or kind." While not all ontological concepts can be directly mapped into OWL constructs, we claim some concepts can be modeled by following specific guidelines for using and combining OWL constructs.

In our discussion, the word *guidelines* refers to informal statements on how to use OWL constructs in principle, and the word *rules* indicates specific ways to implement the guidelines.[1]

4.1 Mapping Guidelines and Rules

In the following, we use the word "substantial thing" to refer to any entity perceived as something that might exist (in space-time). All other concepts, unless otherwise stated, will be considered conceptual, or non-substantial, things. Our first mapping guideline refers to substantial things.

Guideline 1: Substantial things should be modeled as OWL individuals.

OWL does not restrict what can be modeled as individuals. OWL individuals can represent concepts other than substantial things, such as properties and property values. This may create

Figure 1.

```
<owl:Class rdf:about="#Substantial_Thing">
    <owl:disjointWith>
            <owl:Class rdf:ID="Non_Substantial_Thing"/>
    </owl:disjointWith>
</owl:Class>

<owl:Class rdf:about="#Non_Substantial_Thing">
    <owl:disjointWith>
    <owl:disjointWith rdf:resource="#Substantial_Thing"/>
    </owl:disjointWith>
```

A class Non_Substantial_Thing is defined

Non_Substantial_Thing class is made disjoint with Substantial_Thing class

construct overload—where an OWL instance could represent several different types of domain concepts—and can undermine the clarity of conceptual models (Wand & Weber, 1993). It is unrealistic in current OWL syntax to restrict the use of individuals for modeling only substantial things. Thus, we propose to alleviate this problem by using the following guideline.

Guideline 2: When using OWL constructs in conceptual modeling, it is necessary to distinguish OWL instances that represent substantial things from non-substantial things.

To implement this guideline we suggest declaring two upper-level classes (subclasses of the owl:Thing class). First, a class whose members are all substantial things, and second, a class whose instances represent conceptual things. Since a thing cannot be both substantial and non-substantial simultaneously, these two upper-level classes should be declared as disjoint. The following modeling rule implements the first two guidelines.

Modeling Rule 1: An OWL-based conceptual model should include two disjoint upper-level classes:

1 *Substantial_Thing* class – the extension of this class will consist of all OWL individuals that represent substantial things.
2 *Non_Substantial_Thing* class – the extension of this class will consist of all OWL individuals that are used to represent non substantial things.

The OWL statements in Figure 1 demonstrate how the guidelines can be implemented.

These statements can be depicted as in Figure 2.

In the figure, the rounded rectangle is used to denote Non_Substantial_Thing. The links between the classes Substantial_Thing and NonSubstantial_Thing indicate that these classes are disjoint. The minimal representation of a substantial thing, for example, a specific person, John Smith, will require that it is represented as an OWL individual and an instance of the class Substantial_Thing: <owl:Substantial_Thing rdf:ID="John_Smith">. The guidelines have several consequences.

Consequence 1. Substantial things should be modeled as OWL individuals that are instances

Figure 2. Substantial thing class and non-substantial thing class

of the class Substantial_Thing or its subclasses. OWL individuals used for other purposes should be made instances of the Non_Substantial_Thing class or its subclasses.

Consequence 2. Any OWL class, all instances of which are intended to represent substantial things, should be made a subclass of the Substantial_Thing class.

Consequence 3. No OWL individual can represent both a substantial thing and non-substantial thing at the same time.

Consequence 4. Other OWL constructs (such as OWL properties) should not be used to represent substantial things.

If the above guidelines are followed, OWL individuals in the class Substantial_Thing are assigned unambiguous ontological semantics.

The guidelines and rules assume substantial and non-substantial individuals can be clearly distinguished. This distinction is not a question of modeling, but of domain understanding. We suggest some guidance for making the distinction. First, the important aspect is not the actual existence of things, but rather their *perceived possible existence* (in one's mind, or shared by a community of individuals (Smith, 2001)). Second, this should be *existence in time and space* (Bunge, 1977). To determine if a class is of substantial things, one can ask if it has instances that (might) exist in time and space. For example, both dog and unicorn would be considered (classes of) substantial things (assuming a unicorn can be considered a possibly existing animal). In contrast, a bank account exists in time but not in space. All that can exist in space is the (physical) record of the state (or changes) of an account (on paper or in a digital form). This record, however, should not be confused with the account itself. We address the question of modeling an account when discussing interaction (Section 5).

The identification of (classes of) substantial individuals also suggests how to identify some important types of conceptual things. In particular, any statement about the properties of substantial individuals or their changes will be a conceptual thing. Thus, properties and attributes of individuals, changes of properties of individuals, and laws governing possible properties and attributes or their changes, will be considered non-substantial things.[2] It follows that types of attributes (e.g. "color") will be represented by classes of non-substantial things.

Having outlined the guidelines for modeling things in general, we now propose guidelines related to properties. According to Bunge, "every property is possessed by some individual or other; there are no properties that fail to be paired to any individuals" (Bunge, 1977, p. 62). Classes and kinds in Bunge's ontology are defined in terms of properties (Table 3). In OWL, no syntactic restrictions are placed regarding the relationships between individuals, classes, and properties. Hence, no direct support is available in OWL for the above ontological assumptions. Specifically:

- *An OWL individual does not have to possess at least one property*

In OWL, an individual can simply be introduced as an instance of some class or as a minimum, as an instance of the top class owl:Thing. The instance may not possess any properties associated with it (either directly or by virtue of class membership).

- *An OWL class does not have to be associated with at least one property*

In OWL, properties can be associated with classes (via property restrictions). However, OWL also allows defining named classes without using property restrictions.

Figure 3.

```
<owl:DatatypeProperty rdf:ID="hasAge">          } A datatype property hasAge is defined
</owl:DatatypeProperty>
<owl:Thing rdf:ID="John_Doe">                   } An individual John Doe is defined.
        <hasAge rdf:datatype=http://www.w3.org/2001/XMLSchema#int >28</hasAge>

    <!--- The above sentence means the datatype property has Age is assigned to a
predefined XML schema of type integer -->
```

- *OWL does not require that a property be associated with at least one individual*

In OWL, properties are declared as separate constructs, independent of any classes or individuals. That is, in general, OWL syntax does not require properties to be associated with any classes or to be possessed by any individual (even though it might not seem very useful to declare a property which is not used at all).[3]

The above issues enable the creation of OWL statements that do not comply with the fundamental ontological assumptions regarding properties. Therefore, we propose additional guidelines addressing the relationships between properties, classes and individuals in OWL-based conceptual models.

First, we introduce a guideline to reflect that all things possess properties:

Guideline 3: Every OWL individual representing a substantial thing must possess at least one property.

Implementation of this guideline in OWL can be done in one of two ways:

At an instance level: by explicitly declaring a fact that the individual possesses a particular value for a property, or

At a class level; by declaring that an individual is a member of a class which includes at least one property in its class definition.[4]

To illustrate this guideline, consider an individual John_Doe. We associate a property (hasAge)

Figure 4.

```
<owl: Class rdf: ID="Person"/>                  } A class Person is defined

    <owl:DatatypeProperty rdf:ID="hasAge">
        <rdfs:range rdf:resource="http://w3.org/2001/XML Schema#int"/>

        <rdfs:domain rdf:resource="#Person"/>   } The domain of hasAge is the class
                                                  Person and the range is the set of
    <owl:DatatypeProperty                         integer values.

</owl:Class>

<Person rdf:ID="John_Doe">                      } John Doe is defined as an individual of the class Person

    <hasAge rdf:datatype=http://w3.org/2001/XML Schema#int">28</hasAge>

</Person                                        } John Doe inherits the property hasAge with a specific value of 28
```

Figure 5. Implementing guideline 3 at a class level ("IO" means "Instance Of")

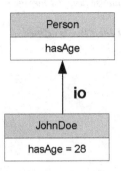

with this individual in one of two ways. In the first case, the individual is associated directly with the property hasAge. The syntax is shown in Figure 3, where the hasAge property is attached to the individual John_Doe and assigned a value 28.

In the second case John_Doe is declared as an individual of the class Person possessing the property hasAge. The syntax is (Figure 4):

The above syntax is also shown visually in Figure 5.

The next guideline assures that every property is possessed by at least one substantial thing:

Guideline 4: Every OWL property that is intended to represent some property of substantial things must be associated with at least one OWL individual representing a substantial thing.[5]

This guideline can be implemented in OWL using one of two ways; at an instance level or at a class level:

At an instance level: explicitly declare a fact about an OWL individual, i.e. a property should be used in at least one assertion about an individual possessing a specific value for the property. For example, to include hasColor as a property in a model, a fact that a substantial individual (John's Car) possesses some value for the property has-Color can be declared as

```
<owl:Car rdf:ID="John'sCar">
<owl:DatatypeProperty
rdf:ID="hasColor">
```

At a class level: at least one substantial OWL individual could be inferred to possess this property by virtue of being a member of a class associated with this property.

For example, the property hasVehicleNumber can be associated with the class Car using a suitable property restriction (e.g. Cardinality =1). Figure 6 describes such a situation where the individual Spider possesses the property hasVehicleNumber by becoming member of the class Car (for simplicity and clarity, we use a visual diagram to replace the long OWL syntax).

4.2 Developing Conceptual Models with the Guidelines

We demonstrate the guidelines by redefining a part of the wine ontology (McGuinness *et al.* 2004) shown in Figure 7 (the original form uses OWL syntax). Wine and WineGrape are modeled as classes because they represent different varieties. CabernetSauvignonGrape is modeled as an instance of the class WineGrape. WineDescriptor is a class that describes wine in terms of its taste and color (therefore modeled as a union of two classes: WineTaste and WineColor).

We now apply the guidelines to this ontology. First, we create two higher-level disjoint classes: Substantial_Thing and Non_Substantial_Thing.

Figure 6. OWL property associated through classes ("IO" means "Instance Of")

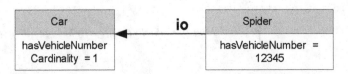

Figure 7. Original wine ontology (based on McGuinness et al. 2004). "IO" means "instance of"; "U" means "union")

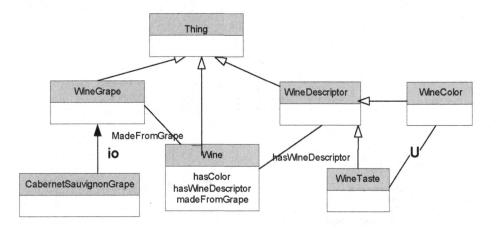

The classes WineGrape and Wine are modeled as subclasses of Substantial_Thing because their instances are real wine grapes and real instances of wine (as stored in containers) respectively. In the original ontology, CabernetSauvignonGrape is modeled as an instance of WineGrape. McGuinness *et al.* (2004) justify this decision by stating that:

"The Grape class denotes the set of all *grape varietals,* and therefore any subclass of Grape should denote a subset of these varietals. Thus CabernetSauvignonGrape should be considered as an instance of Grape and not a subclass. It does not describe a subset of Grape varietals, it *is* [emphasis added] a grape varietal." (p. 11)

However, considering the definition of a substantial individual, CabernetSauvignonGrape cannot be considered as an individual as it does not point towards any actual or possible instance. Rather, it should be modeled as a subclass of WineGrape as it denotes a grape variety (for which physical instances exist). On the other hand, WineDescriptor describes wine and therefore is an attribute and not a class of substantial things. Therefore we model WineDescriptor and its subclasses under Non_Substantial_Thing. Following guideline 3, classes must have properties. Classes WineGrape and Wine should be associated with at least one property each. To see how these properties might be identified, consider that wine can be made of different fruits. The fact that the ontology recognizes grape as the specific fruit and distinguishes among grape types, indicates that there are some characteristics that are common to all grape types (and might distinguish them from other fruits). These characteristics will be modeled as "properties of WineGrape" (e.g. amount of sugar). Note that individual grape types might have different "manifestations" of these properties (the manifestation might be a specific range or a descriptor like "medium"). In short, the ontological guideline "forces" a modeler to provide a *rationale* (in the form of properties of interest) for including a certain class of substantial things (such as "WineGrape"). Without this justification, there might be no reason to include the class. The revised ontology is shown in Figure 8.

Similar to prescribing that each substantial class must have properties, the guidelines also specify that each property should be "owned" by at least one (class of) substantial thing. This implies that in the formal OWL description each property must be used (directly or via a subclass of the property) at least by one substantial class or instance.

Figure 8. Revised wine ontology (rectangles indicate substantial classes; rounded rectangles indicate non-substantial classes)

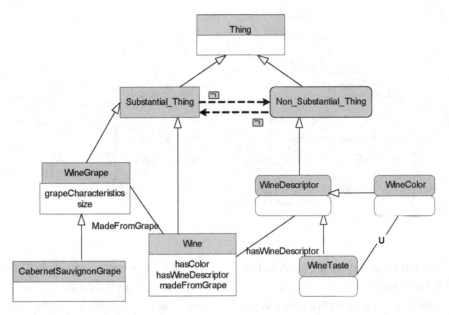

Finally, for substantial things, a clear distinction exists between instances and classes (as discussed above). This, however, is not the case for Non_Substantial things such as properties. We demonstrate this with the WineDescriptor property (Figure 9). The property WineColor (subclass of WineDescriptor) is viewed as a class with instances: White, Rosé and Red. However, Red also has different shades and hence might be conceived as a class. Similarly, individuals of the

Figure 9. WineDescriptor hierarchy

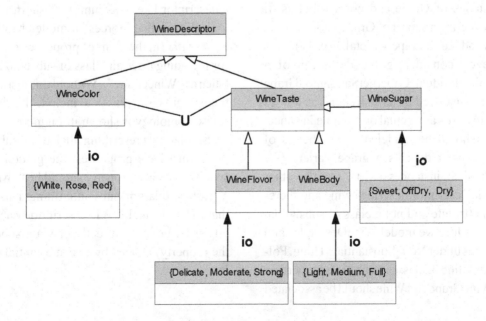

classes WineTaste, WineBody, and WineSugar can also be considered as classes. In the end, the way properties are organized into class and instance hierarchies reflects subjective views, rather than an objective observation of the kind that can be applied to substantial individuals. This, however, might not be a disadvantage, as it points out at how OWL can convey additional domain semantics (as mentioned in Section 2.2).

Assuming we can identify substantial individuals and classes in the modeled domain, we can also identify their properties. The guidelines can then be used to represent the domain facts consistently. If the knowledge about the domain changes and the ontology is modified according to the guidelines, it is unlikely that substantial individuals will become classes or properties, or vice versa. Specifically, new classes of substantial things (such as Fruit) will appear in the hierarchy of classes beginning with Substantial_Thing. As noted above, this, however, will not necessarily be the case for properties. Changes involving properties might cause changes of the types of constructs used to represent specific domain concepts (specifically, instances may become classes).

The above guidelines addressed modeling phenomena that can be directly mapped into OWL constructs. We turn now to modeling phenomena for which no readily available constructs exist in OWL.

5. MODELING INTERACTIONS

5.1 Difficulties in Modeling Some Real-World Phenomena in OWL

OWL has no concept to capture the behaviour or dynamics of instances or classes directly. Because the concept of state does not exist in OWL, a change of state (i.e. event) cannot be represented either. A notion that is related to change of states is *interaction*. We now suggest how to model interaction using OWL constructs. We choose interactions for two reasons. First, interaction conveys how different things in a modeled domain can affect each other. Second, in the context of IS design it has been used to provide ontological meaning to the concept of relationships in entity-relationship diagrams (Wand *et al.*, 1999) and association classes in UML class diagrams (Evermann & Wand, 2005). We first discuss an ontological view of interaction.

5.2 Interaction

Interaction is the ability of a thing to change the "history" (states traversed) by another thing (Bunge, 1977). Changes to things are manifested as changes to properties, modeled as changes of attribute function values, i.e. changes of state (Wand & Weber, 1990b). According to Bunge (1977), interaction can be represented by a *binding mutual property*. Such property indicates that some changes in one thing are related to the existence of another thing. For example, the mutual property "employs" implies that the existence of the (specific) company affects the states of a (specific) person (and vice versa) (Wand *et al.*, 1999). There are also non-binding mutual properties unrelated to interactions, but we are only interested in those that reflect interactions and will eliminate the term "binding."

Guidelines for Modeling Interactions in OWL

Because interactions in Bunge's ontology are manifested by mutual properties, we suggest an explicit distinction between intrinsic and mutual properties. Because domain concepts (which often have multiple instances) are modeled as classes, we refer to class properties.

OWL provides for defining a property termed an *object property,* the value of which is an instance of another class. For example, the object property

Figure 10. Example of OWL object property

Student	enrolledIn	University

"enrolledIn" links *student* class to *university* class (Figure 10).

However, from an ontological point of view, the use of OWL object properties to represent mutual properties has several limitations. First, in Bunge's ontology a property cannot be a thing. Second, several mutual properties are often related to one interaction. For example, relevant properties of *employment* are start date, job title, and salary. Representing an interaction by one mutual property will not allow grouping of mutual properties, and hence might lead to information loss. Third, mutual properties can be shared by more than two things, while OWL object properties can only represent binary mutual properties.[6]

To overcome these problems we follow the suggestions made in Evermann and Wand (2005) and show how to employ these suggestions using OWL constructs. We formulate several guidelines which we illustrate with a running example. Consider a person who becomes a *customer* of a *bank* by opening a *bank account*. Later, the customer may become a *preferred customer* who is entitled to hold a *trading account*. In Figure 11, first, we show the classes and properties that might be included in a typical OWL representation, unguided by ontological considerations.

Figure 11. Unguided OWL representation of the customer/bank domain

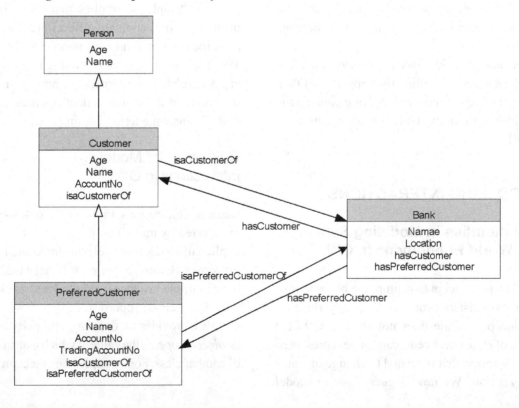

Figure 12. Class hierarchy of the bank-customer domain

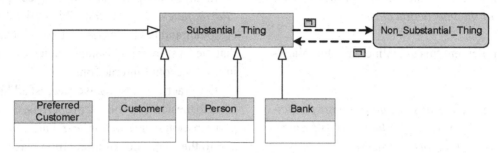

Note, the solid arrows reflect object properties, which can be specified in OWL statements. This cannot be done directly in UML class diagrams or in ER diagrams.

Second, applying the general guidelines for modeling domain concepts, we reorganize the classes as subclasses of two disjoint upper-level classes: Substantial_Thing and Non_Substantial_Thing. Person, Customer, PreferredCustomer, and Bank have substantial instances and thus are modeled as subclasses of Substantial_Thing (Figure 12).

Third, we add interactions to the model. We identify two types of interaction: between the customer and the bank (manifested as BankAccount) and between the preferred customer and the bank (manifested as TradingBankAccount). Each interaction is associated with several mutual properties. BankAccount involves account number, date of opening, and balance. TradingBankAccount involves trading account number, date of opening, and trading limits. To model such interactions and associated mutual properties, we propose the following guidelines.

Guideline 5: Sets of mutual properties of substantial things arising out of the same interaction should be represented as OWL properties of a specially defined OWL non substantial class –interaction.

Guideline 6: Each interaction class represents a set of mutual properties arising out of one interaction.

From the definition of an interaction class it follows that it must be associated with at least one mutual property.

To implement these guidelines in OWL we suggest the following rules.

Rule 2: Interaction classes will be modeled as a subclass of Non_Substantial_Thing and will have at least one OWL property.

Rule 3: Each mutual property of substantial things will be represented as an OWL property of an interaction class.

In our example, we represent the two interactions by two OWL classes (subclasses of Non_Substantial_Thing): BankAccount, and TradingBankAccount.

The rules require that we define OWL properties to represent mutual properties and associate them with interaction classes. For practical reasons, we suggest naming mutual properties with a prefix (e.g. mp_) to differentiate them from other types of properties. The property *bank account number* can be represented by an OWL property *mp_AccountNo* (of the interaction class BankAccount).

Because a mutual property is a property of each of the interacting (substantial) individuals, we propose the following guideline:

Guideline 7: Each interaction should be modeled by a property of a class to which the interacting thing belongs. The value of the property is an instance of the interaction class.

We implement this guideline with the following rule:

Rule 4: Each class of substantial things participating in an interaction will have an OWL object property reflecting this interaction.

To improve the comprehensibility of the model, we suggest that interaction classes should explicitly refer to Substantial_Thing classes that participate in the interaction.

Rule 5: Each interaction class should have a property for each involved class, where the property value is an instance of the involved class.

To demonstrate the rules, Figure 13 shows an example where Customer and Bank are shown explicitly to participate in BankAccount interaction by including the OWL object property "*ParticipatesInBankAccount*" for the customer class.

In this example, the OWL object property "*ParticipatesInBankAccount*" is defined for the customer and bank classes, to indicate explicitly that the Customer and Bank instances participate in BankAccount interactions.

For practical reasons, we suggest adding prefixes to the names of object properties, to indicate participation in interaction (e.g. ParticipatesIn_), and to the properties of interaction classes referring to the involved Substantial_Thing classes (e.g. Involves_). The complete model, including interactions is shown in Figure 14.

Recall that an interaction occurs when one thing affects the changes that occur in another thing. Following the suggested guidelines for modeling of interactions enables explicit modeling of such effects. For example, a customer is a person who participates in the BankAccount interaction. Thus, a Customer possesses all properties of Person, plus the additional properties associated with the interactions that follow from having a bank account. Similarly, a PreferredCustomer participates in the interaction TradingBankAccount, and acquires mutual properties (with the bank) in addition to the properties of a

Figure 13. OWL representation of the bank customer domain showing one interaction: BankAccount

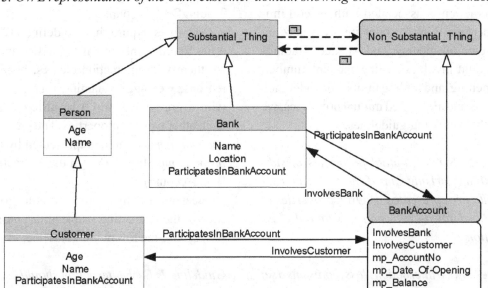

Figure 14. OWL representation of the bank customer domain modified by ontological guidelines

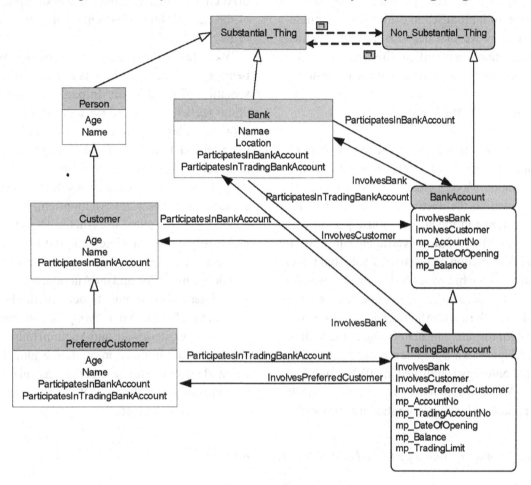

regular customer. We end the above analysis with some additional notes.

1. The guidelines suggest a method to check the models. For each interaction class at least two object properties must exist, linking individuals of the Substantial_Thing class (or one of its subclasses) to the interaction class.

2. When an instance of a class participates in an interaction, it acquires additional properties. This makes it a member of a subclass of the original class (for example – a Preferred Customer is a subclass of Customer).

3. The guidelines imply that all members of a class involved in an interaction *must* possess

the relevant mutual properties. This is in line with the modeling rules which prescribe that when a class instance is involved in an interaction, it becomes a member of a subclass where interaction is mandatory (Wand *et al.*, 1999).

6. EMPIRICAL TESTING

The above examples demonstrate that following the guidelines will result in a different model than otherwise. However, this does not necessarily mean that following the guidelines is advantageous. To test whether following the guidelines results in more understandable domain models than otherwise we conducted an empirical study. In the study we compared a published example with a version of it modified to conform to the guidelines. Below we first describe how the original representation was modified. This description also serves to demonstrate the use of the guidelines.

6.1 The Sample Case

We used the Auction ontology (SchemaWeb, n.d.). An *auction* involves four types of participants: *seller, auction house, bidder,* and *buyer.* The two actors creating the auction are the seller of the *auction item* and the auction house person who runs the auction. A *bidder* is an agent who participates in the auction on behalf of a potential buyer and submits the bid which has an *expiry time.* An auction is initiated when a seller places the items for sale with the auction house. Bidders place bids on an item for sale. The item is sold to the highest bidder. Figure 15 is a graphic representation of the original ontology (published in OWL syntax). In the model, an Auction appears as a class, while Seller and AuctionHouse are shown as properties

of Auction. Similarly, bidder appears as a property of the class Bidding. Participant appears instead of buyer.

We note that the original representation, while being syntactically correct, is not a clear representation of the domain. In particular, physical things (seller, auction house, and bidder) are not shown as classes, while processes and actions (auction and bidding) are considered classes. We now reorganize the domain information following the guidelines. First, classes of substantial things are identified. These are: AuctionItem, ItemSold, Bidder, Buyer, Seller, and AuctionHouse. Next, we identify the relevant interactions in the domain. These are: *auctionedAt* (interaction between the AuctionItem, Seller, and the AuctionHouse); *bidding* (interaction among Bidder, AuctionHouse, and AuctionItem); and *WinningBid* (interaction among Buyer, itemSold, and AuctionHouse). According to the interaction modeling guidelines, we model these three interactions as subclasses of non-substantial things. All classes identified are shown in Figure 16.

Figure 15. Auction ontology (based on SchemaWeb, n.d.)

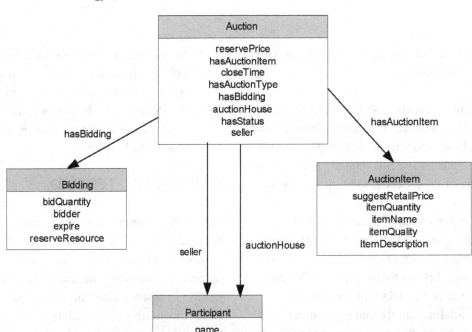

Figure 16. Class hierarchy of the auction domain modified by the modeling guidelines (Right rectangles represent substantial things and round ones interactions)

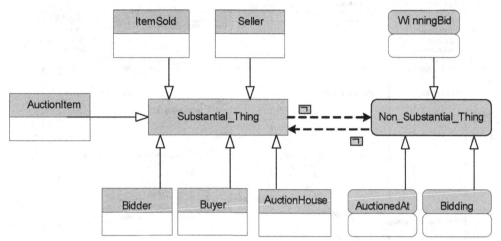

The next step involves identifying the mutual properties related to each of these interactions. Finally, each interaction class is related with the classes of substantial things involved in the interaction. The resulting ontology is depicted in Figure 17.

We briefly note some differences between the two representations. In the original representation (Figure 15), auction is treated as a class. In the new representation (Figure 17), auction is not shown explicitly, but rather is represented by the whole model. On the other hand, the interactions comprising the auction are shown. Note that closing time and reserved price, which are characteristics of an auction, are now mutual properties of the auction house and the auctioned item. The actual process of auctioning and its effects are implied in the modified representation via the interactions among the participants. For example, in the modified representation, it is clear that a bidder becomes a buyer via participating in the WinningBid interaction and thus acquiring the property ParticipatesInWinningBid (which is not a property of the Bidder class). Since a buyer is modeled as a subclass of bidder, it can be inferred that the bidding interaction (involving Bidder) precedes the interaction WinningBid (involving

Buyer). The distinction between AuctionItem and ItemSold is also made explicit in this ontology. As the result of the interaction WinningBid, the ItemSold class acquires additional properties to those of AuctionItem: participatesInWinningBid, and *final price*. FinalPrice is a mutual property of ItemSold, AuctionHouse, and the WinningBidder and thus does not appear in any of these classes.

Earlier (Section 2.2) we noted that one of the advantages of using OWL is the ability to represent rules formally via property restrictions and class axioms. This enables the explicit representation of business rules in conceptual models created in OWL. We demonstrate this using the modified auction model (Figure 17) with two examples. First, assume a bidder cannot be a seller or the auction house. This rule can be implemented using OWL statements indicating that Bidder and Seller classes are disjoint and that Bidder and AuctionHouse classes are disjoint. Second, assume sellers who are organizations are also allowed to sell auction items of high value directly, while this is not the case for individual sellers or for low value items. To implement this business rule, an interaction class "SoldDirectly" can be created reflecting interaction between AuctionItem

Figure 17. Modified auction ontology using interaction modeling guidelines

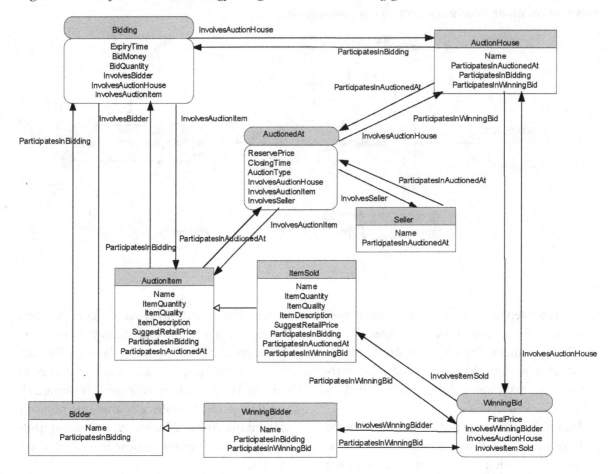

and Organization (as a subclass of Seller). Items can be partitioned to those of "high" and "low" values. This can be done by creating a property value (with values 'high' and 'low') or by using the property Suggested Retail Price). Property restriction can then be used to indicate that only items that have high values can participate in the SoldDirectly interaction.

6.2 A Protocol Analysis Study

In our study, two groups of subjects were each presented with one of the representations and were asked questions about the represented domain. According to the theory of cognitive fit (Vessey & Galletta, 1991), when the information emphasized in a problem representation matches the type of

information used in a task, subjects are expected to perform the task better than otherwise. Accordingly, if following the guidelines results in diagrams that are better representation of a domain, subjects asked questions about the domain will perform better with diagrams constructed with the guidelines (*guided diagrams*) than otherwise. We conducted a protocol analysis study to find out the differences in cognitive difficulties faced by users when they use the two representations of the auction model. Protocol analysis involves subjects verbalizing their thought processes while conducting a task (Ericsson & Simon, 1984).

We first ensured that both representations included similar terms. The guided diagram had a few more classes (such as Winningbid and Item-Sold). These classes were added to the original auction ontology. The modified original ontology (which is an *unguided* diagram) is shown in Appendix B (Figure 19).

We conducted a laboratory study with 10 MIS graduate students from a southern university in the United States as subjects. The subjects had several years of work experience and had taken two courses on IS Analysis and Design, thus being familiar with the use of graphic models. Subjects were first trained on interpreting graphic OWL representations and then given three problem solving questions (see Appendix B) to answer, by using either the guided or unguided representations (five subjects in each group). Problem solving questions require subjects to develop creative solutions that are not directly answerable by viewing the diagrams (Gemino, 1998; Mayer, 1989). Subjects verbalized while answering these questions and their verbalizations were recorded for analysis. The focus of the study was to understand the process of answering the problem solving questions rather than whether the answers to the questions were correct or not.

To analyse the verbal data we coded the difficulties identified when answering problem solving questions (Shanks *et al.*, 2008). The number of difficulties identified in the verbalization served as an indication to cognitive difficulty of performing the task. To narrow the scope of this study we focussed on two phases of difficulty of the six proposed by Shanks *et al.* (2008). *Identification (phase 4)*: "can I identify clearly the subset of the model on which I should focus to answer the problem solving questions?" and *Understanding (phase 5)*: "can I articulate clearly the semantics of the subset of the model that is my focus?" Table 4 relates the two phases to the problem solving questions. For example, to answer the first problem solving question, a subject may face difficulty in identifying bidder, auction, and their relationships. Two MIS graduate students (unaware of the objective of this study) coded the verbal data using Table 4 as guidance.

Examples of difficulties faced by the subjects with unguided diagrams are: "I see auction item and auction to be related but I don't see how it is related to the seller" (identification) and "I don't understand whether the reserve price is decided by the seller or by the auction house" (understanding). In contrast, some subjects given guided diagrams found them useful. For example, "by looking at the diagram I can find that the bidder can directly contact and purchase the item from seller" and "by following the arrows, I can see the bidder is connected to bidding, with property participatingInBidding, which is connected to AuctionHouse, which involves AuctionHouse."

Table 5 shows the number of times subjects had difficulties when answering the questions. The numbers shown are for Coder 1. Coder 2 differed only by one less, in the total number of identification difficulties for unguided models (8 not 9). Subjects using the unguided representation had more difficulties than the subjects using the guided one. This difference is more prominent for understanding. Therefore, we conclude that the guided representations performed better, especially in providing subjects with better understanding than otherwise.

We also found that subjects provided with guided models mentioned where they would like to model additional concepts that appeared in the questions (such as contract and bid cancellation). For example, "with the *contract* the bidder should have a relationship with auction house." In contrast, one subject who was provided with the unguided model expressed the inability to model such new concepts in the existing representation: "I don't know how I would model that *incentive*." In summary, the results support the proposition that guided models provide better domain understanding.

Table 4. Mapping the phases of difficulty with problem solving questions

Phases	Question 1	Question 2	Question 3
Identification: Identify subsets of the models	Difficulty in identifying *bidder, auction*, and their relationships	Difficulty in identifying *auction house*, *bidder*, *seller*, and their relationships	Difficulty in identifying *bidding*
Understanding: Articulate clearly the semantics of subsets	Difficulty in understanding *bidder*, *auction*, and their relationships	Difficulty in understanding *auction house*, *bidder*, *seller*, and their relationships	Difficulty in understanding *bidding*

7. CONCLUSION

Conceptual models are important tools in systems analysis and requirements engineering. Such models should be informative and precise, yet understandable to stakeholders. Ontology languages such as OWL enable forming precise statements, and have some features that can support representation of domain information not readily possible with other techniques. These include, in particular, semantic relationships among domain concepts and domain rules. However, such languages have no clear domain semantics. We suggest using a philosophical ontology to derive guidelines on how OWL constructs can be applied in conceptual modeling.

To test whether the proposed guidelines do indeed result in better models that can be constructed without them, we conducted an experiment to compare the use of an existing domain representation with one modified according to the guidelines. Verbal protocols of subjects asked to reason about the domain, using one of the two types of diagrams, have clearly indicated that the guided diagram led to better domain understanding than the original diagram. Thus, it appears that the guidelines are useful.

We note that the work conforms to the guidelines suggested for Design Science research (Hevner *et al.*, 2004). In particular, the work produces an artifact—a method for conceptual modeling in the form of a set of guidelines for using an existing grammar. This artifact is relevant to a business problem—the need to understand the application domain in the context of information systems development. The research evaluates the artifact using both examples and an empirical study. Rigor is obtained via using an ontological theory for developing the artifact and conducting an experiment based on a theory (cognitive fit).

This research can be extended in several ways. First, other choices of philosophical ontologies can be tested. Second, additional domain phenomena exist, for which there is no direct representation in OWL. These phenomena include, in particular, composites, laws, states and events. Future research can explore mechanisms to model such additional constructs in OWL.

Table 5. Analysis of difficulties

Identification	Question 1					Question 2					Question 3					Total
with guidelines	0	1	0	0	0	0	0	1	0	1	0	0	0	0	1	4
without guidelines	0	2	1	2	0	1	3	0	0	0	0	0	0	0	0	9

REFERENCES

Alter, S. (2005). Architecture of Syspernato: A Model-Based Ontology of the IS Field . *Communications of the Association for Information Systems, 15*, 1–40.

Angeles, P. (1981). *Dictionary of Philosophy*. New York: Harper Perennial.

Bunge, M. (1977). *Ontology I: The Furniture of the World*. New York: D. Reidel Publishing.

Burton-Jones, A., & Meso, P. (2006). Conceptualizing Systems for Understanding: An Empirical Test of Decomposition Principles in Object-Oriented Analysis. *Information Systems Research, 17*(1), 38–60. doi:10.1287/isre.1050.0079

Chisholm, R. (1996). *A Realistic Theory of Categories: An Essay on Ontology*. Cambridge, UK: Cambridge University Press.

Davies, I., Green, P., Rosemann, M., Indulska, M., & Gallo, S. (2006). How do practitioners use conceptual modeling in practice? *Data & Knowledge Engineering, 58*(3), 358–380. doi:10.1016/j. datak.2005.07.007

Ericsson, K., & Simon, H. (1984). *Protocol Analysis: Verbal Reports as Data*. Cambridge, MA: MIT Press.

Evermann, J., & Wand, Y. (2005). Ontology Based Object-Oriented Domain Modelling: Fundamental Concepts. *Requirements Engineering Journal, 10*(2), 146–160. doi:10.1007/s00766-004-0208-2

Evermann, J., & Wand, Y. (2009). Ontology Based Object-Oriented Domain Modeling: Representing Behavior. *Journal of Database Management, 20*(1), 48–77.

Falkenberg, E., Hesse, W., Lindgreen, P., & Nilsson, E. (1998). *A framework of information system concepts: The FRISCO report*. International Federation of Information Processing (IFIP).

Gemino, A. (1998). *Comparing Object Oriented with Structured Analysis Techniques in Conceptual Modeling*. Unpublished doctoral dissertation, University of British Columbia, Vancouver.

Gemino, A., & Wand, Y. (2005). Complexity and clarity in conceptual modeling: Comparison of mandatory and optional properties. *Data & Knowledge Engineering, 55*, 301–326. doi:10.1016/j. datak.2004.12.009

Gomez-Perez, A., Fernandez-Lopez, M., & Corcho, O. (2004). *Ontological Engineering: With examples for the area of knowledge management, e-commerce and the semantic web*. London: Springer-Verlag Limited.

Green, P., & Rosemann, M. (2000). Integrated Process Modeling: An ontological evaluation. *Information Systems, 25*(2), 73–87. doi:10.1016/ S0306-4379(00)00010-7

Gruber, T. (1993). A Translation Approach to Portable Ontology Specification. *Knowledge Acquisition, 5*(2), 199–220. doi:10.1006/knac.1993.1008

Guizzardi, G., Herre, H., & Wagne, G. (2002). *On the General Ontological Foundations of Conceptual Modeling*. In S. Spaccapietra, S. T. March, & Y. Kambayashi (Eds.), *Proceedings of ER 2002* (LNCS 2503, pp. 65-78)

Hevner, A., March, S., Park, J., & Ram, S. (2004). Design Science Research in Information Systems. *MIS Quarterly, 28*(1), 75–105.

Horridge, M., Rector, A., Knublauch, H., Stevens, R., & Wroe, C. (2004). *A Practical Guide to Building OWL Ontologies Using the Protege-OWL Plugin and CO-ODE Tool Edition 1.0*. Retrieved from http://www.co-ode.org/resources/tutorials/ ProtegeOWLTutorial.pdf

Kung, C., & Solvberg, A. (1986). Activity modelling and behavior modelling of information systems. In T. W. Olle, H. G. Sol, & A. A. Verrijn-Stuart, A. A. (Eds.), *Information Systems Design Methodologies: Improving the Practice.* Amsterdam, The Netherlands: North-Holland.

Manola, F., & Miller, E. (2004). *RDF Primer.* Retrieved from http://www.w3.org/TR/ rdf-primer/.

Mayer, R. (1989). Models for Understanding. *Review of Educational Research, 59*(1), 43–64.

McGuinness, D., Smith, K., & Welty, C. (2004). *OWL Web Ontology Language Guide.* Retrieved from http://www.w3.org/TR/owl-guide/

Milton, S. (2000). *An Ontological Comparison and Evaluation of Data Modelling Frameworks.* Unpublished doctoral dissertation, University of Tasmania, Hobart.

Milton, S., & Kazmierczak, E. (2004). An Ontology of Data Modelling Languages: A Study Using a Common-Sense Realistic Ontology. *Journal of Database Management, 15*(2), 19–38.

Mylopoulos, J. (1992). Conceptual modeling and telos. In P. Loucopoulos, & R. Zicari (Eds.), *Conceptual modeling, Databases and CASE: An Integrated View of Information Systems* (pp. 49-68). New York: John Wiley & Sons.

Parsons, J., & Wand, Y. (1997). Using Objects for Systems Analysis. *Communications of the ACM, 40*(12), 104–110. doi:10.1145/265563.265578

Protege. (2003). *Protégé User Guide.* Retrieved from http://protege.stanford.edu/doc/ users_guide/index.html

Scheer, A. (1999). *ARIS: Business Process Frameworks* (2nd ed.). New York: Springer.

SchemaWeb. (n.d.). *SchemaWeb - RDF schemas directory.* Retrieved September 14, 2007, from http://www.schemaweb.info

Shanks, G., Tansley, E., Nuredini, J., Tobin, D., & Weber, R. (2008). Representing Part-Whole Relations in Conceptual Modeling: An Empirical Evaluation. *MIS Quarterly, 32*(3), 553–573.

Shanks, G., Tansley, E., & Weber, R. (2003). Using Ontology to Validate Conceptual Models. *Communications of the ACM, 46*(10), 85–89. doi:10.1145/944217.944244

Sharman, R., Kishore, R., & Ramesh, R. (2004). Computational Ontologies and Information Systems II: Formal specification. *Communications of the Association for Information Systems, 14,* 184–205.

Smith, B. (2001). *Ontology and Information Systems.* Retrieved from http://ontology.buffalo. edu/ ontology%28PIC%29.pdf.

Sowa, J. (2000). *Knowledge Representation: Logical, Philosophical, and Computational Foundations.* Pacific Grove, CA: Brooks Cole.

Uschold, M., & Gruninger, M. (1996). Ontologies: Principles, Methods and Applications. *The Knowledge Engineering Review, 11*(2), 93–136. doi:10.1017/S0269888900007797

Vessey, I., & Galletta, D. (1991). Cognitive Fit: An Empirical Study of Information Acquisition. *Information Systems Research, 2*(1), 63–84. doi:10.1287/isre.2.1.63

Wand, Y., Monarchi, D., Parsons, J., & Woo, C. (1995). Theoretical Foundations for Conceptual Modeling in Information Systems Development. *Decision Support Systems, 15,* 285–304. doi:10.1016/0167-9236(94)00043-6

Wand, Y., Storey, V., & Weber, R. (1999). An Ontological Analysis of the Relationship Construct in Conceptual Modeling. *ACM Transactions on Database Systems, 24*(4), 494–528. doi:10.1145/331983.331989

Wand, Y., & Weber, R. (1990a). Mario Bunge's ontology as a formal foundation for information systems concepts. In P. Weingartner & G. W. D. Dorn (Eds.), *Studies on Mario Bunge's Treatise*. Atlanta, GA: Rodopi.

Wand, Y., & Weber, R. (1990b). An Ontological Model of an Information System. *IEEE Transactions on Software Engineering*, *16*(11), 1282–1992. doi:10.1109/32.60316

Wand, Y., & Weber, R. (1993). On the Ontological Expressiveness of Information Systems Analysis and Design Grammars. *Journal of Information Systems*, *3*, 217–237. doi:10.1111/j.1365-2575.1993.tb00127.x

Wand, Y., & Weber, R. (1997). *Ontological Foundations of Information Systems: Coopers and Lybrand Research Methodology, Vol. 4*. Melbourne, Australia: Coopers and Lybrand Research Methodology.

Wand, Y., & Weber, R. (2002). Research Commentary: Information Systems and Conceptual Modeling— A Research Agenda. *Information Systems Research*, *13*(4), 363–376. doi:10.1287/isre.13.4.363.69

Weber, R. (2003). Conceptual Modelling and Ontology: Possibilities and Pitfalls. *Journal of Database Management*, *14*(3), 1–20.

Weber, R., & Zhang, Y. (1996). An Analytic Evaluation of NIAM's grammar for Conceptual Schema Diagrams. *Information Systems*, *6*(2), 147–170. doi:10.1111/j.1365-2575.1996.tb00010.x

Zhang, H., Kishore, R., & Ramesh, R. (2007). Semantics of the MibML Conceptual Modeling Grammar: An Ontological Analysis Using the Bunge-Wand-Weber Framework. *Journal of Database Management*, *18*(1), 1–19.

ENDNOTES

[1] Rules provide specific constraints for creating OWL statements. Hence, ontology development environments (such as Protégé OWL (Protege, 2003)) can be used to enforce the rules.

[2] Since classes of things are not things, they will be considered conceptual things. The aggregate comprising the instances of a class of substantial things is a substantial thing, but it is not the class.

[3] A property in OWL can be associated with individuals either directly or through defining a class in terms of property restrictions that have to be satisfied by all instances of the class.

[4] Such a definition can also be inherited from another class.

[5] Implicitly every OWL property is attached to the class owl:Thing, but this class is not necessarily related to any substantial thing. Hence, this guideline is necessary.

[6] Representing higher order relationships by binary ones might lead to information loss in a conceptual model (Wand et al., 1999).

APPENDIX A: A BRIEF DESCRIPTION OF OWL

This description is based on the official OWL documentation from the World Wide Web Consortium (W3C) (McGuinness *et al.*, 2004) and a guide to building OWL ontologies (Horridge *et al.*, 2004). OWL is the ontology language recently developed by W3C. It is based on Resource Description Framework (RDF), which is a formal language of meta-data describing any web resources. The key constructs of OWL are *classes*, *individuals*, and *properties*.

Classes in OWL are intended to represent concepts in a domain of discourse and provide a mechanism for grouping resources with similar characteristics. Every OWL class can be associated with a set of *individuals* called the *class extension*. An OWL class owl: Thing is predefined. The class extension of this class is the set of all OWL individuals. Thus, every OWL class is a subclass of owl: Thing. A class in OWL can be defined by declaring a name for it, for example:

```
<owl:Class rdf:ID="Customer">
```

OWL classes are further defined through *class descriptions*. A class description describes an OWL class either by name (as shown above) or by specifying the class extension (set of instances) of an unnamed class. Defining classes in OWL by specifying the class extension means describing the conditions that must be satisfied by an individual for it to be a member of the class. For example, a class in OWL can be described as a set of all individuals which satisfies certain constraints on their properties called property restrictions.

OWL individuals represent objects in the domain of discourse. The individuals in the class extension are called *instances* of the class. It is intended that classes should correspond to naturally occurring sets of things in a domain of discourse, and individuals should correspond to actual entities that can be grouped into these classes. For example, a class Customer can be defined with instances of this class (or individuals) representing some specific customers. An individual can be introduced by declaring it as a member of a class (either of the predefined top class owl:Thing or some other class defined in the ontology), for example:

```
<owl:Thing rdf:ID="SomeBody">
<owl:Human rdf:ID="John_Doe">
```

In the above example, the first statement introduces an individual SomeBody simply as an instance of owl:Thing. The second statement declares another individual, John_Doe, which is stated to be an instance of the class Human. Note that in the second statement, the individual is automatically an instance of owl:Thing since any OWL class is a subclass of owl:Thing.

OWL properties are used to assert general facts about a class and specific facts about individuals. Properties in OWL have direction: a property links *a subject* (an OWL individual) to *an object* (an OWL individual or a data value). The object is considered as a value of the property for the subject. These subjects and objects in OWL are termed *domains* and *ranges* respectively. Properties link individuals from the domain to individuals from the range. There are two main types of properties in OWL: *datatype* and *object*.

Datatype properties link individuals to data values (for example an XML schema of specific types of datatype values such as integers). For example, a datatype property hasAge can be defined to represent the age of a person, i.e. to link an individual (person) to a non-negative integer representing age. In this case the domain of the property hasAge is the class Human and the range is a set of nonnegative integers (represented as an XML Schema datatype). These schemas are assumed to be predefined and stored in specific locations (such as in a website). This is shown below:

```
<owl:Class rdf:ID="Human">
<owl:DatatypeProperty rdf:ID="hasAge">
   <rdfs:domain rdf:resource="#Human"
    <rdfs:range rdf:resource="http://www.w3.org/2001/
XMLSchema#nonnegativeInteger"/>
</owl:DatatypeProperty>
```

Object properties relate individuals to individuals. For example, an ontology that describes persons (as a class), can define an object property hasMother to relate individuals representing persons to other individuals – their mothers. The syntax of this situation (and an equivalent diagram) is shown in Figure 18.

APPENDIX B: REVISED AUCTION ONTOLOGY AS USED IN THE STUDY (FIGURE 19)

Problem Solving Questions

1. What kind of contract should the bidder sign before participating in the auction?
2. How to provide incentives (or rewards) to sellers for letting the auction house know when a bidder directly contacts the seller for buying?
3. How to determine penalties (if any) for the bid cancellation?

Figure 18.

```
<owl:Class rdf:ID=" Perso n"/>
  <owl:Class rdf:ID=" Mother "/>
  <owl:ObjectProperty rdf:ID="  hasMother ">
    <rdfs:domain rdf:resource="#  Mother "/>
    <rdfs:range rdf:resource="#  Person "/>
</owl:ObjectProperty>
```

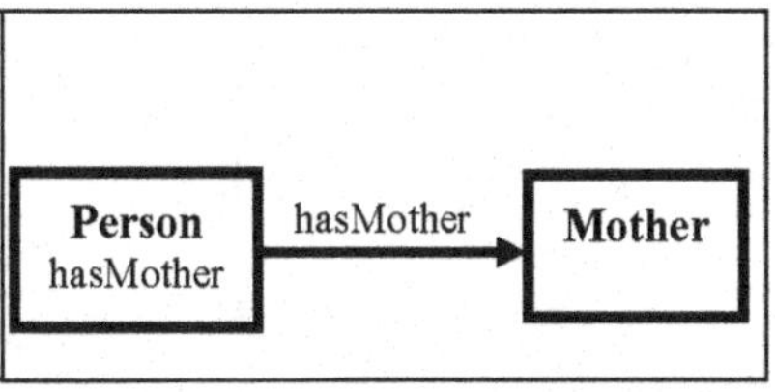

Figure 19. Revised auction ontology without using interaction modeling guidelines

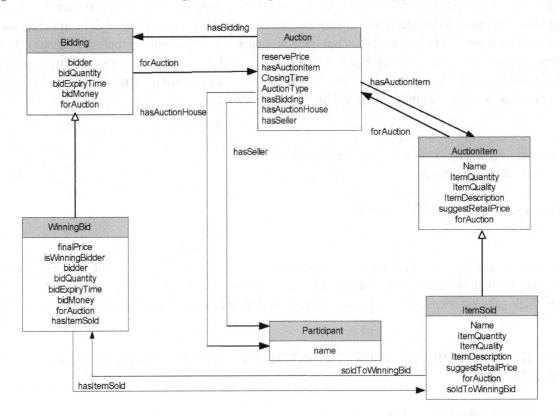

This work was previously published in International Journal of Database Management, Volume 21, Issue 1, edited by Keng Siau, pp. 1-28, copyright 2010 by IGI Publishing (an imprint of IGI Global).

Chapter 2
Modeling Design Patterns for Semi–Automatic Reuse in System Design

Galia Shlezinger
Technion-Israel Institute of Technology, Israel

Iris Reinhartz-Berger
University of Haifa, Israel

Dov Dori
Technion-Israel Institute of Technology, Israel

ABSTRACT

Design patterns provide reusable solutions for recurring design problems. They constitute an important tool for improving software quality. However, correct usage of design patterns depends to a large extent on the designer. Design patterns often include models that describe the suggested solutions, while other aspects of the patterns are neglected or described informally only in text. Furthermore, design pattern solutions are usually described in an object-oriented fashion that is too close to the implementation, masking the essence of and motivation behind a particular design pattern. We suggest an approach to modeling the different aspects of design patterns and semi-automatically utilizing these models to improve software design. Evaluating our approach on commonly used design patterns and a case study of an automatic application for composing, taking, checking, and grading analysis and design exams, we found that the suggested approach successfully locates the main design problems modeled by the selected design patterns.

INTRODUCTION

Patterns are types of themes that specify recurring processes, events, or elements. Commonly used in different engineering fields, patterns can be classified into analysis patterns, design pat-

DOI: 10.4018/978-1-61350-471-0.ch002

terns, organization patterns, process patterns, and domain-specific patterns. Batra (2005) claimed that pattern recognition can be considered as a conceptual modeling technique. He further stated that the main challenge with patterns is "to provide a limited number of patterns at a fairly high level of abstraction and an appropriate level of granularity…" (Batra, 2005, p. 87). Identifying locations in which patterns might be applied can be a tedious task (Eden, 2002). Purao, Storey and Han (2003) described a prototype for automatically generating a conceptual design based on analysis patterns. Their research, which concerns high level analysis and design, aims at producing models automatically from textual requirements. Blomqvist (2005) presented an approach for creating ontology patterns semi-automatically by utilizing knowledge organized as patterns from other areas, like data modeling, knowledge reuse, software analysis, and software design. While these approaches are appropriate for high-level conceptual modeling activities, they are less applicable at the detailed design stage. As the level of design becomes more specific, different parameters, such as code optimization, system limitations, and other non-functional requirements, have to be taken into consideration. These require careful and detailed descriptions of the patterns, their essence, and their exact usages.

In this work, we concentrate on design patterns, which describe reusable solutions for recurring design problems in given contexts (Gamma, Helm, Johnson & Vlissides, 1994). While design patterns may help produce better design and implementation of applications (Prechelt, Unger, Philipssen & Tichy, 2002; Schmidt, 1995), their appropriate use is often hindered due to the inherent ambiguity in the existing ways of description and representation (Taibi & Ngo, 2003). This may impede effective use of design patterns in particular applications, as designers may not be able to appreciate benefits or predict shortcomings associated with their proper use (Dong, Yang & Zhang, 2007). Misuse of design patterns typically results from failure to understand the rationale behind the patterns (Wendorff, 2001) or from difficulties in incorporating the patterns into a specific system design (Abdul Jalil & Azman Mohd Noah, 2007).

In view of these observations, we have developed an approach, accompanied by a tool, for clearly modeling design patterns and applying them semi-automatically to system models. In doing so, we utilize knowledge we have gained from modeling and categorizing design patterns. Our approach supports modeling of the different aspects of design patterns, including their problem and solution specifications, their essence, and their correct usage in particular systems. The design pattern models are specified using Object-Process Methodology (OPM) (Dori, 2002), which enables describing structural and behavioral aspects of design patterns at different granularity and abstraction levels. These design pattern models provide the basis for an algorithm for searching design problems in a given system design and suggesting corrections for them in the form of design patterns. Evaluating our approach and the feasibility of its algorithm using a case study research methodology, we found that the suggested approach successfully locates the main design problems modeled by the selected design patterns.

The structure of the rest of the paper is as follows. First, the relevant literature is reviewed, followed by a section that introduces the suggested design patterns representation method. Then, the algorithm for improving a system's design via the use of design patterns is presented, followed by a report on the evaluation of the approach. Finally, we summarize and propose possible future research directions.

LITERATURE REVIEW: DESIGN PATTERNS REPRESENTATION

Design patterns are widely recognized as an important technique for software design and programming. They are usually described using a template, such as the well known one proposed by Gamma *et al.* (1994). These descriptions are often accompanied by graphical notations. Using UML (Object Management Group, 2002), for example, class diagrams are recruited for modeling the structural aspects of the design patterns, while sequence diagrams are used for specifying their behavioral aspects. Since UML is ill-equipped for precisely representing design patterns (Guennec, Sunye & Jezequel, 2000), different methods and notations have been proposed for representing design patterns. These can be roughly divided into two groups: UML-based methods and proprietary languages.

UML-based methods extend the UML metamodel or define UML profiles in order to represent the different aspects of design patterns. France, Kim, Ghosh and Song (2004) and Kim, France and Ghosh (2004), for example, presented RBML, a UML-based meta-language for specifying design patterns. One of the main drawbacks of RBML is that the designer needs to mentally integrate information from three different design patterns specifications: static, interaction, and state machine. Indeed, Kim *et al.* (2004) indicated that their approach is intended for developers of tools that incorporate patterns into UML models. Gueannec *et al.* (2000) proposed specifying design patterns using OCL (Warmer & Kleppe, 1998) and meta-level collaboration in UML. Furthermore, they suggested using temporal logic to represent the design pattern's behavioral constraints. This kind of abstraction may be too complex for the average designer. Mak, Choy and Lun (2004) extended UML to describe pattern leitmotifs, which are distinguishing structures that define the idea behind design patterns rather than their implementation (Eden, 2002). Lauder and Kent (1998) proposed a three-layered model to describe design patterns in UML. Although this work captures the essence of a design pattern solution, it does not express the pattern's intent or problem description. Pickin and Manjarrés (2000) addressed the need to describe information about how and when to use design patterns. They suggested adding a summary of the informal parts of the design pattern description to a formal description of the patterns using a markup language called PCML (Object Venture Inc., 2002). While this approach may be useful for building tools that support design patterns, markup languages are machine-understandable

and require development and implementation of dedicated tools. Dong *et al.* (2007) presented an extension to UML that may help identify patterns in the system model, but it does not add information about the pattern itself.

DPML (Mapelsden, Hosking & Grundy, 2002) is a proprietary language that enables modeling and reusing design pattern solutions. However, this notation does not support specifying the locations within the system model in which the design patterns should be used. Furthermore, a designer using DPML has to deal with more than one language in order to use design patterns. LePUS (Eden, 2002) is a formal specification language based on a theory of object-oriented design in mathematical logic. The level of abstraction of LePUS is high, its visual representation is quite complex, and the symbolic representation is formal, making it difficult for designers to work with. Dong, Alencar, Cowan and Yang (2007) suggested Object-Z and first order logic for representing design pattern structure and composition, and temporal logic for describing their behavioral aspect. This method is used for design pattern composition and verification rather than for their straightforward implementation in a system model.

In summary, the reviewed UML-based methods are implementation-oriented, and they concentrate on the solutions proposed by the different design patterns. Furthermore, they model behaviors as encapsulated in object classes, complicating the task of reusing design patterns in different contexts that crosscut the system's structure. UML-based methods do not convey the essence of the design pattern as a complete problem-solution pair. Most proprietary languages, on the other hand, are too formal and complex for practical use by average software designers, a factor that discourages their adoption (Kim *et al.*, 2004).

A LAYERED DESIGN PATTERN FRAMEWORK AND ITS IMPLEMENTATION

Catering to a number of abstraction levels, the classical OMG framework for metamodeling (Object Management Group, 2003) consists of four layers: the information layer (M0), the model layer (M1), the metamodel layer (M2), and the meta-metamodel layer (M3). France *et al.* (2004) and Kim *et al.* (2004) defined the notion of model roles at level M2 and explained how they are used for describing design patterns in RBML. Reinhartz-Berger and Strum (2007) referred to domain models in the context of the classical four-layered framework: domain models specify the commonality and allowed variability of application families.

Inspired by these ideas, we define three layers of abstraction for representing design patterns: the system layer, the design pattern layer, and the meta-design pattern layer. At the most concrete layer, the system layer, a specific design pattern is implemented within the context of a system model. This implementation adapts the solution part of the selected design pattern model to fit into the specific context of the system. The design pattern itself belongs to the second layer of abstraction, the design pattern layer, where all the design patterns are modeled. The most abstract layer in this framework, the meta-design pattern layer, defines a metamodel of the design pattern concept, which conceptualizes the commonality and possible variability among all the design patterns.

This three-layered framework can be used in conjunction with different modeling languages. We have chosen Object-Process Methodology (OPM) (Dori, 2002) as the modeling language in this work due to the following reasons. First, OPM views objects and processes as equally important first-class entities, enabling concurrent specification of both structure and behavior. Second, the refinement-abstraction mechanisms in OPM help maintain an OPM model consistent among the different abstraction levels and provide for comparing models at different abstraction levels. The OPM models of the design patterns are problem-oriented, unlike the solution orientation of UML design pattern models, which has been criticized as being too close in its abstraction level to programming languages (Pickin & Manjarrés, 2000). Finally, OPM provides tools for classifying elements based on elements in other models (Strum, Dori & Shehory, 2006). This capability is important when different layers are involved, as in our proposed design pattern framework. Each OPM entity—object, process, or state—exhibits two associated features: role and multiplicity indicator. Like UML stereotypes, a *role* is a kind of a model entity whose information content and form are the same as those of the basic model entity, but its meaning and usage are different. Roles, which are specified in the upper left corner of the entity frame, are used within a system model in order to associate an entity to its design pattern counterpart. A *multiplicity indicator*, specified in a design pattern model, constrains the number of system entities that can be instantiated from the same design pattern entity in any system that applies this design pattern. The multiplicity indicator appears in the right lower corner of an entity frame and is optionally many (0..n) by default. Cardinality of links is used for constraining multiplicities of structural and behavioral relationships. A quick guide of OPM notation is provided in Appendix A.

The Meta-Design and Design Pattern Layers

In the meta-design pattern level, each design pattern is specified by three models: problem, solution, and correction models. A *problem model* represents a recurring design problem that the design pattern aims to solve, while a *solution model* represents the proposed solution for that recurring design problem. A *correction model* helps the designer, or an automated tool, correct the problem in the spirit of the suggested solution. In other words, the correction model is a mapping between the problem model and the solution model

Figure 1. The observer design pattern specification of Gamma et al. (1994, p. 294): (a) the class diagram, and (b) the sequence diagram

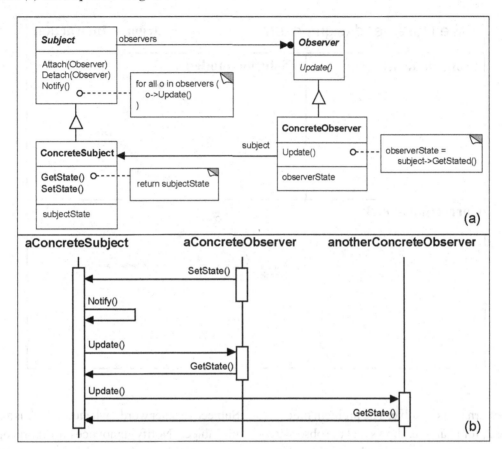

of the same design pattern. A single design pattern may have several problem models, but it can have only one solution model, independently of the system to which the pattern is applied. The result of applying this solution model to a specific system may take different variations, guided by the various correction models associated with the specific design pattern.

As an example, consider the *observer* design pattern. This pattern, which is specified in the design pattern layer using the three aforementioned model types defined in the meta-design pattern layer, offers a solution to a problem of notifying a set of objects when some change in the state of another object takes place. A one-to-many relationship exists between the "subject" object, whose

state is changed, and the "observer" objects that need to be notified. Figure 1 is the observer design pattern specification of Gamma *et al.* (1994, p. 294). This solution model, expressed in terms of UML class and sequence diagrams, specifies how a change in the state of a (concrete) subject is sent to the different observers, using their *notify* operations. Spanning two abstraction levels, it explicitly describes how the abstract classes *Observer* and *Subject* are respectively inherited by *Concrete Subject* and *Concrete Observer*. Furthermore, informal notes are required in order to convey the full meaning of this design pattern.

In contrast to UML, the observer pattern is expressed in OPM in three separate models. The problem model represents the essence of what the

Figure 2. The observer design pattern models: (a) the problem model, (b) the solution model, and (c) the correction model

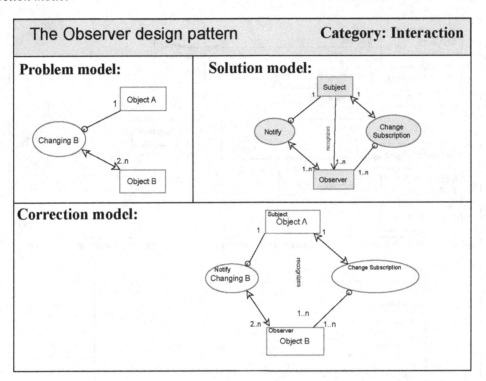

design pattern aims to solve. The problem model in Figure 2, for example, shows that the observer pattern deals with situations in which a change in an object of type A triggers the Changing B process, which may modify at least two different objects of type B. The problem to be solved here is that the Changing B processes should know all types of Object B that can be influenced by a certain change in Object A. The most severe manifestation of this problem is a design in which Object A and Object B are both implemented by the same class.

The design pattern solution model specifies the solution to the recurring design problem. In the observer case, the solution model depicted in Figure 2 includes two processes: Notify, in which a change in the Subject may affect the Observer, and Change Subscription, in which an Observer is added to or removed from the observer list – a list of potentially affected objects associated with Subject. In other words, whenever there is a change in Subject, Notify announces all its recognized Observers. To be included in or removed from the observers list, Observer has to trigger the Change Subscription process. This process generalizes the methods *Attach* and *Detach* in the UML model of Figure 1.

Finally, the correction model maps the design pattern solution model onto the problem model. This is done by employing the OPM role mechanism: when applicable, the entity names in a correction model are taken from the problem model, while their roles are taken from the corresponding solution model. Similarly, the link cardinalities are taken first from the problem model, and only later, new links from the solution model are added. This use of the OPM role mechanism clearly identifies which design patterns were used in the system model and in what way. This solves problems resulting from loss of information regarding the applied design patterns in particular systems (Dong *et al.*, 2007).

The correction model of the observer design pattern, depicted in Figure 2, states that the process Changing B plays the role of Notify, Object A plays the role of Subject, and Object B plays the role of Observer. Object A triggers the Changing B process, which informs the relevant Objects B whenever Object A is modified. In order to actually inform only the "relevant" Objects B, a new process, which plays the Change Subscription role, maintains the relevant set of Objects B that are recognized by Object A. This process is not named in the correction model as it is introduced by the solution model and should be named by the designer.

Comparing the UML and OPM solution models, one can notice that while the UML model of the observer design pattern contains two types of diagrams, class and sequence diagrams, the OPM model is represented with one diagram type, which displays both the static and the dynamic aspects of the model. Furthermore, while the UML solution model spans two abstraction levels, explicitly describing how the abstract classes

Observer and Subject are respectively inherited by Concrete Subject and Concrete Observer, the corresponding OPM model describes only one abstraction level, which models the relations between Subject, Observer, Notify, and Subscribe. The correction models are the ones that hold the information on how to integrate design patterns into system models. Note that the essence of the design pattern, as expressed in the OPM problem model, is not described at all in the UML model.

Appendix B provides problem, solution, and correction models of seven other commonly used design patterns which have different purposes (Gamma *et al.*, 1994).

The System Layer

The system layer is the most concrete one, as it includes design models of different systems and applications. Figure 3 describes an OPM model of a system that displays time in both analog and digital formats. It does not apply any design pattern. The main process in this system, Time Processing, zooms into three processes: Counter Updating, which updates the Time Counter, as well

Figure 3. A partial OPM model for a time display system

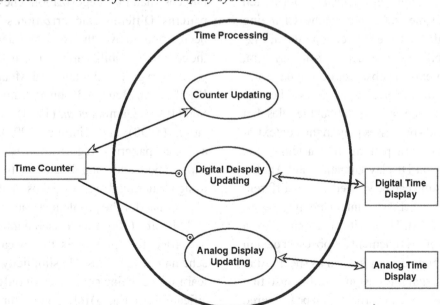

Figure 4. The OPM top level model of the time display system: (a) before applying the observer design pattern and (b) after applying it

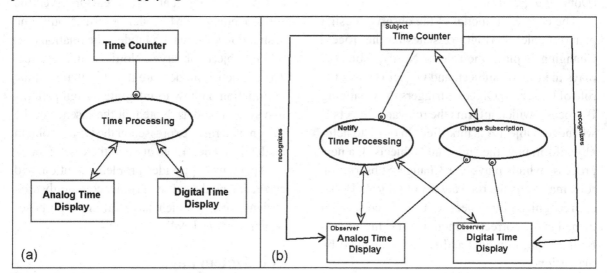

as Digital Display Updating and Analog Display Updating, which change Digital Time Display and Analog Time display, respectively.

Examining this model, one can miss the observer problem model at first glance. Nevertheless, zooming out of Time Processing, Figure 4(a) specifies the system top level, where the observer problem model is clearly noticeable, as Time Counter matches Object A, Digital Time Display and Analog Time Display both match Object B, and Time Processing matches Changing B. Applying the observer correction model, Figure 4(b) specifies the time processing system, which implements the observer design pattern.

Analyzing the lower, detailed level of the time display system, one can argue about the roles that the different sub-processes play in the context of the observer design pattern. In particular, the processes Digital Display Updating and Analog Display Updating can be viewed as two different Notify processes, while Counter Updating has no role in this context. Hence, it is reasonable for a human designer to implement the observer design pattern in the time display system as specified in Figure 5. Note that this design specifies also that the Change Subscription process can be triggered

by Analog Time Display *or* by Digital Time Display (as there may be cases where only one is required for a single subscription).

A Naturally-Induced Categorization Schema for Design Patterns

One of the important features of our proposed design patterns representation approach is that it induces a natural categorization schema of design patterns. Different categorization schemes have been proposed over the years in order to improve the comprehensibility and correct usage of design patterns, e.g., Buschmann and Meunier (1995), Buschmann, Meunier, Rohnert, Summerland and Stal (1996), Gamma *et al.* (1994), Helm (2005), Noble (1998), and Zimmer (1995). Generally, a design pattern categorization schema should support both understanding of the function of the design pattern and retrieving those patterns that are appropriate for the problem at hand. Buschmann and Meunier (1995) and Buschmann *et al.* (1996) identified five properties that a categorization schema must possess: (1) simplicity and ease of learning, (2) being comprised of only a few classification criteria, (3) reflecting natural properties

Figure 5. The time display system model after correctly applying the observer design pattern

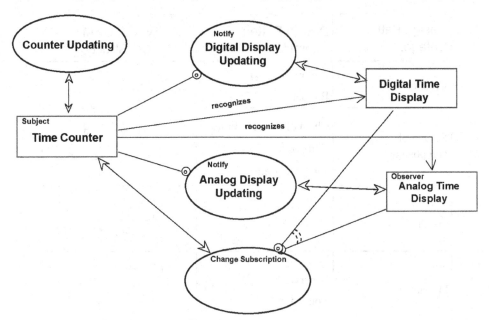

of patterns for each categorization criterion, (4) providing a roadmap that leads users to several possible patterns, and (5) being extensible in order to provide for new patterns to be easily integrated.

Analyzing the different OPM models of the design patterns presented in Gamma *et al.* (1994), we identified common fundamental OPM constructs that appear in several design patterns and help explain their essence. Although the common OPM constructs sometimes appear in the design pattern problem models, the pattern solution models naturally specify the design pattern's intention better than their problem model counterparts. For clarity purposes, these OPM constructs are marked in grey in the models in Figure 2 and Appendix B. The remarkable commonality we have observed induces a design patterns categorization schema, which satisfies the five properties identified by Buschmann and Meunier (1995) and Buschmann *et al.* (1996). This categorization schema includes four groups, which are summarized in Figure 6, but can be extended and refined as new design patterns are introduced.

The first group in our schema is *creational design patterns*, which is similar to the creational group in Gamma *et al.* (1994). It is characterized by the OPM construct of *process – result link – object* (see Figure 6). This construct purely conveys the idea of a process creating an object.

The second group, *structural composition design patterns*, shares in common the abstract characterizing construct of two elements that are connected via a structural relation of some type. The common construct that characterizes structural composition design patterns consists of two processes. However, there may be cases in which the common construct consists of two objects connected by a structural relation. While we did not identify such a construct in any of the design patterns listed in Gamma *et al.* (1994), if such a construct is found, this group may be further divided into two sub-groups: static structural composition and dynamic structural composition. The OPM constructs of these groups will be quite similar. However, static structural composition patterns will refer to objects and their structural

Figure 6. Categorization of design patterns according to their OPM models

Design Pattern Category	Design Pattern Examples	Typical OPM Construct
Creational	Factory Method Builder	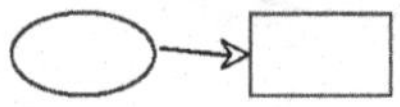
Structural composition	Chain of Responsibility Composite Template Method	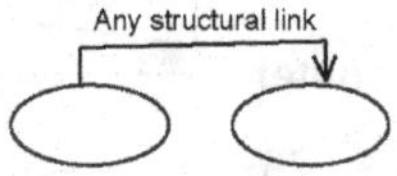 Any structural link
Wrapper	Decorator	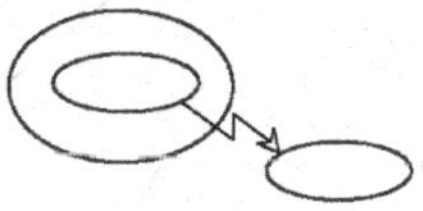
Interaction	Observer Command	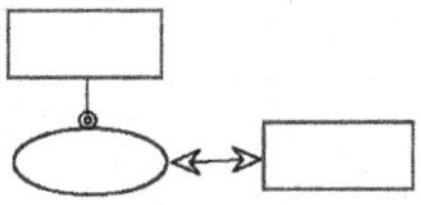

links, while dynamic structural composition will refer to processes and their structural links.

The patterns in the third group are classified as *wrapper design patterns* since they solve their stated problems by wrapping the original functionality. Such design patterns have already been recognized as wrappers in Gamma *et al.* (1994) and Shalloway and Trott (2001). Their common characterizing OPM construct justifies both the existence of this category and its name.

Finally, the fourth group is the *interaction design patterns* group. The patterns in this group focus on the interaction between structural and behavioral aspects of the solution. In OPM terms, these patterns emphasize procedural links, namely effect and event links, which are responsible for updating objects and for triggering processes, respectively. In the observer design pattern solution model, this construct appears twice: one for notifying the subjects and the other for changing their subscription.

AUTOMATICALLY IMPROVING SOFTWARE DESIGN WITH DESIGN PATTERNS

Utilizing the knowledge gained from modeling and categorizing different design patterns in our approach, we present in this section an algorithm that scans system design models, expressed in OPM, searches for different embedded problem models, and suggests the application of relevant design pattern solutions using their correction models. The OPM design models, which are the inputs of this algorithm, can be either created manually by designers or reverse-engineered from code. They are represented as data structures internal to OPCAT (OPCAT Systems), the OPM-based modeling software environment.

The algorithm, called Pattern Candidate Finder, searches for system model portions that are structurally equivalent to design pattern problem models. Here, we use the ability to compare OPM models at different abstraction levels, since usually the system model is concrete, while a design pat-

Figure 7. The Pseudo-code of the Run method of the Pattern Candidate Finder class

```
Run (system model μ) {
       For each pair of problem model Pᵢ and correction model Sᵢ in the repository {
              Candidates =Search (Pᵢ, μ)      // searches for candidate parts in μ that are equivalent to Pᵢ
              For each M in Candidates {
                     Display (M, Sᵢ)      // Sᵢ is a possible solution for the candidate part
              }
       }
}
```

tern problem model is general and more abstract. When a match is found, the tool suggests that the designer replace the system model portion with the corresponding design pattern solution model. It further suggests how to do this by presenting the corresponding correction model. The designer can choose whether to accept the suggestion, reject it, or manually apply the design pattern into the system, taking into consideration factors such as the semantics of the system model and the optimization of code. Figure 7 presents the pseudo-code of the main method, Run, of the Pattern Candidate Finder class. This class has two additional methods, Search, which is presented in Figure 7, and Display, which textually displays the design problems that were found and ways to solve them.

In the search method, we adapted the structural equivalence algorithm presented in Soffer (2005) and modified it to support the different layers at which the design pattern and system models reside. We treat an OPM diagram as a directed graph whose nodes are things (objects or processes) and edges are links. The search method finds a path between two nodes that is structurally (but not necessarily semantically) equivalent to a direct link between these things. This equivalence is deduced primarily according to the dominance of OPM links, which is determined using the link semantics and the abstraction order (Reinhartz-Berger & Dori, 2005). This abstraction order defines for each two procedural links a third procedural link which replaces

the two when a thing (process or object) is abstracted (folded, out-zoomed, or state-suppressed). Each link in a design pattern problem model is considered as a query model, which is searched for equivalent paths in the system model, discarding combinations of paths that do not create a valid OPM model. A more detailed description of the algorithm can be found at http://mis.hevra. haifa.ac.il/~iris/research/DP/ImproverAlg.pdf.

Due to the refinement/abstraction mechanisms of OPM that preserve consistency between the different diagrams of the same model, a particular design problem may appear at various abstraction levels. In order to report each design problem only once, a post processing stage is added to the Pattern Candidate Finder algorithm (Figure 8). At this stage, a candidate is discarded if one of its elements is not at its lowest level of abstraction and the associated design problem model does not explicitly contain different abstraction levels. As an example to this rule, consider Figure 4(a) and Figure 3. Time Processing from Figure 4(a) is refined (in-zoomed) in Figure 3. The observer design problem appears in these two diagrams twice, as presented in Table 1. However, the first case is an abstraction (zooming-out) of the second one. Thus, we wish that the algorithm reports only one design problem that correspond to the observer design pattern in this case. However, if the design problem model itself requires different abstraction levels, such as in the case of the Command pattern problem model, then candidates that include elements which are not at the lowest

Figure 8. Pseudo-code of the search procedure of the Pattern Candidate Finder algorithm

```
Search (problem model P, system model μ) {
        Matches = new MatchGroup()
        linksInP = P.Get_Links ();          //creates a group of all the links in the problem model P
        For each l in linksInP {
        sourcesInSystemModel = μ.Get_Same_Type_System_Model_Entities(l.getSource());
        //finds all entities in the system model that are of the same type (object, process, or
        //state) as the link source
        destinationsInSystemModel = μ.Get_Same_Type_System_Model_Entities(l.getDestination());
        //finds all entities in the system model that are of the same type (object, process, or
        //state) as the link destination
        For each source in sourcesInSystemModel {
                For each destination in destinationsInSystemModel {
                        l.paths.Add(StructuralEquivalence(l, source, destination, μ));
                        //adds the found path to the collection of equivalent paths of this link
                }
        }
        Matches = BuildMatches(linksInP); // builds valid OPM models which match the problem model
                                    // P by choosing one equivalent path for each link in P.
        return Matches;
}
```

Table 1. The appearance of the observer design patterns in Figure 3 and Figure 4(a)

Case #		Changing B	Object A	Object B
	Figure 4(a)	Time Processing	Time Counter	Digital Time Display, Analog Time Display
	Figure 3	Time Processing (through Digital Display Updating and Analog Display Updating)	Time Counter	Digital Time Display, Analog Time Display

level of abstraction and occur in the structure of the design problem model will be reported.

The complexity of the structural equivalence algorithm is $O(n_\mu)$ (Soffer, 2005) and the complexity of the entire Pattern Candidate Finder algorithm is $O(n_\mu l_p)$, where n_μ is the number of things (objects and processes) in model μ and l_p is the overall number of links in all the problem models in the algorithm's repository.

EVALUATION OF THE PATTERN CANDIDATE FINDER ALGORITHM

In order to evaluate the suggested Pattern Candidate Finder algorithm, we applied a case study research methodology (Yin, 1994). This type of research methodology is adequate where (1) the research attempts to answer "how" or "why" questions, (2) the investigator has a little or no possibility to control the events, and (3) the research concerns a contemporary phenomenon in a real-life context. Our research satisfies these three conditions: (1) the research question is whether and how the suggested algorithm might help improve system designs, (2) system design is a mental process, over which we have virtually no control, and (3) system design is a common contemporary phenomenon in a real-life context of organizations such as software companies.

Following the case study research methodology, we run the suggested algorithm on several system designs, the largest of which is ExamPal. ExamPal is an automatic application for composing, taking, checking, and grading analysis and design exams. Its design model consists of 11 Object-Process Diagrams (OPDs) with a maximum of five detail (in-zooming) levels. The nature of this system leads us to believe that design patterns would be applicable. However, we did not instruct the creators of this system model how to design the system. Neither did we deliberately insert design problems to the system model. Since the system is not concerned with distribution and reusability, we thought that wrapper or interaction design patterns were not relevant.

The system was modeled in OPM by a group of graduate and experienced undergraduate students who took an advanced information systems engineering course, called "Methodologies for Information Systems Development", at the Technion, Israel Institute of Technology. All students in this course took several analysis and design courses, carried out annual information systems projects, and some of them have already worked as software designers. Thus, this population is comparable to industry junior designers. However, none of the students was experienced with design patterns. As part of their final grades, the students were required to develop a system for composing, taking, checking, and grading analysis and design exams, including specifying its requirements and analyzing them, designing feasible solutions that satisfy the requirements, implementing their design, and testing the system they had developed.

The eight design patterns used for running the Pattern Candidate Finder algorithm were the Factory Method, Builder, Decorator, Composite, Observer, Command, Chain of Responsibility, and Template Method. These patterns were selected as representatives of all the categories defined in Gamma *et al.* (1994) and are considered commonly used patterns (Hahsler, 2003, 2004). The models of these patterns are given in Appendix B, while the system model of ExamPal is given in Appendix C.

To evaluate the algorithm results, two experienced software designers, who are not the authors of this paper, were requested to specify which of the eight design patterns they would use to improve the ExamPal design model. These experienced designers were further asked to indicate the exact places in which these design patterns should be applied. Comparing the results obtained from the experienced software designers with those proposed by the algorithm, we classified the pattern candidates into three groups: (1) hits, i.e., cases which the algorithm discovered design pattern candidates that were also recommended by the experts, (2) false positives, i.e., cases where the algorithm discovered design pattern candidates that were not recommended by the experts and should not be applied according to them, and (3) false negatives, i.e., cases which were recommended by the experts but were not found by the Pattern Candidate Finder algorithm. When contradictions between the design experts were discovered, the candidate was considered as not applicable in that context.

For the Builder, Factory Method, Composite, Decorator, Chain of Responsibility, and Template Method design patterns, we found no false positives, no false negatives, and no hits. These findings are in line with our expectations of the design model, since the system does not possess characteristics that suggest using these patterns: it does not contain a general framework user interface specification, nor does it models a change in an existing system or deal with composite objects. Table 2 summarizes the results we got for the other two design patterns, namely Observer and Command.

Regarding the Observer design pattern, one hit and two false positives were found. No false

Table 2. Design experts vs. the suggested Pattern Candidate Finder algorithm

Design Pattern	Hits	False Positives	False Negatives
Observer	1	2	0
Command	4	4	2

negatives were found for this design pattern. The found false positives do indeed match the Observer problem model, but are not necessarily appropriate for implementing the Observer design pattern. This finding indicates the need for semantics-based techniques in addition to the structural (syntactic) ones, raising potential for future research.

Analyzing the Command design pattern, the algorithm originally found eight candidates, of which four were hits. Two design pattern candidates were missed by the algorithm in the ExamPal system.

To summarize, the suggested algorithm found the main places where design patterns have to be applied, however it also raised some false positives and in the Command case—two false negatives were detected as well. Analyzing the places where false negatives and false positives occur, we concluded that the algorithm accuracy and effectiveness in terms of the manual operations required from the designers depend on the following factors:

1. The application of the structural equivalence algorithm in general and its selection rules in particular,
2. The generality of the design pattern problem models, and
3. The completeness or detail level of the system models.

SUMMARY

We have introduced a three-layered framework for modeling design patterns. The layers are the meta-design pattern layer, the design pattern layer, and the system layer. The meta-design pattern layer includes specifications of commonalities among design patterns, allowing for variability among the different design patterns. This layer includes the different templates for documenting design patterns. We focused on a template that defines three model types for each design pattern: problem models, solution models, and correction models. The correction models map problem models to solution models. The design pattern layer hosts design pattern models in a complete and coherent way, which helps understand and use these patterns correctly in software system models. Finally, the concrete system layer includes specific system models that implement the various design patterns. The elements in the system layer are mapped to the roles they play in the more abstract representation of the design pattern solution models (in the design pattern layer).

Evaluating the approach on eight commonly used design patterns and several case studies, we found that the suggested approach and algorithm successfully locates the main design problems modeled by the selected design patterns. However, the algorithm detects a manageable amount of false positives, requiring a reasonable amount of human designers' involvement for deciding whether a design pattern suggested by the algorithm should be applied or rejected. This outcome is in line with Yacoub and Ammar (2003) who state that experienced designers argue that "patterns are mental building blocks that are more related to human understanding than to automatic usage" (p. 352). The combination of the proposed design pattern models and the Pattern Candidate Finder algorithm may help users understand design problems and consequences of their solutions.

The contribution of the work is twofold. First, the suggested representation approach offers a comprehensive design pattern categorization schema, which includes creational design patterns, structural compositions, wrappers, and interactions. This categorization schema is intuitive and extensible, as it relies on common OPM constructs that are identified in the patterns' models. Furthermore, establishing the categorization on a simple visual feature of the patterns makes the schema comprehensible and usable as a design pattern catalog reference. Second, our approach makes the development of a design improver feasible, as it enables extracting the knowledge gained from modeling and analyzing design patterns to find specific locations in a system model where design patterns can be embedded to improve the design. This mechanism may be helpful not only for novice designers, but also for experts who are not familiar with the ever-growing vocabulary of design patterns.

Possible extensions of our work include studying design patterns composition (Dong *et al.*, 2007) and improving the Pattern Candidate Finder algorithm by incorporating semantic techniques or learning mechanisms, as presented in Purao *et al.* (2003). Additional research should further empirically test the value of our approach in terms of its cost-effectiveness by comparing standard designs to those done with our approach of enhancing the design with semi-automatically suggested design patterns.

REFERENCES

Abdul Jalil, M., & Azman Mohd Noah, S. (2007). The difficulties of Using Design Patterns among Novices: An Exploratory Study. In M. L. Gavrilova & O. Gervasi (Eds.), *Proceedings of the 2007 International Conference on Computational Science and its Applications – ICCSA 2007* (pp. 97-103). Washington, DC: IEEE Computer Society.

Batra, D. (2005). Conceptual Data Modeling Patterns: Representation and Validation. *Journal of Database Management, 16*(2), 84–106.

Blomqvist, E. (2005). Fully Automatic Construction of Enterprise Ontologies Using Design Patterns: Initial Method and First Experiences. In R. Meersman, Z. Tari, M-S. Hacid, J. Mylopoulus, B. Pernici, O.,Babaoglu, *et al.* (Eds.), *On the Move to Meaningful Internet Systems 2005: CoopIS, DOA, and ODBASE* (LNCS 3761, pp. 1314-1329). Berlin-Heidelberg, Germany: Springer.

Buschmann, F., & Meunier, R. (1995). A System of Patterns. In J. O. Coplien & D. C. Schmidt (Eds.), *Pattern Language for Program Design* (pp. 325-343). New York: Addison-Wesley.

Buschmann, F., Meunier, R., Rohnert, H., Sommerland, P., & Stal, M. (1996). *Pattern-Oriented Software Architecture: A System of Patterns.* Chichester, UK: John Wiley & Sons.

Dong, J., Alencar, P. S. C., Cowan, D. D., & Yang, S. (2007). Composing pattern-based components and verifying correctness. *Journal of Systems and Software, 80*(11), 1755–1769. doi:10.1016/j.jss.2007.03.005

Dong, J., Yang, S., & Zhang, K. (2007). Visualizing Design Patterns in their Applications and Composition. *IEEE Transactions on Software Engineering, 33*(7), 433–453. doi:10.1109/TSE.2007.1012

Dori, D. (2002). *Object-Process Methodology – A Holistic System Paradigm.* London: Springer.

Eden, A. H. (1999). *Precise Specification of Design Patterns and Tool Support in Their Application.* Unpublished PhD thesis, University of Tel Aviv.

Eden, A. H. (2002). A Visual Formalism for Object-Oriented Architectures. In J. C. Peterson, B. Kraemer, & B. Enders (Eds.), *Proceedings of the 6th World Conference on Integrated Design and Process Technology (IDPT'2002).* Pasadena, CA: Society for Design and Process Science.

France, R. B., Kim, D.-K., Ghosh, S., & Song, E. (2004). A UML-Based Pattern Specification Technique. *IEEE Transactions on Software Engineering*, 30(3), 193–206. doi:10.1109/TSE.2004.1271174

Gamma, E., Helm, R., Johnson, R., & Vlissides, J. (1994). *Design Patterns: Elements of Reusable Object-Oriented Software*. Reading, MA: Addison-Wesley.

Guennec, A. L., Sunye, G., & Jezequel, J.-M. (2000). Precise Modeling of Design Patterns. In A. Evans, S. Kent, & B. Selic (Eds.), *<<UML>> 2000 – The Unified Modeling Language. Advancing the Standard* (LNCS 1939, pp. 482-496). Berlin-Heidelberg, Germany: Springer.

Hahsler, M. (2003). *A Quantitative Study of the Application of Design Patterns in Java* (Working Papers on Information Processing and Information Management No. 01/2003). Wien, Austria: Institute of Information Processing and Information Management.

Hahsler, M. (2004). A Quantitative Study of the Adoption of Design Patterns by Open Source Software Developers. In S. Koch (Ed.), *Free/Open Source Software Development*. Hershey, PA: Idea Group.

Helm, R. (2005). Patterns in Practice. In R. E. Johnson & R. P. Gabriel (Eds.), *Proceedings of the 10th Annual Conference on Object-Oriented Programming Systems, Languages, and Applications (OOPSLA'2005)* (pp. 337-341). New York: ACM Publishing.

Kim, D. K., France, R. B., & Ghosh, S. (2004). A UML-based language for specifying domain-specific patterns. *Journal of Visual Languages and Computing*, 15(3-4), 265–289. doi:10.1016/j.jvlc.2004.01.004

Lauder, A., & Kent, S. (1998). Precise Visual Specification of Design Patterns. In E. Jul (Ed.), *ECOOP'98 – Object Oriented Programming* (LNCS 1445, pp. 114-136). Berlin-Heidelberg, Germany: Springer.

Mak, J. K. H., Choy, C. S. T., & Lun, D. P. K. (2004). Precise Modeling of Design Patterns in UML. In A. Finkelstein, J. Estublier, & D. S. Rosenblum (Eds.), *Proceedings of the 26th International Conference on Software Engineering (ICSE'04)* (pp. 252-261). Washington, DC: IEEE Computer Society.

Mapelsden, D., Hosking, J., & Grundy, J. (2002). Design Pattern Modeling and Instantiation using DPML. In J. Noble & J. Potter (Eds.), *Proceeding of TOOLS Pacific 2002 – Objects for Internet, Mobile and Embedded Applications. Conference in Research and Practice in Information Technology* (Vol. 10, pp. 3-11). Darlinghurst, Australia: ACS.

Noble, J. (1998). Classifying relationships between Object-Oriented Design Patterns. In *Proceedings of the Australian Software Engineering Conference* (pp. 98-108). Washington, DC: IEEE Computer Society.

Object Management Group. (2002). *UML 2.0 Superstructure FTF convenience document*. Retrieved from http://www.omg.org/docs/ptc/04-10-02.zip

Object Management Group. (2003). *Meta Object Facility (MOF™) version 1.4*. Retrieved from http://www.omg.org/docs/formal/02-04-03.pdf

Object Venture Inc. (2002). *Pattern and Component Markup Language*. Retrieved from http://www.objectventure.com/pcml.html

Pickin, S., & Manjarrés, A. (2002). Describing AI Analysis Patterns with UML. In A. Evans, S. Kent, & B. Selic (Eds.), *<<UML>> 2000 – The Unified Modeling Language. Advancing the Standard* (LNCS 1939, pp. 466-481). Berlin-Heidelberg, Germany: Springer.

Prechelt, L., Unger, B., Philipssen, M., & Tichy, W. (2002). Two Controlled Experiments Assessing the Usefulness of Design Pattern Documentation in Program Maintenance. *IEEE Transactions on Software Engineering*, *28*(6), 595–606. doi:10.1109/TSE.2002.1010061

Purao, S., Storey, V. C., & Han, T. (2003). Improving Analysis Pattern Reuse in Conceptual Design: Augmenting Automated Processes with Supervised Learning. *Information Systems Research*, *14*(3), 244–268. doi:10.1287/isre.14.3.269.16559

Reinhartz-Berger, I., & Dori, D. (2005). A Reflective Metamodel of Object-Process Methodology: The System Modeling Building Blocks. In P. Green & M. Rosemann (Eds.), *Business Systems Analysis with Ontologies* (pp. 130-173). Hershey, PA: Idea Group.

Reinhartz-Berger, I., & Sturm, A. (2007). Enhancing UML Models: A Domain Analysis Approach. *Journal of Database Management*, *19*(1), 74–94.

Schmidt, D. (1995). Experience Using Design Patterns to Develop Reusable Object-Oriented Communication Software. *Communications of the ACM*, *38*(10), 65–74. doi:10.1145/226239.226255

Shalloway, A., & Trott, J. (2001). *Design Patterns Explained: A New Perspective on Object-Oriented Design*. Reading, MA: Addison-Wesley.

Soffer, P. (2005). Structural Equivalence in Model-Based Reuse: Overcoming Differences in Abstract Level. *Journal of Database Management*, *16*(3), 21–39.

Sturm, A., Dori, D., & Shehory, O. (2006). Domain Modeling with Object-Process Methodology. In Y. Manolopoulos, J. Filipe, P. Constantopoulos, & J. Cordeiro (Eds.), *Proceedings of the 8th International Conference on Enterprise Information Systems (ICEIS'2006)* (pp. 144-151). Paphos, Cyprus: ICEIS.

Systems, O. P. C. A. T. *OPCAT web site*. Retrieved from http://www.opcat.com/

Taibi, T., & Ngo, D. C. L. (2003). Formal Specification of Design Patterns – A Balanced Approach. *Journal of Object Technology*, *2*(4), 127–140.

Warmer, J., & Kleppe, A. (1998). *The Object Constraint Language: Precise Modeling with UML*. Reading, MA: Addison-Wesley.

Wendorff, P. (2001). Assessment of design patterns during software reengineering: Lessons learned from a large commercial project. In *Proceedings of the 5th Conference on Software Maintenance and Reengineering* (pp. 77-84). Los Alamitos, CA: IEEE Computer Society Press.

Yacoub, S., & Ammar, H. (2003). *Pattern-oriented analysis and design: Composing patterns to design software systems*. Boston: Addison-Wesley.

Yin, R. K. (1994). *Case Study Reaserch. Design and Methods* (2nd ed.). Thousand Oaks, CA: Sage.

Zimmer, W. (1995). Relationships between Design Patterns. In J. O. Coplien & D. C. Schmidt (Eds.), *Pattern Language for Program Design* (pp. 345-364), New York: Addison-Wesley.

APPENDIX A: A QUICK GUIDE TO THE SYNTAX AND SEMANTICS OF OPM

Object-Process Methodology (OPM) (Dori, 2002, Reinhartz-Berger and Dori, 2005) is a holistic approach to the modeling, study, development, and evolution of systems. Structure and behavior coexist in the same OPM model to enhance the comprehension of the system as a whole. The OPM elements, which are summarized along with their symbols and meanings in Figure 9, are entities and links. Entities generalize objects, processes, and states. Objects and processes, the two basic building blocks of an OPM system model, are first-order classes of things. Objects are things that exist, while processes are things that transform objects by creating or destroying them or by changing their states. Links, which connect entities, are structural or procedural. Structural links express static, structural relations between pairs of objects or processes. Aggregation, generalization, characterization, and instantiation are the four fundamental structural links in OPM. General structural relations can take on any semantics, which is expressed textually by their user-defined tags.

The behavior of a system is manifested in three major ways: (1) processes can transform (generate, consume, or change the state of) objects, (2) objects can enable processes without being transformed by them, and (3) objects can trigger events that invoke processes. These ways are specified using different types of OPM procedural links (see Figure 9).

The complexity of an OPM model is controlled through three refinement/abstraction processes: *in-zooming/ out-zooming*, in which the entity being refined is shown enclosing its constituent elements; *unfolding/ folding*, in which the entity being refined is shown as the root of a directed graph; and *state expressing/ suppressing*, which allows for showing or hiding the possible states of an object. These mechanisms enable the user to recursively specify and refine the system under development to any desired level of detail without losing legibility and comprehension of the complete system. Furthermore, these mechanisms include consistency rules among the different granularity and abstraction levels, so that a low-level OPM specification is consistent with the higher level specifications (Dori, 2002).

APPENDIX B: ADDITIONAL EXAMPLES OF OPM MODELS OF DESIGN PATTERNS (Figures 10, 11, 12, 13, 14, 15 and 16)

APPENDIX C: THE EXAMPAL SYSTEM MODEL

The ExamPal system is an automatic application for composing, taking, checking, and grading analysis and design exams. The OPM design model of this system is given below. All candidates found by the Pattern Candidate Finder algorithm for the Command design pattern are marked by a dashed line, whereas all candidates for the Observer design pattern are marked by a dotted line. (Figures 17, 18, 19, 20, 21, 22, 23, 24, 25, 26 and 27)

Figure 9. OPM concepts, symbols, and meaning

Concept Name	Symbol	Concept Meaning
Informatical, systemic object	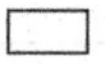	A piece of information
Informatical, environmental object	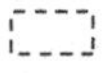	A piece of information which is external to the system
Process		A pattern of transformation that objects undergo
Initial/Regular/Final state		An initial/regular/final situation at which an object can exist for a period of time
Exhibition-Chracterization		A fundamental structural relation representing that an element exhibits a thing (object/process)
Aggregation-Participation		A fundamental structural relation representing that a thing (object/process) consists of one or more things
Generalization-Specialization		A fundamental structural relation representing that a thing is a subclass (refinement) of another thing (object/process)
Classification-Instantiation		A fundamental structural relation representing that a thing (object/process) consists of one or more things
General structural link	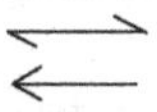	A bidirectional or unidirectional association between things that holds for a period of time, possibly with a tag denoting the association semantics
Enabling event link		A link denoting an event (such as data change or an external event) which triggers (tries to activate) a process. Even if activated, the process does not change the triggering object.
Consumption event link	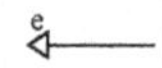	A link denoting an event which triggers (tries to activate) a process. If activated, the process consumes the triggering object.
Condition link		A link denoting a condition required for a process execution, which is checked when the process is triggered. If the condition does not hold, the next process (if any) tries to execute.
Agent link		A link denoting that a human agent (actor) is required for triggering a process execution
Instrument link		A link denoting that a process uses an object without changing it. If the object is not available (possibly in a specific state), the process waits for its availability.
Effect link		A link denoting that a process changes an object
Consumption/Result link		A link denoting that a process consumes/yields an object
Invocation link	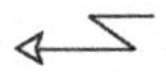	A link denoting that a process triggers (invokes) another process when it ends
XOR relation		A connection between structural or procedural links denoting that exactly one of the links is applicable (i.e., active in a single instance of the object or the process)
OR relation		A connection between structural or procedural links denoting that at least one of the links is applicable (i.e., active in a single instance of the object or the process)

Figure 10.

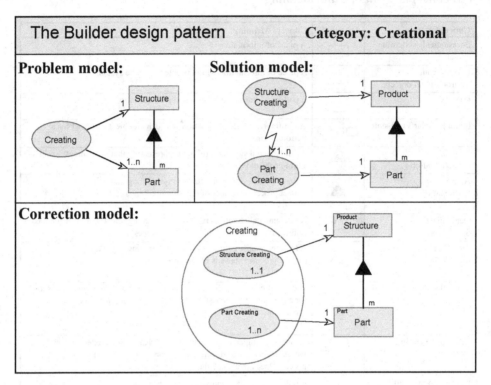

Figure 11.

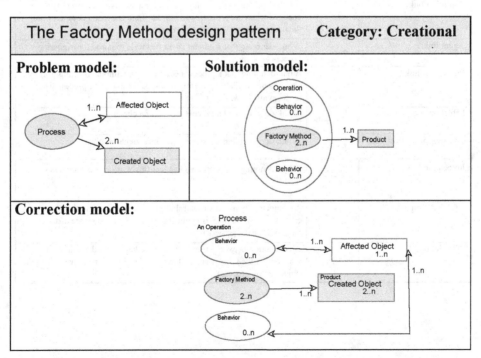

Figure 12.

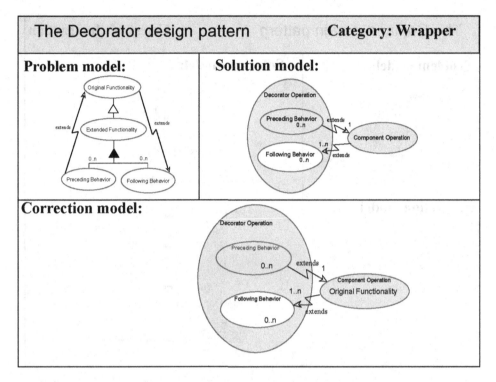

Figure 13.

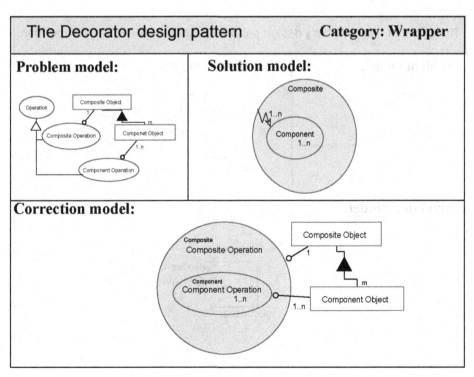

Figure 14.

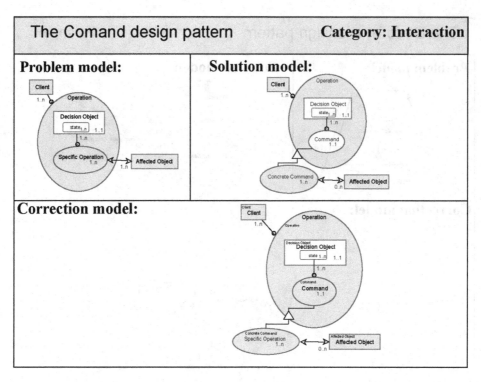

Figure 15.

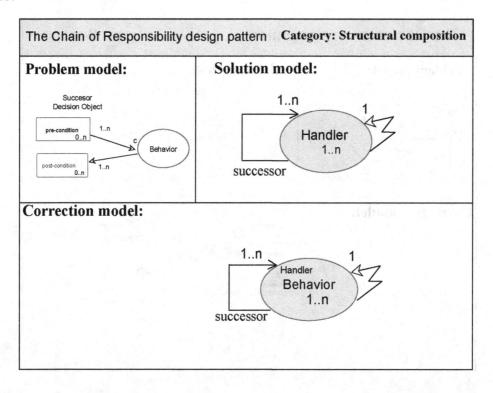

Figure 16.

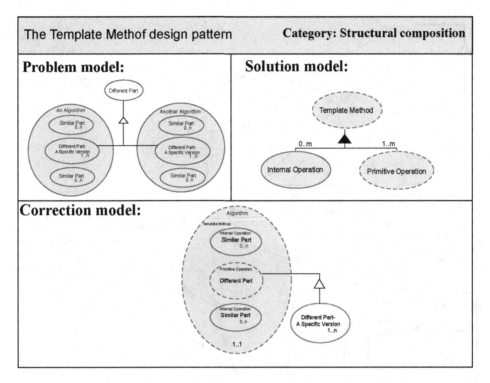

Figure 17. ExamPal top level diagram

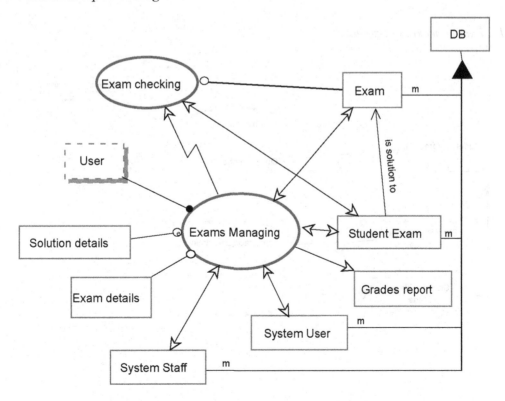

Figure 18. Exams managing in-zoomed

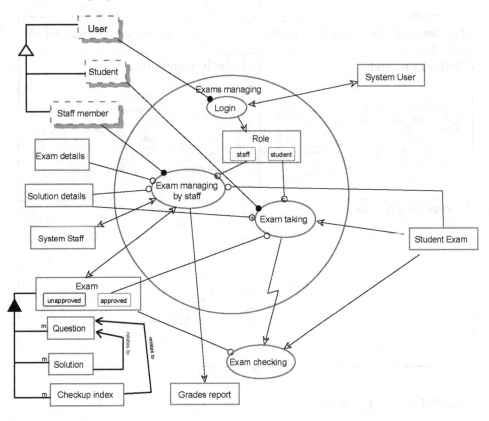

Figure 19. Exam checking in-zoomed

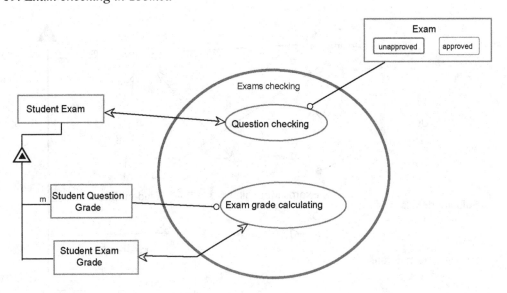

Figure 20. Exam taking in-zoomed

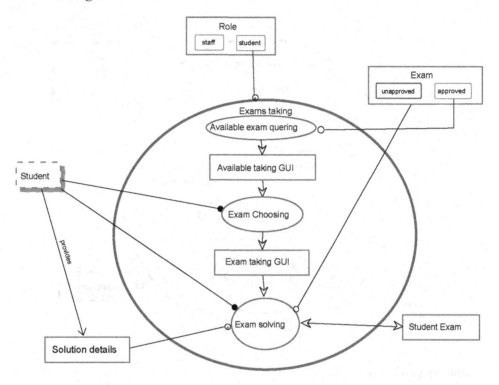

Figure 21. Question checking in-zoomed

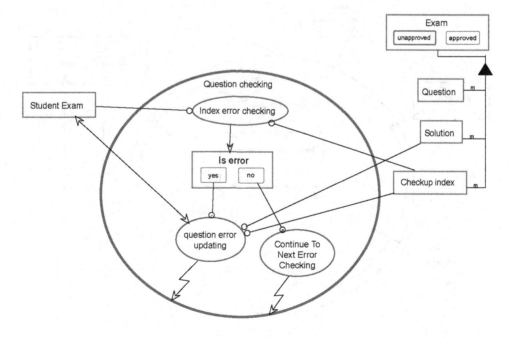

Figure 22. Exam solving in-zoomed

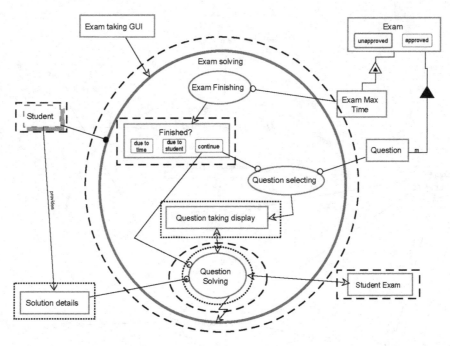

Figure 23. Exam composing in-zoomed

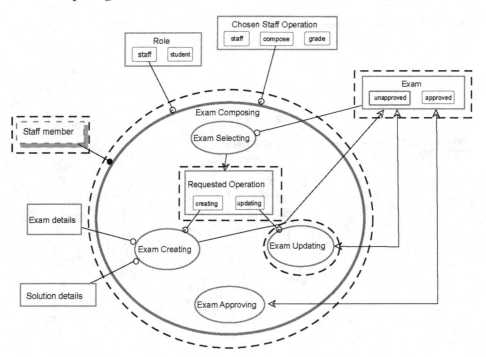

Figure 24. Grade report generating in-zoomed

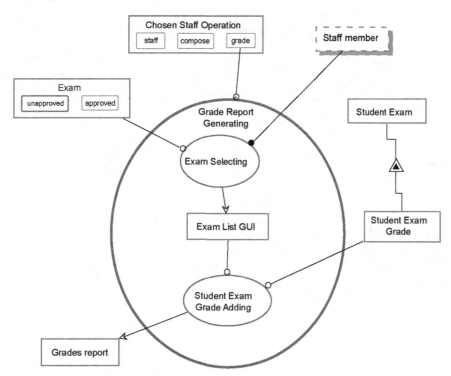

Figure 25. Question error updating in-zoomed

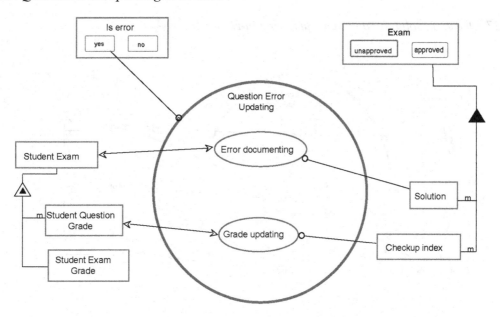

Figure 26. Exam creating in-zoomed

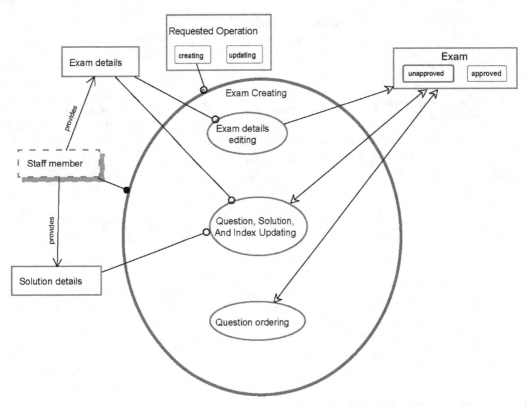

Figure 27. Question, solution, and index updating in-zoomed

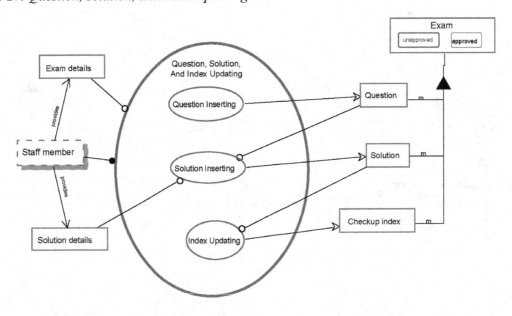

Chapter 3
Energy and Latency Efficient Access of Wireless XML Stream

Jun Pyo Park
Korea University, Korea

Chang-Sup Park
Dongduk Women's University, Korea

Yon Dohn Chung
Korea University, Korea

ABSTRACT

In this article, we address the problem of delayed query processing raised by tree-based index structures in wireless broadcast environments, which increases the access time of mobile clients. We propose a novel distributed index structure and a clustering strategy for streaming XML data that enables energy and latency-efficient broadcasting of XML data. We first define the DIX node structure to implement a fully distributed index structure which contains the tag name, attributes, and text content of an element, as well as its corresponding indices. By exploiting the index information in the DIX node stream, a mobile client can access the stream with shorter latency. We also suggest a method of clustering DIX nodes in the stream, which can further enhance the performance of query processing in the mobile clients. Through extensive experiments, we demonstrate that our approach is effective for wireless broadcasting of XML data and outperforms the previous methods.

INTRODUCTION

As wireless communication technologies are rapidly gaining in popularity, the mobile computing paradigm has been realized in the industry, where mobile clients communicate by using hand-held devices such as laptops, PDAs, and cellular phones while they are moving (Acharya, Alonso, Franklin, & Zdonik, 1995; Imielinski, Viswanathan, & Badrinath, 1997). In wireless and mobile environments, data broadcasting is an effective method for data dissemination because it provides the benefits of bandwidth efficiency, scalability, and energy-efficiency. Meanwhile, mobile clients use battery-powered mobile devices in wireless broadcast environments, and thus, selective access

DOI: 10.4018/978-1-61350-471-0.ch003

Figure 1. An example of XML document and its tree representation

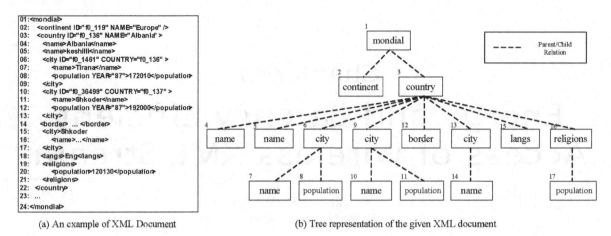

(a) An example of XML Document   (b) Tree representation of the given XML document

of broadcast data is necessary for energy conservation in the devices. The overall query processing time must be also minimized in order to provide fast response to the users. The former is related to energy-efficiency and the latter is related to latency-efficiency (Imielinski, Viswanathan, & Badrinath, 1994). When a mobile device tunes in to and receives data from the broadcast stream in the *active mode*, it consumes much more energy than when it is in the *doze mode*. The tuning time is the sum of the elapsed times when the mobile client is in the active mode, and thus serves as a criterion for measuring the energy-efficiency. Meanwhile, the access time is the time elapsed from when a query is issued by a mobile client to when the target data is completely retrieved from the stream, and thus serves as a measure of the latency-efficiency.

In this article, we consider efficient streaming and access of XML data in a wireless mobile environment. With the successful development and proliferation of various related technologies, XML (eXtensible Markup Language) (W3C Recommendation-XML, 2006) has been popularly used as a standard means to facilitate the representation and sharing of structured data across different information systems not only in the wired Internet environment but also in the

wireless broadcast environment (Fong & Wong, 2004). Figure 1 shows an example of an XML document (a) and its tree representation (b). This XML document will be used as a running example throughout the article.

Currently, wireless broadcasting of XML data is used in emerging applications such as the Electric Program Guide (EPG) of Digital Audio/ Video Broadcasting services (DVB, 2004), and the Traffic and Travel information (TTI) over a wireless broadcast channel in T-DMB (Terrestrial Digital Multimedia Broadcasting) services (TPEG, 2006). Especially, data is not static but continuously updated in such applications. Thus, there should be support for a query processing algorithm that allows mobile clients to start evaluation of a given query as soon as they tune in to the broadcast channel in order to satisfy the users' information needs quickly and efficiently.

Park, Kim, and Chung (2005) and Park, Choi, and Lee (2006) proposed methods to stream XML data in the wireless broadcast environment in an energy-efficient manner. However, their approaches are based on a tree-structured index inserted in the stream, and query processing in a mobile client is performed by following the location paths from the XML document root to the desired data. And the mobile client cannot seek

Figure 2. An example of delayed query processing

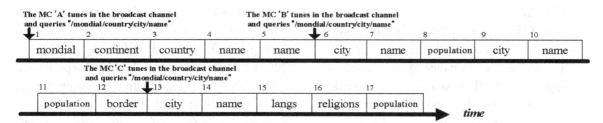

backward in the stream unless the streamed data is buffered at the client. Therefore, if the mobile client tunes in to the broadcast channel after the XML root has been passed over, it should wait until the next broadcast cycle begins, and this waiting time results in a long access time. We refer to this as the *Delayed Query Processing Problem*, which is described in the following example.

Example 1. Figure 2 shows a broadcast stream of the example XML document in Figure 1. The broadcast server organizes XML data in *document order*, i.e. the order in which the XML elements appear in the document, and broadcasts them repeatedly on the air. In a conventional approach to processing an XML path expression query over the stream, mobile clients search the nodes in the stream satisfying the location steps in the location path of the query in a sequential manner (i.e., *mondial*, *country*, *city*, and *name* in sequence). Assume that a mobile client 'A' tunes in to the broadcast channel before the XML root is broadcast, while mobile clients 'B' and 'C' tune in to the middle of broadcast stream (i.e., after the XML root has been passed over). The mobile client 'A' can start query processing within the current broadcast cycle, but 'B' and 'C' must wait until the next broadcast cycle starts.

To solve the problem, we need a new broadcasting and query processing strategy which can answer queries without exploring the stream from the XML root element in the beginning of the broadcast cycle. In this article, we propose an effective streaming scheme for XML data that can provide mobile clients with energy and laten-

cy-efficient access to XML data. To this end, we present a novel distributed index structure for an XML data stream, called *DIX*. In our method, an XML data stream is a sequence of nodes that have the attributes and content of an XML element and links to the other subsequent nodes in the stream. The node structure also contains the *Location Path Information* of an element which allows a mobile client to start query processing as soon as it tunes in to the broadcast channel without waiting until a node for the document root element is broadcast. Moreover, we suggest a clustering strategy to further enhance the performance of query processing. By clustering XML elements of the same depth within the stream, mobile clients can find target data by searching only a bounded and sequential part of the stream, and thus energy and latency efficiency can be improved. The main contributions of this article are summarized as follows:

- We define a DIX node structure to implement a fully distributed index for XML data. The DIX node structure contains a location path encoded as a 4-bytes length bit string, called LPI. Unlike the previous XML data broadcast methods, our approach allows mobile clients to start query processing on the stream without exploring it from the root node. To the best of our knowledge, the proposed scheme is the first approach that stores location path information for XML elements in each node in the stream. Furthermore, our concept of storing self-identifiable index information (i.e., LPI) can applicable not only for wireless XML stream but also for other wireless broadcasting applications.

- For the best performance of query processing on the XML broadcast stream, we designed two key indices called Clone node Link (CL) and Foreign node Link (FL), which are stored in each DIX node. The CL is used to access the candidate answer nodes of the query selectively while the FL is used to skip nodes irrelevant to the query. These link indices, together with LPIs, can support energy-efficient processing of XPath queries having various features such as descendent axes and wild-cards.

- We propose a clustering strategy to confine the search range to part of DIX nodes broadcast in the stream. Since the previous methods generate and broadcast XML data stream in document order, a mobile client must search the entire XML data stream in order to retrieve all of the result data. In our clustering strategy, the nodes of elements of the same depth are clustered together within the stream, and thus a mobile client can retrieve the desired data by searching only part of the stream (i.e., the clustering region having the same depth as the given query). Consequently, both the access and tuning time performances can be further improved.

- We evaluate the performance of our approach by extensive experiments. We present the performance results of our approach compared with previous XML broadcasting methods. The experimental results show that the proposed index structure and clustering strategy can reduce the access and tuning times effectively, and it outperforms the previous approaches in wireless broadcast environments.

A number of researches have been conducted on compression of XML data (Liefke & Suciu, 2000; Tolani & Haritsa, 2002; Min, Park, & Chung, 2003; Arion, Bonifati, & Manolescu, 2007), filtering streamed XML data for publisher/subscriber system (Diao, Altinel, Franklin, Zhang, & Fischer, 2003; Chan, Felber, Garofalakis, & Rastogi, 2002; Gupta & Suciu, 2000; Candan, Hsiung, Chen, Tatermura, & Agrawal, 2006; Moro, Bakalov, & Tsotras, 2007; Silvasti, Sippu, & Soisalon-Soininen, 2009; Choi & Wong, 2009), and querying streaming XML data in wired environments (Lam, Ng, Wood, & Levene, 2003; Barton, Charles, Goyal, Raghavachari, Fontoura, & Josifovski, 2003; Wong, Chan, & Leong, 2004; Avila-Campillo *et al.*, 2002; Ludascher, Mukhopadhyay, & Papakonstantinou, 2002; Peng & Chawathe, 2003; Olteanu, 2007; Koch, Scherzinger, & Schmidt, 2007; Han, Jiang, Ho, & Li, 2008). These approaches are not suitable for the wireless broadcasting of XML data because they considered neither energy issues nor the restricted computing capability of mobile devices. However, we consider that the distributed indexing strategy and clustering technique proposed in our work can be exploited to enhance query processing performance of general XML streaming systems.

The rest of this article is organized as follows. Some related work is presented in the next section. In the section titled "DIX: THE PROPOSED INDEX STRUCTURE," we define the structure of an XML data stream including distributed indices, and describe the XML stream generation algorithm. In "QUERY PROCESSING OVER XML DATA STREAM," we present the query processing algorithm over the XML data stream constructed by our method. In the section titled "CLUSTERING STRATEGY," we propose a clustering method of streaming XML data based on the depth of XML elements. The revised algorithms for the generation of the clustered stream and the corresponding query processing are also described in this section. The results of performance evaluation by various experiments are presented in "PERFORMANCE EVALU-ATION." Finally we draw our conclusions and future work in "CONCLUSIONS."

RELATED WORK

Much work has been conducted on compressing, filtering, streaming, and wireless broadcasting of XML data.

- *XML Compression.* The researches on XML compression have been proposed to reduce storage space and network bandwidth. Liefke and Suciu (2000) proposed an XML compressor, XMill, to minimize the size of XML data. XMill reduces the size of XML data by exploiting the library function for gzip. However, it does not support querying compressed XML data. Several approaches for querying compressed XML data have been proposed in the literature (Lam *et al.*, 2003; Tolani & Haritsa, 2002; Min *et al.*, 2003). XCQ (Lam *et al.*, 2003) requires partial decompression of data in order to evaluate queries over compressed XML data. Meanwhile, XGrind (Tolani & Haritsa, 2002) and XPRESS (Min *et al.*, 2003) support querying compressed XML data without decompression. XQueC (Arion *et al.*, 2007) provides a full-fledged data management system for compressed XML data. XQueC separates the structure and content of an XML document and binds up similar values into one container. Consequently, XQueC reduces documents storage costs and supports efficient query process in the compressed data domain. None of these approaches, however, has an index for selective access to the stream in wireless broadcast environments.
- *XML Filtering.* XML Filtering methods are proposed to identify and deliver documents satisfying given queries in a collection of stored XML data objects. They are mainly used to support publisher/subscriber environments. YFilter (Diao *et al.*, 2003) is a Non-deterministic Finite Automaton (NFA) based filtering scheme that reduces the number of states of a path expression generated by a Finite State Machine (FSM). YFilter employs shared processing of queries and supports predicate conditions in the queries. XTrie (Chan *et al.*, 2002) supports complex XPath queries and both ordered and unordered matching of XML data. XTrie indexes common substrings to reduce unnecessary index probes and redundant matchings. XPush (Gupta & Suciu, 2003) constructs a single deterministic pushdown automaton in a lazy manner to avoid redundant predicate evaluations. However, the number of states increases exponentially in the worst case in the XPush automaton. AFilter (Candan *et al.*, 2006) employs both prefix and suffix sharing to reduce matching cost. Moreover, a lazy mechanism using trigger conditions and an on-demand prefix caching mechanism are used in AFilter to reduce the number of active states and minimize filtering time. BoxFilter (More *et al.*, 2007) have been proposed to prune out queries in advance. In the BoxFilter approach, documents and queries are transformed into a sequence and pruned out by the lower and upper bound estimation. Silvasti *et al.* (2009) addresses the problem of filtering in a managerial view, and proposes a query optimization method, *filter pruning*. Filter pruning eliminates as many occurrences of wildcard("*") and descendant axis("//") by using a given DTD. In addition, they propose a new filtering algorithm using a deterministic automaton based on the Aho-Corasick pattern-matching automaton. Choi and Wong (2009) propose an efficient and scalable filtering approach for high performance XML data service. They classify similar branch queries into groups and analyze common paths. And then it executes join operations and shares

intermediate join results, thus significantly reducing the number of join operations and computation costs. It should be noted that the energy-efficiency issue was not considered in the studies of compression and filtering of XML data.

•*XML Streaming.* A number of approaches to streaming XML data have been proposed in the literature. They support querying streamed XML data and disseminate the part of the stream satisfying the given queries. XMLTK (Avila-Campillo *et al.*, 2002) is a toolkit for highly scalable XML data processing, which consists of stand-alone XML tools and a scalable XPath processor for XML streams. XMLTK generates constant throughput immediately, but does not support predicate conditions in XPath expressions. In the literature, XSM (Ludascher *et al.*, 2002), XSQ (Peng & Chawathe, 2003), and SPEX (Olteanu, 2007), streaming methods based on memory efficient transducers have been proposed. SPEX supports one pass and progressive evaluation over an XML stream. XSM uses transducers with buffers but does not support descendant axes traversal. XSQ supports evaluation of branch conditions and predicates, however it requires an exponential amount of memory space to process queries. HAOS (Barton *et al.*, 2003) supports reverse axes using a matching structure, but it does not support progressive evaluation. That is, HAOS must process the entire stream in order to retrieve results. Particularly, Xstream (Wong *et al.*, 2004) is a middleware system which provides fragmentation and packetizing strategies based on the semantic and structural characteristics of XML documents in wireless environments. GCX (Koch *et al.*, 2007) is the main-memory based streaming XQuery engine which enables them to purge and minimize main memory consumption when evaluating an XQuery. GCX combines static analysis and dynamic buffer management. That is, XQuery expressions are statically rewritten at runtime and useless nodes are removed from the buffer by *active garbage collection*. StreamTX (Han *et al.*, 2008) adopts the holistic twig joins for tuple-extraction queries on an XML stream. StreamTX blocks cursors which do not have associated elements and immediately prunes an element if it does not satisfy the query path in order to provide efficient tuple-extraction with minimal buffer sizes. However, none of the previous work has considered the energy-efficiency issue in the wireless broadcast environments. These works does not focus on the energy and latency efficient query processing but high throughput and memory efficient query processing.

•*Wireless Broadcasting of XML data.* Park *et al.* (2005) and Park *et al.* (2006) proposed energy-efficient stream organization and query processing methods for broadcasting XML data in wireless environments. Park *et al.* (2005) defined a streaming unit for XML data broadcasting, called S-node, and proposed a tree-style index structure consisting of S-nodes. Each S-node contains two kinds of sibling addresses, same-tag and different-tag sibling links. The same-tag sibling link in the S-node is a pointer to the nearest sibling node having the same tag name while the different-tag sibling link is a pointer to the nearest sibling node having the different tag name. Park *et al.* (2006) utilized path summaries as a stream index. In this scheme, the structure information and text values of an XML document are separated, which reduces the entire stream size by eliminating redundant label paths. The separated structure information is used as an XML stream index. Each index node contains the location information of all the child index nodes and text nodes. A mobile client can access the broadcast XML stream selectively by using the location information. In this scheme, however, the order of elements is ignored and predicate conditions are not considered. Also, this approach provides indices only to child nodes and hence wild-card conditions and descendant axes are not fully supported. Our proposed scheme, on the contrary, contains attributes in each DIX node and the mobile client can identify its label path by decoding LPI. Therefore, our scheme supports many XPath features including descendant axes and predicates on XML attributes. Detailed explanations for processing wildcards and descendant axes are presented in the section titled "QUERY PROCESSING OVER XML DATA STREAM."

DIX: THE PROPOSED INDEX STRUCTURE

XML data stream construction involves transforming the contents of the source XML document into an alternative representation for XML data dissemination over a wireless broadcast stream. In this section, we present a novel distributed indexing scheme for XML, which can support efficient query processing over the XML stream at mobile clients, as well as a stream generation algorithm for the proposed approach. We first define the *DIX* (Distributed Index for XML broadcast) node structure to implement a fully distributed index for XML data broadcasting. In the proposed index structure, each node has its index segment, so the mobile client does not wait for a specific part of

the stream (i.e., the mobile client can start query processing at any part of the stream). In the following subsections, we will provide a detailed explanation of the three important components involved in constructing the index segment of a DIX node: *LPI*, *CL*, and *FL*. Finally, we will explain our XML stream organization algorithm.

Node Structure

The DIX node has a unified structure including data related to an XML element (i.e., *the data segment*) and its corresponding index information (i.e., *the index segment*).

Definition 1. The *DIX* node is described as $DIX_i = \{DS_i, IS_i\}$, where DIX_i is DIX a structure for the ith element e_i of the source XML document in *document order*, DS_i is the *data segment* of DIX_i, and IS_i is the *index segment* of DIX_i. DS_i contains the depth, tag name, attribute lists, and text contents of e_i. IS_i consists of the *Location Path Information* (LPI) for e_i and two additional index information, the *Clone node Link* (CL) and the *Foreign node Link* (FL).

Figure 3 shows the structure of a DIX node generated from the first element satisfying "/mondial/country/name" in the example XML document in Figure 1(a) (Line 4). Since the DIX node contains indices with a depth, tag name, attribute lists, and text of an XML element, the mobile client does not need to access indices and data separately. Particularly, by using the LPI and tag name, the mobile client can identify the

Figure 3. The structure of the DIX node

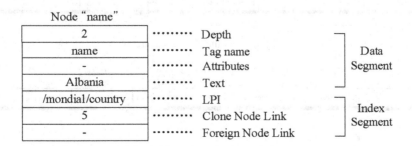

63

location path of any node in the stream without exploring the XML stream from the root element.

Definition 2. The Location Path Information (LPI) of an XML element e_i is a sequence of tag names of its ancestors, i.e. from the document root to the parent element. Specifically, it can be described as $LPI_i = "/T_0/T_1/.../T_{n-1}$," where $T_0 \sim T_{n-1}$ are the tag names of its ancestors, from the document root (T_0) to the parent element (T_{n-1}). That is, the path specification of this element can be described as $Path_i = "/T_0/T_1/.../T_{n-1}/T_n$," including the tag name of the element itself.

From the LPI and tag name, the mobile client can identify its path (i.e., "/mondial/country/ name") without exploring the XML stream from the root node. In the meantime, broadcasting the LPI as a form of text string might increase the size of the XML stream significantly. It is known that the access time performance is directly dependent on the size of the stream (Imielinski *et al.*, 1994). In this article, we use a hashing technique to transform a variable size character string into a fixed size value which is much shorter than the original string (Rivest, 1992). We encode and transport an LPI as a form of a 4-bytes length bit string by using a predefined hash function. Note that by using a 4-bytes length bit string, we can identify up to 2^{32} different LPIs in a source XML document. However, the length of bit string can be extended to cope with large XML documents. By comparing the hash value of an LPI in a DIX node appearing in the stream with that of the query, the mobile client can efficiently identify whether or not the location path of the node matches that of the query.

Definition 3. The Clone node Link (CL) in a DIX node n_i is the address of the nearest DIX node which has the same depth, LPI, and tag name as those in n_i (see Figure 4(b)). The Foreign node

Figure 4. Clone node Link and Foreign node Link

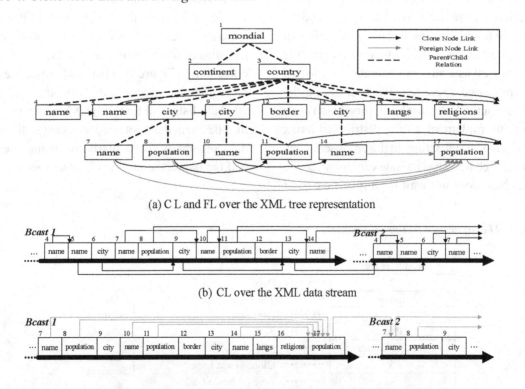

(a) C L and FL over the XML tree representation

(b) CL over the XML data stream

(c) FL over the XML data stream

Link (FL) in a DIX node n_i is the address of the nearest DIX node which has the same depth as n_i but has a different LPI than n_i (see Figure 4(c)).

The Clone node Link and Foreign node Link in the DIX node structure are indices for selective access of an XML stream. In the query processing steps, the CL in an answer node satisfying the query is used to find the next answer node directly. The FL is used to efficiently skip irrelevant nodes (i.e., nodes having different location paths from that of the query) until a node having the same LPI as that of the query appears in the stream.

XML Data Stream Generation

In this article, we generate the proposed DIX node stream by using the SAX (SAX, 2004), an event-driven API for parsing XML documents. Stream organization can be considered a two-phase process. The first phase is concerned with construction of the data segment and LPIs of DIX nodes. In this phase, the stream generator extracts the tag name, attributes, and text content from the XML elements, and encodes the LPI of the elements. In the second phase, the stream generator computes the CL and FL of each DIX node and constructs the stream of DIX nodes in document order.

Figure 5 presents the XML data stream generation algorithm. At first, the stream generator is

Figure 5. XML data stream generation algorithm

```
01: Algorithm Stream_Generator
02: Input: A well-formed XML document D
03: Output: XML Data Stream DS
04: ContentHandler.startDocument()
05: begin
06:        Path Stack PS = Ø              // initialization
07:        Node Queue Q = Ø
08:        int depth = - 1
09: end
10:
11: ContentHandler.startElement()
12: begin
13:        depth = depth + 1
14:        Construct a DIX node DN with Depth, Tag name, and Attribute List
15:        LPI of DN = encoding(PS)
16:        Push Tag name into PS
17:        Push DN into Q
18: end
19:
20: ContentHandler.endElement()
21: begin
22:        depth = depth - 1
23:        Pop an top entry from PS
24: end
25:
26: ContentHandler.characters()
27: begin
28:        Get the top entry DN in Q
29:        Initialize Text Data of DN
30:        Increase Node Size by the length of Text Data
31: end
32:
33: ContentHandler.endDocument()
34: begin
35:        Generate Clone node Link and Foreign node Link of all the DN in Q
36:        Flush all the DN in Q into the XML data stream DS
37: end
```

initialized at the start of XML document parsing (Line 4~9). Whenever a start tag of an element is encountered during document parsing, the stream generator executes the *startElement()* event handler and extracts the tag name, as well as the attributes list, if any, of the element (Line 14). It also constructs a hashed LPI of 4-byte length using the sequence of tag names stored in the path stack and the predefined hash function, and then it stores the DIX node in the queue (Line 15~17). If an element contains text content, the stream generator adds the text string into the data segment of the relevant DIX node in the queue by executing the *characters* event handler (Line 26~31). Finally, the stream generator computes the CL and FL of the stored nodes when it encounters the end of the XML document (Line 35) and then it flushes all the nodes in the queue into the XML data stream (Line 36).

QUERY PROCESSING OVER XML DATA STREAM

In this section, we present a method for a mobile client to process queries over the DIX node stream described earlier, which can skip irrelevant nodes by exploiting the proposed index structure. Figure 6 shows the query processing algorithm.

Given a user query, the mobile client tunes in to the broadcast channel and reads the DIX nodes on the air until a node having the same depth as that of the query appears in the stream (Line 6). Then, the query processor compares the LPIs and tag names of the node and query, respectively (Line 8~9) and adds the node to the result set if they match. If the given query contains predicate conditions over attributes or text content, the query processor.

also investigates whether the node satisfies the conditions (Line 10~12). After finding the first node satisfying the query, the mobile client selectively accesses the other nodes having the same LPI and tag name by following the CLs contained

in the nodes (Line 13~16). On the other hand, if a node and query of the same depth have different LPIs, none of nodes having the same LPI as that of the node satisfy the given query, and thus, the mobile client jumps to the nearest node which is of the same depth and has a different LPI by using the FL in the node (Line 30~32). That is, once the mobile client receives a node having the same depth as that of the query, it can efficiently skip a large number of irrelevant nodes in the stream.

Example 2. Figure 7 illustrates examples of selective access by using the CL and FL. Assume that a given query is "/mondial/country/city/name," and a mobile client tunes in to the broadcast channel when Node 5 is on the air (see Figure 7(a)). The mobile client can find the location path of this node from its LPI and tag name. Since the depth of Node 5 is different from that of the given query, the mobile client continues to download data. After reading Node 7 and comparing the LPIs and tag names of the node and query, the mobile client finds that Node 7 satisfies the given query and thus adds it to the result set. From the CL of Node 7, the mobile client can know the time when the next answer node (i.e., Node 10) will be broadcast, and thus, the mobile client switches to the doze mode to conserve its battery power. When Node 10 is on the air, the mobile client wakes up and downloads the node. In the same manner, the mobile client selectively accesses Node 14 and terminates query processing. Meanwhile, suppose that a given query is "/mondial/country/religions/population" (see Figure 7(b)). In this case, the mobile client finds the depth of Node 7 is equal to that of the given query but the LPI of Node 7 is different from the LPI of the given query. Since none of the nodes having the same LPI as Node 7 (i.e., nodes 10 and 14) can be the result of the given query, the mobile client can effectively skip irrelevant nodes broadcast in the stream by using the FL in Node 7, which points to a node (i.e., node 17) that has a different LPI and is of the same depth as Node 7. Then, the mobile client finds the first answer at

Figure 6. Query processing algorithm

```
01: Algorithm Query_Processing_Algorithm_over_XML_Stream
02: Input a XML stream S, XML path query Q
03: Output result set R satisfying Q
04: begin
05:     while(access latency of client <= the length of the stream)
06:         Read currentNode from the Stream S
07:         if(depth of query == the depth of currentNode) then
08:             if(LPI of currentNode == LPI of the query) then
09:                 if(tagName of currentNode == tagName of the query) then
10:                     if(currentNode satisfies Predicate of the query) then
11:                         Insert currentNode into result set R
12:                     endif
13:                     if(CL of currentNode is not NULL) then
14:                         if(access latency including the CL node <= the length of the stream) then
15:                             Wait in doze mode until the CL node arrives on the air
16:                         else
17:                             return R
18:                         endif
19:                     else
20:                         return R
21:                     endif
22:                 else
23:                     if(access latency of client < the length of the stream) then
24:                         Wait until the next node arrives on the air
25:                     else
26:                         return R
27:                     endif
28:                 endif
29:             else
30:                 if(FL of currentNode is not NULL) then
31:                     if(access latency including the FL node <= the length of the stream) then
32:                         Wait in doze mode until the FL node arrives on the air
33:                     else
34:                         return R
35:                     endif
36:                 else
37:                     return R
38:                 endif
39:             endif
40:         else
41:             if(access latency of client < the length of the stream) then
42:                 Wait until the next node arrives on the air
43:             else
44:                 return R
45:             endif
46:         endif
47:     endwhile
48: end
```

Node 17, since it has the same LPI and tag name as the query.

Wildcard queries can be classified into two types. One represents queries that have a wildcard in the middle of the location path (e.g., /mondial/country/*/name) and the other type includes queries that have a wildcard at the end of the location path (e.g., /mondial/country/city/*). In the former case, after the first answer node is retrieved, the closer link from among the CL and FL is used to find the next answer node having the same depth. The CL of the answer node is used to directly find the next answer node which has the same LPI and tag name, while the FL is

Figure 7. Examples of selective access by using indexes in the DIX

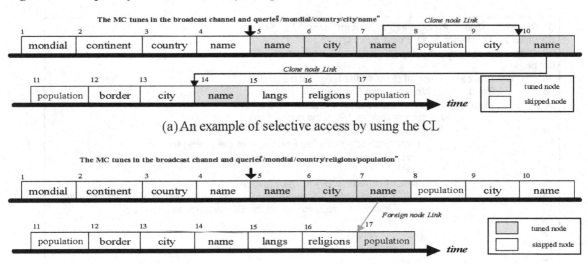

(a) An example of selective access by using the CL

(b) An example of selective access by using the FL

used to find out the next answer node having a different LPI and the same tag name (see Example 3). In the latter case, when the first answer node of the given query is found, the mobile client continues to read all its sibling nodes and then searches for the next answer node by following the CL in the parent of the previous one. By following the CL of the parent node, the mobile client can skip all irrelevant nodes having different LPIs from the given query. In the meantime, a descendant axis query can be considered as the union of a simple path query and multiple queries having a wildcard in a different location step. For example, assume that a given query is "/mondial/country//name." Since the maximum depth of the example document is 3, the result of the given

query can be obtained by calculating the union of the result of a simple query "/mondial/country/name" and a wildcard query "/mondial/country/*/name."

Example 3. Figure 8 illustrates an example of a wildcard query. Assume that a given query is "/mondial/country/*/name," where a mobile client tunes in to the broadcast channel when Node 5 is on the air. After the mobile client retrieves the first answer node, i.e., Node 7, it can skip exploring irrelevant nodes by using the CL in Node 7 because its target node (i.e., Node 10) is closer than the target of the FL in Node 7 (i.e., Node 17). In the same manner, the mobile client can skip Node 11-13 by using the CL in Node 10. Then,

Figure 8. An example of wildcard query processing

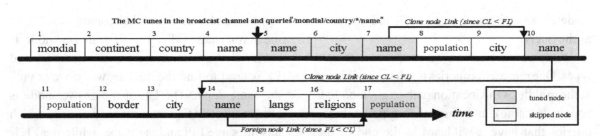

Figure 9. Non-clustered and clustered XML data stream

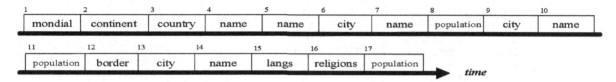

(a) Non-clustered XML data stream

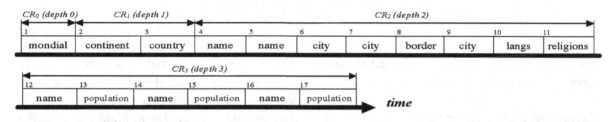

(b) Clustered XML data stream

the mobile client continues exploring the answer nodes by using the FL in Node 14.

CLUSTERING STRATEGY

Concept of Clustering

The distributed index structure proposed in the previous section can enhance the access time performance of the mobile client over the XML stream since it enables the client to start query processing within the current broadcast cycle without necessarily waiting for the next broadcast cycle. However, in a DIX node stream constructed from a general XML document in the document order, the nodes of elements with the same location path are often distributed over the entire broadcast stream. Thus, the mobile client must access a large part of a broadcast stream to retrieve the answer nodes to the given query. If the nodes of elements having the same properties are clustered in the stream, the mobile client can retrieve the desired data by accessing a limited part of the stream. This means that the mobile client

can further reduce the access and tuning times. From this observation, we propose a *clustering strategy* based on the depth of the XML elements

Definition 4. The Clustering Region (CR) is a logical section of XML data stream, which is partitioned by the depth of nodes. A Clustering Region of depth d is described as $CR_d = \{DIX_i \mid DIX_i$ is the DIX node for an element of depth d\}. □

Whereas Figure 9(a) shows a non-clustered XML data stream generated in document order by performing a depth-first traversal of the XML tree in Figure 1, Figure 9(b) presents a clustered XML data stream partitioned by CRs which are arranged in increasing order of their depths.

Example 4. Assume that the mobile client processes a query "/mondial/country/city/name." As we mentioned earlier, elements of the same tag name can appear multiple times over the entire stream. In Figure 9(a), the mobile client must explore the stream from Node 1-14 to retrieve all the answer nodes. On the contrary, in Figure 9(b), the mobile client can retrieve the desired data by

Figure 10. Extended DIX node structure

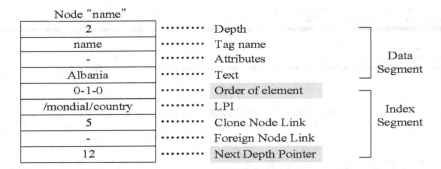

searching only CR_3 (Node 12 ~ 17) because the depth of the given query is 3.

Extended Index Structure for Clustered Stream

The order of XML elements in a clustered XML data stream is different from that of the document. In this regard, we use the Dewey ordering (Online Computer Library Center, 2007) to denote the document order of the element in each DIX node. Dewey ordering is an effective way to maintain structural information (Gou & Chirkova, 2007; Harder, Haustein, Mathis, & Wagner, 2007; Haustein & Harder, 2007). The stream generator computes the Dewey order of elements and records them in the field of *Order of element* in DIX nodes while parsing the source XML document.

Meanwhile, as shown in the proposed query processing method, a mobile client can efficiently search for desired data by exploiting the CL and FL in each DIX node. However, another problem of the DIX node stream is that when the mobile client tunes in to the stream, it must continue to receive DIX nodes until a node having the same depth as that of the query is encountered in the stream, regardless of whether the stream was clustered or not. In order to reduce this kind of tuning time overhead by skipping more irrelevant nodes, we add to the DIX node structure a new index link which points to the beginning of the next CR in the clustered DIX node stream. In other words, to help find the CR having the same depth as that of the given query in the mobile client, we add the *Next Depth Pointer* field to the DIX node structure, which stores the address of the next CR in the stream. The mobile client can efficiently move to subsequent CRs by using this information in DIX nodes. Figure 10 shows the DIX node structure extended from the previous one in Figure 3: it contains two additional fields, *Order of element* and *Next Depth Pointer*, in the index segment.

In subsection titled "XML Data Stream Generation," we described an algorithm to generate a stream of DIX nodes which are in document order. In order to cluster the DIX nodes by depth, the *endDocument()* event handler presented in Figure 5 (in Line 33~37) should be rewritten as follows:

```
33: ContentHandler.endDocument()
34: begin
35: depth = 0
36: Calculate CL, FL, and Next Depth
Pointer of DN
37: while(Q is not empty)
38:     while(the end of Q is not de-
tected)
39:             Get the top entry
DN in Q
40:             if(depth of DN equals
```

Figure 11. Query processing over clustered XML data stream

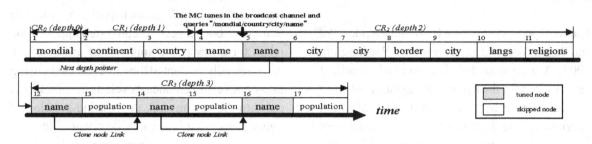

depth)

```
41:                Flush current DN
in Q into the XML data stream DS
42:        else
43:                Move to the next
entry DN in Q
44:        endif
45:    endwhile
46:    depth = depth + 1
47: endwhile
48: end
```

Query Processing over clustered XML data stream

Since each node of the clustered XML data stream has a Next Depth Pointer, the mobile client can easily find a target CR that has the same depth as that of the query. In order to implement this, the following segment of algorithm must be added between Line 6 and 7 of the original query processing algorithm in Figure 6. The clustering approach also allows query processing to finish immediately after the investigation of the target CR.

```
07: if(depth of currentNode != depth
of the query)
08:    Read Next Depth Pointer of
currentNode
09:    Move to the next CR of cur-
rentNode
10: endif
```

Example 5. Figure 11 shows the query processing steps over the clustered XML data stream. Assume that the mobile client tunes in to the broadcast channel when Node 5 is on the air, and the query specified as "/mondial/country/city/name." Since the depth of the query is 3, nodes in CR_2 (i.e., nodes of depth 2) cannot be the result of the query. Thus, the mobile client skips the irrelevant nodes from Node 6-11, by using the Next Depth Pointer of Node 5. Then the mobile client downloads Node 12 (i.e., the first node of CR_3). From the LPI and tag name of Node 12, the mobile client can identify that Node 12 satisfies the given query, and thus, the mobile client adds it to the result list. Also, from the CL of Node 12, the mobile client retrieves the next desired data, Node 14. Finally, the mobile client retrieves the last desired data, Node 16, by using the CL of Node 14.

PERFORMANCE EVALUATION

In this section, we present the results of our experiments to evaluate the performance of the proposed scheme. We have performed the experiments using XPath queries with various features and compared the performance of our approach with the previous S-node stream organization scheme (Park *et al.*, 2005) and the path summary technique (Park *et al.*, 2006).

Experiment Setting

For the experiments we used two datasets, *mondial* and *SigmodRecord* (University of Washington, 2007). We generated their associated broadcast data streams for the datasets using the considered approaches and then evaluated six types of XPath queries over the streams. Query type 1 and 2 were used for testing simple XPath queries. Character and attribute condition predicates were tested by using query type 3 and 4, respectively. Query type 5 was used for testing a wildcard condition. Finally, queries with a descendant axis were tested by using query type 6. The sizes of the datasets and the example test queries on each dataset are shown in Table 1.

Among the experimental approaches, the path summary technique ignores the order of XML elements and, furthermore, does not support various XPath features such as descendant axes and predicate conditions. For that reason, the performance experiment on the path summary technique was conducted only for the simple XPath queries (i.e., query type 1 and 2).

We assumed that stream data are broadcast and accessed in units of a fixed size bucket containing multiple DIX nodes and thus we measured access and tuning times in processing user queries by the number of buckets. Without loss of generality, the number of buckets can be converted into the *time* taken for query processing. In the experiments, we repeatedly evaluated the same test query using every bucket in a broadcast cycle as the first access point to the stream, i.e., the starting position of query processing in the mobile client. The average access and tuning times measured for each test query are presented in the following figures that show the results of the experimental results.

In order to measure the effect of the bucket size, we have experimented with three different bucket sizes: 128, 256, and 512 bytes. Since the results are similar irrespective of the bucket size, we present only the results of the 256 bytes bucket for brevity of presentation.

The experimental results show that clustered DIX outperforms the previous methods in most cases. The reduction in the access time can be explained by the following observations. 1) Query processing in S-node and Path Summary is performed by following the location paths of the elements in the document. Therefore, a mobile client which tunes in to the middle of the broadcast stream must wait until the next broadcast cycle starts. This waiting time increases the access time by an

Table 1. Datasets and test XPath queries

Dataset	Size (Bytes)		Test Query
mondial (ver. 3.0)	1,784,825	M1	/mondial/country/province/city/name
		M2	/mondial/organizations
		M3	/mondial/country/name[text()="Finland"]
		M4	/mondial/country/province[@name="Tyrol"]
		M5	/mondial/country/*/name
		M6	/mondial/country//city
SigmodRecord	478,416	S1	/SigmodRecord/issue/articles/article
		S2	/SigmodRecord/issue/articles/article/title
		S3	/SigmodRecord/issue/articles/article/author[text()="Nita Goyal"]
		S4	/SigmodRecord/issue/articles/article/author[@position="00"]
		S5	/SigmodRecord/issue/articles/*/title
		S6	/SigmodRecord/issue/articles//author

average of half a broadcast cycle. On the contrary, the proposed scheme starts query processing as soon as the mobile client tunes in to the broadcast channel, since each DIX node contains LPI. So, the proposed method outperforms the S-node approach in terms of the access time, though its stream size is bigger than the S-node data stream. 2) The previous methods must search the entire stream to find the desired data dispersed over the stream. The clustered DIX, on the contrary, effectively restricts the search range by using the node clustering strategy. Thus, the access time can be reduced if a mobile client tunes in to the broadcast channel before a target CR containing the desired data is broadcast.

EXPERIMENTAL RESULTS

In this section, we present the experimental results. Figure 12 shows the sizes of the XML data streams generated by the six methods: *Path Summary*, *SL*, *SD*, *SP*, *DIX*, and *clustered DIX*, where the SL, SD, and SP methods are from the S-node approach. Since Path Summary eliminates redundant tags of the XML document, the size of

the result XML stream is smaller than the others. Particularly, the *SigmodRecord* document has a large number of elements, most of which do not contain attributes or text contents. Therefore, the result data stream generated by Path Summary is significantly smaller. In the meantime, the XML data streams generated by our methods contain various indices representing structural information of XML data and hence its stream size is relatively larger. In particular, since the clustered DIX data stream has two additional index fields, *Order of Element* and *Next Depth Pointer*, in the nodes, its size is slightly larger than that of the non-clustered DIX data stream.

Figure 13 shows the access time evaluation results. As shown in the figure, the access time of DIX is reduced by an average of 29.3%, 22.7%, and 22.6%, respectively, compared to SL, SD, and SP. DIX has achieved a smaller access time than S-node because DIX starts query processing as soon as the mobile client tunes in to the broadcast channel. In addition, DIX guarantees that query processing is completed within a broadcast cycle in the worst case. In comparison with Path Summary, DIX shows similar access time performance for the M1 and M2 queries over the *mon-*

Figure 12. Comparison of stream sizes

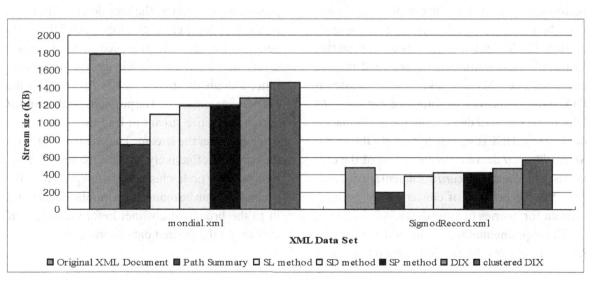

Figure 13. Access time comparison

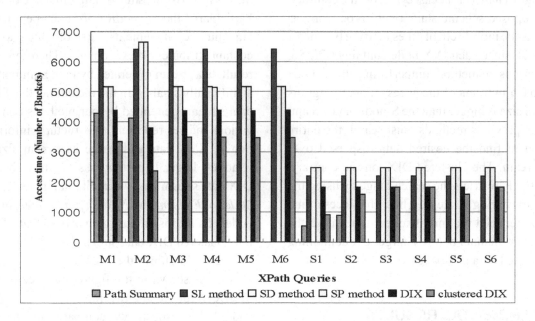

dial dataset. For the queries S1 and S2, however, the access time performance of DIX is worse than Path Summary, since the size of the Path Summary data stream is significantly smaller. In the meantime, the access time performance of clustered DIX is further improved than DIX. The access time of clustered DIX is reduced by an average of 43.5%, 38.3%, and 38.2%, respectively, compared to SL, SD, and SP. Particularly, in the case of M2, clustered DIX shows the best performance because the depth of M2 is lower than the other queries. So, query processing of clustered DIX can terminate earlier. For queries with predicate conditions, wildcards, and descendant axes (i.e., M3~M6 and S3~S6), clustered DIX shows improved performance compared to DIX in the *mondial* dataset, but the performance of clustered DIX is similar to that of DIX in the *SigmodRecord* dataset, because most of the elements in the *SigmodRecord* document are of depth 3~5. So, the benefits of clustering are not significant for queries of large depth.

The experimental results show that clustered DIX outperforms the previous methods in most

cases. The reduction in the access time can be explained by the following observations. 1) Query processing in S-node and Path Summary is performed by following the location paths of the elements in the document. Therefore, a mobile client which tunes in to the middle of the broadcast stream must wait until the next broadcast cycle starts. This waiting time increases the access time by an average of half a broadcast cycle. On the contrary, the proposed scheme starts query processing as soon as the mobile client tunes in to the broadcast channel, since each DIX node contains LPI. So, the proposed method outperforms the S-node approach in terms of the access time, though its stream size is bigger than the S-node data stream. 2) The previous methods must search the entire stream to find the desired data dispersed over the stream. The clustered DIX, on the contrary, effectively restricts the search range by using the node clustering strategy. Thus, the access time can be reduced if a mobile client tunes in to the broadcast channel before a target CR containing the desired data is broadcast.

Figure 14. Tuning time comparison

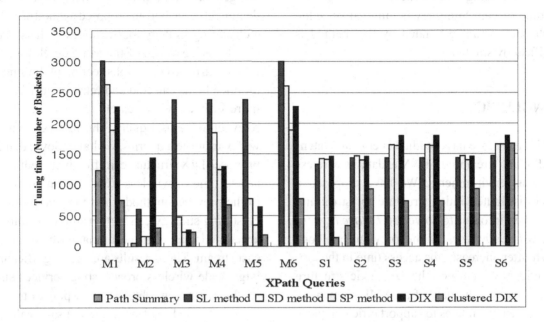

Figure 14 shows the tuning time evaluation results. The tuning time of DIX is reduced by 19.6% compared to SL. However, it is increased by 0.8% and 20.3% compared to SD and SP, respectively because DIX continuously accesses the data stream until the first node having the same depth as that of the query is delivered on the air. This overhead may result in deterioration of the tuning time performance of the proposed method. In the experiments with the query M2, for example, since the "organization" elements are located in the last part of the document, the mobile client must access numerous elements having the same depth as the query until an "organization" element is broadcast.

In the meantime, the tuning time of clustered DIX is reduced by an average of 63.9%, 53.8%, and 46.0%, respectively, compared to SL, SD, and SP. The reason can be explained as follows: 1) The nodes contained in the clustered DIX have Next Depth Pointers, and thus, the tuning time required to find a node having the same depth as that of the query can be minimized. 2) Clustered DIX can reduce the tuning time required to search

the location path 3) Since the DIX nodes having the same depth are clustered in the stream, the mobile client can retrieve much more answer nodes per bucket read.

As shown in the figure, except for M2 and S6, the tuning time performance of clustered DIX is always better than S-node because clustered DIX effectively skips the irrelevant nodes by using the FL and CL. For M2, the tuning time of clustered DIX is slightly larger than SD and SP because the "organization" elements appear at the end of the document, and thus, clustered DIX continuously downloads the CR_l nodes until an "organization" element is broadcast. SD and SP, on the contrary, find "organization" elements more efficiently by using different tag links. For S6, clustered DIX is slightly worse than the S-node approach because it must access almost all the buckets having a depth higher than 2. In comparison with Path Summary, clustered DIX outperforms Path Summary for M1. For M2 and S1, however, the tuning time of the Path Summary method is extremely small since the target elements do not contain any text content (i.e., query processing can be performed by only accessing index nodes). For S2, the tuning time of Path Summary is minimal since the result data stream generated by the method is significantly smaller.

CONCLUSION

In this article, we have studied energy and latency-efficient streaming of XML data in wireless broadcast environments. We have proposed a novel distributed index structure for streaming XML data in order to solve the *Delayed Query Processing Problem* of the previous methods which often increases the access time in the mobile client. We defined the *DIX* node structure which contains the data of an XML element as well as various indices to support efficient query processing. We also provided stream generation and query processing algorithms for the proposed stream organization. Since the DIX node contains the *Location Path Information*, the mobile client can start query processing without waiting for the document root element in the next broadcast cycle. In addition, it can skip irrelevant nodes by using the *Clone node Link* and *Foreign node Link* contained in each node. Moreover, we have proposed a *clustering strategy* for DIX nodes to enhance access and tuning time performances.

Our proposed method is fundamentally different to the previous wireless XML broadcasting schemes. *Firstly*, to support energy-efficient processing of user queries, our approach provides a fully distributed index structure in which each DIX node has a location path encoded as a bit string, as well as two kinds of link addresses to various relevant nodes of the same depth in the stream. The previous XML broadcasting methods are based on tree-structured indices, hence mobile clients must wait until the root data of the XML document is broadcast. On the contrary, the index components in our scheme are distributed over all the nodes in the stream, and thus mobile clients can start query processing as soon as it tunes in to the broadcast channel. *Secondly*, the previous methods generate and broadcast XML data streams in document order, but our proposed method provides a clustering strategy for the nodes in the stream. By clustering nodes of the same depth together into a restricted continuous section of the stream, mobile clients can find and retrieve desired data more efficiently by searching only the cluster relevant to the user query. Through experiments with various test queries, we have shown that the proposed DIX structure can effectively reduce the access time of wireless XML stream compared to the previous methods, and that the proposed clustering strategy can further improve both the access and tuning time performances of the broadcast stream. Those results are very significant in large-scale wireless broadcasting services since all the clients can obtain fast responses to their queries on the broadcast data, and save valuable energy of their mobile devices.

Currently, XML data broadcasting is supported in many applications over wireless digital broadcast systems, such as TPEG and EPG services. In such applications, not only the tuning time but also the access time is an important criterion to measure the efficiency of query processing since broadcast data changes moment-by-moment. Unlike the previous XML broadcasting methods, our method minimizes the access time and thus can achieve quick response time in the mobile clients to search the updated data. For example, tpegML is used to deliver TPEG applications via wireless digital broadcast bearers such as ARIB (Association of Radio Industries and Businesses), DVB, and T-DMB, which have layered structures and carousel delivery mechanisms. The TPEG-RTM (Road Traffic Message) provides information on traffic accidents, road repairs, weather, and street demonstrations, which affects the speed of vehicles. Since these types of information change rapidly and continuously, our proposed method can be exploited to provide more efficient and qualified services by eliminating the delayed query processing that is often associated with the existing approaches and satisfying users' information need quickly.

In the future, we plan to investigate several problems which were not fully addressed in this article. Firstly, we will propose an optimal clustering strategy considering various XML features such as the depth, tag name, location path, attributes, and content of XML elements. Secondly, we will leverage the benefits of a filtering technique within clustering regions. This could improve the access (i.e., tuning) time performance further. Thirdly, packet losses and network failures, which have not been addressed in the previous XML data broadcasting approaches, should be considered in the wireless broadcast environments. Finally, we will extend our query processing algorithm to support more complex XML queries including twig queries.

ACKNOWLEDGMENT

This work was supported by the Korea Science and Engineering Foundation (KOSEF) grant funded by the Korea government (No. R01-2008-000-20564-0).

REFERENCES

W3C Recommendation. (2006). *Extensible Markup Language (XML) 1.0* (4th ed.). Retrieved from http://www.w3.org/XML

Acharya, S., Alonso, S., Franklin, M. J., & Zdonik, S. B. (1995). Broadcast Disks: Data Management for Asymmetric Communication. In *Proceedings of the ACM SIGMOD Conference* (pp. 199-210).

Arion, A., Bonifati, A., Manolescu, I., & Pugliese, A. (2007). XqueC: A Query-Concious Compressed XML Database. *ACM Transactions on Internet Technology, 7*(2). doi:10.1145/1239971.1239974

Avila-Campillo, I., Green, T. J., Gupta, A., Onizuka, M., Raven, D., & Suciu, D. (2002). *XMLTK: An XML Toolkit for Scalable XML Stream Processing*. Paper presented at PLANX.

Barton, C., Charles, P., Goyal, D., Raghavachari, M., Fontoura, M., & Josifovski, V. (2003). Streaming Xpath Processing with Forward and Backward Axes. In *Proceedings of the International Conference on Data Engineering* (pp. 455-466).

Candan, K. S., Hsiung, W.-P., Chen, S., Tatemura, J., & Agrawal, D. (2006). *AFilter: Adaptable XML Filtering with Prefix-Caching and Suffix-Clustering*. In Paper presented at the VLDB Conference.

Chan, C.-Y., Felber, P., Garofalakis, M., & Rastogi, R. (2002). *Efficient Filtering of XML Documents with XPath Expressions*. Paper presented at the International Conference on Data Engineering.

Chen, M. S., Wu, K. L., & Yu, P. S. (2003). Optimizing Index Allocation for Sequential Data Broadcasting in Wireless Mobile Computing. *IEEE Transactions on Knowledge and Data Engineering, 15*(1), 161–173. doi:10.1109/TKDE.2003.1161588

Choi, R. H., & Wong, R. K. (2009). Efficient Filtering of Branch Queries for High-Performance XML Data Services. *Journal of Database Management, 20*(2), 58–83.

Chung, Y. D., & Kim, M. H. (2000). An Index Replication Scheme for Wireless Data Broadcasting. *Journal of Systems and Software, 51*(3), 191–199. doi:10.1016/S0164-1212(99)00123-5

Clark, J., & Derose, S. (1999). XML Path Language (XPath), Version 1.0. *W3C Recommendation*. Retrieved from http://www.w3c.org/TR/XPath

Cowan, J., & Tobin, R. (2004). XML Information Set. *W3C Recommendation*. Retrieved from Web: http://www.w3.org/TR/2001/ CR-xml-infoset-20010514/

Data Repository, X. M. L. (2007). Retrieved from the World Wide Web: http://www.cs.washington.edu/ research /xmldatasets

Diao, Y., Altinel, M., Franklin, M., Zhang, H., & Fischer, P. (2003). Path Sharing and Predicate Evaluation for High-Performance XML Filtering. *ACM Transactions on Database Systems, 28*(4), 467–516. doi:10.1145/958942.958947

DVB Document A081. (2004). *Digital Video Broadcasting (DVB) Transmission System for Handheld Terminals DVB-H.*

Ericson, J., & Siau, K. (2008). Web Services, Service-Oriented Computing, and Service-Oriented Architecture: Separating Hype from Reality. *Journal of Database Management, 19*(3), 42–54.

Fong, J., & Wong, H. K. (2004). XTOPO: An XML-Based Topology for Information Highway on the Internet. *Journal of Database Management, 15*(3), 18–44.

Gou, G., & Chirkova, R. (2007). Efficiently querying large XML data repositories: A survey. *IEEE Transactions on Knowledge and Data Engineering, 19*(10). doi:10.1109/TKDE.2007.1060

Gupta, A. K., & Suciu, D. (2003). *Stream Processing of XPath Queries with Predicates.* Paper presented at the ACM SIGMOD Conference.

Han, W.-S., Jiang, H., Ho, H., & Li, Q. (2008). StreamTX: Extracting Tuples from Streaming XML Data. In *Proceedings of the VLDB Endowment* (pp. 289-300).

Harder, T., Haustein, M., Mathis, C., & Wagner, M. (2007). Node labeling schemes for dynamic XML documents reconsidered. *Data & Knowledge Engineering, 60*(1), 126–149. doi:10.1016/j.datak.2005.11.008

Haustein, M., & Harder, T. (2007). An efficient infrastructure for native transactional XML processing. *Data & Knowledge Engineering, 61*(3), 500–523. doi:10.1016/j.datak.2006.06.015

Imielinski, T., & Badrinath, B. R. (1993). Data Management for Mobile Computing. *SIGMOD Record, 22*(1), 34–39. doi:10.1145/156883.156888

Imielinski, T., Viswanathan, S., & Badrinath, B. R. (1994). Energy Efficient Indexing on Air. In *Proceedings of the ACM SIGMOD Conference* (pp. 25-36).

Imielinski, T., Viswanathan, S., & Badrinath, B. R. (1997). Data on Air: Organization and Access. *IEEE Transactions on Knowledge and Data Engineering, 9*(3), 353–372. doi:10.1109/69.599926

Josifovski, V., Fontoura, M., & Barta, A. (2004). Querying XML Streams. *The VLDB Journal, 14*(2), 197–210. doi:10.1007/s00778-004-0123-7

Kaushik, R., Shenoy, P., Bohannon, P., & Gudes, E. (2002). Exploiting Local Similarity for Indexing of Paths in Graph-Structured Data. In *Proceedings of International Conference on Data Engineering* (pp. 129-140).

Koch, C., Scherzinger, S., & Schmidt, M. (2007). The GCX System: Dynamic Buffer Minimization in Streaming Xquery Evaluation. In *Proceedings of the VLDB Conference* (pp. 1378-1381).

Lam, W. Y., Ng, W., Wood, P. T., & Levene, M. (2003). *XCQ: XML Compression and Querying System.* Paper presented at the International WWW Conference.

Liefke, H., & Suciu, D. (2000). XMill: An Efficient Compressor for XML Data. In *Proceedings of the ACM SIGMOD Conference* (pp. 153-164).

Ludascher, B., Mukhopadhyay, P., & Papakonstantinou, Y. (2002). A Transducer-based XML Query Processor. In *Proceedings of the VLDB Conference* (pp. 227-238)

Min, J.-K., Park, M.-J., & Chung, C.-W. (2003). XPRESS: A Queriable Compression for XML Data. In *Proceedings of the ACM SIGMOD Conference* (pp. 122-133).

Moro, M., Bakalov, P., & Tsotras, V. J. (2007). Early Profile Pruning on XML-aware Publish-Subscribe Systems. In *Proceedings of the VLDB Endowment* (pp. 866-877).

Nestorov, S., Ullman, J., Weiner, J., & Chawathe, S. (1997). Representative Object: Concise Representations of Semi-structured, Hierarchical Data. In *Proceedings of the International Conference on Data Engineering* (pp. 79-90).

Olteanu, D. (2007). SPEX: Streamed and Progressive Evaluation of XPath. *IEEE Transactions on Knowledge and Data Engineering, 19*(7), 934–949. doi:10.1109/TKDE.2007.1063

Online Computer Library Center. (2007). *Introduction to the Dewey Decimal Classification*. Retrieved from http://www.oclc.org/dewey/about

Park, C.-S., Kim, C. S., & Chung, Y. D. (2005). Efficient Stream Organization for Wireless Broadcasting of XML Data. In *Proceedings of the Asian Computing Science Conference* (pp. 223-235).

Park, S. H., Choi, J. H., & Lee, S. (2006). An Effective, Efficient XML Data Broadcasting Method in Mobile Wireless Network. In *Proceedings of the DEXA Conference* (pp. 358-367).

Peng, F., & Chawathe, S. S. (2003). XPath Queries on Streaming Data. In *Proceedings of the ACM SIGMOD Conference* (pp. 431-442).

Revest, R. L. (1992). *The MD5 Message Digest Algorithm* (RFC 1321). IETF.

SAX. (2004). *Simple API for XML*. Retrieved from http://www.saxproject.org/

Shiu, H., & Fong, J. (2009). Reverse Engineering from an XML Document into an Extended DTD Graph. *Journal of Database Management, 20*(2), 38–57.

Silvasti, P., Sippu, S., & Soisalon-Soininen, E. (2009). Schema-Conscious Filtering of XML Documents. In *Proceedings of the International Conference on Extending Database Technology* (pp. 970-981).

Sundaresan, N., & Moussa, R. (2001). Algorithm and Programming Models for Efficient Representation of XML for Internet Application. In *Proceedings of the international WWW Conference* (pp. 366-375).

Tolani, P. M., & Haritsa, J. R. (2002). *XGRIND: A Query-Friendly XML Compressor*. Paper presented at the International Conference on Data Engineering.

Transport Protocol Experts Group. (2006). *Traveller Information Services Association*. Retrieved from http://www.tpeg.org/

University of Washington. (2007). *XML Data Repository*. Retrieved from http://www.cs.washington.edu/ research/xmldatasets

Wong, E. Y. C., Chan, A., & Leong, H. (2004). Xstream: A Middleware for Streaming XML Contents over Wireless Environments. *IEEE Transactions on Software Engineering, 30*(12), 918–935. doi:10.1109/TSE.2004.108

This work was previously published in International Journal of Database Management, Volume 21, Issue 1, edited by Keng Siau, pp. 58-79, copyright 2010 by IGI Publishing (an imprint of IGI Global).

Chapter 4
Toward a Unified Model of Information Systems Development Success

Keng Siau
University of Nebraska-Lincoln, USA

Yoanna Long
Colorado State University Pueblo, USA

Min Ling
University of Nebraska-Lincoln, USA

ABSTRACT

Information systems development (ISD) is a complex process involving interconnected resources, stake holders, and outcomes. Understanding factors contributing to ISD success has attracted keen interest from both researchers and practitioners, and many research studies have been published in this area. However, most studies focus on one or two factors affecting ISD success. A holistic view of factors impacting ISD success is missing. This paper synthesizes past research on the topic and proposes a unified model on ISD success through a systematic and comprehensive literature review. The unified model highlights that ISD is a complex and interactive process involving individual, team, and organization factors, as well as ISD methodology. These factors impact the ISD process as well as its success.

1. INTRODUCTION

Information systems development (ISD) is a complex process involving interconnected resources, stake holders, and outcomes. An ISD project can be time consuming and expensive to undertake. A better understanding of ISD and the factors

DOI: 10.4018/978-1-61350-471-0.ch004

impacting ISD success is crucial for both practitioners and researchers to ensure the success of ISD projects. Understanding ISD success requires the recognition of the: (a) ISD process, (b) ISD product (outcome), (c) ISD participants, (d) ISD groups, (e) ISD organizational environment, (f) ISD methodology, and (g) interaction between these entities. Due to the intricate and interactive nature of the ISD, past studies usually focused on one or two factors, such as individual personality (e.g., Kaiser & Bostrom, 1982), task complexity (e.g., McKeen *et al.*, 1994), and top management support (e.g., Etton *et al.*, 2000; Sauer, 1993). Although much research has been done, a holistic view of the factors contributing to ISD success is missing. This research synthesizes existing literature on ISD and proposes a unified model depicting factors identified in the literature that affects ISD success.

In this research, we developed an integrated and comprehensive unified model for ISD success. The unified model involves three levels of input variables—individual, team, and organization. The ISD process is affected by the ISD methodology. The output variable is ISD success.

The paper is organized as follows. First, a systematic literature review of factors impacting ISD performance is discussed. Based on the syntheses of the literature review, the paper proposes a unified model on ISD success. Finally, the paper concludes with a discussion on the implications of the unified model on research and practice, and suggests future research directions.

2. LITERATURE REVIEW

This section first introduces the Input-Process-Output model, which forms the foundation of the unified model. The section reviews literature on input factors from three levels (i.e., individual, team, and organizational factors), process factors (i.e., knowledge sharing, innovation, and systems development methodology), and output factors (i.e., systems usage and user satisfaction).

2.1. Input-Process-Output Model

The classic Input-Process-Output model (Hackman, 1987; McGrath, 1984) provides a systematic way to view general working processes. The Input-Process-Output model presents the basic idea that inputs lead to processes that, in turn,

lead to outcomes. This classic framework has been widely used in the IS/IT area and provides the conceptual underpinnings to develop the unified model on ISD success in this research.

Information systems development (ISD) is a complex, adaptive, and dynamic process. Information Systems (IS) literature has long studied factors impacting ISD success. However, different researchers address different research issues focusing on different factors. There is a need to provide a holistic view of the factors impacting ISD success and to provide a unified model to guide future research.

To investigate the research question of ISD success in a systematic way, we shall follow the conceptual framework of the Input-Process-Output model, and develop a unified ISD success model by identifying three sets of factors associated with input, process, and output.

2.2. Input Variables

Three levels of factors—individual, team, and organization—emerged from the literature review.

2.2.1. Individual Factors

A number of individual characteristics such as personality, cognitive style, problem-solving style, skills, experience, expectations, as well as user participation and involvement, have been suggested in the literature as factors affecting the success of ISD. The following provides a discussion on these factors:

Personality

Personality type theory is based on the work of Jung (1923). According to personality type theory, people who possess more accepting personalities are more willing to consider different perspectives. Some people are risk-averse while others are stimulated by taking risks. Still others are motivated by the challenge of an unsolved problem, while others are easily overwhelmed and slip into inaction. Some people have personalities that make them natural leaders while others are more comfortable as followers. Certain people are natural communicators while others find it very difficult to express themselves. Each personality type, however, can act as a positive contribution toward the overall effectiveness of the team. Therefore, a balance of personality types should be sought. Individuals are predisposed to one of the four preference alternatives in their behavior (Bradley & Hebert, 1997):

A. How a person is energized – designated by extroverts versus introverts

B. What information a person perceives – designated by sensing versus intuition

C. How a person decides – thinking versus feeling, and

D. The lifestyle a person adopts – judging versus perceiving.

Individuals can adopt other personality types if they are aware of personality-type differences and make a conscious effort to change. However, these individuals need to be monitored carefully (Bradley & Hebert, 1997).

Several studies have used Jung's typology (1968) to evaluate the personality types represented in project teams. For example, Kaiser and Bostrom (1982) examined the characteristics of individuals involved in systems development and suggested that these characteristics impact the way IS designers perceive the organization, organizational members, and the functioning of an IS system. They found that personality styles of the systems design team affect the nature and direction of group interaction process and systems development. Further, individuals exhibiting the personality type representing "feeling" were missing from teams that were involved in project failure. In summary, this research has suggested that teams exhibiting the full range of personality characteristics were associated with project success to a greater extent than when one or more

of the personality types were missing from the team. Trimmer *et al.* (2002) examined the impact of personality diversity on different forms of conflict in the ISD team process. Bradley *et al.* (1997) highlighted the impact of personality type on team productivity and proposed a model that could be used to analyze the personality-type composition of an IS development team.

Cognitive Style

The effective design and implementation of an information system are complex undertakings, which require skillful management to anticipate the possible effects of different psychological dispositions on task performance. Cognitive styles have been derived from Jung's (1923) theory of psychological types. Jung contended that people have distinctive differences in the way they gather and process data. Some people take in information by sensing, stressing facts and details (what is in actuality), and others by intuition, stressing possibilities (what might be) as well as environmental and contextual factors.

Cognitive styles are defined as characteristic modes of functioning that people show throughout their perceptive and intellectual activities in a highly consistent and pervasive way (Witkin, 1973). Benbasat and Taylor (1978) explored the nature of cognitive styles and the effects of different cognitive styles on information systems usage and design. Cognitive style perceptions are suggested as possible explanations for the communication barrier that is often found between system specialists and the users (Zmud, 1979). In his research, Zmud (1979) demonstrated that (a) perceptual differences could be observed between subjects with contrasting educational backgrounds, (b) no apparent relationship exists between cognitive style perceptions and cognitive behaviors, and (c) consistent differences were shown in the manner in which subjects perceive the analytic (more potent) and heuristic (less potent) cognitive styles.

Bariff and Lusk (1977) proposed that the measurement and evaluation of the users' cognitive styles and related personality traits provide an effective means to attain successful IS modifications. They suggested that two aspects of cognitive and personality traits are relevant to user adaptive behavior: cognitive style and implementation apprehension. Spence *et al.* (1997) used inconclusiveness of cognitive style to explain human interaction with computer systems, and used the cognitive process to explain differences in human performances across multiple tasks.

Problem-Solving Style

Problem solving occurs when individuals in conflict try to satisfy the concerns of all parties (Barkin & Hartwick, 1994). In IS development, Newman and Sabherwal (1989) defined problem solving as a cooperative process between users and IS professionals who are working together towards an information system that meets organizational goals. They also noted that such behaviors are more likely to occur in cases where users perceive the project as a benefit to their work. Newman and Sabherwal (1989) developed a process model to portray the dynamics of ISD using problem-solving style.

Skills

White and Leifer (1986) examined how a mixture of technical and process skills of individuals impacts the success of the systems design process. In their research, technical skills refer to the "what" aspect of task accomplishment, which include possessing technical knowledge, being analytical, and understanding the business. Process skills, on the other hand, refer to the "how" aspect of task accomplishment, the manner in which people proceed to deal with their tasks. While technical skills are often the most obvious, process skills are part of the repertoire of skills that team members should also acquire, especially when they

need to interact with users outside teams. White and Leifer (1986) found that the top five skills perceived as critical factors impacting systems success across the overall systems design phases are: business knowledge, good communication skills, technical expertise, analytic skills, and good organizational skills.

Henry *et al.* (1973) surveyed 981 managers, users, and systems analysts from fourteen firms regarding the usefulness of a set of 111 skills in seven skill categories, *performance skills, people skills, systems skills, organizational skills, computer skills, society skills, and model skills.*

In IS development teams, skill is believed to be directly related to increased team performance (Rash & Tosi, 1992). Boehm (1987) stressed the importance of selecting the most highly skilled people to work on a particular project, since the productivity difference between exceptional performers and average performers is significant. Guinan *et al.* (1998) suggested that group processes were important predictors of team performance in requirement determination, and in addition, skills have had a major influence on group processes and team performance. Thompson (1999) suggested that inadequate team member skills and means of performing work led to dysfunctions and poor team outcomes. Oz and Sosik (2000) found that the element of having inadequate skills was one of the factors which contributed to the failure of information systems development projects.

The complexity of IS development projects requires skills and methods that enhance team members' awareness of hidden problems facing the project (Keil & Robey, 1999). Without such skills and work procedures, it is unlikely that project management practices such as scheduling and budgeting, can be completed successfully.

Experience

Experience entails rehearsal of known judgment strategies, generation of new strategies in the face of new situations, general learning by trial and error, and an increasing awareness and familiarity with the types of domain problems and their structures (Schank, 1982). Hardgrave *et al.* (1999) found that a developer's experience with prototyping is one of the variables that affects system success. Also, a user's experience with prototyping should be considered when choosing a prototyping strategy, because users who are not familiar with prototyping often have unrealistic expectations which can be translated into dissatisfaction with developers and can lead to failure of the final systems (Hardgrave *et al.*, 1999). Schenk *et al.* (1998) provided insight into similarities and differences in how novice and expert systems analysts approach the requirements analysis task. The results suggest that the major differences between a novice and an expert systems analyst's approach to requirements analysis lie in the areas of domain-specific knowledge (Siau *et al.* 1997), problem structuring, hypothesis management, goal setting and strategy use. Senn (1987) found that previous experience with computer systems influenced user satisfaction.

Expectation

Two primary components of expectation include future time expectation and degree of uncertainty (Szajna & Scamell, 1993). A user's expectation of an information system is proposed as a set of beliefs associated with the eventual performance of the IS and his/her experience using the system (Szajna & Scamell, 1993). User expectations are positioned between pre-implementation factors (e.g., user involvement, management support, and user training) and indicators of IS success (Sanders, 1984). Aronson and Carlsmith (1962) suggested that performance on a task is influenced by expectations. DeSanctis (1983) measured a user's expectation and found it to be related to systems use. In addition, Rushinek and Rushinek (1986) found that user expectations exhibit a strong association with overall satisfaction.

User expectations concerning the systems benefit are associated with user satisfaction (Hirschheim & Newman, 1988). An end-user's high expectations for the systems are positively correlated with high user satisfaction (Lawrence & Low, 1993). In studies of electronic messaging systems, expectations about the outcomes of electronic messaging systems were found to endure and influence later evaluations of that medium (e.g., Rice *et al.*, 1990). Ginzberg (1981) found that the realism of user expectations: (a) was significantly correlated with user attitudes and the usage of information systems and (b) explained the success or failure of an information system better than several other pre-implementation factors.

The dynamic nature of the systems development process can benefit from an awareness of user expectations. Assessing expectations at different stages of the process enables developers to diagnose and deal with problem areas before they become ingrained in the systems (Szajna & Scamell, 1993).

User Participation and User Involvement

The terms user participation and user involvement have been used interchangeably in MIS literature. User participation has been widely touted by the MIS community as a means to improve user satisfaction within systems development. Barki and Hartwick (1994) suggested that the term user participation refer to "the various design related behaviors and activities that the target users or their representatives perform during the system development process" and the term user involvement refer to "a subjective psychological state of the individual and defined as the importance and personal relevance that users attach either to a given system or to MIS in general".

The importance of user participation in the systems development process has been widely recognized in the literature (Ives & Olson, 1984; Kappelman & McLean, 1991). For example, researchers stress that decision support systems (DSS) development requires a high level of user involvement (Vitalari, 1985). Alter (1978), Gallagher (1974), Guthrie (1974), and Swanson (1974) found positive relationships between user involvement and system success. Tait and Vessey (1988) studied factors affecting user involvement and the role of user involvement on success of systems implementation. Mckeen and Guimaraes (1997) demonstrated that increased user participation improves a user's satisfaction with systems. Mckeen *et al.* (1994) analyzed 151 independent systems development projects in eight different organizations and concluded that user participation has a direct relationship with user satisfaction. Their results help explain the relationship between user participation and user satisfaction by suggesting the nature of the relationship under different sets of conditions. The implications are relevant to systems developers and to academicians seeking to explain how, when, why, and where user participation is needed.

2.2.2. Team Factors

Factors at the team level such as decision making, resource, task and system complexity, conflict, and trust are found to influence ISD processes, which in turn affect ISD success.

DECISION MAKING

Decision making is required throughout the ISD. At the beginning of a project, team leaders should establish the system's goals. During the development procedure, the decision to continue or abandon a troubled project is another dilemma. These decisions are no doubt closely related to the failure or success of an ISD project.

Abdel-Hamid *et al.* (1999) studied the association between goals and project actions. Through a role-playing project simulation game (in which participants were asked to play team leaders with different goal settings), the researchers inves-

tigated the impact of different goal settings (in this case, cost/schedule and quality/schedule) on decision-making behavior, resource allocations, and project performance. The research result shows that cost/schedule leads to lower cost, while quality/schedule leads to higher quality. The findings suggest that with a given project goal, team managers have the ability to make planning and resource allocations in order to meet their goal.

Other researchers (Keil, 1995; Keil *et al.*, 2000) addressed the decision-making process during the systems development process. They investigated factors that influence the manager's decision on the escalation of a project. Keil (1995) employed a case study to explore IT project escalation. He found that escalation is promoted by combined factors including project (referring to cost/benefit, difficulty, and expected duration related to a project), psychology (referring to psychological factors impacting a manager's tendency to continue a project), social (referring to competitive rivalry, need for external justification, and norms of consistency), and organization (referring to structural and political environment).

Keil *et al.* (2000) further studied the factors impacting the managerial decision of continuing or abandoning a project. Based on the sunk-cost and risk-taking theory, the researchers conducted a cross-cultural laboratory experiments in three countries. They found that the level of sunk-cost and decision-makers' risk-perception significantly contribute to their tendency to continue a project. Moreover, the risk propensity (referring to the tendency to take risky actions) is inversely related to the risk perception. This inverse relationship is significantly stronger in Singapore than in two other countries (i.e., Finland and Netherlands). The researchers hypothesized that behind decision making, cultural factors also play an essential role in influencing a decision-maker's behavior.

In summary, factors such as goal setting, sunk cost, risk perception, and culture have been found to influence a team manager's decision making. These decisions, in turn, affect the project performance and success of an ISD project.

RESOURCES

The availability of resources is a critical factor impacting ISD success (Ein-Dor & Segev, 1977; Tait & Vessey, 1988; McConnell, 1996) and is deemed a critical element of the software development project (Sommerville, 1996; Pressman, 1997). Resources typically refer to people, money, materials, and time that are required to complete an ISD project successfully. Ein-Dor and Segev (1978) identified two major types of resource constraints for information systems development: internal versus external resources. Internal resources refer to constraints internal to the organization such as time and funds limitation. External resources refer to constraints external to the organization such as professionals, software, and hardware. The constraints of resources contribute to the failure of ISD. That is, with insufficient resources, the developers are unable to follow the planned procedures of ISD, and therefore, will increase the likelihood of ISD failure (Ein-Dor & Segev, 1978). On the contrary, the availability of resources leads to a better chance of overcoming organizational obstacles and achieving organizational commitment (Tait & Vessey, 1988). Several other studies also suggested that there is a close relationship between resources and ISD success. Tait and Vessey (1988) testified the factors impacting user involvement, and those impacting systems development. They found a significant negative relationship between resource constraints and the success of systems development. They argued that when financial and time constraints exist, the chances for success of a system implementation is low. McConnell (1996) argued that when given an identified task, the timeline of a project would be affected by the amount of available time and professionals. Therefore, resources influence the accomplishment of milestones during systems implementation.

Task and Systems Complexity Task and systems complexity have been found to be important factors influencing ISD success. According to Daft

et al. (1987), complexity arises from ambiguity and the lack of structure in tasks and sub-tasks involved. Two types of complexity are important in systems development—task complexity and systems complexity (McKeen et al., 1994). Task complexity stems from the user's environment and refers to the ambiguity and uncertainty of the business practice, while systems complexity stems from the developer's environment and refers to the ambiguity and uncertainty of systems development. Thus, task complexity relates to a user's understanding or perception of the task while systems complexity relates to a developer's understanding or perception of the systems development. An increase in project complexity decreases the assurance of achieving project goals (Nauman et al., 1980). With a complex project, ambiguity and uncertainty arise during the specification, design, and implementation of an information system, thus increasing the likelihood of system failure. Other Factors Conflicts as well as conflict management have been studied as factors influencing ISD performance and success (Barki & Hartwick, 2001; Robey et al., 1993). Conflict refers to the disagreement and incompatible goals among group members (Robey et al., 1993). In their research, Robey et al. (1993) found a negative relationship between conflict and ISD success.

Trust has long been regarded as an important issue in team project, especially in virtual teams (Brown, 2004; Piccoli & Ives, 2003; Jarvenpaa et al., 1998; Eschenbrenner et al. 2008) and e-commerce (McKnight et al., 2002; Torkzadeh & Dhillon, 2002; Siau & Shen 2003).

Learning and training has been regarded as being important in ISD, especially for ISD methodology (Lee & Truex, 2000; Siau & Loo, 2006; VanderMeer & Dutta, 2009). In their research, Lee and Truex (2000) examined the relationship between the formal training of systems development methods and the cognitive change of systems developers. They found that training facilitates the evolvement of cognitive complexity of systems developers.

Other factors, such as team size and timeline, have also been found to be important during ISD.

2.2.3. Organization Factors

Information Systems Development is a complex and interactive process among individuals, teams, and organizations. The organizational implications of ISD are usually so extensive that it is natural to view ISD process from a wide context of organizational change and organizational design (Sillince & Mouakket, 1997). Based on the perspective of the organization, the success of an information system depends on whether it facilitates or impedes organizational learning, evolvement, and adaptation (Sillince & Mouakket, 1997; King, 2006).

Several factors, such as IS strategic planning, top management support, IT governance style, and organization learning environment play an important role during the process of integrating an information system into an organization. These factors are discussed below.

IS Strategic Planning

IS strategy is a comprehensive set of plans of systems objectives, constraints, and design strategies (King & Teo, 1997). IS/IT strategic planning (Brancheau & Wetherbe, 1987) as well as the alignment between IT strategy and organization objectives have long been regarded as top issues in ISD success (Reich & Benbasat, 1996; Lederer & Mendelow, 1986).

Numerous studies have highlighted the relationship between IS strategy and IS effectiveness (Earl, 1987; Henderson & Sifonis, 1988; Lederer & Mendelow, 1986), as well as the importance of alignment between IT strategy and business strategy on ISD success and business performance (Sabherwal & Chan, 2001; Luftman & Papp, 1999; Segars & Grover, 1998; Chan et al., 1997; King & Teo, 1997; Reich & Benbasat, 1996; Lederer & Mendelow, 1989). These papers focus on differ-

ent perspectives of strategic information systems planning. Some perspectives investigated tools and methodology to develop strategic information systems planning, some highlighted the alignment and the profile of the alignment (e.g., Sabherwal & Chan, 2001; Reich & Benbasat, 1996), and others developed constructs and measurements for strategic information systems planning (e.g., Segars & Grover, 1998). For example, Chan et al. (1997) studied the relationships among IS strategic orientation, business strategic orientation, IS strategic alignment, IS effectiveness, and business performance. Empirical data obtained from their survey suggested that IS strategic alignment significantly impacts IS effectiveness, and further affects business performance.

Although focusing on different perspectives, these papers argue that the strategic information systems planning is an essential factor impacting ISD success, which in turn affects business success.

TOP MANAGEMENT SUPPORT/INVOLVEMENT

Management support refers to the widespread sponsorship for a project such as resource providence and resistance prevention. Top management support is well accepted as a critical success factor in ISD.

Top management support includes several components, such as the clarity of objectives, resource commitment, and objective communication (Etton et al., 2000). Empirical studies highlight the importance of top management support in assuring ISD (such as decision support systems) success (Etton et al., 2000; Sauer, 1993). Management support prevents political resistance, encourages employee participation, and motivates people to adapt to organizational changes accompanying ISD (Markus & Robey, 1988). People have the tendency to accept an information system that follows the management's expectations (Karahanna *et al.*, 1999). In summary, top management support is important for ISD success as it avoids political inconsistency, provides resources, and motivates people's involvement.

IT GOVERNANCE STYLE

IT governance style refers to the pattern of IT authority in an organization. It consists of IT infrastructure, as well as IT use and project management (Sambamurthy & Zmud, 1999). Among those, IT infrastructure focuses on the "physical" arrangement, such as hardware and software platforms, network and database infrastructure, and IT assets deployment and procurement (Sambamurthy & Zmud, 1999). IT use addresses IT application planning, budgeting, and day-to-day operations (Sambamurthy & Zmud, 1999). Project management is concerned with planning, organizing, directing, and controlling an IT project to achieve cost-efficient construct and usage (Felix & Harrison, 1984).

These activities are directed, controlled, and coordinated by IT governance arrangement. There are typically three types of IT governance— centralized, decentralized, and federal modes (Sambamurthy & Zmud, 1999). Sambamurthy and Zmud (1999) empirically studied the factors impacting IT governance modes. The results support that the contingency forces (e.g., reinforcing, conflicting, and dominating) influence IT governance. The pattern of IT governance represents the IT-related authority and resource arrangement of an organization. An appropriate IT governance style, therefore, is closely related to ISD success.

ORGANIZATIONAL KNOWLEDGE AND LEARNING ENVIRONMENT

Organization knowledge and learning environment are essential for ISD. Because organizational knowledge is complex and hard to mimic, it may produce long-term competitive advantages (Alavi & Leidner, 2001). Information systems researchers suggest that organization knowledge is captured through organization technology, structure, and routine (Leonard & Sensiper, 1998).

There is close relationship between information systems and organization knowledge. On one side, information systems facilitate the creation, storage/retrieval, transfer, and application of organizational knowledge (Holzner & Marx, 1979; Pentland, 1995). On the other hand, understanding organization environment and utilizing organizational knowledge for ISD are regarded as pre-requisites for ISD success.

OTHER FACTORS

Other environmental factors such as organization characters (e.g., size, revenue, and industry type), organization infrastructure and process (such as administrative structure, processes, and skills), politics (Smolander & Rossi, 2008), and culture (Sillince & Mouakket, 1997; Ven & Verelst, 2008) have also been found to be important during ISD.

2.3. Process

One component that has received relatively little research attention in prior literature is the ISD process. The ISD process is either skimmed through in literature or treated as a black box. The following review the literature that sheds light on the ISD process.

LEARNING/KNOWLEDGE SHARING

Argyris and Schon (1978) divided *learning* into single-loop and double-loop *learning*. In single-loop learning, individuals, teams, or organizations modify their actions according to the difference between expected and obtained outcomes. In double-loop learning, individuals, teams or organization question the values, assumptions and policies that led to the actions in the first place. If they are able to view and modify those, then second-order or double-loop learning has taken place. Double-loop learning is the learning about single-loop learning. Senge (1990) distinguished between adaptive learning (learning to cope) and generative learning (learning to create). March (1991) characterized learning as the exploitation of old certainties and the exploration of new possibilities.

Systems are typically developed, used, and refined as their developers and users learn more about them. In theory, this iterative process not only enables users to understand what they really need, but also enables developers to modify systems according to users' changing requirements (Stein & Vandernbosch, 1996). Salaway (1987) studied the organizational learning interaction process in ISD. The result shows that the information generated from communication between users and analysts forms the basis for information systems development and is therefore a major determinant of success.

INNOVATION/CREATIVITY

Innovation and creativity are vital components of a successful organization (Siau 1996). Process innovation is defined as any innovation that changes the way a job is performed (Damanpour, 1991). Contingency studies show that a fit between various characteristics and the software process innovation increases systems success (Hardgrave & Johnson, 2003; Siau & Messersmith, 2003). Nilakanta and Scamell (1990) examined the process of diffusion of innovations in the context of database systems development. Fagon (2004) investigated the role of creative style and climate on teams striving to develop innovative IT designs. Seiler *et al.* (1983) examined pressures on design personnel that stifle creativity, and provided suggestions for overcoming those pressures. Couger

(1990) discussed the widespread applicability of the creative theory on information systems design. Couger (1990) classified theories of creativity, phases of the process of creativity, and various techniques to facilitate the creativity process. Couger (1990) also suggested ways to ensure creativity in systems design. In another paper, Cooper (2000) adapted a creativity model from organization theory and used it to develop propositions regarding organizational characteristics that foster IT development creativity in organizations. Cooper's (2000) model attempts to help managers and researchers identify important variables and relationships in IT creative process, determine the degree to which creative IT requirements and logical design are feasible, and plan and execute a creative IT requirement and design process.

In addition to individual, team, and organization factors, systems development methodology is another important factor that affects ISD process.

2.4. Systems Development Methodology

A methodology is regarded as a recommended series of steps and procedures to be followed in the course of developing an information system. Adopting an appropriate methodology involves three main benefits: a better end product, a better development approach, and a standardized process.

PARADIGM

Paradigmatic assumptions can be divided into: ontology (what is assumed to be the nature of IS), epistemology (what is human knowledge and how it can be acquired), research methodology (what are the preferred research methods for development), and ethics (what are the values that ought to guide IS research) (Iivari *et al.*, 1998; Avison & Fitzgerald, 2008).

Ontological theories are intended to provide faithful representations of the general structure and dynamics of the real world as it exists. According to Hirschheim and Klein (1989), ontology is concerned with the essence of things and the nature of the world. Ontology provides a lens that allows people to view the real world so as to make sense of those phenomena. Ontology has been found to facilitate conceptual modeling in three important ways: choosing the conceptual modeling grammar for representing the focal domain, understanding the phenomena represented in conceptual modeling scripts (diagrams), and making sense of ambiguous semantics in conceptual models (Shanks *et al.*, 2003; Evermann & Wand, 2009).

Epistemological assumptions are concerned with the nature of knowledge and the proper methods of inquiry. Two extreme positions are identified as positivism and interpretivism. Positivism implies that the scientific method can be used to investigate the causal relationships, whereas interpretivism implies that there is no single truth that can be proven by such investigation (Avison & Fitzgerald, 2008; Siau & Matti, 2010).

MODEL

The model is the basis of the methodology's view of the world. It has a number of uses: a means of communication, a way of capturing the essence of a problem or a design, and a representation that provides insight into the problem or area of concern. Models have been categorized into four distinct types (Shubik, 1979):

A. Verbal;
B. Analytical or mathematical;
C. Iconic, pictorial, or schematic
D. Simulation.

A model is a form of abstraction (Booch *et al.*, 2005). The abstraction can be viewed as the simplification of systems and objects at three primary levels—conceptual, logical, and physical level. The conceptual model is viewed as the definition of problem structure of an information system. The logical model refers to the description of the information systems without any reference to the detailed technology concerning implementation. The physical model refers to the description of the information systems including the technology of a particular implementation. Studies have been conducted to investigate the effect of various levels of abstractions on users' performance (e.g., Chan *et al.*, 1993; Chan *et al.*, 1994; Chan *et al.*, 1995). The general consensus is that higher abstraction level is easier for users to understand and comprehend. For communication with end users, the analysts should use conceptual level diagrams as much as possible.

TECHNIQUES AND TOOLS

In Iivari *et al.*'s (1998) article, ISD methodology is defined as a codified set of goal-oriented 'procedures', which are intended to guide the work and cooperation of the various parties (stakeholders) involved in the building of an information systems application. Typically, these procedures are supported by a set of preferred techniques and tools, as well as guiding principles. A technique consists of a well-defined sequence of elementary operations that more or less guarantee the achievement of certain outcomes if executed correctly. Many techniques (e.g., DFD, ER diagram, UML diagrams) have been proposed in the past few decades and many studies have been done to evaluate and compared such techniques (e.g., Siau, 2004; Siau & Tan, 2005; Siau *et al.*, 2005; Siau & Tan, 2006; Erickson & Siau, 2007). Studies have shown that many of these techniques are far from ideal and more works need to be done to enhance existing techniques and design better techniques to facilitate the ISD process. For example, Siau and Loo (2006) found that UML is difficult to learn for users. Siau *et al.* (2005) argued that in considering the complexity of modeling languages, one needs to differentiate between the theoretical and practical complexity of a language. Siau and Cao (2001) showed that UML is up to 11 times more complex than other object-oriented techniques. Thus, UML is theoretically very complex. Nevertheless, not all constructs in the language will be used all the times and the practical complexity of the language may be lower.

As ISD methods and methodologies directly impact the ISD process, they affect the success of ISD.

2.5. Information Systems Development Success

There are many ways to view the success of ISD. Several factors that have been used to measure the success of ISD are user satisfaction (Malone, 1990), perceived usefulness or ease of use (Davis, 1989), and service quality (Pitt *et al.*, 1995). ISD success, therefore, can be regarded as a multi-faceted construct (Wixom & Watson, 2001). The choice of the ISD success measurement is based on the research questions and the phenomena under investigation (DeLone & McLean, 1992).

Table 1 summarizes ISD success measurements.

The above mentioned ISD success factors can be broadly classified into two categories—system

Table 1. Summary of ISD success measurements

Article	ISD success/ISD performance measurements/dimensions
DeLone, W. H. and McLean, E. R. (1992). Information systems success: the quest for the dependent variable	• System quality • Information quality • IS use • User satisfaction • Individual impact • Organizational impact
Saarinen, T. and Vepsalainen, A. P. J. (1994). Procurement strategies for information systems.	• Success of the development process • Success of the user process • Quality of the IS product, and • Impact of IS on the organization
Seddon, P.A. (1997). Respecification and Extension of the DeLone and McLean Model of IS Success	• Data quality • System quality • Perceived net benefits

Abdel-Hamid, T. K., Sengupta K., and Swett C. (1999). The Impact of Goals on Software Project Management: An Experimental Investigation	• Product performance
	  o Cost
	  o Duration
	  o Quality

Ravichandran, T. and Rai, A. (2000). Total quality management in information systems development: key constructs and relationships	• Product quality
	  o Portability
	  o Efficiency
	  o Human engineering

Barki, H. and Hartwick, J. (2001) Interpersonal Conflict and Management in Information Systems Development.	• Process efficiency • Process satisfaction • System quality • System attitude • Adhere to budget • Adhere to schedule • Adhere to specifications • Overall success

usage and user perceived satisfaction. The former focuses on the behavior of using a system, while the latter focuses on the attitude toward the system.

System usage is a two-fold measure comprising project success and system success. Project success refers to the measurement related to the project implementation and efficiency, such as cost, duration, specification, and process efficiency. System success refers to the evaluation associated with system usage and effectiveness, such as system quality (including maintainability, agility, and efficiency), information or data quality (including integration, unification, effectiveness, and efficiency), and system usage.

User-perceived satisfaction has long been believed as a critical measurement of ISD success (Kim, 1989; Melone, 1990). User satisfaction could be viewed from different perspectives, such as satisfaction with IS, systems quality, and IS effectiveness (Kim, 1989). It could be generally concluded that user satisfaction is measured by perceived satisfaction with systems, including systems quality, effectiveness, and efficiency.

3. A UNIFIED MODEL ON ISD SUCCESS

Based on the syntheses of literature review, we present a unified model on ISD success, which synthesizes the concepts, factors, and relationships discussed in section 2.

The framework (as shown in Figure 1) addresses three classes of variables—individual, team, and organization, and their impact on ISD process, which in turn, impacts ISD success.

The three classes of input variables—individual, team, and organization—interact with each other. For example, knowledge is distributed across individuals, teams, and organizations. Moreover, knowledge-related actions such as knowledge creation and knowledge management occur interactively between individuals, teams, and organizations. Individual knowledge comprises the psychological and cognitive components for an individual to understand the outside world. Social/organization knowledge is a collective knowledge of routines, cultures, and norms that are publicly available in an organization (Spender, 1996). Team knowledge, according to Griffith *et al.* (2003), is influenced by individual and organization cultures. Researchers and practitioners investigate the translation of tacit/implicit knowledge to explicit knowledge, as well as transfer of knowledge among individuals, teams, and organization (e.g., Nah *et al.*, 2002; Nah *et al.*, 2005; Siau *et al.*, 2007). The learning environment facilitates the dissemination of knowledge across individuals, teams and organizations, and in turn, influences ISD process and success.

Many prior works on ISD success view the ISD process as a black box. They focus on the direct relationship between input factors (e.g., individual, team, and organization characteristics) and output factors (e.g., ISD performance and ISD success). In our unified model, we do not view ISD process as a black box but instead view the ISD process as a process of creation, innovation, and knowledge sharing and learning. Both input factors and systems development methodology impact this process, and affect the ISD success.

Different researchers view ISD success from different perspectives. There is no one standard measurement for ISD success. Based on the literature, we propose a multi-faceted measure of ISD success. We argue that ISD success contains systems usage and user satisfaction. The former refers to the actual behavior of IS usage, while the latter measures the attitude toward systems usage.

4. DISCUSSION

Differences and similarities exist between the unified ISD success model presented in this paper and earlier works. The proposed ISD success framework is not only a summary but also a comprehensive, synthesized, and unified model on ISD success.

Figure 1. Unified Model of ISD success

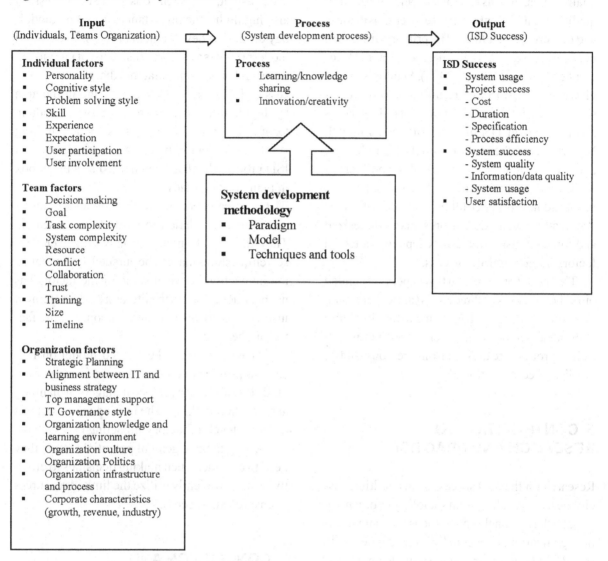

Previous literature proposed models impacting ISD success (or performance) and most models are limited to one or two levels (i.e., individual, team or organization). For example, some researchers focus on the individual level, such as interpersonal conflict (Barki & Hartwick, 2001; Robey *et al.*, 1993), user participation (McKeen *et al.*, 1994), user expectation (Szajna & Scamell, 1993), and user involvement (Tait & Vessey, 1988). Others researchers focus on team and/or organizational levels, such as knowledge in teams (Griffith, 2003), corporation and uncertainty (Nidumolu, 1995) and organizational learning (Stein & Vandenbosch, 1996). The proposed unified model depicts an overall and comprehensive picture of ISD success.

Further, most of the previous models ignore the intermediate role of ISD process and treat the ISD process as a black box. The unified model depicts the importance of ISD process and highlights the role of ISD methodology.

Two of the more comprehensive models in prior research are DeLone and McLean's (1992) and Seddon's (1997) models of information systems (IS) success. These two models regard system quality (measured as ease of use) and information quality as antecedents of IS use, user satisfaction, and perceived usefulness. The primary difference between these two is the definition and placement of IS use (Rai *et al.*, 2000). Seddon's model views the use of IS as a resulting behavior of IS success rather than an inherent trait of IS success as presented in DeLone and McLean's model. Nevertheless, these two models have limited antecedents and outcome variables, and focuses on several primary factors. The unified model proposed in this paper follows the idea of Input-Process-Output model and presents a synthesized and comprehensive framework depicting potential factors impacting ISD success.

The model presented in this paper is grounded on earlier works. The three levels (individual, team, and organization) are based on existing literature in the area. Factors within each of the level as well as ISD process are derived from previous studies (as discussed in section 2).

5. CONTRIBUTION TO RESEARCH AND PRACTICE

Research on the ISD success spans multiple disciplines. Researchers from sociology or organizational behavior background focus their attentions on organizational issues in ISD. Researchers with social psychology training study team issues. Researchers with psychology training pay more attention to individual issues. Theoretical models and empirical techniques from these disciplines have heavily influenced and driven research effort in ISD. These research works have illuminated the issues in ISD success and a unified model on ISD success would further advance the field. The proposed model in this paper serves that purpose by integrating diverse theoretical underpinnings and synthesizes accumulated knowledge.

The proposed unified model contributes to both research and practice. Compared to earlier models, the unified model depicts the Input-Process-Output dimensions of ISD success. It also highlights the importance of ISD methodology during the development process. The unified model provides a comprehensive list of individual, team, and organization factors that affect the success of ISD. It advances knowledge in the area by highlighting the importance of individual, team, and organization factors in determining ISD success, and advocates the importance of ISD process that has been treated as a black box in many prior studies.

For researchers, the unified model provides a conceptual foundation to guide future research. The unified model points to many unanswered research questions that can be pursued. For example, the interaction between some of the factors has not been addressed in the literature. Measurement instruments are also needed for some of the factors in the model.

For practitioners, the unified model on ISD success provides a comprehensive framework to guide ISD and assist project managers in planning and decision-making. The unified model depicts different levels of factors impacting ISD success, suggesting to management potential factors they need to consider when making decisions to effectively and efficiently utilize the limited resources to ensure ISD success.

6. CONCLUSION AND FUTURE RESEARCH

Based on the synthesis of prior research and existing knowledge in the field, this research developed a unified model of ISD success. The unified model enhances our understanding of ISD success and provides guidelines for future empirical studies. Although the proposed unified model may be limited to existing literature and knowledge, it is our contention that the major factors have been included in the model. A unified model on ISD success must depict the complexity and richness of the ISD process and integrate the individual, team, and organization factors.

With this unified model, researchers and practitioners can focus their research interests on specific factors (components) impacting ISD process and contribute to existing knowledge on ISD success. Future research can examine and test the various variables in the model. Subsequent research can also extend the model presented in this paper by demonstrating how individual, team, and organization factors interact in the process. In addition, the model can be extended by studying the relationships between process success and system success. Organizations and their environments change rapidly, and so do critical success factors for systems development.

Further, researchers can address new approaches and paradigms in ISD. For example, there are a variety of new challenges in virtual collaborations and cooperation in ISD success. These need to be investigated. Mobile and ubiquitous applications may challenge the traditional view of ISD as these applications are typically smaller and built quickly. So will new ideas to ISD such as agile development (Erickson *et al.*, 2005), open source approach (Long & Siau, 2007; Brydon & Vining, 2008; Koch & Neumann, 2008), service-oriented architecture (Erickson & Siau, 2008), and cloud computing. Outsourcing of ISD is another emerging trend and the planning, managing, and governance issues related to ISD success in outsourcing circumstances need to be investigated.

REFERENCES

Abdel-Hamid, T. K., Sengupta, K., & Swett, C. (1999). The Impact of Goals on Software Project Management: An Experimental Investigation. *MIS Quarterly*, *23*(4), 531–555. doi:10.2307/249488

Alavi, M., & Leidner, D. E. (2001). Review: Knowledge Management and Knowledge Management Systems: Conceptual Foundations and Research Issues. *MIS Quarterly*, *25*(1), 107–136. doi:10.2307/3250961

Alter, S. (1978). Development Patterns for Decision Support Systems. *MIS Quarterly*, *2*(3), 33–42. doi:10.2307/249176

Argyris, C., & Schon, D. A. (1978). *Organizational Learning: A Theory of Action Perspective*. Reading, MA: Addison-Wesley.

Aronson, E., & Carlsmith, J. M. (1962). Performance Expectancy as a Determinant of Actual Performance. *Journal of Abnormal and Social Psychology*, *65*(3), 178–182. doi:10.1037/h0042291

Avison, D., & Fitzgerald, G. (2008). *Information Systems Development: Methodologies, Techniques and Tools* (4th ed.). New York: McGraw Hill.

Bariff, M. L., & Lusk, E. J. (1977). Cognitive and personality tests for the design of management information systems. *Management Science*, *23*(8), 820–829. doi:10.1287/mnsc.23.8.820

Barki, H., & Hartwick, J. (1994). User Participation, Conflict, and Conflict Resolution: The Mediating Roles of Influence. *Information Systems Research*, *5*(4), 422–438. doi:10.1287/isre.5.4.422

Barki, H., & Hartwick, J. (2001). Interpersonal Conflict and Management in Information Systems Development. *MIS Quarterly*, *25*(2), 195–228. doi:10.2307/3250929

Benbasat, I., & Taylor, R. N. (1978). The Impact of Cognitive Styles on Information System Design. *MIS Quarterly*, *2*(2), 43–54. doi:10.2307/248940

Boehm, B. W. (1987). Improving Software Productivity. *Computer*, (September): 43–57. doi:10.1109/MC.1987.1663694

Booch, G., Rumbaugh, J., & Jacobson, I. (2005). *The Unified Modeling Language User Guide* (2nd ed.). Reading, MA: Addison Wesley.

Bradley, J. H., & Hebert, F. J. (1997). The effect of personality type on team performance. *Journal of Management Development*, 16(5/6), 337–353. doi:10.1108/02621719710174525

Brancheau, J. C., & Wetherbe, J. C. (1987). Key issues in information systems management. *MIS Quarterly*, 11(1), 23–45. doi:10.2307/248822

Brown, H. G., Marshall, S. P., & Rodgers, T. L. (2004). International traits, complementarity and trust in virtual collaboration. *Journal of Management Information Systems*, 20(4), 115–137.

Brydon, M., & Vining, A. R. (2008). Adoption, Improvement, and Disruption: Predicting the Impact of Open Source Applications in Enterprise Software Markets. *Journal of Database Management*, 19(2), 73–94.

Chan, H., Wei, K., & Siau, K. (1993). User-Database Interface: The Effect of Abstraction Levels on Query Performance. *Management Information Systems Quarterly*, 17(4), 441–464. doi:10.2307/249587

Chan, H., Wei, K., & Siau, K. (1994). An Empirical Study on End Users' Update Performance for Different Abstraction Levels. *International Journal of Human-Computer Studies*, 41(3), 309–328. doi:10.1006/ijhc.1994.1061

Chan, H., Wei, K., & Siau, K. (1995). The Effect of a Database Feedback System on User Performance. *Behaviour and Information Technology: An International Journal on the Human Aspects of Computing*, 14(3), 152–162.

Chan, Y. E., Copeland, D. G. D., & Barclay, W. (1997). Business strategy, information systems strategy, and strategic alignment. *Information Systems Research*, 8(2), 125–150. doi:10.1287/isre.8.2.125

Cooper, R. B. (2000). Information Technology Development Creativity: A Case Study of Attempted Radical Change. *MIS Quarterly*, 24(2), 245–276. doi:10.2307/3250938

Couger, J. D. (1990). Ensuring Creative Approaches in Information System Design. *Managerial & Decision Economics*, 11(5), 281–295. doi:10.1002/mde.4090110503

Daft, R., Lengel, R., & Trevino, L. (1987). Message equivocality, media selection, and manager performance. *MIS Quarterly*, 11(3), 355–366. doi:10.2307/248682

Damanpour, F. (1991). Organizational innovation: A meta-analysis of effects of determinants and moderators. *Academy of Management Journal*, 34(3), 555–590. doi:10.2307/256406

Davis, F. (1989). Perceived usefulness, perceived ease of use, and user acceptance of Information technology. *MIS Quarterly*, 13(3), 319–340. doi:10.2307/249008

DeLone, W. H., & McLean, E. R. (1992). Information systems success: The quest for the dependent variable. *Information Systems Research*, 3(1), 60–95. doi:10.1287/isre.3.1.60

DeSanctis, G. (1983). Expectancy Theory as an Explanation of Voluntary Use of a Decision-Support System. *Psychological Reports*, 52(1), 247–260.

Earl, M. J. (1987). Information systems strategy formulation. In R. J. Boland Jr. & R. A. Hirschheim (Eds.), *Critical Issues in Information Systems Research* (pp. 157-178). New York: Wiley.

Ein-Dor, P., & Segev, E. (1978). Organizational Context and the Success of Management Information Systems. *Management Science*, 24(10), 1064–1077. doi:10.1287/mnsc.24.10.1064

Erickson, J., Lyytinen, K., & Siau, K. (2005). Agile Modeling, Agile Software Development, and Extreme Programming: The State of Research. *Journal of Database Management*, 16(4), 88–100.

Erickson, J., & Siau, K. (2007). Theoretical and Practical Complexity of Modeling Methods. *Communications of the ACM, 50*(8), 46–51. doi:10.1145/1278201.1278205

Erickson, J., & Siau, K. (2008). Web Services, Service-Oriented Computing, and Service-Oriented Architecture: Separating Hype from Reality. *Journal of Database Management, 19*(3), 42–54.

Eschenbrenner, B., Nah, F. F. H., & Siau, K. (2008). 3-D virtual Worlds in Education: Applications, Benefits, Issues, and Opportunities. *Journal of Database Management, 19*(4), 91–110.

Etton, P., Martin, A., Sharma, R., & Johnston, K. (2000). A model of Information systems development project performance. *Information Systems Journal, 10*(4), 263–289. doi:10.1046/j.1365-2575.2000.00088.x

Evermann, J., & Wand, Y. (2009). Ontology Based Object-Oriented Domain Modeling: Representing Behavior. *Journal of Database Management, 20*(1), 48–77.

Felix, R. G., & Harrison, W. L. (1984). Project Management Considerations for Distributed Applications. *MIS Quarterly, 8*(3), 161–170. doi:10.2307/248663

Gallagher, C. A. (1974). Perceptions of the Value of a Management Information System. *Academy of Management Journal, 17*(1), 46–55. doi:10.2307/254770

Ginzberg, M. J. (1981). Early diagnosis of MIS implementation failure: Promising results and unanswered questions. *Management Science, 27*(4), 459–478. doi:10.1287/mnsc.27.4.459

Griffith, T. L., Sawyer, J. E., & Neale, M. A. (2003). Virtualness and Knowledge in Teams: Managing the Love Triangle of Organizations, Individuals, and Information Technology. *MIS Quarterly, 27*(2), 265–287.

Guinan, P. J., Cooprider, J. G., & Faraj, S. (1998). Enabling software development team performance during requirements definition: A behavioral versus technical approach. *Information Systems Research, 9*(2), 101–125. doi:10.1287/isre.9.2.101

Guthrie, A. (1974). Attitudes of User-Managers towards Management Information Systems. *Management Informatics, 3*(5), 221–232.

Hackman, J. R. (1987). The design of work teams. In J. W. Lorsch (Ed.), *Handbook of organizational behavior* (pp. 315-342). Englewood Cliffs, NJ: Prentice Hall.

Hardgrave, B. C., & Johnson, R. A. (2003). Toward an Information Systems Development Acceptance Model: The Case of Object-Oriented Systems Development. *IEEE Transactions on Engineering Management, 50*(3), 322–336. doi:10.1109/TEM.2003.817293

Hardgrave, B. C., Wilson, R. L., & Eastman, K. (1999). Toward a Contingency Model for Selecting an Information System Prototyping Strategy. *Journal of Management Information Systems, 16*(2), 113–136.

Henderson, J. C., & Sifonis, J. G. (1988). The value of strategic IS planning: understanding consistency, validity, and IS markets. *MIS Quarterly, 12*(2), 187–200. doi:10.2307/248843

Henry, R. M., Dickson, G. W., & LaSalle, J. (1973). Human resources for MIS: A report of research. In *Proceedings of the Fifth Annual Conference of the Society for Management Information Systems,* Chicago (pp. 21-34).

Hirschheim, R., & Klein, H. K. (1989). Four Paradigms of Information Systems Development. *Communications of the ACM, 32*(10), 1199–1216. doi:10.1145/67933.67937

Hirschheim, R., & Newman, M. (1988). Information Systems and User Resistance: Theory and Practice. *The Computer Journal, 31*(5), 398–408. doi:10.1093/comjnl/31.5.398

Holzner, B., & Marx, J. (1979). *The Knowledge Application: The Knowledge System in Society.* Boston: Allyn-Bacon.

Iivari, J., Hirschheim, R., & Klein, H. K. (1998). A Paradigmatic Analysis Contrasting Information Systems Development Approaches and Methodologies. *Information Systems Research, 9*(2), 164–193. doi:10.1287/isre.9.2.164

Ives, B., & Olson, M. (1984). User Involvement and MIS Success: A Review of Research. *Management Science, 30*(5), 586–603. doi:10.1287/mnsc.30.5.586

Jarvenpaa, S. L., Knoll, K., & Leidner, D. E. (1998). Is anybody out there? Antecedents of trust in global virtual teams. *Journal of Management Information Systems, 14*(4), 29–64.

Jung, C. G. (1923). *Psychological Types.* London: Rutledge and Kegan Paul.

Jung, C. G. (1968). *Analytical Psychology: Its Theory and Practice.* New York: Vintage Press.

Kaiser, K., & Bostrom, R. (1982). Personality Characteristics of MIS Design Project Teams: An Empirical Study and Action-Research Design. *MIS Quarterly, 6*(4), 43–60. doi:10.2307/249066

Kappelman, L., & McLean, E. (1991). The Respective Roles of User Participation and User Involvement in Information Systems Implementation Success. *International Conference on Information Systems*, New York (pp. 339-348).

Karahanna, E., Straub, D. W., & Chervany, N. L. (1999). Information Technology Adoption Across Time: Cross-Sectional Comparison of Pre-Adoption and Post-Adoption Beliefs. *MIS Quarterly, 23*(2), 183–213. doi:10.2307/249751

Keil, M. (1995). Pulling the Plug: Software Project Management and the Problem of Project Escalation. *MIS Quarterly, 19*(4), 421–447. doi:10.2307/249627

Keil, M., Mann, J., & Rai, A. (2000). Why Software Projects Escalate: An Empirical Analysis and Test of Four Theoretical Models. *MIS Quarterly, 24*(4), 631–664. doi:10.2307/3250950

Keil, M., & Robey, D. (1999). Turning Around Troubled Software Projects: An Exploratory Study of the De-escalation of Commitment to Failing Courses of Action. *Journal of Management Information Systems, 15*(4), 63–87.

Kim, K. K. (1989). User satisfaction: A synthesis of three different perspectives. *The Journal of Information Systems, 4*(1), 1–12.

King, W. R. (2006). The Critical Role of Information Processing in Creating An Effective Knowledge Organization. *Journal of Database Management, 17*(1), 1–15.

King, W. R., & Teo, T. S. H. (1997). Integration between business planning and information systems planning: Validating a stage hypothesis. *Decision Sciences, 28*(2), 279–308. doi:10.1111/j.1540-5915.1997.tb01312.x

Koch, S., & Neumann, C. (2008). Exploring the Effects of Process Characteristics on Product Quality in Open Source Software Development. *Journal of Database Management, 19*(2), 31–57.

Lawrence, M., & Low, G. (1993). Exploring Individual User Satisfaction within User-Led Development. *MIS Quarterly, 17*(2), 195–208. doi:10.2307/249801

Lederer, A., & Mendelow, A. (1986). Issues in information systems planning. *Information & Management, 10*(5), 245–254. doi:10.1016/0378-7206(86)90027-3

Lederer, A. L., & Mendelow, A. L. (1989). Coordination of information systems plans with business plans. *Journal of Management Information Systems, 6*(2), 5–19.

Lee, J., & Truex, D. P. (2000). Exploring the impact of formal training in ISD methods on the cognitive structure of novice information systems developers. *Information Systems Journal, 10*(4), 347–367. doi:10.1046/j.1365-2575.2000.00086.x

Leonard, D., & Sensiper, S. (1998). The Role of Tacit Knowledge in Group Innovation. *California Management Review, 40*(3), 112–132.

Long, Y., & Siau, K. (2007). Social Network Structures in Open Source Software Development Teams. *Journal of Database Management, 18*(2), 25–40.

Luftman, J., Papp, R., & Brier, T. (1999). Enablers and inhibitors of business-IT alignment. *Communication of AIS, 1*(11).

March, J. G. (1991). Exploration and exploitation in organizational learning. *Organization Science, 2*(1), 71–87. doi:10.1287/orsc.2.1.71

Markus, M. L., & Robey, D. (1988). Information Technology and Organizational Change: Causal Structure in Theory and Research. *Management Science, 34*(5), 583–598. doi:10.1287/mnsc.34.5.583

McConnell, S. (1996). *Rapid Development*. Redmond, WA: Microsoft Press.

McGrath, J. E. (1984). *Groups: Interaction and Performance*. Englewood Cliffs, NJ: Prentice-Hall.

McKeen, J. D., & Guimaraes, T. (1997). Successful strategies for user participation in systems development. *Journal of Management Information Systems, 14*(2), 133–150.

McKeen, J. D., Guimaraes, T., & Wetherbe, J. C. (1994). The Relationship Between User Participation and User Satisfaction: An Investigation of Four Contingency Factors. *MIS Quarterly,*, 427–451. doi:10.2307/249523

McKnight, D. H., Choudhury, V., & Kacmar, C. (2002). Developing and validating trust measures for e-commerce: an integrative typology. *Information Systems Research, 13*(3), 334–359. doi:10.1287/isre.13.3.334.81

Melone, N. A. (1990). Theoretical Assessment of the User-Satisfaction Construct in Information Systems Research. *Management Science, 36*(1), 76–91. doi:10.1287/mnsc.36.1.76

Nah, F., Siau, K., & Tian, Y. (2005). Knowledge Management Mechanisms of Financial Service Sites. *Communications of the ACM, 48*(6), 117–123. doi:10.1145/1064830.1064836

Nah, F., Siau, K., Tian, Y., & Ling, M. (2002). Knowledge Management Mechanisms in E-Commerce: A Study of Online Retailing and Auction Sites. *Journal of Computer Information Systems, 42*(5), 119–128.

Nauman, J. D., Davis, G. B., & McKeen, J. D. (1980). Determining Information Requirements: A Contingency Method for Selection of a Requirements Assurance Strategy. *Journal of Systems and Software, 1*, 273–281. doi:10.1016/0164-1212(79)90029-3

Newman, M., & Sabherwal, R. (1989). A Process Model for the Control of Information System Development Projects. In *Proceedings of ICIS* (pp. 185-197).

Nidumolu, S. (1995). The Effect of Coordination and Uncertainty on Software Project Performance: Residual Performance Risk as an Intervening Variable. *Information Systems Research, 6*(3), 191–219. doi:10.1287/isre.6.3.191

Nilakanta, S., & Scamell, R. W. (1990). The Effect of Information Sources and Communication Channels on the Diffusion of Innovation in a Data Base Development Environment. *Management Science, 36*(1), 24–40. doi:10.1287/mnsc.36.1.24

Oz, E., & Sosik, J. J. (2000). Why information systems projects are abandoned: a leadership and communication theory and exploratory study. *Journal of Computer Information Systems, 41*(1), 66–88.

Pentland, B. T. (1995). Information Systems and Organizational Learning: The Social Epistemology of Organizational Knowledge Systems. *Accounting . Management and Information Technologies, 5*(1), 1–21. doi:10.1016/0959-8022(95)90011-X

Piccoli, G., & Ives, B. (2003). Trust and the unified effects of behavior control in virtual teams. *MIS Quarterly, 27*(3), 365–395.

Pitt, L., Watson, R. T., & Kavan, C. B. (1995). Service quality: a measure of information systems effectiveness. *MIS Quarterly, 19*(2), 173–187. doi:10.2307/249687

Pressman, R. S. (1997). *Software Engineering: A Practitioner's Approach* (4th ed.). New York: McGraw-Hill.

Rai, A., Lang, S. S., & Welker, R. B. (2000). Assessing the validity of IS Success Models: An empirical test and theoretical analysis. *Information Systems Research, 13*(1), 50–69. doi:10.1287/isre.13.1.50.96

Rash, R. H., & Tosi, H. L. (1992). Factors Affecting Software Developers' Performance: An Integrated Approach . *MIS Quarterly, 16*(3), 395–413. doi:10.2307/249535

Ravichandran, T., & Rai, A. (2000). Total quality management in information systems development: key constructs and relationships. *Journal of Management Information Systems, 16*(3), 119–155.

Reich, B. H., & Benbasat, I. (1996). Measuring the Linkage between Business and Information Technology Objectives. *MIS Quarterly, 20*(1), 55–81. doi:10.2307/249542

Rice, R. E., Grant, A., Schmitz, J., & Torobin, J. (1990). Individual and Network Influences on the Adoption and Perceived Outcomes of Electronic Messaging. *Social Networks, 12*(1), 27–55. doi:10.1016/0378-8733(90)90021-Z

Robey, D., Smith, L., & Vijayasarathy, L. (1993). Perceptions of Conflict and Success in Information Systems Development Projects. *Journal of Management Information Systems, 10*(1), 123–139.

Rushinek, A., & Rushinek, S. F. (1986). What Makes Users Happy? *Communications of the ACM, 29*(7), 594–598. doi:10.1145/6138.6140

Saarinen, T., & Vepsalainen, A. P. J. (1994). Procurement strategies for information systems. *Journal of Management Information Systems, 11*(2), 187–208.

Sabherwal, R., & Chan, Y. E. (2001). Alignment between business and IS strategies: A study of Prospectors, Analyzers, and Defenders. *Information Systems Research, 12*(1), 11–33. doi:10.1287/isre.12.1.11.9714

Salaway, G. (1987). An Organizational Learning Approach to Information Systems Development. *MIS Quarterly, 11*(2), 244–260. doi:10.2307/249370

Sambamurthy, V., & Zmud, R. W. (1999). Arrangements for IT Governance: A Theory of Multiple Contingencies. *MIS Quarterly, 23*(2), 261–290. doi:10.2307/249754

Sanders, G. L. (1984). MIS/DSS Success Measure. *Systems, Objectives . Solutions, 4*(1), 29–34.

Sauer, C. (1993). *Why information systems fall: A case study approach.* Henley-on-Thames, UK: Alfred Waller.

Schank, R. C. (1982). *Dynamic Memory: A Theory of Learning in People and Computers.* Cambridge, UK: Cambridge University Press.

Schenk, K. D., Vitalari, N. P., & Davis, K. S. (1998). Differences between novice and expert systems analysts: What do we know and what do we do? *Journal of Management Information Systems, 15*(1), 9–51.

Seddon, P. A. (1997). Respecification and Extension of the DeLone and McLean Model of IS Success. *Information Systems Research, 8*(3), 240–253. doi:10.1287/isre.8.3.240

Segars, A., & Grover, V. (1998). Strategic information systems planning success: An investigation of the construct and its measurement. *MIS Quarterly, 22*(2), 139–163. doi:10.2307/249393

Seiler, R. E., & Boockholdt, J. L. (1983). Creative Development of Computerized Information Systems. *Long Range Planning, 16*(5), 100–106. doi:10.1016/0024-6301(83)90084-5

Senge, P. M. (1990). The leader's new work: Building learning organizations. *Sloan Management Review, 32*(1), 7–23.

Senn, J. A. (1987). *Information Systems in Management* (3rd ed.). Belmont, CA: Wadsworth Publishing.

Shanks, G., Tansley, E., & Weber, R. (2003). Using Ontology to Validate Conceptual Models. *Communications of the ACM, 46*(10), 85–89. doi:10.1145/944217.944244

Shubik, M. (1979). Computers and Modeling. In M. L. Dertouzos & J. Moses (Eds.), *The Computer Age: A Twenty Year View*. Cambridge, MA: MIT Press.

Siau, K. (1996). Electronic Creativity Techniques for Organizational Innovation. *The Journal of Creative Behavior, 30*(4), 283–293.

Siau, K. (2004). Informational and Computational Equivalence in Comparing Information Modeling Methods. *Journal of Database Management, 15*(1), 73–86.

Siau, K., & Cao, Q. (2001). Unified Modeling Language – A Complexity Analysis. *Journal of Database Management, 12*(1), 26–34.

Siau, K., Erickson, J., & Lee, L. (2005). Theoretical vs. Practical Complexity: The Case of UML. *Journal of Database Management, 16*(3), 40–57.

Siau, K., & Loo, P. (2006). Identifying Difficulties in Learning UML. *Information Systems Management, 23*(3), 43–51. doi:10.1201/1078.10580530/46108.23.3.20060601/93706.5

Siau, K., & Messersmith, J. (2003). Analyzing ERP Implementation at a Public University Using the Innovation Strategy Model. *International Journal of Human-Computer Interaction, 16*(1), 57–80. doi:10.1207/S15327590IJHC1601_5

Siau, K., Nah, F., & Ling, M. (2007). National Culture and its Effects on Knowledge Communication in Online Virtual Communities. *International Journal of Electronic Business, 5*(5), 518–532. doi:10.1504/IJEB.2007.015450

Siau, K., & Rossi, M. (in press). Systems Analysis and Design: Evaluation Techniques for Conceptual and Data Modeling Methods. *Information Systems Journal*.

Siau, K., & Shen, Z. (2003). Building Customer Trust in Mobile Commerce. *Communications of the ACM, 46*(4), 91–94. doi:10.1145/641205.641211

Siau, K., & Tan, X. (2005). Evaluation Criteria for Information Systems Development Methodologies. *Communications of the AIS, 16*, 856–872.

Siau, K., & Tan, X. (2006). Cognitive Mapping Techniques for User-Database Interaction. *IEEE Transactions on Professional Communication, 49*(2), 96–108. doi:10.1109/TPC.2006.875074

Siau, K., Wand, Y., & Benbasat, I. (1997). The Relative Importance of Structural Constraints and Surface Semantics in Information Modeling. *Information Systems, 22*(2-3), 155–170. doi:10.1016/S0306-4379(97)00009-4

Sillince, J. A., & Mouakket, S. (1997). Varieties of Political Process during Systems Development. *Information Systems Research, 8*(4), 368–397. doi:10.1287/isre.8.4.368

Smolander, K., & Rossi, M. (2008). Conflicts, Compromises, and Political Decisions: Methodological Challenges of Enterprise-Wide E-Business Architecture Creation. *Journal of Database Management, 19*(1), 19–40.

Sommerville, I. (1996). *Software Engineering* (5th ed.). Reading, MA: Addison-Wesley.

Spence, J. W., & Tsai, R. J. (1997). On human cognition and the design of information systems. *Information & Management, 32*(2), 66–74. doi:10.1016/S0378-7206(97)00012-8

Spender, J. C. (1996). Making Knowledge the Basis of a Dynamic Theory of the Firm. *Strategic Management Journal, 17*(2), 45–62.

Stein, E. W., & Vandenbosch, B. (1996). Organizational learning during advanced system development: Opportunities and obstacles. *Journal of Management Information Systems, 13*(2), 115–136.

Swanson, E. B. (1974). Management Information Systems: Appreciation and Involvement. *Management Science, 21*(2), 178–188. doi:10.1287/mnsc.21.2.178

Szajna, B., & Scamell, R. W. (1993). The effects of information system user expectations on their performance and perceptions. *MIS Quarterly, 17*(4), 493–516. doi:10.2307/249589

Tait, P., & Vessey, I. (1988). The Effect of User Involvement on System Success: A Contingency Approach. *MIS Quarterly, 12*(1), 91–108. doi:10.2307/248809

Thompson, L. L. (1999). *Making the Team.* Upper Saddle River, NJ: Prentice Hall.

Torkzadeh, G., & Dhillon, G. (2002). Measuring factors that influence the success of internet commerce. *Information Systems Research, 13*(2), 187–204. doi:10.1287/isre.13.2.187.87

Trimmer, K. J., Domino, M. A., & Blanton, J. E. (2002). The Impact of Personality Diversity on Conflict in ISD Teams. *Journal of Computer Information Systems, 42*(4), 7–14.

Vander Meer, D., & Dutta, K. (2009). Applying Learner-Centered Design Principles to UML Sequence Diagrams. *Journal of Database Management, 20*(1), 25–47.

Ven, K., & Verelst, J. (2008). The Impact of Ideology on the Organizational Adoption of Open Source Software. *Journal of Database Management, 19*(2), 58–72.

Vitalari, N. P. (1985). Knowledge as a Basis for Expertise in Systems Analysis: An Empirical Study. *MIS Quarterly, 9*(3), 221–240. doi:10.2307/248950

White, K. B., & Leifer, R. (1986). Information Systems Development Success: Perspectives from Project Team Participants. *MIS Quarterly, 10*(3), 215–223. doi:10.2307/249253

Witkin, H. A. (1973). The role of cognitive style in academic performance and in teacher-student relations. *Educational Testing Service Research Bulletin,* 73-101.

Wixom, B. H., & Watson, H. J. (2001). An Empirical Investigation of the Factors Affecting Data Warehouse Success. *MIS Quarterly, 25*(1), 17–41. doi:10.2307/3250957

Zmud, R. W. (1979). Perceptions of Cognitive Styles: Acquisition, Exhibition and Implications for Information System Design. *Journal of Management, 5*(1), 7–20. doi:10.1177/014920637900500101

This work was previously published in International Journal of Database Management, Volume 21, Issue 1, edited by Keng Siau, pp. 80-101, copyright 2010 by IGI Publishing (an imprint of IGI Global).

Chapter 5
Representing Classes of Things and Properties in General in Conceptual Modelling:
An Empirical Evaluation

Graeme Shanks
University of Melbourne, Australia

Daniel Moody
University of Twente, The Netherlands

Jasmina Nuredini
Simsion and Associates, Australia

Daniel Tobin
University of Melbourne, Australia

Ron Weber
Monash University, Australia

ABSTRACT

How classes of things and properties in general should be represented in conceptual models is a fundamental issue. For example, proponents of object-role modelling argue that no distinction should be made between the two constructs, whereas proponents of entity-relationship modelling argue the distinction is important but provide ambiguous guidelines about how the distinction should be made. In this paper, the authors use ontological theory and cognition theory to provide guidelines about how classification should be represented in conceptual models. The authors experimented to test whether clearly distinguishing between classes of things and properties in general enabled users of conceptual models to better understand a domain. They describe a cognitive processing study that examined whether clearly distinguishing between classes of things and properties in general impacts the cognitive behaviours of the users. The results support the use of ontologically sound representations of classes of things and properties in conceptual modelling.

DOI: 10.4018/978-1-61350-471-0.ch005

1. INTRODUCTION

The notions of classes of things and the properties that things in the class possess (properties in general) have been of interest to philosophers concerned with ontology (the nature of the world) (e.g., Bunge, 1977). They have also been of interest to information systems researchers and practitioners concerned with finding better ways to model the world. For instance, the representation of classes of things and properties in general features in early work on conceptual modelling (Chen, 1976; Nijssen, 1976; Kent, 1978). It also features in more-recent object-oriented conceptual modelling approaches–in particular, the Unified Modelling Language (e.g., Rumbaugh et al., 1999).

For a number of reasons, the notions of classes of things and properties in general and their representation in conceptual models are problematic. First, not all scholars agree that things and properties are distinct phenomena. For instance, nominalist philosophers "dispense with properties, which they regard as Platonic fictions, and attempt to reduce everything to things, their names, and collections of such" (Bunge, 1977, p. 57). Moreover, those philosophers who do sustain a distinction between things and properties face the difficult task of showing how the distinction should be made (e.g., Denkel, 1996).

Second, some information systems scholars argue the distinction between classes of things and properties in general ought not to be sustained in conceptual models, because different users may perceive the same phenomena differently (in short, implicitly these scholars subscribe to a nominalist philosophy). For example, in the object-role approach to conceptual modelling, the distinction between classes of things and properties in general is not maintained (Halpin, 2008). Both are represented using the object symbol in a conceptual model. Similarly, Date (2003, p. 436) eschews the distinction between an entity (thing) and a relationship (type of property of a thing): "In this writer's opinion, any approach that

insists on making such a distinction is seriously flawed, because…*the very same object* can quite legitimately be regarded as an entity by some users and a relationship by others."

Third, even when conceptual modelling approaches allow classes of things to be distinguished from properties in general, how the distinction should be maintained is often unclear. In the entity-relationship (ER) model (Chen, 1976), for example, classes of things are supposed to be represented as entity types, and properties in general are supposed to be represented as attribute types. Nonetheless, entity-type symbols are often used to represent both classes of things and properties in general. For instance, a *preference*, which many individuals would deem to be a property in general of a class of things, might be represented as an entity type that is connected via a relationship type to a *client* entity type (see, e.g., Connolly & Begg, 2005, p. 344).

Fourth, disputes arise about how classes of things and properties in general should be represented in conceptual models if database design considerations are to be taken into account. For example, Simsion and Witt (2001, p. 104) state: "Attributes in an ER model correspond to columns in a relational model." They further suggest that ER models should be "normalized" and repeating groups of attributes removed to form additional entity types. Thus, they argue that representations in a conceptual model ought to be influenced by database design considerations.

A conceptual model is used to discover and document user views of an information system and to provide a basis for informed discernment, reconciliation, and compromise among users and information systems professionals (Hirschheim et al., 1995). Therefore, we argue that the representation of classes of things and properties in general in conceptual models should be based on a sound underlying theory about the structure and dynamics of phenomena in the world (Parsons & Wand, 2008). In this regard, however, little empirical work has been done (Evermann & Wand,

2006; Moody, 2002; Weber, 1996). Consequently, we undertook a theoretically based, empirical evaluation of alternative conceptual-modelling representations of classes of things and properties in general.

Five factors motivated our work. First, it is well recognized that the cost of fixing errors grows exponentially the later they are discovered in the system development process (e.g., Boehm, 1981). Because conceptual modelling work is undertaken early in the system development process, improvements in conceptual modelling practice potentially should lead to high payoffs (Moody & Shanks, 1998).

Second, in the context of implementing, operating, and maintaining enterprise systems, conceptual models are becoming increasingly important. They provide a means of evaluating the "fit" between an organization's needs and the business models embedded within the enterprise application software used to implement such systems (Sia & Soh, 2002). Similarly, in the context of implementing, operating, and maintaining interorganizational information systems, conceptual models provide a means to compare and contrast the different business models that underlie the participants' operations.

Third, we sought to test previous theoretical work undertaken to predict how well different types of representations facilitate or inhibit human understanding of real-world phenomena (e.g., Weber, 1997). If we can make accurate predictions about what types of conceptual modelling practices are likely to work well, we avoid the high costs associated with learning about the strengths and weaknesses of different practices through experience.

Fourth, it is important to determine which type of representation of real-world phenomena in a conceptual model enables humans to better understand the phenomena and why this outcome occurs. When conceptual models are prepared initially (e.g., by systems analysts), users of an information system are asked to evaluate the mod-els to determine how accurately and completely the models represent their perceptual worlds. If users cannot understand a conceptual model clearly in the first place, their ability to validate the model is impaired. Moreover, subsequent users may employ conceptual models to understand the functionality provided by an information system. If these users cannot understand the conceptual models clearly, their ability to engage effectively with the information system is undermined.

Fifth, we sought to contribute to improved conceptual modelling practice. As we discussed above, many different, sometimes-ambiguous guidelines for representing classes of things and properties in general appear in the practitioner literature. For example, the object role model does not distinguish between classes of things and properties in general (Halpin, 2008), whereas proponents of the entity relationship model provide differing guidelines about how the distinction is made (Chen, 1976; Simsion & Witt, 2001). These may confuse rather than assist practitioners (Simsion & Witt, 2001). We have designed our study to enable a comparison of alternative representations of classes of things and properties in general to determine empirically which representation supports better user understanding. If we develop improved conceptual-modelling rules for classes of things and properties in general, the conceptual-modelling tasks that practitioners undertake should be more straightforward.

The remainder of our paper proceeds as follows. The next section discusses the theory and proposition that underpin our empirical work. The third and fourth sections describe the design, conduct, and results of the laboratory experiment and cognitive process tracing study we undertook. The fifth section discusses our empirical results and relates the results of the process tracing study to those of the experiment. The sixth section presents our views on the implications of our results for research and practice. Finally, we discuss some limitations of our research and some directions for future research.

2. THEORY AND PROPOSITION

We base our proposition on two theories. First, we use the ontological theory proposed by Bunge (1977) and adapted for information systems by Wand and Weber (1993) to argue that a distinction between the representation of classes of things and properties in general is essential to avoid construct overload. We also use a theory of cognitive clustering within human information processing (Bousfield, 1953; Miller, 1956; Baddeley, 1994) to argue that clustering properties in general with the classes of things to which they belong helps humans understand complex representations.

The ontological theory we use analyzes the representation of classes of things and properties in general as follows:

1. "The world is made of things that possess properties" (Wand et al., 1999, p. 497). These are the two basic constructs that are needed to describe the world. There can be no bare things; they must possess one or more properties. Properties cannot exist by themselves; they must be attached to one or more things. Furthermore, properties themselves may not have properties (Wand et al., 1999, p. 498).

2. There are two types of properties: intrinsic properties and mutual properties. Intrinsic properties depend on one thing only–for example, the height of a person (Wand et al., 1999, p. 498). Mutual (or relational) properties depend on two or more things–for example, being a university student depends on both a person and a tertiary institution (Wand et al., 1999, p. 498).

3. Things can interact with each other (Wand et al., 1999, p. 503). Two things interact (are coupled) when a history of one thing (manifested as a sequence of the thing's states) would be different if the other thing did not exist. The existence of a mutual property between two things can indicate that they interact with each other. Mutual

properties that manifest interactions between two things are called *binding mutual properties*. For example, the mutual property that a person is a student at a university implies that the existence of the university affects the state of the person (and vice versa). If the university ceases to exist, the state of the person changes from being a student. If the person leaves the university, then the state of the university changes (the list of students will change in value (adapted from Wand et al., 1999, p. 503).

4. Properties (represented by attributes) that belong to the substantial individuals of all members of a set, *S*, are *properties in general* (e.g., age); properties that belong to a specific individual in the set are *properties in particular* (e.g., age is 16 years) (Bunge 1977, p. 63).

In the context of ontological theory we use, a property in general should not be represented as an entity type (or class) in conceptual modelling[1]. This practice leads to construct (semantic) overload because the same grammatical construct (an entity type or class symbol) has been used to represent two ontological constructs (classes of things and properties in general). Under these circumstances, users of the model must employ tacit knowledge to determine the semantics of the model (Wand & Weber, 1993).

It is well known that humans cognitively cluster phenomena that they perceive to be related in some way (Bousfield, 1953; Miller, 1956; Baddeley, 1994). They appear to use clustering as a means of dealing with the complexity they often encounter in their perceptual worlds. By focusing on the cluster rather than each phenomenon that makes up the cluster, they reduce cognitive load and enhance their abilities to make sense of the world. Parsons and Wand (2008a, 2008b) highlight the importance of classification as a cognitive clustering mechanism within science generally.

By sustaining a distinction between classes of things and properties in general, we argue humans invoke a cognitive strategy that allows them to deal with complexity. Properties in general "naturally" cluster with the things in the class to which they belong. Thus, perceiving the world in terms of classes of things and their properties in general helps humans to mitigate the cognitive problems they experience when they perceive phenomena to be complex.

For example, in the context of conceptual modelling, Moody (2002) and Weber (2003) argue information systems analysts and users who have to undertake the often-difficult task of decomposing an application domain into systems and subsystems will achieve a better outcome if the conceptual model developed to represent the domain clearly distinguishes between classes of things and properties in general in the domain. Similarly, Weber (1996) found that students trained in object-role modelling, which does not distinguish between classes of things and their properties in general, still used clusters of things and their properties as a basis for recalling object-role models (obtained from two organizations) that they had studied. He proposes a model based on spreading activation theory (Collins & Quillian, 1969; Anderson, 1983; Anderson & Pirolli, 1984) to account for why clustering of things with their properties will facilitate comprehension and recall of conceptual models.

Although the ontological theory we use provides a means of distinguishing and representing classes of things and properties in general in conceptual modelling, some conceptual modelling approaches do not sustain the distinction–for example object-role modelling (Halpin, 2008). For this reason, we argue that it is important to evaluate empirically the consequences of sustaining or not sustaining a distinction between classes of things and properties in general. Although theories of representation can never be proved correct, we can test falsifiable propositions based upon them (Bacharach, 1989; Popper, 1961).

In light of the ontological theory and the theory of cognitive clustering we use, we contend that conceptual models ought to maintain a distinction between classes of things and properties of things because it will allow their users to better comprehend the perceptual worlds that the models are supposed to represent. Thus, the following proposition motivates the empirical work we undertook:

Proposition: Conceptual models that distinguish between classes of things and properties in general will enable their users to better understand the semantics of the perceptual domains the models are representing than conceptual models that do not sustain this distinction.

3. LABORATORY EXPERIMENT

We employed a laboratory experiment because we sought to (a) manipulate in specific ways those phenomena about a domain that we represented in a conceptual model to try to obtain support for a cause-effect relationship, (b) control for extraneous factors that might confound any impacts of alternative representations of classes of things and properties in general in conceptual models on how well users of the models understood these constructs, and (c) obtain sufficient numbers of participants in our research to test statistically hypotheses motivated by our proposition.

3.1 Design and Measures

A four-group, post-test only experimental design was used with one active between-groups factor. This factor, "type of representation," had four levels. The first, which we term the "ontologically sound" level, represented classes of things as entity types and properties in general as attribute types in an ER diagram. The second, which we term the "partially ontologically sound" level, represented only *mutual* properties in general (properties of *n*-tuples of classes of things) as entity types. *In-*

trinsic properties in general (properties inherent to single class of things) were still represented as attribute types. The third, which we term the "normalized" level, represented mutual properties in general and some intrinsic properties in general as entity types. This level complied with the approach to representing application domains via ER diagrams used by many practitioners (Simsion & Witt, 2001). The fourth, which we term the "entity-only" level, represented both classes of things and properties in general as entity types. This level follows the principles used by object-role modellers (Halpin, 2008).

The dependent variable, performance, was evaluated in three ways: comprehension performance, problem-solving performance, and discrepancy-checking performance. These are all measures of script interpretation in the evaluation framework proposed by Gemino and Wand (2004). *Comprehension* involves someone using a conceptual model to understand the "surface-level" features of a domain. *Problem solving* involves someone using a conceptual model to solve problems that might arise in the domain. We differ from earlier work (e.g., Bodart et al., 2001; Gemino, 1999; Mayer, 1989) in that our problem-solving questions involved using and navigating a conceptual model to understand more-complex aspects of a domain, thereby providing a better indicator than comprehension of someone's "deep" understanding of a conceptual model. We used comprehension and problem-solving tasks to test how well the four conceptual models communicated the semantics of a domain to the participants in our experiment. *Discrepancy checking* involves someone comparing a conceptual model against a textual description of the domain (into which differences or discrepancies have been added) to evaluate whether the conceptual model represents the semantics manifested in the textual description accurately and completely (Moody, 2002). This task provides an alternative to answering questions as a means of testing someone's understanding of a conceptual model.

We measured comprehension, problem-solving, and discrepancy-checking performance in two ways: (a) accuracy, and (b) time taken. *Comprehension accuracy* was measured via the number of comprehension questions answered correctly by a participant. *Problem-solving accuracy* was measured via a score that was based on whether participants obtained a correct answer to the problem and provided a clear explanation of their rationale. *Discrepancy-checking accuracy* was measured via a score that was based on whether participants (a) identified correctly a discrepancy between the conceptual model and some text that described part of the application domain represented by the conceptual model, and (b) provided a clear explanation of the nature of the discrepancy. *Comprehension time*, *problem-solving time*, and *discrepancy-checking time* were all measured via the number of minutes (or part thereof) that participants took to complete each task.

3.2 Materials

Seven sets of materials were developed for the experiment. We present them below in three subsections: profile and training materials, conceptual models, and understanding tasks materials.

3.2.1 Profile and Training Materials

Two sets of profile and training materials were developed. The first comprised a "personal-profile" questionnaire to obtain information about participants' academic qualifications, industry experience, work experience, time in their current position, and modelling experience. We used these materials to ensure participants who received the different treatments had similar academic qualifications, work experience, etc.

The second was a summary of the ER symbols used in the diagrams provided to participants in the experiment. Note, to maximize our contribution to conceptual modelling practice, we decided to base our study on the ER approach to conceptual modelling. This approach is used widely in practice (Rosemann et al., 2003; Simsion & Witt, 2001).

3.2.2 Conceptual Models

Four ER diagrams of alternative conceptual models of a sales order domain (one that is understood widely) were developed. We first prepared a diagram using an approach that is employed widely in practice (Figure 1)–namely, where entity types essentially are third normal form relations (Simsion & Witt, 2001). Using this approach, classes of things are represented as entity types. In addition, multi-valued attributes in general (intrinsic properties in general) are represented as entity types (known as attributive or characteristic entity types–for example, *Customer Contact Person* in Figure 1). Similarly, value domains are also represented as entity types (known as classification entity types–for example, *Customer Industry Type* in Figure 1), and many-to-many relationships (mutual properties in general) are represented as entity types (known as intersection or associative entity types–for example, *Sales Order Item* in Figure 1). In ontological terms, many ontological constructs are represented by one modelling construct, an entity type, which leads to construct overload (Wand & Weber, 1993). In developing the model in Figure 1, we first analyzed a typical model from practice to work out the ratios of the different categories of entity types described above. We ensured our model had similar ratios to increase its external validity.

Next, we developed an ontologically sound model of the sales order domain. In preparing the ER diagram for this model, we adopted a two-stage approach. First, we transformed the "normalized" ER model into a "partially ontologically sound" model (Figure 2) by removing the attributive and classification entity types and folding their attributes in general into the related entity type (e.g., attributes in general from *Customer Contact Person* and *Customer Industry Type* were folded into the *Customer* entity type).

These transformations are consistent with ontological principles for representing intrinsic properties in general.

Third, we transformed the "partially ontologically sound" model into the "ontologically sound" ER model (Figure 3) by removing the associative entity types through folding their attributes in general into both related entity types (e.g., attributes in general from *Sales Order Item* were folded into both the *Order* entity type and the *Product* entity type). This transformation is consistent with ontological principles for representing mutual properties in general[2]. When these transformations are made, minor information losses occur that are associated with constraints on relationships that were deleted. We were careful to avoid involving these aspects of the models in our comprehension, problem-solving, and discrepancy-checking tasks to ensure information equivalence issues did not confound the results (Burton-Jones et al., 2009; Parsons & Cole, 2005; Siau, 2004).

We then developed a model of the sales domain that does not distinguish between things and properties (Figure 4). We transformed the "normalized" ER model by creating a new entity type for each attribute. This transformation is consistent with the philosophy underlying object-role modelling–namely, that no distinction should be made between classes of things and their properties in general. "Facts" that connect classes of things are the key concept. When this transformation was made, a more complex model resulted. Nonetheless, the cardinality constraints on the relationships provided clear semantics.

The four categories of model used in this study constitute four points in a continuum (Figure 5) varying from the "entity-only" ER model, where no distinction is made between classes of things and properties in general, to the "normalized" ER model, where all mutual properties in general but only some intrinsic properties in general are represented as entity types, to the "partially ontologically sound" ER model, where mutual prop-

Figure 1. Normalized ER model

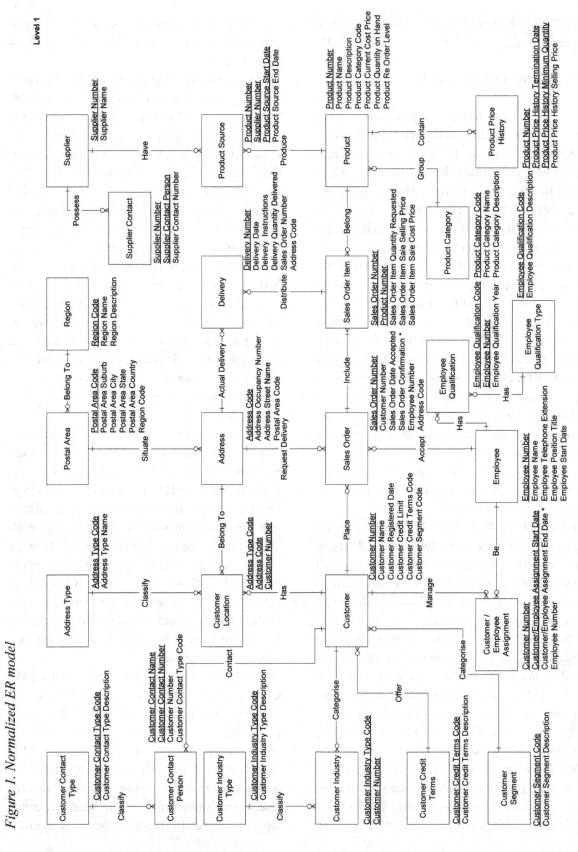

Figure 2. Partially ontologically sound ER model

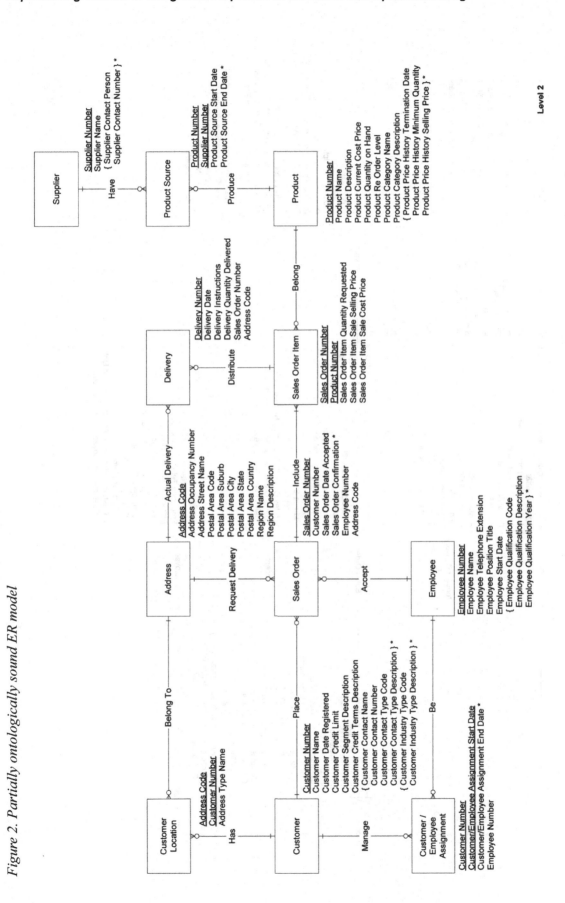

Figure 3. Ontologically sound ER model

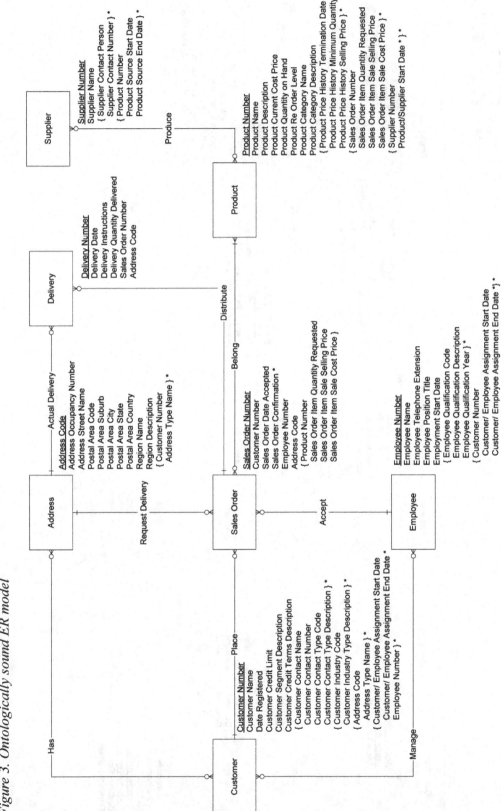

Figure 4. Entity-Only ER model

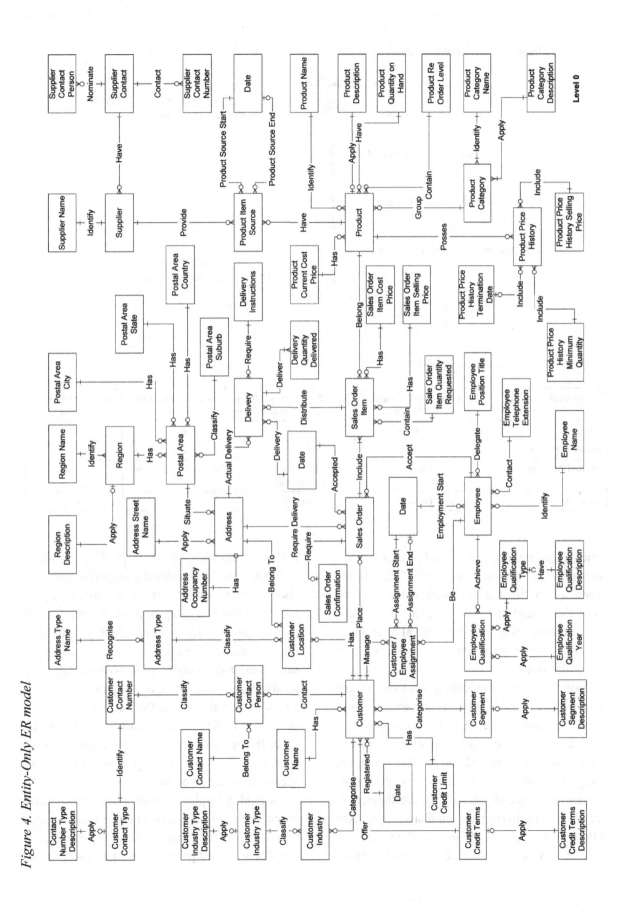

Figure 5. Thing/Property continuum

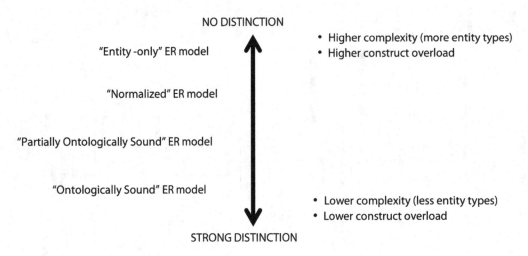

Table 1. Mapping between models

Ontological Concept	Ontologically Sound ER Model	Partially Ontologically Sound ER Model	Normalized ER Model	Entity-Only ER Model
Thing	Entity	Entity	Entity	Entity
Intrinsic Property	Attribute	Attribute	Entity or Attribute	Entity
Mutual Property	Attribute	Entity or Relationship	Entity or Relationship	Entity
Value Domain	Domain	Domain	Domain	Entity

erties in general are represented as entity types, through to the "ontologically sound" ER Model, where a clear distinction is made between classes of things and properties in general[3]. Table 1 shows the mapping from ontological concepts to modelling notation constructs for each of the four types of model.

In preparing these models, a problem we faced was how we should distinguish classes of things from properties in general in our application domain. Clearly, if this task were straightforward, no debate would arise about whether classes of things and properties in general were distinct phenomena in the world. To make the distinction, we used three criteria. First, qualitatively we deem a thing to be a physically independent phenomenon in the world—that is, it satisfies the condition

that it is "capable of existing in physical space, by itself, without requiring the support of anything else" (Denkel, 1996, p. 16). For example, a particular person is a thing because the person is a phenomenon that exists independently in physical space. A skill, however, is a property because it cannot exist independently in physical space–it must inhere in a thing. In this regard, if we move a person in physical space, the fact that the person's skills also move is "gratuitous." If we want to move the person's skills in physical space, however, we have to move the person "in order to" accomplish this outcome.[4]

Second, if the phenomenon when named can be conceived as a function that maps something to a value domain, we deem it to be a property in general. For instance, "person" cannot be conceived as a function that maps something to a value domain. On the other hand, skill is a property in general of the "person" class of things because it can be conceived as a function that maps something to a value domain (e.g., skill can take on the values "programming," "accounting," and "bass playing" for a particular person thing). In short, we cannot assign a thing a value; only its properties can be assigned values.

Third, following Denkel (1996, p. 35), things survive a change of their properties,[5] whereas properties cannot survive changes of things. For instance, a person may have the skill of being a bass player. The skill may be lost, however, if the person fails to practice the instrument for a long period or suffers permanent injury to a hand. Nonetheless, the person survives in spite of the skill being lost. The person's skill of being a bass player cannot simply be transported or given to another person. Note, we are focusing on a *property in particular* (a particular person's particular skill as a bass player) as opposed to a *property in general* (the skill of bass playing that many people possess) (Bunge, 1977, pp. 62-65).

3.3.2 Understanding Tasks Materials

Three sets of materials were developed. The first comprised 10 comprehension questions. They were designed to test a user's ability to access and navigate the model for relatively simple, surface-level tasks. Responses to questions were "yes," "no," or "not sure" (included to minimize guessing). An example is: "Can an employee be assigned to manage more than one customer at a time?" (See Appendix 1 for more examples.)

The second comprised 10 problem-solving questions. They were designed to force participants to use the ER diagrams in deeper ways and to obtain a correct answer based on the diagrams rather than relying on their tacit knowledge of the sales order domain. Responses to questions were "possible," "not possible," or "not sure" (included to minimize guessing). Participants also had to provide a brief explanation of their answer. An

example is: "An Ontological Plastics supplier wishes to send samples of new and improved hoses to customers who regularly order hoses. Can we determine the number of hoses each customer has had delivered in the previous three months and the date of each delivery?" (See Appendix 1 for more examples.)

The third comprised a typed transcript of a fictitious interview between a conceptual modeller and three users. The users described a number of aspects of the sales order domain. For example, a comment made by the second user is: "Yes, well, each of our deliveries consists of a single product but may contain items from multiple sales orders, so we need to know precisely where they all need to go." Beside the transcript was a column where participants could note any discrepancies they identified between the semantics in the conceptual model they had been given and the details of the sales domain described in the transcript. We had seeded the transcript so its semantics differed in eight ways from the conceptual model. Again, participants had to provide a brief explanation of any discrepancy they identified. (See Appendix 1 for an example paragraph from the transcript.)

3.3 Participants

Participants in the experiment were 80 volunteers who either worked in industry or had worked in industry but at the time of the experiment were postgraduate students. None performed or had performed information systems/information technology functions as their primary role within their organization. In essence, in the experiment they acted as surrogate end users. With the exception of one person who had 20 years' work experience, all had at least an undergraduate degree with majors in diverse areas (e.g., arts, architecture, psychology, law, accounting, education, mathematics, information systems, engineering). Forty-two had between one and five years' work experience, and 14 had in excess of 10 years' work experience. Sixty-one had no experience of data models. The remainder had minor experience of one or two modelling techniques like flowcharts or financial models. Each participant was paid $30 to undertake the experiment.

3.4 Procedures

Participants were first assigned randomly to one of the four treatments (20 per treatment). Sixty-nine participants were run singly through the experiment, seven undertook the experiment together in a group, and there were two other groups of two participants[6]. When they arrived to undertake the experiment, they were asked to complete a consent form and the personal-profile questionnaire.

Next they were given the document that explained the ER symbols. Participants were permitted to discuss the symbols with the researchers until they indicated they felt confident in their understanding of the ER symbols. They retained and could refer to the ER summary throughout the experiment.

When participants indicated they were ready to begin, they were given the "ontologically sound" ER diagram, the "partially ontologically sound" ER diagram, the "normalized" ER diagram, or the "entity-only" ER diagram, depending on the treatment to which they had been assigned randomly. They retained and could refer to the diagram throughout the experiment. The times taken to answer each comprehension and problem-solving question were recorded as well as the total time taken to perform the discrepancy-checking task.[7] Notes were also made based on participant reactions, queries, and approaches to each question. With 67 participants, one researcher conducted the experiment, while another took notes, recorded times, and observed the participant's behavior during the experiment. The remaining 13 participants recorded their own times because they undertook the experiment in groups or only one researcher could be present as two participants were undertaking the experiment concurrently in different locations. Overall, the experiment took about 90 minutes to complete.

Note that we did not randomize the order in which participants were given the comprehension, problem-solving, and discrepancy-checking tasks (see, also, Mayer, 1989; Mayer & Gallini, 1990). Rather, we had participants follow a sequence of tasks aimed at testing the different types of understanding we expected they would acquire at different stages as they progressively came to grips with the meaning of the conceptual model they had been given. In this regard, at the outset we expected that participants would first acquire a surface-level understanding of the conceptual model. Hence, we gave them the comprehension task first to test how well they had acquired a surface-level understanding of the domain using the four models. Next, we expected that participants would build on their surface-level understanding to develop a deep-level understanding of the conceptual model. Ideally, we would have split our participant group to then undertake either the problem-solving or the discrepancy-checking task. We lacked the resources to pursue this strategy, however. Thus, we chose to give participants the problem-solving task before the discrepancy-checking task because we thought the former would provide us with a more-valid and more-reliable measure of participants' deep-level understanding of the conceptual model.

3.5 Results

Scores for the individual items on the comprehension, problem-solving, and discrepancy-checking dependent measures were first calculated. Next, a reliability check on the dependent measures was undertaken. Statistical analyses were then performed on the scores for each dependent measure to test the proposition that underlies our research.

3.5.1 Data Scoring

Scores were awarded as follows (and then normalized to a score out of 100):

1. *Comprehension* (10 questions; maximum score 10)

One mark was given if the answer ("possible" or "not possible") was correct; zero was given if a participant selected "not sure" or their answer was incorrect. Participants were encouraged to answer "not sure" rather than guess an answer.

2. *Problem Solving* (10 questions; maximum score 20)

Two marks were given if the answer ("possible" or "not possible") was correct; zero was given if a participant selected "not sure" or their answer was incorrect. Explanations were used to amend the score only if the explanation was inconsistent with the answer given. If the answer was correct but the explanation was unclear and did not support the answer, one mark was subtracted from the score. If the answer was incorrect or "not sure" but the explanation indicated the participant was reasoning coherently about the problem, one mark was added to the score. The two of us who conducted the experiment independently scored the problem-solving measures on pre-formatted scoring sheets.[8] Few differences arose between the two sets of scores. Where they did occur, they were discussed and reconciled.

3. *Discrepancy Checking* (8 discrepancies; maximum score 16)

One mark was given if a participant correctly identified a discrepancy between the text and the conceptual model. A second mark was given if the participant then provided a clear explanation of the nature of the discrepancy. Again, the two of us who conducted the experiment independently scored the discrepancy-checking measure. Few differences arose, and they were discussed and reconciled where they did occur.

3.5.2 Reliability Analysis of Dependent Measures

Cronbach alphas for the comprehension, problem-solving, and discrepancy-checking measures were .56, .42, and .56. Given the complex, multifaceted "understanding" construct that underlies these measures, we believe their reliability is satisfactory (Nunnally, 1978). Deletion of any "item" from the measures neither increased nor decreased alpha markedly.

3.5.3 Tests of Proposition

In this section, we report the results of the tests we undertook of the proposition that "Conceptual models that distinguish between classes of things and properties in general will enable their users to better understand the semantics of the perceptual domains the models are representing than conceptual models that do not sustain this distinction."

For each of the four models (ontologically sound, partially ontologically sound, normalized, and entity-only), we test the accuracy (interpretational fidelity) and time taken (interpretational efficiency) (Burton-Jones et al., 2009) for the comprehension, problem solving, and discrepancy checking tasks. We first report the accuracy and time measures and their correlations. We then explain the statistical analyses we undertook. Finally, we present our significant findings.

1. Accuracy and Time Measures

Table 2 shows the means and standard deviations for the accuracy and time measures associated with the three primary performance constructs (comprehension, problem solving, and discrepancy checking). Table 3 shows the Pearson correlation coefficients among the accuracy and time measures.

Table 2. Means and Standard deviations for comprehension, problem-solving, and discrepancy-checking performance measures

	Comprehension		Problem Solving		Discrepancy Checking	
	Accuracy	Time	Accuracy	Time	Accuracy	Time
Ontologically Sound ER Model	74.50 (16.38)	6.70 (2.89)	59.75 (16.97)	29.27 (13.87)	50.63 (21.55)	16.20 (5.32)
Partially Onto-logically Sound ER Model	62.50 (15.52)	8.11 (3.53)	54.5 (13.85)	28.05 (8.17)	37.97 (19.77)	12.97 (38.33)
Normalized ER Model	66.00 (19.84)	12.88 (5.24)	51.25 (17.24)	36.40 (13.10)	52.5 (21.28)	16.66 (6.46)
Entity-Only ER Model	50.50 (23.72)	11.40 (4.71)	49.25 (16.00)	31.92 (11.46)	43.91 (20.99)	16.23 (5.52)

Table 3. Pearson correlations among comprehension, problem-solving, and discrepancy-checking performance measures

	Comprehension Time	Problem-Solving Accuracy	Problem-Solving Time	Discrepancy-Checking Accuracy	Discrepancy-Checking Time
Comprehension Accuracy	-.177 (.116)	.407 (.000)	.266 (.017)	.338 (.002)	.006 (.955)
Comprehension Time		-.137 (.226)	.397 (.000)	.070 (.537)	.324 (.003)
Problem-Solving Accuracy			.176 (.119)	.452 (.000)	.124 (.273)
Problem-Solving Time				.217 (.053)	.435 (.000)
Discrepancy-Checking Accuracy					.297 (.007)

2. Statistical Analyses

The three accuracy measures and the three time measures are moderately correlated with one another (see Table 3). For this reason, we undertook two separate, single-factor multivariate analyses of variance (MANOVA). In both MA-NOVAs, the factor was type of model at four levels (ontologically sound, partially ontologically sound, normalized, and entity-only). In the first, the dependent measures were comprehension accuracy, problem-solving accuracy, and discrepancy-checking accuracy. In the second, the dependent measures were comprehension time,

problem-solving time, and discrepancy-checking time. Checks of the assumptions underlying both MANOVAs (univariate and multivariate normality, univariate and multivariate outliers, linearity, homogeneity of variance-covariance matrices) revealed no violations.

For the three *accuracy* measures, the model was significant: $F(9, 180.247) = 2.748$, $p = .005$; Wilks' Lambda = . 980, partial eta squared = .099. In this light, we used the Roy-Bargmann stepdown analysis procedure to determine which of the three accuracy measures were statistically significant (Tabachnick & Fidell, 2007, pp. 271-272). We entered the dependent variables into the stepdown analysis following the order in which they had been measured in the experiment (i.e., comprehension accuracy, problem-solving accuracy, and discrepancy-checking accuracy).

We first undertook a univariate analysis of variance (ANOVA) with type of model as the factor and comprehension accuracy as the dependent variable. The model was significant: $F(3,76) = 5.408$, $p = .005$; adjusted R-squared $= .143$. Using a Bonferroni adjusted alpha level of .008 to give a family alpha level of .05, we then undertook six follow-up pairwise comparisons of means. Only one was statistically significant ($p = .001$)—namely, participants who received the entity-only ER model performed less well than participants who received the ontologically sound ER model.

Next, we undertook an analysis of covariance (ANCOVA) with type of model as the factor, problem-solving accuracy as the dependent variable, and comprehension accuracy as the covariate. While comprehension accuracy was statistically significant as a covariate ($p = .001$), type of model was not statistically significant.

We then undertook another ANCOVA with type of model as the factor, discrepancy-checking accuracy as the dependent variable, and comprehension accuracy and problem-solving accuracy as the covariates. On this occasion, problem-solving accuracy was a statistically significant covariate ($p < .001$), but neither comprehension accuracy nor type of model was statistically significant.

For the three *time* measures, the MANOVA was also significant: $F(9, 180.247) = 3.528$, $p < .001$; Wilks' Lambda $= .674$, partial eta squared $= .123$. In this light, we again used the Roy-Bargmann stepdown analysis procedure to determine which of the three time measures were statistically significant. Once more, we entered the dependent variables into the stepdown analysis following the order in which they had been measured in the experiment (i.e., comprehension time, problem-solving time, and discrepancy-checking time).

We first undertook a univariate analysis of variance (ANOVA) with type of model as the

factor and comprehension time as the dependent variable. The model was significant: $F(3,76) = 9.267$, $p < .001$; adjusted R-squared $= .239$. Using a Bonferroni adjusted alpha level of .008 to give a family alpha level of .05, we then undertook six follow-up pairwise comparisons of means. Participants who received the ontologically sound ER model outperformed those who received the entity-only ER model ($p = .004$) and normalized ER model ($p < .001$). Furthermore, those who received the partially ontologically sound ER model outperformed those who received the normalized ER model ($p = .003$).

Next, we undertook an analysis of covariance (ANCOVA) with type of model as the factor, problem-solving time as the dependent variable, and comprehension time as the covariate. While comprehension time was statistically significant as a covariate ($p = .003$), type of model was not statistically significant.

We then undertook another ANCOVA with type of model as the factor, discrepancy-checking time as the dependent variable, and comprehension time and problem-solving time as the covariates. On this occasion, problem-solving time was a statistically significant covariate ($p < .002$), but neither comprehension time nor type of model was statistically significant.

3. Significant Findings

Our results show that the type of model had a significant effect for the comprehension task but not for the problem-solving or discrepancy-checking tasks. In terms of comprehension accuracy (interpretational fidelity), we found that participants who received the ontologically sound ER model outperformed those who received the entity-only ER model ($p = .001$). For comprehension time taken (interpretational efficiency), we found that participants who received the ontologically sound ER model outperformed those who received the normalized ER model ($p < .001$) and entity-only ER model ($p = .004$). Moreover, those who received the partially ontologically sound ER model outperformed those who received the normalized ER model (p = .003).

Although the comprehension *accuracy* results are somewhat muted in terms of support for our proposition, the *time taken* results are strongly supportive. We further explore the reasons why these results were found in the next section.

4. COGNITIVE PROCESS TRACING STUDY

We conducted a process tracing study to better understand the cognitive behaviour patterns of users of conceptual models and to help explain the outcomes we obtained in our laboratory experiment. We focus in particular on the ontological sound and normalized ER models to enable a comparison of the model motivated by our theory with the model most widely used in practice.

4.1 Design and Measures

We collected data about the cognitive processes of individuals who participated in our study using a verbal protocol technique. This technique requires individuals to verbalize their thoughts as they undertake some task (Ericsson & Simon, 1984). Cognitive process tracing is a recognized data gathering technique in cognitive psychology and information systems research. It is based on the assumption that humans consciously construct a representation of a problem and their detailed problem-solving strategies when they solve a problem. It also assumes that humans are able to access these strategies and verbalize them.

In this study we use the concurrent verbal protocol approach. Participants are asked to think aloud during the course of the task, thereby providing the researchers with direct access to their thought processes (Newell & Simon, 1972; Ericsson & Simon, 1984). Using verbal protocols provides a means to trace cognitive processes step by step,

instead of relying on information about task outcomes or querying participants retrospectively about their cognitive processes. Our focus was on (a) understanding the cognitive behaviour of participants for those experimental tasks in which a significant difference was obtained, and (b) explaining why these outcomes occurred.

4.2 Materials

Four sets of materials were used in the study. The first was a "personal-profile" questionnaire to obtain information about participants' backgrounds. The second, third, and fourth sets of materials had been used in our prior laboratory experiment. The second comprised a summary of the ER symbols used in the diagrams provided to participants in the study. The third comprised two ER diagrams of alternative conceptual models of a sales order domain (one that is understood widely). We used only the ontological sound and normalized models from the laboratory experiment because the first model is motivated by our theory and the latter is the most widely used in practice. The fourth comprised five comprehension questions and five problem-solving questions.

4.3 Participants

Twelve participants took part in the study. All had at least three years' industry experience. They were selected on the basis that they would act as surrogate end users. They did not play an information technology role in their organisation, nor did they have previous data modelling experience.

4.4 Procedures

The materials were first pilot tested with two individuals who were not participants in the primary study. No concerns were identified. The primary study then commenced.

Participants in the primary study were first assigned randomly to one of the two alternative representation groups. Within each group, the sequence of tasks was altered for every second participant (comprehension followed by problem solving or problem solving followed by comprehension). Participants were then run singly through the task. When they arrived to undertake the task, they were asked to complete a consent form and the personal-profile instrument. The "speak-aloud" approach to data collection was then explained. A camcorder mounted on a tripod was focused on the ER models and used to (a) videotape participants as they indicated navigation of the models with a pencil, and (b) record participants' verbalizations.

Next, participants were given the document that explained the ER modelling symbols. They were permitted to discuss the symbols with the researchers until they indicated they felt confident with their meaning. Throughout the study, participants retained and could refer to the summary of the ER modelling symbols.

When participants indicated they were ready to begin, they were given either the "ontologically sound" or "normalized" ER diagram. They were then asked to work through the first task (either comprehension or problem solving). If periods of silence occurred, they were prompted to "speak aloud" to explain their cognitive behaviour. After a brief pause at the conclusion of the first task, participants were asked to work through the second task. At the conclusion of this task, participants were thanked and dismissed.

4.5 Coding Scheme

A coding scheme was established using the problem-solving literature (e.g., Newell & Simon 1972) and similar previous studies of data modelling (e.g., Batra & Davis, 1992; Chaiyasut, 1994; Shanks et al., 2008). This coding scheme comprised five cognitive behavior categories:

- *Understanding Question*: Includes reading the question, seeking clarification, iden-

tifying assumptions and constraints, and recognizing the problem posed.
- *Identifying Model Segment*: Includes locating appropriate parts of the model and matching them against key concepts in the question.
- *Articulating Model Semantics*: Includes verifying semantics of symbols in the model and re-reading the symbol summary.
- *Preparing Solution*: Includes developing solutions and simulating and revising solutions against the question.
- *Evaluation*: Includes selection of alternative answers and developing justifications.

4.6 Analysis of Protocol Data

All utterances on the videotapes were transcribed and partitioned into segments based on similar content. Video data was used to help identify start and end times for each segment. Each segment was then assigned to a cognitive behavior category within the coding scheme. Data was coded independently by two of the authors. Differences were reconciled.

Protocol data was further analyzed in three ways. First, the average time that participants spent in each of the five cognitive behavior categories was compared. This comparison indicates in which category the main differences occurred. Second, the proportion of time spent in each cognitive behavior category for each of ten equal time segments was compared. This comparison indicates which categories were prominent at different stages of the comprehension task. Third, the total number of transitions between each of the five categories was compared. This comparison indicates patterns in the sequence of cognitive behavior categories.

Figure 6 shows the average time that participants spent in each cognitive behavior category. Participants who received the ontologically sound model on average took 6.61 minutes to complete all five comprehension questions. Those who received the normalized ER model on average took

Figure 6. Average time spent in each behaviour category

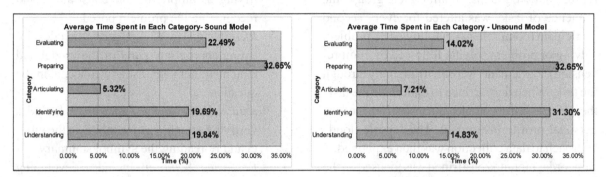

Figure 7. Proportion of time spent in each behaviour category

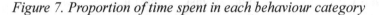

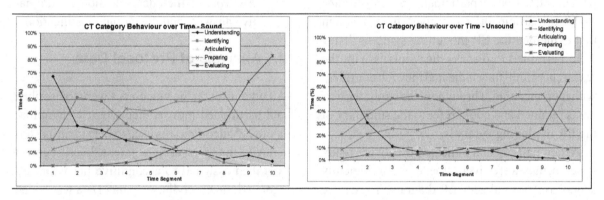

7.68 minutes to complete all five comprehension questions. The average time spent in identifying appropriate parts of the model and articulating model semantics was considerably less for participants who received the ontologically sound ER model. For example, participants who received the ontologically sound ER model spent 19.69 percent (compared to 31.30 percent for participants who received the normalized ER model) of their time in identifying appropriate parts of the model. This outcome suggests that participants found the normalized ER model more difficult to read and navigate. Furthermore, participants who received the ontologically sound ER model spent more of their time in understanding the model and evaluating their solutions, which suggests that they obtained a better comprehension of the model semantics.

Figure 7 shows the proportion of time spent in each cognitive behavior category for each of the ten time segments. The participants who received the ontologically sound ER model were able to identify appropriate parts of the model much earlier in the overall process. For example, in time segments 2 and 3, they spent about 50 percent of their time in the "identify" category, after which the proportion of their time in this category reduced sharply. In contrast, those participants who received the normalized ER model spent about 50 percent of their time in the "identify" category in time segments 3, 4, and 5, after which the proportion of their time in this category reduced at a slower rate. Similarly, preparing and evaluating solutions occurred much earlier for those participants who received the ontologically sound ER model.

Figure 8. Total number of transitions between each behaviour category

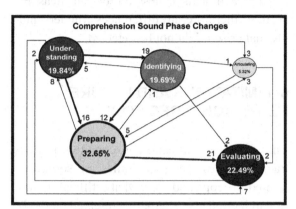

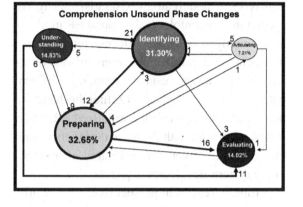

Figure 8 shows the sequential dependencies between the five behaviour categories. The numbers above the dependency arrows are the total number of transitions between two categories. The thickness of the arrows indicates the intensity of the dependency. Overall, the most-common sequence for participants regardless of the type of model they received was to understand the question and to either identify the area in the model or directly prepare the solution before their final evaluation of the answer. Participants who received the ontologically sound model had less transition activity for the identifying model segment cognitive behavior category and more transition activity for the preparing solution cognitive behavior category. For example, they had 20 transitions in and 20 transitions out of the identifying model segment cognitive behavior category compared with 25 transitions in and 25 transitions out for participants who received the normalized ER model. They also had 43 transitions in and 32 transitions out of the preparing solutions model segment cognitive behavior category compared with 26 transitions in and 26 transitions out for participants who received the normalized ER model. This outcome is consistent with participants who received the ontologically sound model focusing more on solution preparation and evaluation rather than identifying appropriate parts of the model.

5. IMPLICATIONS OF THE RESEARCH

Our results provide some support for our proposition that classes of things and properties in general should be modelled explicitly as entity types and attributes. In this light, we argue that practitioners should be cautious when modelling properties in general as entity types and not attribute types. By failing to distinguish between classes of things and properties in general in the conceptual models they construct, they risk undermining users' understanding of the real-world phenomena being represented in the models. This understanding may be important to successfully accomplishing certain types of tasks that users of the models have to perform.

Our results also suggest that practitioners should be cautious about using the same type of model for both conceptual modelling and database-design purposes[9]. In this regard, relative to the normalized ER model, we have some evidence to indicate that the ontologically sound ER model better facilitates users' understanding of a domain. Given the way in which the normalized ER model has been constructed, however, we expect it is more suitable than the ontologically sound ER model as a means of supporting logical database design tasks. Moreover, because we could fairly easily transform an existing normalized ER model into an ontologically sound ER model, we expect that both types of model can co-exist satisfactorily. We predict that the ontologically sound ER model is best employed with users during requirements modelling and validation or comparisons of alternative models embedded within, say, different enterprise systems packages. On the other hand, we predict that the equivalent normalized ER model is best employed with database designers during implementation work carried out at later stages in the system-development process[10].

From a research perspective, our results strengthen a growing body of empirical work that supports the usefulness of ontological theories, particularly Bunge's (1977) ontological theory, as a means of predicting the strengths and weaknesses of alternative conceptual modelling methods (e.g., Weber, 1996; Green and Rosemann, 1996; Gemino, 1999; Opdahl & Henderson-Sellers, 2001; Parsons, 1996; Parsons & Wand, 2000; Bodart et al., 2001; Burton-Jones & Meso, 2006; Shanks et al., 2008). In the past, researchers have compared alternative conceptual modelling methods via omnibus feature comparisons or case studies (e.g., Olle et al., 1983). The results they have obtained using these approaches have been equivocal, which has motivated some researchers to call for better theory (e.g., Floyd, 1986). We argue that ontological theories can be used to address the shortcomings of these approaches because they allow us to pinpoint the strengths and weaknesses of alternative conceptual modelling methods. These predictions can then be tested using empirical research.

Our research also highlights the importance of the methods we employ to measure users' understanding of the phenomena represented by a conceptual model. Like prior research (e.g., Bodart et al., 2001), we found that some measures detected differences in the understanding obtained by users who studied a conceptual model. Other measures, however, detected no differences in user understanding. Presumably, users are eliciting different types of understanding when they study

conceptual models. Unless appropriate measures are used, therefore, any differences in understanding that arise might not be detected.

6. LIMITATIONS AND FUTURE RESEARCH DIRECTIONS

Like most experimental and cognitive process tracing studies, our two studies are somewhat limited in scope and somewhat artificial. Future research might use alternative research methods, such as case studies and action research, to test our proposition in more-realistic settings (Siau & Rossi, 2007).

Our results are also limited by the validity and reliability of our measures. The fundamental construct that underlies our research, human understanding of a domain, is complex and multifaceted. We need better insights into the different types of understanding (e.g., surface-level versus deep-level) that users of conceptual models obtain when they employ a model. We also need better insights into how these different types of understanding support various tasks that users of conceptual models must undertake (e.g., responding to queries about a domain versus solving problems in the domain). Without these types of insights, our measures of user understanding will remain problematic.

Our results also suggest that humans might attend to different generic features of the real world, depending upon the task they must undertake. For instance, Shanks et al. (2008) found that users of a conceptual model attend to how composites and components are represented in the model when they have to solve problems about the domain represented by the model. On the other hand, we found that users of a conceptual model do *not* appear to be attending to whether a distinction is being made between classes of things and properties in general when they have to solve problems about the domain represented by the model. Instead, we found the distinction is important in relation to comprehension tasks that they have to perform. Moody (2002) and Weber (2003) have also argued the distinction is important if users have to undertake decomposition tasks. Thus, future research might examine what sorts of tasks, if any, are best supported by distinguishing between classes of things and properties in general in conceptual models.

ACKNOWLEDGMENT

Earlier and partial reports on the research described in this paper have been published in Shanks et al. (2003a), Shanks et al. (2003b), and Shanks et al. (2004). An Australian Research Council Discovery Grant funded this research. We thank Graeme Simsion for helpful comments on our research

REFERENCES

Andersen, J. R. (1983). A spreading activation theory of memory. *Journal of Verbal Learning and Verbal Behavior, 22*, 261–295. doi:10.1016/S0022-5371(83)90201-3

Anderson, J. R., & Pirolli, P. L. (1984). Spread of activation. *Journal of Experimental Psychology. Learning, Memory, and Cognition, 10*(4), 791–798. doi:10.1037/0278-7393.10.4.791

Bacharach, S. (1989). Organizational theories: Some criteria for evaluation. *Academy of Management Review, 14*(4), 496–515. doi:10.2307/258555

Baddeley, A. (1994). The magical number seven: Still magic after all these years. *Psychological Review, 101*(2), 353–356. doi:10.1037/0033-295X.101.2.353

Bodart, F., Sim, M., Patel, A., & Weber, R. (2001). Should optional properties be used in conceptual modelling? A theory and three empirical tests. *Information Systems Research, 12*(4), 384–405. doi:10.1287/isre.12.4.384.9702

Boehm, B. (1981). *Software Engineering Economics*. Upper Saddle River, NJ: Prentice-Hall.

Bousfield, W. A. (1953). The occurrence of clustering in the recall of randomly arranged associates. *The Journal of General Psychology, 49*(October), 229–240.

Bunge, M. (1977). Treatise on Basic Philosophy: *Vol. 3. Ontology I: The Furniture of the World.* Boston: Reidel.

Burton-Jones, A., & Meso, A. P. (2006). Conceptualizing systems for understanding: An empirical test of decomposition principles in object-oriented analysis. *Information Systems Research, 17*(1), 38–60. doi:10.1287/isre.1050.0079

Burton-Jones, A., Wand, Y., & Weber, R. (2009). Guidelines for Empirical Evaluations of Conceptual Modeling Grammars . *Journal of AIS, 10*(6), 495–532.

Chen, P. P. S. (1976). The entity-relationship model: Toward a unified view of data. *ACM Transactions on Database Systems, 1*(1), 9–36. doi:10.1145/320434.320440

Collins, A. M., & Quillian, M. R. (1969). Retrieval time from semantic memory. *Journal of Verbal Learning and Verbal Behavior, 8*, 240–247. doi:10.1016/S0022-5371(69)80069-1

Connolly, T., & Begg, C. (2005). *Database Systems: A Practical Approach to Design, Implementation, and Management* (4th ed.). Harlow, UK: Addison-Wesley.

Date, C. J. (2003). *An Introduction to Database Systems* (8th ed.). Reading, MA: Addison-Wesley.

Davis, F. D. (1989). Perceived usefulness, perceived ease of use, and user acceptance of information technology. *MIS Quart., 13*, 319–340. doi:10.2307/249008

Denkel, A. (1996). *Object and Property*. Cambridge, UK: Cambridge University Press. doi:10.1017/CBO9780511554575

Evermann, J., & Wand, Y. (2006). Ontological Modelling Rules for UML: An Empirical Assessment. *Journal of Computer Information Systems*, *46*(5), 14–19.

Floyd, C. (1986). A comparative evaluation of system development methods. In Olle, T. W., Sol, H. G., & Verrijn-Stuart, A. A. (Eds.), *Information System Design Methodologies: Improving the Practice* (pp. 19–54). Amsterdam, The Netherlands: North-Holland.

Gemino, A. (1999). *Empirical methods for comparing system analysis modelling techniques*. Unpublished doctorial dissertation, University of British Columbia.

Gemino, A., & Wand, Y. (2004). A framework for empirical evaluation of conceptual modelling techniques. *Requirements Engineering*, *9*, 248–260. doi:10.1007/s00766-004-0204-6

Green, P., & Rosemann, M. (2000). Integrated process modelling: An ontological evaluation. *Information Systems*, *25*(2), 73–87. doi:10.1016/S0306-4379(00)00010-7

Halpin, T. A. (2008). *Information Modeling and Relational Databases* (2nd ed.). San Francisco: Morgan Kaufman.

Hirschheim, R., Klein, H., & Lyytinen, K. (1995). *Information Systems Development and Data Modeling: Conceptual Foundations and Philosophical Foundations*. Cambridge, UK: Cambridge University Press.

Kent, W. (1978). *Data and Reality*. Amsterdam, The Netherlands: North-Holland.

Mayer, R. E. (1989). Models for understanding. *Review of Educational Research*, *59*, 43–64.

Mayer, R. E., & Gallini, J. K. (1990). When is an illustration worth ten thousand words? *Journal of Educational Psychology*, *82*(4), 715–726. doi:10.1037/0022-0663.82.4.715

Miller, G. A. (1956). The magical number seven, plus or minus two: Some limits on our capacity to process information. *Psychological Review*, *63*, 81–97. doi:10.1037/h0043158

Moody, D. (2002). *Dealing with complexity: A practical method for representing large entity-relationship models*. Unpublished doctoral dissertation, University of Melbourne.

Moody, D. L., & Shanks, G. (1998). Improving the quality of entity-relationship models: An action research programme. *The Australian Computer Journal*, *30*, 129–138.

Nijssen, G. M. (1976). *Modelling in Database Management Systems*. Amsterdam: North Holland.

Nunnally, J. (1978). *Psychometric theory*. New York: McGraw-Hill.

Olle, T. W., Sol, H. G., & Tully, C. J. (Eds.). (1983). *Information System Design Methodologies: A Feature Analysis*. Amsterdam, The Netherlands: North-Holland.

Parsons, J. (1996). An information model based on classification theory. *Management Science*, *42*(10), 1437–1453. doi:10.1287/mnsc.42.10.1437

Parsons, J., & Cole, L. (2005). What do the pictures mean? Guidelines for experimental evaluation of representation fidelity in diagrammatical conceptual modelling techniques. *Data & Knowledge Engineering*, *55*, 327–342. doi:10.1016/j.datak.2004.12.008

Parsons, J., & Wand, Y. (2000). Emancipating instances from the tyranny of classes in information modelling. *ACM Transactions on Database Systems*, *25*(2), 228–268. doi:10.1145/357775.357778

Parsons, J., & Wand, Y. (2008a). Using Cognitive Principles to Guide Classification in Information Systems Modeling. *Management Information Systems Quarterly, 32*(4), 839–868.

Parsons, J., & Wand, Y. (2008b). A question of class. *Nature, 455*, 1040–1041. doi:10.1038/4551040a

Popper, K. R. (1961). *The Logic of Scientific Discovery*. New York: Science Editions.

Rosemann, M., Davies, I., & Green, P. (2003). The very model of modern BPM. *Information Age, February/March*, 24-29.

Shanks, G., Nuredini, J., Tobin, D., Moody, D., & Weber, R. (2003a, June). Representing Things and Properties in Conceptual Modelling: an Empirical Evaluation. In *Proceedings of the European Conference on Information Systems,* Naples, Italy.

Shanks, G., Nuredini, J., Tobin, D., & Weber, R. (2003b). Representing Things and Properties in Conceptual Modeling: Understanding the Impact of Task Type. In *Proceedings of the Twenty-Third International Conference on Information Systems,* Barcelona, Spain (pp. 909-913).

Shanks, G., Tansley, E., Nuredini, J., Tobin, D., & Weber, R. (2008). Representing part-whole relationships in conceptual modelling: An empirical evaluation. *Management Information Systems Quarterly, 32*(3), 553–573.

Shanks, G., Weber, R., & Nuredini, J. (2004). Evaluating Conceptual Modelling Practices . In Rosemann, M., & Green, P. (Eds.), *Business Systems Analysis with Ontologies* (pp. 28–55). Hershey, PA: Idea Group Publishing.

Sia, S. K., & Soh, C. (2002). Severity assessment of ERP-organizational misalignment: Honing in on ontological structure and context specificity. In *Proceedings of the Twenty-Third International Conference on Information Systems*, Barcelona, Spain (pp. 723-729).

Siau, K. (2004). Informational and computational equivalence in comparing conceptual modeling methods . *Journal of Database Management, 15*(1), 73–86.

Siau, K., & Rossi, M. (2007). *Evaluation techniques for systems analysis and design modelling methods – A review and comparative analysis.* Information Systems Journal.

Simsion, G., & Witt, G. (2001). *Data Modelling Essentials: Analysis* (2nd ed.). Design and Innovation.

Tabachnick, B. G., & Fidell, L. S. (2007). *Using Multivariate Statistics* (5th ed.). Boston: Allyn and Bacon.

Teorey, T. J., Yang, D., & Fry, J. P. (1986). A logical design methodology for relational databases using the extended entity-relationship model. *ACM Computing Surveys, 18*(2), 197–222. doi:10.1145/7474.7475

Wand, Y., Storey, V., & Weber, R. (1999). An Ontological Analysis of the Relationship Construct in Conceptual Modelling. *ACM Transactions on Database Systems, 24*(4), 494–528. doi:10.1145/331983.331989

Wand, Y., & Weber, R. (1993). On the ontological expressiveness of information systems analysis and design grammars. *Journal of Information Systems, 3*, 217–237. doi:10.1111/j.1365-2575.1993.tb00127.x

Wand, Y., & Weber, R. (2002). Information systems and conceptual modelling: A research agenda. *Information Systems Research, 13*, 363–376. doi:10.1287/isre.13.4.363.69

Weber, R. (1996). Are attributes entities? A study of database designers' memory structures. *Information Systems Research, 7*, 137–162. doi:10.1287/isre.7.2.137

Weber, R. (1997). *Ontological Foundations of Information Systems*. Melbourne, Australia: Coopers & Lybrand.

ENDNOTES

[1] Note that we refer to conceptual (domain) modelling and not logical (e.g., relational database design) modelling.

[2] Note that the "ontologically sound" model is not completely compliant with the principles of Bunge's (1977) ontological theory. In this study, we focus primarily on the distinction between classes of things and properties in general, and we are most concerned with representing intrinsic and mutual properties in general. We decided to retain the "Sales Order" and "Delivery" events in the "ontologically sound" model because the representation of events is a separate issue. Their deletion from the conceptual models might have confounded the results of our experiment.

[3] Note that the conceptual models increase in complexity from the ontologically sound model (relatively simple) to the entity-only model (relatively complex). Although the increasing complexity may make the models more difficult to read and interpret, it is a direct consequence of distinguishing things and properties in the models.

[4] In terms of the notion of "physical independence," see Denkel (1996, pp. 34-35) on ways that things can be distinguished from properties.

[5] We recognize that some changes of properties may result in a change in the "natural kind" of a thing (Bunge, 1977, p. 221).

[6] Note, however, that the participants did not work in groups. Rather, they worked individually in the same room.

[7] It proved impossible to record accurately the time taken for each discrepancy that a participant identified because, for example, participants vacillated back and forth between discrepancies as they attempted to find and articulate them. We ceased timing participants when they indicated they were done with the discrepancy-checking task.

[8] We fully understand that this approach may lead to biases. The benefit, however, is that our scores are based on an in-depth understanding of our notes and our understanding of the participants' reactions as they undertook the experiment. Moreover, some of our scores are objective.

[9] We use the term conceptual model to mean a representation of the data in an information system that is suitable for human understanding and is independent of any particular data management technology. This may be contrasted with a logical data model that represents that data in terms of a particular data management technology (e.g., relational) and a physical data model that takes into account specific storage structures and indexing mechanisms.

[10] Note that these predictions are not based on the results of the experiment reported in this paper. They reflect our understanding of the consequences of the experimental results.

APPENDIX 1: EXPERIMENTAL TASKS

Example Comprehension Questions

1. Can an employee be assigned to manage more than one customer at a time?
   Yes / No / Not Sure
   2. Can a customer belong to many postal area codes?
   Yes / No / Not Sure
   3. Can an address have more than one region?
   Yes / No / Not Sure

Example Problem Solving Questions

1. The area code for all overseas telephone numbers has changed. Can we always identify the customer contact numbers for the customers located overseas?
   1. Possible / Not possible / Not Sure
   Explanation:
   2. An Ontological Plastics supplier wishes to send samples of new and improved hoses to customers who regularly order hoses. Can we determine the number of hoses each customer has had delivered in the previous 3 months and the date of each delivery?
   1. Possible / Not possible / Not Sure
   Explanation:
   3. A customer was delivered industrial piping, which has developed cracks in it 3 days after delivery. The customer wants a refund and the faulty piping collected by Ontological Plastics. Does the model allow an empty delivery truck to be sent to collect the goods?
   Possible / Not possible / Not Sure
   Explanation:

Example Paragraphs from Discrepancy Checking Task

Modeller: Thank you for meeting with me. I was hoping that each of you could identify the requirements of your business area for me so I can start developing a model for you.

User: Sure, happy to help. I'll start, because I work in the customer side of the business. We deal with a number of customers, ranging from companies to individuals. Because of our large customer base, we feel it is important for each customer to have a specific relationship with an employee, whose role is to ensure customer satisfaction.

All our customers have an employee assigned to manage them at a particular point in time. With large customers, multiple employees may be assigned to them.

As part of our customer satisfaction focus, it is imperative that we keep an accurate record of customer details, especially: credit limits, contact numbers, Australian Business Numbers, industry, date of registration etc. Also, when placing sales orders customers sometimes have delivery instructions, which we pass to the delivery team.

Chapter 6
Information Search Patterns in E-Commerce Product Comparison Services

Fiona Fui-Hoon Nah
University of Nebraska-Lincoln, USA

Weiyin Hong
University of Nevada, Las Vegas, USA

Liqiang Chen
University of Nebraska-Lincoln, USA

Hong-Hee Lee
Dankook University, South Korea

ABSTRACT

To facilitate product selection and purchase decisions on e-commerce Web sites, the presentation of product information is very important. In this research, the authors study how disposition styles influence users' search patterns in product comparison services of e-commerce Web sites. The results show that people use relatively more feature paths and less product paths in vertical disposition style than horizontal disposition style. The findings also indicate that there are relatively more feature paths and less product paths in the first half than second half of the information search paths. This is consistent with Gensch's two-stage choice model which suggests that people use attribute processing to derive a consideration set before they apply alternative processing to arrive at a final choice in product comparison services.

INTRODUCTION

Electronic commerce continues to capture market share from brick-and-mortar stores, with US online retailing reaching $175 billion in 2007 and projected to grow to $335 billion by 2012 (Mulpuru, Johnson, McGowan, & Wright, 2008). One of the values of e-commerce is derived from product comparison services (Keeney, 1999; Wan, Menon, & Ramaprasad, 2007) where customers can compare a wide variety of alternative products at their convenience, such as in the comfort of

DOI: 10.4018/978-1-61350-471-0.ch006

their homes. The design of product comparison services in e-commerce Web sites can influence online traffic and sales, as well as the quality of consumers' online purchase decisions (Cai & Xu, 2008; Diehl, 2005; Lohse & Spiller, 1998; Pu, Chen, & Kumar, 2008). E-commerce Web sites that facilitate customers' search for products and the information they need can increase online sales and promote return visits (Nah, Siau, Tian, & Ling, 2002; Tarafdar & Zhang, 2007, 2008; Tarasewich, Pomplun, Fillion, & Broberg, 2005). Hence, the design of product comparison services on e-commerce Web sites is important for success in e-commerce.

Product comparison services in e-commerce Web sites are usually presented in one of two disposition styles: vertical disposition and horizontal disposition. Vertical disposition displays products by columns and features/attributes by rows (see Figure 1). Horizontal disposition displays products by rows and features/attributes by columns (see Figure 2). For example, vertical disposition style is used for product comparison at Dell.com, and horizontal disposition style is used to display different flight options at Travelocity.com.

Research has shown that information presentation format can influence consumers' information acquisition and processing strategies (Bettman & Kakkar, 1977; Biehal & Chakravarti, 1982;

Figure 1. Vertical disposition style in product comparison

	Product 1	Product 2	...	Product N
Image	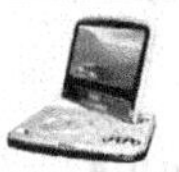	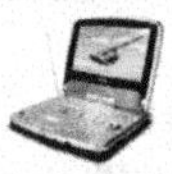	...	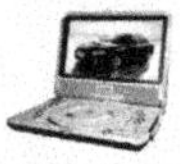
Feature 1 (Ex. Name)	DVD Player 1	DVD Player 2	...	DVD Player N
Feature 2 (Ex. Size)	8.5 inches	7 inches	...	8 inches
...		...	...	...
Feature M (Ex. Weight)	1.3 pound	1.1 pound	...	1.1 pound

Feature Path

Product Path

Figure 2. Horizontal disposition style in product comparison

	Image	Feature 1 (Ex. Name)	Feature 2 (Ex. Size)	...	Feature M (Ex. Weight)
Product 1	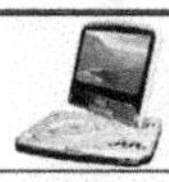	DVD Player 1	8.5 inches	...	1.3 pound
Product 2	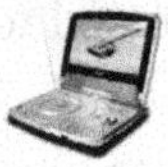	DVD Player 2	7 inches	...	1.1 pound
...	...	...			
Product N	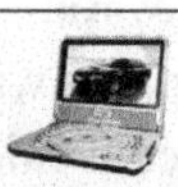	DVD Player N	8 inches	...	1.1 pound

Product Path

Feature Path

Jarvenpaa, 1989). Hence, the disposition style used in online product comparison services can have an impact on consumers' information search patterns and possibly the decisions they make. The objective of this research is to examine the effects of vertical and horizontal disposition styles on users' information search patterns in the e-commerce context.

LITERATURE REVIEW

Human-computer interaction and design issues are important for e-commerce to be successful (Nah & Davis, 2002; Zhang, Nah, & Benbasat, 2005). This section reviews related literature on product presentation in e-commerce Web sites and on decision making.

Presentation Format

The influence of product presentation format on users' browsing and search patterns on Web sites has received significant attention from IS and marketing researchers. A number of product presentation formats have been examined in prior studies, including thumbnails and images (Hong, Thong, & Tam, 2004a; Lam, Chau, & Wong, 2007; Weathers, Sharma, & Wood, 2007), videos and narration (Jiang & Benbasat, 2007; Kim & Lennon, 2008), 3D presentation and rotation (Kim, Kim, & Lennon, 2009; Park, Stoel, & Lennon, 2008).

While most of these studies focus on the presentation of a single product on a Web page, another stream of research examines the comparison of multiple products on the same Web page, which is a popular presentation format on e-commerce Web sites (Nah & Davis, 2002). In fact, comparison-shopping has been a fundamental activity among online consumers due to lower search costs on the Internet (Brynjolfsson, Hu, & Smith, 2003; Wan, Menon, & Ramaprasad, 2007). When reviewing literature on product comparisons, we found that attribute information is either grouped by product

alternatives or organized in a tabular format for easier comparison. For example, Hong, Thong, and Tam (2004b) compared two types of information displays in which attribute information is organized by products, and the products are either presented in a list-format or a matrix format. Using the cognitive fit theory, the 'competition for attention' theory, and the scanpath theory, Hong, Thong, and Tam (2004b) found that the list-format display provides better support for "browsing" tasks while the matrix-format display facilitates "searching" tasks. This is in line with cognitive fit theory, which suggests that when the problem representation (or information representation format) matches the nature of the task, a quicker and more accurate decision-making performance can be achieved. In another study, Lam, Chau, and Wong (2007) examined consumers' information processing of product information organized in a matrix format, i.e., in a 2 by 3 matrix with each cell containing a product image and other attribute information. Using an eye-tracking experiment, they found that consumers' scanning of product information is consistent with their dominant reading direction, which is the reading direction associated with the language a consumer uses most often in reading and writing.

A more direct comparison of products by their attributes can be enabled by presenting attribute information in a tabular format, with each cell containing one attribute of one product (e.g., the price of a particular product). The table may follow either a horizontal or vertical disposition style depending on whether the attributes of a product are presented in rows or columns. Interestingly, existing research using product comparison tables appears to have arbitrarily chosen one disposition style over the other. For example, Haubl and Trifts (2000) examined a decision aid called a comparison matrix, which is operationalized as a table with alternatives presented in rows and attributes presented in columns. Similarly, Pu, Chen, and Kumar (2008) developed an online product search tool, known as example critiquing, which entails a table format with alternatives organized in rows and attributes listed in columns. In a recent study of the effects of product sorting on consumer decision making, Cai and Xu (2008) also used a table to present alternatives in rows and attributes in columns, and examined how consumers' purchase decisions were affected by different sorting of products. It is unclear in the extant literature, however, why one disposition style (horizontal disposition style) was chosen over the other (vertical disposition style), and more importantly, whether the choice has an impact on the outcomes.

The literature suggests that the way in which product information is presented can make a significant impact on consumers' information acquisition and processing strategies (Payne, Bettman, & Johnson, 1993). Specifically, Bettman and Kakkar (1977), Biehal and Chakravarti (1982), and Jarvenpaa (1989) found that decision makers' acquisition and processing strategies were influenced by whether information was organized by alternatives or attributes. Information organized by alternatives can promote processing by products or alternatives whereas information organized by attributes can promote processing by features or attributes. When processing by alternatives, consumers tend to focus on the entire set of attributes associated with an alternative and evaluate these attributes in a holistic manner. On the other hand, when processing by attributes, consumers tend to focus on a specific attribute across multiple alternatives (Russo & Dosher, 1983). In physical stores, information is sorted by products or brands, which encourages alternative (product/brand) processing. But in an online environment, attribute processing is made feasible by online product comparison tables. Web designers can potentially use horizontal or vertical disposition style to promote different types of processing in an online environment. Hence, in this research, we examine the impact of vertical versus horizontal disposition style on user's information acquisition and search pattern behaviors.

Decision-Making Process

According to Gensch's (1987) two-stage disaggregate attribute choice model, there are two stages involved in making a final choice (such as in product selection). The first stage is attribute-processing which is to screen and narrow down the number of alternatives for consideration. The second stage is alternative-processing which considers the attributes simultaneously and allowing for tradeoffs among them. In the first stage, several products are excluded by an initial screening process, and in the second stage, a compensatory analysis is used to derive the final decision (Lehtinen, 1974). In other words, people tend to use a conjunctive strategy to eliminate unacceptable alternatives before they apply a compensatory strategy to evaluate the remaining acceptable alternatives and derive a final choice (Lussier & Olshavsky, 1979). Payne, Bettman, and Johnson (1993) indicated that decision makers have a tendency to remove items or conditions that they are not interested in (i.e., through elimination/simplifying) before they evaluate the remaining options in a more holistic manner (i.e., making explicit tradeoffs). Figure 3 shows the decision-making process involved in online product comparison and selection.

THEORETICAL BACKGROUND AND HYPOTHESES

This section presents the theoretical background for this research and explains the development of the hypotheses.

Disposition Styles and Information Paths

The two commonly used disposition styles for online product comparison services are *vertical* and *horizontal* disposition styles. In the vertical disposition style, products are displayed by columns and features/attributes by rows (see Figure

Figure 3. Decision-making process for product comparison service

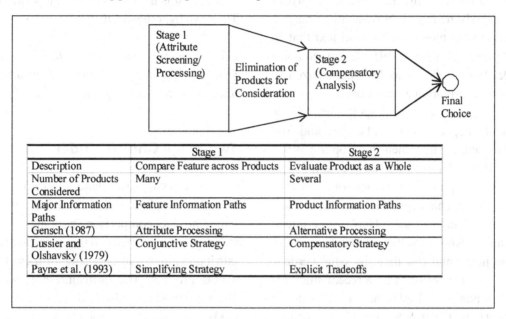

	Stage 1	Stage 2
Description	Compare Feature across Products	Evaluate Product as a Whole
Number of Products Considered	Many	Several
Major Information Paths	Feature Information Paths	Product Information Paths
Gensch (1987)	Attribute Processing	Alternative Processing
Lussier and Olshavsky (1979)	Conjunctive Strategy	Compensatory Strategy
Payne et al. (1993)	Simplifying Strategy	Explicit Tradeoffs

1). Hence, the attribute information about each product is presented vertically. In the horizontal disposition style, products are displayed by rows and features/attributes by columns (see Figure 2). Hence, attribute information about a product is displayed horizontally. The disposition style is expected to influence users' information search patterns in online product comparison services.

In this research, a user's information search pattern is captured by information paths, which refer to the movement of his or her visual attention from one cell to another, where each cell presents a specific feature (or attribute) of a particular product (or alternative). Three types of information paths are possible when users examine alternatives on a product comparison page: feature path, product path, and crossed path. When a user moves his/her attention between the same feature of different products (e.g., comparing the sizes of two different products), the user is following the *feature* path (see Figures 1 and 2). On the other hand, when a user moves his/her attention from one attribute to another for the same product (e.g., examining the size followed by the weight of a particular

product), the user is following the *product* path (see Figures 1 and 2). When a path is neither a feature nor a product path, it is a *crossed* path, which refers to the movement of visual attention to a different feature of a different product. The two information paths that are of interest in this research are feature and product paths.

Effects of Disposition Styles on Information Paths

People acquire information through spatial patterns they have been accustomed to (Lohse, 1997). In the western context, which is the focus of this research, readers and writers are accustomed to the horizontal format in reading and writing. Hence, there is a tendency for people to bind information horizontally than vertically. Furthermore, since perceptual span in a vertical direction is more limited than in a horizontal direction, readers have better control of their eye movements in a horizontal direction (Ojanpaa, Nasanen, & Kojo, 2002; Rayner, 1998; Rayner & Pollatsek, 1989), and therefore users are more likely to carry out horizontal search patterns than vertical search patterns. Similarly, text that is horizontally arranged tends to be read more quickly than text that is vertically arranged (Tinker, 1955; Laarni, Simola, Kojo, & Risto, 2004), thus favoring horizontal patterns of information acquisition.

Eye movement research suggests that reading begins in the upper left corner of the text and proceeds from left to right, then from top to bottom (Rayner, 1998). This reading habit, coupled with the larger perception span of horizontal vision, increases one's tendency to browse information horizontally than vertically. Thus, users' attention is more likely to shift to another target on the same horizontal row than the same vertical column. This is confirmed by a recent study on using thumbnails to display product images on Web sites (Lam, Chau, & Wong, 2007). Using an eye-tracking experiment, Lam, Chau, and Wong (2007) found that when a number of product images are organized in an array format (e.g., a 2 by 3 array for six product thumbnails), consumers scan the array in a manner similar to their reading of text, or so called dominant reading direction.

Applying the above notion and explanation to users' search patterns in online product comparison shopping, we expect more feature paths to take place in the vertical disposition style than in the horizontal disposition style because feature information across products is organized horizontally in the vertical disposition style but vertically in the horizontal disposition style. Hence, we hypothesize that:

H1: E-commerce users are inclined to use more feature paths in the vertical disposition style than in the horizontal disposition style.

Product information is displayed horizontally in the horizontal disposition style and vertically in the vertical disposition style. Given the tendency to scan information horizontally than vertically, the horizontal disposition style will yield more product paths than the vertical disposition style. Thus, we hypothesize that:

H2: E-commerce users are inclined to use more product paths in the horizontal disposition style than in the vertical disposition style.

Two-stage Choice Model

Gensch's (1987) two-stage choice model can be used to explain product and feature paths in online product comparison shopping. In the first stage, consumers focus on the important features (attributes) by comparing each of these features across products (i.e., attribute-processing) to eliminate products (alternatives) that are considered unacceptable or inferior. Hence, feature paths are used to narrow down the number of products (alternatives) for consideration. In the second stage, customers examine and assess each of the remaining products by making "explicit tradeoffs" among them (Payne, Bettman, & Johnson, 1993). Hence, product paths are used to bind attributes together (alternative-processing) so they can be considered simultaneously in making the final product selection.

Gensch's two-stage choice model suggests that feature paths (attribute-processing) are used more extensively in the first stage than the second stage. Hence, we hypothesize that there are more feature paths (attribute-processing) in the first stage than in the second stage of the decision making search paths. Thus,

H3: E-commerce users are inclined to use more feature paths in the first stage than the second stage of their decision-making search paths.

In the second stage, a more holistic approach is expected where consumers consider multiple attributes of each product simultaneously. For example, a particular product may be more expensive but has better quality, whereas an alternate product could be less expensive but has lower quality. Hence, greater use of product paths is expected in the second stage than in the first stage. Thus, we hypothesize that there are more product paths (alternative-processing) in the second stage than in the first stage of the decision-making search paths.

H4: E-commerce users are inclined to use more product paths in the second stage than the first stage of their decision-making search paths.

Figure 4 shows the research model. The independent variable in H1 and H2 is disposition style (horizontal/vertical), representing two different information presentation formats for online product comparison services. The independent variable in H3 and H4 refers to the first stage and second stage of the user's search paths. H1 and H3 examine the number of feature paths as the dependent variable, and H2 and H4 examine the number of product paths as the dependent variable.

RESEARCH METHODOLOGY

A within-subject experimental design was used to test the hypotheses. In other words, each subject was exposed to both conditions – one with vertical disposition style and the other with horizontal disposition style – thus serving as his/her own control. We chose the within-subject design for this study because it reduces the number of subjects required, increases statistical power, and reduces the error variance associated with individual differences (Keppel & Wickens, 2004). The potential carry-over (or order) effect of a within-subject design was controlled by randomizing the order of disposition styles given to the subjects. We invited student volunteers from business and computer science to participate in the experiment. 24 graduate and undergraduate students volunteered for the study. Two-thirds of these subjects were male, and the age of the subjects ranged from 19 to 45.

The product comparison matrix used in this study is 5×5 representing 5 products by 5 attributes of these products. The matrix format was used for online product comparisons because it facilitates searching tasks (Hong, Thong, & Tam, 2004b). To control for the positioning of the products in the matrix, a randomized procedure was used, where 5 of 10 products were randomly selected for the first condition (or disposition style) and the remaining 5 products were used for the second condition (or disposition style). The 5 products in

Figure 4. Research model

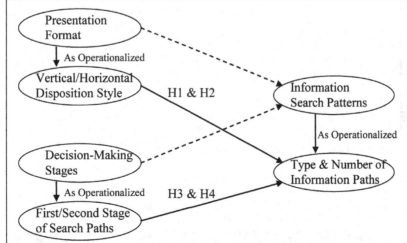

each disposition style were also randomly ordered for each subject and session. In other words, for each experimental session with a subject, the total set of 10 products was randomly divided into two sets, with each set of 5 products used for each disposition style. These products were then displayed in a completely randomized order in the product comparison table of each disposition style. In this way, the placement of products was completely randomized for each subject.

The product type used in this study was PDAs. We felt that an appropriate product type for this study was one that was of interest to the subjects (to encourage search behaviors) and yet was not familiar to them (to avoid recognition of products *a priori*). PDAs fit these criteria for our subjects.

A control validation showed that none of our subjects owned a PDA during the time of the study.

Each subject was shown two product comparison tables (one using vertical disposition style and the other using horizontal disposition style) on PDAs and was asked to select a PDA that he/she would like to purchase from each of the two product comparison tables. Figure 5 shows a screen shot depicting the vertical disposition style. Each cell in the product comparison table contained information about a feature (or value of an attribute) of a PDA. At the beginning of the experiment, the information in every cell was hidden. To view the information in a particular cell, the subject needed to click on the cell to have the information displayed. When the subject clicked on another cell, the information displayed on the

Figure 5. Screen shot for vertical disposition style

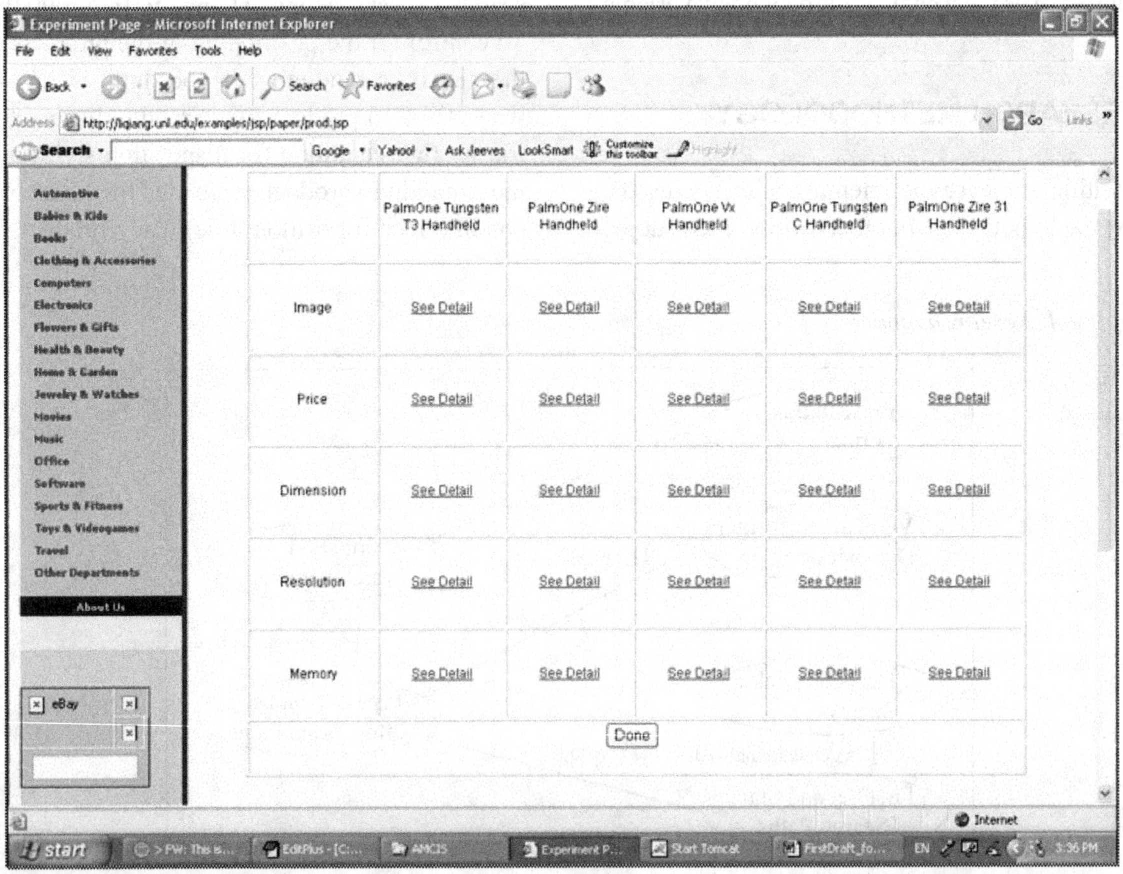

previously opened cell was hidden again (as was done in other studies on consumer choice such as Payne (1976) in order to precisely track which information was being attended to at any one time and to derive the complete information search paths. This process-tracing method, known as the information display board, has been widely used in studies on consumer choice (Painton & Gentry, 1985; Todd & Benbasat, 1987). Using this method, the visual attention of each subject was tracked using computer logs of the click patterns. The subject was allowed to click on any cell as many times as he/she needed until a product (PDA) was selected for purchase. Upon completion of the task (i.e., when the product to be purchased had been determined), the subject clicked on the "Done" button at the bottom of the screen (see Figure 5).

The experimental Web pages were developed using Java Server Pages (JSP). JSPs were connected to an Apache Web server to make the pages available on the Web and to MySQL to record all data generated by subjects during the experiment. The search paths of each subject in each condition were logged, which showed the chronological list of cells clicked during the product comparison process.

Operationalization of Independent and Dependent Variables

The information presentation format was operationalized as vertical and horizontal disposition styles (see Figures 1 and 2). The decision-making stage was operationalized as the first and second halves of all search paths for each comparison shopping page. Since it is not possible to deter-

mine an exact cut-off between the first and second stages of Gensch's (1987) model because these two stages overlap around the transition point, we operationalized decision making stages as the first and second halves of the total search paths. For example, if a subject made a total of 24 search paths in a shopping trip, then we operationalized the first 12 search paths as the first stage and the next 12 search paths as the second stage. If a subject made an odd number of search paths in a shopping trip, we discard the one in the middle. This operationalization offers a feasible way to test Gensch's two-stage model.

The dependent variable, information search patterns, refers to feature and product paths. If the movement of cells took place from one feature (or attribute) to another feature (or attribute) of the *same* product, we called it a *product* path. For example, if a subject clicks on the 'resolution' attribute of product A followed by the 'dimension' attribute of the same product, a product path is recorded. If the movement of cells took place from one feature (or attribute) of a product to the *same* feature (or attribute) of another product, then we called it a *feature* path. For example, if a subject clicks on the 'resolution' attribute of Product A followed by the 'resolution' attribute of Product B, a feature path is recorded. Any search path that is neither a product or feature path is considered a crossed path, which is not of interest in this study.

DATA ANALYSIS

The hypotheses were analyzed using repeated-measures ANOVA. Tables 1 and 2 show the de-

Table 1. Descriptive statistics for hypotheses 1 and 2

Hypothesis	Disposition Style	Information Path	Mean of # of Information Paths	Std. Dev.
H1	Vertical	Feature	18.23	13.52
	Horizontal		13.18	8.45
H2	Vertical	Product	5.55	5.74
	Horizontal		8.14	7.53

Table 2. Results for hypotheses 1 and 2

Effect	F	Sig. (1-tailed)
H1: Disposition Style => Feature Information Paths	4.91	.02
H2: Disposition Style => Product Information Paths	2.86	.05

Table 3. Descriptive statistics for hypotheses 3 and 4

Hypothesis	Stage	Information Path	Mean of # of Information Paths	Std. Dev.
H3	First	Feature	18.46	11.99
	Second		15.29	7.90
H4	First	Product	6.67	6.04
	Second		9.50	6.87

Table 4. Results for hypotheses 3 and 4

Effect	F	Sig. (1-tailed)
H3: Stage => Feature Information Paths	6.86	.01
H4: Stage => Product Information Paths	5.90	.01

Table 5. Results for interaction effect

Interaction Effect	Dependent Variable	F	Sig. (2-tailed)
Disposition Style and Stage	# of Feature I. P.	1.054	.16
Disposition Style and Stage	# of Product I. P.	.142	.36

scriptive statistics and the results for H1 and H2. The mean numbers of feature and product paths for vertical and horizontal disposition styles and their standard deviations are presented in Table 1. As presented in Table 2, both H1 and H2 are supported (p<=0.05).

Tables 3 and 4 show the descriptive statistics and the results of H3 and H4. The mean numbers of feature and product paths for the first and second stages of information search paths and their standard deviations are presented in Table 3. As presented in Table 4, both H3 and H4 are supported (p<=0.05).

As shown in Table 5, we also examined whether there is an interaction effect between disposition styles (vertical/horizontal) and stages (first/second). The results show that there is no moderating or interaction effect.

DISCUSSION AND IMPLICATIONS

The results support all four hypotheses. H1 and H2 suggest that people have a greater tendency to search for information horizontally than vertically, which is in line with the reading habits in the western or English culture where this study was conducted. Given the horizontal search bias, feature paths are used more often in vertical than horizontal disposition style, whereas product information paths are used more often in horizontal than vertical disposition style. On the other hand, H3 and H4 suggest that attribute processing or feature paths are used more frequently in the first half than second half of the product comparison process. The results also suggest that alternative processing or product paths are employed more often in the second half than first half of the product comparison process. These findings are in line with Gensch's two-stage disaggregate attribute choice model, where the first stage involves mainly the use of attribute processing to screen or eliminate products (alternatives) to narrow down to a smaller consideration set and the second stage involves the use of alternative processing to derive at a final choice.

Since information presentation format can bias online users' patterns of information acquisition, an appropriate information presentation format that is congruent with the desired (e.g., most natural or most effective) method of processing can be presented to users to promote the use of that processing method. For example, if processing by attributes is desired for a certain kind of product (either because it is more effective or is a better fit) for a decision-making task, then the vertical disposition style is recommended.

Since the first stage of decision-making in product comparisons relies more on feature paths (i.e., attribute processing) and providing an effective form of decision support for this initial stage is essential (to minimize information overload), the vertical disposition style is recommended in online product comparison services to support this first stage, which demands the highest cognitive load from users due to the larger number of products being considered. In other words, since the initial stage involves the greatest amount of information to be processed and vertical disposition style provides a better cognitive fit for the first stage, e-commerce vendors may find it desirable to use vertical disposition style for supporting online product comparison services. This reasoning is also in line with the Cognitive Fit

theory (Vessey, 1991; Vessey & Galletta, 1991), which suggests that decision-making can be best achieved when there is a cognitive fit between the decision-making task and the presentation format. In reality, we also notice that many online product comparison services in e-commerce Web sites use vertical disposition style to promote attribute processing across products, thus providing further support for our analysis. After users have further narrowed down on their choices, Web sites may adopt a horizontal disposition style for the selected products to facilitate more holistic product comparisons[1].

CONCLUSIONS, LIMITATIONS, AND FUTURE RESEARCH

The effects of disposition styles on users' search patterns in online product comparison services were examined in this research. Prior research on multiple product comparisons appears to have arbitrarily chosen one disposition style over another. Failure to recognize the potential impact of vertical versus horizontal disposition style may lead to a biased or inaccurate understanding of users' decision making preferences in online product comparisons. The results of this study show that disposition styles can bias consumers' online information search patterns in product comparisons. When making product comparisons in the vertical disposition style, users use relatively more feature paths or attribute processing and less product paths or alternative processing than in the horizontal disposition style. Making attribute-based comparisons can be difficult in physical stores, but is made feasible by online product comparison services.

According to Payne, Bettman, and Johnson's (1993) decision-making theory and Gensch's (1987) two-stage choice model, consumers will first compare the feature/attribute information (such as price) of a list of available products to eliminate the undesirable products and to arrive at a smaller set of products for consideration. Next, consumers make their final decision by binding the features of each product together for making comparisons among the products. Our results support this two-stage process, where more feature paths and less product paths are present in the first stage than second stage of product comparison process. In the first stage, consumers rely on feature information to carry out attribute processing, which can be well supported by vertical disposition style. In the second stage, consumers use more alternative processing than in the first stage to make a final choice, which can be better supported by horizontal disposition style

There are some limitations in this research which call for future research. First, in this study, we focused on information acquisition rather than information processing in decision-making. To understand users' decision-making process in online product comparison services, we tracked and recorded subjects' movement of visual attention using the information display board method that is used widely in consumer choice research. This method opens up the decision-making "black box" by capturing the user's visual attention in order to determine the information paths used in decision-making. However, we acknowledge that not all visual attention might translate into information processing. This is a limitation of the information display board method, which focuses on information acquisition rather than information processing. In future research, we are also interested to use the 'think-aloud' protocol (i.e., by asking subjects to think aloud during the process) to examine information processing in online product comparison services.

Second, we have limited the number of attributes and number of products to 5 in this study because they fit within the 7±2 rule which represents the short-term capacity of human information processing (Miller, 1956). In future research, we are interested in extending this study to examine product comparison services for a larger set of products and attributes, as well as to assess the effect of different numbers of features and/or products (e.g., product comparison services with 3, 5, and 7 products) to determine an optimal size for online product comparison services. Another possible study is to investigate different designs for product comparison services. For example, Canon.com allows users to delete or insert products in the comparison table whenever they want, which could support more effective comparisons.

Third, the generalizability of the study may be limited by subjects' familiarity with the product, the nature of the product, and the cultural context. First, the information search paths of subjects may be influenced by their expertise or product familiarity, as noted by Bettman and Kakkar (1977). They found that experts might favor alternative (holistic) processing while novices might focus more on attribute (dimensional) processing due to their lack of familiarity with the products. In this study, we control for expertise by using products (i.e., PDAs) that were not familiar to the subjects. It would be interesting to replicate the study with products that are familiar to the subjects to see if alternative processing (or horizontal disposition style) will be preferred. Another possibility is that certain product type may trigger more feature (attribute) processing or product (alternative) processing. Future research may also examine the effect of product type on information acquisition and search patterns in online product comparison services.

Lastly, the current research focuses on the western context where people's reading habit is horizontal (i.e., from left to right). In some eastern contexts, people are used to reading vertically (such as in Traditional Chinese). The findings of this research apply to people whose dominant reading direction is horizontal, and the results could be different for people whose dominant reading direction is vertical. Thus, it would be interesting to replicate the study in an eastern context where the reading direction is different.

In summary, this study provides an empirical investigation on how disposition styles impact users' information search patterns in online product comparison services. It also shows that disposition styles can be used to influence the information acquisition strategies of decision makers. That is, if there is a desired method of processing information (i.e., an easier or more effective method), the information can be presented in a disposition style that is congruent with that method of processing to promote its usage. Last but not least, this research provides some useful insights to researchers and practitioners in understanding decision-making in online product comparison services and on the design of product comparison services on e-commerce Web sites.

REFERENCES

Bettman, J. R., & Kakkar, P. (1977). Effects of information presentation format on consumer information acquisition strategies. *The Journal of Consumer Research*, *3*(4), 233–240. doi:10.1086/208672

Biehal, B., & Chakravarti, D. (1982). Information-presentation format and learning goals as determinants of consumers' memory retrieval and choice processes. *The Journal of Consumer Research*, *8*(4), 431–441. doi:10.1086/208883

Brynjolfsson, E., Hu, Y., & Smith, M. D. (2003). Consumer surplus in the digital economy: Estimating the value of increased product variety at online booksellers. *Management Science*, *49*(11), 1580–1596. doi:10.1287/mnsc.49.11.1580.20580

Cai, S., & Xu, Y. (2008). Designing product lists for e-commerce: The effects of sorting on consumer decision making. *International Journal of Human-Computer Interaction*, *24*(7), 700–721. doi:10.1080/10447310802335730

Diehl, K. (2005). When two rights make a wrong: Searching too much in ordered environment. *JMR, Journal of Marketing Research*, *42*(3), 313–322. doi:10.1509/jmkr.2005.42.3.313

Gensch, D. H. (1987). A two-stage disaggregate attribute choice model. *Marketing Science*, *6*(3), 223–239. doi:10.1287/mksc.6.3.223

Haubl, G., & Trifts, V. (2000). Consumer decision making in online shopping environments: The effects of interactive decision aids. *Marketing Science*, *19*(1), 4–21. doi:10.1287/mksc.19.1.4.15178

Hong, W., Thong, J. Y. L., & Tam, K. Y. (2004a). Designing product listing pages on e-commerce websites: An examination of presentation mode and information format. *International Journal of Human-Computer Studies*, *61*(4), 481–503. doi:10.1016/j.ijhcs.2004.01.006

Hong, W., Thong, J. Y. L., & Tam, K. Y. (2004b). The effects of information format and shopping task on consumers' online shopping behavior: A cognitive fit perspective. *Journal of Management Information Systems*, *21*(3), 149–184.

Jarvenpaa, S. L. (1989). The effect of task demands and graphical format on information processing strategies. *Management Science*, *35*(3), 285–303. doi:10.1287/mnsc.35.3.285

Jiang, Z., & Benbasat, I. (2007). The effects of presentation formats and task complexity on online consumers' product understanding. *Management Information Systems Quarterly*, *31*(3), 475–500.

Keeney, R. L. (1999). The value of Internet commerce to the customer. *Management Science*, *15*(4), 533–542. doi:10.1287/mnsc.45.4.533

Keppel, G., & Wickens, T. D. (2004). *Design and Analysis: A Researcher's Handbook*. Upper Saddle River, NJ: Pearson Prentice Hall.

Kim, J.-H., Kim, M., & Lennon, S. J. (2009). Effects of web site atmospherics on consumer responses: Music and product presentation. *Direct Marketing*, *3*(1), 4–19. doi:10.1108/17505930910945705

Kim, M., & Lennon, S. (2008). The effects of visual and verbal information on attitudes and purchase intentions in internet shopping. *Psychology and Marketing*, *25*(2), 146–178. doi:10.1002/mar.20204

Laarni, J., Simola, J., Kojo, I., & Risto, N. (2004). Reading vertical text from a computer screen. *Behaviour & Information Technology*, *23*(2), 75–82. doi:10.1080/01449290310001648260

Lam, S. Y., Chau, A. W.-L., & Wong, T. J. (2007). Thumbnails as online product displays: How consumers process them. *Journal of Interactive Marketing*, *21*(1), 36–59. doi:10.1002/dir.20073

Lehtinen, O. (1974). A brand choice model: Theoretical framework and empirical results. *Journal of European Research*, *2*, 51–68.

Lohse, G. L. (1997). Consumer eye movement patterns on yellow pages advertising. *Journal of Advertising*, *26*(1), 62–74.

Lohse, G. L., & Spiller, P. (1998). Electronic shopping. *Communications of the ACM*, *41*(7), 81–87. doi:10.1145/278476.278491

Lussier, D. A., & Olshavsky, R. W. (1979). Task complexity and contingent processing in brand choice. *The Journal of Consumer Research*, *6*(2), 154–165. doi:10.1086/208758

Miller, G. A. (1956). The magical number seven plus or minus two: Some limits on our capacity for processing information. *Psychological Review*, *63*, 81–97. doi:10.1037/h0043158

Mulpuru, S., Johnson, C., McGowan, B., & Wright, S. (2008). US eCommerce Forecast: 2008 To 2012: B2C eCommerce expected to top $300B in five years. *Forrester Research*.

Nah, F., & Davis, S. (2002). HCI research issues in electronic commerce. *Journal of Electronic Commerce Research*, *3*(3), 98–113.

Nah, F., Siau, K., Tian, Y., & Ling, M. (2002). Knowledge management mechanisms in e-commerce: A study of online retailing and auction sites. *Journal of Computer Information Systems*, *42*(5), 119–128.

Ojanpaa, H., Nasanen, R., & Kojo, I. (2002). Eye movements in the visual search of word lists. *Vision Research*, *42*(12), 1499–1512. doi:10.1016/S0042-6989(02)00077-9

Painton, S., & Gentry, J. W. (1985). Another look at the impact of information presentation. *The Journal of Consumer Research*, *12*(2), 240–244. doi:10.1086/208512

Park, J., Stoel, L., & Lennon, S. J. (2008). Cognitive, affective and conative responses to visual simulation: The effects of rotation in online product presentation. *Journal of Consumer Behaviour*, *7*(1), 72–87. doi:10.1002/cb.237

Payne, J. W. (1976). Task complexity and contingent processing in decision making: An information search and protocol analysis. *Organizational Behavior and Human Performance*, *16*(2), 366–387. doi:10.1016/0030-5073(76)90022-2

Payne, J. W., Bettman, J. R., & Johnson, E. J. (1993). *The Adaptive Decision Maker*. New York: Cambridge University Press.

Pu, P., Chen, L., & Kumar, P. (2008). Evaluating product search and recommender systems for e-commerce environments. *Electronic Commerce Research*, *8*(1-2), 1–27. doi:10.1007/s10660-008-9015-z

Rayner, K. (1998). Eye movements in reading and information processing: 20 years of research. *Psychological Bulletin*, *124*(3), 372–422. doi:10.1037/0033-2909.124.3.372

Rayner, K., & Pollatsek, A. (1989). *The Psychology of Reading*. Englewood Cliffs, NJ: Prentice-Hall.

Russo, J., & Dosher, B. (1983). Strategies for multiattribute binary choice. *Journal of Experimental Psychology: Learning and Memory, 9*(4), 676–696. doi:10.1037/0278-7393.9.4.676

Tarafdar, M., & Zhang, J. (2007/2008). Determinants of reach and loyalty - A study of website performance and implications for website design. *Journal of Computer Information Systems, 48*(2), 16–25.

Tarasewich, P., Pomplun, M., Fillion, S., & Broberg, D. (2005). The enhanced restricted focus viewer. *International Journal of Human-Computer Interaction, 19*(1), 35–54. doi:10.1207/s15327590ijhc1901_4

Tinker, M. A. (1955). Perceptual and oculomotor efficiency in reading materials in vertical and horizontal arrangements. *The American Journal of Psychology, 68*(3), 444–449. doi:10.2307/1418529

Todd, P., & Benbasat, I. (1987). Process tracing methods in decision support systems research: Exploring the black box. *Management Information Systems Quarterly, 11*(4), 493–512. doi:10.2307/248979

Vessey, I. (1991). Cognitive fit: A theory-based analysis of the graphs versus tables literature. *Decision Sciences, 22*(2), 219–240. doi:10.1111/j.1540-5915.1991.tb00344.x

Vessey, I., & Galletta, D. (1991). Cognitive fit: An empirical study of information acquisition. *Information Systems Research, 2*(1), 63–85. doi:10.1287/isre.2.1.63

Wan, Y., Menon, S., & Ramaprasad, A. (2007). A classification of product comparison agents. *Communications of the ACM, 50*(8), 65–71. doi:10.1145/1278201.1278208

Weathers, D., Sharma, S., & Wood, S. L. (2007). Effects of online communication practices on consumer perceptions of performance uncertainty for search and experience goods. *Journal of Retailing, 83*(4), 393–401. doi:10.1016/j.jretai.2007.03.009

Zhang, P., Nah, F., & Benbasat, I. (2005). Human-computer interaction research in management information systems. *Journal of Management Information Systems, 22*(3), 9–14. doi:10.2753/MIS0742-1222220301

ENDNOTE

[1.] Another possibility is to provide both vertical and horizontal presentation styles and allow users to choose their preferred format. While this approach provides users with some flexibility, it also requires more development effort as well as additional effort from users to make the selection. So, the pros and cons of this approach need to be carefully evaluated.

This work was previously published in International Journal of Database Management, Volume 21, Issue 2, edited by Keng Siau, pp. 26-40, copyright 2010 by IGI Publishing (an imprint of IGI Global).

Chapter 7
Antecedents of the Closeness of Human–Avatar Relationships in a Virtual World

Yi Zhao
City University of Hong Kong, China

Weiquan Wang
City University of Hong Kong, China

Yan Zhu
Tsinghua University, China

ABSTRACT

Virtual worlds (e.g., Second Life), where users interact and form relationships with other users' virtual identities represented by avatars (i.e., human-avatar relationships), are increasingly influential in today's businesses and society. Nevertheless, the sustainability and impact of virtual worlds depend largely on the closeness of human-avatar relationships. This study investigates the antecedents of the closeness of such relationships. The authors conceptualize human-avatar relationship closeness as composed of interaction frequency, activity diversity, and relational influence. They identify its antecedents (perceived needs fulfillment, relationship irreplaceableness, and resource investment) by extending Rusbult's invest-ment model of interpersonal relationship commitment to the domain of human-computer interaction. The authors test the hypotheses through an online survey of Second Life users and find that (1) resource investment is positively associated with all three human-avatar relationship closeness dimensions; (2) needs fulfillment is positively associated with interaction frequency and relational influence; and (3) relationship irreplaceableness is positively associated with relational influence.

INTRODUCTION

Virtual worlds (e.g., Second Life and HipiHi), which are defined as computer-simulated digital social environments (Messinger *et al.*, 2009), have become increasingly popular and influen-tial in today's businesses and in people's lives (Mennecke *et al.*, 2008; Wolfendale, 2007). In such digital social environments, users interact and form relationships with other users' virtual "identities," which are represented by two- or three-dimensional (2D or 3D) avatars (For con-venience, we call this kind of relationship formed

DOI: 10.4018/978-1-61350-471-0.ch007

Figure 1. Screen shot of avatars that are socializing in Second Life

between one user and another user's avatar as "human-avatar relationship." See Figure 1 for an example of a Second Life avatar) (Kim, 2007; Wolfendale, 2007). However, in the absence of *close* human-avatar relationships in a virtual world, people cannot fully enjoy the convenience of socialization enabled by avatars, cannot utilize avatars as an effective relationship marketing tool, and cannot obtain enough exposure to the virtual world. This indicates that there is limited impact of virtual worlds on users. Therefore, this research focuses on the *closeness* of human-avatar relationships in virtual worlds.

Previous research has investigated the attributions of interpersonal relationship closeness (Berscheid, Snyder, & Omoto, 1989; Rusbult, Olsen, Davis, & Hannon, 2001); however, the antecedents of the closeness of people's relationships with other users' avatars (as representations of virtual "others") remain unexplored. While people in the real world normally interact with other people's *real identities,* and these interactions are subject to strong *social norms*, people in the virtual world interact with other users'

virtual identities represented by avatars, and real world social norms such as politeness and honesty may no longer be salient (Wolfendale, 2007). In addition, the activities that people engage in with other users' avatars are not the same as those in the real world. For instance, when users have dinners with other users' avatars, it is not the delicious food but the interaction and engagement that they truly enjoy. Hence, it is unknown whether theories in the interpersonal domain still hold in the human-avatar relationship domain.

In virtual worlds, an avatar is the primary embodiment of a user's entire virtual identity and is an independent "social actor" in-world (Junglas, Johnson, Steel, Abraham, & Loughlin, 2007). The use of avatars in a virtual world brings considerable influences and benefits to its end users, organizations, and the virtual world itself. For end users, avatars provide a user-friendly interface and a rich social context. As virtual worlds become increasingly sophisticated, many users are likely to become frustrated with complex interfaces (Alty, Knott, Anderson, & Smyth, 2000). The use of avatars can address this challenge as they enable end users to navigate easily and conveniently within a virtual world and to interact with the virtual identities of other users in a way similar to that of the real world (England & Gray, 1998). For instance, users could initiate a conversation with another user's avatar by moving their own avatars into the neighborhood of that avatar and greeting it, just as they do in the real world. Furthermore, avatars allow users to express verbal information and to convey many non-verbal cues such as gestures and postures, rendering a rich simulation of the real world.

For organizations, avatars engender a new way of doing business. In Web-based business-to-consumer (B2C) ecommerce, using avatars as sales advisors may provide stronger social support and more favorable shopping experiences to customers (Holzwarth, Janiszewski, & Neumann, 2006; Keeling, Mcgoldrick, & Beatty, 2007), ultimately increasing their purchase intentions

(Wood, Solomon, & Englis, 2006). Similarly, this same potential of avatars has been observed in the emerging virtual world businesses (Scott, 2007). For instance, retailers may adopt avatars to be salespersons in their virtual stores who can then effectively recommend products to customers (Hemp, 2006), provide customized trainings and consultations on product usage (Jennings & Collins, 2007), conduct after-sales interviews with customers to gather feedback on the product, and handle customer complaints and appeals.

Moreover, close human-avatar relationships are vital to sustain a virtual world. The rapid development of information technology (IT) has made the construction of a virtual world less difficult. However, preventing it from declining becomes a challenge, and many virtual worlds have become idle after some time following their establishment (Kazmer, 2007). Even in Second Life, one of the world's largest and most influential 3D virtual worlds, only 575,604 (Linden Research Inc., 2009) registered residents are active users[2], accounting for only 3.33% of its whole population of 17,273,295 residents (SL Name Watch, 2009). Although many factors may contribute to the decline of a virtual world (Bruckman & Jensen, 2002), if individuals have close relationships with other users' avatars, their need for socialization, which is one of the people's primary motivations to using virtual worlds (Messinger *et al.*, 2009), will be better satisfied. Hence, they will have stronger motivation to stay in a virtual world, and as a result, the virtual world will be less likely to decline.

In spite of the aforementioned substantial benefits of avatars, the realization of these merits depends largely on the extent to which users can establish close relationships with other users' avatars. As a first step in promoting close human-avatar relationships, this research explores users's attributions of the closeness of their relationships with other users' avatars in a virtual world by not only extending theories in the human-human relationship domain to the human-avatar relationship

domain but also by taking the specific features of human-computer interaction into consideration. The research topic is important because it will enrich the theories on relationship closeness in an emerging context of human-artifact (specifically, human-avatar) interactions and shed light on how effective human-avatar interactions in virtual worlds should be designed to promote close human-avatar relationships, which consequently contributes to the success of virtual worlds (De Souza & Preece, 2004; Preece, 2001).

The paper proceeds as follows. The next section proposes the research model after a review of the relevant literature. Following that, we discuss the research methodology. The empirical results are then presented and discussed, followed by a discussion on the implications and limitations of the study. The last section summarizes the conclusion of this research.

THEORETICAL BACKGROUND AND HYPOTHESES DEVELOPMENT

The current research focuses on a user's relationships with someone else's avatar, and the term "human-avatar relationship" refers exclusively to this type of relationships[3]. In virtual worlds that are virtual social systems *per se*, socialization is among the most important activities (Messinger *et al.*, 2009; Social Research Foundation, 2008). Users socialize with others by interacting and building relationships with other users' virtual identities represented as *avatars*, analogous to their interactions with other human beings in the real world. In this sense, users' relationships with other users' avatars are especially worthy of investigation.

Social Responses toward Computers

An avatar is an IT artifact created with computing technologies; thus, the exploration of users' attributions of the closeness of their relationships with other users' avatars warrants theoretical insights from the nature of human-computer interaction. In human-computer interaction, people *directly* respond to computing technologies *socially* (Reeves & Nass, 1996; Wang & Benbasat, 2007, 2008, 2009). Media equation theory suggests that human-computer interaction is *social* in nature (Reeves & Nass, 1996). When interacting with computing technologies such as computers, people unconsciously equate computers with real life, and thus they respond *socially* and apply social rules in interactions with computing technologies just as they do in interpersonal interactions (Nass & Moon, 2000; Reeves & Nass, 1996). Even if people are IT professionals and believe it inappropriate to apply social rules in human-computer interaction, they still unconsciously respond in a social manner. This theory has been tested and supported by numerous empirical studies. For instance, users are reluctant to give negative evaluations to a computer when asked by the same computer about its performance directly (Nass & Moon, 2000) and are more cooperative with a computer labeled as his/her teammate than with a computer not labeled as teammate (Reeves & Nass, 1996).

The reason why people respond *socially* is that the aforementioned social response is *directly* oriented to the computer itself. People *directly* interact with the computer and *behaviorally* treat it *as if* it were an independent social actor (Computers as Social Actors [CASA] paradigm) (Reeves & Nass, 1996; Sundar, 1994; Sundar & Nass, 2000). Compared with traditional non-interactive mass media (e.g., television) and interactive communication conduits (e.g., telephone), today's computing technologies can simulate many social cues originally unique to human beings such as interactivity, language, and gestures. The human brain has evolved from an old-world scenario in which only human beings exhibit social cues, and thus people usually *unconsciously* treat these social cues generated by technologies *as if* they were a part of their real lives (Reeves & Nass, 1996). Facing these social cues, people *mind-*

lessly and *automatically* resort to the schemata of human-human interaction and respond *directly* to the computer as an independent social actor (Nass & Moon, 2000; Sundar & Nass, 2000). As people's social response is *automatic* and *unconscious*, the simulations of the social cues needed to elicit social responses do not need to be sophisticated. Empirically, even merely labeling a computer as a human being is enough to elicit people's social responses toward that computer (Aharoni & Fridlund, 2007). This *direct* and *automatic* orientation to the computer itself has also been empirically confirmed by numerous studies (Aharoni & Fridlund, 2007).

In virtual worlds, avatars are technological artifacts implemented with computing technologies, such as virtual reality and 3D rendering (Kanade, Rander, & Narayanan, 1997). They are created and controlled by the users (Eschenbrenner, Nah, & Siau, 2008). Although avatars are not exactly the same as real human beings in terms of their appearances, they can still display human-like social cues such as interactivity, gestures, and postures. These human-like social cues may make people treat avatars as social actors.

The availability of flexible avatar creation and customization tools in virtual worlds (see Figure 2 for an example of the avatar customization tool in Second Life) has allowed users to create one or more avatars with various appearances. These can be true representations of their real identities, representations of entirely different identities (Chan, 2007; Galanxhi & Nah, 2007), or something in between, lying in the different positions in a continuum from the most genuine to the most artificial (Wood *et al.*, 2006). For example, in virtual worlds, a female may create an avatar that represents a male and then act as a man (Ashford, 2008); an old man may use an avatar that looks like a handsome boy to date an avatar that looks like a pretty girl, which in turn can also be artificial. As such, in human-avatar interaction, users interact with other users' virtual identities (genuine or artificial) represented in the

Figure 2. The avatar customization tool of Second Life

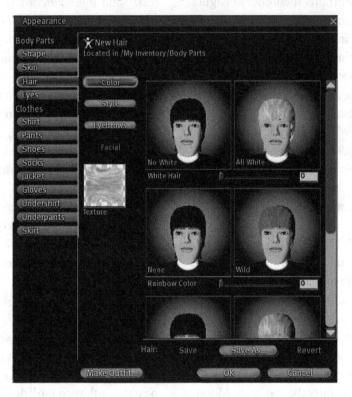

form of avatars (for convenience, we call them avatars) rather than the human beings that create and control the avatars.

In summary, human-avatar interaction in virtual worlds follows the theory of media equation and the CASA paradigm (Reeves & Nass, 1996; Sundar & Nass, 2000). When interacting with other users' avatars, people treat them *as if* they were real social actors and apply social rules guiding human-human interactions *directly* and *mindlessly*, even though the avatars are artificial. Through these interactions, people establish relationships with other users' avatars similar to interpersonal relationships (Al-Natour & Benbasat, 2009). Thus, the rationale of this research is to borrow theories on relationship closeness in the interpersonal domain and extend them to the context of human-avatar relationships. Due to the unique characteristics of human-computer interaction (e.g., the activities people engage in with IT artifacts are not the same as those in interper-

sonal interaction), factors leading to relationship closeness might differ in different contexts. This is an empirical question explored in the present study.

Relationship Closeness

Kelley *et al.* (1983) proposed that a close relationship should have four characteristics: (1) the relationship partners have frequent impact on each other; (2) the impact should be strong; (3) the impact should involve a variety of activities; and (4) the aforementioned three characteristics should exist for a long period.

Based on Kelly *et al.*'s conceptualization, Berscheid *et al.* developed a 3D model of relationship closeness. The three dimensions are interaction frequency, activity diversity, and relational strength. Interaction frequency refers to the number of interactions between relationship partners during a fixed period. Activity diversity refers to the range of activity domains that relationship partners engage in. For instance, people normally engage in a relatively limited range of activities with their colleagues compared with their interactions with family members. Relational strength describes the extent to which the relationship partners influence each other's work, life, decision making, goals, plans, and so on. People, like our parents, may have a stronger influence on our lives than others (e.g., sales representatives in a shopping mall). Therefore, the strengths of people's relationships with different entities may vary. In this research, we adapt Berscheid *et al.*'s conceptualization and contend that the closeness of a user's relationship with another user's avatar comprises three dimensions: interaction frequency, activity diversity, and relational influence[4].

Investment Model of Interpersonal Relationship

Generally, relationships need maintenance, and they will become increasingly close as they continue and improve. People's actions to continue and improve their current relationships are mainly determined by their intentions to do so (Ajzen, 1991; Ajzen & Fishbein, 1973). From the perspective of an interpersonal relationship,

these intentions can be identified with the concept of interpersonal relationship commitment, which is used to describe people's tendency to stay in a certain relationship and try to maintain and improve it (Ballard-Reisch & Weigel, 1999; Hendrick, 2004). Based on this logic, we contend that human-avatar relationship closeness is mainly determined by people's relationship commitment with other users' avatars.

Prior studies have examined the antecedents of interpersonal relationship commitment, and a summary is provided in Table 1. Based on a review of these previous studies, we found that the investment model of interpersonal relationship commitment provides an appropriate theoretical grounding for the current research (Rusbult, 1983). This model includes three determinants of interpersonal relationship commitment, namely, satisfaction level, quality of alternatives, and investment size. Satisfaction level is an overall evaluation of one's experiences in a relationship, and this evaluation is based on the degree to which the relationship fulfills an individual's needs (Rusbult, Martz, & Agnew, 1998). Quality of alternatives refers to people's perceived desirability of alternatives to the current relationship. The evaluation of the desirability is based on a comparison between the current and the alterna-

Table 1. Previous studies on antecedents of interpersonal relationship commitment

Studies	Antecedents of Relationship Commitment		
	Satisfaction Level	**Quality of Alternatives**	**Investments Size**
Rusbult, Wieselquist, Foster, and Witcher (1999)	√[a]	√	√
Stanley and Markman (1992)	√ (Termed "dedication")	√ (Termed "constraint")	
Baumeister and Leary (1995)	√ (Involve the need to belong)	×[b]	×
Bendapudi and Berry (1997)	√ (Termed "dedication")	√ (Termed "constraint")	
Kurdek (2000)	√ (Termed "attraction")	√ (Termed "constraint")	
Schutz (1966) and Corrigan (2001)	√ (Involve the senses of inclusion, control and affection)	×	×

[a] √ means the antecedent (i.e., satisfaction level, quality of alternatives, or investments size) of interpersonal relationship commitment was investigated in the study.

[b] × means the antecedent was not investigated.

Figure 3. Research model

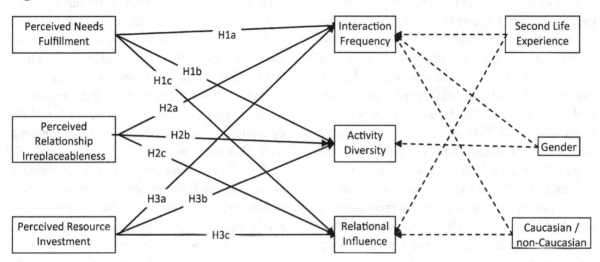

tive relationships. Investment size refers to the resources (e.g., time, effort, money, and affection) people invest in a relationship.

We used Rusbult's (1983) investment model in this research for three reasons. First, it is a comprehensive model that integrates most of the antecedents of relationship closeness identified in previous research. Second, compared with other dichotomic models (Bendapudi & Berry, 1997; Kurdek, 2000; Stanley & Markman, 1992), the investment model identifies a set of concrete and specific reasons for interpersonal relationship commitment (e.g., the quality of alternatives). Therefore, the model possesses practical value in promoting a close relationship. Third, the investment model has been extensively tested in various interpersonal relationship contexts (e.g., romantic and business relationships) (Rusbult, 1983), and it has consistently demonstrated a strong predictive power (Le & Agnew, 2003). As human-avatar relationships in virtual worlds involve various types of relationships, a generic model applicable to different relationship types is needed.

In this research, we adapted the aforementioned investment model to the context of human-avatar relationships and contend that people's perceived needs fulfillment[5], perceived relationship irreplaceableness[6], and perceived resource investment

contribute to human-avatar relationship closeness. The research model is depicted in Figure 3. Perceived needs fulfillment refers to the extent to which people perceive that their needs are fulfilled through the interaction with other users' avatars. Perceived relationship irreplaceableness refers to the extent to which people feel that relationships with avatars cannot be replaced by those with other avatars. Perceived resource investment refers to the degree to which people think that they have spent resources (e.g., time, effort) in the relationship with avatars.

Virtual world users build relationships with other users' avatars through a series of human-avatar interactions (Al-Natour & Benbasat, 2009). When a user socializes with another user's avatar, he/she will have some initial interactions with the avatar. During these interactions, the user obtains impressions and forms beliefs about the characteristics of the avatar and his/her interactions with the avatar. For instance, how his/her needs are satisfied in the interactions with the avatar, how irreplaceable the avatar is, and how much time and effort he or he has invested in the interactions with the avatar. These beliefs will in turn lead to the user's subjective judgment regarding the closeness of his/her relationship with the avatar (Al-Natour & Benbasat, 2009).

Perceived Needs Fulfillment

Perceived needs fulfillment is based on people's overall evaluation of their interaction with avatars where they may have many needs to be fulfilled. In the interpersonal domain, people interact and form relationships with others for different purposes, among which acquiring a sense of inclusion, a sense of control, and a sense of affection are the three most fundamental needs of people involved in the relationships (Corrigan, 2001; Schutz, 1966). A sense of inclusion means a feeling of being included in the community; a sense of control refers to a feeling of having power to control one's interpersonal interactions; finally, a sense of affection describes a feeling of gaining affection from relationship partners (Corrigan, 2001).

A virtual world is a social system where people socialize with other avatars through their own avatars and seek to fulfill the three types of needs. For instance, in a virtual world, people may get married with other avatars to acquire a sense of affection from their "spouses" (Cable News Network, 2008); they may join certain special interest groups (e.g., education, see http://slurl.com/secondlife/ISTE%20Island/93/83/30) where all the avatars share the same hobbies to obtain a sense of inclusion. They may buy "land," play the role of a governor, and control the activities of avatars entering their land by imposing rules, thereby obtaining a sense of control (Scoble, 2006).

When people's various needs are well satisfied in the previous interactions with an avatar, they may form an impression that the interactions are beneficial and enjoyable. People are prone to extend their existing experience and impression to new circumstances as a shortcut in decision making (Bettman & Park, 1980). Thus, they are likely to believe that future interactions with that avatar are equally beneficial and enjoyable, and the avatar may provide benefits in other activities that they currently do not engage in. As such, to acquire more benefits, people will be motivated to interact more frequently and engage in a wider range of activities with the avatar. Therefore, we posit the following hypotheses.

H1a: Perceived needs fulfillment has a positive effect on the *interaction frequency* of human-avatar relationships.

H1b: Perceived needs fulfillment has a positive effect on the *activity diversity* of human-avatar relationships.

With respect to relational influence, it can be demonstrated by people's compliance with the request or suggestions from other users' avatars (Cialdini & Trost, 1998). Due to the social nature of the human-avatar relationship, people's compliance behaviors are motivated by human beings' goal of affiliation, that is, their desires to maintain good social relationships with others (Cialdini & Goldstein, 2004). To have good relationships with others, people must follow a set of social norms, among which the norm of reciprocation is the most pervasive one across all cultures; people tend to repay others from whom they obtain benefits (Cialdini & Goldstein, 2004). If an avatar can fulfill their needs well in previous interactions, people will gradually form an obligation to reciprocate. When requested by the avatar in some situations, compliance is more likely to take place as a result of reciprocation. In this sense, people are more likely to be influenced by that avatar.

On the other hand, an avatar's good performance in satisfying people's needs leaves an impression that the avatar possesses expertise in certain domains, and this impression contributes to people's perceived credibility of that avatar (Giffin, 1967). When the avatar attempts to exert an influence on people (e.g., offering suggestions), the people's perceived credibility of the avatar will serve as an important heuristic that induces them to accept the attempt to influence (O'keefe, 2002). Therefore, the following hypothesis is proposed.

H1c: Perceived needs fulfillment has a positive effect on the *relational influence* of human-avatar relationships.

Perceived Relationship Irreplaceableness

When people believe that their relationship with an avatar cannot be easily replaced, they will be forced to stay in it (Stanley & Markman, 1992) even if they may not be willing to do so. Hence, we contend that perceived relationship irreplaceableness contributes to the closeness of a human-avatar relationship.

When a particular human-avatar relationship is considered irreplaceable, it becomes a scarce resource. People usually regard a scarce resource as more valuable, attractive, and favorable (Suri, Kohli, & Monroe, 2007). As the human-avatar relationship is a *non*-consumable resource, people are inclined to have more frequent interactions with that avatar. In addition, people are prone to treat the scarcity of a resource as a threat; thus, they may try their best to hold on to the resource to reduce this threat (Clee & Wicklund, 1980). One way to hold on to the scarce resource is to acquire more access to it. In this research context, more access to the irreplaceable human-avatar relationship can be achieved by having more frequent interactions with the avatar. Thus, we posit the following hypothesis.

H2a: Perceived relationship irreplaceableness has a positive effect on the *interaction frequency* of human-avatar relationships.

Another way to hold on to a scarce resource (i.e., an irreplaceable human-avatar relationship) is to protect the relationship from being terminated, specifically, by preventing that avatar from getting out of the relationship. Exposing an avatar to diverse activity domains will disperse and reduce the risk that the avatar will get out of the relationship. When the avatar loses interest

in doing a certain activity with an individual, if they interact in other activities, it is possible that some other activities can still attract the avatar in the relationship. As a result, people are likely to engage in more diverse activities with an avatar when they perceive their relationship as irreplaceable. Hence, we posit the following hypothesis.

H2b: Perceived relationship irreplaceableness has a positive effect on the *activity diversity* of human-avatar relationships.

In addition, when a certain human-avatar relationship is perceived to be irreplaceable, people may believe that the avatar is in control of some unique expertise and resources. These unique abilities of the avatar make people consider it as very powerful (French & Raven, 2001). As people are prone to accept the influence attempt exerted by powerful entities, they are more likely to comply with the influence from irreplaceable avatars (Yukl, Kim, & Falbe, 1996). Hence, we propose the following hypothesis.

H2c: Perceived relationship irreplaceableness has a positive effect on the *relational influence* of human-avatar relationships.

Perceived Resource Investment

Nowadays, it is common to see many users invest considerable resources in a virtual world (Taylor, 2003), especially in their relationships with avatars. For instance, in gaming virtual worlds, it sometimes takes users considerable efforts to maintain collaborative relationships with other avatars in order to level up (Klimmt, 2009). These substantial investments will cause an inertia effect on the motivation of people to engage in their current relationships with these avatars (Klimmt, 2009).

When people have already invested many resources in a human-avatar relationship, they are likely to expect a return in the future; the more the investment, the greater is the expectation. However, if the relationship is terminated, the prior investment will become the sunk cost that cannot return any benefits (Garland & Newport, 1991). Therefore, the more the investment, the more concern people will have on the security of their investment. People will try their best to secure their relationships with the avatar, and acquire the expected return of the investment. Hence, with more resources invested in an avatar, the interactions will be more frequent, as frequent interactions can increase the possibility of gaining benefits and enable people to monitor closely the status of the relationships with the avatar to ensure the security of the relationship. Similarly, compared with staying in a single activity with an avatar, being involved in multiple activities can also increase the possibility of gaining benefits. This is because if people cannot acquire benefits from one activity, they can still resort to other activities to seek benefits. In this way, the risk of losing in the relationship investment is dispersed. Therefore, we have the following two hypotheses.

H3a: Perceived resource investment has a positive effect on the *interaction frequency* of human-avatar relationships.

H3b: Perceived resource investment has a positive effect on the *activity diversity* of human-avatar relationships.

Moreover, when people have already invested a large quantity of resources (e.g., time) in their relationship with another user's avatar, they must have exposed to that avatar heavily. In these previous exposures, people's subsequent work, life, and decision making are likely to be affected by both consciously accepting the avatar's suggestions or persuasion (Wood, 2000), and unconsciously imitating the avatar's behaviors (Freedman, Birsky, & Cavoukian 1980) through social learning (Bandura, 1969). The higher the exposure, the higher the possibility of the avatar influencing the user both overtly and covertly.

On the other hand, the resources an individual possess are limited. When the individual has invested many of his/her extant resources in the relationship with a certain avatar, resources originally needed to conduct other activities can no longer be sufficiently assigned. These activities include both interactions with other avatars in the virtual world and his/her real life activities. Therefore, these original activities are likely to be out of order from lack of necessary resources (e.g., time). Consequently, people's work and life will be affected by the large investment. Actually, the emergence of virtual worlds, especially gaming virtual worlds, has many power gamers who have invested so much in the virtual environment that they become socially isolated and inept and feel uncomfortable in the real life (Taylor, 2003). Hence, we propose the following hypothesis.

H3c: Perceived resource investment has a positive effect on the *relational influence* of human-avatar relationships.

METHODOLOGY

Data Collection Platform

To test the hypotheses, an online survey was conducted to collect data on people's relationship closeness and its three antecedents in the specific context of Second Life, a 3D virtual world established in 2003. The reasons why we chose Second Life can be summarized as follows. First, it is one of the world's most popular virtual worlds, with 17,273,295 registered accounts (SL Name Watch, 2009). Second, it has prominent economic implications. It is an independent social economic system with its own residents, estates, currency, shopping malls, and schools (Eschenbrenner *et al.*, 2008). In July 2009, 27,840,722 transactions were made and 67,056 users earned revenue through Second Life (Linden Research Inc., 2009). Third, although it is usually considered as mainly containing social elements, it also has some gaming elements (Messinger *et al.*, 2009), which means people form various human-avatar relationships there. The human-avatar relationships in Second Life are typical of relationships in today's virtual worlds.

Measures

In this research, the three dimensions of human-avatar relationship closeness together with their three antecedents were measured. However, no extant measurement scales could be adopted directly in this research context, the human-avatar relationship in a virtual world. Thus, after referring to the measures in an interpersonal relationship context (Berscheid *et al.*, 1989; Rusbult *et al.*, 1998), we developed items for all six constructs following the scales development procedures of Moore and Benbasat (1991) with minor adjustments.

We first created an initial pool of 28 items for all six constructs following a comprehensive literature review (e.g., (Berscheid *et al.*, 1989; Rusbult *et al.*, 1998)) and through brainstorming among four Information Systems research students in a focus group interview (Parasuraman, Zeithaml, & Berry, 1988). This method ensures the content validity of the measures from the start (Straub, Boudreau, & Gefen, 2004). The items for the three human-avatar relationship closeness dimensions (activity diversity, interaction frequency, and relational influence) are statements about the status of the participants' relationships with an avatar. The items for the other constructs (i.e., perceived needs fulfillment, relationship irreplaceableness, and resource investment) are specific reasons for human-avatar relationship closeness. All the items went through two rounds of card sorting. In each round, a panel of four Information Systems professionals (professors and research students) was recruited as judges to sort the items into categories. In the first round, the definition of each construct and the number of constructs that should be identified were not revealed to the judges. In

the second round, the intended constructs and their definitions were disclosed in advance. After each round of card sorting, the items were checked and revised one by one based on (a) the disagreements on categorization among the judges and (b) the comments raised by the judges regarding the wording, length, and ambiguity of the items. At the end of the card sorting, 18 items remained covering the six constructs (see Appendix for the detailed results of the card sorting exercises).

All constructs were measured by reflective items except for perceived needs fulfillment. Each of the three basic needs (i.e., senses of inclusion, affection, and control) describes only one aspect of people's needs in a human-avatar relationship. These needs do not need to correlate with one another. In addition, perceived needs fulfillment is only one of the six constructs under investigation. To make the whole model parsimonious and to capture the nature of the construct, it was modeled as a three-item formative construct with one item measuring each of the three basic needs respectively (Petter, Straub, & Rai, 2007)[7]. To validate further this formative construct prior to data collection, we invited three Information Systems research students in a panel to review all three items under perceived needs fulfillment (Straub *et al.*, 2004). In the panel discussion, we double checked and ensured that (1) the construct is predicted by its items; (2) the items measuring different needs do not conceptually co-vary with one another and have different antecedents and consequences; (3) they cover the full domain of the construct; and (4) they can be consistently sorted into the intended categories in the card sorting by the judges (Petter *et al.*, 2007).

Procedures

An online questionnaire was set up, and each respondent's Internet Protocol (IP) address and the start/end time of the corresponding survey session were recorded automatically. Survey invitations with the questionnaire hyperlink were posted on several online Second Life discussion forums and were distributed through the public mailing lists at https://lists.secondlife.com/cgi-bin/mailman/listinfo. At the beginning of the survey, the respondents were asked to recall an avatar with which they had recent contact and with which they still had a relationship. The survey is composed of three sections. Section 1 measures the closeness of the human-avatar relationship using the seven-point Likert-type scales. Section 2 informs the respondents that the listed items are specific reasons for keeping the relationship with the avatar, and asks the subjects to assess all these reasons using also the seven-point Likert-type scales. Section 3 deals with background questions including Second Life experience, age, gender, and ethnicity. The respondents were informed that a lucky draw would be conducted at the end of the survey, and the winners would be awarded Amazon Coupons and Linden Dollars.

RESULTS

A total of 162 completed responses were received between March and May 2008. Two responses were excluded owing to the duplication of IP addresses, and two other responses were removed because they were made in a period of less than two minutes, which was regarded as the minimum time for a person to read all survey questions. We also conducted casewise diagnostics to identify cases whose standardized regression residues lie beyond the three standard deviations from zero (Field, 2009). Five such cases were detected, which might distort our data analysis (Wiggins, 2000). After careful examination of these five cases, we found that they were typical of outliers (e.g., almost the same response to different questions throughout the whole questionnaire, indicating that the respondents did not treat the questions seriously), and thus they were removed. This resulted to 153 answers remaining valid for data analysis.

The data collected was analyzed using partial least squares (PLS) implemented in the SmartPLS 2.0.M3 (Ringle, Wende, & Will, 2005). PLS is suitable for research that is still at the theory building stage (Barclay, Higgins, & Thompson, 1995). It can handle both reflective and formatives items (Gefen, Straub, & Boudreau, 2000). Moreover, both the measurement model and structural model can be examined concurrently (Barclay *et al.*, 1995).

Demographic Data

Of the 153 valid responses, 142 indicated gender information: 72 responses were from males, while 70 were from females. This gender ratio conforms to the results of the 2008 Second Life Survey conducted by the Social Research Foundation (Social Research Foundation, 2008), which shows that "the gender ratio is about even among the most active Second Life residents" (p. 4). Table 2 shows that a large portion of the respondents (62.09%) are residents of Second Life for more than one year, and about half (47.06%) of the respondents are between 30 and 50 years old. This is aligned with the results of the 2008 Second Life Survey, which reveals that "Second Life is not overwhelmingly populated by teens and young adults" (p. 5). Nowadays, there is a dedicated version of Second Life (i.e., Teen Second Life) for teens aged 13-17 (Linden Lab, 2010). Table 2 suggests that majority of the respondents (at least 80.39%) are Caucasians; this is also supported by the 2008 Second Life Survey, which shows that most Second Life residents are from Europe and North America (Social Research Foundation, 2008).

There was no significant difference in the respondents' human-avatar relationship closeness (p>0.05) between subjects who did not disclose their demographic data (i.e., age, gender, and ethnicity group) and those who did. Subjects' responses to human-avatar relationship closeness were further compared across age, gender, ethnicity groups, and Second Life experience. We found

Table 2. Respondents' Second Life experience, gender, age, and ethnicity

SL Experience	≤0.5 Yr.	0.5-1 Yr.	1-2 Yr.	2-3 Yr.	3-4 Yr.	>4 Yr.	Total		
No. of Respondents	22	36	63	18	13	1	153		
Percentage	14.38%	23.53%	41.18%	11.76%	8.50%	0.65%	100.00%		
Sex	Male	Female	Did not indicate	Total					
No. of Respondents	72	70	11	153					
Percentage	47.06%	45.75%	7.19%	100.00%					
Age	≤20	20-30	30-40	40-50	50-60	>60	Did not indicate	Total	
No. of Respondents	5	25	32	40	38	6	7	153	
Percentage	3.27%	16.34%	20.92%	26.14%	24.84%	3.92%	4.58%	100.00%	
Ethnicity	Asian	White	Black	Chinese	Mixed	Others	Did not indicate	Total	
No. of Respondents	3	123	1	6	3	3	14	153	
Percentage	1.96%	80.39%	0.65%	3.92%	1.96%	1.96%	9.15%	100.00%	

that age had no significant effect on relationship closeness ($p>0.05$). However, Caucasians responded differently from others on interaction frequency ($p<0.05$) and relational influence ($p<0.05$). Males responded differently from females on activity diversity ($p<0.05$) and interaction frequency ($p<0.05$). People's Second Life experience was positively associated with the interaction frequency ($p<0.001$) and relational influence ($p<0.001$). Hence, we included ethnicity (Caucasian vs. Non-Caucasian), gender, and

Second Life experience into our research model as control variables.

Measurement Model

The basic statistics, including the mean and standard deviation of each construct, are listed in Table 3. As both reflective and formative indicators were adopted to assess all six constructs, we used different evaluation criteria for these two types of measures. For perceived needs fulfillment, a formative construct with three indicators,

Table 3. Means, standard deviations, composite reliabilities, correlations of constructs

Construct	Mean	SD	Composite Reliability	Activity Diversity	Interaction Frequency	Relational Influence	Perceived Relationship Irreplaceableness	Perceived Resource Investment
Activity Diversity	4.830	1.390	0.846	0.804[c]				
Interaction Frequency	5.368	1.517	0.947	0.505	0.926[c]			
Relational Influence	4.174	1.747	0.906	0.457	0.597	0.873[c]		
Perceived Relationship Irreplaceableness	4.582	1.613	0.883	0.477	0.485	0.586	0.847[c]	
Perceived Resource Investment	4.839	1.529	0.940	0.536	0.718	0.681	0.676	0.916[c]
Perceived needs fulfillment[d]	4.460	1.145						

[c] The diagonal elements are square roots of the average variance extracted (AVE).

[d] Perceived needs fulfillment was measured with formative items.

the evaluation method for reflective items is not applicable. Therefore, we based the assessment of the perceived needs fulfillment construct on the procedure of Diamantopoulos and Winklhofer (2001) and Petter *et al.* to ensure the quality of the formative items.

First, the content validity and indicator specification of perceived needs fulfillment were checked before data collection (i.e., in the measurement development stage). Second, the variance inflation factor (VIF) of each indicator of perceived needs fulfillment was calculated as a measure of multicollinearity. The VIF for all items ranged from 1.05 to 1.45, all well below even the most strict cut-off value of 3.30 (Petter *et al.*, 2007). Therefore, multicollinearity is not a prob-

lem. Third, the model weights of formative items were examined, and those of the sense of affection and sense of inclusion are significant, while that of the sense of control is insignificant (see Table 4). As our study is explorative, and the removal of any item will make the content validity suffer, we follow the suggestion of Bollen and Lennox (1991) to retain all these three items in the data analysis.

All other constructs used reflective indicators, and we assessed these measurement scales by (1) individual item reliability, (2) internal consistency, and (3) discriminant validity (Barclay *et al.*, 1995). Individual item reliability was checked by examining the factor loading of each item on its corresponding latent variable. Table 4 shows

Table 4. Loadings, cross loadings, and weights of measures [e]

Items	Activity Diversity (DVST)	Interaction Frequency (FREQ)	Relational Influence (INFL)	Perceived Relationship Irreplaceableness (ALTR)	Perceived Resource Investment (IVST)	Perceivd Needs Fulfillment [f] (NDFL)
DVST1	**0.844****	0.481	0.447	0.372	0.512	
DVST2	**0.812****	0.352	0.303	0.430	0.448	
DVST3R	**0.755****	0.376	0.343	0.350	0.299	
FREQ1	0.430	**0.916****	0.533	0.450	0.631	
FREQ2	0.458	**0.902****	0.551	0.404	0.640	
FREQ3	0.511	**0.958****	0.573	0.489	0.718	
INFL1	0.506	0.592	**0.919****	0.542	0.662	
INFL2	0.410	0.514	**0.884****	0.482	0.550	
INFL3R	0.272	0.451	**0.815****	0.507	0.565	
ALTR1	0.470	0.490	0.567	**0.907****	0.630	
ALTR2	0.368	0.299	0.425	**0.813****	0.505	
ALTR3	0.362	0.417	0.480	**0.817****	0.571	
IVST1	0.491	0.639	0.657	0.665	**0.904****	
IVST2	0.444	0.685	0.599	0.612	**0.920****	
IVST3	0.536	0.650	0.615	0.581	**0.924****	
AFEC1						**0.624****
CTRL2						**0.098**
INCL2						**0.497****

[e] scores for perceived needs fulfillments are weights, and scores for other constructs are loadings.
[f] Perceived needs fulfillment was measured with formative items.
** p<0.01, *p<0.05

that the loadings of all items are significant and above the rule of thumb, which is 0.707 (Barclay *et al.*, 1995). Internal consistency was evaluated using the composite reliability of each latent variable. Table 3 shows that the composite reliabilities of all constructs are above the 0.70 threshold (Barclay *et al.*, 1995). Discriminant validity was verified using two criteria. First, the square root of the average variance extracted (AVE) for each construct was greater than its correlations with all other constructs (Table 3). Second, the loading of each item on its target construct was greater than its cross-loadings on other constructs (Table 4). Thus, all scales using reflective indicators are reliable and valid.

Common Method Bias

Three measures were taken to address potential concerns of common method bias. First, in the survey questionnaire, instead of placing the items of the same construct together, the presentation order of all items within the same session was counterbalanced to reduce the bias related to the question context (Podsakoff, Mackenzie, & Podsakoff, 2003).

Second, we conducted Harmon's one-factor test, which assumes that if the common method bias exists, a single factor emerges or a significant factor explaining the majority of the variance is present in factor analysis with the principal axis factoring extraction method (Podsakoff & Organ, 1986). The results of Harmon's one-factor test suggests that there is little common method bias in our online survey in that none of the four factors extracted in the factor analysis can account for more than half of the total covariance of the sample.

Third, we statistically modeled a common method factor into the PLS structural model (for the detailed procedure, see (Liang, Saraf, Hu, & Xue, 2007)). In the model, a common method factor, whose indicators are all items in the study, was introduced[8]. This can explain the variance of

an item by both its corresponding factor and the common method factor. Table 5 shows that the average variance explained by the items' corresponding factors is much larger than that explained by the common method factor (73.4:1), and only one of the items' loadings on the common method factor is significant. In addition, all originally (in)significant paths in the structure model are still (in)significant. Therefore, we are confident that the common method bias is not a problem in the current research.

Structural Model

The results of the structural model are reported in Figure 4. These include the path coefficient, the significance of each hypothesized path based on t-statistics (one-tailed), and the value of R square for each dependent variable.

Perceived needs fulfillment has significant positive effects on both the interaction frequency and relational influence of human-avatar relationships, but it does not exert any significant influence on activity diversity. Thus, H1a and H1c were supported, but H1b was not. Perceived relationship irreplaceableness has a significant positive impact on the relational influence of human-avatar relationships, but it does not have any significant influence on either interaction frequency or activity diversity. Hence, H2c was supported, but H2a and H2b were not. Perceived resource investment has positive impacts on all three human-avatar relationship closeness dimensions, including interaction frequency, activity diversity, and relational influence. Thus, H3a~c were all supported.

DISCUSSION

Discussion of Findings

Overall, our research model performed very well in explaining the closeness of human-avatar rela-

Table 5. Common method bias analysis

Construct	Item	Substantive Factor Loading (R1)	R1²	Method Factor Loading (R2)	R2²
Activity Diversity	DVST1	0.742**	0.550	0.113	0.013
	DVST2	0.817**	0.667	-0.017	0.000
	DVST3R	0.864**	0.747	-0.103	0.011
Interaction Frequency	FREQ1	0.965**	0.930	-0.056	0.003
	FREQ2	0.921**	0.849	-0.024	0.001
	FREQ3	0.894**	0.799	0.075	0.006
Relational Influence	INFL1	0.82**	0.672	0.12	0.015
	INFL2	0.979**	0.959	-0.104	0.011
	INFL3R	0.824**	0.679	-0.024	0.001
Perceived Relationship Irreplaceable-ness	ALTR1	0.821**	0.674	0.098	0.010
	ALTR2	0.983**	0.966	-0.196*	0.038
	ALTR3	0.748**	0.559	0.083	0.007
Perceived Resource Investment	IVST1	0.75**	0.562	0.167	0.028
	IVST2	0.981**	0.963	-0.065	0.004
	IVST3	1.015**	1.030	-0.1	0.010
Perceived needs fulfillment	AFEC1	0.785**	0.616	0.068	0.005
	CTRL2	0.454	0.206	-0.144	0.021
	INCL2	0.887**	0.787	-0.016	0.000
	Average	0.847	0.734	-0.007	0.010

** p<0.01, *p<0.05

Figure 4. Structural model results

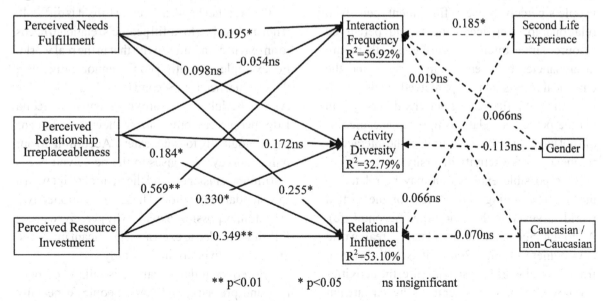

** p<0.01   * p<0.05   ns insignificant

161

Table 6. f Squares between independent/control variables and dependent variables

	Perceived Needs Fulfillment	Perceived Relationship Irreplaceableness	Perceived Resource Investment	SL Experience	Gender	Ethnicity
Activity Diversity	0.006	0.020	0.069	0.000	0.019	0.000
Interaction Frequency	0.039	0.006	0.276	0.075	0.009	0.001
Relational Influence	0.061	0.038	0.094	0.009	0.000	0.009
Average	0.035	0.021	0.146	0.028	0.009	0.003

tionships in virtual worlds. The data of this study showed that it accounted for 56.92%, 32.79%, and 53.10% of the variance of the three dimensions of human-avatar relationship closeness (i.e., interaction frequency, activity diversity, and relational influence), respectively. We also calculated the f square between each independent variable and dependent variable, which is another measure of an independent variable's explorative power (Chin, 1998). Table 6 shows that while perceived needs fulfillment and perceived relationship irreplaceableness have a small effect, perceived resource investment has a medium effect (Chin, 1998).

As theoretically predicted, we found that human-avatar relationship closeness, which involves interaction frequency, activity diversity, and relational influence, can be largely attributed to people's perceived needs fulfillment, perceived relationship irreplaceableness, and perceived resource investment. Nevertheless, there are discrepancies between our hypotheses and the empirical results: (1) the perceived needs fulfillment did not influence the activity diversity, and (2) the perceived relationship irreplaceableness did not have any influence on either the interaction frequency or the activity diversity.

One possible explanation may be related to the specific setting and context of the virtual world surveyed in this study (i.e., Second Life). Although Second Life simulates a real world environment (White, 2008), it is still different from the real world. In Second Life, the activities people engage in with other users' avatars are not the same as those in the real world. Due to the limitation of current technologies, the activities in Second Life are quite limited. For instance, in the real world, many people play basketball to keep fit, during which they may build relationships with their teammates. However, in Second Life, it is difficult for people to achieve the goal of keeping fit through playing "basketball" in-world. Therefore, not so many people are willing to do exercises in-world. Thus, it is possible that people interact with other users' avatars only in a limited set of activities (e.g., chatting), and they cannot engage in all types of activities that they may wish to. This argument is also supported by the result of our online survey indicating that the standard deviation of activity diversity is the lowest among all three human-avatar relationship closeness dimensions.

On the other hand, in Second Life, it is difficult, if not impossible, to fulfill people's relational needs to an extent comparable with that in the real world. For example, currently, people cannot really fulfill their sexual needs in Second Life physiologically. Although adult services are very popular in Second Life, people can only satisfy their sexual needs psychologically to some extent. According to our online survey, responses to the perceived needs fulfillment cluster around the neutral point with a low standard deviation. The aforementioned two aspects may possibly explain why perceived needs fulfillment failed to exert any significant influence on activity diversity in this study.

Moreover, today's real life is full of competition and pressure, and many people (especially the middle-aged who took up a large portion of our sample) are busy with work (Ng, Phillips, & Lee, 2002). They may not have enough time to be fully involved in a virtual world and completely enjoy their virtual lives. Thus, even if people perceive that a certain human-avatar relationship is irreplaceable and scarce, the scarcity of this human-avatar relationship is far from being a threat to people. As such, the corresponding threat reaction behaviors (e.g., getting more exposure to the relationship) cannot be easily induced. This could explain why perceived relationship irreplaceableness did not have any significant effect on interaction frequency or activity diversity in this study.

Implications

Theoretically, in this study, we explained the attributions of human-avatar relationship closeness from the perspective of interpersonal relationship investment. In virtual worlds, it is very salient and prevalent that users establish relationships with other users' virtual identities represented as avatars through their interactions with these avatars. By building relationships with other users' avatars, people can achieve a major objective of using virtual worlds, that is, socialization (Messinger *et al.*, 2009; Social Research Foundation, 2008). Organizations can conduct relationship marketing and customer relationship management in-world. However, users' relationships with other users' avatars vary in terms of the level of closeness, which influences the success of socialization and business activities in-world. Nevertheless, this phenomenon has seldom been investigated. Our research is among the first to explain and articulate the underlying reasons for the human-avatar relationship closeness, which will help us better understand this important phenomenon.

Furthermore, the successful identification of the three antecedents of human-avatar relationship closeness enriches the theories on relationship closeness. Human-avatar interaction has become the basic interaction mode in today's virtual worlds. It provides end users with a natural and

favorable online experience, offers organizations many business opportunities, and is helpful in the sustainable development of a virtual world. Personalized avatars enable virtual world users to create virtual identities represented as avatars, which can be entirely different from their real identities (Galanxhi & Nah, 2007). These artificial identities represented by avatars are the entities people interact with.

According to the prevailing media equation theory and the CASA paradigm, people *directly* interact and build relationships with IT artifacts (Sundar, 1994). This phenomenon is especially salient in today's virtual worlds, where real-world characteristics are simulated, and avatars are widely utilized to help people navigate virtual worlds. As a type of human-computer interaction (Van Vugt, Konijn, Hoorn, Keur, & Eliens, 2007), human-avatar interaction contributes to the success of a virtual world (De Souza & Preece, 2004). However, to realize the advantages of human-avatar interaction in a virtual world, the building of close human-avatar relationships is essential.

Nevertheless, there have been few studies conducted to investigate the mechanism behind the building of human-avatar relationships or the factors contributing to the closeness of these relationships. Prior research on relationship closeness focused on human-human interaction, while this research extended the investment model of interpersonal relationship to the context of human-avatar interaction. We found that human-avatar relationship closeness could be largely attributed to people's perceived needs fulfillment, relationship irreplaceableness, and relationship investment. Moreover, we found something unique to the human-avatar interaction in virtual worlds. The activity diversity and interaction frequency of a human-avatar relationship cannot be so easily induced as relational influence. This might be due to the limitations of virtual worlds (e.g., only limited activities can be conducted) and the fast pace of modern life.

Practically, the results of this study can provide a set of guidelines for practitioners to design effective human-computer interactions to sustain the prosperity of virtual worlds. Several useful virtual world design principles emerged for promoting a close human-avatar relationship.

First, virtual world designers should try to satisfy people's needs, including the sense of inclusion, affection, and control; the first two needs are more important. Specifically, virtual worlds can offer simple facilities for users to easily create and join special interest groups in which they can enjoy a sense of inclusion with people sharing the same interest. Typical intimate behaviors (e.g., kiss, hug, and touch) can be implemented and added to the avatar's options of actions. These options will make it easier and straightforward for avatars to show and for users to sense affection. Ranking mechanisms based on the avatar's attributes (e.g., Second Life experience, activeness, and sophistication) can be introduced where avatars with a high ranking can control certain activities of those with a low ranking, inducing a sense of control.

Second, virtual world designers should make each avatar unique so that users will perceive them to be irreplaceable. This can be achieved by providing user-friendly avatar customization tools, where all attributes of an avatar can be customized and personalized.

Third, designers should make users realize that they have already invested plenty of resources in certain human-avatar relationships. In particular, the relationship investment can be visualized by automatically recording user's interactions with avatars and dynamically displaying the resources (e.g., total time of interaction and Linden Dollars paid to the avatar) they have invested.

In addition, our research results provide some guidance for people, especially sales managers, to build close relationships between their own avatars (e.g., sales avatars) and other users. First, people can use their own avatars to satisfy other users' various needs, involving the sense of inclusion, affection, and control, especially the first two needs. For instance, a company can make its sales avatars dress similarly to its customers' avatars so

that the customers can feel a sense of inclusion; an individual can make his/her own avatars smile sweetly in front of other users to convey affection; a person can provide other users with a sense of control by making his/her avatar look like a good listener (e.g., nod during conversation). Second, people should differentiate their avatars from other avatars by making full use of the customization tool provided by virtual worlds and innovatively adding some scripts if possible. In this way, other users will perceive these avatars to be unique and irreplaceable. Third, when interacting with others, an individual can use his/her avatars to tell the interaction partner that plenty of resources have been invested in their relationship.

Limitations and Future Research

Our research has some limitations. First, it did not explicitly relate the antecedents of human-avatar relationship closeness to the specific technological features of a virtual world. How technological design features influence people's attributions of human-avatar relationship closeness remains unknown. For instance, both the avatars and entire social environment in Second Life are cartoon like and are low in realism. However, with the rapid development of virtual reality technologies, the avatar and the immersive social environment will become much more similar to real life. The uncanny valley literature indicates that with an increase in realism, the positivity of users' emotional responses to an agent will increase to a point and then decrease dramatically, When the agent is perfect in realism, the positivity of the user's response will increase again (Mori, 1970). People's emotional states may influence their social relationships with other avatars. Therefore, how the realism of avatars influences people's relationship building with avatars is worthy of investigation in future research.

Second, the anonymous avatar-represented virtual identities in Second Life are not so closely related to users' real life identities as those in other non-anonymous virtual communities, such as Facebook, where users disclose much authentic personal information (e.g., name, gender, and affiliation) (Sagayama *et al.*, 2008). Therefore, in this anonymous environment, people may not trust other users' virtual identities represented with avatars and would not want to maintain relationships with them. Hence, trust is a very salient issue in virtual worlds and is expected to influence people's relationship building with avatars. However, in this research, we did not investigate the trust issue explicitly, and we recommend future research to look into this area.

Third, the measurement employed by the current research is newly developed due to the lack of extant scales. Although we adopted a rigorous scales development method (Moore and Benbasat, 1991), there is still room for improvement. Therefore, future research can contribute by further refining and validating our measurement.

Fourth, in addition to the human-avatar relationship discussed in the current study, there are other types of relationships in virtual worlds, including a user's relationship with his/her own avatar and the relationship between two users' avatars. The attributions of the closeness of these relationships may be different from the attributions of users' relationships with other users' avatars, and thus they deserve future research.

Fifth, there could be many types of human-avatar relationships, such as romantic relationships, seller-buyer relationships, and teacher-student relationships. People are likely to make different attributions of relationship closeness for different types of human-avatar relationships because of their distinct natures. However, in this study, we investigated human-avatar relationships as a whole and did not distinguish between the diverse types of relationships. Possible differential attributions of various human-avatar relationships need further exploration.

CONCLUSION

Based on the media equation theory and the CASA paradigm, this study identifies users' attributions of human-avatar relationship closeness in virtual worlds by extending the investment model of interpersonal relationships to the domain of human-avatar interaction. By examining a particular type of virtual worlds, namely, Second Life, we confirmed the similarity between human-avatar relationship closeness and human-human relationship closeness. Therefore, future research investigating human-avatar relationship closeness may rely on the abundant research on interpersonal relationship closeness; otherwise fundamentally new theories are needed. Specifically, the closeness of the human-avatar relationship can be largely attributed to people's perceived needs fulfillment, relationship irreplaceableness, and resource investment. By articulating the antecedents of human-avatar relationship closeness, practitioners can invest design resources on the aspects associated with such attributions to retain the virtual world residents effectively and to sustain the stable development of virtual worlds.

ACKNOWLEDGMENT

The authors would like to thank the special issue Editor, Shu Schiller, and the anonymous referees for their valuable comments on the earlier versions of the paper. The work described in the paper was partially supported by grants from the Research Grants Council of Hong Kong S.A.R. (Project No. CityU 150207) and from the National Natural Science Foundation of China (NSFC) under grants #70890082 and #70872059.

REFERENCES

Aharoni, E., & Fridlund, A. J. (2007). Social reactions toward people vs. Computers: How mere labels shape interactions. *Computers in Human Behavior, 23*(5), 2175–2189. doi:10.1016/j.chb.2006.02.019

Ajzen, I. (1991). The theory of planned behavior. *Organizational Behavior and Human Decision Procedures, 50*(2), 179–211. doi:10.1016/0749-5978(91)90020-T

Ajzen, I., & Fishbein, M. (1973). Attitudinal and normative variables as predictors of specific behaviors. *Journal of Personality and Social Psychology, 27*(1), 41–57. doi:10.1037/h0034440

Al-Natour, S., & Benbasat, I. (2009). The adoption and use of IT artifacts: A new interaction-centric model for the study of user-artifact relationships. *Journal of the Association for Information Systems, 10*(9), 661–685.

Alty, J. L., Knott, R. P., Anderson, B., & Smyth, M. (2000). A framework for engineering metaphor at the user interface. *Interacting with Computers, 13*(2), 301–322. doi:10.1016/S0953-5438(00)00047-3

Ashford, R. (2008, June 16). *About my Second Life avatar gender identity*. Retrieved from http://librarianbydesign.blogspot.com/2008/06/about-my-second-life-avatar-identity.html

Ballard-Reisch, D. S., & Weigel, D. J. (1999). Communication process in marital commitment: An integrative approach. In Adams, J. M., & Jones, W. H. (Eds.), *Handbook of interpersonal commitment and relationship stability* (pp. 407–424). New York: Kluwer Academic / Plenum Publishers.

Bandura, A. (1969). Social-learning theory of identificatory processes. In Goslin, D. A. (Ed.), *Handbook of socialization theory and research* (pp. 213–262). Chicago: Rand McNally.

Barclay, D., Higgins, C., & Thompson, R. (1995). The partial least square (PLS) approach to casual modeling: Personal computer adoption and use as an illustration. *Technology Studies, 2*(2), 285–309.

Baumeister, R. F., & Leary, M. R. (1995). The need to belong: Desire for interpersonal attachments as a fundamental human motivation. *Psychological Bulletin, 117*(3), 497–529. doi:10.1037/0033-2909.117.3.497

Bendapudi, N., & Berry, L. L. (1997). Customers' motivations for maintaining relationships with service providers. *Journal of Retailing, 73*(1), 15–37. doi:10.1016/S0022-4359(97)90013-0

Berscheid, E., Snyder, M., & Omoto, A. M. (1989). The relationship closeness inventory: Assessing the closeness of interpersonal relationships. *Journal of Personality and Social Psychology, 57*(5), 792–807. doi:10.1037/0022-3514.57.5.792

Bettman, J. R., & Park, C. W. (1980). Effects of prior knowledge and experience and phase of the choice process on consumer decision processes: A protocol analysis. *The Journal of Consumer Research, 7*(3), 234–248. doi:10.1086/208812

Bollen, K., & Lennox, R. (1991). Conventional wisdom on measurement: A structural equation perspective. *Psychological Bulletin, 110*(2), 305–313. doi:10.1037/0033-2909.110.2.305

Bruckman, A., & Jensen, C. (2002). The mystery of the death of MediaMOO. In Renninger, K. A., & Shumar, W. (Eds.), *Building virtual communities: Learning and change in cyberspace* (pp. 21–33). New York: Cambridge University Press. doi:10.1017/CBO9780511606373.006

Cable News Network. (2008, November 14). *Second Life affair ends in divorce*. Retrieved from http://www.cnn.com/2008/WORLD/europe/11/14/second.life.divorce/index.html

Chan, M. J. (2007, June 14). *Identity in a virtual world*. Retrieved from http://edition.cnn.com/2007/ TECH/06/07/virtual_identity/ index.html

Chin, W. W. (1998). The partial least squares approach to structural equation modeling . In Marcoulides, G. A. (Ed.), *Modern methods for business research* (pp. 295–336). Hillsdale, NJ: Lawrence Erlbaum Associates.

Cialdini, R. B., & Goldstein, N. J. (2004). Social influence: Compliance and conformity. *Annual Review of Psychology*, *55*, 591–621. doi:10.1146/annurev.psych.55.090902.142015

Cialdini, R. B., & Trost, M. R. (1998). Social influence: Social norms, conformity, and compliance . In Gilbert, D. T., Fiske, S. T., & Lindzey, G. (Eds.), *The handbook of social psychology* (*Vol. 2*, pp. 151–192). New York: Random House.

Clee, M. A., & Wicklund, R. A. (1980). Consumer behavior and psychological reactance. *The Journal of Consumer Research*, *6*(4), 389–405. doi:10.1086/208782

Corrigan, M. W. (2001). *Social exchange theory, interpersonal communication motives, and volunteerism: Identifying motivation to volunteer and the rewards and costs associated*. Unpublished master's thesis, West Virginia University, Morgantown, WV.

De Souza, C. S., & Preece, J. (2004). A framework for analyzing and understanding online communities. *Interacting with Computers*, *16*(3), 579–610. doi:10.1016/j.intcom.2003.12.006

Diamantopoulos, A., & Winklhofer, H. M. (2001). Index construction with formative indicators: An alternative to scale development. *JMR, Journal of Marketing Research*, *38*(2), 269–277. doi:10.1509/jmkr.38.2.269.18845

England, D., & Gray, P. (1998). Temporal aspects of interaction in shared virtual worlds. *Interacting with Computers*, *11*(1), 87–105. doi:10.1016/S0953-5438(98)00033-2

Eschenbrenner, B., Nah, F. F.-H., & Siau, K. (2008). 3-D virtual worlds in education: Applications, benefits, issues, and opportunities. *Journal of Database Management*, *19*(4), 91–110.

Field, A. (2009). *Discovering statistics using SPSS* (3rd ed.). London: SAGE.

Freedman, J. L., Birsky, J., & Cavoukian, A. (1980). Environmental determinants of behavioral contagion: Density and number . *Basic and Applied Social Psychology*, *1*(2), 155–161. doi:10.1207/s15324834basp0102_4

French, J. R. P., & Raven, B. (2001). The bases of social power . In Asherman, I., Bob, P., & Randall, J. (Eds.), *The negotiation sourcebook* (2nd ed., pp. 61–74). Amherst, MA: Human Resource Development Press.

Galanxhi, H., & Nah, F. F.-H. (2007). Deception in cyberspace: A comparison of text-only vs. Avatar-supported medium. *International Journal of Human-Computer Studies*, *65*(9), 770–783. doi:10.1016/j.ijhcs.2007.04.005

Garland, H., & Newport, S. (1991). Effects of absolute and relative sunk costs on the decision to persist with a course of action. *Organizational Behavior and Human Decision Processes*, *48*(1), 55–69. doi:10.1016/0749-5978(91)90005-E

Gefen, D., Straub, D. W., & Boudreau, M.-C. (2000). Structural equation modeling and regression: Guidelines for research practice. *Communications of the Association for Information Systems*, *4*, 1–77.

Giffin, K. (1967). The contribution of studies of source credibility to a theory of interpersonal trust in the communication process. *Psychological Bulletin*, *68*(2), 104–120. doi:10.1037/h0024833

Hemp, P. (2006). Avatar-based marketing. *Harvard Business Review, 84*(6), 48–57.

Hendrick, S. S. (2004). *Understanding close relationships*. Boston: Allyn & Bacon.

Holzwarth, M., Janiszewski, C., & Neumann, M. M. (2006). The influence of avatars on online consumer shopping behavior. *Journal of Marketing, 70*(4), 19–36. doi:10.1509/jmkg.70.4.19

Jennings, N., & Collins, C. (2007). Virtual or virtually u: Educational institutions in Second Life. *International Journal of Social Sciences, 2*(3), 180–186.

Junglas, I. A., Johnson, N. A., Steel, D. J., Abraham, D. C., & Loughlin, P. M. (2007). Identity formation, learning styles and trust in virtual worlds. *The Data Base for Advances in Information Systems, 38*(4), 90–96.

Kanade, T., Rander, P., & Narayanan, P. J. (1997). Virtualized reality: Constructing virtual worlds from real scenes. *IEEE MultiMedia, 4*(1), 34–47. doi:10.1109/93.580394

Kazmer, M. M. (2007). Beyond C U L8R: Disengaging from online social worlds . *New Media & Society, 9*(1), 111–138. doi:10.1177/1461444807072215

Keeling, K., Mcgoldrick, P., & Beatty, S. (2007). Virtual onscreen assistants: A viable strategy to support online customer relationship building? *Advances in Consumer Research. Association for Consumer Research (U. S.), 34*, 138–144.

Kelley, H. H., Berscheid, E., Christensen, A., Harvey, J. H., Huston, T. L., & Levinger, G. (1983). *Close relationships*. New York: W.H. Freeman.

Kim, D. J., Ferrin, D. L., & Rao, H. R. (2009). Trust and satisfaction, two stepping stones for successful e-commerce relationships: A longitudinal exploration. *Information Systems Research, 20*(2), 237–257. doi:10.1287/isre.1080.0188

Kim, Y. J. (2007). An exploratory study of social factors influencing virtual community members' satisfaction with avatars. *Communications of the Association for Information Systems, 20*, 1–44.

Klimmt, C. (2009). Key dimensions of contemporary video game literacy: Towards a normative model of the competent digital gamer. *Journal for Computer Game Culture, 3*(1), 23–31.

Kurdek, L. A. (2000). Attractions and constraints as determinants of relationship commitment: Longitudinal evidence from gay, lesbian, and heterosexual couples. *Personal Relationships, 7*(3), 245–262. doi:10.1111/j.1475-6811.2000.tb00015.x

Le, B., & Agnew, C. R. (2003). Commitment and its theorized determinants: A meta-analysis of the investment model. *Personal Relationships, 10*(1), 37–57. doi:10.1111/1475-6811.00035

Liang, H., Saraf, N., Hu, Q., & Xue, Y. (2007). Assimilation of enterprise systems: The effect of institutional pressures and the mediating role of top management. *Management Information Systems Quarterly, 31*(1), 59–87.

Linden Lab. (2010). *What is teen Second Life?* Retrieved from http://teen.secondlife.com/whatis

Linden Research Inc. (2009, December 8). *Economic statistics*. Retrieved from http://secondlife.com/whatis/ economy_stats.php

Mennecke, B. E., Mcneill, D., Ganis, M., Roche, E. M., Bray, D. A., & Konsynski, B. (2008). Second Life and other virtual worlds: A roadmap for research. *Communications of the Association for Information Systems, 22*, 371–388.

Messinger, P. R., Stroulia, E., Lyons, K., Bone, M., Niu, R., & Smirnov, K. (2009). Virtual worlds—past, present, and future: New directions in social computing. *Decision Support Systems, 47*(3), 204–228. doi:10.1016/j.dss.2009.02.014

Moore, G. C., & Benbasat, I. (1991). Development of an instrument to measure the perception of adoption an information technology innovation. *Information Systems Research, 2*(3), 192–222. doi:10.1287/isre.2.3.192

Mori, M. (1970). The uncanny valley. *Energy, 7*(4), 33–35.

Name Watch, S. L. (2009, December 10). *Site statistics.* [Online]. Retrieved December 10, 2009, http://slnamewatch.com/

Nass, C., & Moon, Y. (2000). Machines and mindlessness: Social responses to computers. *The Journal of Social Issues, 56*(1), 81–103. doi:10.1111/0022-4537.00153

Ng, A. C. Y., Phillips, D. R., & Lee, W. K.-M. (2002). Persistence and challenges to filial piety and informal support of older persons in a modern Chinese society a case study in Tuen Mun, Hong Kong. *Journal of Aging Studies, 16*(2), 135–153. doi:10.1016/S0890-4065(02)00040-3

O'keefe. D. J. (2002). *Persuasion: Theory and research.* Thousand Oaks, CA: SAGE.

Parasuraman, A., Zeithaml, V. A., & Berry, L. L. (1988). SERVQUAL: A multiple-item scale for measuring consumer perceptions of service quality. *Journal of Retailing, 64*(1), 12–40.

Petter, S., Straub, D., & Rai, A. (2007). Specifying formative constructs in information systems research. *Management Information Systems Quarterly, 31*(4), 623–656.

Podsakoff, P. M., Mackenzie, S. B., & Podsakoff, N. P. (2003). Common method biases in behavioral research: A critical review of the literature and recommended remedies. *The Journal of Applied Psychology, 88*(5), 879–903. doi:10.1037/0021-9010.88.5.879

Podsakoff, P. M., & Organ, D. W. (1986). Self-reports in organizational research: Problems and prospects. *Journal of Management, 12*(4), 531–544. doi:10.1177/014920638601200408

Preece, J. (2001). Sociability and usability in online communities: Determining and measuring success. *Behaviour & Information Technology, 20*(5), 347–356. doi:10.1080/01449290110084683

Reeves, B., & Nass, C. I. (1996). *The media equation: How people treat computers, television, and new media like real people and places.* Stanford, CA: CSLI Publications.

Ringle, C. M., Wende, S., & Will, S. (2005). *SmartPLS (Version 2.0 (M3) Beta).*

Rusbult, C. E. (1983). A longitudinal test of the investment model: The development (and deterioration) of satisfaction and commitment in heterosexual involvements. *Journal of Personality and Social Psychology, 45*(1), 101–117. doi:10.1037/0022-3514.45.1.101

Rusbult, C. E., Martz, J. M., & Agnew, C. R. (1998). The investment model scale: Measuring commitment level, satisfaction level, quality of alternatives, and investment size. *Personal Relationships, 5*(4), 357–387. doi:10.1111/j.1475-6811.1998.tb00177.x

Rusbult, C. E., Olsen, N., Davis, J. L., & Hannon, P. A. (2001). Commitment and relationship maintenance mechanism . In Harvey, J. H., & Wenzel, A. (Eds.), *Close romantic relationships: Maintenance and enhancement* (pp. 87–114). Mahwah, NJ: Lawrence Erlbaum Associates, Inc.

Rusbult, C. E., Wieselquist, J., Foster, C. A., & Witcher, B. S. (1999). Commitment and trust in close relationships: An interdependence analysis . In Adams, J. M., & Jones, W. H. (Eds.), *Handbook of interpersonal commitment and relationship stability* (pp. 427–449). New York: Kluwer Academic / Plenum Publishers.

Sagayama, K., Kanenishi, K., Matsuura, K., Kume, K., Miyoshi, Y., Matsumoto, J., et al. (2008). Application of campus SNS for supporting students and their behavior. In *Proceedings of the 16th International Conference on Computers in Education,* Taipei, Taiwan.

Schutz, W. (1966). *The interpersonal underworld.* Palo Alto, CA: Science & Behavior Books.

Scoble, R. (2006, May 5). *Rules and rule breaking in Second Life.* Retrieved from http://scobleizer.com/2006/05/05/ rules-and-rulebreaking-in-second-life/

Scott, D. M. (2007). Marketing a Second Life. *EContent, 30*(2), 56–56.

Social Research Foundation. (2008). *2008 Second Life survey.* New York: Social Research Foundation.

Stanley, S. M., & Markman, H. J. (1992). Assessing commitment in personal relationships. *Journal of Marriage and the Family, 54*(3), 595–608. doi:10.2307/353245

Straub, D., Boudreau, M.-C., & Gefen, D. (2004). Validation guidelines for is positivist research. *Communications of the Association for Information Systems, 13,* 380–427.

Sundar, S. S. (1994). *Is human-computer interaction social or parasocial?* Paper presented at the Annual Convention of the Association for Education in Journalism and Mass communication, Atlanta, GA.

Sundar, S. S., & Nass, C. (2000). Source orientation in human-computer interaction: Programmer, networker, or independent social actor? *Communication Research, 27*(6), 683–703. doi:10.1177/009365000027006001

Suri, R., Kohli, C., & Monroe, K. B. (2007). The effects of perceived scarcity on consumers' processing of price information. *Journal of the Academy of Marketing Science, 35*(1), 89–100. doi:10.1007/s11747-006-0008-y

Taylor, T. L. (2003). *Power gamers just want to have fun?: Instrumental play in a MMOG.* Paper presented at the Digital Games Research Conference (Level Up), Utrecht, the Netherlands.

The authors would like to thank the special issue Editor, Shu Schiller, and the anonymous referees for their valuable comments on the earlier versions of the paper. The work described in the paper was partially supported by grants from the Research Grants Council of Hong Kong S.A.R. (Project No. CityU 150207) and from the National Natural Science Foundation of China (NSFC) under grants #70890082 and #70872059.

Van Vugt, H. C., Konijn, E. A., Hoorn, J. F., Keur, I., & Eliens, A. (2007). Realism is not all! User engagement with task-related interface characters. *Interacting with Computers, 19*(2), 267–280. doi:10.1016/j.intcom.2006.08.005

Wang, W., & Benbasat, I. (2007). Recommendation Agents for Electronic Commerce: Effects of Explanation Facilities on Trusting Beliefs. *Journal of Management Information Systems, 23*(4), 217–246. doi:10.2753/MIS0742-1222230410

Wang, W., & Benbasat, I. (2008). Attributions of Trust in Decision Support Technologies: A Study of Recommendation Agents for E-Commerce. *Journal of Management Information Systems, 24*(4), 249–273. doi:10.2753/MIS0742-1222240410

Wang, W., & Benbasat, I. (2009). Interactive Decision Aids for Consumer Decision Making in e-Commerce: The Influence of Perceived Strategy Restrictiveness. *Management Information Systems Quarterly, 33*(2), 293–320.

White, B. A. (2008). *Second Life: A guide to your virtual world.* Indianapolis, IN: Que Publishing.

Wiggins, B. C. (2000). *Detecting and deleting with outliers in univariate and multivariate context.* Paper presented at the Annual Meeting of the Mid-South Educational Research Association, Bowling Green, KY.

Wolfendale, J. (2007). My avatar, my self: Virtual harm and attachment. *Ethics and Information Technology, 9*(2), 111–119. doi:10.1007/s10676-006-9125-z

Wood, N. T., Solomon, M. R., & Englis, B. G. (2006). Personalization of the web interface: The impact of web avatars on users' responses to e-commerce sites. *Journal of Website Promotion, 2*(1/2), 53–69.

Wood, W. (2000). Attitude change: Persuasion and social influence. *Annual Review of Psychology, 51,* 539–570. doi:10.1146/annurev.psych.51.1.539

Yukl, G., Kim, H., & Falbe, C. M. (1996). Antecedents of influence outcomes. *The Journal of Applied Psychology, 81*(3), 309–317. doi:10.1037/0021-9010.81.3.309

ENDNOTES

[1] An early version of the paper has appeared in the Proceedings of First World Summit on Knowledge Society, Athens, September, 2008, Greece (M.D. Lytras *et al.* (Eds.): WSKS 2008, LNAI 5288, pp. 61-69, 2008.)

[2] Active users were those who logged in Second Life during the last seven days before December 8, 2009.

[3] When navigating a virtual world, a user normally interacts with two types of avatars (i.e., virtual identities): his/her own avatar and someone else's avatar. Therefore, a user can establish a relationship with his/her own avatar, and the user can also build relationships with someone else's avatars.

[4] In this research, the term "relational influence" is used instead of "relationship strength" because the term "relationship strength" may be intuitively confused with "relationship closeness." Additionally, "strength" in Berscheid *et al.*'s relationship closeness inventory (RCI), which is the theoretical lens we rely on, actually deals with the influence that one relationship partner can impose on the other. Berscheid *et al.* assessed relationship strength in RCI by presenting subjects with a variety of activity domains and then asking them to evaluate the influence their relationship partner exerts on them in each activity domain. Therefore, the term "relational influence" does not change the nature of the construct "relationship strength" in RCI but makes its underlying meaning unambiguous and straightforward. Thus, "relational influence" is adopted in the current research.

[5] "Perceived needs fulfillment" is used instead of "satisfaction level." "Satisfaction level" in the investment model is evaluated with a criterion that taps the extent to which people's needs in relationships are fulfilled (Rusbult *et al.*, 1998). Rusbult *et al.* assessed the satisfaction level of a relationship by items such as "My partner fulfills my needs for intimacy." However, current information systems literature generally conceptualizes satisfaction differently from that of Rusbult *et al.* For example, Kim, Ferrin, and Rao (2009) defined satisfaction as an emotional reaction to previous experience. Therefore, to avoid confusion with the current literature on the conceptualization of satisfaction, we adopted the term "perceived needs fulfillment" in this study. "Perceived needs fulfillment" does not change the nature of the construct "satisfaction level" in the investment model but makes its underlying meaning unambiguous and straightforward.

6   "Perceived relationship irreplaceableness" is used instead of "quality of alternatives" because the definition of the latter in the investment model is based on the comparison between the current relationship and alternative relationships (Rusbult *et al.*, 1998). If the current relationship can be replaced by an alternative relationship (e.g., the alternative is perceived to be more attractive than the current), the alternative relationship is considered high quality.

7   Although perceived needs fulfillment was modeled as a formative construct rather than a multidimensional construct, in the initial items pool, multiple items were created for each of the three basic needs. After a series of item purification procedures prior to the data collection, only one item for each need ultimately remained. The three items remaining were consistently categorized into their corresponding dimensions under perceived needs fulfillment in the card sorting (aka Q-Sort). In this way, the content validity is partially confirmed (Petter *et al.*, 2007; Straub *et al.*, 2004).

8   Each item was re-modeled as a second-order construct with a single reflective item because the SmartPLS does not allow one item to be determined by more than one latent variable (Liang *et al.*, 2007).

9   At the beginning of the survey, the respondents were given the following instructions: "Before you answer the survey questions, please think of an avatar with which you have contacts recently".

APPENDIX: CARD SORTING DETAILS

Item Pool[9]
(Initial Item Pool: 28 items, After 1st Round Card Sorting: 26 items, Final Version: 18 items)
Interaction Frequency (FREQ)
FREQ1: I often interact with this avatar.
FREQ2: I interact with this avatar many times per week.
FREQ3: I interact with this avatar frequently.
FREQ4R: I seldom interact with this avatar.(*) (dropped after 2nd round card sorting)

Activity Diversity (DVST)

DVST1: The type of activities I took part in with this avatar is diverse.
DVST2: When I interact with this avatar, we usually engage in different activities.
DVST3R: Normally, I interact with this avatar in only one activity.(*)
DVST4R: For me, this avatar always plays a single role.(*) (dropped after 2nd round card sorting)

Relational Influence (INFL)

INFL1: This avatar has significant influence on my life.
INFL2: This avatar influences the way I handle my work or life.
INFL3R: My life will not be influenced if my relationship with this avatar is suspended. (*)
INFL4: I will feel lost if my relationship with avatar is suspended. (dropped after 1st round card sorting)

Perceived Relationship Irreplaceableness (ALTR)

ALTR1: Currently, there is no other avatar that can replace this avatar in my relationship network in Second Life.
ALTR2: I cannot find a new avatar as an alternative to this avatar.
ALTR3: For me, this avatar is unique and is difficult to find elsewhere.

Perceived Resource Investment (IVST)

IVST1: I have put much time in the relationship with this avatar.
IVST2: I have put much effort in the relationship with this avatar.
IVST3: I have taken great effort to establish and maintain the relationship with this avatar.

Perceived Needs Fulfillment --- Sense of Affection (AFEC)

AFEC1: This avatar always cares for me. AFEC2: This avatar is considerate to me. (dropped after 2nd round card sorting) AFEC3: This avatar treats me sincerely. (dropped after 2nd round card sorting)

Perceived Needs Fulfillment --- Sense of Inclusion (INCL)

INCL1: Keeping the relationship with this avatar reduces my sense of loneliness. (dropped after 2nd round card sorting) INCL2: The relationship with this avatar gives me a sense of belonging. INCL3: Keeping the relationship with this avatar makes me feel connected in the virtual community. (dropped after 2nd round card sorting)

Perceived Needs Fulfillment --- Sense of Control (CTRL)

CTRL1: I am dominant in my interactions with this avatar. (dropped after 2nd round card sorting) CTRL2: I lie in a position of authority in my interaction with this avatar.
CTRL3: I feel free in the interaction with this avatar. (dropped after 1st round card sorting) CTRL4: I can control the process of interaction with this avatar. (dropped after 2nd round card sorting)
(*) this item needs reverse coding.

Table A-1. Inter-Judge Reliability of 1st Round Sorting (Cohen's Kappa)

Judge	A	B	C	D
A	1.000			
B	0.681	1.000		
C	0.519	0.561	1.000	
D	0.714	0.718	0.522	1.000

Table A-2. Actual-Target Matrix of 1st Round Sorting

Target Dimension	Actual Dimension									Total	Hit Ratio
	INCL	CTRL	AFEC	IVST	ALTR	FREQ	DVST	INFL	N/A		
INCL	12	0	0	0	0	0	0	0	0	12	100.00%
CTRL	1	13	1	0	0	0	0	0	1	16	81.25%
AFEC	0	0	12	0	0	0	0	0	0	12	100.00%
IVST	0	0	0	12	0	0	0	0	0	12	100.00%
ALTR	0	0	0	0	8	0	0	0	4	12	66.67%
FREQ	0	0	0	0	0	16	0	0	0	16	100.00%
DVST	0	1	0	1	0	3	8	0	3	16	50.00%
INFL	2	0	0	0	4	0	0	6	4	16	37.50%
								Overall Hit Ratio		=	79.43%

Table A-3. Inter-Judge Reliability of 2ⁿᵈ Round Sorting (Cohen's Kappa)

Judge	Judge E	Judge F	Judge G	Judge H
Judge E	1.000			
Judge F	0.825	1.000		
Judge G	0.913	0.782	1.000	
Judge H	0.956	0.739	0.956	1.000

Table A-4. Actual-Target Matrix of 2ⁿᵈ Round Sorting

Target Dimension	Actual Dimension									Total	Hit Ratio
	AFEC	ALTR	CTRL	DVST	FREQ	INCL	IVST	INFL	N/A		
AFEC	12	0	0	0	0	0	0	0	0	12	100.00%
ALTR	0	12	0	0	0	0	0	0	0	12	100.00%
CTRL	0	0	12	0	0	0	0	0	0	12	100.00%
DVST	0	0	1	13	0	0	0	0	2	16	81.25%
FREQ	0	0	0	0	16	0	0	0	0	16	100.00%
INCL	1	0	0	0	0	11	0	0	0	12	91.67%
IVST	0	0	0	0	0	0	12	0	0	12	100.00%
INFL	0	0	0	0	0	0	0	10	2	12	83.33%
								Overall Hit Ratio	=		94.53%

Chapter 8

Antecedents of Online Game Dependency:
The Implications of Multimedia Realism and Uses and Gratifications Theory

Kaunchin Chen
Western Michigan University, USA

Jengchung V. Chen
National Cheng Kung University, Taiwan

William H. Ross
University of Wisconsin, La Crosse, USA

ABSTRACT

Massively Multiplayer Online Game (MMOG) dependency has been widely studied but research results suggest inconclusive antecedent causes. This study proposes and empirically tests three predictive models of MMOG dependency using a survey of online gaming participants. It finds multimedia realism for social interaction serves as an original antecedent factor affecting other mediating factors to cause MMOG dependency. These mediating factors derive from Uses and Gratifications theory and include: (1) participation in a virtual community, (2) diversion from everyday life, and (3) a pleasant aesthetic experience. Of these, participation in a virtual community has a strong positive relationship with MMOG dependency, and aesthetics has a modest negative relationship. Moderator analyses suggest neither gender nor "frequency of game playing" are significant but experience playing online games is a significant moderating factor of MMOG dependency.

INTRODUCTION

Massively Multiplayer Online Games (MMOGs) have attracted much attention from industry analysts (e.g., Zackariasson & Wilson, 2008) as the revenues generated are enormous. For example, the MMOG *Second Life* has more than 15 million players, spending more than US $1.5 billion in 2007 on virtual goods and services (Sayre, 2008). MMOGs must successfully address privacy concerns because they run on multiple databases and user authentication is critical to the prosperity of

DOI: 10.4018/978-1-61350-471-0.ch008

the game (Kumar et al., 2008; Krotoski, Cezanne, Rymaszewski, Rossignol, & Au, 2008).

MMOG and virtual world applications offer a wealth of opportunities beyond just merely tools that offer activities for the purpose of personal leisure. For example, MMOGs may be used for distance education. Eschenbrenner, Nah, and Siau (2008) conducted an extensive assessment of such opportunities in education. They caution that behavioral, health, and safety issues should not be overlooked. Others (Chen & Park, 2005) have also cited behavioral problems including over-indulgence or psychological dependency on such games (Golub and Lingley, 2008). Such dependency may have negative implications for individuals and for society (Sattar and Ramaswamy, 2004), as when employees feel a compulsion to play MMOGs instead of working. Early research on computer addiction used pathological definitions and behavioral models (Young, 1996). However, recent studies suggest non-pathological dependency behaviors may also develop (Chen, Tarn, & Han, 2004).

Aside from behavioral issues in the virtual world, scholars also observe that the realistic imitation of a player's physical environment may enhance the gaming experience (Garau et al., 2003); others (e.g., Cheng & Cairns, 2005) suggest that this effect may be valid only in certain domains. For example, if a gap exists between the user interface/functionality and players' skills, players have to learn to master the user interface. Those who do not quickly master these skills could suffer (Dickey, 2005).

Thus, while many observers assume that realistic MMOGs lead to a positive user experience, others suggest that realistic MMOGs may lead to psychological changes including dependency. Given the richness of Internet media generally and MMOGs specifically, the theoretical foundations for MMOG dependency must be examined. Such theoretical foundations for MMOG dependency will help both those who are concerned about video game addiction and the video game industry

to understand the underpinnings of dependency formation. The relationship between a realistic representation of one's physical environment and one's psychological experience with such artificial virtual environment offers some insights as to the extent to which user interface realism has an effect on use experience and user dependency. The present study investigates antecedent factors affecting such dependency.

The motivation of the present study is to explore the linkages between (1) software design characteristics (Multimedia Realism for Social Interaction -- MRSI), (2) psychological factors that are enhanced by those design characteristics, such as participation in a virtual community, and (3) users' psychological dependency upon online games. While others write about each of these topics separately, few authors write about their linkages (see Olson & Olson, 2003; Carroll, 1997 for historical reviews of this literature). The present paper seeks to fill this gap in the literature by exploring these linkages. Figure 1 shows possible linkages. For example, software design characteristics such as MRSI may influence a user's aesthetic experience, sense of diversion, and sense of participation in a 'virtual community' with other users; these psychological experiences, may, in turn, affect MMOG dependency either directly or indirectly. We will briefly review the literature and offer testable hypotheses regarding these possible linkages derived from 'Uses & Gratifications' theory. Then, we will proceed to test these hypotheses.

PRIOR RESEARCH AND THEORETICAL BACKGROUND

Addiction and Dependency

Excessive Internet use such as playing games has been associated with psychological or behavioral problems, including poor college adjustment (Lanthier and Windham, 2004), depression (Ybarra,

Figure 1. Candidate roles of Multimedia Realism for Social Interactions (MRSI)

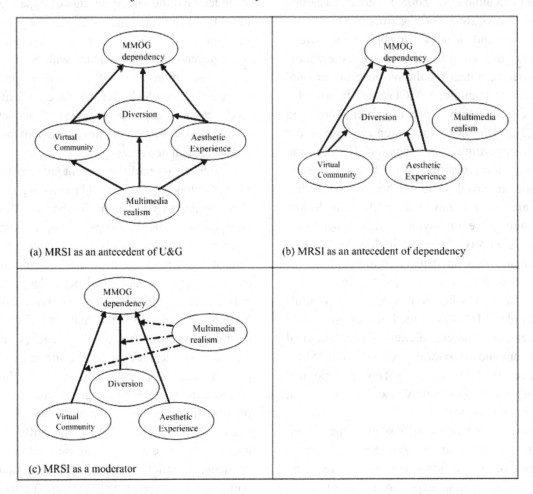

Alexander, & Mitchell, 2005; Golub and Lingley, 2008), and interpersonal and financial problems (Yang & Tung, 2007). The detrimental effects to one's life, work, or relationships intensify if extensive Internet use becomes addictive. *Internet addiction* is defined "as a psychological dependence on the Internet, regardless of the type of activity once logged on" (Kandell, 1998, p. 12). Such a concept has been operationalized and investigated by Young (1996, 1997, 1998b). Chen, Chen, and Paul (2001) and Chen, Tarn, and Han (2004) have also examined behavioral patterns in electronic commerce activities among Internet addicts as well as non-dependent users. Their results confirm a distinctive set of usage patterns in various forms of electronic commerce activities.

Internet dependency is a closely-related concept (Scherer, 1997), differing only in degree; generally, this type of negative psychological dependency is seen as only slightly less pathological than Internet addiction. In many studies (e.g., Soule, Shell, & Kleen, 2003), the terms are used interchangeably (notice the use of the term 'dependence' in the above definition of Internet addiction), and most researchers measure Internet dependency using Young's Internet addiction measure. Because the present investigation focuses on negative psychological and behavioral aspects of Internet overuse, the present study treats dependency in this manner. However, a few scholars define Internet dependency as a concept without connotations of a psychological disorder. For example, Mafe' and Blas (2006) define Internet dependency as "a relation where the individual's capacity to reach his or her objectives, depends to a certain extent on the Internet information resources" (p. 382). Such definitions focus on practical or functional dependency (rather than psychological dependency) and are the exceptions in the research literature. Therefore we use the two terms, dependency and addiction, interchangeably throughout the paper.

Internet dependency can be costly to both work organizations and individuals. The employee who engages in non-work activities like playing online MMOGs wastes company resources, and also deprives the firm of the productivity that the employee owes the organization. Misuse of the Internet may also lead to employee discipline, including suspension without pay or dismissal (Lichtash, 2004). In addition to lost productivity, internet abuse can lead to overpaid wages, a tarnished reputation (e.g., Ashmore and Herman, 2006), and/or the unintentional release of confidential information (Phillips, 1999). Finally, some employees may need therapeutic psychological interventions (Young, 2007), often at the employer's expense.

Just as one can become addicted to the Internet generally, one can become addicted to or psychologically dependent upon specific computer applications (e.g., chat rooms; online gambling sites). People become addicted to non-online video games; it is possible to become psychologically dependent upon online games (including MMOGs) as well. To date, research has emphasized personality correlates of Internet or video game addiction (e.g., Pawlak, 2002; Chak & Leung, 2004) as well as psychological needs that the Internet may satisfy (e.g., Stanton, 2002). Little research has investigated design features and how they interact with psychological variables to influence dependency. Further, much of the literature has

investigated the Internet generally or aspects of the Internet (e.g., search engines, gambling sites) that may be very different from the immersive dynamics found in MMOG (Lee, et al., 2007). One exception is a set of studies by Choi and Kim (2004) who report that several game features (e.g., explanations about the background and/or characters of the game and having both numerical and graphical information about the status of the player's character) facilitate a feeling of goal accomplishment. Further, the ability to select the type of feedback one receives, being able to restart the game, and being able to select a character's ability levels affect the perceived quality of interaction with the game. These factors, as well as social interaction with other players increase players' willingness to play the game. The present study adds to this current knowledge base by further focusing on the interplay between design features and psychological variables as they specifically affect MMOG dependency.

Uses and Gratifications Theory

The Uses and Gratifications (U & G) theory from the field of Communication Studies is characterized by the idea that people select and use media to receive gratification from having needs or goals fulfilled (Stafford, 2008). Rather than treating people as a passive audience for media, this theory acknowledges that needs drive individuals' motivations to use certain media and that media use often fulfils these needs (Katz, Blumler, & Gurevitch, 1974). This theory assumes that people are goal-oriented active media users; therefore, they actively take initiatives to evaluate their needs and select media that seem likely to fulfill these needs. The result of such a self-assessment affects their current level of gratification, which serves as the basis for evaluating future needs. Uses and gratifications theory has a long history of field tests and many have confirmed its applicability to various areas, including television (Conway & Rubin, 1991), e-mail (Dimmick, Kline, & Stafford, 2000), and the World Wide Web (Eighmey, 1997; Papacharissi & Rubin, 2000).

Process and Content Gratifications

The line of U & G research suggests that gratifications may be channeled through at least two processes: (1) being engaged in an aesthetically-pleasing medium (e.g., the diversion of playing a game or surfing the Internet), and/or (2) the content of the medium (e.g., the excitement received from learning something new, or becoming knowledgeable in some way). The former is termed *process gratifications* that concern primarily the experience during the use of a medium, while the latter is termed *content gratifications* that are aroused by the message or the information that a medium delivers (Cutler & Danowski, 1980).

User interactions with a medium may generate both process and content gratifications. Research suggests that both process and content gratifications may be important. For example, early Internet studies (e.g., McDonald, 1997) indicate that users are attracted to web sites primarily because of the content of the sites. Song, Larose, Eastin, and Lin (2004) suggest that process gratifications are also important. Process-oriented use of the Internet may include using various forms of services to pass time, while content-based use of the Internet is delivered through the informational content and knowledge-enhancement. One reason for differences in research findings using the same medium lies in the fact that the medium in question actually evolved from text-based content-central web sites to multimedia web sites in the past decade. Therefore, a true classification of gratification type relies heavily on the current capabilities of the medium in question.

Although the Internet offers a multi-facet collection of services, collectively both types of gratifications are possible. However, certain individual Internet services, (e.g., discussion forums and skill training sites) are more likely to deliver content gratifications as opposed to process gratifications. In addition, most users do not visit a regular web site for its nice-looking user interface design – although multimedia features may enhance user satisfaction with the web site. Rather, users typically visit a web site to fulfill their information needs (Stafford, 2008). This is the reason that Stafford, Stafford, and Schkade (2004) recommend that the distinction between process gratifications and content gratifications that a medium offers "must be defined *in context*, with operational definitions and resulting measures that are specific to the medium" (pp. 267-268).

Process Gratifications Through Interaction With Games

Process gratifications come from interacting with the media itself. As stated by Song et al. (2004), "Process gratification bears no direct link to characteristics of the messages. The individual receives gratification from being involved in the process of communication, rather than message content." (p. 385). They empirically identified seven gratification-related dimensions pertaining to general Internet use. However, some of their factors – for instance, monetary compensation (e.g., finding bargains and improving one's job prospects) are irrelevant for most MMOGs. So which of their dimensions are relevant for process gratifications within such games? We suggest two: Diversion and Aesthetic experience.

Diversion. Many people consider computer games to be simply a way to pass time – an entertaining diversion. The concept of MMOG as *diversion* here refers to a broad attitude of having fun, feeling excited, and feeling entertained by playing MMOG, which take the person's mind off of the mundane or problematic aspects of their real life. Wu and Liu (2007) report that enjoyment of online gaming is positively related to intentions to play MMOGs. Kim et al. (2002) demonstrate that for many online game users, diversion, (operationalized as "escape from reality") is a primary motive for participating in online games. This suggests that diversion may predict MMOG dependency directly, as shown in Figures 1(a) and 1(b)in ways consistent with Young (1998a).

Aesthetic experience. Like other visual web sites (Huang, 2008), consumers prefer games that are visually interesting and easy to use, resulting in many programmers continually striving to improve the aesthetic qualities (e.g., realistic graphical appearance) of their games (Kim et al, 2002). Such attitudes suggest that MMOGs provide process gratifications. Song et al. (2004) tested seven types of Internet gratifications, including member participation in a virtual community, information seeking, aesthetic experience, monetary compensation, diversion, personal status and relationship maintenance. According to their study, attractive features, pleasing multimedia schemes, ease of use, and "cool" interactions characterize the general aesthetic experience of the Internet. These aesthetic features are also available in MMOGs Similarly, Wu, Li, and Rao (2008) demonstrate that aesthetic features such as interesting visual graphics and sound are related to online gaming enjoyment, consistent with Figures 1(a) and 1(b). Therefore, MMOG's rich aesthetic features offer a set of process gratifications, engaging players in the game. If such engagement is excessive, dependency may result. This logic suggests the following hypothesis:

Hypothesis 1: (a) The attitude that MMOGs are a pleasant diversion and (b) positive attitudes about the aesthetic qualities of MMOGs will be positively related to MMOG dependency.

Content and Social Gratifications Through Participation in a Virtual Community

MMOG offer capabilities for user-to-user interactions beyond the simple user-to-machine interactions found in single-user video games. Such user-to-user interactions may range from simple one-on-one interactions to group interactions. A variety of software technologies exist for such interactions (Wagner, 2005). The result is a dynamic entertainment arena where players may exchange various types of information.

In an MMOG environment, communication takes one of two forms: system messages from the software to the player and human messages from one player to another. An example of the latter form of message is the communication messages among players within the *virtual community* environment of MMOG. The actual messages (or content) during a communication of a virtual community are supplied by humans using other computers, thereby forming human-to-human communication. Virtual communities have proven to be very popular in other contexts, like work settings (Guru & Siau, 2008). In the context of MMOGs, communication software becomes a "tool" or a channel that facilitates human-to-human communication within a virtual community. In addition, this form of virtual community becomes an integrated component of the whole MMOG experience, rather than a separate component requiring additional effort to activate. The virtual community interactions provide people with new, useful information (e.g., how to succeed in the game), status recognition, and positive emotional affirmation; they also allow players to engage in impression management activities (Rosenfeld, Giacalone, & Riordan, 2001). Therefore, the integrated virtual community in MMOG offers substantial opportunities for content gratifications.

The scientific literature has not been consistent in terms of the type of gratifications that virtual community generates. Song et al. (2004) treat "virtual community" as a source for process gratifications, because a virtual community offers a combination of "social-integrative and personal-integrative gratifications." However, they consider a similar factor called "relationship management" to offer content gratifications, because the latter construct gives opportunities to maintain relationships with existing acquaintances. Stafford and Stafford (2001) suggest that virtual communities offer a new form of motivation to interact with the media. This form is neither process nor content dominant. Similarly, in Stafford (2008), a factor analysis of America Online (AOL) users derived three factors: process, content, and social factors, with the last factor consisting of characteristics of a virtual community (chatting, interacting with friends, etc.).

One can argue that participation in virtual communities within MMOG satisfy primarily 'content' and 'social' needs as well as some 'process' needs. For example, players frequently glean information from other players (e.g., how to overcome specific obstacles within the game). Thus, the virtual community becomes a primary source of useful information in a MMOG, providing content gratifications. However, in some games, players may develop friendships, interact in teams, and have social status with other players. Thus, the virtual community may satisfy social needs that are distinct from content gratifications. The purpose of the present paper is not to resolve the issue of how to best classify various psychological variables. Rather it is to employ the Uses & Gratifications literature to identify relevant and distinct variables for investigation that may predict MMOG dependency. Participation in virtual communities appears to be such a variable.

The multiple gratifications satisfied by virtual communities are similar to chat rooms where people exchange information and develop relationships. Young (1997, 1998) has identified chat rooms as an application that promotes Internet dependency. This logic suggests a second hypothesis:

Hypothesis 2: Participation in virtual communities within MMOGs will be positively related to MMOG dependency.

The Effect of Virtual Community and Aesthetics on a Sense of Diversion

As stated earlier, MMOG players experience gratifications through interactions with the game (human-to-game interaction) and with other people at other locations (human-to-human interaction). The two forms of interaction, are likely to provide sources of enjoyment, offering entertaining and exciting experiences. In some cases, the pleasure begins with process gratifications (e.g., realistic three-dimensional graphics), elevated by content and social gratifications through human interactions, and then fed back to another possibly higher level of process gratifications. For example, a player's initial experience with the game (process gratification) may be enhanced after consulting or chatting with the existing virtual community for new game strategies or new hidden powers (content and social gratification). In some other cases, the virtual community provides the primary source of fun and excitement (Pisan, 2007). These linkages between aesthetic experience, virtual community, and a sense of diversion are shown in Figures 1(a) and 1(b)

Interpersonal attraction develops due to affective bonds among members in a small community that share the same goals (Henry, Arrow, & Carini, 1999). Such bonding, as Pisan puts it, will cause members to "... enjoy each other's company ... spend more time together and achieve goals together." As a result, gratifications are achieved with group members working towards a similar set of goals using MMOG as a vehicle. Therefore, the process gratification of a sense of diversion, operationalized as fun, exciting, and relaxing feelings, may very likely be an intermingled effect, resulting from other process (e.g., aesthetics) and content (e.g., virtual community) gratifications. We postulate the following hypotheses.

Hypothesis 3: Participation in virtual communities within MMOGs will be positively related to diversion gratifications.
Hypothesis 4: Positive attitudes about the aesthetic qualities of MMOGs will be positively related to diversion gratifications.

Multimedia Realism for Social Interactions (MRSI)

Early online social interactions (e.g., chat rooms) were popular as a separate stream of human activities on the Internet. Most of the tools that facilitated such interactions were in text-only mode. Even so, reports (e.g., Young, 1998) have documented cases that people were "hooked" on the Internet, staying in chat rooms for hours or even days. An early work (Dourish, 1998) using text-based Multi-User Domains (MUDs, also called Multi-User Dungeons) suggests that a rich and immersive environment may not always be a prerequisite for a compelling social experience. After most MMOGs incorporated chat capabilities, players engaged in communications through the graphical user interface of the MMOG software. As a result, the communication quality may largely be affected by the user interface of the software, realism of the virtual environment and commonly accepted cues of gathering places (Choi and Kim, 2004; Ducheneaut, Moore, and Nickell, 2007). Multimedia realism used in the present study extends Slater et al.'s (2001) "Graphical Realism" to represent not just realism of lighting, shadows, shape of the objects, but also other multimedia representations (e.g., auditory cues) of the objects.

Until recently, researchers have primarily focused on ways to improve game realism, assuming that game realism has a generally positive effect on gaming experience by improving the aesthetic experience (Kücklich, 2007). Such realism in the forms of graphic representation (i.e., realism in images) and others encourage the players to perform actions in the game (Galloway, 2004). If dependency is possible without an immersive, realistic environment, it may be even more likely when one exists. Results from Choi and Kim's (2004) study show that Multimedia Realism for Social Interactions (MRSI; a key component in what they term "communication place") fosters better social interaction, which in turn is related to a willingness to play the game again. Social communications inside and outside of the games are known to be predictors of game commitment (Seay, Jerome, Lee, & Kraut, 2004). In some MMOG environments, such communications are a prerequisite so that a player is required to communicate, bargain, or even collaborate with other players in order to achieve the player's next goal. Therefore, experience with high levels of multimedia realism in the environment for social interactions is an increasingly common encounter. Together, these studies imply that MRSI will influence continued use and perhaps even MMOG dependency through intervening variables such as the quality of the social interactions found in a virtual community. Social interaction also boosts the overall online sense of diversion, causing what they term a "flow" experience. They define "flow" as an "optimal level of experience...If somebody enters the flow state while playing an online game, this means that he/she is interested in playing the game, is curious about the game, has full control over the game and is focused on playing the game with no other distraction." (pp. 12-13; also see Koufaris, 2002). Chou and Ting (2003) demonstrate that flow experience relates to internet addiction. Together, these findings suggest that MRSI influences MMOG dependency indirectly, through intervening psychological variables.

The scientific literature does not offer clear guidance in this area. Based on the above literature review, it seems likely that MRSI effects may be moderated by intervening variables. MRSI may have a direct psychological link with each of the three Uses & Gratifications Theory variables discussed in this paper (diversion, aesthetic experience, and virtual community) and these influence MMOG dependency. This implies that MRSI will influence dependency through intervening variables such as the quality of the social interactions found in a virtual community, as shown in Figure 1 (a). Alternatively, one can posit direct effects of MRSI on MMOG dependency, as shown in Figure 1 (b). Finally, it is possible that MRSI acts as a moderator variable, altering the otherwise direct relations between the U & G dimensions (virtual community, diversion, and aesthetic experience) and MMOG dependency. These types of indirect effects are shown in Figure 1 (c). Thus, whether and how MRSI influences MMOG dependency remains an empirical question.

As described above, the literature suggests two possible types of relationships between MRSI and MMOG dependency: direct effects and indirect effects. This leads to the following hypothesis:

Hypothesis 5: Multimedia realism for social interactions (MRSI) will be positively related to MMOG dependency, as follows:

Hypothesis 5a: MRSI positively affects MMOG dependency through participation in a virtual community, a sense of diversion, and a pleasant aesthetic experience.

Hypothesis 5b: MRSI directly affects MMOG dependency.

Demographic Mediators

Investigators have long studied gender differences in computer use. Many early studies on computer knowledge and use (e.g., Durndell & Thomson, 1997) report that males tend to be more active computer users. Even among computer users, gender differences occur across different types of software. Odell et al. (2000) report that females are attracted to communication activities, including chat rooms and online communities; males are more likely to play computer games (Rosen & Weil, 1995). Because of equal opportunities for computer education and the general social norms that support computer use, the gender gap in general computer use is narrowing (Vandenbroeck, Verschelden, & Boonaert, 2008). Willoughby (2008) also suggests that the gender gap in computer use is narrowing, but reports that boys still play computer games more frequently than girls.

Other demographic variables also have certain effects on MMOG dependency. For example,

Internet dependent users tend to be online longer and more frequently compared to non-dependent users (Chen, Chen, and Paul, 2001). Other findings from Chen et al. support that Internet dependent users are not newcomers to the Internet and they are likely the users of interactive features, such as games and chat rooms. Chen, Tarn, and Han (2004) divide Internet dependency level into three categories: (1) positive dependency (where the internet is used frequently as a tool for self-improvement), (2) negative, pathological dependency (where the internet is used to temporarily relieve anxiety, depression, or frustration, but produces detrimental effects on users' lives), and (3) little dependency. They report that the negative dependent group frequently uses highly interactive features (e.g., Internet Relay Chats and chat rooms) compared to the other two groups. Users in the two dependency groups (positive and negative) have been on the Internet longer than the little dependency group. Other studies (e.g., Yang and Tung, 2007; Chou and Hsiao, 2000) also point to the correlation between Internet addiction and online gratifications for entertainment and social reasons. Therefore, a distinct demographic profile or use pattern may be associated with those who are psychologically dependent upon the Internet and/or its applications.

These research findings suggest that several demographic variables may moderate relationships between the various predictors described above and MMOG dependency. Specifically, gender differences in game play may moderate these relationships. The pattern of relationships may be stronger for men who may look to these games for gratification whereas women may look to other applications (e.g., social networking websites). Experience and frequency of playing MMOGs may also moderate these relationships. For these latter variables, long-time and frequent players may experience stronger effects from participation in virtual communities within MMOGs. As interpersonal relationships are developed, they may influence both a sense of diversion (e.g., they become a greater component in the "fun" of the game) and MMOG dependency. This logic suggests the following hypotheses:

Hypothesis 6: Gender will moderate the effects of uses and gratifications on MMOG dependency.

Hypothesis 7: Experience will moderate the effects of uses and gratifications on MMOG dependency.

Hypothesis 8: Play frequency will moderate the effects of uses and gratifications on MMOG dependency.

In summary, three possible roles of MRSI in MMOG dependency are considered; these are shown in Figure 1. Figure 1(a) shows MRSI influencing the three U & G dimensions of virtual community, diversion, and aesthetic experience, which, in turn, influence MMOG dependency. Figure 1(b) shows MRSI affecting MMOG dependency directly and independently of the three U & G variables. Finally, Figure 1(c) shows MRSI as a moderator variable, influencing the relations between the three U & G variables and MMOG dependency. We tested each of these models along with the accompanying hypotheses.

RESEARCH METHODS

Measures

This study examined relationships among variables found within existing theories. Therefore, the questionnaire was derived from the relevant literature. Questions to measure Uses and Gratifications of MMOGs were adapted from Song, Larose, Eastin, and Lin (2004). As Song et al., concerned Internet gratifications, care was taken to remove questions that did not apply to most MMOGs. For example, questions regarding general Internet information-seeking activities and monetary compensation (locate bargain products, receive free product samples, save money on phone calls, etc.) were either not the main concern of MMOG gamers, or were least applicable in the MMOG environment. The resulting instrument measuring Uses and Gratifications included questions about participation in a Virtual Community (with items such as, "Get people to think I'm 'cool.'", "Meet new friends.", "Improve my standing in the world.", and "Find companionship."); questions about the Aesthetic Experience (with items such as, "Find cool new Web pages.", "See attractive graphics.", "Find cool animated backgrounds.", and "See pleasing color schemes."), and questions about Diversion (with items such as, "Feel excited.", "Have fun." "Feel relaxed." and "Feel entertained."). Each question was measured using a five-point Likert-type scale that ranges from 1 (strongly disagree) to 5 (strongly agree).

Two questions regarding characteristics of multimedia realism for online social interactions were adopted from Choi and Kim (2004). These two questions measured perceptions of game design offering "real world impressions" and a "harmonious atmosphere" for social interaction. Both were measured using a five-point Likert-type scale too.

Young's (Young, 1996, 1997, 1998b) Internet addiction instrument was the basis for measuring MMOG dependency. As with the scale used in the above two constructs, the scale for measuring MMOG dependency was a five-point Likert-type scale ranging from 1 (strongly disagree) to 5 (strongly agree).

As part of the procedure to validate the instrument, we first sent the questionnaire to several content experts to eliminate problems that might result from wording, content coverage, and other details. The questionnaire was revised accordingly. Thirty online game players were recruited to pretest the instrument. The resulting scales showed acceptable reliability (as (Cronbach's alphas > .70).

Procedure

Subjects were recruited via online game forums using procedures similar to other studies (e.g., Griffiths, Davies, & Chappell, 2004; Ha, Yoon, & Choi, 2007; Yee, 2006; Kim, Namkoong, Ku, & Kim, 2008). A short message inviting people to participate an online survey for research was posted in dozens of popular online game forums. Online gamers gather together on these forums for various reasons like exchanging information, exchanging online game treasurers, making teams, looking for advices, etc. It was ideal to recruit real online gamers on those Web forums. Whoever wanted to participate the survey could click the hyperlink of the message and they were directed to the questionnaire survey. The questionnaire was administered online via a secure website. To encourage participation, a lottery was held for cash prizes as well as products that the youth would like to have such as Web camera and USB memory. To prevent multiple participation by the same person, two means were adopted: 1. only one entry per e-mail address was allowed; 2. researchers carefully examined the server log file for repeating IP addresses. We did not find answers provided by the same email addresses, nor did we find repeating IP addresses in this study. Finally computer scripts reminded respondents of missing answers while they were taking the survey.

RESULTS

Subject Profile

Respondents included 250 males (84.45%) and 46 females (15.54%) (see Table 1). This gender distribution of more males than females was consistent with existing online game research (Griffths, Davies, and Chappell, 2004; Williams, 2006; Wang and Wang, 2008). In Griffths et al. (2004), the sample of 540 subjects, mostly from North America, had 81% male and 19% female. Williams (2006) collected a similar composition of the sample: 84% male and 16% female. Wang and Wang's (2008) study in Taiwan also had roughly 75% male and 25% female. Interestingly, studies on Internet addiction and Internet dependency had about the same sample and composition (such as Griffiths, 1998; Morathan-Martin & Schumacher, 2000; Chen, Chen, & Paul, 2001). Online gaming experience of the respondents leaned toward the high side with more than two thirds (68.24%) of respondents playing online games for two years or more. This was followed by the second highest category of 6-12 months of online gaming experience (13.85%). The majority of respondents (81.76%) played online games at home. Some played at school (9.12%) or coffee shops / Internet cafes (5.74%). The majority played less than 20 hours a week (59.80%); one third (33.44%) played less than 10 hours a week; 26.35% played between 10 to 20 hours a week). About seventeen percent (17.22%) played between 20 and 30 hours a week.

Confirmatory Factor Analysis and Construct Validity

In order to test structural equation models it is necessary to have distinct and homogeneous factors. Therefore, a confirmatory factor analysis (CFA) using AMOS version 16 was first conducted for all constructs, including the three dimensions of Uses and Gratifications, online dependency and perceived multimedia reality. Items with low factor loadings (< .50) were dropped to arrive at the final measurement model. Most items were retained in the final model except for two items from the MMOG Dependency scale, two from the Aesthetic Experience measure and one from the Virtual Community scale. The fit indices of the final CFA model (χ^2 = 264.69, d.f. = 160, GFI = .92, AGFI = .89, CFI = .96, NFI = .91, RMR = .05, RMSEA = .05) were acceptable. The final list of variables and reliability measured in Cronbach's alpha and composite reliability appears in Table 2. All reliabilities ranged between .72 and .94, exceeding the generally accepted threshold of .70.

Table 1. Demographics of online gamers

Attribute		Count
Gender	Male	250
	Female	46
Education	Grade school	4
	High school	31
	College	207
	Graduate degree	54
Age	14 or below	1
	14 – 20	42
	20 – 25	169
	25 – 30	65
	30 or more	19
Online Gaming Experience	6 months or less	22
	6 – 12 months	41
	12 – 18 months	18
	18 months – 2 years	13
	2 years – 2.5 years	13
	2.5 years – 3 years	9
	3 years or more	180
Location where games were played	Home	242
	School	27
	Work	2
	Coffee shop / book store	17
	Other	8
Time spent on online games per week	< 10 hours	99
	10 – 20 hours	78
	20 – 30 hours	51
	30 – 40 hours	30
	40 – 50 hours	13
	> 50 hours	25

We also examined the fit of a CFA model where all indicators were loaded in one single factor, an approach recommended by (Podsakoff & Organ, 1986) to partly address concerns of common method variance (or same method bias) regarding measures used in a study. The logic behind this single-factor analysis, termed "Harman's Single-Factor Test" in (Podsakoff & Organ, 1986), was that a single factor would emerge when a substan- tial amount of common method variance was present. In other words, if the Harman's Single-Factor Test resulted in a single factor that fits the data well, method variance was likely responsible for the covariance among the measures (Moss-holder, Bennet, Kemery & Wesolowski, 1998). The one-factor CFA model did not fit well (GFI = .48, CFI = .39, RMSEA = .188).

Table 2. Construct reliability

Construct	Cronbach's alpha	Composite reliability	Factor loading
MMOG dependency	.89	.94	
(1) Feel preoccupied with the MMOG			.72
(2) Unsuccessful efforts to control or cut back			.67
(3) Restless, moody or depressed when attempting to cut down			.80
(4) Play games longer than originally intended			.79
(5) Lie to others to conceal the involvement with MMOG			.84
(6) Play MMOG as a way of escape from problems			.71
U & G – virtual community	.84	.75	
(1) Get people to think I'm "cool"			.71
(2) Find companionship			.67
(3) Meet new friends			.75
(4) Improve my standing in the world			.75
(5) Get support from others			.69
U & G – Aesthetic Experience	.87	.87	
(1) Find cool animated background			.84
(2) See attractive graphics			.91
(3) See pleasing color schemes			.74
U & G – Diversion	.86	.87	
(1) Have fun			.84
(2) Feel excited			.80
(3) Feel entertained			.89
(4) Feel relaxed			.64
Multimedia realism for social interactions	.72	.75	
(1) Characters and background provide "real world impressions of places"			.72
(2) Communication place provides an overall harmonious atmosphere			.82

Convergent validity refers to the idea that indicator variables of a construct should at least moderately correlate to each other. This was tested by checking factor loadings of the CFA model if they were indeed significant and greater than .50. The factor loadings ranged from .67 to .91, thereby offering some basis for convergent validity. In addition, convergent validity was checked by calculating Averaged Variance Extracted (AVE) for all constructs involved in the CFA model. AVEs ranged from .50 to .70 exceeding the cut-off point of .50 suggested in Fornell and Larcker (1981).

Discriminant validity refers to the idea that indicator variables of different constructs should not be highly correlated with the indicator variables of a construct leading one to conclude that the two constructs are measuring the same thing. Discriminant validity was assessed using the guidelines

Table 3. Construct correlations and AVE

	AVE	Multimedia Realism	UG - Aesthetics	UG – Virtual Community	UG - Diversion	MMOG Dependency
Multimedia Realism	.60	**0.77**				
UG - Aesthetics	.70	0.55	**0.84**			
UG – Virtual Community	.64	0.52	0.44	**0.80**		
UG - Diversion	.51	0.30	0.26	0.41	**0.71**	
MMOG Dependency	.54	0.10	-0.04	0.20	0.44	**0.73**

suggested by Fornell and Larcker (1981) in that the squared root of the AVE for a given construct should be greater than the correlation between the construct and others in the same model. Table 3 shows correlations among constructs in the model, with the square root of AVE on the diagonal line. All diagonal values exceed correlations among constructs listed under their respective columns. Therefore, the result of discriminant validity test is considered acceptable.

Effects of Multimedia Realism for Social Interactions (Hypotheses 1 – 5)

Although multimedia realism may benefit social interactions directly, it may also be the source of other, indirect, effects. For example, prior research demonstrated that Multimedia Realism for Social Interactions (MRSI) leads to enhanced use experience, "flow" experience, which leads to customer loyalty (Choi and Kim, 2004). In this section, MRSI was tested using structural equation modeling (SEM) in AMOS for its effect on related

constructs shown in Figure 1. Figure 1 proposed three types of relationships of MRSI with the other constructs. The first model (Figure 1a) included MRSI as the antecedent of Uses and Gratifications constructs. The result in Table 4 shows that all major fit indices were over .90 (GFI = .92; NFI = .92; CFI = .96, RMSEA = .05) for this model except AGFI, which was also very close to .90. All these fit indexes were above the conventional thresholds (GFI > .90, AGFI > .80, NFI > .90, CFI > .90, and RMSEA < .08) (Gefen, et al., 2000), offering evidence of acceptable model fit.

When MRSI was treated as the direct antecedent of MMOG dependency in the second model (Figure 1b), the model fit worsened. Most major fit indices for the second model fell below commonly recommended cut-offs. Comparing the second model with the first one, the degradation in model fit was significant ($\Delta \chi^2$/ Δd.f. = 82.93, p < .05). AIC (Akaike Information Criterion) and ECVI (Expected Cross Validation Index) have been widely used to compare non-nested models. The lower AIC and ECVI values of model one (Figure 1a) indicated a better model fit than

Table 4. Different roles of MRSI

Roles of MRSI	χ^2	d.f.	GFI	NFI	CFI	RMSEA	AIC	ECVI	$\Delta \chi^2$/ Δd.f.
Model 1: MRSI as antecedent of Uses and Gratifications constructs	267.42	162	.92	.92	.96	.05	363.42	1.23	N/A
Model 2: MRSI as antecedent of MMOG dependency	378.02	164	.89	.88	.93	.07	470.02	1.59	82.93*

* p < .05

Figure 2. MRSI as antecedent of Uses and Gratifications

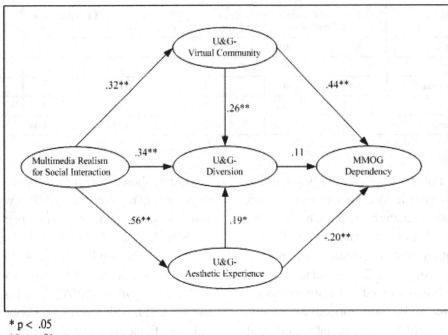

* p < .05
** p < .01

model two (Figure 1b), thereby offering some rationale for choosing model one as the preferred model.

Figure 2 shows the resulting path coefficients of model one. The virtual community dimension of the Uses and Gratifications construct was most influential on MMOG dependency (supporting hypothesis 2). This was followed by aesthetic experience, which had an inverse but significant effect on MMOG dependency. Diversion, on the other hand, had the smallest effect (a non-significant effect) on MMOG dependency. These two effects provide only partial support for hypothesis 1. Participation in a virtual community was positively related to a sense of diversion (supporting hypothesis 3). A positive attitude toward the aesthetics of the computer game was also related to a sense of diversion (supporting hypothesis 4). MRSI had a positive effect on all three Uses and Gratifications dimensions, with most of its effect on the aesthetic experience. Its effect on virtual community and diversion were approximately the

same between the two. In the section below, we further detail the mediation effect of the three U & G dimension on the relationship between MSRI and MMOG dependency.

Mediation Analysis

Baron and Kenny's (1986, p. 1177) pioneering study that looked at moderators versus mediators suggested that the following conditions must hold in order to establish statistical mediation: (1) the independent variable (X) must be shown to affect the dependent variable (Y), (2) the independent variable (X) must affect the mediating variable (M), and (3) M must affect the dependent variable (Y). As a result, a series of independent multiple regressions measured the magnitude of the mediation effect. The mediation model assumes that one unit change in X is related to a change of *a* units in M; a unit change of M is associated with *b* units of change in Y when X is controlled (Shrout and Bolder, 2002). The magnitude of the indirect effect is therefore calculated as $a \times b$. Studies have since been conducted to revise Baron and Kenny's criteria for mediation as well as their recommendation for measuring mediation.

1. The requirement of the second condition.

Studies have been recommending dropping the first requirement of Baron and Kenny's mediation criteria in favor of not to establish a relation between the independent variable (X) and the dependent variable (Y) before the mediation analysis. For example, Shrout & Bolder (2002) suggest that the effect of mediation may be proximal or distal. The former suggests that the effect of X leads to a new value of Y "shortly after." When the mediation effect becomes more distal, one would expect that the effect of X on Y be smaller or even zero. Therefore, they recommend mediation analysis proceed on the basis of theoretical argument, rather than the statistical test of X on Y. Other researchers (e.g., MacKinnon et al., 2000 and Preacher & Hayes, 2008) also recommend dropping this requirement for the reason of suppression effects, where multiple indirect effects that go in different directions causing the total effect to disappear. Following the recommendations of the above studies, we do not specifically consider an existing direct effect of X on Y as a prerequisite for conducting mediation analysis.

2. Reliance on the assumption of normal distribution for indirect effects

Although the assumption of normal distribution may hold for a and b separately, it may not necessarily be true for the indirect effect computed as $a \times b$ (Shrout & Bolder, 2002). The possibility for a skewed distribution of the indirect effect has been reported in the literature (e.g., Bollen & Stine, 1990; Stone & Sobel, 1990). As a result of a skewed distribution, the usual test for indirect effects may lack statistical power to reject the null

hypothesis that $a \times b = 0$ (MacKinnon, et al., 2002). Bollen & Stine recommended using the bootstrap procedure to calculate the non-symmetric bounds for the confidence interval of $a \times b$, Shrout & Bolder's experiment show that the statistically insignificant indirect effect under the standard normal distribution turn out to be statistically significant under the bootstrap procedure because of, again, the underlying distribution of $a \times b$ is far from the normal distribution.

3. Suppression Effect

Suppression occurs when indirect effect ($a \times b$) runs in a different direction of the direct effect (c') between X and Y (Tzelgov and Henik, 1991). MacKinnon, Krull, and Lockwood (2000) point out that the scenario of indirect and direct effects entirely cancelling each other out may be rare, it is realistic to expect a situation where the indirect and direct effects both have the similar magnitudes and opposite signs. The result of this latter effect is a nonzero but nonsignificant total effect between X and Y.

Our mediation analysis proceeds with the above cautions in mind. We started by performing the bootstrap procedure that generated 2000 sub-samples. The result of mediation analysis is presented in Table 5. The direct effect from MSRI (independent variable) to the three U&G dimensions are significant (.41 for Virtual Community, .36 for Diversion and .78 for Aesthetic Experience), thereby confirming the effect of the independent variable on mediating variables (Baron and Kenny's second criterion). The table also shows that two mediating variables (Aesthetic Experience and Virtual Community) also have an effect on the dependent variable. Therefore, Baron and Kenny's third criterion is also confirmed for these variables. The direct effect, total indirect effect, and total effect between MSRI and MMOG dependency are small and statistically insignificant (failing to support hypothesis 5b). Upon examining Aesthetic Experience alone as

Table 5. Mediation analysis: Effects decomposition

	U & G - Virtual Community			U & G - Diversion			U & G – Aesthetic Experience			MMOG Dependency		
	Unst.	SE	St.	Unst.	SE	St.	Unst.	SE	St.	Unst.	SE	St.
MSRI												
Direct effect	.41**	.12	.32**	.36**	.13	.34**	.78**	.10	.56**	.05	.14	.03
Total indirect effects	.00	.00	.00	.20*	.09	.19*	.00	.00	.00	.10	.11	.07
Total effect	.41**	.12	.32**	.56**	.10	.53**	.78**	.10	.56**	.14	.10	.11
U & G -Aesthetic Experience												
Direct effect	---	---	---	.14	.10	.19	---	---	---	-.20*	.08	-.21*
Total indirect effects	---	---	---	.00	.00	.00	---	---	---	.02	.02	.02
Total effect	---	---	---	.14	.10	.19	---	---	---	-.18*	.08	-.19*
U & G - Virtual Community	---	---	---				---	---	---			
Direct effect	---	---	---	.22**	.06	.26**	---	---	---	.45**	.09	.43**
Total indirect effects	---	---	---	.00	.00	.00	---	---	---	.03	.02	.03
Total effect	---	---	---	.22**	.06	.26**	---	---	---	.48**	.09	.46**
U & G - Diversion	---	---	---	---	---	---	---	---	---	.00		
Direct effect	---	---	---	---	---	---	---	---	---	.12	.11	.10
Total indirect effects	---	---	---	---	---	---	---	---	---	.00	.00	.00
Total effect	---	---	---	---	---	---	---	---	---	.12	.11	.10

Note: *Unst.* = unstandardized; *SE* = Standard Error; *St.* = standardized.
* p < .05; ** p < .01

a mediator, the smaller total effect than the direct effect between MSRI and MMOG Dependency, and the negative indirect effect together confirm a case of suppression effect (MacKinnon, et al., 2000) making Aesthetic Experience a suppression variable. Both MacKinnon, et al. (2000), and Shrout and Bolger (2002) recommend that the procedure for mediation analysis be followed (as we did in this study) for the suppression effect.

The path leading from MSRI to MMOG dependency through Virtual Community suggests a mediation effect. The indirect effect through Virtual Community is 0.19 (0.41 × 0.45), while the indirect effect through Aesthetic Experience is -0.16 (0.78 × -0.20). Both are close to each

other in magnitude, but their signs are different. Because of the magnitude of the mediating effect being similar to that of the suppression effect, the total indirect effect between MSRI and MMOG dependency turns out to be statistically insignificant. As Preacher and Hayes (2008) suggested, this is a case that a significant total indirect effect between the independent variable and the outcome/ dependent variable should not be treated as the prerequisite to investigate individual indirect effects. The results from this mediation analysis empirically supported the structure of our first model in Figure 1, supporting hypothesis 5a.

Effects of Moderating Variables (Hypotheses 6 – 9)

Multimedia Realism for Social Interactions (MRSI)

In the third model of Figure 1, MRSI is proposed to moderate the effect of Uses and Gratifications on MMOG dependency. Since MRSI is a ratio variable, the sample was divided into two groups (high versus low MRSI) based on the median of all MRSI variables summed together. Using median to split samples to test moderating effects is not an uncommon practice in research (e.g., Im, Kim, and Han, 2008). The resulting two groups allow us to apply multi-group SEM analysis, which simultaneously fits multiple models with various levels of constraints to the sample for the two groups.

One hundred and twenty six cases were classified as low MRSI, while the remaining one hundred and seventy cases were classified into the high MRSI group. To test the moderating effect of this and other proposed moderating variables, four constraint models were examined with each imposing an equality constraint in its respective area. The first model was the baseline model that allows all parameters to vary freely. The second model constrained all factor loadings to be equal between the two MRSI groups. The third model further added an additional constraint on equal structural weights between the groups. The last model constrained error variances for endogenous variables. The four models were labeled A, B, C, and D as follows.

1. Model A: the unconstrained model with all parameters free to vary.
2. Model B: all factor loadings were constrained to be equal across the two gender groups.
3. Model C: all structural weights are constrained across the two gender groups.
4. Model D: error variances for endogenous variables were constrained across the two gender groups.

The result shown in Table 5 indicated that MRSI's moderating effect was rather weak. Models B and C were not statistically different from model one ($\Delta \chi^2 / \Delta$d.f. = 1.17 for model B, $\Delta \chi^2 / \Delta$d.f. = 1.33 for model C, p > .05). The only exception was model D, which seemed to be different from model A ($\Delta \chi^2 / \Delta$d.f. = 1.80, p < .05). As a result, the data did not support treating MRSI as a moderator as shown in Figure 1c.

Gender

It was hypothesized that gender had some moderating effect on the relationships among constructs in the present study. Table 6 shows the result of the comparison. Invariance of parameter values was supported as the four models were not significantly different from each other for the two gender groups. Most major fit indices were similar across the four models. Therefore, the moderating effect of gender could not be confirmed, leading to a rejection of hypothesis 6.

Experience with MMOG

Experience was measured in terms of number of years that a respondent has been playing MMOGs. Since the variable is not categorical, the sample was split into long and regular MMOG experience using the median. This resulted in one hundred and sixteen regular players versus one hundred and eighty long-time players. The sample was then subject to the four-model analysis outlined in the previous sections. As Table 6 shows, models B, C, and D were significantly different from the unconstrained model (p < .01). This shows that the two groups were different in terms of their path coefficients among constructs and factor loadings for each construct. Therefore, hypothesis 7 was supported.

The moderating effect of MMOG experience took the form of path diagram shown in Figure 3. MRSI's effect on the three Uses and Gratifications dimensions appeared to be quite heavy for the regular user group, but only so on the aesthetic

Table 6. Moderating effects

Model	χ²	d.f.	χ²/d.f.	AGFI	NFI	CFI	RMSEA	Δ χ²/ Δd.f.	p
(1) Multimedia realism for social interactions									
A	405.09	260	1.56	.83	.86	.94	.04	N/A	N/A
B	421.17	274	1.54	.83	.85	.94	.04	1.17	.31
C	427.43	277	1.54	.83	.85	.94	.04	1.33	.17
D	441.00	281	1.57	.83	.85	.94	.04	1.80	.02
(2) Gender									
A	541.56	324	1.67	.82	.84	.93	.05	N/A	N/A
B	560.01	339	1.65	.82	.84	.93	.05	18.45	.24
C	567.23	345	1.64	.82	.83	.93	.05	25.67	.22
D	574.92	350	1.64	.82	.83	.93	.05	33.35	.15
(3) MMOG gaming experience									
A	526.72	324	1.63	.81	.85	.93	.05	N/A	N/A
B	546.49	339	1.61	.82	.84	.93	.05	4.37	.00
C	572.72	345	1.66	.81	.83	.93	.05	4.14	.00
D	579.13	350	1.66	.81	.83	.92	.05	2.97	.00
(4) MMOG play frequency									
A	495.24	324	1.53	.82	.85	.94	.04	N/A	N/A
B	513.09	339	1.51	.82	.85	.94	.04	1.19	.27
C	521.78	345	1.51	.82	.85	.94	.04	1.26	.19
D	523.86	350	1.50	.82	.84	.94	.04	1.10	.33

Figure 3. Regular players vs. Long-time players

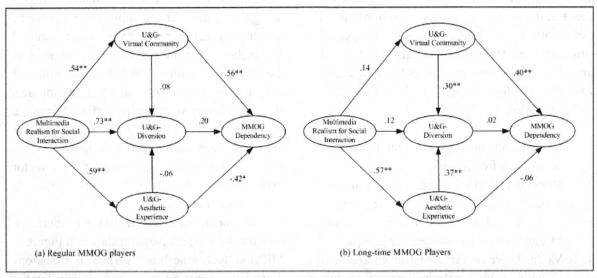

(a) Regular MMOG players   (b) Long-time MMOG Players

* p < .05
** p < .01

experience for the long-time user group. Again, this could also be evidence that long-time players were looking for less of enjoyment through game playing, but rather more for the human interactions through the games. Also, the effect of virtual community and aesthetic experience on diversion was confirmed for the experienced group, but not for the less experienced group.

Aesthetic experience had a minor and statistically insignificant role on MMOG dependency for the more experienced group, but it had a significant negative effect on MMOG dependency for the regular player group. Diversion was not statistically significant as an antecedent for MMOG dependency for either group.

MMOG Play Frequency

MMOG play frequency was measured in six categories of hours per week spent on playing MMOG. The categories range from less than or equal to 10 hours a week to over fifty hours. The median split classifies one hundred and seventy-seven respondents into the "less frequent users" group, while the rest of one hundred and nineteen respondents into the "more frequent users" group. It was hypothesized that play frequency had a significant effect on construct relationships, but Table 6 seems to suggest otherwise. The four models were compared and there did not seem to be any significant difference among the four models. There was not a significant degradation of model fit either. Therefore, it is evident that play frequency's moderating effect on parameter values were minor and not statistically significant. Hypothesis 8 was not supported. The results of hypothesis testing are summarized in Table 7.

Table 7. Summary of hypothesis testing

Hypothesis	Result
Hypothesis 1a: the attitude that MMOGs are a pleasant diversion will be positively related to MMOG dependency.	Rejected
Hypothesis 1b: positive attitudes about the aesthetic qualities of MMOGs will be positively related to MMOG dependency.	Rejected
Hypothesis 2: Participation in virtual communities within MMOGs will be positively related to MMOG dependency.	Supported
Hypothesis 3: Participation in virtual communities within MMOGs will be positively related to diversion gratifications.	Supported
Hypothesis 4: Positive attitudes about the aesthetic qualities of MMOGs will be positively related to diversion gratifications.	Supported
Hypothesis 5 Multimedia Realism for Social Interaction (MRSI) will be positively related to MMOG dependency. **Hypothesis 5a: MRSI positively affects MMOG dependency through participation in a virtual community, a sense of diversion, and a pleasant aesthetic experience** **Hypothesis 5b: MRSI directly affects MMOG dependency.**	Partially Supported Supported Rejected
Hypothesis 6: Gender will moderate the effect of uses and gratifications on MMOG dependency.	Rejected
Hypothesis 7: Experience will moderate the effect of uses and gratifications on MMOG dependency.	Supported
Hypothesis 8: Play frequency will moderate the effect of uses and gratifications on MMOG dependency.	Rejected

DISCUSSION

MMOGs and related types of games are not simply a way to pass time. They are used for entertainment, social interactions, learning, or even conducting businesses (e.g., Terdiman, 2007). Yet many authors have expressed concern that people may develop a dependency upon MMOGs that has a negative impact upon their lives (Kelly, 2004). In our study, we examined multimedia realism for social interactions as well as other moderating variables for their effects on factors derived from existing psychological and communication theories, including Uses and Gratifications theory and research investigating Internet dependency. Virtual community, aesthetic experience and diversion were identified based on existing theories as the three main forms of gratifications for MMOG. Three models of construct relationships were identified and tested with each model proposing a different role of multimedia realism for social interactions (MRSI) with other constructs. Results showed that MRSI is an antecedent of Uses and Gratifications constructs. This MRSI relationship with other theoretical constructs was our baseline model used to further test moderating effects of other related constructs.

In spite of the intuitively straightforward links between multimedia realism and both visual aesthetic experience and an overall sense of diversion, the effect of the latter two on MMOG dependency is mixed (failing to support hypothesis 1). Diversion was not significantly related to MMOG dependency (failing to support hypothesis 1a). Aesthetic experience had a negative but significant impact on MMOG dependency (hypothesis 1b). In fact, aesthetic experience was more of an inhibitor of MMOG dependency as exemplified by its negative path coefficient with MMOG dependency. One possible explanation is that players experienced novelty with the aesthetic design when they first saw the scene but the novelty effect faded as a stimulus during continued use. As many game studies point out, players are

drawn to the games largely because of the challenges and potential "unknowns" of the game. The negative path coefficient also indicates that there was a possibility that the aesthetic design "overwhelmed" or distracted players as they undertook these cognitively complex tasks (Allison & Polich, 2008) – in which case the players had to learn to ignore these distracting features. Another plausible explanation comes from Grohol's (2005) model for internet addiction, where he postulates that internet addiction goes through three stages: enchantment, disillusionment and balance. Users are likely to be fully immersed by the activity during the enhancement stage. This is followed by the disillusionment stage with a decline in usage, and then by the balance stage. The negative path coefficient between aesthetic effect and dependency in our present study is statistically significant, while the positive coefficient between virtual community and dependency is even stronger. Therefore, this group has likely gone through the first stage of the Grohol's model, where the initial excitement coming from visual or auditory effects of the game no longer becomes a significant reason for them to keep coming back to the game. As Grohol (2005) postulates, it is possible for a user to find a new activity or discover a new meaning of their gaming experience from some existing services already present in the game. This latter idea seems to support the model for regular players since they have developed a stronger relationship between virtual communication and dependency. As such, visual and auditory effects are less of an incentive anymore, or perhaps they have become more of a hindrance to their experience of person-to-person relationships in the virtual community. For long-time players, aesthetic experience is no longer a relevant factor in MMOG dependency; rather, dependency is predicted by virtual community.

In this final baseline model, virtual community had the largest effect of the variables studied and thus emerged as a key antecedent for MMOG dependency. The more realistic the virtual environment, the more likely players were to interact with other players as part of a virtual community, which, in turn, was an important component of MMOG dependency. This finding supported hypothesis 2 and was consistent with research looking at Internet addiction in other contexts (e.g., Leung, 2004). This body of research suggested that the Internet could satisfy social needs, which contributed to dependency and addiction.

Diversion was measured as a macro-level variable after playing MMOG. It was hypothesized that the content gratifications (i.e., virtual community) and process gratifications (i.e., aesthetic experience) could both significantly influence such after-play impressions. The moderate but statistically significant effect of virtual community participation (hypothesis 3) and aesthetic experience (hypothesis 4) on diversion offer some preliminary evidence that sources of gratifications may be inter-related. As the diversion variable is operationalized as "have fun", "feel excited", "feel entertained", and "feel excited", all characterize the effect after a gamer has experienced gratifications from other sources (e.g., virtual community participation and the game's aesthetic effects). This finding of inter-related gratifications extends Song et al.'s (2004) work, where they discovered moderate correlations among the three gratification variables without further investigating their relationships.

Our findings from mediation analysis and structural model support that multimedia realism might magnify the effects on dependency indirectly by facilitating conditions where informational, psychological, and social needs were satisfied through the different forms of gratifications. Hypothesis 5a postulates an indirect relationship between MRSI and MMOG dependency through variables that reflect various Uses & Gratifications: participation in a virtual community, a sense of diversion, and a pleasant aesthetic experience. Hypothesis 5b postulates a direct relationship between MRSI and dependency. Although hypothesis 5b is rejected based on the statistical significance of the direct effect between the two variables, the result

from mediation analysis uncovers more insights regarding significant indirect effects between the two variables (supporting hypothesis 5a). The mediation effect (path from MRSI to MMOG dependency through virtual community) and suppression effect (path from MRSI to MMOG dependency through aesthetic experience) are similar in magnitude but different in sign, thus cancelling each other. The net result is non-significant total indirect effects between MRSI and MMOG dependency, but taken individually the indirect effects from the two paths are significant (see MacKinnon et al., 2000, and Preacher & Hayes, 2008). Taken together, multimedia realism was directly related to aesthetic user interface design and to a sense of diversion, it was also an antecedent to foster a better communication experience in the virtual community. It was through the virtual community experience of sharing information and finding social support that MMOG dependency was fostered.

To test the moderating effect of various variables (e.g., gender, experience, and play frequency), the models were constrained in various areas, such as measurement weights, structural weights and structural residuals. As a result, three additional sub-models were compared with the unconstrained baseline model for each moderating variable. The only moderating effect was confirmed for gaming experience (supporting hypothesis 7). All three sub-models were comparatively different from the unconstrained model, indicating that the two gaming experience groups (long-time players versus regular players) were different in many aspects. For both groups, the virtual community experience predicted MMOG dependency. However, for regular players, there was a significant negative relationship between the aesthetic experience and MMOG dependency; for long-time players, the relationship was not significant. This is consistent with the explanation that regular players found high multimedia realism to be aesthetically pleasant, but distracting (reducing MMOG dependency), whereas long-time players had become habituated to such realism (resulting in no relationship between aesthetic experience and dependency).

There was also a moderating effect for experience playing MMOG. The relationships were significant for the more experienced group with both process and content gratifications having an approximately equal effect on diversion; they were not significant for less-experienced players. For long-time players, MRSI was a prerequisite condition to trigger a better aesthetic experience, which, in turn, influenced their sense of diversion. Multimedia realism had no statistical effect on the other two uses and gratifications dimensions for this group. This implies that two different processes were at work for long-time players. First, multimedia realism influenced aesthetic experience, which influenced a sense of diversion. Second, as discussed earlier, the sense of virtual community influenced MMOG dependency. This differed from the relationships that emerged for regular MMOG players. For regular players, multimedia realism influenced a sense of diversion, a pleasant aesthetic experience, and a feeling of belonging to a virtual community – and the latter two U & G variables predicted MMOG dependency, as discussed earlier. Together, these findings support hypotheses 5a and 7. They also suggested three conclusions: First, long-time players experienced MMOGs in a qualitatively different psychological way than regular players. Second, factors that predicted a sense of diversion were not necessarily the same factors as those that predicted MMOG dependency. Third, being a long-time player is not the same as being high in MMOG dependency – there was variability in dependency scores among both long-time and regular MMOG players. Researchers would be wise to bear these conclusions in mind when investigating online games.

Multimedia realism, a target that game designers and researchers aim to improve, has a multifaceted effect on gamers. A large body of existing gaming literature operates under the assumption that such realism fosters positive experience equally in all contexts of use. Our study contributes to the body of knowledge in terms of how multimedia realism is related to gamers' psychological states for game play. One benefit derived from our findings lies in possible areas of cost reduction for game designers. For example, the realistic representation of places for social interactions is helpful in general, but such an effect gradually diminishes to only aesthetic effects for the more experienced long-time users. The suppression effect in our mediation analysis between MRSI and dependency suggests that achieving a better aesthetic effect (through graphics, multimedia and the like) may hamper the capabilities of MRSI in engaging users.

This study also offers contributions to the literature in terms of the relationships among Uses and Gratifications dimensions. In Song et al.'s (2004) study, the three variables were assumed to represent two distinct types of gratifications dimensions (process and content gratifications). The variables were also assumed to be independent from each other and independent from other Internet gratifications variables. As the diversion variable of the U & G theory was constructed as a way to measure after-play perceptions, it is likely that such perceptions may be the result from one's aesthetic experience in the game and communication experience in the virtual community. Our study relaxed the mutually exclusive relationship among U & G dimensions and proposed that the psychological experience of diversion was influenced by the other two U & G variables of aesthetic experience and a sense of virtual community. The result of such construction was supported for the more experienced group. Song et al.'s independency assumption for the three U & G variables was partially supported for the less experienced group only. Therefore, our findings augment our understanding in different patterns of gaming factor structure.

Dependency on technology is a double-edged sword. On one side, an individual's experience with a particular type of technology may be used to one's advantage. On the other, dependency to the degree of indulgence that causes detrimental effects on one's personal life, productivity or on society is certainly an unwanted effect. Although it is not the focus of the present study to examine the psychological transformations between the healthy side and negative side of dependency, our findings highlight that MMOG dependency does not just come from the "thrill" of player-game interactions. The human-to-human interaction through the virtual world also encourages a gamer to play, thereby offering some evidence of social, process, and content gratifications. Our findings in this area for the whole sample and for different moderator groups offer some preliminary understanding of antecedents of MMOG dependency, which supplements the majority of dependency studies that focus on measuring dependency, delineating patterns of dependency, and identifying treatments, .

Uses & Gratifications theory guided the design of the present study. This is a theory that has been used extensively in the field of Communication Studies to predict whether people will select a particular medium for a particular purpose. This theory is increasingly being used in the field of Information Systems, as it is well suited for predicting whether people will use the Internet for specific purposes (Liang, Lai, & Ku, 2006; Stafford, Stafford, & Schkade, 2004). Other theoretical perspectives could have been taken to guide this research. For example, the Technology Acceptance Model (TAM; Davis, 1989) or the Theory of Planned Behavior (TPB; Ajzen, 1991) from which TAM was derived, could have been used. The reason that TAM was not used is that twofold: First, TAM is most frequently used to predict initial adoption, or acceptance of a particular type of technology or system by an organization or individual rather than ongoing use of that technology or system. Second, TAM focuses heavily on "perceived ease of use" and "perceived usefulness" as predictors of adoption; by contrast,

some MMOGs are neither particularly easy to learn or use, nor useful to one's work or life. TPB extending Theory of Reasoned Action is a general psychological model of decision-making that focuses on perceived behavioral control. While the present study could have used this model, it did not; that was because the model measured multiple concepts (e.g. perceived control) that did not seem necessary to measure in order to explain MMOG dependency. Thus, in the interest of parsimony, Uses & Gratifications theory offered a reasonable theoretical perspective for guiding the present investigation. Perhaps future research might design 'critical tests' comparing the efficacy with which TAM and TPB predict MMOG dependency relative to Uses & Gratifications Theory.

The present paper also uses concepts from "flow" theory (Csikszentmihalyi, 1988; Koufaris, 2002) which suggests that people can enjoy the immersion experience (e.g. flow state) given their skills and challenges faced are matched. Uses & Gratifications Theory states that people select a certain medium because of their needs which is mostly for enjoyment (Sherry, 2004). The enjoyment is the result of the immersion experience- flow state. In other words, what people want, based on Uses & Gratifications Theory, is the final product from a balance of skill and challenge. While Internet-based MMOG game characteristics like MRSI may increase the likelihood of a flow state, the present investigation shows that MRSI also indirectly increases the likelihood of MMOG dependency. Immersion through realistic and engaging games may lead to overwhelming indulgence in those games, a phenomenon similar to the "flow" state (Cheng & Cairns, 2005). Although "flow" and "dependence" may be theoretically two different concepts, some evidence (Thatcher, Wretschko, & Fridjhon, 2008) suggests that a game user may move directly from the flow state to dependency on the game. Prior research demonstrates that MRSI affects "flow" (Choi & Kim, 2004); prior research also shows that "flow" is related to dependency (Chou & Ting,

2003). The present study offers a complementary view in demonstrating that MRSI also influences MMOG dependency through another route, i.e., through users experiencing a virtual community. Future research may investigate other possible routes through which MRSI influences MMOG dependency.

LIMITATIONS

There are several limitations of this study. First, we did not develop measurement instruments specifically designed for this research study. We used Young's (1996) questionnaire; this instrument treats Internet dependency as similar to a clinical substance addiction. The subjects responding to this questionnaire might have been influenced by the questions treating frequent or extended Internet use as "pathological". However, this limitation means that we used a proven instrument with known validity and reliability. It also enhances the comparability of this study with other published research (e.g., Chen, Tarn & Han, 2004).

Secondly, we surveyed the subjects through Internet and therefore there was no control over the responses. The questionnaire was posted on several online game forums in order to elicit more responses from real players. A few respondents, however, could be non-players who were attracted by the rewards we provided. Also a real player could repeatedly fill in the questionnaire in order to get higher chance to be rewarded. Though we asked them to provide email address in order to minimize such deceit, they could always use multiple email addresses. The overwhelming predominance of males in the sample may have also limited our ability to detect gender effects. These may have emerged had a larger and more diverse sample of females participated in the study.

Third, this was not a controlled experiment – it was a survey. Not every person had played the same game or experienced the same stimuli within the games that they had played. Thus, one cannot

conclude from this study that the multimedia realism of Game X enhanced the diversion experience or MMOG dependency compared to Game Y. However, the naturally-occurring variability in game experiences enhances the external validity of the findings. In fact, it would be difficult to do a controlled experiment with MMOGs because so many players are needed to participate in the games and because players interact with each other in so many varied ways. We chose to emphasize external validity over internal validity. In addition, surveying respondents at the same time with the same instrument may pose concerns about common method variance (CMV). Although some scholars suggest that CMV is not a serious concern (e.g., Lance & Vandenberg, 2008), we have followed recommendations from previous studies to examine common method variance through a CFA model. The result suggests that CMV may not be a concern; the moderating models examined in this study also provide some support to mitigate the CMV problem. Even with great care taken through the above post hoc statistical tests, one would also greatly benefit from other procedural means (e.g., collecting measures at different times or from different sources) to alleviate the CMV problem.

Finally, Uses and Gratifications theory assumes that individuals are goal-oriented, active media consumers. For persons with clinical Internet addictions who may be depressed, this assumption may not always hold. However, other theoretical models make similar assumptions. For those who are not clinically depressed, the assumption that people consciously choose specific media for specific purposes is a reasonable one, particularly for an Internet-based survey where participants self-selected.

IMPLICATIONS

For game developers, multimedia realism for social interaction enhances the gaming experience in varied ways based on U & G theory and consistent with prior research (e.g., Choi & Kim, 2004). This suggests that developers would find it beneficial to enhance multimedia realism. Additional research needs to be conducted to discover what additional components enhance the gaming experience.

This study has implications for other institutions as well, as they must recognize that the sense of virtual community is predictive of MMOG dependency. Social institutions have taken different responses to the development of MMOGs. Parents, high school counselors, and college officials have viewed the growth of MMOGs with some concern as studies link MMOG addiction to academic and social problems (Ng and Weimer-Hastings, 2004). The business community has taken mixed approaches. Some businesses, for example, recognize that MMOG addiction may hamper productivity and so they filter employee access to MMOG websites. Others advertise in online games, including *Second Life,* hoping to attract new customers. At other organizations, Human Resource managers are creating a "presence" in MMOGs for training and orientation activities because it is cheaper than flying new employees to training sites (Crush, 2008; Arnold, 2009). However, such an approach may be short sighted as side effects such as a tendency to develop some form of dependency or abuse may develop through gaming experiences. If firms use these games to create a "virtual community" among employees in the belief that this will enhance their *esprit de corps,* they may be setting the stage for MMOG dependency among some employees, for the sense of virtual community was the single best predictor of MMOG dependency in the present study. Ironically, as the amount of time spent playing online games increases, the quality of interpersonal relationships actually decreases (Lo, Wang, & Fang, 2005). Therefore, the role of the management is crucial when an engaging experience (through virtual community or other factors) may possibly lead to some form

of dependency. While identifying opportunities of using 3D worlds and games for educational purposes, Eschenbrenner et al. (2008) reported that safety issues (such as ocular and behavioral problems) must be controlled. They cautioned that these online activities may be more playful than educational, challenging the true value of delivering education using online games. In our view, playfulness of the technology (especially the creation of virtual communities within games) can easily lead to dependency, thereby making it more important to study the intrinsic motivational factors that may lead to dependency. Although beyond the scope of the present study, organizations would perhaps be well-advised to consider developing a "sense of community" among organizational members in reality, so that people do not feel they must turn to virtual communities (either within or outside of the organization) to find information and acceptance. Another approach to prevent Internet addiction is to cut down use by adopting gaming intermittently for some isolated business activities only.

CONCLUSION

The present study suggests that Multimedia Realism for Social Interaction is related to dependency among players of Massively Multiplayer Online Games. However, this relationship is not a simple, straightforward one; it is not simply that more realistic games foster dependency. Instead, MRSI is positively related to a sense of diversion, a positive aesthetic experience, and a sense of virtual community, as suggested by Uses & Gratifications theory. These intervening psychological variables were related to MMOG dependency in different ways: Diversion was unrelated to dependency, aesthetic experience was negatively related, and virtual community was positively related to dependency. Further, participation in a virtual community and a pleasant aesthetic experience predicted a sense of diversion. These findings suggest that variables that predict a pleasant sense of diversion are not always the same variables that predict MMOG dependency. MMOG dependency seems to depend primarily on the information and social support obtained from a virtual community. Also, these general relationships were moderated by how long a person had played MMOGs, suggesting that long-time players became habituated to the aesthetic experiences that resulted from MRSI and these were unrelated to MMOG dependency. Thus, as research continues in the areas of game design and MMOG dependency, it will be important for investigators to distinguish between long-time game players and regular players, because the psychological experiences of the two groups with the games may be qualitatively different.

REFERENCES

Ajzen, I. (1991). The theory of planned behavior. *Organizational Behavior and Human Decision Processes*, *50*, 179–211. doi:10.1016/0749-5978(91)90020-T

Allison, B. Z., & Polich, J. (2008). Workload assessment of computer gaming using a single-stimulus event-related potential paradigm. *Biological Psychology*, *77*(3), 277–283. doi:10.1016/j.biopsycho.2007.10.014

Arnold, J. T. (2009). Gaming technology used to orient new hires. *HR Magazine, 54*(1), 36-37. Beard, J. W. (Ed.). (1996). *Impression management and information technology.* Greenwich, CT: Quorum.

Ashmore, R. W., & Herman, B. (2006). Managing the risk of employee blogging. *Risk Management*, *53*(4), 40–43.

Baron, R. M., & Kenny, D. A. (1986). The moderator–mediator variable distinction in social psychological research: Conceptual, strategic, and statistical considerations. *Journal of Personality and Social Psychology*, *51*, 1173–1182. doi:10.1037/0022-3514.51.6.1173

Bollen, K. A., & Stine, R. (1990). Direct and indirect effects: Classical *and bootstrap esti*mates of variability. *Sociological Methodology*, *20*, 115–140. doi:10.2307/271084

Carroll, J. M. (1997). Human-computer interaction: Psychology as a science of design. *Annual Review of Psychology*, *48*, 61–83. doi:10.1146/annurev.psych.48.1.61

Chak, K., & Leung, L. (2004). Shyness and Locus of Control as predictors of Internet addiction and Internet use. *Cyberpsychology & Behavior*, *7*(5), 559–570.

Chen, J. V., & Park, Y. (2005). The differences of addiction causes between massive multiplayer online game and multi user domain. *International Review of Information Ethics*, *4*, 53–60.

Chen, K., Chen, I., & Paul, H. (2001). Explaining online behavioral differences: an Internet dependency perspective. *Journal of Computer Information Systems*, *41*(3), 59–63.

Chen, K., Tarn, J. M., & Han, B. (2004). Internet dependency: its impact on online behavioral patterns in e-commerce. *Human Systems Management*, *23*(1), 49–58.

Cheng, K., & Cairns, P. A. (2005). Behaviour, realism and immersion in games. In *Proceedings of the Conference on Human Factors in Computing Systems* (pp. 1272-1275).

Choi, D., & Kim, J. (2004). Why people continue to play online games: in search of critical design factors to increase customer loyalty to online contents. *Cyberpsychology & Behavior*, *7*(1), 11–24. doi:10.1089/109493104322820066

Chou, C., & Hsiao, M.-C. (2000). Internet addiction, usage, gratification, and pleasure experience: the Taiwan college students' case. *Computers & Education*, *35*(1), 65–80. doi:10.1016/S0360-1315(00)00019-1

Chou, T. J., & Ting, C. C. (2003). The Role of Flow Experience in Cyber-Game Addiction. *Cyberpsychology & Behavior, 6*(6), 663–675. doi:10.1089/109493103322725469

Conway, J. C., & Rubin, A. M. (1991). Psychological Predictors of Television Viewing Motivation. *Communication Research, 18*(4), 443–463. doi:10.1177/009365091018004001

Crush, P. (2008). Virtually speaking. *Human Resources,* 38- 41. Retrieved from http://www.humanresourcesmagazine.com/ news/search/864791/E-learning-Virtual-worlds---Virtually-speaking/

Csikszentmihalyi, M. (1988). *Optimal Experience: Psychological Studies of Flow in Consciousness.* Cambridge, UK: Cambridge University Press.

Cutler, N. E., & Danowski, J. A. (1980). Process gratification in aging cohorts. *The Journalism Quarterly, 57,* 269–277.

Davis, F. D. (1989). Perceived usefulness, perceived ease of use, and user acceptance of information technology. *Management Information Systems Quarterly, 13*(3), 319–340. doi:10.2307/249008

Dickey, M. D. (2005). Brave new (interactive) worlds: A review of the design affordances and constraints of two 3D virtual worlds as interactive learning environments. *Interactive Learning Environments, 13*(1-2), 121–137. doi:10.1080/10494820500173714

Dimmick, J., Kline, S., & Stafford, L. (2000). The Gratification Niches of Personal E-mail and the Telephone. *Communication Research, 27*(2), 227–248. doi:10.1177/009365000027002005

Dourish, P. (1998). Introduction: The state of play. *Computer Supported Cooperative Work: The Journal of Collaborative Computing, 7*(1/2), 1–7. doi:10.1023/A:1008697019985

Ducheneaut, N., Moore, R., & Nickell, E. (2007). Virtual "Third places": a case study of sociability in massively multiplayer games. *Computer Supported Cooperative Work, 16,* 129–166. doi:10.1007/s10606-007-9041-8

Durdell, A., & Thomson, K. (1997). Gender and computing: a decade of change? *Computers & Education, 28*(1), 1–9. doi:10.1016/S0360-1315(96)00034-6

Eighmey, J. (1997). Profiling User Responses to Commercial Web Sites. *Journal of Advertising Research, 37*(3), 59–66.

Eschenbrenner, B., Nah, F. F.-H., & Siau, K. (2008). 3-D Virtual Worlds in Education: Applications, Benefits, Issues, and Opportunities. *Journal of Database Management, 19*(4), 91–110.

Fornell, C., & Larcker, D. F. (1981). Evaluating structural equation models with unobservable variables and measurement error. *JMR, Journal of Marketing Research, 18*(1), 39–50. doi:10.2307/3151312

Galloway, A. (2004). Social Realism in Gaming. *International Journal of Computer Game Research, 4*(1). Retrieved from http://www.gamestudies.org/ 0401/galloway/.

Garau, M., Slater, M., Vinayagamoorthy, V., Brogni, A., Steed, A., & Sasse, M. A. (2003). The impact of avatar realism and eye gaze control on perceived quality of communication in a shared immersive virtual environment. In *Proceedings of the SIGCHI conference on Human factors in computing systems,* Ft. Lauderdale, FL (pp. 529-536).

Gefen, D., Straub, D., & Boudreau, M. (2000). Structural equation modeling and regression: Guidelines for research practice. *Communications of the Association for Information Systems, 4*(5), 1–77.

Golub, A., & Lingley, K. (2008). 'Just like the Qing Empire': Internet addiction, MMOGs, and moral crisis in contemporary China. *Games and Culture: A Journal of Interactive Media, 3*(1), 59-75.

Griffiths, M. (1998). Internet addiction: Does it really exist? In Gackenback, J. (Ed.), *Psychology and the Internet: Intrapersonal, interpersonal and transpersonal implications* (pp. 61–75). New York: Academic Press.

Griffiths, M. D., Davies, M. N. O., & Chappell, D. (2004). Demographic factors and playing variables in online computer gaming. *Cyberpsychology & Behavior, 7*(4), 479–487. doi:10.1089/cpb.2004.7.479

Grohol, J. M. (2005). *Internet Addiction Guide*. Retrieved from http://psychcentral.com/ netaddiction/

Guru, A., & Siau, K. (2008). Developing the IBM virtual community: iSociety. *Journal of Database Management, 19*(4), 1–13.

Ha, I., Yoon, Y., & Choi, M. (2007). Determinants of adoption of mobile games under mobile broadband wireless access environment. *Information & Management, 44*(3), 276–286. doi:10.1016/j.im.2007.01.001

Henry, K. B., Arrow, H., & Carini, B. (1999). A Tripartite Model of Group Identification: Theory and Measuremen. *Small Group Research, 30*(5), 555–581. doi:10.1177/104649649903000504

Huang, E. (2008). Use and gratification in e-consumers. *Internet Research, 18*(4), 405–426. doi:10.1108/10662240810897817

Im, I., Kim, Y., & Han, H.-J. (2008). The effects of perceived risk and technology type on users' acceptance of technologies. *Information & Management, 45*(1), 1–9.

Kandell, J. J. (1998). Internet addiction on campus: The vulnerability of college students. *Cyberpsychology & Behavior, 1*(1), 11–17. doi:10.1089/cpb.1998.1.11

Katz, E., Blumler, J., & Gurevitch, M. (1974). *The Use of Mass Communication*. Beverly Hills, CA: Sage.

Kelly, R. V. (2004). *Massively Multiplayer Online Role-Playing Games: The people, the addiction, and the playing experience*. Jefferson, NC: McFarland & Company.

Kim, E. J., Namkoong, K., Ku, T., & Kim, S. J. (2008). The relationship between online game addiction and aggression, self-control, and narcissistic personality traits. *European Psychiatry, 23*(3), 212–218. doi:10.1016/j.eurpsy.2007.10.010

Kim, K. H., Park, J. Y., Kim, D. Y., Moon, H. I., & Chun, H. C. (2002). E-lifestyle and motives to use online games. *Irish Marketing Review, 15*(2), 71–77.

Koufaris, M. (2002). Applying the technology acceptance model and flow theory to online consumer behavior. *Information Systems Research, 13*(2), 205–223. doi:10.1287/isre.13.2.205.83

Krotoski, A., Cezanne, P., Rymaszewski, M., Rossignol, J., & Au, W. J. (2008). *Second Life: The Official Guide* (2nd ed.). New York: Wiley.

Kücklich, J. (2007, September 24-28). MMOGs and the Future of Literature. In *Situated Play: Proceedings of [Digital Games Research Association] DiGRA 2007 Conference*, Tokyo (pp. 319- 326).

Kumar, S., Chhugani, J., Kim, C., Kim, D., Nguyen, A., & Dubey, P. (2008). Second Life and the New Generation of Virtual Worlds. *Computer, 41*(9), 46–53. doi:10.1109/MC.2008.398

Lance, C. E., & Vandenberg, R. J. (2008). *Statistical and methodological myths and urban legends: Doctrine, verity, and fable in organizational and social sciences*. London: Taylor & Francis.

Lanthier, R. P., & Windham, R. G. (2004). Internet use and college adjustment: The moderating role of gender. *Computers in Human Behavior, 20*(5), 591–606. doi:10.1016/j.chb.2003.11.003

Lee, M. S., Ko, Y. H., Song, H. S., Kwon, K. H., Lee, H. S., & Nam, M. (2007). Characteristics of Internet use in relation to game genre in Korean adolescents. *Cyberpsychology & Behavior, 10*(2), 278–285. doi:10.1089/cpb.2006.9958

Leung, L. (2004). Net-generation attributes and seductive properties of the Internet as predictors of online activities and Internet addiction. *Cyberpsychology & Behavior, 7*(3), 333–348. doi:10.1089/1094931041291303

Liang, T. P., Lai, H. J., & Ku, Y. C. (2006). Personalized Content Recommendation and User Satisfaction: Theoretical Synthesis and Empirical Findings. *Journal of Management Information Systems, 23*(3), 45. doi:10.2753/MIS0742-1222230303

Lichtash, A. E. (2004). Inappropriate use of e-mail and the Internet in the workplace: The arbitration picture. *Dispute Resolution Journal, 59*(1), 26–36.

Lo, S. K., Wang, C. C., & Fang, W. (2005). Physical interpersonal relationships and social anxiety among online game players. *Cyberpsychology & Behavior, 8*(1), 15–20. doi:10.1089/cpb.2005.8.15

MacKinnon, D. P., Krull, J. L., & Lockwood, C. M. (2000). Equivalence of the mediation, confounding and suppression effects. *Prevention Science, 1*(4), 173–181. doi:10.1023/A:1026595011371

MacKinnon, D. P., Lockwood, C. M., Hoffman, J. M., West, S. G., & Sheets, V. (2002). A comparison of methods to test mediation and other intervening variable effects. *Psychological Methods, 7*(1), 83–104. doi:10.1037/1082-989X.7.1.83

Mafé, C. R., & Blas, S. S. (2006). Explaining Internet dependency: An exploratory study of future purchase intention of Spanish Internet users. *Internet Research, 16*(4), 380–397. doi:10.1108/10662240610690016

McDonald, S. C. (1997). The once and future web; Scenarios for advertisers. *Journal of Advertising Research, 37*(2), 21–28.

Morahan-Martin, J., & Schumacher, P. (2000). Incidence and correlates of pathological Internet use. *Computers in Human Behavior, 16*(1), 13–29. doi:10.1016/S0747-5632(99)00049-7

Mossholder, K. W., Bennett, N., Kemery, E. R., & Wesolowski, M. A. (1998). Relationships between bases of power and work reactions: The mediational role of procedural justice. *Journal of Management, 24*(4), 533–552. doi:10.1016/S0149-2063(99)80072-5

Ng, B., & Wiemer-Hastings, P. (2004). Addiction to massively multiplayer online role-playing games. *Annual Review of Cybertherapy and Telemedicine, 2*, 97–101.

Odell, P. M., Korgen, K., Schumacher, P., & Delucchi, M. (2000). Internet use among female and male college students. *Cyberpsychology & Behavior, 3*(5), 855–862. doi:10.1089/10949310050191836

Olson, G. M., & Olson, J. S. (2003). Human-computer interaction: Psychological aspects of the human use of computing. *Annual Review of Psychology, 54*, 491–516. doi:10.1146/annurev.psych.54.101601.145044

Papacharissi, Z., & Rubin, A. M. (2000). Predictors of Internet Use. *Journal of Broadcasting & Electronic Media, 44*(2), 175–196. doi:10.1207/s15506878jobem4402_2

Pawlak, C. (2002). Correlates of Internet use and addiction in adolescents. *Dissertation Abstracts International, Section A: Humanities and Social Sciences, 63*(5-A), 1727.

Phillips, T. (1999, March). The enemy within. *Director (Cincinnati, Ohio), 54,* 89.

Pisan, Y. (2007, December 3-5). My guild, my people: role of guilds in massively multiplayer online games. In *Proceedings of the 4th Australasian conference on Interactive Entertainment,* Melbourne, Australia. Retrieved from http://portal.acm.org/toc.cfm?id= 1367956&type=proceeding&coll=ACM&dl= ACM&CFID=27655947&CFTOKEN=58909698

Podsakoff, P. M., & Organ, D. W. (1986). Self-Reports in Organizational Research: Problems and Prospects. *Journal of Management, 12*(4), 531–544. doi:10.1177/014920638601200408

Preacher, K. J., & Hayes, A. F. (2008). Asymptotic and resampling strategies for assessing and comparing indirect effects in multiple mediator models. *Behavior Research Methods, 40*(3), 879–891. doi:10.3758/BRM.40.3.879

Rosen, L. D., & Weil, M. M. (1995). Adult and teenage use of consumer, business, and entertainment technology: Potholes on the information superhighway? *The Journal of Consumer Affairs, 29*(1), 55–84.

Rosenfeld, P., Giacalone, R. A., & Riordan, C. (2001). *Impression management: Building and enhancing reputations at work.* Florence, KY: Cengage Learning Business Press.

Sattar, P., & Ramaswamy, S. (2004). Internet gaming addiction. *Canadian Journal of Psychiatry, 49*(12), 871–872.

Sayre, C. (2008, December 1). Imaginary Trends. *Time,* 22.

Scherer, K. (1997). College life on-line: healthy and unhealthy Internet use. *Journal of College Student Development, 38*(6), 655–665.

Seay, A. F., Jerome, W. J., Lee, K. S., & Kraut, R. E. (2004, April 24-29). *Project massive: A study of online gaming communities.* Paper presented at the Computer-Human Interaction conference, Vienna, Austria.

Sherry, J. L. (2004). Flow and media enjoyment . *Communication Theory, 14*(4), 328–347. doi:10.1111/j.1468-2885.2004.tb00318.x

Shrout, P. E., & Bolder, N. (2002). Mediation in experimental and nonexperimental studies: New procedures and recommendations. *Psychological Methods, 7*(4), 422–445. doi:10.1037/1082-989X.7.4.422

Slater, M., Steed, A., & Chrysanthou, Y. (2001). *Computer Graphics and Virtual Environments: From Realism to Real-Time.* Reading, MA: Addison Wesley.

Song, I., Larose, R., Eastin, M. S., & Lin, C. A. (2004). Internet gratifications and Internet addiction: On the uses and abuses of new media. *Cyberpsychology & Behavior, 7*(4), 384–394. doi:10.1089/cpb.2004.7.384

Soule, L. C., Shell, L. W., & Kleen, B. A. (2003). Exploring Internet addiction: Demographic characteristics and stereotypes of heavy Internet users. *Journal of Computer Information Systems, 44*(1), 64–73.

Stafford, T. F. (2008). Social and usage-process motivations for consumer Internet access. *Journal of Organizational and End User Computing, 20*(3), 1–21.

Stafford, T. F., & Stafford, M. R. (2001). Identifying motivations for the use of commercial Web sites. *Information Resources Management Journal, 14*(1), 22–30.

Stafford, T. F., Stafford, M. R., & Schkade, L. L. (2004). Determining uses and gratifications for the Internet. *Decision Sciences, 35*(2), 259–288. doi:10.1111/j.00117315.2004.02524.x

Stanton, J. M. (2002). Company profile of the frequent internet user. *Communications of the ACM, 45*(1), 55–59. doi:10.1145/502269.502297

Stone, C. A., & Sobel, M. E. (1990). The robustness of estimates of total indirect effects. *Psychometrika, 55*(2), 337–352. doi:10.1007/BF02295291

Terdiman, D. (2007). *The entrepreneur's guide to Second Life: Making money in the metaverse.* Hoboken, NJ: Sybex.

Thatcher, A., Wretschko, G., & Fridjhon, P. (2008). Online flow experiences, problematic Internet use and Internet procrastination. *Computers in Human Behavior, 24*(5), 2236–2254. doi:10.1016/j.chb.2007.10.008

Tzelgov, J., & Henik, A. (1991). Suppression situations in psychological research: Definitions, implications, and applications. *Psychological Bulletin, 109*(3), 524–536. doi:10.1037/0033-2909.109.3.524

Vandenbroeck, M., Verschelden, G., & Boonaert, T. (2008). E-learning in a low-status female profession: The role of motivation, anxiety, and social support in the learning divide. *Journal of Computer Assisted Learning, 24*(3), 181–190. doi:10.1111/j.1365-2729.2007.00252.x

Wagner, C. (2005). Supporting Knowledge Management in Organizations with Conversational Technologies: Discussion Forums, Weblogs, and Wilds. *Journal of Database Management, 16*(2), 1–8.

Wang, C.-C., & Wang, C.-H. (2008). Helping others in online games: Prosocial behavior in cyberspace. *Cyberpsychology & Behavior, 11*(3), 344–346. doi:10.1089/cpb.2007.0045

Williams, D. (2006). Groups and goblins: The social and civic impact of an online game . *Journal of Broadcasting & Electronic Media, 50*(4), 651–670. doi:10.1207/s15506878jobem5004_5

Willoughby, T. (2008). A short-term longitudinal study of Internet and computer game use by adolescent boys and girls: prevalence, frequency of use and psychosocial predictors. *Developmental Psychology, 44*(1), 195–204. doi:10.1037/0012-1649.44.1.195

Wu, J., Li, P., & Rao, S. (2008). Why do they enjoy virtual game worlds? An empirical investigation. *Journal of Electronic Commerce Research, 9*(3), 219–231.

Wu, J., & Liu, D. (2007). The effects of trust and enjoyment on intention to play online games. *Journal of Electronic Commerce Research, 8*(2), 128–140.

Yang, S. C., & Tung, C.-J. (2007). Comparison of Internet addicts and non-addicts in Taiwanese high schools . *Computers in Human Behavior, 23*(1), 79–96. doi:10.1016/j.chb.2004.03.037

Ybarra, M. L., Alexander, M. P. H., & Mitchell, K. J. (2005). Depressive symptomatology, youth Internet use, and online interactions: A national survey. *The Journal of Adolescent Health, 36*(1), 9–18. doi:10.1016/j.jadohealth.2003.10.012

Yee, N. (2006). Motivations for play in online games. *Cyberpsychology & Behavior, 9*(6), 772–775. doi:10.1089/cpb.2006.9.772

Young, K. S. (1996, August, 15). *Internet addiction: The emergence of a new clinical disorder.* Paper presented at the 104th annual meeting of the American Psychological Association, Toronto, Canada. Retrieved from http://www.netaddiction.com/ articles/newdisorder.htm

Young, K. S. (1997). *What Makes the Internet Addictive? Potential Explanations for Pathological Internet Use.* Paper presented at the 105th annual conference of the American Psychological Association. Retrieved from http://www.healthyplace.com/Communities/ Addictions/netaddiction/ articles/ habitforming.htm

Young, K. S. (1998a). *Caught in the Net: How to recognize the signs of Internet addiction and a winning strategy for recovery.* New York: Wiley.

Young, K. S. (1998b). Internet addiction: The emergence of a new clinical disorder . *Cyberpsychology & Behavior*, *1*, 237–244. doi:10.1089/cpb.1998.1.237

Young, K. S. (2007). Cognitive Behavior Therapy with Internet Addicts: Treatment Outcomes and Implications . *Cyberpsychology & Behavior*, *10*(5), 671–679. doi:10.1089/cpb.2007.9971

Zackariasson, P., & Wilson, T. L. (2008). Game on: Competition and competitiveness in the video game industry. *Competition Forum*, *6*(1), 43–52.

This work was previously published in International Journal of Database Management, Volume 21, Issue 2, edited by Keng Siau, pp. 69-99, copyright 2010 by IGI Publishing (an imprint of IGI Global).

Chapter 9
Assigning Ontological Meaning to Workflow Nets

Pnina Soffer
University of Haifa, Israel

Maya Kaner
Ort Braude College, Israel

Yair Wand
University of British Columbia, Canada

ABSTRACT

A common way to represent organizational domains is the use of business process models. A Workflow-net (WF-net) is an application of Petri Nets (with additional rules) that model business process behavior. However, the use of WF-nets to model business processes has some shortcomings. In particular, no rules exist beyond the general constraints of WF-nets to guide the mapping of an actual process into a net. Syntactically correct WF-nets may provide meaningful models of how organizations conduct their business processes. Moreover, the processes represented by these nets may not be feasible to execute or reach their business goals when executed. In this paper, the authors propose a set of rules for mapping the domain in which a process operates into a WF-net, which they derived by attaching ontological semantics to WF-nets. The rules guide the construction of WF-nets, which are meaningful in that their nodes and transitions are directly related to the modeled (business) domains. Furthermore, the proposed semantics imposes on the process models constraints that guide the development of valid process models, namely, models that assure that the process can accomplish its goal when executed.

1. INTRODUCTION

Process models are widely used to model how an organization conducts its activities to accomplish its goals. In that sense, process models are a widely used type of conceptual models. Process modeling

is a complicated task and, hence, error-prone (e.g., Sadiq & Orlowska, 1997; Mendling, 2007). The syntax of process modeling languages specifies how to compose their constructs (which often have graphical notation) into process models. However, syntactically correct process models are not necessarily meaningful in terms of conveying the way the business conducts its activities.

DOI: 10.4018/978-1-61350-471-0.ch009

Moreover, a syntactically correct model might not even be feasible to execute, and even if it is, it cannot always be assured to reach its goal, namely, produce its required outcome. Some meaning can be represented in a process model via the semantics of the modeling language used. These semantics are believed to represent some real-world phenomena, and can be defined textually or mathematically. Either representation may have shortcomings. Textual definitions are typically semi-formal or informal (e.g., "An event is something that "happens" during the course of a business process" (Object Management Group, 2006)), and therefore do not provide representations that are sufficiently precise for formal analysis. In contrast, mathematically-based process representations (e.g., Petri nets (Petri, 1962), YAWL (van der Aalst & ter Hofstede, 2005), Pi Calculus (Milner, Parrow & Walker, 1992)), allow formal analysis and automated verification of models, but their semantics may not be readily associated with the problem domain.

Much effort has been devoted to the formal analysis and verification of process models, leading to methods and tools for analyzing structural properties of process models and for detecting logical problems in them. In particular, Workflow nets (WF-nets)—a special case of Petri nets—have been proposed as tools for modeling the dynamics of processes (van der Aalst, 1998). A Workflow net is a Petri net which (1) has one input place and one output place; and (2) does not contain dangling transitions or places (namely, transitions that might not fire or places that might not be populated). This is equivalent to the net being strongly connected if the output place is interlinked to the input place via an additional transition (van der Aalst, 1998). Workflow nets employ a small set of constructs, yet possess an impressive expressive power and can be used to represent precisely the entire set of workflow patterns (van der Aalst et. al, 2003, Russel et al., 2006).

An extensive body of work exists regarding the mathematical, structural, and behavioral proper-

ties of Petri nets, such as free choice, liveness, boundedness and strong connectedness (e.g., Esparza & Silva, 1990; Jensen, 1990; Desel & Esparza, 1995). These properties have been adapted for WF nets, and additional properties (such as soundness, relating to the process dynamics) have been defined (e.g., van der Aalst, 2000). Furthermore, these properties serve for formalizing and analyzing models in other process modeling languages (such as in EPC (van der Aalst, 1999) and in general workflow (van Hee et al., 2008).

The mathematical semantics of Petri nets (and of WF-nets) is based on the dynamics of tokens that propagate through the net. While supporting formal analysis of process dynamics, Petri net token-based models have several disadvantages. First, they provide abstraction of transitions that can occur during the process. However, being abstract, the transitions in a net do not necessarily convey clearly the real world (dynamic) phenomena that occur in the domain in which the process operates. In other words, a transition does not necessarily reflect a change in the domain that has a clear meaning to stakeholders. In particular, no rules exist for mapping of the real world domain (part of an organization or a business) in which the process takes place into a WF-net beyond the general requirements of WF-nets. Hence, such models are not necessarily meaningful to stakeholders and, beyond that, processes represented by WF-nets might not even be feasible to execute in practice or might not be able to accomplish stakeholders' goals. Second, an important advantage of WF-nets is that they possess several structural or behavioral properties which can be useful in formal analysis. Structural properties relate to the structure of the net, independent of its specific marking and include, in particular, free choice and well-structuredness (van der Aalst, 1998). Behavioral properties are initial marking dependent and include, in particular, soundness, separability and serialisability (van der Aalst, 1998; van Hee, Sidorova & Voorhoeve, 2008; Salimifard & Wright, 2001). However, without well-defined domain semantics assigned to places and transitions, the practical meaning of these properties, namely, what they imply about the domain phenomena they stand for, and their implication to process design is unclear. Finally, the formal analysis and verification of the above properties can be successfully applied to already developed models and identify potential problems in executing these models. However, without a clear mapping of these properties to the process domain, such analysis does not provide guidance to process designers on how to develop valid process models.

In summary, while WF-nets have well-defined formal semantics, this semantics might not necessarily convey the actual business meaning of components of a model. Consequently, the various formally-defined properties of WF-net do not necessarily translate to phenomena that are meaningful to stakeholders. As well, the formal semantics does not provide guidance for constructing useful process models. In short, the use of WF-nets to model business processes might tend to sacrifice the understandability and meaningfulness expected from conceptual models for formality.

We propose that the above disadvantages of WF-nets can be overcome, at least in part, by attaching "real world" meaning to their main constructs – places, transitions, and tokens, and by constraining how actual process domains should be represented using these constructs. To accomplish this objective, we follow a line of research that analyzes conceptual models in general, and process modeling languages and their constructs in particular, using ontological concepts. Ontological models represent beliefs about what exists and might happen in the world. Hence, ontological concepts can be used to convey real-world semantics. Specifically, we use the Generic Process Model (GPM) which provides a process specification semantics based on ontological constructs and is intended as a framework for reasoning about process models in terms of their

real-world meaning. GPM was used to define the notion of goals in business processes, to analyze process model validity, and to suggest an interpretation of control flow structures (Soffer & Wand, 2007; Soffer, Wand & Kaner, 2007).

In this paper we show how the combination of the formal power of WF-nets and the "real world" semantics provided by ontology can lead to better-designed process models. We use GPM concepts to add ontological semantics to WF-nets and to generate necessary conditions for creating semantically meaningful WF-nets. In addition, we propose modeling rules to guide the development of models of processes that reach their goals when executed.

In the following, Section 2 summarizes the main WF-net concepts and motivates our work; Section 3 introduces GPM and its control flow interpretation; Section 4 maps GPM concepts into WF-net constructs; Section 5 analyzes some useful properties of GPM-mapped WF-net; Section 6 presents rules for constructing valid process models; Section 7 demonstrates the application of the proposed rules; Section 8 discusses related work; Section 9 discusses our proposition in a broader context of conceptual modeling, and Section 9 is a conclusion.

2. PETRI-NETS AND WORKFLOW-NETS

This section provides some definitions of Petri-nets in general and Workflow-nets in particular, and their properties which are relevant for our discussion.

A Petri-net is a directed bipartite graph with two node types called places (designated by circles) and transitions (designated by rectangles), connected by arcs. Connections between two nodes of the same type are not allowed.

Definition 1 (Petri net): A Petri-net is a triple (P, T, F):

○ P is a finite set of places;

○ T is a finite set of transitions ($P \cap T = \emptyset$)

○ $F \subseteq (P \times T) \cup (T \times P)$ is a set of arcs.

At any time a place contains zero or more tokens (designated as black dots inside the place circle). The state of the net is defined by the distribution of tokens over places. A place p is termed as *input* of transition t if it has an arc directed from it to t, and an *output* of t if there is an arc directed to it from t. The notations •t, t•, •p, p• indicate the sets of input (preset) and output (postset) places of transition t and the sets of transitions of which p is an output and input place, respectively.[1]

The state of a Petri net changes through its execution according to the following firing rules:

1. A transition t is enabled if each input place p of t contains at least one token.
2. An enabled transition may fire. If transition t fires, then t consumes one token from each input place p of t and produces one token for each output place p of t.

A firing sequence is a sequence of transitions that occur where each one generates tokens in its output places so the next transition is enabled. Given two states M_1 and M_n, $M_1 \xrightarrow{\sigma} M_n$ denotes that M_n is reachable from M_1 through a firing sequence σ.

The syntax of Petri nets is almost free of restrictions, except for the alternating nature of places and transitions. Hence, the fact that a Petri net is syntactically correct does not imply that it represents some real system. Nevertheless, the mathematical basis of Petri nets enabled precise definitions of structural properties which may imply the behavior of systems that can be modeled through Petri nets. Some of these properties, relevant for our discussion, are defined below.

Definition 2 (bounded): A Petri net is *bounded* if for each place p there is a natural number n such that for every reachable state the number of tokens in p is less than n.

The meaning of boundedness is there cannot be a transition or a loop in the net that will cause the number of tokens in a place to increase indefinitely.

Definition 3 (free choice): A Petri net is a *free choice* Petri net if, for every two transitions t_1 and t_2, $•t_1 \cap •t_2 \neq \emptyset$ implies $•t_1 = •t_2$.

Free choice means that if p is an input to t then every input place of t is also an input to every transition for which p is an input. Under such conditions all transitions that share p as input place are enabled when p is populated, and can fire independently of the state of the rest of the net (hence the name "free choice"). In a Petri net which is not free choice cases of combined concurrency and conflict arise. Such cases are hard to analyze and considered inappropriate (van der Aalst, 2000, 2003). Most of the mathematically-based properties identified and analyzed with respect to Petri nets relate to free-choice Petri nets only.

Petri nets can be used for representing various kinds of systems. A specific form of Petri net, specifically intended for workflow modeling is a *Workflow net* (WF net, van der Aalst, 1998).

Definition 4 (Workflow net): A Petri net (P, T, F) is a *Workflow net* (WF-net) if:

i. There is one source place $i \in P$ such that $•i = \emptyset$.

ii. There is one sink place $o \in P$ such that $o• = \emptyset$.

iii. Every node $x \in P \cup T$ is on a path from i to o.

An activation of a WF-net is interpreted as representing the life-cycle of a single workflow case in isolation (van der Aalst, 1998). For a given case it has an initial state following the generation of a case, where only one token exists in place *i*, and a final state *o* after which the case is deleted.

Several properties of interest are defined for WF-nets. Of particular importance is *soundness* which is considered desirable and for which WF-nets are expected to be verified.

Definition 5 (sound): A procedure modeled by a WF-net PN= (*P, T, F*) is *sound* if:

i. For every state M reachable from state *i*, there exists a firing sequence leading from state M to state *o*.

ii. *o* is the only state reachable from state *i* with at least one token in place *o*.

iii. There are no dead transitions in (PN, *i*).[2]

Soundness means that the modeled procedure will terminate eventually, and properly (i.e. no further transition will occur after the sink has been populated). It can be verified in polynomial time for free-choice WF-nets (van der Aalst, 2000).

Another property, closely related to soundness, is *well-structuredness*. In a well-structured WF-net a splitting point and a merging point which

correspond to each other are of the same type, namely, a split at a place (transition) corresponds to a merge at a place (transition). More specifically, in a well-structured WF-net, when a place is an input to more than one transition – a choice occurs into two sequences. The two possible sequences must merge on a place that can be populated by transitions from either sequence. When a transition populates several places, this can cause parallel sequences that eventually lead to one transition, where the parallel sequences synchronize.

Soundness as well as other properties are useful for verifying a predictable behavior of the represented process (or workflow), and in particular, its ability to complete its execution. According to these properties, the prediction of behavior strictly relies on the net structure, regardless of the domain assumed to be represented. The implicit assumption is that the WF-net truthfully represents the domain under consideration. However, since the token semantics is detached from the real-world business semantics of the domain, this assumption is not straightforward, as shown in the example in Figure 1.

Figure 1. WF-net examples

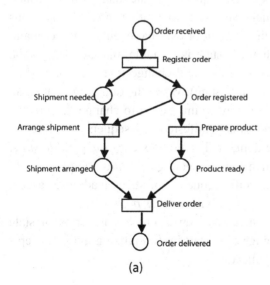

(a)

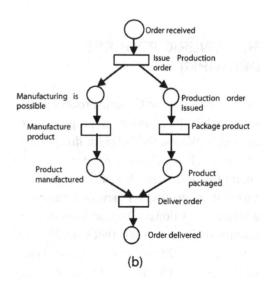

(b)

The WF net in Figure 1(a) is syntactically correct. However, when executed, only one of the transitions that follow the place *Order registered* can be fired, either *Prepare product* or *Arrange shipment*. As a result, the transition *Deliver order* will not be able to fire, and the net will be in a deadlock situation. This problem can be identified based on the token dynamics of the net: only one token can reach either the *Product ready* or the *Shipment arranged* places, while *Deliver order* requires tokens in both places. Note that this net is not sound, not free-choice, and not well-structured. Considering the (syntactically correct) WF net of Figure 1(b) in terms of token dynamics, no problem can be identified. The net is free choice, well structured, and sound. However, in terms of the domain semantics, it is not possible to concurrently manufacture a product and package it. Apparently, token-based semantics, which is not anchored in real-world concepts, cannot deal with this kind of modeling problems. Our aim in this work is to propose an alternative semantic interpretation of WF-nets, which will be able to account for both the identification and the prevention of both types of problems. To this end, we anchor the proposed semantics in the Generic Process Model (GPM), whose basis is a generic ontology, consisting of basic real world concepts, as presented in the following section.

3. THE GENERIC PROCESS MODEL (GPM)

This section presents the Generic Process Model (GPM), which is the basis for our proposed WF-net semantics. We use the GPM for this purpose for two reasons. First, a WF-net can be considered as depicting state changes that can or must occur. GPM formalizes an abstract view of a process in terms of state transitions that occur rather than using common notions such as activities and control flows. Second, the GPM affords an integrated view of a goal as part of the process definition. Since

incorporation of goals can support validity analysis of process models, we will use it to motivate or interpret desired characteristics of WF-nets.

The focus of GPM analysis is a *domain*, which is a part of the world consisting of interacting *things*. We describe the behavior of the domain using concepts from Bunge's ontology (Bunge, 1977; Bunge, 1979) as adapted to information systems and to the evaluation of conceptual modeling (Wand & Weber, 1993, 1995; Weber, 2004) and to process modeling (Soffer & Wand, 2005, 2007). A domain is represented by a set of *state variables*, each representing a *property* of the domain and its value at a moment in time. These properties are either inherited - properties of things in the domain, or emergent – properties that reflect interactions of things in the domain. The state of the domain can change either due to actions within the domain (*internal events*) or by stimuli from outside the domain (*external events*). An *unstable state* is a state that must change due to actions in the domain (manifested as internal events). A *stable state* is a state that only changes due to actions of the environment on the domain (manifested as external events). Internal events are governed by *transformation (transition) laws* that define the allowed (and sometimes necessary) state transitions (the internal events). A successful *process* is a sequence of state changes in the domain which can result from either internal transitions in the domain or external events to the domain. When the state is unstable, the law defines the transition that will change it (to an unstable or to a stable state). When the domain is stable, an external event must exist to change it. Thus the process is manifested as a sequence of *states* of the domain. The process ends on a *stable state*, which is in the set of *goal states* (simply – *goal*). A specific sequence of states leading to a goal state is termed a *process path*.

Since we view a process in terms of state changes, we start by formalizing these concepts as follows:

Definition 6(domain model, state variables): A *domain model* is a set of state functions $D=\{f_1(t)...f_n(t)\}$. The value of $f_k(t)$ at a given time is termed a *state variable*, denoted x_k.

The set of state variables for domain D is denoted by $X^D=\{x_k; k \in I=\{1...n\}\}$. The state of the domain at a given time is $s(D)=<x_1,...x_n>$ (or simply s). The set of possible states of the domain D is denoted by S(D).

For example, assume the domain refers to production in an industrial company. The domain comprises various workstations. The state variables can describe, at a given time, for each machine, the product it processes and the status of unprocessed and processed components near each machine.

Domain dynamics is described in terms of state changes. We describe state changes that can occur due to actions within the domain in terms of *transformation law*:

Definition 7(transformation law): A *transformation law* on D is a mapping $L_D:S(D) \rightarrow S(D)$

For example, the law can specify that when a machine is not busy and there is a supply of unprocessed components available, the machine will change state to "busy, working on the specific components". For some states there are no possible actions that can change them. Such states are mapped into themselves and are termed *stable states*.

Definition 8(stable / unstable state): A domain will be said to be in a *stable state* if $L_D(s)=s$ and in an *unstable state* if $L_D(s) \neq s$.

For example, when a machine is idle, and there is no available supply of components to be processed by it, the machine is in a stable state.

The above definitions do not limit the mapping defined by the transition law. In particular, it is possible that one state will map into several states. For example, if several types of components are available for an idle machine, the next state might involve working on any of these types. However, when designing business processes, we are usually interested in predictable behavior. Hence we define:

Definition 9(well-defined law): A law will be said to be *well-defined* if it is a function. [3]

Considering the machine example, assume the rule is that the machine will always begin working on the items that take the shortest amount of time. Assuming there are always differences in time to process different items, if the state information includes the number of items of each type available to be processed, then the transition law from "idle" to "busy" is a function.

Often, several domain states can be considered equivalent. For example, for no charge on transactions a bank account might only need to be above a minimal balance. Hence, the transformation law can be represented as a mapping between sets of states. Such a set can sometimes be specified by a predicate on values of the state variables - C(s) (as in the bank example above). In particular, often the process goal is a set of stable states, specified by a predicate that manifests business objectives to be fulfilled by the process.

The notion of the transformation law ($L_D(s)$) is of particular importance to our analysis. Since the transformation law defines the state changes that can or must occur, it determines the possible sequences of states – namely process paths. In this sense, the task of the process designer can be described as implementing a transformation law so that the process can accomplish its goal.

In GPM, a process in an abstract fashion is a sequence of states in a domain. However, in practice, processes typically comprise actions that impact only part of the domain at a time. For example, in a production process, different machines might process different components at different times. Each machine can be considered as an independently operating part of the domain. We formalize this view by considering a domain as comprising *sub-domains*, each represented by a subset of the domain state variables. The partitioning of a domain to sub-domains provides the bridge between the (abstract) view of a process in terms of state changes of a domain and the actual implementation of the process in terms of active elements of the domain. Identification of such elements provides the business meaning of the state transitions that occur in a process. In our analysis of WF-nets, partitioning to sub-domains will be key to attaching business meaning to places and transitions. Hence, we explore the relationships between the behavior of the domain and its sub-domains.

When the state of the domain changes the state of at least one sub-domain must change. We say that the domain behavior is *projected* on its sub-domains. State changes that occur in a sub-domain when the domain changes state, are termed the *projections* of the state changes of the domain. Since the possible changes are defined in terms of the domain (transformation) law, the projections of these changes on a sub-domain can be viewed as defining a transformation law on the sub-domain. We term the latter the *projection* of the domain law on the sub-domain. In the following, definitions 10-13 formalize the concept of projection.

Definition 10(sub-domain): A *sub-domain* is part of the domain described by a subset of the set of domain state variables X^D.

Notation: A sub-domain D^1 of D is described in terms of $X^D1 \subset X^D$; $X^D1 = \{x_k ; k \in I^1 \subset I\}$. The state of D^1 is $s(D^1) = <x_{k1}, \ldots x_{k|I1|}>$, $k_j \in I^1$ and $k_j \neq k_l$ for $j \neq l$.

For example, in a job shop production environment, the state variables describing each machine can be viewed as describing a sub-domain of the full work in process (which comprises the states of all machines, workers, and products in processing).

We note that there might be many ways to partition a given domain into sub-domains. Different partitions can reflect different views of the process domain, and not all partitions will be meaningful to process stakeholders.

Definition 11(state projection): Let the state of D be $s = <x_1 \ldots x_n>$. The *projection* of s on the sub-domain D^1 is $s/D^1 = <y_1 \ldots y_{|I|}1>$ where $y_k = x_{I1(k)}$, $k = 1, \ldots |I^1|$

In the job shop example, a possible sub-domain is a cluster of machines and workers. The projection of the job-shop state on this sub-domain is the part of the work-in process that occurs in the cluster.

It is possible that several domain states will map on the same state of the sub-domain. When considering this state of the sub-domain, it might appear as transforming in different ways, depending on the state of the whole domain. To see this point, consider the job shop example. Different states of the overall work-in-process might appear the same within the specific cluster. However as the work in process changes differently (e.g., different components completed), the cluster state might change in different ways (different components will arrive for processing).

It follows, that to understand the actual change of state in a sub-domain, we need to know the state of the whole domain. We therefore define:

Definition 12(projecting set): Let v be a state of D^1. The *projecting set* of v in D is the set of states of D that project into v in D^1: $S(v;D) = \{s \in S(D) \mid s/D^1 = v\}$

In the example above, other clusters might change state, while a given cluster will stay in the same state. Thus, many work-in-process states will be mapped into one state in the cluster.

As noted above, key to our analysis is the view of domain state changes in terms of changes in sub-domains. The former are determined by the domain law. Consider a sub-domain state. There might be several domain states projecting to this sub-domain state. Each of these domain states might map differently. Each mapped state will have a projection in the sub-domain. Observing the sub-domain, it might appear that the original state can change in different ways. However, all are determined by the domain·law. We define the effect of the domain law (L) on a sub-domain, D^1 as follows.

Definition 13(law projection): Let $v \in S(D^1)$ and let $s(v;D)$ be the projecting set of v in D. The *law projection* of L_D on D^1 (denoted L/D^1) for v is defined by the mapping $L_D/D_1 : S(D^1) \to S(D^1)$ such that $L_D/D_1(v) = \cup \{L(s)/D^1 \mid s \in s(v;D)\}$.

In words, each state, v, of the sub-domain is mapped into the union of projections of all states in the projecting set of v. For example, let the states in D projecting to state v of D_1 be s_1 and s_2. Assume $L_D(s_k) = s'_k$, k=1,2. Then, $L_D/D_1(v) = \{s_1', s_2'\}$. In the job shop case, a worker can be in a state "assigned to task A" while other activities are being performed in the job shop. However, when each of these activities changes or is completed, the worker might be reassigned differently.

In general, the effect of the projected law will appear as unpredictable changes in the state of the sub-domain. It is possible, however, that the projected behavior of the whole domain on a sub-domain creates a well-defined function in the sub-domain. In other words, a given unstable state of the sub-domain will always map in the same way, independent of the state of the whole domain, and hence independent of the states of other sub-domains. In the job shop case this would mean that the worker will be always reassigned the same way after performing a given task (independent of what else is happening in the workshop). We will then say that the sub-domain behaves *independently* or that it is *independent*. Partitioning of the domain into independently-behaving sub-domains is often a consequence of different

actors acting in the domain. These actors can be people, departments, machines, computers and combinations of those. Hence, such partitioning is of special interest. It is possible that independent behavior of a sub-domain occurs for only a subset of domain states. For example, workers are assigned in the same way only when there are slack production resources. Formally, we define:

Definition 14(independent sub-domain): A sub-domain D^1 of D will be called an *independently behaving* (or *independent*) in a given state (of the sub-domain) if the law projection on D^1 is a function for this state.
Corollary: For an independent sub-domain the law projection is a function that depends only on state variables of the sub-domain.

Consider now a process as a set of states the domain traverses. Assume that for these states a set of sub-domains behaves so that each sub-domain, is independent and ends on a stable state (of the sub-domain). When a sub-domain reaches stability, there are three possibilities. First, the whole domain might reach a (stable) goal state. Second, the whole domain reaches a stable state not in the goal. An external event must then occur for the process to continue. Third, some other independent sub-domains will become unstable and will begin transforming. Thus, a sequence of state changes occurs, some as a result of well-defined transformations within sub-domains and some as a result of external events. This sequence comprises a process. Note that the decomposition of a domain into sub-domains is not usually a partition, in that sub-domains would usually share state variables.

To demonstrate, assume a sales department comprises two units – one that deals with order taking and one responsible for order fulfilling. An example for a process is that after order taking completes and the first sub-domain becomes stable, the fulfillment unit becomes unstable and starts planning how to fulfill the order.

Process models usually include split and merge points, which reflect either concurrency or choice between possible alternative paths. We now interpret these in GPM terms. First, it is possible that a set of states arrived at can be partitioned so the next transformation is defined differently for each subset of states. Such partitioning might occur because the law becomes "sensitive" to a certain state variable. Consider, for example, a process where a standard product is manufactured, and then packaged according to each customer's requirements. Manufacturing does not depend on the customer (even when the customer is known). When manufacturing is completed, customer information will determine a choice between packaging actions (such approach is termed postponement). This situation is an exclusive choice (an XOR split) between two paths of the process. The different actions may lead to states which are again equivalent for determining the next action (the law will not distinguish between different packaging options), for example, transferring the products to finished goods inventory. This is the point where the paths merge. For example, the merge point in the fulfillment process will occur when the product is packaged and is ready for shipment.

Formally, a choice between two process paths can be defined as follows:

Definition 15 (exclusive choice): S_{sp} is an *exclusive choice* splitting point if there exist sets of states $S_1, S_2 ... S_n$ such that $S_i \subset S_{sp}$, $S_j \cap S_k = \varnothing$, and $\forall s, t s \in S_i t \in S_j L(s) \neq L(t) \Leftrightarrow i \neq j, i, j = 1...n$.

In words, all states within a subset of states transform in the same way, and states from different subsets transform into different states.

The corresponding form of a merge (sometimes termed simple merge) is when a single set of states is reachable by law from different sets of states.

Definition 16 (simple merge): Let S_1, S_2, and S_{me} be non empty sets of states, such that $S_1 \cap S_2 = \varnothing$,

$S_k \cap S_{me} = \varnothing$; s_k states such that $s_k \in S_k$. S_{me} is a *simple merge* if $L(s_k) \in S_{me}$. $(k=1,2)$.

In words, a simple merge occurs when two different paths can reach states that map into the same given set of states. Note that this definition assumes the merge set is given. In particular, it enables defining a merge for any union of states that can be mapped into by the law from S_1 and S_2. However, we will be interested only in such unions where the states in S_{me} have some common characteristics. Specifically, this is the case when they are considered equivalent for the purpose of determining the next state changes in the domain. This means they are similar with respect to the domain law. For instance, in the product packaging example – the different packaging options end in states which are the same with respect to the next activity – shipping.

Also related to splitting and merging is *concurrency*. Since one domain cannot have concurrent transformations, concurrency should relate to transformations in different sub-domains. Concurrency means that each sub-domain proceeds independently through a sequence of (projected) states. All combinations of the projected states of the different sub-domains are possible (in principle). These combinations can be viewed as a "swarm" of states the decomposed domain undergoes. For example, in a domain comprising two machines that work in parallel, each going through three steps – setup, production, cleaning, the combined state can have different combinations. However, for such situations to occur a condition should be satisfied:

Lemma 1: Two sub-domains can transform concurrently only if they are independent.

Proof: Assume that two sub-domains are not independent. Then the transitions in one can depend on the state of the other. In this case, only some combinations of states of each sub-domain are possible.

It follows that a split leading to concurrency must be related to a decomposition of the domain into independently behaving sub-domains. In such a split, for the process to continue, at least one sub-domain must be unstable with respect to its (projected) law. If all these sub-domains are in unstable states for all states in the split, then this is a parallel split. Otherwise, several possibilities exist, depending on the number of the unstable sub-domains (see Soffer et al., 2007). In particular, if exactly one sub-domain can be in an unstable state, then, based on Definition 15, this is an exclusive choice. Formally, a parallel split is defined as follows:

Definition 17(parallel split): S_{sp} is a *parallel split* if there exist at least two sub-domains such that for every state in S_{sp} each sub-domain is independent and is in an unstable state.

For example, in the production and fulfillment process discussed above, once products are ready, the process domain can be decomposed into two independent sub-domains: one where shipment is arranged for some products, and one where the other products are transferred into the warehouse. These two sub-domains are independent and in an unstable state, thus they operate concurrently.

A decomposable domain may entail different types of merge points (see Soffer, Wand & Kaner, 2007). In particular, in a simple merge the completion of action of any sub-domain causes the process to proceed. In Petri Nets all input places for a transition have to be populated for the transition to "fire", thus, of particular interest is a *synchronizing merge*, where process continuation requires that all active sub-domains complete their tasks prior to continuation of the process. Consider a set of states in a merge point. These states should be unstable to enable the process to continue. They should be reachable from the split and hence for each sub-domain, the projected state at the merge should be reachable from the projected state at the split. In a synchronizing

merge, each sub-domain becomes stable at the merge ("waiting" for the other sub-domains). Once all sub-domains reach the merge, the process can continue. For this, another sub-domain must become unstable. We term this the *continuation* sub-domain. This sub-domain must share some state variables with each of the synchronizing sub-domains. Otherwise, the state of the sub-domain will not affect the continuation sub-domain and synchronization will not occur. Formally:

Definition 18(synchronizing merge): Let $D^k \subset D$, k=1...n be independent sub-domains operating concurrently following a split point S_{sp}. S_{me} is a *synchronizing merge* if a sub-domain D^C exists, which shares state variables with each of the sub-domains ($D^C \cap D^k \neq \varnothing \ \forall k$) such that:

$$\forall s \in S_{me} : s/D^C \text{ is unstable} \Leftrightarrow \forall k=1...n$$
$$\exists u_k \in S(D^k), u_k = s/D^k, u_k \text{ stable } \& \ \exists v_k \in S(D^k),$$
$$v_k \neq s/D^k.$$

The definition implies three things: (1) Each sub-domain has at least two states. One state is stable (u_k) and projected to from a domain state where the continuation sub-domain D^C is unstable. The other state (v_k) does not project onto an unstable state of D^C (otherwise, there will be no path in the sub-domain). (2) For each sub-domain, there is at least one u_k that projects onto the same unstable state of D^C as all other sub-domains. (3) There are no other unstable states of the D^C projected into by a state in the merge set (S_{me}). The stability in (1) assures each sub-domain will "wait" for the others. Point (3) assures that D^C will only begin changing when all sub-domains have "arrived" at their "appropriate" states (u_k). Together, these conditions assure synchronization.

To demonstrate the definition, consider a process where several parts need to be manufactured for a product to be assembled. When the need to assemble the product arises, the domain enters a split state where each part is made by a separate production cell. When each cell has completed making the part, the cell "rests". Only when all cells completed (hence each is at rest – in a stable state), the domain enters a state where the product can be assembled. Beginning of production for each cell is the projection of the split state onto an unstable state of the cell. End of production is the projection of the continuation state onto a stable state of the cell.

Finally, the explicit representation of process goal in GPM can be used to support the analysis of process models for goal reachability. A process whose design ensures its goal will always be achieved under a certain set of events external to the domain is termed *valid* (Soffer & Wand, 2007) with respect to this set of events.

4. GPM AS A SEMANTIC BASIS FOR WF-NETS

In this section we propose a GPM-based semantics to WF- nets. For convenience, we first present an informal overview of the GPM interpretation of WF-net constructs and then provide formal definitions and an in-depth discussion of the consequences of this semantics. The main principles underlying the added semantics are:

1. A place in the net represents a set of states of a sub-domain. This sub-domain is represented by a sub-set of state variables of the domain in which the process operates). Below, we will refer to "input" or "output" sub-domains when a place is an input to or an output of a transition, respectively.
2. A populated place indicates that the sub-domain corresponding to the place is in one of the states represented by the place. If the place can have more than one token, this indicates the set of states represented by it can be partitioned.
3. A transition indicates a change of state of a sub-domain. Since the transition depends on the input places and modifies the output places, the sub-domain in which it occurs

must overlap (in terms of state variables) with the sub-domains of the input and output places.

We note that this semantics allows for different places on the net to represent states of the same sub-domain. Also, the sub-domain can be the whole domain. This is the case for the source and the sink nodes of a WF-net. We present an informal description of the semantics of the basic building blocks of WF-nets in Table 1.

We focus our discussion on WF-nets, since these have a distinct termination place, which may correspond to GPM's goal concept. Nevertheless, most of the discussion is applicable to Petri nets in general. As shown in Table 1, every basic WF-net construct and building block can be assigned a GPM-based interpretation. We do not attempt to do a reverse mapping, namely interpret GPM terms using WF-nets, since GPM addresses issues beyond the control flow of the process, which are not in the scope of WF-nets. However, considering the proposed control flow mapping, this interpretation assumes certain domain semantics assigned to the places and transitions of a WF-net. This semantics poses requirements which do not exist in the WF-net syntax. If these requirements are not met, a WF-net cannot be transformed into a meaningful GPM specification. It can thus be claimed that the expressive power of WF-nets exceeds the expressive power of GPM with respect to control flow, in that the former enables structures not possible in the latter. Alternatively, it can be argued that WF-net syntax, being anchored in mathematical semantics of graphical symbols, allows structures which are not necessarily possible in reality.

We now proceed to formally define the proposed GPM-based semantics for WF-net and resulting restrictions on the models. We define the following class of WF-nets which are consistent with the GPM-based semantics.

Table 1. GPM interpretation of WF-Net constructs and basic building blocks (the word "state" in the table refers to a state of a sub-domain)

WF-net construct / building block	GPM interpretation
Place p	A set of states of a sub-domain (the projection of a set of states over a sub-domain)
A populated place	A sub-domain is in one of the states represented by the place
Transition t	A possible transformation in a sub-domain
Arc	An arc into a transition means the transformation law uses the values of the state variables of the input sub-domains. An arc into a place means the transformation can change the states of the output sub-domains.
Initial place *i*	The initial set of states I
Final place *o*	The goal set (of domain states) G
Sequence	t_1 is a transformation in a sub-domain, from a set of states p_1 into a set of states p_2
A parallel split	t_1 is a transformation after which the domain becomes decomposable, where p_1 and p_2 are state projections over different sub-domains. Note, if the domain is not decomposable, the places would be shown as one place (sequence).
A synchronizing merge	t_1 is a transformation whose initial set of states is $p_1 \cap p_2$[4] p_1 and p_2 refer to different sub-domains.
An exclusive choice	p_1 is a set of states in which one of two sub-domain transformations is possible. These transformations can be in the same sub-domain or in different sub-domains.
A simple merge	p_1 is a set of states reachable by two transformations, t_1 and t_2, separately[5]

Definition 19 (well-mapped domain representation): A WF-net is a *well-mapped domain representation* if it can be mapped to a GPM specification. Specifically:

1. Each place can be associated with a set of states of a sub-domain.
2. Each transition can be associated with a change of state of a sub-domain.
3. The initial place represents unstable states of the domain.
4. The sink place represents the goal states of a process in the domain.

While a well-mapped domain representation WF-net (well-mapped WF-net in short) can be understood using the traditional token-based semantics, its underlying semantics is based on GPM. This semantics imposes some restrictions on the model. We will now elaborate this semantics and its resulting restrictions. We start by assigning a meaning to WF-net places.

Definition 20 (populated place): A populated place in a well mapped WF-net represents a set of states of a sub-domain. Let $p_k \in P$, then $\exists D_k \subseteq D$ such that p_k is active if D_k is in a given set of states $S_{pk} \subseteq S(D)/D_k$.

As an example, a place where an order has arrived represents a set of states of the sub-domain of order management. We denote the sub-domain by D_{pk}, its state variables as $X^p k$ and the set of states indicated by the place by S_{pk}. To indicate that D_k is in a state in S_{pk} we can use a *place predicate* - $C(X^p k)$ defined by: $C(X^p k)=$'True' $\Leftrightarrow$ s/ $D_k \in S_{pk.}$ Thus, p_k is active if $C(X^p k)$ is TRUE. Sometimes $C(X^p k)$ can be defined by a function on some state variables of D_k. For example, the sub-domain D_k might represent the state of a machine. The predicate will be true if the machine is idle.

As indicated, $C(X^p k)$=TRUE is equivalent to the existence tokens in p_k. Consider what having more than one token might mean. From the input view of the place, adding a token to an already populated place means a change in the state of the sub-domain without a change in the value of its predicate (which was already TRUE). From the output perspective, an active place p_k implies that the sub-domain D_k is in a state which is necessary (and sufficient if it is the only input) for a transition to fire. After the transition has fired, if there was more than one token, the input place is still populated. This means that the domain D_k, although having changed its state, is still in one of the states defining the place. Hence, this implies the set of states represented by p_k can be partitioned. One possible way to represent such partitioning is to decompose the predicate $C(X^p k)$ to components, each true if is Dk is in one of the subsets of states. Clearly, $C(X^p k)$ must be a conjunction of these components.

If these sub-predicates are based on state variables expressions, then the place predicate is of the form *<Expression OR Expression OR...>*. As an example, consider an order delivery process, where the customer orders several items which can be manufactured concurrently, and each item is delivered once it is ready. This can be modeled by a single place prior to delivery, whose predicate would be ((Item A=ready) OR (Item B=ready) OR...). The arrival of each item can be modeled as adding a token to that place, triggering the delivery transition. The transition can fire again for each item.

Using the above interpretation, the maximal number of tokens in a place is the number of atomic expressions related by an OR in the predicate that defines it. If the place predicate cannot be decomposed, then the maximal number of tokens allowed in that place is 1. Also, it is clear that an infinite partitioning of the states associated with p_k is impractical. Hence, the number of token should be bounded. Hence:

Lemma 2: A well mapped WF-net is bounded.

The dynamics of a well mapped WF-net is established by the transitions, each transforming the state of a defined sub-domain. According to the Petri net semantics, transitions are *enabled* by the existence of tokens in their input places, and they pass a token to each of their output places. According to the GPM view, a transition occurs in a sub-domain once it arrives at an unstable state and hence must transform it to a new state. If the process is to continue, the transition must cause a new sub-domain to reach a new state (which would be unstable unless it is the sink state). For this to happen, the affected sub-domain should share state variables with the one that has transformed. The above means that both input sub-domains and output sub-domains must share state variables with the transition domain. We formalize all this as follows:

Definition 21(transition sub-domains): Let $t \in T$ be a transition, •t its input places, and t• its output places. The *input sub-domain* of t is $D_{•t}$ defined by $X^{•t} = \cup \{X^p, p \in •t\}$, the *output sub-domain* of t is $D_{t•}$ defined by $X^{t•} = \cup \{X^p, p \in t•\}$. The *transformed sub-domain* D_t is the sub-domain changed by t, and its set of state variables is denoted X^t

For example, a delivery transition has the customer order and the availability of goods in its input places; it transforms the order status and the inventory level state variables, so their new values should be reflected in the output place(s).

Definitions 19, 20 and 21 address structural properties of the net. However, the net should also represent the dynamics of the domain. Hence, based on the definition of a well-mapped WF-net, and on the GPM dynamics, the following can be formulated (equivalent to the Petri net firing rules).

Dynamics rule: Let t be a transition in a well mapped WF-net.

    A. $D_{•t}$ is in an unstable state if $C(X^p k)=$TRUE $\forall p_k \in •t$.

B. "Firing" t results in $C(X^{p}k)=TRUE$ $\forall p_{k} \in t\bullet$.

We have now defined the rules about structure and dynamics of a well-mapped WF-net. Each element in such a net has a well defined domain meaning. However, when modeling processes in GPM various relationships exist between transition laws and the definitions of sub-domains. In particular, a sub-domain is "meaningful" if the domain law projects on it a well-defined (i.e. a function) transition law. As well, the process goal must be a set of stable states. It follows, that when places and transitions in a WF-net are assigned domain meaning, certain constraints on the net must hold, so domain relationships will be correctly represented. This leads to four requirements on well-mapped WF-nets. These requirements are intended to assure four conditions:

1. Each transition operates in, and only in, the sub-domains associated with its input and output places.
2. Each transition represents a well defined law.
3. For any concurrent decomposition – the sub-domains are independent.
4. The sink place of the net represents only stable states.

Below we formulate these requirements in terms of four necessary conditions.

Necessary condition 1 (transition domain structure): $\forall t \in T$:
   A. The input, output, and transformed sub-domains satisfy $X^{t} \subseteq X^{\bullet t}$ and $X^{t} \subseteq X^{t \bullet}$.
   B. Let $X^{*} = \mathbf{X}^{\bullet t} \cap \mathbf{X}^{\bullet t}$ and let $X^{diff} \subseteq X^{*}$ be the set of state variables whose values in the input places and in the output places are different. X^{diff} cannot be empty, because otherwise t will have no effect. Then $X^{diff} \subseteq X^{t}$.

For example, assume a transition represents manufacturing a product. Its input places indicate when raw materials and resources are available and a finished product is required. This is an unstable state. The transition should "use" only state variables from its inputs (e.g., raw materials and resources), transform their state (e.g., raw material is consumed, finished product is manufactured), so its output places (e.g., where the product is ready for packaging) become active. It is not possible for an unrelated state variable (e.g., delivery arrangement) to change its state through this transition. Note, the output places of this transition may still represent an unstable state, in case they serve as input places of other transitions (e.g. packaging and shipping the ready product).

For a transition to act within a sub-domain, the sub-domain must be independent (i.e. its law is a function) for the set of states represented by the transition's input places. Hence, we formalize the following condition:

Necessary condition 2 (transition independence): $\forall t \in T$, $\bullet t$ represents a set of states in which $D_{\bullet t}$ is independent.

The dynamic rule and the transition independence condition have certain important implications. First, according to Necessary condition 2, if a place is the only input place of a transition, then it represents a set of states in which its sub-domain is independent. It follows that a place cannot be the sole input place of a transition and part of a set of input places of another one at the same time. If this could happen then it would be possible the other place will fire first, and the present transition will be unpredictable. This structure is often used in WF-nets and is sometimes associated with situations which are hard to analyze. As an example, consider two workers performing tasks in parallelEach worker, when completing the task, checks on the other worker and decides whether to wait for the other to finish so they can have coffee together, or continue independently with a new task. Such a situation is sometimes modeled as a decision between a transition of "having coffee" synchronizing the two sub-domains and a transition of "next task" with just one input place (worker finished previous task). However, this decision is not made independently of the other sub-domain – "next task" will be chosen if the other worker is still busy and not otherwise. Second, consider a set of places which are inputs for a transition. The transition can fire only when all places are populated. When this happens, at least one of the sub-domains must change its state (see the dynamic rule above). Hence, the input places cannot behave as independent sub-domains.

We now turn to address the notion of path. As opposed to the path definition in Petri nets, which relates to any sequence of connected elements, we relate to *domain paths* (D-paths), which correspond to selected sequences of states of the domain. GPM defines a path as a set of states the domain goes through, via a sequence of transitions, determined by the law and by external events (see Section 2). Petri nets (and specifically, WF-nets) do not explicitly address external events, assuming they will occur as expected (van der Aalst, 1998). The state of a WF-net (considering the process as operating over one domain) is defined as the distribution ("marking") of tokens at a given moment in time. According to our view, we may look at the entire process domain or at any of its sub-domains. In the WF-net the state of a given (sub)domain is reflected by the predicate values of its places. Considering a sub-domain D_a, its state is the distribution of active places $(p_j, C(X^p j)=\text{TRUE})$ at a given moment in all the places p_j that satisfy $X^p j \subseteq X^{Da}$. We denote the state of sub-domain D_a by M^{Da}. The above indicates that as the network undergoes transitions, the sub-domain will be changing states. We formalize this as follows:

Definition 22: Let D_a be a sub-domain in a WF-net.[6] A *domain path* (abbreviated to D-path) of D_a is a sequence of states of D $<M^D_1,$ $M^D_2,...M^D_K>$, such that a sequence of transi-

tions $<t_1, t_2,...t_{k-1}>$ exists that satisfies $M^D_i \underset{t_1}{\rightarrow}$ $M^D_{i+1} \underset{t_{l+1}}{\rightarrow} \cdots \underset{t_{k-1}}{\rightarrow} M^D_k$, for $1 \leq i \leq k\text{-}1$.

For clarity, we hereafter relate to domain paths as D-paths and to "ordinary" (or "traditional") Petri net paths simply as paths.

D-paths are demonstrated with respect to the WF-net in Figure 2, which includes four D-paths: (1) $p1 \rightarrow p6 \rightarrow p7$, (2) $p1 \rightarrow p2+p3 \rightarrow p4+p5 \rightarrow p7$, (3) $p1 \rightarrow p2+p3 \rightarrow p2+p5 \rightarrow p4+p5 \rightarrow p7$, and (4) $p1 \rightarrow p2+p3 \rightarrow p3+p4 \rightarrow p4+p5 \rightarrow p7$. These are not equivalent to the three "ordinary" paths of the net. When examining the four D-paths, it is clear that three of them (D-paths 2, 3, and 4) relate to different orderings in which the concurrent transitions can be performed, while D-path 1 specifies a different way for reaching p7. This can be formalized in the following definition:

Definition 23 (distinct D-path): Let Ac be the set of places that become active in D-path C. Two D-paths C_1 and C_2 are termed *distinct* if $Ac_1 \nsubseteq Ac_2$ and $Ac_2 \nsubseteq Ac_1$.

Figure 2 demonstrates a significant difference between D-paths and "ordinary" paths. In concurrent threads that follow parallel splits (for example, the transition to p_2 and p_3 in Figure 1) the domain is decomposed into independently transforming sub-domains. In the graphical Petri net representation the sequence of elements in each sub-domain forms a different "path". Considering the sequences of states the (entire) domain may traverse in such situation, the number of D-paths is combinatorial. However, none of them is distinct with respect to the others (see for example

Figure 2. D-paths example

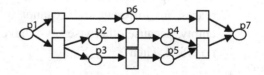

three combinations of the sequences beginning on p_2 and p_3). It follows, that distinct D-paths of the same domain are formed where decisions are made (in Figure 1 – the decision between the two transitions at p_1). Finally, note that considering the entire process domain, every D-path is equivalent to a path in the reachability graph[7] of the net, going from the source node to the sink node.

We now turn to address concurrency. Based on Lemma 1 (Section 2), concurrently operating threads must operate over independent sub-domains. To behave independently, no transition in the sub-domain should be affected by state variables that can be changed in other domains. This implies that if two sub-domains share a state variable, then if this variable is changed in one sub-domain, it should have no impact on the transitions in the other sub-domain. For example, assume a manuscript is sent to a number of reviewers who review it in parallel. Each reviewer can be notified when another reviewer sends a review, but the decisions of each reviewer are independent. This can be modeled as independent sub-domains, sharing some state variables, transforming state variables which are not affected by the shared state variable. Finally, when all review reports are sent, a decision can be made about the paper. This can be considered synchronization of the sub-domains. The above idea is formalized in the following necessary condition.

Necessary condition 3 (concurrency): Let D_1 and D_2 be two sub-domains that may operate concurrently. There should be no state variable $x_i \in X^D j$ that changes in D_k such that the value of x_i affects the state changes occurring in D_k, $k \neq j$, k,j=1,2.

Note that while Necessary condition 3 addresses concurrency situations, we make no similar requirement with respect to choice-related splits (namely, several transitions sharing an input place). Since these may relate to both decomposable and non-decomposable domains (the transi-tions that are activated can occur in the same sub-domain or in different sub-domains), no strict rules can be formed.

While concurrency relates to independent sub-domains, we also take interest in the situation where sub-domains stop being independent. The following Lemma shows that this can only happen through synchronization.

Lemma 3: In a well-mapped WF-net two concur-rent sub-domains will stop being indepen-dent if a transition exists that depends on the states of both.

Proof: (1) By Necessary Condition 1 (transition domain structure), if such a transition exists, then it depends on the states of both sub-domains and affects at least one. Hence the sub-domains are not independent any more. (2) Assume one of the sub-domains reached a state in which it is not independent with respect to the other. This means, by defi-nition, that the law for that state depends on the state of the other sub-domain. In a well-mapped WF-net this can only be shown by a transition that has as input places the states of the two sub-domains, namely, a synchronizing merge.

One of the basic concepts in GPM is the goal of a process. The definition of well-mapped WF-net indicates that the sink place should represent the set of goal states of the process described by the net (condition (4) in definition 19). Since theses states should be stable, for a well-mapped WF-net the sink should represent a set of stable states. It follows that:

Necessary condition 4 (Stability): The sink place in a well-mapped WF net *o* marks a set of stable states of the entire process domain.

Consider now what stability at the goal means for a well-mapped WF-net. When the domain reaches the goal state, the process completes and there are no more transitions that can happen. This means that no sub-domain can be in an unstable state when the process reaches its goal. In the net, this would mean that no transition can "fire". For a transition to fire all its input places need to be active which means that the associated sub-domains must be in the states matching the input places. Thus, for no transition to be activated at least one input place for each transition should be empty. The following Lemma formalizes this:

Lemma 4: Let the set of domain states that match the sink place be S_{Sink}. A necessary and sufficient condition for a well-mapped net to be in a stable state at the sink is: $\forall s \in S_{Sink}$, $\forall t$, $\exists p \in \bullet t$ such that $s/D_p \notin S_p$.

A special case applies to loops in which action continues in parallel to the continuation of the process, namely, loops whose exit point is a parallel split, as formulated in the following corollary.

Corollary: Let a WF-net be well-mapped, and consider a transition t and three places p_1, p_2, and p_3, such that $p_1 = \bullet t$, $\bullet p_2 = \bullet p_3 = t$. Then p_1 is not reachable from p_2 or from p_3.

Proof: Assume p_1 is reachable from p_2. When t fires, p_2 and p_3 become active, and while p_3 may lead to o, p_2 will lead infinitely to the sequence that activates t. This means that o may be reached while the loop sub-domain is unstable, in contradiction to Necessary condition 4 (stability).

5. INTERPRETING WORKFLOW-NET PROPERTIES

Much of the research devoted to Petri nets in general, and WF-nets in particular, has addressed particular properties (such as free choice and well-structuredness) defined for these models. While these properties are well-defined in terms of model structure, their behavioral consequences are not well understood. In general, they are claimed to be associated with "good" process behavior (van der Aalst, 2000), but this claim is typically made in an informal manner and is not theoretically grounded. In this section we use the GPM-based semantics in order to explain the behavior associated with these properties. Furthermore, we show that the proposed semantics enables a more fine-grained distinction between "good" and "bad" behaviors of the structures under consideration. We focus on three known properties of WF-nets: being free- choice, well-structured, and S-coverable.

5.1 Free Choice

A Petri net is said to be free choice if, for every two transitions t_1 and t_2, $\bullet t_1 \cap \bullet t_2 \neq \emptyset$ implies $\bullet t_1 = \bullet t_2$ (Definition 3). A Petri net which is not free-choice usually involves a mixture of choice and parallelism, which is hard to analyze and considered inappropriate (albeit syntactically possible). Many of the properties identified and analyzed for Petri nets relate to free-choice Petri nets only (see Desel & Esparza, 1995).

We now analyze the meaning of free choice in a well-mapped WF-net. We will show, by example, that the real issue is not the topology of the net, but rather the independence of sub-domains that are associated with the nodes in the net. To understand what non free choice might mean for well-mapped WF-nets consider the non free-choice structures depicted in Figures 3(a) and 4(b). We assume the diagrams are part of a well-mapped WF-net.

In Figure 4(a) the two places – p1 and p2 – are input places of the transition t1 hence this transition synchronizes their sub-domains. In addition,

Figure 3. Non free-choice structures

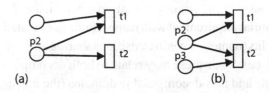

(a)   (b)

Figure 4. Non well-structured examples

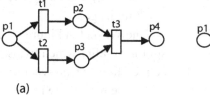

(a)

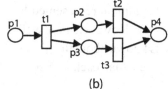

(b)

place p2 is a sole input place of transition t2. By Necessary condition 2 – transition independence – p2 must be independent. However, what happens to the p2 sub-domain depends also on p1. It is impossible for one set of states to have an independent law and to depend on synchronization with another sub-domain at the same time. Hence, this structure is not possible in a well-mapped WF-net.

In contrast, consider the non free-choice structure in Figure 3(b). First – to attach sub-domain semantics to it, assume that p1 and p3 are different sets of states of sub-domain D_1[8] (reached by different distinct D-paths of that sub-domain), and that p2 is defined over sub-domain D_2. D_1 and D_2 are synchronized either by t1 or by t2 and hence are not independent at the states represented by p1 and p3 for D_1 and by p2 for D_2. This does not contradict sub-domain independence as neither domain is expected to behave independently due to synchronization by either transition. While this structure is not allowed in a free-choice WF-net, it is meaningful in the GPM semantics. Hence, it should be allowed in a well-mapped WF-net.

This analysis demonstrates how the use of ontological semantics can provide meaning to topological properties that have been formalized but not necessarily well-justified. Specifically, the difficulty faced by non free-choice models is not the (topological) combination of choice and parallelism. In practical situations such a combination can occur. Rather, the difficulty reflects the inability to distinguish independent sub-domains from dependent ones (where the dependence re-

flects the need to synchronize sub-domains that were independent prior to synchronization).

To resolve this difficulty, we suggest replacing the original definition of free choice property by a new one which we term *relaxed free-choice*.

Definition 24 (relaxed free choice): A WF-net is *relaxed free choice* if for every two transitions t_1, t_2, $\bullet t_1 \cap \bullet t_2 \neq \varnothing$ implies $D_{\bullet t1} = D_{\bullet t2}$.

In a relaxed free choice WF-net, when two transitions share inputs the domains of their inputs are associated with the same sub-domain. The intuitive meaning is as follows: each transition can synchronize the common sub-domain with the other input domains it has. Hence, the common sub-domain and the other input should be viewed as one joint sub-domain. Since they share a sub-domain, the joint sub-domains for both are the same.

Due to the conditions imposed on a well-mapped WF-net it should reflect correctly the independence of sub-domains. This is reflected in the following lemma:

Lemma 5: A well-mapped WF-net is relaxed free-choice.

Proof: from Necessary condition 2 – transition independence. If the network was not a relaxed free choice, then some transitions could be shown to operate in sub-domains that are not independent (namely, the transitions could "fire" differently under the same conditions).

Note, in WF-nets which are not free choice it is possible that transitions are not independent as the exact states of the domain represented by a marking are not known. However, in a well-mapped WF-net more is known about the places. They are configured such that each transition operates independently.

Note that every free choice WF-net is also relaxed free choice. This is because the topology of the free choice net proscribes the possibility of transitions that are not independent.

5.2 Well-Structuredness

A WF-net is said to be well-structured if, for any pair of nodes x and y such that one is a place and the other a transition and for any pair of elementary paths P_1 and P_2 leading from x to y, $P_1 \cap P_2 = \{x,y\}$ implies that $P_1 = P_2$.

As mentioned in Section 3, well-structuredness requires a parallel split (a transition leading into several places) to be complemented by a synchronizing merge (several places leading to a transition), and an exclusive choice split (a place leading to several transitions) to be complemented by a simple merge (several transitions leading to a place). To understand this property in GPM terms, let us examine the examples in Figure 4. We assume the net is well-mapped and thus use GPM concepts to discuss the meaning of situations that do not satisfy the well-structureness requirement.

Figure 4(a) includes a WF-net in which an exclusive choice is taken in place p1. Recall, an exclusive choice may stand for two situations. First, the entire domain may select one of two (or more) different D-paths. Since the domain is not decomposable, Necessary condition 3 (concurrency) does not hold, hence synchronization in t3 is not possible. Second, the domain may be decomposable into different sub-domains, and the choice is which one of them becomes active. Since only one sub-domain can become active, it is impossible for p2 and p3 to be active at the same time and activate t3. Hence, this is a case

of deadlock (this case will be revisited in the next section) and can prevent the process from reaching its goal.

The WF-net in Figure 4(b) includes a parallel split in t1, after which two sub-domains become active. However, no synchronization is made, and p4 can be reached twice. Unlike the example of Figure 4(a), this situation is possible in practical situations, and is included in the workflow patterns collection as a "discriminator" (van der Aalst et al., 2003). As an example, consider two teams competing for a trophy, which is awarded to the winning team once it arrives at the finish line. A problem may arise if the winner is already announced and the trophy is given, while the other team is still on its way, unaware that the game is over. According to Necessary condition 4 (stability), the goal of the process (the sink place of the net) should be a stable state of the entire domain, which is not the case if one team is still active. Some action is required for notifying the losing team that the game is over, before the goal of the process is reached. Such action entails a synchronization of the actions of the two teams. This is formalized in the following lemma.

Lemma 6: In a well-mapped WF-net for every two concurrent sub-domains D_1, D_2 represented by net places there exist two places $p_k \in D_k$, k=1,2, and a transition t such that $\bullet t = \{p_1, p_2\}$.

Proof: In a well mapped WF-net, from Necessary condition 4 (stability), once the sink is reached, no more transitions can happen, namely, no sub-domain is unstable. Consider two independent sub-domains D_1 and D_2 represented by the net that are concurrently active. If D_1 reached the sink, D_2 cannot be unstable. It follows that the two sub-domains must stop being independent before the sink. By Lemma 3, there is a transition t synchronizing D_1, D_2 before the sink.

Note that Lemma 6 does not proscribe non well-structured nets like the one in Figure 4(b), which may be useful from a business point of view. Yet, it requires some synchronization of the sub-domains to be made. It is possible that the continuation of the process does not depend on the arrival of both sub-domains at the merge (namely, no synchronization at the merge, as required in well-structured WF-nets). However, in this case synchronization must be made elsewhere, before the goal of the process can be reached.

5.3 S-Coverability

The property of S-coverability in WF-nets relies on the following definitions (van der Aalst, 1998).

Definition 25 (state machine): A Petri net is a state machine if every transition has exactly one input and one output place.

Definition 26 (S-component): A subnet $PN_s=(P_s, T_s, F_s)$ is called an S-component of a Petri net $PN=(P, T, F)$ if $P_s \subseteq P$, $T_s \subseteq T$, $F_s \subseteq F$, PN_s is strongly connected, PN_s is a state machine, and for every $q \in P_s$ and $t \in T$: $(q,t) \in F$ implies that $(q,t) \in F_s$ and $(t,q) \in F$ implies that $(t,q) \in F_s$.

Definition 27 (S-coverable): A Petri net is S-coverable if for any node there exists an S-component which contains this node.

Finally, a WF-net is S-coverable if the short-circuited net[9] is S-coverable.

S-coverability is perceived as some kind of generalization of well-structuredness and free choice (van der Aalst, 2000) (although a net can satisfy any of these properties without satisfying the others (Jianchun & Dongqing, 2002). Van der Aalst (2003) argues that although it is possible to construct sound WF-nets which are not S-coverable, from a practical point of view it should be avoided. He proposes an intuitive interpretation of this property by using a metaphor of document flows, where each such flow corresponds to an S-component.

Consistently with this metaphor, we interpret each S-component as the projection of the process into a sub-domain. To be an S-component, two conditions must hold with respect to the sub-domain. First, it should be possible to view the behavior of the sub-domain as a separate stand-alone process (or WF-net). Like every process, it has a law which acts independently, and it may have some transitions which depend on external events (events outside the sub-domain). Second, an S-component stands for a non-decomposable sub-domain.

Since an S-component should be possible to view as a stand-alone process, all its places must relate only to the sub-domain under consideration. For example, the WF-net in Figure 4(b) is not S-coverable, because the sub-domain of p4 includes state variables from both the sub-domains of p2 and p3 (Necessary condition 1).

While the strong decomposability of the domain which is reflected in an S-coverable WF-net makes its behavior predictable and relatively easy to analyze, we do not consider it a mandatory property of a process. Rather, we rely on the restrictions that are posed on a well-mapped WF-net to achieve this predictability. In particular, Necessary conditions 2 (transition independence) and 3 (concurrency) as well as Lemma 6 (which assures that concurrent sub-domains must synchronize) resolve some of the problems typical to WF-nets which are not S-coverable. To demonstrate that, we make an analogy to the corollary presented by van der Aalst (2000), who showed that a sound well-structured WF-net is S-coverable. In analogy to that, we propose the following Lemma.

Lemma 7: A well-mapped and well-structured WF-net is S-coverable.

Proof: Consider a well-mapped and well-structured WF-net. Assume first, that the process domain is not decomposable, then the entire net is an S-component (there is no concurrency in the domain, hence no transition leading to more than one place). Second, assume the process domain is decomposable at some set of states to at least two independently transforming sub-domains. Consider the sub-net PN_s, depicting the behavior of one. PN_s is not included in an S-component if (a) there is a place $p \in P_s$ and a transition $t \notin T_s$, such that $t \in \bullet p$, or (b) there is a place $p \in P_s$ and a transition $t \notin T_s$, such that $t \in p \bullet$. (a) is not possible for the following reason: t must be in another independent sub-domain (Necessary condition 3 – concurrency); hence, there must be a parallel split on the paths from i to p and from i to t, where the decomposition took place. Since the net is well-structured, p is a place and t is a transition, this is not possible. (b) is not possible since it is in violation of Necessary condition 2 (independence).

Note that a well-mapped WF-net is not necessarily sound, hence Lemma 7 is more general than the result presented by van der Aalst (2000).

6. PROCESS VALIDITY AND SOUNDNESS

In this section we address the GPM concept of process validity on one hand, and the WF-net property of soundness on the other hand. According to GPM, validity of a process model can only be assessed with respect to a set of expected external events and to a defined goal (Soffer & Wand, 2007). How these are determined is outside the scope of the current analysis. We consider only the reachability of the process termination state, assuming that it represents the process goal. Assuming that all the expected external events occur, validity relates to completeness of the internal law definition (which relates to internal events) and to its consistency with the goal definition (Soffer & Wand, 2007).

Incompleteness reflects potential deadlock situations. Following Kiepuszewski, ter Hofstede

and van der Aalst (2003), a process instance is in deadlock if it is not in the goal and no transition is enabled. GPM also allows for a process execution "hanging" when external events fail to occur, but we assume here no such failure happens. Thus, deadlock means that the process is in a state for which the law is not defined. In a well mapped WF-net this may occur when a transition has more than one required input place (i.e., it is a synchronizing merge which joins different sub-domains) and it is possible the net reaches a state where not all input places can be populated. Two situations are possible:

1. Not all sub-domains have been activated at the split point.
2. At least one of the sub-domains took a D-path which does not lead to the input place of the merge transition.

We will specify modeling rules to avoid each of these cases. Case (1) is only possible if an exclusive choice (i.e., a place leading to more than one transition) is followed by a synchronizing merge. As discussed in Section 5.2, this is only possible if the domain is decomposable. While such structures do not appear in a well-structured WF-net 0(van der Aalst, 1998, 2000), we do not require well-structuredness. Instead, we only require that every synchronizing merge be preceded by a split, where all branches would be activated. This may be a parallel split (transition) or an exclusive choice (place) activated at least once for each branch. Note, following Lemma 6 (synchronization of sub-domains), if the split is an exclusive choice, it should be activated exactly once for every branch. As opposed to well structuredness, we leave simple merges (merges in a place) unconstrained as to the type of split they should be preceded by. is the above considerations (including the result of Lemma 6) is formalized in Modeling rule 1:

Table 2. Allowed split / merge combinations

split	merge	When possible
Place	Place	Always allowed
Place	Transition	Allowed only if the possible number of activations of the place is equal to the number of elementary paths to the transition.
Transition	Place	Always allowed
Transition	Transition	Always allowed

Modeling requirement: In a well-mapped WF-net a place can only be connected to a transition by two or more elementary paths if each elementary path is activated exactly once.

A corollary of the modeling requirement is that the possible number of activations of the place (its maximal number of tokens) should be equal to the number of the elementary paths.

Following the modeling requirement, the combinations listed in Table 2 are possible.

We are interested in practical rules that can guide the construction of a WF-net that satisfies the modeling requirements. To do that, we will use the fact that a WF-net has only one initial place. This implies that for any place to be activated a given number of times, there should be enough parallel splits in the net to enable the creation of the required number of tokens. We therefore conclude that for a place to be activated a given number of times it must be preceded (not necessarily immediately) by the same number of parallel net paths (which represent the same number of concurrently active sub-domains). We can use the following construction rule to assure

that each path leading from the split (place) under consideration is activated once. In each path leading from the split place there should be a transition also conditioned by exactly one of the parallel paths that must be active to assure the required number of activations of the place. Formally:

Modeling Rule (MR) 1: Let p be a place connected by $n \geq 1$ elementary paths to a transition t.

A. If p can be activated at most once (its maximal number of tokens is 1) then the net should satisfy n=1.

B. Else, for n>1 let D_k, k=1..n, be concurrently operating sub-domains prior to place p. Let $t_k \in p\bullet$. Then the net should satisfy the following: for each k, $\exists p_k$ in D_k such that $p_k\bullet = t_k$.

Part (b) of MR1 is sketched in Figure 5, focusing on the domain D_k, where the rest appear in dashed lines without details.

To avoid the case (2), the modeler needs to make sure that if two sub-domains that have alternative distinct D-paths need to synchronize, then every possible combination of these D-paths

Figure 5. Illustration to MR1 (part b)

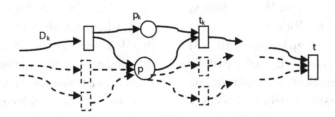

Figure 6. D-path combinations

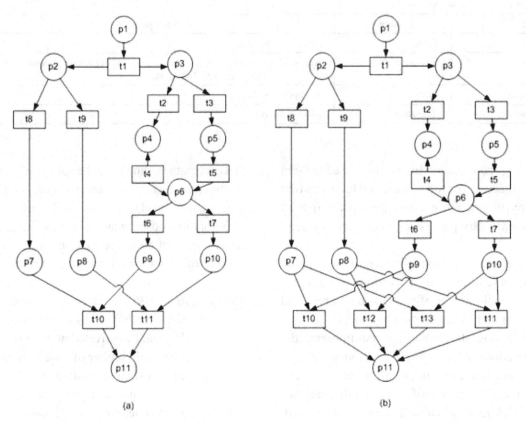

(a)   (b)

has a merging transition defined for it. To illustrate the idea, consider the examples of Figure 6.

In Figure 6(a), the process domain is split in t1 to two concurrently active sub-domains, and both these sub-domains have different D-paths that can be selected. The process may clearly deadlock, if one sub-domain takes a D-path leading to p7 while the other reaches p10, or if one sub-domain reaches p8 while the other takes a D-path that leads to p9. There are more combinations of D-paths that can be taken than combinations that lead to the goal of the process. The sub-domain on the left side has two distinct D-paths: (1) p2→p7, and (2) p2→p8. The sub-domain on the right side has four distinct D-paths: (1) p3→p4→p6→p9, (2) p3→p4→p6→p10, (3) p3→p5→p6→p9, and (4) p3→p5→p6→p10. To eliminate the possible deadlock, we need to define action in every possible situation the process may

reach. We may look for a place which is reached from all D-paths. Considering the right side sub-domain, p6 is reachable in all the distinct D-paths. Hence, it is guaranteed to be reached. Let us examine a possible correction, where p6 is connected to t11. Then t6, t7, and t11 would share p6 as an input place, while t11 is also preceded by p8 (whose domain is different). This is in contradiction to the relaxed free choice requirement that if two transitions share some input places, then the sub-domains of the inputs are the same. Following this analysis, p9 and p10, which are reachable in two distinct D-paths each and together "cover" all the four D-paths, do not represent states where the sub-domain is independent (since they lead to a merge). A complete solution, addressing every possible situation, requires the net, to include a transition defined for every possible combination of non-independent places in the two sub-domains, namely, $(p7, p8) \times (p9, p10)$, as shown in Figure 6(b).

The above analysis is formalized in Modeling rule (MR) 2 that requires that if a transition depends on a combination of states of two sub-domains, and that combination is not guaranteed to happen, there must be other transitions specified for all other possible state combinations.

Modeling rule (MR) 2: Let D_1, D_2 be two sub-domains, and t a transition such that $\bullet t = \{p_1, p_2\}$, where p_k is associated with sub-domain D_k.

Let, for each D_k (k=1,2) PM_k be set of places for which D_k is not independent and are on distinct D-path in D_k. Then for every $p \in PM_1$ and $q \in PM_2$, there must be a transition $t_{p,q}$ such that $\bullet t_{p,q} = \{p,q\}$.

Note: D_1 and D_2 can be identified by backtracking paths from p_1 and p_2 until the first transition which is included in both paths. Inconsistency between the law and the goal definition relates to infinite loops. In WF-nets, since every element must be on a path from i to o, loops must have (at least one) exit points. These may be parallel splits or exclusive choice splits. According to the corollary of Lemma 4, parallel splits cannot be exit points of loops in a well-mapped domain representation WF-net. We shall hence examine the possible structures in which loops whose exit point is an exclusive choice may become infinite. When a loop has an exclusive choice as an exit point at place p, two cases are possible:

1. The next transition has only one input place ($\bullet t = \{p\}$). Then the exit depends on one sub-domain only. Structurally, this is not an infinite loop. The exit from the loop depends on the decision criteria defined by the analyst (based on the actual state that is reached in the set of states represented by the place).

2. The next transition has more than one input place (i.e., it merges a number of concurrent sub-domains). In this case, if

the merge deadlocks, the loop will continue infinitely. However, merging deadlocks can be eliminated by using modeling rules 1 and 2. Hence, if the modeling rules are used in a well-mapped WF-net, it does not include infinite loops.

Theorem 1: A well-mapped WF-net which satisfies Modeling rules 1 and 2 is sound.

Proof: soundness has three requirements. We first address conditions (ii) and (iii).

ii. Proper termination – follows directly from Necessary condition 4 (stability) and Lemma 6. (iii) no dead transitions – follows from Necessary condition 2 which requires the input domain of every transition to be independent, and from MR1, which ensures that if more than one sub-domain is required for enabling a transition, they all will be activated. To prove (i), namely that *o* is reachable from every state reachable from *i*, we will show that for any state M reachable from *i* there is a transition t that can be fired. Since all the elements in a WF-net are on a path from *i* to *o* and no infinite loops are possible, if any arbitrary state M transforms, *o* will be reached.

We will show that in a given state M every transition is either (a) within an independent sub-domain, or (b) a result of a merge between two (or more) sub-domains. In the first case, a transition will be fired with certainty. In the second case, by MR1, all the required sub-domains should be active, and by MR2 there is a transition defined for every possible combination of D-paths of the sub-domains. Hence a transition will be fired.

Formally: Let P(M) be the set of active places in M, and consider a place $p_i \in P(M)$ and a transition $t_1 \in p_1 \bullet$. Two cases are possible: (1) $\bullet t_1 \subseteq P(M)$, then t_1 fires at M. (2) $\bullet t_1 \not\subseteq P(M)$, then t_1 cannot fire at M. We will show that when Rules 1 and 2 hold, there exists a transition t_2 that can fire at M.

Having more than one input place, t_1 merges two or more independent sub-domains with at least one having a place which is not active in M. Let this place be $p_2 \in \bullet t_1$, $p_2 \notin P(M)$. By the definition of a well-mapped WF-net p_2 represents states in a sub-domain D_2 and is active for at least one marking M'. Now, t_1 synchronizes p_1 and p_2 and due to MR 1, prior to t_1 there are two independent and necessarily activated sub-domains D_1 and D_2 (which are the domains whose states are represented by p_1 and p_2). According to our assumption, when the net is in M, D_2 is not in a state corresponding to p_2 (otherwise, t_1 could fire). However, since D_2 is part of the input of t_1, it cannot be independent at the domain state for M. Due to MR 2, a transition t_2 should exist to synchronize D_2 with an active domain in M (concurrent to D_2). This transition can fire.

In summary, following the necessary conditions and modeling rules, it is possible to construct a sound and meaningful WF-net.

7. APPLYING THE RULES IN CONSTRUCTING PROCESS MODELS

This section demonstrates the application of the ideas presented in this paper for the construction of well-mapped WF-nets. We will demonstrate the application using the following order fulfillment process in a company which sells and installs communication systems.

To fulfill an order, components need to be sourced (either by in-sourcing or by outsourcing) and delivered to the customer's site. Concurrently, infrastructure should be prepared at the customer's site. The infrastructure preparation as well as the delivery of the ready components to the customer's site can be done by the customer or by the company. When the infrastructure is ready and the components delivered, the communications system can be installed. The common practice is either that the customer takes responsibility for both infrastructure installation and component delivery or both are done by the company. This is captured in Figure 6(a), which corresponds to the case by assigning the place and transition meanings listed in Table 3.

However, in some cases the customer may only take responsibility for the infrastructure installation or the delivery. These cases would lead to deadlock in Figure 6(a) (as there are no transitions that can occur when these situations arise). An alternative model, in which such combinations are feasible (i.e., can lead to project completion) is shown in Figure 6(b).

We now use this example to demonstrate the guidelines to be followed when constructing a sound well-mapped WF-net. Table 4 provides a summary of these guidelines. The table indicates the origin of each guideline in the formal part of the paper, and provides examples from the communication company order fulfillment process.

8. RELATED WORK

The basic formalism of Petri nets (Petri, 1962) has been assigned numerous extensions that are intended to add semantics to the net, serving a variety of purposes over the years (Salimifard & Wright, 2001). Examples are timed Petri nets (e.g., Zuberek, 1991), stochastic Petri nets (e.g., Bause & Kritzinger, 1996), reset nets (e.g. Dufourd, Finkel & Schnoebelen, 1998) and hierarchical Petri nets (e.g. Chrastowski-Wachtel et al., 2003). While in this paper we specifically address WF-nets, which are a restricted class of the traditional Petri nets, our approach can be viewed as being similar to Colored Petri nets (CPN) (Jensen, 1990). CPN appear graphically as Petri nets, where tokens have "colors", representing different types of data. Places are associated with color sets which

Table 3. Place and transition labels for Figure 6

Place	Label		Transition	Label
p1	Order status: received		t1	Order fulfillment initiation
p2	Infrastructure status: to be installed		t2	Issue outsourcing order for components
p3	Components status: to be sourced		t3	Issue production order for components
p4	Components status: ordered from supplier		t4	Receive components from supplier
p5	Components status: manufactured		t5	Receive components from production
p6	Components status: all are available		t6	Coordinate delivery by customer
p7	Infrastructure status: installed (by customer)		t7	Coordinate delivery by company
p8	Infrastructure status: installed (by company)		t8	Infrastructure installation by customer
p9	Customer delivery coordinated		t9	Infrastructure installation by company
p10	Company delivery coordinated		t10	Install system (infrastructure and delivery handled by customer)
p11	System status: installed		t11	Install system (infrastructure and delivery handled by company)
			t12 (b only)	Install system (infrastructure handled by company, delivery by customer)
			t13 (b only)	Install system (infrastructure handled by customer, delivery by company)

determine the types of data they may contain. This is analogous to the place sub-domain in our terminology, where the state variables of the sub-domain represent information (about the state). The marking (state) of a CPN is the distribution of tokens in places. It is changed by the occurrence of transitions, which consume and create the tokens according to expressions specified on the arcs. These expressions determine the number and colors of the tokens that should be moved along each arc. The expressions can be compared to our notion of transformation laws which govern the transitions.

While the colors used in CPN incorporate domain information into the model, similarly to our state variables, there are major differences between our approach and CPN. First, CPN is aimed at formally representing certain information about the domain for execution purposes (Liu et al., 2002). In contrast, we aim at understanding how the nature of this information affects the structure of the model and the behavior of processes. Second, CPN uses the Petri net syntax and adds more information to it. We use the Petri Net syntax, and rely on an ontological model to provide meanings to the syntactical constructs. From this meaning we derive restrictions on the types of nets that can be constructed. These rules can be viewed as semantic rules intended to make the models consistent with ontological principles. The information conveyed by CPN and by our model can be similar; still, its implications are completely different. Third, CPN entails verification procedures (Jensen, 1997), to be applied to a complete model. Our approach, in contrast, is intended to support the process designer in the construction of semantically (i.e., ontologically) meaningful models, and by implication, to assure the models are valid, in being able to reach their goals.

To produce a WF net that is an actual representation of the modeled domain, overcoming possible

Table 4. Modeling guidelines that follow the formal discussion

	Guideline	Derived from	Example
	Basic modeling		

1	Each place should match a set of states of a sub-domain.
	  In practice: The set of states can be defined by a condition on state variables.
		Definition 20 (meaning of a populated place)	Place: p6
			Sub-domain: state variables describing the components.
			  Condition: components status='all are available'

2	Transitions should transform values of state variables from initial values (at input places) to final values (at output places)	Necessary condition 1 (transition domain structure)	Transition: t4 From components status: 'ordered from supplier' (p4) to components status: 'all are available' (p6)

3	Define the sink place as the goal of the process.
	  In practice: a condition defining a set of desired stable domain states.
		Necessary condition 4 (stability)	Sink is Place p11.
			  Domain states: system status = 'installed'

	Splits		

4	Consider a split transition:
	  For each branch: the state variables that change in the branch do not affect changes that occur in the other branches.
		Necessary condition 3 (concurrency)	Split transition: order fulfillment initiation (t1).
			Branches "obtain and deliver components" and "prepare infrastructure" change different state variables.
			  Note, there might be common state variables which do not change (e.g. customer ID).

5	A split at a place should lead to a set of transitions that (a) All have only the place as an input OR (b) All synchronize the place with at least one other place.	Necessary condition 2 (independence), Lemma 5 (relaxed free choice)	Place: p6 (components status: "all are available"). Transitions t6 ("coordinate delivery by customer") and t7 ("coordinate delivery by company") have only p6 as input. Note: each transition represents a different decision in the "components" sub-domain. Place p10 (in Figure 6 (b)) splits to t13 (delivery by company, infrastructure by customer) and t11 (delivery and infrastructure by company). Each synchronizes the "components" and the "infrastructure" sub-domains.
6	There should be no loop where the only exit is on a transition split.	Corollary of Necessary condition 4 (stability)	
	Merges		
7	For concurrently changing sub-domains, when the next transition of at least one cannot be determined independently, a merge is needed at that point (with one of the others).	Necessary condition 3 (concurrency)	For p9 and p10 (components status='delivered') installation (t10...t13) can only take place when the other concurrent sub-domain - infrastructure - is ready (p7 and p8).
8	The sub-domains merged at a transition should satisfy for each branch: the state variables that change in the branch do not affect changes that occur in the other branches.	Necessary condition 3 (concurrency)	Install system (t10...t13) synchronize "components" and "infrastructure".
9	A merge at a transition: (1) All input places must be synchronized at all their output transitions OR (2) All output transitions of an input place must have the same input domain.	Necessary condition 2 (independence), Lemma 5 (relaxed free choice)	Transitions t10 and t11 (in the original model) synchronize the infrastructure and components sub-domains. They both satisfy condition (1).

continued on following page

gaps between the model and the process reality, a possible approach is process mining (van der Aalst & Weijters, 2004; van der Aalst et al., 2007). Process mining starts by gathering the informa-tion of the real process based on the event log of an information system, and develops the process model (e.g. WF-net) based on this information. Although this approach supports representation of

Table 4. Continued

	Guideline	Derived from	Example
10	When a merge at a transition corresponds to a split at a place (1) the number of possible activations of the place should be equal to the number of branches. (2) Each branch contains a transition that depends on the split place and on preceding independent branch*	Modeling rule 1	Assume that upon completion and verification of either components delivery or infrastructure a supervisor is notified, and sends experts to sign off and approve quality. Installation can be carried out only after both approvals have been obtained. This is depicted in the diagram in Figure 7. The place Supervisor notified will be activated twice. The activation of each of the outgoing branches is assured by two additional places, one in the component domain and the other in the infrastructure domain.
11	If concurrent sub-domains are merged in a place (namely, the place is populated whenever one sub-domain "reaches" it), the sub-domains should be synchronized after the place (by one or more transitions).	Lemma 6 (synchronization of sub-domains)	Referring to the example in the above cell, the components and infrastructure sub-domains are synchronized at installation.
12	When two sub-domains synchronize at a transition, there should be merging transitions for all the combinations of possible states each sub-domain can reach (final places of distinct D-paths).	Modeling rule 2	In the original model (Figure 6 (a)), the possibility existed that both components and infrastructure were ready and installation could not be done. For example, when infrastructure was done by company (p8) and delivery by customer (p9). Similarly, for p7 and p10). This is resolved by adding transitions t12 and t13.

* This rule can also be categorized under "split". For brevity the full condition is not included, see MR1.

Figure 7. Addition to the order fulfilling process, demonstrating guideline 11

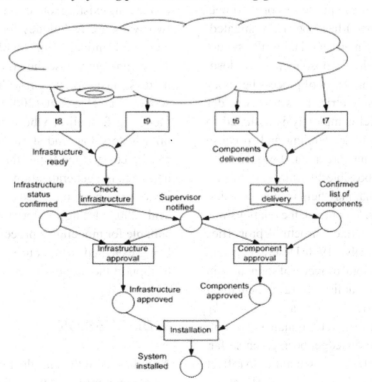

an existing real world system, it does not employ some generic semantics for this purpose. Rather, following actual process events, process mining avoids process design difficulties that may result in erroneous process models. Nevertheless, process mining cannot be used for the design of new non-existing processes.

A mapping of Petri nets to the ontological model of Bunge has already been performed by Recker and Indulska (2007). The purpose of this mapping was to evaluate the expressive power of Petri nets rather than to enhance their semantics. As such, their mapping is done on a construct-by-construct basis in a technical manner, not attempting to achieve a coherent semantic model. The basis of this mapping is the general ontological framework adapted to information systems (also known as BWW ontology), and not GPM, which specializes the ontological model for business processes. Finally, since no coherent semantic model is established, no modeling rules can be derived from their mapping.

Over the years, many properties of Petri nets (and later of WF-nets) have been investigated. Process complexity metrics relate to the syntax of the model (e.g., the Cardoso metric, Cardoso, 2005) and to the complexity of process behavior (e.g., structuredness metric, Lassen & van der Aalst, 2009). Model complexity is assumed to hamper designer's understanding and to cause difficulties in model interpretation. However, these metrics only reflect possible difficulties, and do not lead to principles that may help resolve possible modeling problems. In contrast, the relationships between precisely defined structural properties (see, e.g., Esparza & Silva, 1990; Desel & Esparza, 1995) and the behavioral property of soundness in WF-nets have been established on a mathematical basis. However, a rigorous explanation for *why* these properties are related to soundness has not, to the best of our knowledge, been given so far. Our enhancement of WF-net semantics to reflect domain concepts provides such an explanation. Moreover, this enhancement reveals that in some cases possessing a structural property is not the reason for the "good" behavior of the modeled process. Rather, it reflects, for a well-mapped WF-net, domain properties such as decomposability and independent sub-domain behavior[10]. These domain properties, in turn, are the real cause for the "good" behavior achieved. Based on this understanding, we showed that it is possible to define properties which are less restrictive than the pure structural properties (e.g., relaxed free choice), yet overcoming the unpredictable behavior the structural properties are intended to prevent when fulfilled by a WF-net.

Using our proposed semantics, we show how sound process models can be constructed. Soundness by construction has been claimed to be achieved by other works as well. Chaudron et al. (2003) propose two ways for constructing sound WF-nets: (a) *Top down*: by stepwise refinement of places and transitions of a given start net, where the start net as well as the refinement fragments should be sound; and (b) *Bottom up*: by connecting existing sound component nets. These two ways are techniques for creating a sound composite model from simpler sound models. They apparently ease the task of creating sound models, but do not support such construction from scratch. Van Hee et al. (2008) propose a generic modeling formalism whose semantics is based on a history log, and show how sound models can be constructed using this formalism. Their approach is a generalization of the top-down and bottom-up operations discussed above (Chaudron et al., 2003). Using a history log as a basis is more suitable for modeling a process which is already being executed, while our approach is intended to support the design of new processes.

9. DISCUSSION

As indicated in the introduction, process models are a commonly used type of conceptual models (Wand & Weber, 2002). Specifically, the purpose of process models is to represent the behavior of business domains. On a more general note, conceptual models are intended to enable stakeholders and business and systems analysts communicate about a business domain. Thus, they should clearly convey the meaning of the represented domain. However, formal Process models, in particular WF-Nets, do not directly and clearly convey this meaning.

To overcome this limitation, this work aims at providing a clear domain meaning to WF-Nets. This is done by assigning ontological semantics to the modeling constructs and by imposing certain rules on models to be considered acceptable (in that they provide a direct mapping of domain phenomena). This is in line with approaches that analyze conceptual modeling techniques and suggest ways to apply or improve them based on ontological considerations. Therefore, to place this work in a wider context, we now briefly discuss approaches to analyzing conceptual modeling grammars in general.

In the conceptual modeling literature, ontology-based frameworks have mainly been applied for evaluating the representational capabilities of modeling grammars (Wand & Weber, 1993; Opdahl & Henderson-Sellers, 2001, 2002; Green & Rosemann, 2004). In addition, there have also been attempts to use ontology as a basis for deriving modeling rules, intended to achieve a consistent representation of domain phenomena in a model (Guizzardi, Ferreira & van Sinderen, 2005; Evermann & Wand, 2005, 2009; Bera, Krasnoperova, & Wand, in press). This line of work is very closely related to the approach presented in this paper. However, there are clear differences between our set of rules and the ontology-based rules for conceptual modeling in the above works. These differences stem from differences in the purposes the models may serve. While conceptual models mainly serve for communication and understanding (Mylopoulos, 1992), process models may also serve as a basis for workflow execution (Dussart, Aubert & Patry, 2004). As a first consequence,

the models expected to be created with grammars used or suggested for conceptual modeling (e.g., UML) are not required to be as formal as the models created with the grammar addressed here (WF-nets). A second consequence of these different purposes is the different quality criteria proposed for conceptual models in comparison to those defined for process models. Quality dimensions of conceptual models include semantic quality, namely the correspondence between the conceptual model and the domain, syntactic quality, namely the correspondence between the model and the modeling language, and pragmatic quality, which relates to the audience's interpretation of the model or its understandability (Lindland, Sindre & Solvberg, 1994). In contrast, although recently some quality criteria of process models relate to their understandability (Mendling & Strembeck, 2008), the most commonly addressed criteria, such as soundness, serve the purpose of executability.

The rules presented in the paper, similarly to conceptual modeling ontology-based rules, are concerned with the semantic quality of the model. This quality aspect has not been addressed so far with respect to formal process models, in particular those that apply token-based semantics. Not only it provides for more meaningful models, but it also reveals the meaning of net qualities so far considered mostly technical in nature (such as free choice). Furthermore, an important result shown in the paper is that addressing semantic quality also supports the executability purpose through soundness.

10. CONCLUSION

Most process modeling techniques do not provide the degree of formality needed to mathematically analyze process model characteristics. To enable such analysis, Petri Net models of process dynamics, in particular Workflow Nets, can be used. However, while supporting the analysis of workflow behavior, WF-nets do not possess well-defined and clear domain semantics. Hence, there are no rules on how to model a given domain using WF-nets or how to interpret a given net in domain terms. Moreover, the use of WF nets might lead to process models which do not directly convey the semantics of the domain in which they operate.

To support formal analysis and to enable the construction of semantically meaningful models, we propose to assign ontologically-based semantics to Petri Net constructs. We base our semantics on GPM, which is an adaptation to process modeling of a general ontological model proposed by Bunge. Based on GPM, we suggest a specific assignment of semantics to Petri Net constructs. We show how modeling guidelines, based on this semantics, can assist in constructing process models to avoid problems that traditionally could only be detected by verification of the completed models.

Existing verification algorithms for WF-nets can analyze in polynomial time only specific classes of models (free-choice or well-structured). The modeling rules suggested here can lead to the creation of sound WF-nets which are not necessarily free-choice or well-structured. The modeling rules do not constitute a verification approach. Rather, they form a *construction* approach, which yields sound models when applied. We have also shown that net properties such as free choice and S-coverability can be explained using the ontological semantics.

Based on the ontological semantics, we also suggest modeling rules for constructing process models that are assured to reach their goals when executed. The essence of the analysis is in mapping common situations that can occur when a domain undergoes state transitions, into a WF-net representation. For a process to be guaranteed to reach its goal, its definition should fulfill three conditions: (1) no situations should arise where it "hangs", (2) completeness: all possible states should have defined transitions, and (3) infinite loops should not be possible. Process "hanging" can happen when several conditions need to be

fulfilled for the process to continue – i.e. in merge situations. Merges occur because a split has occurred earlier in the process. By choosing only appropriate combinations of splits and merges, the process can be guaranteed to proceed. This was the purpose of Modeling Rule 1. Completeness requires that the process model will specify continuation for all possible states – this was the purpose of Modeling Rule 2. Both rules and the incorporation of goal definition into the model ensure the absence of infinite loops. Constructing models that conform to these two rules, assures therefore that the process, when executed, can always complete (in the sense of reaching its goal). It is important to note that the rules can be used to guide the actual construction of process models, rather than being applicable only to already existing models.

Besides the contribution to process modeling, the paper also makes a theoretical contribution regarding GPM and Bunge's ontology. The modeling rules and restrictions proposed here are strictly based on the ontological analysis of domain behavior. Nevertheless, we showed that following these restrictions leads to sound models, namely, models that satisfy a specific mathematically defined property. Since the usefulness of ontologies can only be determined empirically (Wand & Weber, 2002), this result provides an evidence supporting the usefulness of GPM and its underlying ontology.

This work can be extended in several ways. First, as GPM concepts are generic, they can be applied to other modeling languages. This can help provide techniques for mapping process models created in other languages into well-mapped Workflow nets. This application would require mapping of a process modeling grammar to GPM and deriving appropriate restrictions and modeling rules for models constructed in the grammar. Second, the modeling rules can be tested empirically to examine their effectiveness in creating WF-nets of realistic situations. The resulting models can be evaluated for their quality. Finally, since the rules are well formalized, they can be used as the basis for computerized tools to support the development of meaningful and valid process models.

ACKNOWLEDGMENT

The authors are indebted to very helpful suggestions made by W.M.P. van der Aalst at CAiSE 2008. This work was supported in part by a grant from the Natural Sciences and Engineering Research Council of Canada to one of the authors.

REFERENCES

Bause, F., & Kritzinger, P. S. (1996). *Stochastic Petri Nets, An introduction to the Theory*. Berlin: Verlag-Vieweg.

Bera, P., Krasnoperova, A., & Wand, Y. (2010). Using Ontology Languages for Conceptual Modeling. *Journal of Database Management*, *21*(1), 1–28.

Bunge, M. (1977). Treatise on Basic Philosophy: *Vol. 3. Ontology I: The Furniture of the World*. Boston: Reidel.

Bunge, M. (1979). Treatise on Basic Philosophy: *Vol. 4. Ontology II: A World of Systems*. Boston: Reidel.

Cardoso, J. (2005). Control-flow complexity measurement of processes and Weyuker's Properties . In *Transactions on Informatika, Systems Sciences and Engineering, Budapest 2005* (*Vol. 8*, pp. 213–218). Berlin: Springer Verlag.

Chaudron, M., van Hee, K., & Somers, L. (2003). Use cases as workflows. In W. M. P. van der Aalst et al. (Eds.): *Business Process Modeling 2003* (LNCS 2678, pp. 88-103).

Chrastowski-Wachtel, P., Benatallah, B., Hamadi, R., O'Dell, M., & Susanto, A. (2003). A top-down Petri net-based approach for dynamic workflow modeling. In W. M. P. van der Aalst et al. (Eds.), *Business Process Modeling* 2003 (LNCS 2678, pp. 336-353).

Desel, J., & Esparza, J. (1995). Free Choice Petri Nets . In *Cambridge Tracts in Theoretical Computer Science* (*Vol. 40*). Cambridge, UK: Cambridge University Press.

Dufourd, C., Finkel, A., & Schnoebelen, P. (1998). Reset nets between decidability and undecidability. In K. Larsen, S. Skyum, & G. Winskel (Eds.), *Proceedings of the 25th International Colloquium on Automata, Languages and Programming* (LNCS 1443, pp. 103-115).

Dussart, A., Aubert, B. A., & Patry, M. (2004). An evaluation of inter-organizational workflow modeling formalisms. *Journal of Database Management*, *15*(2), 74–104.

Esparza, J., & Silva, M. (1990). Circuits, Handles, Bridges and Nets. In G. Rozenberg (Ed.), *Advances in Petri Nets 1990* (LNCS 483, pp. 210-242).

Evermann, J., & Wand, Y. (2005). Ontology Based Object-Oriented Domain Modelling: Fundamental Concepts. *Requirements Engineering Journal*, *10*(2), 146–160. doi:10.1007/s00766-004-0208-2

Evermann, J., & Wand, Y. (2009). Ontology based object-oriented domain modeling: Representing behavior. *Journal of Database Management*, *20*(1), 48–77.

Green, P., & Rosemann, M. (2004). Applying ontologies to business and systems modelling techniques and perspectives: Lessons learned. *Journal of Database Management*, *15*(2), 105–117.

Guizzardi, G., Ferreira, P. L., & van Sinderen, M. (2005). An ontology-based approach for evaluating the domain appropriateness and comprehensibility appropriateness of modeling languages. In *ACM/IEEE 8th International Conference on Model Driven Engineering Languages and Systems,* Montego Bay, Jamaica (LNCS 3713).

Jensen, K. (1990). Coloured Petri Nets: A High Level Language for System Design and Analysis. In G. Rozenberg (Ed.), *Advances in Petri Nets 1990* (LNCS 483, pp. 342-416).

Jensen, K. (1997). *Coloured Petri Nets. Basic Concepts, Analysis Methods and Practical Use* (*Vol. 1*). Berlin: Springer-Verlag.

Jianchun, S., & Dongqing, Y. (2009). Process mining: Algorithm for S-Coverable workflow nets. In *WKDD 2009: Proceedings of the Second International Workshop on Knowledge Discovery and Data Mining* (pp. 239-244). Washington, DC: IEEE Computer Society.

Kiepuszewski, B., ter Hofstede, A. H. M., & van der Aalst, W. M. P. (2003). Fundamentals of control flow in workflows. *Acta Informatica,* *39*(3), 143–209. doi:10.1007/s00236-002-0105-4

Lassen, K. B., & van der Aalst, W. M. P. (2009). Complexity metrics for workflow nets. *Information and Software Technology, 51,* 610–626. doi:10.1016/j.infsof.2008.08.005

Lindland, O. I., Sindre, G., & Solvberg, A. (1994). Understanding quality in conceptual modeling. *IEEE Software, 11*(2), 42–49. doi:10.1109/52.268955

Liu, D., Wang, J., Chan, S., Sun, J., & Zhang, L. (2002). Modeling workflow processes with colored Petri nets. *Computers in Industry, 49,* 267–281. doi:10.1016/S0166-3615(02)00099-4

Mendling, J. (2007). *Detection and Prediction of Errors in EPC Business Process Models.* Unpublished PhD thesis, Vienna University of Economics and Business Administration.

Mendling, J., & Strembeck, M. (2008). Influence Factors of Understanding Business Process Models. *Business Information Systems.* (*LNBIP,* *7,* 142–153.

Milner, R., Parrow, J., & Walker, D. (1992). A calculus of mobile processes. *Information and Computation, 100*(100), 1–40. doi:10.1016/0890-5401(92)90008-4

Mylopoulos, J. (1992). Conceptual modeling and telos . In Locoupoulos, P., & Zicari, R. (Eds.), *Conceptual modeling, databases, and cases.* New York: John Wiley & Sons, Inc.

Object Management Group (OMG). (2006). *Business Process Modeling Notation Specification.* Retrieved from http://www.bpmn.org

Opdahl, A., & Henderson-Sellers, B. (2001). Grounding the OML meta-model in ontology. *Journal of Systems and Software, 57*(2), 119–143. doi:10.1016/S0164-1212(00)00123-0

Opdahl, A., & Henderson-Sellers, B. (2002). Ontological evaluation of the UML using the Bunge-Wand-Weber model. *Software and Systems Modeling, 1*(1), 43–67.

Petri, C. A. (1962) *Kommunikation mit Automaten.* PhD thesis, Fakult¨at f¨ur Mathematik und Physik, Technische Hochschule Darmstadt, Darmstadt, Germany.

Recker, J., & Indulska, M. (2007). An Ontology-Based Evaluation of Process Modeling with Petri Nets. *Journal of Interoperability in Business Information Systems, 2*(1), 45–64.

Russell, N., ter Hofstede, A. H. M., van der Aalst, W. M. P., & Mulyar, N. (2006). *Workflow Control-Flow Patterns: A Revised View* (BPM Center Rep. No. BPM-06-22). BPMcenter.org.

Sadiq, W., & Orlowska, M. E. (1997). On Correctness Issues in Conceptual Modeling of Workflows. In *Proceedings of the 5th European Conference on Information Systems,* Cork, Ireland (pp. 943-964).

Salimifard, K., & Wright, M. (2001). Petri net-based modeling of workflow systems: An overview. *European Journal of Operational Research, 134,* 664–676. doi:10.1016/S0377-2217(00)00292-7

Soffer, P., & Wand, Y. (2005). On the notion of soft goals in business process modeling. *Business Process Management Journal, 11*(6), 663–679. doi:10.1108/14637150510630837

Soffer, P., & Wand, Y. (2007). Goal-Driven Multi-Process Analysis. *Journal of the Association for Information Systems, 8*(3), 175–203.

Soffer, P., Wand, Y., & Kaner, M. (2007). Semantic Analysis of Flow Patterns in Business Process Modeling. In *Proceedings of Business Process Management (BPM'07)* (LNCS 4714, pp. 400-407).

van der Aalst, W. M. P. (1998). The application of petri nets to workflow management. *The Journal of Circuits. Systems and Computers, 8*(1), 21–66.

van der Aalst, W. M. P. (1999). Formalization and verification of Event-driven Process Chains. *Information and Software Technology, 41*(10), 639–650. doi:10.1016/S0950-5849(99)00016-6

van der Aalst, W. M. P. (2000). Workflow Verification: Finding Control-Flow Errors Using Petri-Net-Based Techniques, In W.M.P. van der Aalst, J. Desel, & A. Oberweis (Eds.), *Business Process Management: Models, Techniques, and Empirical Studies* (LNCS 1806, pp. 161-183).

van der Aalst, W. M. P. (2003). Challenges in business process management: Verification of business processes using Petri nets. *Bulletin of the EATCS, 80,* 174–199.

van der Aalst, W. M. P., & ter Hofstede, A. H. M. (2005). YAWL: Yet Another Workflow Language. *Information Systems, 30*(4), 245–275. doi:10.1016/j.is.2004.02.002

van der Aalst, W. M. P., ter Hofstede, A. H. M., Kiepuszewski, B., & Barros, A. P. (2003). Workflow Patterns. *Distributed and Parallel Databases, 14*(1), 5–51. doi:10.1023/A:1022883727209

van der Aalst, W. M. P., van Dongen, B. F., Herbst, J., Maruster, L., Schimm, G., & Weijters, A. J. M. M. (2007). Workflow mining: A survey of issues and approaches. *Information Systems, 32*(5), 713–732.

van der Aalst, W. M. P., & Weijters, A. J. M. M. (2004). Process mining: a research agenda. *Computers in Industry, 53*(3), 231–244. doi:10.1016/j.compind.2003.10.001

van Hee, K., Oanea, O., Serebrenik, A., Sidorova, N., & Voorhoeve, M. (2008). History-based joins: semantics, soundness and implementation. *Data & Knowledge Engineering, 64,* 24–37. doi:10.1016/j.datak.2007.06.005

van Hee, K., Sidorova, N., & Voorhoeve, M. (2008). Soundness and separability of workflow nets in the stepwise refinement approach. In W.M.P. van der Aalst & E. Best (Eds.), *ICATPN 2003* (LNCS 2679, pp. 337-356).

Wand, Y., & Weber, R. (1993). On the ontological expressiveness of information systems analysis and design grammars. *Journal of Information Systems, 3,* 217–237. doi:10.1111/j.1365-2575.1993.tb00127.x

Wand, Y., & Weber, R. (1995). Towards a theory of deep structure of information systems. *Journal of Information Systems, 5*(3), 203–223. doi:10.1111/j.1365-2575.1995.tb00108.x

Wand, Y., & Weber, R. (2002). Research Commentary: Information Systems and Conceptual Modeling – a Research Agenda. *Information Systems Research, 13*(4), 363–378. doi:10.1287/isre.13.4.363.69

Weber, R. (2004). Conceptual modelling and ontology: Possibilities and pitfalls. *Journal of Database Management, 14*(3), 1–20.

Zuberek, W. M. (1991). Timed Petri nets – definitions, properties and applications. *Microelectronics and Reliability . Special Issue on Petri Nets and Related Graph Models, 31*(4), 627–644.

ENDNOTES

[1] More generally, •u = {v| (v,u)∈F}, u• ={v| (u,v) ∈F}.

[2] The notation (PN, *i)* indicates a "marking" of a token in (the initial) place *i*.

[3] In definition 7, since L(s) enables the mapping to be into a set of states for an unstable state, L(s)≠{s}. When the law is a function we omit the set symbol: L(s)=s'∈S(D).

[4] GPM merge relates to the states, while Petri-net relates to the transition that follows the states.

[5] In WF-nets two different types of merge exist – on a place (simple) and on a transition (synchronizing).

[6] This means that there is at least one place or one transition whose state variables match those of the sub-domain.

[7] The reachability graph of a WF net is a directed graph whose nodes represent possible markings (states) of the net and whose arcs specify possible transitions between these markings.

[8] This is possible because they are not synchronized by any transition.

[9] The short-circuited net is the Petri net resulting from adding a transition connecting the sink place to the initial place

[10] As, for example, is formalized by Necessary Conditions 2 and 3 in Section 4,

This work was previously published in International Journal of Database Management, Volume 21, Issue 1, edited by Keng Siau, pp. 1-28, copyright 2010 by IGI Publishing (an imprint of IGI Global).

Chapter 10
Maintaining Mappings between Conceptual Models and Relational Schemas

Yuan An
Drexel University, USA

Xiaohua Hu
Drexel University, USA

Il-Yeol Song
Drexel University, USA

ABSTRACT

This paper describes a round-trip engineering approach for incrementally maintaining mappings between conceptual models and relational schemas. When either schema or conceptual model evolves to accommodate new information needs, the existing mapping must be maintained accordingly to continuously provide valid services. In this paper, the authors examine the mappings specifying "consistent" relationships between models. First, they define the consistency of a conceptual-relational mapping through "semantically compatible" instances. Next, the authors analyze the knowledge encoded in the standard database design process and develop round-trip algorithms for incrementally maintaining the consistency of conceptual-relational mappings under evolution. Finally, they conduct a set of comprehensive experiments. The results show that the proposed solution is efficient and provides significant benefits in comparison to the mapping reconstructing approach.

INTRODUCTION

There are many data-centric applications relying on some kinds of mappings between conceptual models and relational schemas—*conceptual-relational mappings*. The mappings are used to

DOI: 10.4018/978-1-61350-471-0.ch010

achieve interoperability (An, Borgida, Miller, & Mylopoulos, 2007) or to overcome the well-known *impedance mismatch* problem (Elmasri & Navathe, 2006), that is, the differences between the data model used by databases and the modeling capabilities and programmability needed by the application. Essentially, a conceptual-relational mapping specifies a particularly meaningful relationship between a conceptual model (hereafter, CM) and a relational schema. Most often, a mapping specifies a *semantically consistent relationship*. Informally, a semantically consistent relationship between a CM and a relational schema specifies that, despite the differences between the constructs and abstraction levels of the modeling languages, both the CM and relational schema will describe the same "semantics" of an application. A CM describes an application in terms of entities, relationships, and attributes, while a relational schema describes information in terms of relational tables; each table has one or more columns with a primary key, and zero or more foreign key constraints. A *semantically consistent relationship* that associates relationships/entities in a CM with relational tables in a relational schema satisfies the following condition: The constraints imposed on the relationships/entities, such as cardinality/participation constraints, encode the same semantic requirements as that described by the key and foreign key constraints in the relational tables. For instance, a many-to-one relationship from an entity E_1 to an entity E_2 in an Entity-Relationship diagram will be mapped using some mapping formalism to a relational table that uses the identifier of E_1 as the key and referring to the identifier of E_2 as a foreign key (Elmasri & Navathe, 2006). The key and foreign key constraints reflect the semantics encoded in the many-to-one relationship.

However, conceptual models and relational schemas evolve over time to accommodate changes in the information they represent. Such evolution may cause existing conceptual-relational mappings to become inconsistent. For example, the database administrator (DBA) in charge of the aforementioned relational table might change the key of the table from the identifier of E_1 to the combination of the identifiers of E_1 and E_2. Consequently, the many-to-one relationship from E_1 to E_2 in the ER diagram would be *semantically inconsistent* with the new table. The reason is that some instances of the table might violate the many-to-one relationship. When conceptual models and schemas change, the conceptual-relational mappings between conceptual models and schemas must be updated. This process is called *conceptual-relational mapping maintenance under evolution*, or *mapping maintenance* for short.

A typical solution to the mapping maintenance problem is to regenerate the conceptual-relational mapping. However, there are two major problems. First, regenerating the mapping alone sometimes cannot solve the inconsistency problem, because the semantics of the conceptual model and the schema are out of synchronization. Second, the mapping generation process, even with the help of mapping generation tools (An, Borgida, & Mylopoulos, 2005a, 2005b), can be costly in terms of human effort and expertise. Especially, complex CMs and schemas that were developed independently require a great deal of effort for reconciliation. A better solution would be to design algorithms that synchronize CMs and schemas, and reuse the original semantics. The algorithms should be able to *incrementally* update the mappings into a set of new mappings. The new mappings should be consistent with respect to the new CMs and schemas.

The process of synchronizing models by keeping them consistent is called *Round-Trip Engineering* (RTE) (Knublauch & Rose, 2000; Sendall & Kuster, 2004). RTE offers a bi-directional exchange between two models. Changes to one model must at some point be reconciled with the other model. In this paper, we propose a round-trip engineering process for maintaining the consistency of conceptual-relational mappings. Notice that round-trip engineering is not forward engineering, for example, generating a relational schema from a CM, plus reverse engineering (Hainaut, 1998), for example, generating a new CM from an existing schema. RTE focuses on synchronization.

Motivation

We begin with a number of applications and environments in which conceptual-relational mappings are used extensively and a solution to the mapping maintenance problem will greatly benefit the applications.

Database Design: A typical database design process begins with the development of a conceptual model such as an ER diagram and ends up with a logical database schema. Although the process of generating a logical schema from a CM is mostly automated, the translation mappings between CMs and logical schemas are not kept in automated tools. The CMs and logical schemas may evolve independently causing the "legacy data" problem. Saving and maintaining the mappings between CMs and logical schemas implied by the database design process will help reduce "legacy data."

Data-Centric Applications: To increase the productivity of the developers of data-centric applications, there are a number of middleware mapping technologies such as Hibernate (Bauer & King, 2006), DB Visual Architect, Oracle TopLink, and Microsoft ADO.NET (Adya, Blakeley, Melnik, & Muralidhar, 2007). They provide an easy-to-use environment for generating conceptual-relational mappings. In these middleware mapping tools, when the object/conceptual models and the database schemas change, a solution is needed for maintaining the conceptual-relational mappings.

Data Integration: In data integration, a set of heterogeneous data sources are queried and accessed through a unified global and virtual view (Lenzerini, 2002; Zhao & Siau, 2007). There are many ontology-based data integration applications which use ontologies as their global views. For these applications, the mappings between ontologies and local data sources are the main vehicles for data integration. Early studies have been focused on integration architectures, query answering capabilities, and global view integration. What has been missing is a solution to maintaining the mappings between ontologies and local data sources when ontologies and database schemas evolve.

The Semantic Web: On the Semantic Web, data is annotated with ontologies having precise semantics. For the "deep Web" where data is stored in backend databases, the semantic annotation of the data is achieved through the mappings between Web ontologies and schemas of backend databases. However, maintaining mappings on the Semantic Web has not yet been considered.

Although conceptual-relational mapping maintenance is important and necessary for many applications, solutions to the problem are rare. The scarcity of solutions is due to many challenges including: how to define consistency of mapping and detect inconsistency of a mapping; what is a right mapping language; how to capture changes to CMs and database schemas; how to devise a plan for reconciling the CMs and schemas according to the intent and expectation of the user; and what are the principles for systematic reconciliation. In this paper, we address these challenges and offer a systematic study and a comprehensive evaluation of how round-trip engineering can be applied to solve the mapping maintenance problem.

The rest of the paper presents our approach. In summary, we explore the approach of using correspondences for capturing changes. We develop a novel round-trip engineering approach for maintaining *consistent* conceptual-relational mappings. We demonstrate the effectiveness and efficiency of our algorithms by conducting a set of experiments.

The remaining content is organized as follows. The "Literature Review" section reviews studies on related work. The "Formal Preliminaries" section presents the formal notation used in later sections. The section entitled "Mappings between Conceptual Models and Relational Schemas" introduces our formalism for conceptual-relational mappings. The section entitled "Changes to Schemas and CMs" characterizes schema and CM evolution. The section entitled "Maintaining Conceptual-Relational Mappings" describes a solution to the problem of mapping maintenance and provides formal results of the proposed algorithms. The "Experience" section presents our evaluation results. The "Discussion" section highlights the contributions and discusses limitations. Finally, the last section concludes the paper.

LITERATURE REVIEW

We conduct a comprehensive literature review in this section. The areas we reviewed are directly related to the work in this paper. These areas include *mappings, view maintenance, schema mapping adaptation, schema evolution for object-oriented databases, conceptual models, reverse engineering, round-trip engineering, data integration,* and *the Semantic Web.*

Mappings. Mapping is the problem of finding a "meaningful" relationship from one data model/representation to another data model/representation (Evermann, 2008; Madhavan, Bernstein, Domingos, & Halevy, 2002). The relationship is expressed in terms of logical formulae. A mapping is often used for data integration, exchange, and translation. Mappings are fundamental to many applications. To study them in a general, application independent way, Madhavan et al. (2002) proposed a general framework for mappings between domain models. A domain model denotes a representation of a domain in a formal language, such as a relational schema in the relational formalism. Given two domain models T_1 (in a language L_1) and T_2 (in L_2), a mapping between T_1 and T_2 may include a helper domain model T_3 (in language L_3), and consists of a set of formulae each of which is over (T_1, T_2), (T_1, T_3), or (T_2, T_3). A mapping formula over a pair of domain models (T_1, T_2) is of the form $e_1 o p e_2$, where e_1 and e_2 are expressions over T_1 and T_2, respectively, and op is a well-defined operator. For example, both e_1 and e_2 can be query expressions over two relational databases T_1 and T_2. The query results of e_1 and e_2 should be compatible, and op can be a subset relationship between the two queries. The semantics of the mapping is given by the interpretations of all domain models involved such that these interpretations together satisfy all the mapping formulae.

Given two data models/representations—either relational schemas or conceptual models such as Entity-Relationship diagrams, finding the mapping between the two representations is a difficult problem. Nevertheless, people have striven to develop tools for helping users in deriving mappings. Example tools are TranSem (Milo & Zohar, 1998), Clio (Miller, Haas, & Hernandez, 2000; Popa, Velegrakis, Miller, Hernández, & Fagin, 2002), HePToX (Bonifati, Chang, Ho, Lakshmanan, & Pottinger, 2005), MQG (Kedad & Bouzeghoub, 1999), the XML data integration system presented in (Kedad & Xue, 2005), and MAPONTO (An, Borgida, & Mylopoulos, 2006). Such a tool usually adopts a two-step paradigm: First, specify some simple correspondences between schema elements; there are a number of tools supporting this task (Melnik, Garcia-Molina, & Rahm, 2002; Rahm & Bernstein, 2001). Then derive plausible declarative mapping expressions. Users need to select the final mappings from the list of candidates. The selection process may be assisted using the actual data stored in the database (Yan, Miller, Haas, & Fagin, 2001). In addition to tools for schema mapping, a considerable body of work exists for discovering mappings between ontologies (Kalfoglou & Scholemmer, 2003; Shvaiko & Euzenat, 2005).

In this paper, we assume that mappings have been established between CMs and relational schemas. We are concerned with maintaining the properties of the original mappings when changes occur to CMs or schemas. Our assumption is that an incremental maintenance approach would outperform the mapping reconstructing approach that uses a mapping discovery tool. We verify the assumption at the end of this paper in the section about experimental results.

View Maintenance. In a database, a view is a derived relation defined in terms of base (stored) relations. A view, thus, defines a mapping from a set of base tables to a derived table. A view can be materialized by storing the tuples of the view in the database. Index structures can be built on the materialized view. Consequently, database accesses to the materialized view can be much faster than re-computing the view. Incremental view maintenance (Ceri & J.Widom, 1991; Huang, Yen, & Hsueh, 2007; Mumick, Quass, & Mumick, 1997) is the problem of dealing with the methods for efficiently updating materialized views when the base schema data are updated. This problem is closely related to the mapping maintenance problem. View adaptation (Gupta, Mumick, & Ross, 1995; Mohania & Dong, 1996) is a variant of view maintenance that investigates methods of keeping the data in a materialized view up-to-date in response to changes in the view definition itself. However, view adaptation may be required after mapping maintenance; hence, we view this work as complementary to mapping maintenance.

Schema Mapping Adaptation. The directly related work is the study on schema mapping adaptation (Velegrakis, Miller, & Popa, 2004; Yu & Popa, 2005). The goal of schema mapping adaptation is to automatically update a schema mapping by reusing the semantics of the original mapping when the associated schemas change. Yu & Popa (2005) explore the schema mapping composition approach. Schema evolutions are captured by formal and accurate schema mappings, and schema adaptation is achieved by composing the evolution mapping with the original mapping. On the other hand, the schema change approach proposed by Velegrakis et al. (2004) incrementally changes

mappings each time a primitive change occurs in the source or target schemas. Both solutions focus on reusing the semantics encoded in existing mappings for merely adapting the mappings without considering the synchronization between schemas. Adaptation without synchronization is due to the nature of the adaptation problems where schema mappings are primarily used for *data exchange*, that is, translating a data instance under a source schema to a data instance under a target schema. If a schema mapping connects two schemas which are semantically inconsistent, then the data exchange process simply does not always produce a target instance. Our approach is different from these solutions in that we aim to maintain the semantic *consistency* of conceptual-relational mappings through model synchronization.

Schema Evolution. In object-oriented databases (OODB), the problem of schema evolution (Rahm & Bernstein, 2006) is to maintain the consistency of an OODB when its schema is modified. The challenges are to update the database efficiently and minimize information loss. A variety of solutions, (e.g., (Banerjee, Kim, Kim, & Korth, 1987; Claypool, Jin, & Rundensteiner, 1998; Ferrandina, Ferran, Meyer, Madec, & Zicari, 1995) have been proposed in the literature. Our problem is different from the schema evolution problem in OODB in that we are concerned with the semantic consistency between a schema and a CM. In AutoMed (Brien & Poulovassilis, 2002; Fan & Poulovassilis, 2004), schema evolution and integration are combined in one unified framework. Source schemas are integrated into a global schema by applying a sequence of primitive transformations to them. The same set of primitive transformations can be used to specify the evolution of a source schema into a new schema. In our approach, we do not ask users to specify a sequence of transformations. The EVE (Lee, Nica, & Rundensteiner, 2002) investigates the view synchronization problem, which supports a limited set of changes. The work in (Colazzo & Sartiani, 2005) describes techniques for maintaining mapping in XML peer-to-peer databases which is different from our problem. Another mapping maintenance problem studied in (McCann et al., 2005) mainly focuses on detecting inconsistency of simple correspondences between schema elements when schemas evolve. This problem is complementary to the problem we consider here.

Conceptual Models. Conceptual modeling is concerned with the construction of computer-based symbol structures which model some part of the real world directly and naturally (Mylopoulos, 1998). In Database, conceptual modeling produces *semantic data models* which are used to directly and naturally model an application before proceeding to a logical and physical database design. For data management, semantic data models offer more semantic terms and abstraction mechanisms for modeling an application than logical data models.

The fundamental concern for all conceptual models is the abstraction mechanisms. In the following, we summarize some common abstraction mechanisms used in conceptual modeling.

- *Classification,* sometimes called instanceOf, classifies instances under one or more generic classes. Instances of a class share common properties.
- *Generalization,* referred to as ISA, organizes all classes in terms of a partial order relation determined by their generality/specificity. Inheritance is a functional inference rule of generalization mechanism.
- *Aggregation,* also called partOf, views objects as aggregates of their components or parts. A strong form of aggregation states that a component can be a part of only one aggregate.

  Reverse Engineering: Because many databases and their operational environments evolve constantly, maintaining these databases has long been recognized as a painful and complex activity. An important aspect of database maintenance is the recovery of a CM that represents the meaning of the logical schema. Database reverse engineering (Hainaut, 1998) is defined as the process of recovering such a CM by examining an existing database system to identify the database's contents and their interrelationships. Database reverse engineering is relevant to round-trip engineering, but substantially different.

Round-Trip Engineering: Round-trip engineering (Henriksson & Larsson, 2003) has been applied to and studied in software engineering and knowledge management applications (Demeyer, Ducasse, Tichelaar, & Tichelaar, 1999; Knublauch & Rose, 2000). There are commercial software engineering tools for implementing round-trip engineering between Unified Modeling Language models and source code. In software engineering, round-trip engineering is a process for converting a piece of program code to a design and generating the original code from the design.

While reverse engineering can be defined as the process of reconstructing the design of a program from the program itself, round-trip engineering can recover the original program from the reverse-engineered design. In particular, assume that there is a reverse engineering procedure that is always able to give the design of a given program. Now assume that there is a procedure that will always generate the program from a given design. If a design is reverse engineered from a program, used to generate a program, and the generated program is identical to the original program, then this is a round-trip engineering process.

In maintaining mappings between CMs and relational schemas, a round-trip engineering process is employed to synchronize CMs/schemas when changes occur to them. The process implies that the synchronization will propagate changes of the model on one side to the model on the other side. The propagated changes can be converted back to the original changes.

Data Integration: Data integration is the problem of combining data from disparate sources and provides users with a unified view of these data (Lenzerini, 2002). The typical architecture of a data integration system consists of a global schema, a set of data sources (local schemas), and mappings between the sources and the global schema. The sources provide the real data, while the global schema is an integrated and reconciled view of the real data. Sometimes, a middleware infrastructure (Bouguettaya, Malik, Rezgui, & Korff, 2006) is needed to support data integration.

As ontologies have gained growing attention over the past decade, many people have used an ontology as the global schema for a data integration system, building so-called ontology-based information integration systems, for example, Carnot (Collet, Huhns, & Shen, 1991), SIMS (Arens, Knoblock, & Shen, 1996), OBSERVER (Mena, Illarramendi, Kashyap, & Sheth, 1996), Information Manifold (Levy, Srivastava, & Kirk, 1996), InfoSleuth (Bayardo et al., 1997), PICSEL (Goasdoue, Lattes, & Rousset, 1999), and DWQ (Calvanese, Giacomo, Lenzerini, Nardi, & Rosati, 2001). In these systems, mappings are specified from data sources to an ontology acting as a global schema. One of the important problems associated with ontology-based information integration systems is to maintain the mappings between ontologies and source databases when ontology or database schemas change. In this paper, we study a solution to the problem.

Semantic Web: Recently, the Semantic Web was proposed for improving information gathering and integration on the Web (Berners-Lee, Hendler, & Lassila, 2001). Data on the Semantic Web promises to be machine-understandable by being attached through semantic annotations. These annotations can be based on formal ontologies with, hopefully, widely accepted vocabulary and definitions. Data on the Semantic Web could be database-resident data or HTML Web pages. The annotations to database-resident data can be viewed as mappings between the data and ontologies. For the purpose of describing and publishing ontologies on the Semantic Web, the W3C consortium has proposed the RDF (Klyne & Carroll, January 2003) data model and the OWL ontology language (McGuinness & v. Harmelen, 2004). In this paper, we use a general term *conceptual model* to refer to a wide range of data representations including Web ontologies.

FORMAL PRELIMINARIES

In this section, we describe some formal notation about the relational schema and CM studied in this paper.

Relational Schema: A relational database consists of a set of relational tables (or relations) each of which contains a set of tuples. The schema for a table specifies the name of the table, the name of each column (or attribute or field), and the type of each column. Furthermore, we can specify *integrity constraints*, which are conditions that the tuples in tables must satisfy. Here, we consider the *key* and *foreign key* (abbreviated as f.k. henceforth) constraints. A key in a table is a subset of the columns of the table that uniquely identifies a tuple. An f.k. in a table T is a set of columns F that *references* the key of another table T' and imposes a constraint that the projection of T on F is a

Figure 1. Relational tables

biosample					person		
sampleID	species	organ	donorID*		**pID**	age	address
s0001	x1	x2	d0001		d0001	25	xyz
s0002	y1	y2	d0001		d0002	36	abc
....	....	....	....		....	....	....

subset of the projection of *T'* on the key of *T'*. A relational schema thus consists of a set of relational schemes (or tables). Formally, we use R=(R, Σ_R) to denote a relational schema R with a set of tables R and a set Σ_R of key and f.k. constraints.

Figure 1 shows two relational tables: biosample and person. The biosample table has 4 columns: biosample.sampleID, biosample.species, biosample.organ, and biosample.donorID*; the person table has 3 columns: person.pID, person.age, and person.address. We use a dot notation such as tableName.columnName to indicate a column "columnName" of the table "tableName."

Each table contains a number of tuples consisting of values drawn from the domains of the columns. An underlined column such as biosample.sampleID is the key of a table. The column annotated with "*" represents a foreign key (f.k.). For instance, the column biosample.donorID* of the table biosample is a foreign key referencing the key person.pID of the table person. A relational table T with columns $c_1, c_2, ..., c_n$ is written as $T(c_1, c_2,.., c_n)$, for example, biosample (sampleID, species, organ, donorID*).

Conceptual Model. A conceptual model (CM) describes a subject matter in terms of concepts, relationships, and attributes. In this paper, we do not restrict ourselves to any particular language for describing CMs. Instead, we use a generic conceptual modeling language (CML), which has the following specifications. The language allows the representation of *classes/concepts/entities* (unary predicates over individuals), *object prop-*

erties/relationships (binary predicates relating individuals), and *datatype properties/attributes* (binary predicates relating individuals with values such as integers and strings); attributes are single valued in this paper. Concepts are organized in ISA hierarchy, that is, generalization/specialization hierarchy. Relationships and their inverses (which are always present) are subject to cardinality constraints each of which consists of two numbers: a lower bound cardinality and an upper bound cardinality. If the lower bound cardinality for a relationship is 1, then the relationship is called a *total* relationship. If the upper bound cardinality for a relationship is 1, then the relationship is called a *functional* relationship. If the upper bound cardinalities of a relationship and its inverse are greater than 1, then the relationship is called a *many-to-many* relationship. In addition, a subset of attributes of a concept is specified as the identifier of the concept. As in the Entity-Relationship model, a strong entity has a global identifier, while a weak entity is identified by an identifying relationship plus a local identifier. We use C=(C, Σ_C) to denote a CM C with a set C of concepts, attributes, and relationships and a set Σ_C of identification and cardinality constraints.

Figure 2 shows a conceptual model having 4 concepts and several relationships. In the figure, a relationship and its inverse are represented as a single line. For instance, the line between the concepts Biosample and Person represents the relationship donor from Biosample to Person and its inverse donation from Person to Biosample.

The concept Person is a specialized concept of the more general concept Donor. These two

Figure 2. A conceptual model

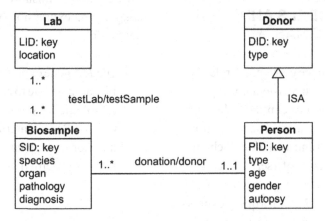

concepts are organized in an ISA hierarchy. The lower bound cardinality of the donation relationship is 1. This indicates that the donation relationship is total, that is, each donor donates at least one Biosample instance. The upper bound cardinality of the donor relationship is 1. This indicates that the donor relationship is a functional relationship, that is, a given Biosample instance has a unique donor. Both upper bound cardinalities of the relationship testLab and its inverse testSample are greater than 1. This indicates that the relationship is a many-to-many relationship. The keyword "key" indicates the identifier of a concept.

Figure 3 illustrates a conceptual model with a weak entity, Sample concept. A weak entity in a CM diagram is represented as a double-lined rectangle. The identifying/ownership relationship is represented by a dashed line in the CM, that is, the screenedIn relationship. The ownership relationship indicates that a sample cannot be globally identified by its local identifier sid. To globally identify a sample, the combination of the identifier, tid, of the owner entity, Test, and the local identifier, sid, of the weak entity, Sample,

must be used together. An identifying/ownership relationship from a weak entity to its owner entity is always functional, that is, each weak entity has a unique owner entity.

We can represent a given CM as a graph called a *CM graph*. We construct the CM graph from a CM by considering concepts and attributes as nodes and relationships as edges. There are also edges between a concept node and the attribute nodes belonging to the concept. For the sake of succinctness, we sometimes use UML-like notations, as in Figures 2 and 3, to represent the CM graph. Note that in such a diagram, instead of drawing separate attribute nodes, we place the attributes inside the rectangle concept nodes; and relationships and their inverses are represented by a single undirected edge. A many-to-many relationship p between concepts C_1 and C_2 will be written in text as C_1---p---C_2. For a functional relationship q, ones with upper bound cardinality of 1, from C_1 to C_2, we write C_1---q->--C_2. In a CM graph, we will treat an ISA relationship as a 1:1 functional edge.

Figure 3. A weak entity in a conceptual model

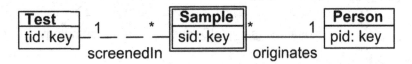

MAPPINGS BETWEEN CONCEPTUAL MODELS AND RELATIONAL SCHEMAS

In this section, we introduce conceptual-relational mappings and define a consistent conceptual-relational mapping. A conceptual-relational mapping specifies a particularly meaningful relationship between a CM and a relational schema. Formally, a mapping consists of a set of statements each of which relates a query expression $\Phi(X,Y)$ in a language L_1 over the CM with a query expression $\Psi(X,Y)$ in a language L_2 over the relational schema. In such a statement, the shared variables X give rise to the query results. In this paper, we consider conjunctive formulae over concepts, attributes, and relationships in a CM and conjunctive formulae over relational tables. A conjunctive formula over relational tables can be translated into equivalent select, join, and project (SJP) query expressions. Queries are evaluated in the usual way.

In the sequel, we will use the terms "mapping" and "mapping statement" interchangeably when the context is clear. Generally, we represent a conceptual-relational mapping (or mapping statement) between a CM and a relational schema as an expression $\Phi(X,Y) \ll \Psi(X,Y)$, where $\Phi(X,Y)$ and $\Psi(X,Y)$ are conjunctive formulae. The following example illustrates the mapping formalism using a gene expression database and a conceptual model.

Example 1: A gene expression database contains a biosample table to record information about a biological sample which can be a tissue, cell, or RNA material that originates from a donor of a given species. The biosample table is specified as follows:

```
biosample(sampleID, species, organ,
pathology,..., donorID*),
```

Formally, a mapping between a CM and a relational table is represented as an expression in the form of $\Phi(X,Y) \ll \Psi(X,Y)$. In this example, the conceptual-relational mapping between the relational table biosample and the CM shown in Figure 4 is represented in the following expression:

$M : Biosample(x_1) \wedge SID(x_1, sampleID) \wedge$
$species(x_1, species) \wedge ... \wedge Person(x_2) \wedge$
$donation(x_1, x_2) \wedge PID(x_2, donorID) \leftrightarrow$
$biosample(sampleID, species, ..., donorID),$

Figure 4. A conceptual model, a relational schema, and value correspondences

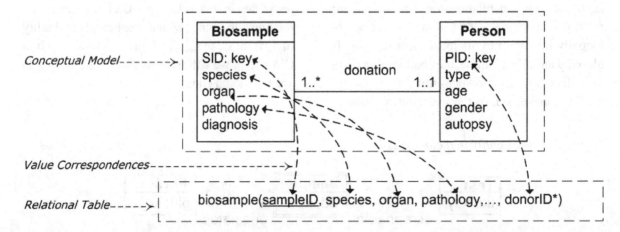

where, the prefix *M:* indicates that the expression is a mapping, the predicates *Biosample* and *Person* represent the concepts in the CM, the predicates *SID, species,...,* represent the attributes of the concepts and the relationship, and the shared variables *sampleID, species,...,* give rise to query results on both sides. +

Consistent Conceptual-Relational Mappings: The semantics of a mapping expression $\Phi(X, Y)$ « $\Psi(X, Y)$ is given through data instances. Three possibilities have been considered in the literature (Lenzerini, 2002), *sound, complete,* and *exact.* A sound or complete mapping $\Phi(X, Y)$ « $\Psi(X, Y)$ means that the answers provided by one query, for example, $\Phi(X, Y)$, is contained in the answers provided by another query, for example, $\Psi(X, Y)$. An exact mapping means that these two sets of answers are equivalent, that is, both sound and complete. We define a *consistent* mapping as an exact mapping over all *legal* instances of the two related models. We write such a consistent mapping as $\Phi(X, Y) = \Psi(X, Y)$.

Specifically, we define a *consistent* conceptual-relational mapping $\Phi(X, Y) = \Psi(X, Y)$ between a CM and a relational schema in terms of *legal instances* of the CM and the relational schema. An *instance* of a model contains values drawn from the element domains specified by the model definition. An element domain contains a set of permissible values. Generally, for a given model we can construct multiple instances. However, in defining a consistent conceptual-relational mapping, we are more interested in *legal instances* of models. Formally, for a CM C=(C, Σ_c), a legal instance I is an instance of C which satisfies the constraints Σ_c, denoted as $I ' \Sigma_c$. We use I to denote the set of all legal instances of C, that is, I={$I \mid I$ is an instance of C and $I ' \Sigma_c$}. Likewise, for a relational schema R=(R, Σ_R),

we use J to denote the set of all legal instances of R, i.e., J={$J \mid J$ is an instance of R and $J ' \Sigma_R$}.

For a query expression $\Phi(X, Y)$ over C, we use I^F to denote the query results over the instance *I*. We use J^Y to denote the query results of the query expression $\Psi(X, Y)$ over the instance *J* of R. We say that a pair of legal instances <*I, J*> satisfies a mapping statement $M: \Phi(X, Y) = \Psi(X, Y)$ between C and R, if and only if $I^F = J^Y$, denoted as <*I, J*>' *M*.

Definition 1 [Consistent Conceptual-Relational Mapping]:For a CM C=(C, Σ_c) and a relational schema R=(R, Σ_R), a mapping M: $\Phi(X, Y) = \Psi(X, Y)$ between C and R is consistent if and only if for every legal instance IÎI, there is a legal instance JÎJ such that <I, J> ' M, and for every legal instance J' Î J, there is a legal instance I' Î I such that <I', J'> ' M.

Essentially, the consistency of a mapping dictates that the constraints in the CM and the schema are *consistent*. For example, if a relationship in a CM is mapped to a relational table in a relational schema, then the cardinality constraints imposed on the relationship are consistent with the key and foreign key constraints defined over the columns of the table.

CHANGES TO SCHEMAS AND CMS

A user can change a schema (or CM) in different ways: either through modifying the original schema (or CM) or by generating a new schema (or CM) directly. If a user changes a schema (or CM) by modifying the original schema (or CM), a possible way to capture the changes is to classify them into a set of primitive actions. An example set of primitive actions (Velegrakis et al., 2004) includes (1) adding/deleting elements, (2) merging/splitting elements, (3) moving/copying elements, (4) renaming elements, and (5) modifying constraints. On the other hand, if a user changed a schema (or CM) through generating a new schema (or CM), it would be difficult to ask the user to provide a sequence of primitive actions for capturing the changes. In this case, it is probably easier to ask the user to draw a set of simple correspondences between the elements in the new schema (or CM) and the elements in the original schema (or CM). In this paper, we use a set of correspondences between columns in schemas (or attributes in CMs) to capture the commonality/differences between a new schema (or CM) and an original schema (or CM).

Simple Correspondences: A simple correspondence is a link/relationship *between a single element e_1 in a model M_1 and a single element e_2 in another model M_2.* We represent such a correspondence as $M_1{:}e_1$ Ï $M_2{:}e_2$ or a simple line in a graph, where the prefixes M_1 and M_2 distinguishes elements in the two models. For example, $R_1{:}T_1.f$Ï $R_2{:}T_2.e$ represents the simple correspondence between the column f of the table T_1 in the relational schema R_1 and the column e of the table T_2 in the relational schema R_2. The following example illustrates that changes to a schema are captured by a set of simple correspondences specified as dashed lines.

Example 2: Figure 5 shows on the top an original schema R_1 consisting of a single table biosample. At the bottom of the figure is a new schema R_2 containing two tables biosample and tissue. R_2 evolved from R_1. The dashed lines between columns in R_1 and the columns in R_2 capture the commonality/differences between the original schema and the new

schema. The open arrow indicates that the column tissue.bsid* is a foreign key referring to the key biosample.bsid +.

MAINTAINING CONCEPTUAL-RELATIONAL MAPPINGS

As introduced earlier, conceptual models and schemas evolve over time to accommodate changes in the information they represent. Such evolution may cause existing conceptual-relational mappings to become inconsistent. The focus of this paper is to deal with the problem of maintaining conceptual-relational mappings under evolution. The solution we develop is a round-trip engineering approach that synchronizes the schema and CM, and keeps the mapping consistent. To achieve the goal of synchronization, the algorithm in the round-trip engineering approach must first "understand" the existing semantics in the original mapping and then systematically update the associated schema and CM.

We begin with exploring the knowledge encoded in the standard forward engineering process. The forward engineering process designs relational schemas from CMs. We then develop the algorithms in the round-trip engineering approach by utilizing that knowledge.

Knowledge about the Conceptual-Relational Mappings in Standard Database Design Process

In relational database design, a standard technique (we refer to this as ER-to-Relational schema

Figure 5. Capturing schema change

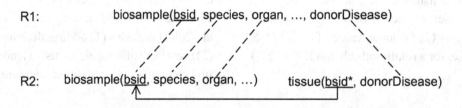

design) which is widely covered in undergraduate database courses (Elmasri & Navathe, 2006) derives a relational schema from an Entity-Relationship diagram. The ER-to-Relational design implies a set of conceptual-relational mappings in the form $\Phi(X,Y)=T(X)$, where $\Phi(X,Y)$ is a conjunctive formula encoding a tree structure called *semantic tree or s-tree* (An et al., 2006) in a CM, and $T(X)$ is a relational table with columns X. Such a conceptual-relational mapping is also used in the middleware mapping technologies.

In this paper, we choose to design our solution for synchronizing models and maintaining mappings in a systematic manner by considering the behavior of our algorithm based on the conceptual-relational mappings encoded in the ER-to-Relational design process. In our previous work (An et al., 2006), we have carefully analyzed the knowledge encoded in the ER-to-Relational design. We summarize the knowledge related to our study in this paper as follows.

The ER-to-Relational design methodology is defined by a function t(O) returning a relational table scheme for every CM component O, where O is either a concept/entity or a relationship. We use key(T) to refer to the key of a relational table T; therefore, key(t(O)) refers to the key of the table generated from the object O in a CM. In listing the results of applying the function t(O) to an Entity-Relationship diagram, we use several functions for referring to the components of the ER diagram. Specifically, for an entity set E (called just "entity" here), function attribs(E) returns the attributes of the entity. A strong entity S has some attributes that act as identifier. We shall refer to these using unique(S) when describing the rules of schema design. A weak entity W has instead localUnique(W) attributes, plus a functional total binary relationship p denoted as idRel(W) to an identifying owner entity denoted as idOwn(W). Table 1 illustrates the application of the function

Table 1. ER-to-relational design

ER Diagram Object O		Relational Table t(O)
Strong Entity S Let X = attribs(S) Let K = unique(S) Let y be the variable used in the mapping for the entity S	*columns:* *primary key:* *foreign key:* *anchor:* *mapping:*	X K none S $T(X) = S(y)$ÙhasAttribs(y,X)
Weak Entity W Let E = idOwn(W), P = idRel(W) Z = attribs(W), X = key$(t(E))$ U = localUnique(W), $V = Z - U$ Let y_1 and y_2 be the variables used in the mapping for W and E, respectively.	*columns:* *primary key:* *foreign key:* *anchor:* *mapping:*	ZX UX X W $T(U,X,V) = W(y_1)$ÙhasAttribs(y_1,Z)Ù$E(y_2)$Ù$P(y_1,y_2)$ Ùidentify$_E(y_2,X)$.
Functional Relationship F from E_1 to E_2 Let $X_i = t(E_i)$ for $i = 1, 2$ Let y_1 and y_2 be the variables used in the mapping for E_1 and E_2, respectively.	*columns:* *primary key:* *foreign key:* *anchor:* *mapping:*	X_1X_2 X_1 X_1 referencing $t(E_1)$ E_1 $T(X_1,X_2) = E_1(y_1)$ Ù identify$_{E1}(y_1,X_1)$ Ù$F(y_1,y_2)$ Ù $E_2(y_2)$ Ù identify$_{E2}(y_2,X_2)$.
Many-to-Many Relationship M between E_1 and E_2 Let $X_i = t(E_i)$ for $i = 1, 2$ Let y_1 and y_2 be the variables used in the mapping for E_1 and E_2, respectively.	*columns:* *primary key:* *foreign key:* *anchor:* *mapping:*	X_1X_2 X_1X_2 X_i referencing $t(E_i)$ for $i = 1,2$ none $T(X_1,X_2) = E_1(y_1)$ Ù identify$_{E1}(y_1,X_1)$ Ù $M(y_1,y_2)$ Ù$E_2(y_2)$ Ù identify$_{E2}(y_2,X_2)$.

t(O) to the Entity-Relational model that only contains binary relationships.

In addition to the schema (columns, key, f.k.s), Table 1 also associates with a relational table T(X) a number of additional notions:

- An anchor, which is the central object in the CM from which T is derived, and which is useful in explaining our algorithm (it will be the root of the semantic tree);

- A formula for the semantic mapping for the table, expressed as a formula in the form of $T(X) = \Phi(X, Y)$ (this is what our algorithm should be maintaining); in the body of the formula, the function hasAttribs(x, Y) returns conjuncts $attr_j(x, Y[j])$ for the individual columns $Y[1], Y[2], \ldots$ in Y, where $attr_j$ is the attribute name corresponded by column $Y[j]$.

- The predicate $identify_C(x, Y)$ which can be expanded into a conjunctive formula, showing how object x in (strong or weak) entity C can be identified by values in Y.

Another important step of the ER-to-Relational schema design methodology suggests that the schema generated using t(O) can be modified by (repeatedly) *merging* into the table T_0 of an entity E the table T_1 of some functional relationship involving the same entity E (which has a foreign key reference to T_0). Consequently, tables for multiple functional relationships can be merged into the table for the single entity involved in these functional relationships. Graphically, the merged table represents the information from a tree structure connecting all participating entitles. In fact, as illustrated in Table 1, all of the objects that the ER-to-Relational design function t applies to are trees: either a single node tree, for example, a strong entity, or a tree connecting multiple entities, for example, a many-to-many relationship. Trees also correspond to the tables derived from ER models containing n-ary relationships (An et

al., 2006). We call the trees that are associated with the relational tables generated by the ER-to-Relational design *semantic tree (s-tree)* in a CM.

If a relational table T contains foreign keys, then the table also represents information about some relationships. To further capture the fine-grained knowledge about the ER-to-Relational design process, we can decompose an s-tree into several sub-trees: a sub-tree corresponding to the key of the table, sub-trees corresponding to f.k.s of the table, and sub-trees corresponding to the rest of the columns of the table. This decomposition is not a simple decomposition of the entire s-tree into its nodes and edges because some sub-trees are not trivial (i.e., not single nodes). For example, if a table represents a many-to-many relationship between two *weak entities*, then the key of the table is the combination of the keys of the tables for the two weak entities. The keys of the tables for the two weak entities correspond to trees representing the identifying/owner relationships between the weak entities and their owner entities. We call the sub-trees corresponding to key and foreign keys *skeleton trees* of an s-tree. The semantic and skeleton trees have the following more characteristics:

1. Each skeleton tree has a root which is the anchor entity illustrated in Table 1.

2. To satisfy the semantics of the key in a table, the s-tree is connected by functional paths from the anchor of the skeleton tree corresponding to the key to the anchors of the skeleton trees corresponding to the foreign keys as well as anchors of other skeleton trees.

   Example 3: Figure 6 shows a relational table sample(sid, test*, donor*) and the associated s-tree: Test --<-screenIn-- Sample –originates->- Person. As the diagram indicates, the Sample concept is a weak entity connecting to the owner entity Test by the identifying relationships --<-screenIn--. The anchor of

Figure 6. S-tree and skeleton trees

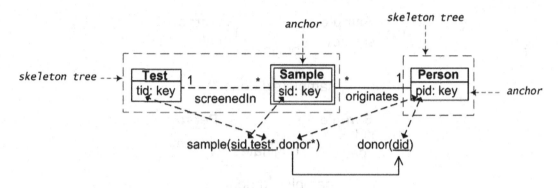

the s-tree is the Sample concept. The sample.donor* column is a foreign key referencing the key donor.did of the table donor(did) which is associated with the s-tree consisting of a single node Person.

The s-tree associated with the table sample(sid, test*, donor*) is decomposed into two skeleton trees: The skeleton tree Test --<-screenIn-- Sample corresponds to the key {sample.sid, sample.test} of the table. The second skeleton tree Person corresponds to the foreign key sample.donor* of table. The anchor of the first skeleton tree is the Sample node and the anchor of the second skeleton tree is the Person node.+

Sketch of the Maintenance Algorithm

We now turn to the problem of maintaining a conceptual-relational mapping under evolution. We first outline the maintaining algorithm for round-trip engineering through the mappings in the form of $\Phi(X, Y) = T(X)$. We develop the complete algorithm later. Given a relational schema R, a CM C, a set of existing consistent conceptual-relational mappings $M = \{ \Phi(X, Y) = T(X) \}$ between R and C, a new schema R' (or CM C'), and a set of correspondences M' between R and R' (or between C and C'), the algorithm works in

several steps for fulfilling the goals of model synchronization and mapping maintenance:

1. Analyze the existing semantics in the original mapping in terms of skeleton trees and connections between roots (i.e., anchors) of skeleton trees.
2. Discover changes through the correspondences between the new schema/CM and the original schema/CM.
3. Synchronize the associated CM/schema and adapt the mapping accordingly.

   Illustrative Examples: Before fleshing out the above steps, we illustrate the algorithms using several examples on *schema evolution*. Through these examples, we lay out our principles for mapping maintenance and model synchronization.

*Example 4 [Adding a Column]:*Figure 7 (a) shows a mapping which is specified in the following statement:

$$M : Sample(x_1) \wedge sid(x_1, sid) \wedge Person(x_2) \wedge$$
$$originates(x_1, x_2) \wedge pid(x_2, donor) = sample(sid, donor)$$

Figure 7 (b) shows that a column species was added to the table sample(sid, donor*). *For adding an element in the schema, our goal of mapping maintenance is to add a corresponding element in the CM to maximize the coverage of*

Figure 7. Adding a column to a schema

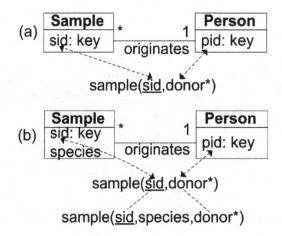

the schema elements. Because the key column sid corresponds to the identifier attribute of the Sample concept and the column sample.donor* is a foreign key referring to the key donor.did of a table donor(did) (not shown in the figure) for the Person concept, we synchronize the CM through adding an attribute sample.species to the Sample concept which is the anchor of the skeleton tree corresponding to the key sample.sid +.

The *first principle* for mapping maintenance under schema evolution is to locate, through correspondences, the appropriate elements in the CM for adding new attributes. The location process is guided by analyzing the key and foreign key information in the original and new schemas.

Adding a new column to the schema associated with a mapping may have different effects on the mapping. As we illustrated in Example 4, if the new column is not a foreign key, a new attribute

is added to the anchor of the skeleton tree in the CM, where the skeleton tree corresponds to the key of the schema. However, if a newly added column is a foreign key, a functional relationship needs to be discovered or added for achieving the goal of mapping maintenance. Because an f.k. represents a functional relationship between two elements in the CM, adding foreign key columns in the schema means that the semantics of the schema covers a new functional relationship. The original mapping needs to accommodate the new semantics. The following example illustrates the situation when a foreign key column is added to the schema associated with a mapping.

Example 5: Figure 8 shows an original mapping between a table sample(sid,test,donor*) and an s-tree:

Figure 8. An original mapping

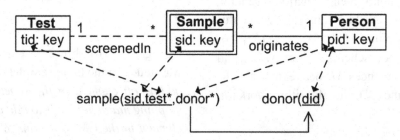

$M : Test(x_1) \wedge tid(x_1, test) \wedge Sample(x_2) \wedge sid(x_2, sid) \wedge$
$screenedIn(x_1, x_2) \wedge Person(x_3) \wedge$
$originates(x_2, x_3) \wedge pid(x_3, donor) =$
$saple(sid, test, donor).$

In the CM, Sample is modeled as a weak entity with an identifying functional relationship screenedIn connecting to the owner entity Test. Accordingly, the key of the table sample(sid,test*,donor*) is the combination of columns sample.sid and sample.test* with sample. test* being a foreign key referring to a table test(tid) for the Test concept (not shown in the figure.)

In Figure 9, the table sample(sid, test*, donor*) is changed to sample(sid,test*,disease*,donor*) with the new column sample.disease* being a foreign key referring to the key disease.dsid of the table disease(dsid). The foreign key constraint is shown as the open arrow. To update the mapping between the new sample table and the CM, we analyze the key and foreign key structure of the table and recognize that Sample class is the *anchor* of the skeleton tree S: Test -<--screenIn--- Sample for the key of the original table sample(sid,test*,donor*) . Sample is a weak entity which must be identified by the owner entity Test through the identifying relationship screenIn. But Sample is the anchor

of the skeleton tree corresponding to the key of the table sample(sid,test*,donor*).

The newly added foreign key sample.disease* represents a functional relationship from the anchor of the s-tree S to the anchor of the s-tree corresponding to the key of the table disease(dsid). The anchor of the s-tree S is the Sample class, while the anchor of the s-tree corresponding to the key of the table disease(dsid) is the Disease_Stage class. Therefore, we update the original mapping between sample(sid,test*,donor*) and the CM to a new mapping between sample(sid,test*,disease*,donor*) and the CM where the s-tree which is associate with sample(sid,test*,d isease*,donor*) covers a new functional relationship from Sample to Disease_Stage. The new mapping expression is as follows:

$M : Test(x_1) \wedge tid(x_1, test) \wedge Sample(x_2) \wedge sid(x_2, sid) \wedge$
$screenedIn(x_1, x_2) \wedge Person(x_3) \wedge$
$originates(x_2, x_3) \wedge pid(x_3, donor) \wedge$
$Disease\_Stage(x_4) \wedge dsid(x_4, disease) \wedge$
$disease(x_2, x_4) = sample(sid, test, disease, donor).$

Note that with the key and foreign key structures, we correctly identified a functional relationship from the weak entity Sample to the

Figure 9. Adding a foreign key column to a schema

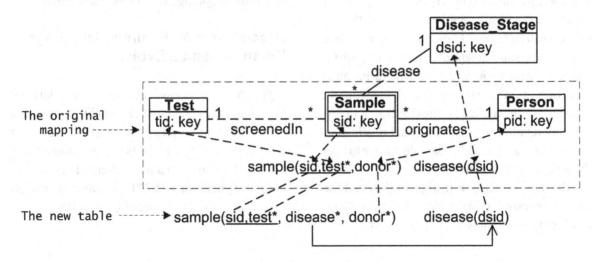

Disease_Stage concept rather than some other relationship from other concepts, for example, the owner entity Test concept, to the Disease_Stage concept. +

Our *second principle* is to locate, through the correspondences, the anchors of the appropriate skeleton trees for discovering/adding relationships. The location process is guided by using key and foreign key structure in the schemas.

Primitive changes to schemas include adding columns, deleting columns, and changing constraints. We have illustrated the situations about adding different types of columns. For deleting columns, it is easier to update the mapping by deleting any references to the deleted columns in the mapping expression. The next example illustrates the case when a constraint is changed in the schema associated with a mapping.

Example 6 [Changing Constraints]: The following existing mapping associates a relational table treat(tid*, sgid*) with a CM Treatment---appliesTo---Sample_Group:

$$M : Treatment(x_1) \wedge tid(x_1, tid) \wedge Sample\_Group(x_2) \wedge$$
$$appliesTo(x_1, x_2) \wedge sgid(x_2, sid) = treat(tid, sgid)$$

where, the relationship appliesTo is many-to-many.

Later, the database administrator obtained a better understanding of the application by realizing that each treatment only applies to one sample group. Consequently, the DBA changed the key of the treat(tid*, sgid*) table from the combination of columns {treat.tid*, treat.sgid*} to the single column treat.tid*, so the table becomes treat(tid*, sgid*). Having the change on the schema, we update the appliesTo from a many-to-many relationship to a functional relationship Treatment---appliesTo->--Sample_Group to keep the mapping consistent.

The *third principle* is to align the key and foreign key constraints in the (new) schema with the cardinality constraints in the (new) CM.

Round-Trip Engineering Algorithm for Mapping Maintenance

In this paper, we develop a round-trip engineering algorithm for maintaining *consistent mappings*. In particular, the input to the maintenance algorithm is a set of conceptual-relational mapping statements $\{\Phi(X, Y) = T(X)\}$. Each statement is consistent and associates a relational table $T(X)$ with a semantic tree in a CM. The semantic tree is encoded in the formula $\Phi(X, Y)$. In general, conceptual-relational mappings may associate graphs with conjunctive formulae over schema. For a mapping associating a graph with a conjunctive formulae over a schema, we can first convert the graph into a tree by replicating nodes (An et al., 2007). Then we either decompose the mapping into mappings between semantic trees (s-trees) and single tables or treat the entire conjunctive formula over the schema as a big table. The details for converting general mappings into mappings between semantic trees and tables are beyond the scope of this paper and will be realized in future work.

The maintenance algorithm has two components. The first component deals with changes to schemas, and the second component deals with changes to CMs. We first focus on schema changes. The following Procedure 1 synchronizes models and maintains the consistency of conceptual-relational mappings when schemas evolve.

Procedure 1 Maintaining Mappings When Schemas Evolve

Input: A set of consistent conceptual-relational mappings $M=\{\Phi(X, Y) = T(X)\}$ between a CM C and a relational schema R; a set of correspondences M' between columns in R and columns in a new schema R'.

Output: Synchronized CM C'' and a set of updated mappings M'' between C'' and R'.

Steps:

1. Mark skeleton trees: for each mapping statement in *M*, decompose the semantic tree in the CM into several skeleton trees based on the key and foreign key structures of the table; mark the associations between keys/f.k.s and skeleton trees.

2. Apply the principles we have laid out above to each of the following cases for synchronizing the CM and updating the mapping (we ignore the renaming change in our algorithm):

    a. *Case 1:* A new table is obtained by adding columns, deleting columns, or changing constraints to a single original table.

    b. *Case 2:* A new table is obtained by adding columns, deleting columns, or changing constraints from several original tables.

    c. *Case 3:* Multiple new tables are obtained by adding columns, deleting columns, or changing constraints from a single original table.

We now elaborate on each case.

- If a new table is obtained from a single table, then columns which are not foreign key components have been changed or a foreign key has been deleted. Otherwise, the change would involve multiple original tables, which is covered in Case 2. If a new column is added, then the algorithm adds a new attribute to the anchor of the key skeleton tree (see Example 4). If the column becomes part of the key, then the new attribute becomes part of the identifier of the anchor. If a column is deleted, we only update the mapping by removing the reference to the deleted column in the mapping. If the key constraint has been changed, then synchronize the identifier of the anchor of the key's skeleton tree ac-

cordingly. Finally, if a foreign key is deleted, then update the mapping by removing the corresponding functional relationship referenced in the mapping.

- If a new table *T* is obtained from several tables $\{T_1, T_2, ..., T_n\}$, then we focus on the following two situations: (1) foreign keys are modified in the table *T* and (2) multiple tables are merged. When new foreign keys are added to the new table *T*, we consider merging the semantic trees which correspond to the original tables $\{T_1, T_2, ..., T_n\}$ to obtain a larger tree. Suppose that the key of the table *T* comes from the key of table T_1. Let the skeleton trees $\{S_1, S_2, ..., S_n\}$ correspond to the keys of $\{T_1, T_2, ..., T_n\}$. Connect the anchor of S_1 to the anchors of $\{S_2, ..., S_n\}$ by *functional edges*. The new table is mapped to the larger tree. Example 5 illustrates the case where a new table sample(sid, test*, disease*, donor*) evolved from two original tables sample(sid, test*, donor*) and disease(dsid). The new table is mapped to a larger semantic tree by connecting the two anchors Sample and Disease_Stage using a functional edge ---disease-->.

We now continue the above illustration. If multiple tables are merged into the new table *T* *through the same key,* we merge the corresponding s-trees by connecting them using ISA relationships from the anchor of S_1 to the anchors of $\{S_2, ..., S_n\}$. If the s-trees are the same because the original tables store the split information about the same s-tree, we update the mapping by merging the original mapping expressions into a larger one.

If existing foreign keys are updated in the table *T,* we proceed as follows. If a foreign key is deleted, then it is handled by Case 1. If a foreign key becomes part of the key, we identify the corresponding functional relationship in the CM. Whether we modify the functional relationship depends on the semantics of the key structure. If the original key is also a foreign key, update the relationship from functional to non-functional. Otherwise, the functional relationship remains unchanged because it indicates an identifying relationship for a weak entity.

- Multiple tables $\{T_1, T_2, ..., T_n\}$ are obtained from a single table T. There are two subcases: (1) creating new tables connecting to the original table through foreign keys and (2) splitting an original table. For case (1), if new tables are created and connect to the original table through foreign keys, we create new concepts and functional relationships in the CM. For case (2), splitting an original table into multiple tables primarily means two things: (i) storing the information about a structure of a CM in different relational tables and (ii) storing the information about an ISA (i.e., generalization/specialization) hierarchy into separate tables, each table corresponds to a single concept in the hierarchy. In both case (i) and case (ii), the set of new tables should have the same key. Among the set of tables, the key of one table is not a foreign key, while the keys of the rest of the tables are foreign keys referencing the key of the first table. We focus on the case of splitting the information about an ISA hierarchy here.

The ability to represent ISA hierarchies, such as the one in Figure 2, is a hallmark of modern conceptual modeling languages. If two classes are involved in an ISA relationship, we usually call the more general class *superclass* and the specialized class *subclass*. Almost all textbooks (e.g., Elmasri & Navathe, 2006) describe several techniques for designing relational schemas in the presence of ISA hierarchies:

1. Map each class/concept into a separate table following the standard ER-to-Relational rules. Each table for a subclass must have the same key as the table for the single superclass. The key of a subclass table is also a foreign key referencing the key of the superclass table.

2. Expand inheritance, so that all attributes and relations involving a class C appear on all its subclasses. Then generate tables as usual for the subclasses, though not for C itself. This approach is used only when the subclasses cover the superclass.

3. Some researchers also suggest a third possibility: "Collapse up" the information about subclasses into the table for the superclass. The "collapse-up" can be viewed as the result of merging the subclass tables generated at case 1.

When an original table is split into several tables, each of which has the same key as the original table and the key is also a foreign key, then we can consider it as the result of the following process: Splitting the information about an ISA hierarchy into individual tables. The original table might be generated by design (3.). In the CM, it could be imagined that the entire ISA hierarchy was "collapsed up." Then the "collapsed up" table gets split into tables as generated by design (1.). Accordingly, we should create separate subclasses in the CM corresponding to the separate tables.

For multiple tables $\{T_1, T_2, ..., T_n\}$ that are obtained from a single table T, we assume that one of the tables inherits the key of T. Without losing generality, suppose T_1 inherits the key of T. We then create new concepts $\{C_2, ..., C_n\}$ in the CM for the new tables $\{T_2, ..., T_n\}$, respectively. Let S_1 be the original s-tree associated with T. Some attributes of S_1 are moved to concepts $\{C_2, ..., C_n\}$, if the attributes are associated with those columns in T such that the columns are split into tables $\{T_2, ..., T_n\}$. Let C_1 be the anchor of the skeleton tree in S_1 corresponding to the key of T_1. For tables T_i $(i=2..n)$, if there is a foreign key constraint from the column $T_i.f$ to the key of T_1, then we connect

C_i to C_1 by a functional edge in the CM. If the column $T_i.f$ is also the key of the table T_1, then we connect C_i to C_1 by an ISA relationship.

Example 7 [Adding New Tables]: In Figure 10, a new schema R_2 containing two tables biosample and tissue evolved from the original schema R_1 with a single table biosample. The original mapping associates R_1 with the concept Biosample. On the top of the figure is a new CM, where a new concept Tissue is added and connected to Biosample by an ISA relationship according to the f.k. constraint between the keys tissue.bsid* and biosample.bsid of the tissue and biosample tables in the new schema R_2. +

The following proposition states the desired property of the Procedure 1 for maintaining a conceptual-relational mapping through synchronizing the CM and schema when the associated schema evolves.

Proposition 1:Let the input of the Procedure 1 be (1) $M=\{\Phi(X,Y)=T(X)\}$ which is a set of consistent conceptual-relational mappings between a CM C and a relational schema R, and (2) M' which is a set of identity correspondences between columns in R and columns in a new schema R' evolved from R. Each mapping in the set of conceptual-relational mappings returned by the Procedure 1 is consistent.

Proof (Sketch): The proof of the proposition is almost straightforward but tedious. The following is a lengthy sketch of the proof.

By the Definition 1, a mapping M: $\Phi(X,Y)=T(X)$ between a CM C=(C, Σ_C) and a relational schema R=(R, Σ_R) is consistent, if and only if for every legal instance I of R, there is a legal instance J of C such that <I, J> ' M, and vice versa. To prove Proposition 1, we consider the set of mappings $M¢=\{\Phi'(X,Y)=T¢(X)\}$ between a new CM C¢ and a new schema R¢ returned by the Procedure 1. We need to prove that for any

Figure 10. Add a new concept for a newly added table

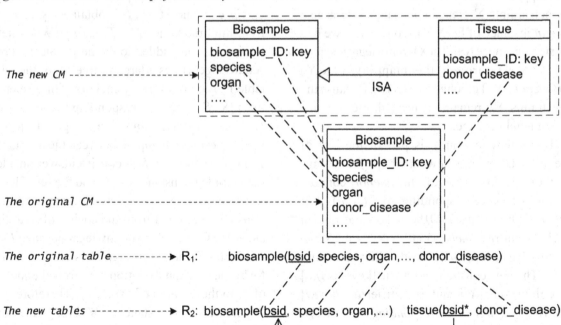

mapping statement $\Phi'(X,Y)=T¢(X)$ in $M¢$, *for* a legal instance of $C¢$, we can find a legal instance of $R¢$ such that the two instances together satisfy the statement, and vice versa.

We conduct the proof for each case in Procedure 1 as follows.

Case 1: A new table is obtained from a single table. Let T be the original table with mapping $F(X,Y) = T(X)$. Let $T¢$ be the new table with mapping $F¢(X,Y)=T¢(X)$. If $T¢$ is obtained from T by adding a new column c which is not a foreign key, then Procedure 1 adds a new attribute f to the anchor of the s-tree corresponding to F(X,Y). In particular, $F¢(X,Y)=F(X,Y)Ùf(anchor, c)$ and $T¢(X)=T¢(columns(T(X),c)$, where the variable *anchor* denotes the anchor of the s-tree corresponding to F(X,Y), and columns(T(X)) denotes the columns of the table T(X). For a legal instance $I¢$ of $T¢$, $I¢$ contains new values for the new column c and values corresponding to a legal instance I of T. We can create an instance $J¢$ of $F¢(X,Y)$ through the mapping $F(X,Y)Ùf(anchor, c)$ $=T¢(columns(T(X),c)$ as follows. First, we map the legal instance I of T(X) to the legal instance J of F(X,Y). Second, the values for the column c are mapped to the values of the attribute f. Because the constraints Σ_c remain unchanged, $J¢$ is also a *legal* instance of $F¢(X,Y)$. Conversely, we can create an instance $I¢$ of $T¢(X)$ from a legal instance of $F¢(X,Y)$ through the mapping F(X,Y) $Ùf(anchor, c)$ $=T¢(columns(T(X),c)$. Because the constraints Σ_R remain unchanged, the instance $I¢$ is a legal instance.

If the new column c is part of the key of the new table, the new attribute f becomes part of the identifier of the *anchor* concept of the s-tree corresponding to F(X,Y). Let key$(T(X))$®columns$(T(X))$ be the key constraint in S_R. Let identifier$(anchor)$®attributes*(s-tree S cor-responding to F(X,Y))* be the identifier constraint in S_C. The new constraints become [key$(T(X))$,c] ® columns$(T¢(X))$ and [identifier$(anchor)$,f] ®attributes*(s-tree S¢ corresponding to F¢(X,Y))*.

By the consistency of the mapping $F(X,Y) = T(X)$, key$(T(X))$ corresponds to identifier*(anchor)* and columns$(T(X))$ corresponds to attributes*(s-tree S)*. By the mapping $F(X,Y)Ùf(anchor, c)$ $=T¢(columns(T(X),c)$, columns$(T¢(X))$ corresponds to attributes*(s-tree S¢)* and the values of f correspond to the value of c. Therefore, the two constraints are [key*(T(X))*,c] ®[columns*(T(X)*,c] and [identifier*(anchor)*,f] ®[attributes*(s-tree S corresponding to F(X,Y))*,f] . It is easy to show that for a legal instance of $T¢(X)$, we can create a legal instance of $F¢(X,Y)$, the new semantic tree, and vice versa.

If the column c is deleted from the table $T(X)$, the mapping becomes $F(X,Y)\backslash Y(X¢,Y¢) = T¢(columns(T(X))-c)$, where $Y(X¢,Y¢)$ contains the atoms referencing the attribute f corresponding to the column c. If c is not a key or foreign key column, we can create a legal instance of $T'(X)$ for each legal instance of $F'(X,Y)$ and vice versa. If c is a key column, the corresponding identifier constraint corresponding to the key constraint referencing c is deleted from the CM as well. Therefore, the mapping $F(X,Y)\backslash Y(X¢,Y¢) = T¢(columns(T(X))-c)$ is consistent. Similarly, we have consistent mapping if c is a foreign key.

Case 2: A new table T' is obtained by changes from multiple tables $\{T_1, T_2, ..., T_n\}$. When new foreign keys are added to the new table T', Procedure 1 generates a larger s-tree S' for the new table T' by connecting the anchors of the skeleton trees $\{S_1, S_2, ..., S_n\}$ corresponding to the keys of $\{T_1, T_2, ..., T_n\}$ using functional edges. To prove that the resultant mapping between the new table T' and the new s-tree S' is consistent, we consider the set of legal instances of T' and the set of legal instances of S'. Suppose that the functional relationships are added from the anchor of S_1 to the anchors of $\{S_2 ...,S_n\}$. For any legal instance I' of T', the newly added foreign keys are accounted for by the functional relationships from the anchor of S_1 to the anchors of $\{S_2 ...,S_n\}$. Therefore, we can create a legal instance of S' through the new mapping. Conversely, the functional relationships in the s-tree S' are accounted for by the foreign key constraints in T'. Consequently, for any legal instance of S' we can create a legal instance of T' through the new mapping. Putting them together, we prove that the new mapping is consistent.

If multiple tables are merged into the new table *T through the same key*, Procedure 1 generates a new s-tree S' by merging the corresponding s-trees by connecting them using ISA relationships. To prove that the resultant mapping between the new table T' and the new s-tree S' is consistent, we consider the set of legal instances of T' and the set of legal instances of S'. Suppose that the ISA relationships are added from the anchor of S_1 to the anchors of $\{S_2, ..., S_n\}$. For any legal instance I' of T', the same key and merged columns are accounted for by the ISA relationships from the anchor of S_1 to the anchors of $\{S_2, ..., S_n\}$. Conversely, the ISA relationships in the s-tree S' are accounted for by the key and merged columns in T'. Therefore, we can create legal instances for both cases. Putting them together, we prove that the new mapping is consistent.

If a foreign key becomes part of the key, Procedure 1 generates a new s-tree S' by identifying the corresponding functional relationship in the CM, and updating the relationship from functional to non-functional if the original key is also a foreign key. To prove that the resultant mapping between the new table T' and the new s-tree S' is consistent, we consider the set of legal instances of T' and the set of legal instances of S'. Suppose that the key of table T corresponds to the skeleton tree S_1 and the foreign key corresponds to the skeleton S_2, and the functional relationship is from the anchor of S_1 to the anchor of S_2. The key of T' is the combination of two foreign keys. The combination is accounted for by the non-functional relationship which is newly updated. Conversely, the non-functional relationship is accounted for by the key of the table T' in which the key is the combination of two foreign keys. Therefore, for any legal instance I' of T', we can create a legal instance of S', and

vice versa. Putting them together, we prove that the new mapping is consistent.

Case 3: Multiple tables $\{T_1, T_2, ..., T_n\}$ are obtained from a single table T. There are two sub-cases: splitting a table and creating new tables connecting to the original table through foreign keys. Without losing generality, suppose T_1 inherits the key of T. Procedure 1 creates new concepts $\{C_2, ..., C_n\}$ in the CM for the new tables $\{T_2, ..., T_n\}$, respectively; and connects C_i to C_j by a functional edge in the CM if there is a foreign key constraint from the column $T_i.f$ to the key of T_j, or connects C_i to C_j by an ISA relationship if the column $T_i.f$ is also the key of the table T_i. To prove that the resultant mappings between the new tables $\{T_1, T_2, ..., T_n\}$ and the new s-trees are consistent, we consider the set of legal instances of each table T_i and the set of legal instances of each s-tree S_i. The foreign key of T_i referencing the key of T_1 is accounted for by the functional relationship from the anchor of S_i to the anchor of S_1. If the key of T_i is the same as the key of T_1, then the ISA relationships between the anchor of S_i and the anchor of S_1 accounts for the semantics. Conversely, the foreign key and key constraints in the table T_i account for the functional/ISA relationship in the skeleton tree. Therefore, for any legal instance I' of T_i, we can create a legal instance of S_i, and vice versa. Putting them together, we prove that the new mappings are consistent. +

We now turn to the procedure dealing with changes to CMs. Intuitively, synchronizing schemas when associated CMs change is more costly than synchronizing CMs when schemas change. The reason is that synchronizing schema often results in data translation. Two strategies can be considered for maintaining mappings when CMs change. The first strategy is to design a procedure in the same fashion as in Procedure 1. The second is to adapt mappings to maintain consistency without automatic synchronization. We take the second approach in this paper and leave the first approach to future work.

Specifically, for a mapping M={ $\Phi(X,Y) = T(X)$ } between a CM C=(C, Σ_C) and a relational schema R=(R, Σ_R), when the CM evolves, we update those mapping statements $\Phi(X,Y) = T(X)$ that are directly affected by the changes in the CM. For a mapping $\Phi(X,Y) = T(X)$, let S be the s-tree corresponding to the formula $\Phi(X,Y)$. S may change due to several actions: deleting some elements from S, changing the identifier of the anchor, changing the cardinality constraints of some relationships of S, and restructuring S. If an element is deleted from S, we update the mapping expression by deleting the atoms referencing the element. If S is restructured, we update the mapping expression by generating a new conjunctive formula from the new s-tree (An et al., 2006). If the cardinality constraints of a specific relationship of S are changed, for example, from one to many or from many to one, then we drop the atoms in the mapping expression which reference the relationship. Finally, if the identifier of the anchor of S is changed, we have to drop the mapping or mark the mapping as inconsistent.

The following Procedure 2 updates conceptual-relational mappings when the CMs evolve.

Procedure 2 Maintain Mappings When CMs Evolve

Input: A set of consistent conceptual-relational mappings M={ $\Phi(X,Y) = T(X)$ } between a CM C and a relational schema R; a set of correspondences M' between attributes in C and attributes in a new CM C'

Output: Update M to a new set of mappings M'' between R and C'.

1. Mark skeleton trees: the same as in the first step of Procedure 1.
2. For a mapping statement in M associating a semantic tree S with a table T
   a. *If* the skeleton tree corresponding to the key of T has changed such that identifier attributes of the

anchor were added/deleted or a cardinality constraint in the skeleton tree has changed from one to many, then drop the mapping. /* changes to the identifier information of either a strong or a weak entity will result in inconsistent mapping to the original table.*/

   b. *Else if* a cardinality constraint imposed on a relationship p in S has changed from many to one or from one to many, then remove from S the relationship edge p and the rest part which connects to the anchor through p. Update the mapping so that T is mapped to the new smaller tree.
   c. *Else if* an element is deleted from the s-tree, then delete the atoms from M which reference the element.
   d. *Else if* s is restructured, generate a new conjunctive formula from the s-tree with the existing algorithm. /* see (An et al., 2006) for the algorithm.*/

Example 8 [Change Cardinality Constraint]: The following original mapping M is a consistent mapping between a relational schema biosample(bsid, disease*, donor*) and an s-tree consisting of two functional relationships as shown in Figure 11.

$M : Biosample(x_1) \wedge bsid(x_1, bsid) \wedge Person(x_2) \wedge$
$originates(x_1, x_2) \wedge pid(x_2, donor) \wedge Disease(x_3) \wedge$
$dsid(x_3, disease) \wedge disease(x_1, x_3) =$
$biosample(bsid, disease, donor).$

In the table, the columns bisosample.disease* and biosample.donor* are two foreign keys referencing the keys of the tables corresponding to the

Figure 11. A relational table encoding two functional relationships

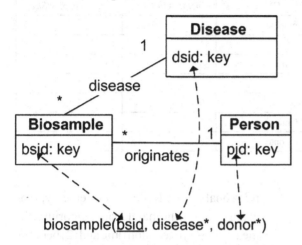

concepts Person and Disease. The foreign key constraints are consistent with the functional relationships between Biosample and the other two concepts, that is, Person and Disease .

If the upper bound cardinality imposed on the relationship disease from Biosample to Disease gets changed from 1 to many, then the mapping M is updated, according to *step 2.b* of *Procedure 2*, to the following expression by dropping the disease relationship in order to maintain the property of consistency:

$$M : Biosample(x_1) \wedge bsid(x_1, bsid) \wedge Person(x_2) \wedge$$
$$originates(x_1, x_2) \wedge pid(x_2, donor)$$
$$= biosample(bsid, \_, donor).$$

The following proposition states the desired property of the Procedure 2 for maintaining a conceptual-relational mapping through updating the mapping when the associated CM evolves.

Proposition 2: Let the input of the Procedure 2 be (1) M={Φ(X,Y) =T(X)} which is a set of consistent conceptual-relational mappings between a CM C and a relational schema R, and (2) M' which is a set of identify corre-

spondences between attributes in C and attributes in a new CM C¢ evolved from C. Each mapping in the set of conceptual-relational mappings returned by the Procedure 2 is consistent.

Proof (Sketch): We prove the proposition in a similar fashion as we did for Proposition 1.

By the definition of mapping consistency, a mapping M: $\Phi(X,Y) = T(X)$ between a CM C=(C, Σ_C) and a relational schema R=(R, Σ_R) is consistent, if and only if for every legal instance I of R, there is a legal instance J of C such that <I, J> ' M, and vice versa. To prove the Proposition 2, we consider the set of mappings M¢={Φ'(X,Y) =T(X)} between the new CM C¢ and the original schema R returned by the Procedure 2.

First of all, if M¢={Φ'(X,Y) =T(X)} is a subset of the original mapping by dropping the inconsistent mapping statements due to changes to the identifier in the s-tree, then M¢={Φ'(X,Y) =T(X)} is still consistent.

Let the mapping $F¢(X,Y) = T(X)$ be a mapping updated from an original mapping $F(X,Y)=T(X)$. If $F¢(X,Y)$ is a sub formula of $F(X,Y)$ by deleting some atoms, then $F¢(X,Y) = T(X)$ is still consistent.

Suppose $F¢(X,Y)$ is a formula generated from the new s-tree S¢ which is restructured from the original s-tree S. For a legal instance of S¢, we can create an instance of the table $T(X)$ through the new mapping $F¢(X,Y) = T(X)$. Conversely, for a legal instance of $T(X)$, we can create an instance of the s-tree S¢ through the new mapping $F¢(X,Y) = T(X)$. Because the constraints for both $T(X)$ and the s-tree remain unchanged, the instance of S¢ created from a legal instance of $T(X)$ still satisfies the constraints in S¢. Conversely, the instance of $T(X)$ created from a legal instance of S¢ still satisfies the constraints in $T(X)$. Therefore, $F¢(X,Y) = T(X)$ is consistent.

Overall, we prove that each mapping returned by Procedure 2 is consistent.

Table 2. Characteristics of test data

Schema	#Tables	Avg. # Cols Per Table	CM	#Nodes in CM	Avg. Mapping Size
DBLP	22	9	Bibliographic	75	9
Mondial	28	6	Factbook	52	7
Amalgam	15	12	Amalgam	26	10
3Sdb	9	14	3Sdb ER	9	6
CS Dept.	8	6	KA onto.	105	7
Hotel	6	5	Hotel Onto	7	7
Network	18	4	Network onto.	28	6

EXPERIENCE

To evaluate the performance of our round-trip engineering approach for maintaining conceptual-relational mappings, we applied the algorithm to a set of conceptual-relational mappings drawn from a variety of domains. The purpose of our evaluation is two-fold: (1) to test the efficiency of the algorithm and (2) to measure the benefits of mapping maintenance over reconstructing consistent mappings using mapping discovery tools.

Data Sets: We selected our test data from a variety of domains. Our previous work (An et al., 2006) on the development of the MAONTO mapping tools generated conceptual-relational mappings for many of the test data. Subsequently, our other previous work (An et al., 2007) used the conceptual-relational mappings for improving traditional tools on constructing direct mappings between database schemas. It follows naturally to continue using this set of data for measuring the benefits of mapping maintenance. Table 1 summarizes the characteristics of the test data. The size of a mapping is measured by the size of the semantic tree—the number of nodes including attribute nodes.

Methodology: Our experiments focused on maintaining the consistency of tested mappings under *schema evolution*. For each mapping, we applied different types of changes to the

relational table (Table 2). For each type of change, we ran the maintenance algorithm for measuring (1) execution time and (2) benefits of the round-trip engineering approach. The types of changes to a table include: (a) adding/deleting ordinary columns, (b) adding/deleting key columns, (c) splitting a table, (d) merging two tables, (e) add/deleting f.k. columns, (f) moving columns from one table to another table, and (g) changing existing key and f.k. constraints.

For measuring benefits, we compared the round-trip engineering process with the mapping reconstructing approach which discovers a new mapping from scratch. In our experiment, we used the MAPONTO (An et al., 2006) tool for the comparison. We adopted the approach for measuring how much "user effort" can be saved when schemas evolved and a new *consistent* mapping has to be established. Both Velegrakis et al. (2004) and Yu & Popa (2005) applied a similar approach for measuring the benefits of mapping adaptation. Specifically, the "user effort" for obtaining a consistent mapping through mapping maintenance after the schema evolved is compared to the same type of "user effort" spent for reconstructing the mapping.

Intuitively, user effort is related to the difficulty of a task. The more difficult a task is, the more effort a user has to put into performing the task. For the task of mapping maintenance/discovery, two quantities would be related to "difficulty." The first is the number of correspondences a user has to specify before starting the maintenance/discovery algorithm, and the second is the number of candidate mappings that the maintenance/discovery algorithm generates for a user to select the final ones. In our study, we used these two quantities for measuring "difficulty" or "user effort." For a mapping $\Phi(X,Y) = T(X)$ associating a semantic tree with a relational table, let T' be the new table that evolved from T. For mapping maintenance, the user specifies a set of simple correspondences between T' and T. Then the maintenance algorithm generates a new mapping between T' and, probably, an updated semantic tree. On the other hand, to reconstruct a mapping using the MAPONTO tool, the user also needs to specify a set of correspondences between T' and the CM. However, the MAPONTO tool may be unable to generate the expected mappings because the CM is out of synchronization. If the expected mapping is generated by the maintenance algorithm while it is missing from the results of MAPONTO, then we assign 100% to the benefit of maintenance. Otherwise, we use the following expression to measure the benefit:

$$1 - \frac{\# \text{mapping}_{\text{maintenance}}}{\# \text{mapping}_{\text{MAPONTO}} + \# \text{correspondences}}$$

where the quantity $\# \text{mapping}_{\text{maintenance}}$ is the number of candidate mappings generated by the round-trip engineering approach, the quantity $\# \text{mapping}_{\text{MAPONTO}}$ is the number of candidate mappings generated by the MAPONTO mapping discovery tool, and the quantity $\# \text{correspondences}_{\text{MAPONTO}}$ is the number of correspondences a user has to specify before starting the MAPONTO mapping tool. Because specifying correspondences between a schema and CM is much more costly than specifying correspondences between an evolved schema and

the original schema, we omit the quantity for specifying evolution correspondences, that is, $\# \text{correspondences}_{\text{maintenance}}$, from the above expression.

Results: First of all, the times used by the maintenance algorithm for synchronizing CMs and updating mappings are insignificant. For all the tested mappings, the round-trip maintenance algorithm took less than one second to generate the results. This is comparable with the MAPONTO tool for discovering mappings between schemas and CMs. Next, in terms of benefits, Figure 12 presents the average benefits for the tested cases. The results show that the round-trip engineering process provides significant benefits in terms of maintaining the consistency of conceptual-relational mappings under schema evolution.

DISCUSSION

Database schemas play a critical role in data management. In practice, changes almost always occur to database schemas that have been popu-

Figure 12. Benefits of mapping maintenance approach in comparison to mapping reconstruction approach

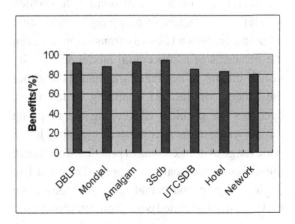

lated with data instances. Previous study has been focused on the problem of data transformation (Haas et al., 1999), that is, migrating the data instances structured under an old schema to new data instances that conform to a new schema. Little attention has been paid to the problem of adopting the conceptual model associated with a database schema when the schema changes. In this paper, we have identified a number of practical applications where adopting conceptual models associated with schemas under schema evolution is important and has deep implications.

A common feature of these applications is that database schemas are associated with conceptual models through mappings. Mappings are expressed in terms of logical formulae. Such a mapping specifies a particularly meaningful relationship between a database schema and a conceptual model, and is a key component in these applications. For example, object-relational mappings play a key role in many modern data-centric applications. When schemas or conceptual models evolve in order to accommodate new information needs, previously existing mappings often lose their "meanings" and need to be regenerated. In this paper, we proposed a novel approach for incrementally maintaining mappings under schemas and conceptual models evolution. The goal is to keep the mappings remain "meaningful" after the changes. Our hypothesis was that incrementally maintaining mappings would be more efficient and have "better" results than regenerating mappings from scratch.

We focused on a type of relationship which we define as *consistent* mapping. A consistent mapping permits a two-way translation between the instances of a conceptual model and a relational schema. When there are changes to either the schema or the CM, mapping maintenance becomes the problem of keeping the mapping remain consistent. A consistent mapping has a wide range of applications in practice. To achieve the maintenance goal, we proposed a round-trip engineering approach that can synchronize the CM/schema associated with a consistent mapping when either one evolves. We developed synchronization algorithms based on a careful study on the knowledge encoded in standard database design methodology.

The contributions of this research are manifold. Theoretically, we explicated the hidden knowledge encoded in the process of standard database design. The knowledge was largely ignored in previous studies and applications. We demonstrated in our round-trip algorithms that the explication of the knowledge provided opportunities of developing systematic approaches for dealing with mapping maintenance. We believe that the explicit knowledge can be leveraged in many problems involving database schemas and conceptual models. Practically, we studied an important problem to many applications. We proposed an effective and useful solution to the problem of maintaining object-relational mappings under schemas/CMs evolution. As opposed to current mapping regeneration practice, our experiments showed that the incremental maintenance approach provided significant benefits.

As the first study on maintaining mappings between conceptual models and database schemas, this research bears some limitations and points to several interesting future research directions.

The main limitation is that the paper addresses only one side of the problem caused by changes to database schemas, that is, the problem of synchronizing conceptual models and database schemas. We do not address the problem of data transformation when schemas change. If changes first occur to schemas, we will assume that underlying data has already been migrated and we focus on adopting the associated conceptual model and mapping. However, if changes occur to conceptual models, we only modify the mapping for maintaining consistency, leaving the schema unchanged to avoid data transformation. This limitation indicates that there is more work to do for synchronizing schemas when CMs evolve. It involves not only schema synchronization but also data transformation.

The second limitation of the current work is that it considers the common and relatively simple constraints such as primary and foreign key constraints and their corresponding conceptual counterparts. More complex constraints can be found in the literature such as in ORM conceptual schemas or in advanced ER schemas (Halpin & Morgan, 2008). It is also recognized in the literature that data transformation is, in general, nontrivial (Halpin & Morgan, 2008). Extending the current work to consider more complex constraints is listed in the future work directions. Moreover, as discussed above, combining CM/schema synchronization and data transformation is an interesting problem and will be investigated in the future as well.

CONCLUSION

A conceptual-relational mapping specifies a particularly meaningful relationship between a conceptual model (CM) and a relational schema. In this paper, we studied an important problem which is to maintain a *consistent* conceptual-relational mapping when the associated CM and schema evolve. We considered the need for synchronizing the CM and relational schema associated by a conceptual-relational mapping. We presented a novel round-trip engineering framework and developed algorithms that automatically and incrementally maintain conceptual-relational mappings as schemas/CMs evolve. Our solution is unique in that we carefully compile the knowledge encoded in the widely covered methodology for database design into our approach. Theoretically, our results showed that the process achieved desired properties for maintaining mappings. Experimental analysis demonstrated that the solution was efficient and provided significant benefits for maintaining conceptual-relational mappings in dynamic environments.

Future research directions include extending the round-trip engineering approach to more general conceptual-relational mappings such that a mapping statement may involve a sub-graph (not necessarily a tree) in a conceptual model and multiple tables in a relational schema. In addition, we also plan to extend the round-trip engineering approach by taking the following two situations into consideration: (1) relational schemas with other types of constraints such as general inclusion constraint, in addition to key and foreign key constraints; and (2) synchronizing relational schemas when the associated CMs change.

ACKNOWLEDGMENT

Yuan An is partially supported by NSF CCF-0905291. Xiaohua (Tony) Hu is supported by NSF CCF-0905291.

REFERENCES

Adya, A., Blakeley, J., Melnik, S., & Muralidhar, S. (2007). Anatomy of the ADO.NET Entity Framework. *In Proceedings of ACM SIG Conference on Management of Data*, 877-888.

An, Y., Borgida, A., Miller, R. J., & Mylopoulos, J. (2007). A Semantic Approach to Discovering Schema Mapping Expressions. *In Proceedings of International Conference on Data Engineering (ICDE)*, 206-215.

An, Y., Borgida, A., & Mylopoulos, J. (2005a). Constructing Complex Semantic Mappings between XML Data and Ontologies. In *Proceedings of the International Conference on Semantic Web (ISWC)* (pp. 6-20).

An, Y., Borgida, A., & Mylopoulos, J. (2005b). Inferring Complex Semantic Mappings between Relational Tables and Ontologies from Simple Correspondences. In *Proceedings of International Conference on Ontologies, Databases, and Applications of Semantics (ODBASE)* (pp. 1152-1169).

An, Y., Borgida, A., & Mylopoulos, J. (2006). Discovering the Semantics of Relational Tables through Mappings. *Journal on Data Semantics, VII*, 1–32.

Arens, Y., Knoblock, C. A., & Shen, W. (1996). Query reformulation for dynamic information integration. *Journal of Intelligent Information Systems, 6*(2-3), 99–130. doi:10.1007/BF00122124

Banerjee, J., Kim, W., Kim, H.-J., & Korth, H. F. (1987). Semantics and Implementation of Schema Evolution in Object-Oriented Databases. *SIGMOD Record, 16*(3), 311–322. doi:10.1145/38714.38748

Bauer, C., & King, G. (2006). *Java Persistence with Hibernate*. Greenwich, CT . *Manning Publications., ISBN-10*, 1932394885.

Bayardo, R. J., Bohrer, W., Brice, R., Cichocki, A., Fowler, G., Helai, A., et al. (1997). InfoSleuth: Agent-based semantic integration of information in open and dynamic environments. In *Proceedings of ACM SIGMOD* (pp. 195-206).

Berners-Lee, T., Hendler, J., & Lassila, O. (2001). The Semantic Web. *Scientific American, May*.

Bonifati, A., Chang, E. Q., Ho, T., Lakshmanan, V. S., & Pottinger, R. (2005). HePToX: Marring XML and Heterogeneity in Your P2P Databases. In *Proceedings of International Conference on Very Large Data Bases (VLDB)* (pp. 1267-1270).

Bouguettaya, A., Malik, Z., Rezgui, A., & Korff, L. (2006). A Scalable Middleware for Web Databases. *Journal of Database Management, 17*(4), 20–46.

Brien, P. M., & Poulovassilis, A. (2002). Schema Evolution in Heterogeneous Database Architectures, A Schema Transformation Approach. In *Proceedings of Conference on Advanced Information Systems Engineering (CAiSE)* (pp. 484-499).

Calvanese, D., Giacomo, G. D., Lenzerini, M., Nardi, D., & Rosati, R. (2001). Data integration in data warehouse. *Cooperative Information Systems, 10*(3), 237–271. doi:10.1142/S0218843001000345

Ceri, S., & Widom, J. (1991). Deriving Production Rules for Incremental View Maintenance. In *Proceedings of International Conference on Very Large Data Bases (VLDB)* (pp. 277-289).

Claypool, K. T., Jin, J., & Rundensteiner, E. (1998). SERF: Schema Evolution through an Extensible, Re-usable, and Flexible Framework. In *Proceedings of Int. Conf. on Information and Knowledge Management (CIKM)* (pp. 314-321).

Colazzo, D., & Sartiani, C. (2005). Mapping Maintenance in XML P2P Databases. In *Database Programming Languages* (LNCS 3774, pp. 74-89).

Collet, C., Huhns, M. N., & Shen, W.-M. (1991). Resource integration using a large knowledge base in Carnot. *IEEE Computer, 24*, 55–62.

Demeyer, S., Ducasse, S., Tichelaar, S., & Tichelaar, E. (1999). Why Unified is not Universal - UML Shortcomings for Coping with Round-trip Engineering. *Proceedings UML'99 (The Second International Conference on The Unified Modeling Language), volume 1723 of LNCS, 630-645*.

Elmasri, R., & Navathe, S. B. (2006). *Fundamentals of Database Systems* (5th ed.). Upper Saddle River, NJ, USA: Addison Wesley.

Evermann, J. (2008). Theories of Meaning in Schema Matching: A Review. *Journal of Database Management, 19*(3), 55–82.

Fan, H., & Poulovassilis, A. (2004). Schema Evolution in Data Warehousing Environments: a schema transformation-based approach. *In Proceedings of International Conference on Conceptual Modeling (ER)*, 639-653.

Ferrandina, F., Ferran, G., Meyer, T., Madec, J., & Zicari, R. (1995). Schema and Database Evolution in the O2 Object Database System. *In PRoceedings of International Conference on Very Large Databases (VLDB)*, 170-181.

Goasdoue, F., Lattes, V., & Rousset, M. (1999). The Use of Carin Language and Algorithm for Information Integration: The PICSEL Project. *International Journal of Cooperative Information Systems, 9*(4), 383–401. doi:10.1142/S0218843000000181

Gupta, A., Mumick, I., & Ross, K. (1995). Adapting Materialized Views After Redefinition. *In Proceedings of ACM SIG Conference on Management of Data*, 211-222.

Haas, L. M., Miller, R. J., Niswonger, B., Roth, M. T., Schwarz, P. M., & Wimmers, E. L. (1999). Transforming Heterogeneous Data with Database Middleware: Beyond Integration. *A Quarterly Bulletin of the Computer Society of the IEEE Technical Committee on Data Engineering, 22*(1), 31–36.

Hainaut, J.-L. (1998). Database reverse engineering [online]. Available: http://citeseer.ist.psu.edu/article/ hainaut98database.html.

Halpin, T., & Morgan, T. (2008). *Information Modeling and Relational Databases, 2nd edition*. San Fransisco: Morgan Kaufmann.

Henriksson, A., & Larsson, H. (2003). *A Definition of Round-trip Engineering*. Linköping, Sweden: Department of Computer and Information Science, Linköpings Universitet.

Huang, S.-M., Yen, D. C., & Hsueh, H.-Y. (2007). A Space-Efficient Protocol for Consistency of External View Maintenance on Data Warehouse Systems: A Proxy Approach. *Journal of Database Management, 18*(3), 21–47.

Kalfoglou, Y., & Scholemmer, M. (2003). Ontology Mapping: The State of the Art. *The Knowledge Engineering Review, 18*(1), 1–31. doi:10.1017/S0269888903000651

Kedad, Z., & Bouzeghoub, M. (1999). Discovering View Expressions from a Multi-Source Information Systems. *In Proceedings of International Conference on Cooperative Information Systems (CoopIS)*, 57-68.

Kedad, Z., & Xue, X. (2005). Mapping Discovery for XML Data Integration. In *Proceedings of International Conference on Cooperative Information Systems (CoopIS)* (pp. 166-182).

Klyne, G., & Carroll, J. J. (2003). *Resource Description Framework (RDF): Concepts and Abstract Syntax*. Retrieved from http://www.w3.org/ TR/rdf-concepts

Knublauch, H., & Rose, T. (2000). Round-Trip Engineering of Ontologies for Knowledge-based Systems. In *Proceedings of the Twelfth International Conference on Software Engineering and Knowledge Engineering (SEKE)* (pp. 239-247).

Lee, A., Nica, A., & Rundensteiner, E. (2002). The EVE Approach: View Synchronization in Dynamic Distributed Environment. *IEEE Transactions on Knowledge and Data Engineering, 14*(5), 931–954. doi:10.1109/TKDE.2002.1033766

Lenzerini, M. (2002). Data Integration: A Theoretical Perspective. In *Proceedings of the ACM Symposium on Principles of Database Systems (PODS)* (pp. 233-246).

Levy, A. Y., Srivastava, D., & Kirk, T. (1996). Data Model and Query Evaluation in Global Information Systems. *Journal of Intelligent Information Systems, 5*(2), 121–143. doi:10.1007/BF00962627

Madhavan, J., Bernstein, P., Domingos, P., & Halevy, A. (2002). Representing and reasoning about mappings between domain models. In *Proceedings of Eighteenth National Conference on American Association Artificial Intelligence* (pp. 80-86).

McCann, R., AlShebli, B., Le, Q., Nguyen, H., Vu, L., & Doan, A. (2005). Maveric: Mapping Maintenance for Data Integration Systems. In *Proceedings of International Conference on Very Large Databases (VLDB)* (pp. 1018-1029).

McGuinness, D. L., & v. Harmelen, F. (2004). *OWL Web Ontology Language Overview*. Retrieved from http://www.w3c.org/ TR/owl-features

Melnik, S., Garcia-Molina, H., & Rahm, E. (2002). Similarity flooding: a versatile graph matching algorithm and its application to schema matching. In *Proceedings of the International Conference on Data Engineering (ICDE)* (pp. 117-128).

Mena, E., Illarramendi, A., Kashyap, V., & Sheth, A. P. (1996). OBSERVER: An approach for query processing in global information systems based on interoperation across pre-existing ontologies. In . *Proceedings of CoopIS*, *96*, 14–25.

Miller, R. J., Haas, L. M., & Hernandez, M. A. (2000). Schema Mapping as Query Discovery. In *Proceedings of the 26th International Conference on Very Large Data Bases* (pp. 77-88).

Milo, T., & Zohar, S. (1998). Using Schema Matching to Simplify Heterogeneous Data Translation. In *Proceedings of International Conference on Very Large Data Bases (VLDB)* (pp. 122-133).

Mohania, M., & Dong, G. (1996). Algorithms for adapting materialized views in data warehouses. In *Proceedings of the International Symposium On Cooperative Database Systems for Advanced Applications* (pp. 62-69).

Mumick, I. S., Quass, D., & Mumick, B. S. (1997). Maintenance of Data Cubes and Summary Tables in a Warehouse. In *Proceedings of ACM SIG Conference on Management of Data* (pp. 100-111).

Mylopoulos, J. (1998). Information Modeling in the Time of the Revolution. *Information Systems*, *23*, 127–155. doi:10.1016/S0306-4379(98)00005-2

Popa, L., Velegrakis, Y., Miller, R. J., Hernández, M. A., & Fagin, R. (2002). Translating Web Data. In *Proceedings of the International Conference on Very Large Data Bases (VLDB)* (pp. 598-609).

Rahm, E., & Bernstein, P. (2006). An On-line Bibliography on Schema Evolution. *SIGMOD Record*, *35*(4), 30–31. doi:10.1145/1228268.1228273

Rahm, E., & Bernstein, P. A. (2001). A Survey of Approaches to Automatic Schema Matching. *The VLDB Journal*, *10*, 334–350. doi:10.1007/s007780100057

Sendall, S., & Kuster, J. (2004). Taming Model Round-Trip Engineering. In *Proceedings of the Workshop on Best Practices for Model-Driven Software Development*.

Shvaiko, P., & Euzenat, J. (2005). A Survey of Schema-Based Matching Approaches. *J. Data Semantics*, *IV*, 146–171.

Velegrakis, Y., Miller, R., & Popa, L. (2004). Preserving mapping consistency under schema changes. *The VLDB Journal*, *13*(3), 274–293. doi:10.1007/s00778-004-0136-2

Yan, L. L., Miller, R. J., Haas, L., & Fagin, R. (2001). Data-Driven Understanding and Refinement of Schema Mappings. In *Proceedings of the ACM SIGMOD* (pp. 485-496).

Yu, C., & Popa, L. (2005). Semantic Adaptation of Schema Mappings when Schema Evolve. In *Proceedings of the International Conference on Very Large Data bases (VLDB)* (pp. 1006-1017).

Zhao, L., & Siau, K. (2007). Information Mediation Using Metamodels: An Approach Using XML and Common Warehouse Metamodel. *Journal of Database Management*, *18*(3), 69–82.

This work was previously published in International Journal of Database Management, Volume 21, Issue 3, edited by Keng Siau, pp. 36-68, copyright 2010 by IGI Publishing (an imprint of IGI Global).

Chapter 11
Impact of Flow and Brand Equity in 3D Virtual Worlds

Fiona Fui-Hoon Nah
University of Nebraska-Lincoln, USA

Brenda Eschenbrenner
University of Nebraska-Lincoln, USA

David DeWester
University of Nebraska-Lincoln, USA

So Ra Park
University of Nebraska-Lincoln, USA

ABSTRACT

This research is a partial test of Park et al.'s (2008) model to assess the impact of flow and brand equity in 3D virtual worlds. It draws on flow theory as its main theoretical foundation to understand and empirically assess the impact of flow on brand equity and behavioral intention in 3D virtual worlds. The findings suggest that the balance of skills and challenges in 3D virtual worlds influences users' flow experience, which in turn influences brand equity. Brand equity then increases behavioral intention. The authors also found that the impact of flow on behavioral intention in 3D virtual worlds is indirect because the relationship between them is mediated by brand equity. This research highlights the importance of balancing the challenges posed by 3D virtual world branding sites with the users' skills to maximize their flow experience and brand equity to increase the behavioral intention associated with the brand.

INTRODUCTION

Earmarking the next development in the Internet, 3D virtual worlds (3DVWs) are providing significant potential for marketing and branding. Companies that have created a presence in 3DVWs, such as Second Life, include Adidas,

NTT DoCoMo, Sony, Reuters, Cisco Systems, IBM, Dell, Sun Microsystems, Mazda, Nissan, Pontiac, and Warner Brothers. Figure 1 shows examples of virtual sites in Second Life created and owned by businesses.

3DVWs are characterized by 3D space in computer-generated environments where users interact and navigate in the space through their avatars, which are digital, simulated representa-

DOI: 10.4018/978-1-61350-471-0.ch011

Figure 1. 3DVW Sites of IBM (Left) and Dell (Right)

tions of themselves. Through their avatars, users can navigate freely in the space, create and manipulate objects in the space, and interact and collaborate with other avatars in the shared space (Davis, Murphy, Owens, Khazanchi, & Zigurs, 2009; Eschenbrenner, Nah, & Siau, 2008; Ives & Junglas, 2008; Park, Nah, DeWester, Eschenbrenner, & Jeon, 2008).

Many of the activities that are conducted on the 2D Web can also take place in 3DVWs, and, in some instances, with enhanced capabilities being offered by 3DVWs. For example, customers can view and interact with virtual products. They can find relevant information on products and services, and interact with customer service representatives whose avatars are online. Also, they can customize and order virtual products and services.

3DVWs, however, are not just an extension of the 2D Web because the capabilities of 3DVWs can far exceed those of the 2D Web. For example, Dell's 2D Web site allows visitors to customize a computer before purchasing it, but it does not provide a way for them to see exactly what the computer looks like. In Second Life, however, a visitor can not only customize a computer, but can also view a virtual copy of the computer that is the same size, shape and color as the real product (Brandon, 2007). Visualization of products is a key strength of 3DVWs (Ives & Junglas, 2008).

For example, Coldwell Banker offers 3D tours through virtual models of real-world homes (Burselm, 2007) and Pontiac allows test driving of automobiles in Second Life (Brandon, 2007).

Although extensive business opportunities may exist with this new medium, to generate the greatest return on investment in 3DVWs, it is important for businesses to understand how to maximize customers' experiences and provide the ultimate experiences for them. In other words, businesses need to understand how to engage customers in this new, experiential environment and, in particular, in their 3DVW sites. For example, companies are creating innovative branding activities, such as games and interactive demonstrations, on their 3DVW sites to involve and engage customers in the branding experience (Park et al., 2008). However, they may not be capitalizing on the appropriate set of affordances offered by the 3DVW environment to provide the best experience for maximizing profitability.

Park et al. (2008) provide a list of such potential affordances in 3DVWs that can be used by companies to create positive user experiences to enhance branding. Companies can capitalize on these affordances in their 3DVW branding sites to engage customers for extended periods of time. These experiences can assist in enhancing branding opportunities, which include creating interest in the brand, increasing awareness of the brand, and strengthening association with the brand.

Drawing on the work of Hoffman and Novak (1996), Park et al. (2008) highlight three key characteristics – control characteristics, content characteristics, and process characteristics – that can be used to provide the optimal experience for customers to enhance brand equity. This research will test Park et al.'s (2008) model by examining the first set of characteristics, user's control characteristics, to understand the impact of these characteristics on customers' optimal experience (also termed flow) and their subsequent effects on brand equity and the intention to use the brand.

BACKGROUND AND LITERATURE REVIEW

3DVWs are attracting a tremendous amount of attention from the business world (Arakji & Lang, 2007). For example, in Second Life, Adidas and Reebok sell virtual shoes, and Toyota and Nissan sell virtual cars. The Westin and Sheraton chains tested their new hotels, Aloft, in Second Life before rolling them out to the real-world in 2008. Many other businesses and corporations such as BBC, Fox, MTV, PA Consulting, and Telus Mobility also have a presence in Second Life. Hence, businesses are taking advantage of 3DVWs to explore business opportunities including experiential and viral marketing. For example, Coke used viral marketing by promoting a vending machine design contest in Second Life, MySpace, and YouTube (Lewis, 2007) to increase brand awareness. Both Coke and Pepsi (Lafayette, 2007) have capitalized on the interactivity offered by 3DVWs by allowing avatars to acquire and enjoy their beverages.

Barnes (2007) suggests that virtual worlds are designed to entertain as well as provide an experience that engages users or customers in the business context. As noted by Linda Zimmer, president and CEO of the consultancy firm, MarCom:interactive (Leggatt, 2007):

"The point that's been made over and over again is that these worlds are seriously engaging. The other point is that you (the marketer) have to engage, too."

Businesses can use the 3DVW environment to promote virtual versions of their existing products to increase brand image or the perceived value of the brand. Also, the high degree of involvement and engagement that one can experience in 3DVWs, coupled with the creative characteristic and richness of the environment, provide businesses with ample opportunities to carry out marketing activities. For instance:

- Customers can find out information about Kraft's products at Phil's supermarket in Second Life (Steinriede, 2007).
- A simulated version of a real-life hospital that is being built in California provides patients and the health care community the opportunity to visit and experience some of the amenities of the real-life hospital in Second Life (McGee, 2008).
- For a discounted price during a limited time promotion, H&R Block provided visitors in Second Life with an access code to the Web-based Tango online tax preparation software that normally costs US$70 (Brandon, 2007). This bundle included access to virtual scooters, dance shoes, a T-shirt, and other paraphernalia to attract customers to its sites. H&R Block also provided free tax advice for two hours a week until the tax deadline.
- Best Buy Geek Squad positioned their representatives as avatars on their site in Second Life to assist visitors with computer and technology related questions (Brandon, 2007). Strong links or integration between the Geek Squad virtual site and physical stores allow delegation of customer issues to physical locations.

- Businesses use the 3DVW environment to co-create or collaborate with customers to strengthen customer relationships (Goel & Mousavidin, 2007).

The affordances of 3DVWs allow users to experience a high level of interactivity and presence (Hecht & Reiner, 2007; Hobson, 2006; Lok, 2004; Mikropoulos & Strouboulis, 2004; Park et al., 2008; Riva et al., 2007; Venezia, 2007). The sense of immersion in a 3DVW can be enhanced with an increased number of sensory inputs and outputs, which in turn increases the sense of presence (Steuer, 1992). Real-world-like activities, objects, and interactions enhanced with quality 3D graphics and audio allow users to interact with one another and their environment through their avatars. Such environments are highly creative and dynamic in that users can own and design their virtual lands (e.g., corporate buildings and sites), create and design objects including a virtual equivalence of real-world products (e.g., ATMs by Wells Fargo and automobiles by Toyota), and organize activities such as hosting events (e.g., conventions, training, corporate meetings, and parties).

Businesses are leveraging on the immersive environment of 3DVWs to enrich and enhance customers' experiences. The engagement of optimal experience, termed flow by Csikszentmihalyi (1975, 1990, 1993, 1997), can have significant implications on business and marketing activities by enhancing consumer learning, brand equity, and exploratory behavior (Finneran & Zhang, 2005; Hoffman & Novak, 1996; Park et al., 2008). Hence, studying the phenomenon of flow in 3DVWs is warranted. In this paper, we use the flow theory (Csikszentmihalyi 1975, 1990, 1993; 1997; Csikszentmihalyi & Csikszentmihalyi, 1988; Csikszentmihalyi & Lefavre, 1989) to study the impact of users' characteristics on their flow experience in a 3DVW site, and the subsequent effects of the flow experience on their perceived brand equity and intention to use the brand.

THEORETICAL FOUNDATION AND HYPOTHESES

The theoretical foundation for this research includes the use of: (i) flow theory, or theory of optimal experience, by Csikszentmihalyi (1975, 1990, 1993, 1997) to understand the impact of users' control characteristics on their flow experience, (ii) broaden-and-build theory of positive emotions by Fredrickson (2001) to explain the relationship between flow and brand equity, and (iii) brand equity theory by Keller (1993) to understand the impact of brand equity on behavioral intention associated with the brand.

Flow Theory

Flow is "the holistic sensation that people feel when they act with total involvement" (Csikszentmihalyi, 1975, p. 36). It refers to an optimal state of experience where one is completely absorbed and engaged in an activity (Csikszentmihalyi, 1975, 1990, 1993, 1997). Flow is characterized by the following elements (Csikszentmihalyi, 1975, 1990, 1993, 1997): clear goals, immediate feedback, balance of skills and challenges, focused concentration, distorted sense of time, sense of control, loss of self-consciousness, merging of action and awareness, and self-rewarding or autotelic experience.

Various researchers have used the flow theory to study and understand online experiences of users, which have been found to influence learning, attitudes, intentions, and behaviors (Chen, 2006; Fortin & Dholakia, 2005; Ghani, 1995; Hoffman & Novak, 1996; Hsu & Lu, 2004; Klein, 2003; Koufaris, 2002; Luna, Peracchio, & de Juan, 2003; Nel, van Niekerk, Berthon, & Davies, 1999; Skadberg & Kimmel, 2004; Trevino & Webster, 1992; Webster, Trevino, & Ryan, 1993; Siekpe, 2005; Shin, 2006). Table 1 summarizes the literature on application of flow theory in the online environments.

Table 1. Summary of literature on flow theory in online environments

Reference	Flow Antecedents	Flow Experience	Flow Outcomes	Research Setting	Method
Ghani et al. **(1991)**	Skills, Control, Challenge	Enjoyment, Concentration		Virtual versus Face-to-face Groups	Survey
Trevino & Webster (1992)	Technology Type, Tech Char. (Ease of Use), Ind. Diff. (Computer Skill), Organizational Factors (Management Support, Partners' Medium Use)	Control, Attention Focus, Curiosity, Intrinsic Interest	Attitude, Effectiveness, Quantity, Barrier Reduction	Communication Technologies (E-mail, Voice Mail) in Work Setting	Survey
Webster et al. **(1993)**		Control, Attention Focus, Cognitive Enjoyment (Curiosity and Intrinsic Interest)	User Control, Attention, Positive Attitude, System Use, Positive Work Outcome	Software Usage in the Work Setting	Survey
Ghani & Deshpande (1994)	Control, Challenge	Enjoyment, Concentration	Exploratory Use	Computer Use	Survey
Ghani (1995)	Task Challenges and Perceived Control, Cognitive Spontaneity	Enjoyment, Concentration	Focus on Process, Learning, Creativity	Work Communication	Survey
Hoffman & Novak (1996)	Control Characteristics (Skills, Challenges), Content Characteristics (Interactivity, Vividness), Process Characteristics (Goal-Directed, Experiential), Involvement, Focused Attention, Tele-presence	Flow	Consumer Learning, Perceived Behavioral Control, Exploratory Behavior, Subjective Experience (Pleasure, Future Voluntary Computer Interaction, and Time Distortion)	Hypermedia Computer Mediated Environment	Conceptual
Lombard & Ditton (1997)	Vividness (through type and various sensory outputs), Interactivity, Contents, Media User Variables	Presence (or Tele-presence)	Arousal, Enjoyment, Involvement, Task Performance, Skills Training, Desensitization, Persuasion, Memory, Social Judgment, Para-social Interaction, Relationship	Virtual Environment	Conceptual
Nel et al. **(1999)**		Content, Attention Focus, Curiosity, Intrinsic Interest	Website Re-visit	Web Navigation	Experiment
Agarwal & Karahanna (2000)	Personal Innovativeness, Playfulness	Cognitive Absorption (Curiosity, Control, Temporal Dissociation, Focused Immersion, Heightened Enjoyment)	Perceived Ease of Use, Perceived Usefulness, Intention to Use	World Wide Web	Survey
Chen et al. **(2000)**	Clear Goals, Immediate Feedback, Potential Control, Merger of Action and Awareness	Concentration, Time Distortion, Loss of Self Consciousness, Tele-presence	Auto-telic Experience, Positive Affect	Web Navigation	Survey using online ESM (Experience Sampling Method)

continued on following page

Table 1. Continued

Reference	Flow Antecedents	Flow Experience	Flow Outcomes	Research Setting	Method
Novak et al. **(2000)**	Skill/Control, Interactive Speed, Importance, Challenge/Arousal, Focused Attention, Tele-presence/Time Distortion	Flow	Positive Affect, Exploratory Behavior	Web Navigation	Survey
Rettie (2001)	Goals, Feedback, Skills, Challenge	Merging of Action and Awareness, Focused Concentration, Sense of Control, Loss of Self-Consciousness, Time Distortion, Autotelic Experience		Internet Use	Focused groups
Koufaris (2002)	Product Involvement, Web Skills, Value-Added Search Mechanism, Challenge	Shopping Enjoyment, Concentration	Intention to Return	Online Shopping	Survey
Luna et al. **(2002)**	Balance – Challenges/Skills, Perceived Control, Unambiguous Demands, Focused Attention, Attitude toward Site	Flow	Revisit Intention, Purchase Intention	Web Sites	Experiment
Huang (2003)	Complexity, Novelty, Interactivity	Control, Attention, Curiosity, Interest	Utilitarian Performance, Hedonic Performance	Web Sites	Survey
Klein (2003)	Media Richness, User Control	Tele-presence	Persuasion, Attitude Belief Strength, Attitude Intensity	Computer–mediated Environment	Experiment
Korzaan (2003)		Flow	Exploratory Behavior, Attitude	Online Shopping	Survey
Luna et al. **(2003)**	Attention, Challenge, Interactivity, Attitude towards the Site	Flow	Purchase Intent, Revisit Intent	Web Sites	Survey
Novak et al. **(2003)**	Goal-directed vs. Experiential Activities, Skill, Challenge, Novelty, Importance	Flow		Online Shopping Experience	Survey
Hsu & Lu (2004)	Perceived Ease of Use	Flow	Attitude, Intention	Online Game	Survey
Jiang & Benbasat (2004)	Visual Control, Functional Control	Flow		Shopping Web Sites	Experiment
Pace (2004)	Goals and Navigation Behavior, Challenge and Skills, Attention	Duration, Frequency and Intensity, Joy of Discovery, Reduced Awareness of Irrelevant Factors, Distorted Sense of Time, Merging of Action and Awareness, Sense of Control, Mental Alertness, Tele-presence		Web Browsing	Grounded Theory (Theoretical Sampling, Semi-Structured Interview)
Pilke (2004)	Immediate Feedback, Clear Rules/Goals, Complexity, Dynamic Challenges			World Wide Web	Interviews

continued on following page

Table 1. Continued

Reference	Flow Antecedents	Flow Experience	Flow Outcomes	Research Setting	Method
Reid (2004)	Cognitive Ability, Volitional Control, Self-Efficacy	Flow and Playfulness	Competence, Creativity, User Satisfaction	Virtual Reality	Interviews, Experiment, Observation
Skadberg & Kimmel (2004)	Speed, Ease of Use, Attractiveness, Interactivity, Domain Knowledge/Skill, Information on the Web Site/Challenge	Enjoyment, Time Distortion, Tele-presence	Increased Learning, and Subsequent Attitude Change and Behavior Change	Web Browsing	Survey
Fortin & Dholakia (2005)	Interactivity, Vividness	Arousal, Involvement, Social Presence	Attitude towards Ad, Attitude towards Brand, Purchase Intention	Product Web Site	Experiment and Survey
Kim et al. **(2005)**	Skills, Challenges, Focused Attention	Flow		Online Games	Survey
Siekpe (2005)		Challenges, Concentration, Curiosity, Control	Intention to Purchase, Intention to Return	Web sites	Survey
Chen (2006)	Clear Goal, Potential Control, Immediate Feedback, Merger of Action and Awareness	Tele-presence, Time Distortion, Concentration, Loss of Self-Consciousness	Positivity of Affects, Enjoyable Feeling	Web Browsing	Digitalized Experience Sampling Method
Li & Browne (2006)	Need for Cognition, Mood	Focused Attention, Control, Curiosity, Temporal Dissociation		General Online Experience	Survey
Shin (2006)	Skill, Challenge, Individual Differences	Enjoyment, Tele-presence, Focused Attention, Engagement, Time Distortion	Achievement, Satisfaction	Virtual Learning Environment	Survey
Tung et al. **(2006)**	Involvement	Flow	Mood, Attitudes	Web Sites	Survey
Park et al. **(2008)**	Content Characteristics (Skills, Challenges), Content Characteristics (Interactivity, Vividness), Process Characteristics (Extrinsic/Intrinsic Motivation)	Flow	Brand Equity	3D Virtual World	Conceptual
Guo & Poole (2009)	Website Complexity, Clear Goal, Immediate Feedback, Congruence of Challenge and Skill	Concentration, Control, Mergence of Action and Awareness, Transformation of Time, Transcendence of Self, Auto-telic Experience		Web Sites	Experiment
Hoffman & Novak (2009)	Skill, Challenge, Interactivity, Vividness, Tele-presence, Motivation, Involvement, Attention, Usage, Attractiveness, Novelty, Playfulness, Personal Innovativeness, Content/Interface, Ease of Use	Flow	Learning, Control / Perceived Behavioral Control, Exploratory Behavior / Curiosity / Discovery, Positive Subjective Experience / Attitude, Ease of Use, Perceived Usefulness, Purchase / Behavioral Intention, Purchase / Use, Addictive Behavior	Internet	Conceptual

continued on following page

Table 1 presents numerous antecedents of the flow experience. In this research, we focus on one of the characteristic dimensions or requirements of the flow experience, balance of skills and challenges (Csikszentmihalyi, 1975, 1990, 1993, 1997). In the context of 3DVWs, one is more likely to experience a state of flow when the opportunities for action (i.e., challenges imposed by a 3DVW site) are evenly matched by the capabilities (i.e., skills of the users) (Csikszentmihalyi, 1975). If one's skill level is inadequate, frustration or anxiety will develop and a state of flow cannot be achieved. Thus, when a user is on a 3DVW site where there are multiple opportunities that challenge them to act, whether he or she has the skills and capacity to cope with the demands imposed by the site will be a key factor that determines the degree of flow experience. Therefore, we hypothesize that the balance of skills and challenges will positively impact flow.

H1: Balance of skills and challenges will have a positive effect on flow.

Broaden-and-Build Theory of Positive Emotions

Broaden-and-build theory of positive emotions proposes that when people feel positive emotions, they become associated with greater feelings of 'self-other' overlap and "oneness" (Fredrickson, 2001; Fredrickson, Tugade, Waugh, & Larkin., 2003; Waugh & Fredrickson, 2006). When one experiences positive emotions, autonomic arousal takes place which leads to cognitive broadening where one's attention, thinking, and behavioral repertoires (e.g., explore, play) are broadened or expanded (Fredrickson et al., 2003). The flow experience can be intrinsically rewarding or considered an auto-telic experience (Heckman, 1997). According to Heckman (1997), "When people approach challenging physical and/or mental tasks matched with high personal skill they not only enjoy the experience, they stretch their capabilities and increase the likelihood that they will learn or achieve new and higher skill levels" (p. 24). Therefore, the positive emotions that can arise from the flow experience of interacting with a 3DVW branding site can increase consumer

learning about the brand as well as strengthen association with the brand.

A brand is a "name, term, sign, design, or a unifying combination of them intended to identify and distinguish a product or service from its competitors" (McDowell & Sutherland, 2000). Drengner, Gaus, and Jahn (2008) found that flow can influence brand image through positive emotions. Similarly, Nowak, Thach, and Berthon (2006) found that positive emotions associated with winery tasting room experiences led to higher levels of brand equity of the winery. Brand equity is conceptualized as the added value of a brand to a customer (Aaker, 1991) or the perceived value of a brand beyond its functional value (Keller, 1998). Other researchers have also demonstrated positive outcomes of flow experiences in terms of increased learning and attitude change (Hsu & Lu, 2004; Klein, 2003; Shin, 2006; Skadberg & Kimmel, 2004; Trevino & Webster, 1992; Webster, 1993), both of which can also contribute to higher brand equity when interacting with a 3DVW branding site.

Thus, building on the broaden-and-build theory of positive emotions and the empirical findings from the literature on the relationship between positive emotions and brand equity, we hypothesize that the positive emotions that emerge from the flow experience of interacting with a 3DVW branding site can have a positive impact on brand equity.

H2: Flow will have a positive effect on brand equity.

Various researchers have demonstrated a direct relationship between flow and behavioral intentions (Hsu & Lu, 2004; Koufaris, 2002; Luna, Peracchio, & de Juan, 2002; Luna et al., 2003; Siekpe, 2005). Gupta and Kim (2007) found that pleasure or enjoyment in online experiences influenced online repurchase intentions. Pleasure experienced during on-line customer visits also influences consumer satisfaction and number of items purchased (Mummalaneni, 2005). Hence, we hypothesize that flow influences behavioral intention.

H3: Flow will have a positive effect on behavioral intention.

Brand Equity Theory

Brand equity theory proposes that consumers prefer to associate themselves with products and services with a strong brand (Allen, Mahto, & Otondo, 2007, citing Keller, 1993). Brand equity can influence attitudes and behaviors (Allen et al., 2007; Keller, 1998) and attract customers for (repeat) visits and purchases (Mummalaneni, 2005). Brand equity has been shown to influence consumer preferences and purchase intentions (Cobb-Walgren, Ruble, & Donthu, 1995). Brand equity has also been shown to influence brand loyalty intentions in the service industry (Taylor, Hunter, & Lindberg, 2007). Thus, we hypothesize that brand equity has a positive effect on behavioral intention.

H4: Brand equity will have a positive effect on behavioral intention.

RESEARCH METHODOLOGY

We utilized a survey approach where subjects filled out a questionnaire before and after they experienced a 3DVW branding site. We recruited undergraduate business students who were taking 'Introduction to MIS' classes at a large midwestern university to participate in the study and gave them extra credit for their participation. To control for possible confounding factors in their visit to the 3DVW branding site, subjects participated in the study in a university computer lab.

A 3DVW branding site was selected for this study after a comprehensive review and thorough search in one of the leading 3DVWs, Second Life. The site hosts a virtual hospital that is a replica-

tion of a future, real-world hospital[1]. The virtual hospital provides visitors the opportunity to tour the facilities and enjoy an immersive experience combining video, scripting, and architectural innovation. The reasons for choosing this site are: (i) it is one of the most technologically advanced branding sites in Second Life, (ii) branding is one of the main goals of the site, and (iii) the hospital walkthrough or tour at the site involves highly structured activities, thus ensuring that all subjects experienced the same script during the virtual tour which helped to maintain consistency and control across subjects.

Every subject took part in a virtual tour of the branding site and completed pre-tour and post-tour questionnaires. The entire session, which included introduction and training (3-5 minutes), completion of pre-tour and post-tour questionnaires (about 5 and 10 minutes respectively), and the tour itself (20 minutes), took approximately 40 minutes. Subjects were scheduled for the study in the computer lab at intervals of 5-10 minutes apart to avoid meeting their fellow peer avatars in Second Life during the standard scripted tour of the branding site.

Demographic variables were captured in the pre-tour questionnaire, while the four variables – balance of skills and challenges, flow, brand equity, and behavioral intention (i.e., intention to visit or patronize the physical site, which is one of the key goals of this branding site) – were captured in the post-study questionnaire using 12 items adapted from the existing literature (see Table 2). These 12 items were measured using a 7-point Likert scale.

Balance of skills and challenges items were adapted from Guo and Ro (2008). Flow items were adapted from Novak, Hoffman, and Yung (2000). Brand equity items were adapted from Yoo and Donthu (2001). Intention items were developed by the authors based on the work of Koufaris (2002) and Mummalaneni (2005). The appendix presents all the 12 items for these four variables.

Table 2. Source of measurement for constructs

Construct	Source	# of Items
Balance of Skills and Challenges	Guo & Ro (2008)	2
Flow	Novak et al. (2000)	4
Brand equity	Yoo & Donthu (2001)	3
Intention	Koufaris (2002); Mummalaneni (2005)	3

Table 3. Sample demographics

Variable	Frequency (%)
Gender	
Male	131 (62%)
Female	80 (38%)
Age	
19-25	200 (95%)
26-35	9 (4%)
36-45	2 (1%)
Over 45	0 (0%)

DATA ANALYSIS

The sample size for this study is 211. The data collection started in January 2008 and was conducted over multiple semesters with undergraduate business students enrolled in MIS classes.

The demographics of the sample are presented in Table 3. Of the subjects participating in the study, 62% are male and 38% are female. Their ages range from 19 to 45, with 95% of them between the ages of 19-25. The majority of the subjects reported not having any virtual world experience although 52 (25%) of the 211 subjects indicated that they have at least two years of 3DVW experience. These subjects also indicated that nearly all of their 3DVW experience was in online role-playing games such as World of WarCraft.

Measurement Model

Factor analysis and reliability analysis were performed on the four variables: balance of skills and challenges (BSC), flow (F), brand equity (BE), and intention (INT). Table 4 shows the factor loadings of the items. All items load onto their intended factors with a loading of at least 0.8. The four factors account for 84 percent of the variance in the data. Table 5 shows the Cronbach's Alpha coefficients and Table 6 shows the descriptive statistics of the items.

Convergent and Discriminant Validity

Convergent validity was assessed using several methods. First, Table 4 shows the factor analysis of the items. Each item loads on its factor with a weight of at least 0.8 and all items load only on their corresponding construct. Second, a general rule used in SEM (e.g., Hulland, 1999) states that the loading of each indicator on its construct should have a path weight of at least 0.7. One item (F3) has a weight of 0.68 and all other items have weights between 0.72 and 0.97. Third, the Cronbach's Alpha coefficients for the constructs

Table 4. Loadings and cross-loadings of measures

	Flow	Intention	Brand Equity	Balance of Skills & Challenges
F1	**.914**	.112	.179	.100
F2	**.899**	.071	.131	.043
F3	**.835**	.030	-.023	.000
F4	**.824**	.070	.221	.101
INT1	.025	**.917**	.149	.026
INT2	.086	**.912**	.196	.103
INT3	.139	**.879**	.260	.124
BE1	.221	.232	**.884**	-.010
BE2	.102	.226	**.862**	.045
BE3	.109	.139	**.862**	.002
BSC1	.063	.100	-.006	**.944**
BSC2	.101	.091	.032	**.943**

* Principal components analysis with varimax rotation and Kaiser normalization

Table 5. Reliability analysis results

Variable	Cronbach's Alpha
Balance of Skills and Challenges (BSC)	0.89
Flow (F)	0.90
Brand Equity (BE)	0.89
Intention to Visit (INT)	0.91

Table 6. Descriptive statistics

Item	Mean	Standard Deviation
F1	4.66	1.49
F2	4.43	1.55
F3	4.75	1.69
F4	4.07	1.55
INT1	4.14	1.76
INT2	4.56	1.63
INT3	4.48	1.64
BE1	4.32	1.38
BE2	4.30	1.30
BE3	4.55	1.42
BSC1	6.00	0.99
BSC2	6.02	0.89

Table 7. Correlations of constructs and average variances extracted

Construct	F	INT	BE	BSC
Flow	**0.81**			
Intention to Visit	0.23	**0.88**		
Brand Equity	0.36	0.48	**0.86**	
Balance of Skills & Challenges	0.16	0.04	0.06	**0.90**

(*Diagonal represents Square Root of Average Variance Extracted)

are 0.89 and above, as shown in Table 5. Hence, they are substantially higher than the threshold of 0.8 recommended by Cohen (1988). Fourth, Fornell and Larcker (1981) recommend that all average variance extracted (AVE) be greater than 0.5. According to Table 7, the smallest AVE is 0.65 where its square root is 0.81. Hence, the above statistics show that there is strong convergent validity in the data.

Discriminant validity is demonstrated both through the factor analysis shown in Table 4 and by following the AVE rule from Chin, Marcolin, and Newsted (2003), which states that the square root of the AVE for each of the constructs should be greater than that construct's correlations with

the other constructs. As shown in Table 7, the smallest square root of AVE is 0.81, which is larger than any of the inter-construct correlations.

Hypothesis Testing

Covariance-based Structural Equation Modeling (SEM) was used for the data analysis because it allows us to examine theory and measures simultaneously (Fornell & Bookstein, 1982). We used Mplus 5.1 for the SEM data analysis. Figure 2 shows the model with the results and Table 8 summarizes the results of hypothesis testing.

Figure 2. Model

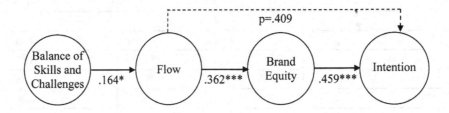

Table 8. Results of hypothesis testing

Hypothesis	Supported?
H1: Balance of skills and challenges → Flow	Yes
H2: Flow → Brand equity	Yes
H3: Flow → Behavioral intention	No
H4: Brand equity → Behavioral intention	Yes

Table 9. Fit statistics of path analyses

X² (df)	72.0 (51)
CFI	0.99
TLI	0.98
RMSEA	0.04
SRMR	0.05

Table 10. Variance accounted

Variable	Variance Accounted For
Flow	3%
Brand Equity	13%
Intention to Visit	23%

Fit Indices and Variance Explained

Table 9 shows the fit statistics which suggest excellent model fit. The variance accounted for by each variable, which refers to the amount of variance explained by each variable divided by the total variance in the model, is presented in Table 10.

DISCUSSION

The theories of flow, positive emotions, and brand equity were utilized to study online experiences in a 3DVW branding site, and the subsequent effects of these experiences on perceptions of brand equity and behavioral intention. The results suggest that the flow experience in a 3DVW site is directly influenced by the balance of one's skills and the challenges posed by the activities on the site. The flow experience on a 3DVW branding site influences perceptions of brand equity, which in turn influences behavioral intention associated with the brand. However, the flow experience has no direct influence on behavioral intention. Instead, the influence of flow on behavioral intention takes place through brand equity.

The results suggest that one's perceived skill level, in comparison to the challenges perceived from the site, influences the degree to which flow is being experienced. Hence, if an individual perceives that his/her skills are inadequate to overcome the challenges of the tasks on a 3DVW site, he/she is less likely to experience flow. In the same regard, if an individual perceives the challenges to be far below his/her level of skills, or is too easy, he/she is also unlikely to experience flow. Therefore, a good match or balance between a user's skill level and the challenges posed by the activities on the site is important to experience flow.

In addition, the results suggest that users who are able to achieve a state of flow in a 3DVW branding site will perceive higher brand equity. Therefore, their perceptions of the brand are enhanced. With heightened levels of brand equity, these users are more likely or inclined to use the brand associated with the site. It is important to note that enhancing the brand equity is important to increasing behavioral intention because flow experience does not directly influence behavioral intention.

In summary, the results suggest that organizations need to carefully consider the design of their 3DVW sites such that the skills required to navigate their site or engage in their site's activities are appropriately matched to the user's skill level.

This careful designing of the site can promote greater opportunities for users to become engaged in interacting with a 3DVW branding site. This engagement, or flow experience, can then improve users' perceptions of the brand or brand equity, which can ultimately result in a greater intention to use the brand.

CONCLUSION

There are a few limitations in this study. First, undergraduate college students were utilized for this study. The research participants may be unique in their skill level and experiences with technology and hence, generalizability of the results to other demographic groups is cautioned. Second, this research is only a partial test of Park et al.'s (2008) model. Other antecedents such as content/media characteristics, process characteristics (e.g., type of motivation), and other dimensions or antecedents of the flow construct will be reported in subsequent research. Third, this study pertained to a specific branding site. Further research is needed to determine the applicability of the findings to other types of brands and branding sites.

Opportunities to generate sales leads, market through increased brand equity, and manage customer relationships abound in 3DVWs. The immersive 3DVW environment provides a business the ability to interact with customers at a more personal level. Our research specifically examines the effects of balance of skills and challenges on one's ability/inability to engage in the flow experience. We utilized the theories of flow, positive emotions, and brand equity to understand this online phenomenon and assess the effect of user characteristics on the flow experience, and the resulting impact on brand equity as well as behavioral intention associated with the brand.

Therefore, we have partially tested Park et al.'s (2008) model to evaluate the relationship between flow and brand equity and their impact in 3D virtual worlds. Our findings demonstrate that flow is directly influenced by a user's perception of the match between skills and challenges posed by the environment and the task. Brand equity is not only an outcome of the flow phenomenon but it also influences the behavioral intention to use the brand. The flow experience, by itself, did not directly influence behavioral intentions.

This research highlights the importance of flow in 3DVW experiences. Our research findings and model provide guidance to businesses who are interested in enhancing users' flow experience, increasing brand equity, and motivating potential customers to use a brand. In particular, the results suggest that businesses should focus on the level of skills of their potential customers as well as the challenges that interacting with the site posed to them. 3DVW branding sites should provide enough help and flexibility to adapt to users' abilities to participate and interact in the environment to enhance users' flow experience. Hence, businesses will want their 3DVW sites to be easily navigated but yet enticing through challenges such as games or events.

In conclusion, 3DVW environments provide new opportunities to engage users in the flow experience, but also present unique aspects for further research and practical considerations. Our research study addresses this question using the theories of flow, positive emotions, and brand equity. Organizations will benefit from this research by developing their 3DVW sites and the activities within these sites around the factors identified in this study to engage their users in the flow experience. Future research will also benefit from the comprehensive review of the online flow literature in this paper (see Table 1) and the theoretical framework in this study to understand the flow phenomenon in 3DVW environments and various aspects of its development, such as creating flow in multiple product comparisons in 3D virtual worlds (Nah, Hong, Chen, & Lee, 2010) and in interacting using different forms of avatars (Zhao, Wang, & Zhu, 2010), as well as understanding how multimedia realism in 3D virtual worlds can impact flow (Chen, Chen, & Ross, 2010). Overall, 3DVW environments present new customer touch points that may prove to be one of the most engaging. Hence, such 3DVW environments provide significant potential to enhance perceived brand equity and appeal in the minds of customers.

ACKNOWLEDGMENT

We acknowledge research funding from the Jane Robertson Layman Fund (2008-2009) from the University of Nebraska-Lincoln Research Council and the Lattanze Grant (2008-2009) from Loyola University Maryland. We also acknowledge the opportunity to present this completed research at the IS seminar at National University of Singapore on October 9, 2008 and to present a completed extension of this research at the Virtual Worlds Conference at University of Texas-Austin on April 2, 2009.

REFERENCES

Aaker, D. A. (1991). *Managing brand equity*. New York: Free Press.

Agarwal, R., & Karahanna, E. (2000). Time flies when you are having fun: Cognitive absorption and beliefs about information technology usage. *Management Information Systems Quarterly*, *24*(4), 665–694. doi:10.2307/3250951

Allen, D. G., Mahto, R. V., & Otondo, R. F. (2007). Web-based recruitment: Effects of information, organizational brand, and attitudes toward a Web site on applicant attraction. *The Journal of Applied Psychology*, *92*(6), 1696–1708. doi:10.1037/0021-9010.92.6.1696

Arakji, R. Y., & Lang, K. R. (2007). The virtual cathedral and the virtual bazaar. *The Data Base for Advances in Information Systems*, *38*(4), 33–39.

Barnes, S. (2007). Virtual worlds as a medium for advertising. *The Data Base for Advances in Information Systems*, *38*(4), 45–55.

Brandon, J. (2007, May 2). The top eight corporate sites in Second Life. *Computer World*.

Burslem, J. (2007). Future of real estate marketing. *Inman News*. Retrieved May 6, 2008, from http://www.futureofrealestatemarketing.com/coldwell-banker-tours-a-home-in-cyberspace

Chen, H. (2006). Flow on the net-detecting Web users' positive affects and their flow states. *Computers in Human Behavior*, *22*(2), 221–233. doi:10.1016/j.chb.2004.07.001

Chen, H., Wigand, R. T., & Nilan, M. (2000). Exploring Web users' optimal flow experiences. *Information Technology & People*, *13*(4), 263–281. doi:10.1108/09593840010359473

Chen, K., Chen, J. V., & Ross, W. H. (2010). Antecedents of online game dependency: The implications of multimedia realism and uses and gratifications theory. *Journal of Database Management*, *21*(2), 69–99.

Chin, W. W., Marcolin, B. L., & Newsted, P. R. (2003). A partial least squares latent variable modeling approach for measuring interaction effects: Results from a Monte Carlo simulation study and an electronic-mail emotion/adoption study. *Information Systems Research*, *14*(2), 189–217. doi:10.1287/isre.14.2.189.16018

Cobb-Walgren, C. J., Ruble, C. A., & Donthu, N. (1995). Brand equity, brand preference, and purchase intent. *Journal of Advertising*, *24*(3), 25–40.

Cohen, J. (1988). *Statistical power for the behavioral sciences* (2nd ed.). Hilldale, NJ: Lawrence Erlbaum Associates.

Csikszentmihalyi, M. (1975). *Beyond boredom and anxiety*. San Francisco: Jossey-Bass.

Csikszentmihalyi, M. (1990). *Flow: The psychology of optimal experience*. New York: Harper & Row.

Csikszentmihalyi, M. (1993). *The evolving self: A psychology for the third millennium*. New York: HarperCollins.

Csikszentmihalyi, M. (1997). *Finding flow: The psychology of engagement with everyday life*. New York: HarperCollins.

Csikszentmihalyi, M., & Csikszentmihalyi, I. S. (1988). *Optimal experience: Psychological studies of flow in consciousness*. New York: Cambridge University Press.

Csikszentmihalyi, M., & Lefavre, J. (1989). Optimal experience in work and leisure. *Journal of Personality and Social Psychology*, *56*(5), 815–822. doi:10.1037/0022-3514.56.5.815

Davis, A., Murphy, J., Owens, D., Khazanchi, D., & Zigurs, I. (2009). Avatars, people, and virtual worlds: Foundations for research in metaverses. *Journal of the Association for Information Systems*, *10*(2), 90–117.

Drengner, J., Gaus, H., & Jahn, S. (2008). Does flow influence the brand image in event marketing. *Journal of Advertising Research*, *48*(1), 138–147. doi:10.2501/S0021849908080148

Eschenbrenner, B., Nah, F. F.-H., & Siau, K. (2008). 3-D virtual worlds in education: Applications, benefits, issues, and opportunities. *Journal of Database Management*, *19*(4), 91–110.

Finneran, C. M., & Zhang, P. (2005). Flow in computer-mediated environment: Promises and challenges. *Communications of the Association for Information Systems*, *15*, 82–101.

Fornell, C., & Bookstein, F. L. (1982). Two structural equation models: LISREL and PLS applied to consumer exit-voice theory. *Journal of Marketing*, *19*(4), 440–452. doi:10.2307/3151718

Fornell, C., & Larcker, D. F. (1981). Evaluating structural equation models with unobservable variables and measurement error. *JMR, Journal of Marketing Research*, *18*(1), 39–50. doi:10.2307/3151312

Fortin, D. R., & Dholakia, R. R. (2005). Interactivity and vividness effects on social presence and involvement with a Web-based advertisement. *Journal of Business Research*, *58*(3), 387–396. doi:10.1016/S0148-2963(03)00106-1

Fredrickson, B. L. (2001). The role of positive emotions in positive psychology: The broaden-and-build theory of positive emotions. *The American Psychologist*, *56*(3), 218–226. doi:10.1037/0003-066X.56.3.218

Fredrickson, B. L., Tugade, M. M., Waugh, C. E., & Larkin, G. R. (2003). What good for positive emotions in crises? A prospective study of resilience and emotions following the terrorist attacks on the United States on September 11th, 2001. *Journal of Personality and Social Psychology*, *84*(2), 365–376. doi:10.1037/0022-3514.84.2.365

Ghani, J. A. (1995). Flow in human computer interactions: Test of a model . In Carey, J. (Ed.), *Human factors in information systems: Emerging theoretical bases* (pp. 291–311). New York: Ablex Publishing.

Ghani, J. A., & Deshpande, S. P. (1994). Task characteristics and the experience of optimal flow in human-computer interaction. *The Journal of Psychology*, *128*(4), 381–391.

Ghani, J. A., Supnik, R., & Rooney, P. (1991). The experience of flow in computer-mediated and in face-to-face groups. In *Proceedings of the Twelfth International Conference on Information Systems* (pp. 229-236).

Goel, L., & Mousavidin, E. (2007). vCRM: Virtual customer relationship management. *The Data Base for Advances in Information Systems*, *38*(4), 56–60.

Guo, Y. M., & Poole, M. S. (2009). Antecedents of flow in online shopping: A test of alternative models. *Information Systems Journal, 19*(4), 369–390. doi:10.1111/j.1365-2575.2007.00292.x

Guo, Y. M., & Ro, Y. K. (2008). Capturing flow in the business classroom. *Decision Sciences Journal of Innovative Education, 6*(2), 437–462. doi:10.1111/j.1540-4609.2008.00185.x

Gupta, S., & Kim, H. (2007). The moderating effect of transaction experience on the decision calculus in on-line repurchase. *International Journal of Electronic Commerce, 12*(1), 127–158. doi:10.2753/JEC1086-4415120105

Hecht, D., & Reiner, M. (2007). Field dependency and the sense of object-presence in haptic virtual environments. *Cyberpsychology & Behavior, 10*(2), 243–251. doi:10.1089/cpb.2006.9962

Heckman, F. (1997). Designing organizations for flow experiences. *Journal for Quality and Participation, 20*(2), 24–33.

Hobson, N. (2006). Is it time you got a Second Life? *Strategic Communication Management, 11*(1). Retrieved September 14, 2008, from http://www.nevillehobson.com/ resources/ is-it-time-you-got-a-second-life/

Hoffman, D. L., & Novak, T. P. (1996). Marketing in hypermedia computer-mediated environment. *Journal of Marketing, 60*(3), 50–68. doi:10.2307/1251841

Hoffman, D. L., & Novak, T. P. (2009). Flow Online: Lessons Learned and Future Prospects. *Journal of Interactive Marketing, 23*(1), 23–34. doi:10.1016/j.intmar.2008.10.003

Hsu, C.-L., & Lu, H.-P. (2004). Why do people play on-line games? An extended TAM with social influences and flow experience. *Information & Management, 41*(7), 853–868. doi:10.1016/j.im.2003.08.014

Huang, M.-H. (2003). Designing website attributes to induce experiential encounters. *Computers in Human Behavior, 19*(4), 425–442. doi:10.1016/S0747-5632(02)00080-8

Hulland, J. (1999). Use of partial least squares (PLS) in strategic management research: A review of four recent studies. *Strategic Management Journal, 20*(2), 195–204. doi:10.1002/(SICI)1097-0266(199902)20:2<195::AID-SMJ13>3.0.CO;2-7

Ives, B., & Junglas, I. (2008). APC forum: Business implications of virtual worlds and serious gaming. *MIS Quarterly Executive, 7*(3), 151–156.

Jiang, Z., & Benbasat, I. (2005). Virtual product experience: Effects of visual and functional control of products on perceived diagnosticity and flow in electronic shopping. *Journal of Management Information Systems, 21*(3), 111–148.

Keller, K. L. (1993). Conceptualizing, measuring, and managing customer brand equity. *Journal of Marketing, 57*(1), 1–30. doi:10.2307/1252054

Keller, K. L. (1998). *Strategic brand management: Building, measuring and managing brand equity*. Upper Saddle River, NJ: Prentice Hall.

Kim, Y. Y., Oh, S., & Lee, H. (2005). What makes people experience flow? Social characteristics of online games. *International Journal of Advanced Media and Communication, 1*(1), 76–92. doi:10.1504/IJAMC.2005.007724

Klein, L. R. (2003). Creating virtual product experiences: The role of telepresence. *Journal of Interactive Marketing, 17*(1), 41–55. doi:10.1002/dir.10046

Korzaan, M. L. (2003). Going with the flow: Predicting online purchase intentions. *Journal of Computer Information Systems, 43*(4), 25–31.

Koufaris, M. (2002). Applying the technology acceptance model and flow theory to online consumer behavior. *Information Systems Research, 13*(2), 205–223. doi:10.1287/isre.13.2.205.83

Lafayette, J. (2007). Life's a virtual beach for Pepsi. *Television Week, 26*(17), 29–30.

Leggatt, H. (2007, March 29). Second Life citizens want engaging marketing and brands. *BizReport*. Retrieved September 14, 2008, from http://www.bizreport.com/2007/03/ second_life_citizens_want_engaging_ marketing_and_brands.html

Lewis, J. (2007, April 17). Coke Expands Viral Marketing Efforts Online. *WebProNews*. Retrieved September 14, 2008, from http://www.webpronews.com/topnews/ 2007/04/17/coke-expands-viral- marketing-efforts-online

Li, D., & Browne, G. J. (2006). The role of need for cognition and mood in online flow experience. *Journal of Computer Information Systems, 46*(3), 11–17.

Lok, B. C. (2004). Toward the merging of real and virtual spaces. *Communications of the ACM, 47*(8), 48–53. doi:10.1145/1012037.1012061

Lombard, M., & Ditton, T. (1997). At the heart of it all: The concept of presence. *Journal of Computer Mediated Communication, 3*(2). Retrieved September 14, 2008, from http://jcmc.indiana.edu/vol3/ issue2/lombard.html

Luna, D., Peracchio, L. A., & de Juan, M. D. (2002). Cross-cultural and cognitive aspects of Web site navigation. *Journal of the Academy of Marketing Science, 30*(4), 397–410. doi:10.1177/009207002236913

Luna, D., Peracchio, L. A., & de Juan, M. D. (2003). Flow in individual Web sites: Model estimation and cross-cultural validation. *Advances in Consumer Research. Association for Consumer Research (U. S.), 30*, 280–281.

McDowell, W., & Sutherland, J. (2000). Choice versus chance: Using brand equity theory to explore TV audience lead-in effects, a case study. *Journal of Media Economics, 13*(4), 233–247. doi:10.1207/S15327736ME1304_3

McGee, M. K. (2008). Hospital takes its grand opening to Second Life. *InformationWeek*. Retrieved February 25, 2008, from http://www.informationweek.com/news/ internet/ebusiness/showArticle.jhtml? articleID=206801783

Mikropoulos, T. A., & Strouboulis, V. (2004). Factors that influence presence in educational virtual environments. *Cyberpsychology & Behavior, 7*(5), 582–591.

Mummalaneni, V. (2005). An empirical investigation of Web site characteristics, consumer emotional states and on-line shopping behaviors. *Journal of Business Research, 58*(4), 526–532. doi:10.1016/S0148-2963(03)00143-7

Nah, F. F.-H., Hong, W., Chen, L., & Lee, H.-H. (2010). Information search patterns in e-commerce product comparison services. *Journal of Database Management, 21*(2), 26–40.

Nel, D., van Niekerk, R., Berthon, J., & Davies, T. (1999). Going with the flow: Web sites and customer involvement. *Internet Research, 9*(2), 109–116. doi:10.1108/10662249910264873

Novak, T. P., Hoffman, D., & Yung, Y. (2000). Measuring the customer experience in online environments: A structural modeling approach. *Marketing Science, 19*(1), 22–44. doi:10.1287/mksc.19.1.22.15184

Novak, T. P., Hoffman, D. L., & Duhachek, A. (2003). The influence of goal-directed and experiential activities on online flow experiences. *Journal of Consumer Psychology, 13*(1/2), 3–16.

Nowak, L., Thach, L., & Olsen, J. E. (2006). Wowing the millennials: Creating brand equity in the wine industry. *Journal of Product and Brand Management, 15*(5), 316–323. doi:10.1108/10610420610685712

Pace, S. (2004). A grounded theory of the flow experiences of Web users. *International Journal of Human-Computer Studies, 60*(3), 327–363. doi:10.1016/j.ijhcs.2003.08.005

Park, S. R., Nah, F. F.-H., DeWester, D., Eschenbrenner, B., & Jeon, S. (2008). Virtual world affordances: Enhancing brand value. *Journal of Virtual Worlds Research, 1*(2), 1–18.

Pilke, E. M. (2004). Flow experiences in information technology use. *International Journal of Human-Computer Studies, 61*(3), 347–357. doi:10.1016/j.ijhcs.2004.01.004

Reid, D. (2004). A model of playfulness and flow in virtual reality interactions. *Presence (Cambridge, Mass.), 13*(4), 451–462. doi:10.1162/1054746041944777

Rettie, R. (2001). An exploration of flow during Internet use. *Internet Research, 11*(2), 103–113. doi:10.1108/10662240110695070

Riva, G., Mantovani, F., Capideville, C. S., Preziosa, A., Morganti, F., & Villani, D. (2007). Affective interactions using virtual reality: The link between presence and emotions. *Cyberpsychology & Behavior, 10*(1), 45–56. doi:10.1089/cpb.2006.9993

Shin, N. (2006). Online learner's 'flow' experience: An empirical study. *British Journal of Educational Technology, 37*(5), 705–720. doi:10.1111/j.1467-8535.2006.00641.x

Siekpe, J. S. (2005). An examination of the multidimensionality of flow construct in a computer-mediated environment. *Journal of Electronic Commerce Research, 6*(1), 31–43.

Skadberg, Y. X., & Kimmel, J. R. (2004). Visitors' flow experience while browsing a Web site: Its measurement, contributing factors and consequences. *Computers in Human Behavior, 20*(3), 403–422. doi:10.1016/S0747-5632(03)00050-5

Steinriede, K. (2007). Virtual world, real awareness: Kraft sees future in Second Life. *Stagnito's New Products Magazine.* Retrieved November 13, 2007, from http://www.allbusiness.com/manufacturing/ food-manufacturing/ 4510733-1.html

Steuer, J. (1992). Defining virtual reality: Dimensions determining telepresence. *The Journal of Communication, 42*(4), 73–93. doi:10.1111/j.1460-2466.1992.tb00812.x

Taylor, S. A., Hunter, G. L., & Lindberg, D. L. (2007). Understanding (Customer-based) Brand Equity in Financial Services. *Journal of Services Marketing, 21*(4), 241–252. doi:10.1108/08876040710758540

Trevino, L. K., & Webster, J. (1992). Flow in computer-mediated communication. *Communication Research, 19*(5), 539–573. doi:10.1177/009365092019005001

Tung, W., Moore, R., & Engelland, B. (2006). Exploring attitudes and purchase intentions in a brand-oriented, highly interactive Web sites setting. *Marketing Management Journal, 16*(2), 94–106.

Venezia, P. (2007). Virtualization. *InfoWorld, 29*(1), 16–17.

Waugh, C. E., & Fredrickson, B. L. (2006). Nice to know you: Positive emotions, self-other overlap, and complex understanding in the formation of a new relationship. *The Journal of Positive Psychology, 1*(2), 93–106. doi:10.1080/17439760500510569

Webster, J., Trevino, L. K., & Ryan, L. (1993). The dimensionality and correlates of flow in human-computer interactions. *Computers in Human Behavior*, *9*(4), 411–426. doi:10.1016/0747-5632(93)90032-N

Yoo, B., & Donthu, N. (2001). Developing and validating a multidimensional consumer-based brand equity scale. *Journal of Business Research*, *52*(1), 1–14. doi:10.1016/S0148-2963(99)00098-3

Zhao, Y., Wang, W., & Zhu, Y. (2010). Antecedents of the Closeness of Human-avatar relationships in a virtual world. *Journal of Database Management*, *21*(2), 41–68.

ENDNOTE

[1]   Hospital name intentionally excluded to maintain confidentiality.

This work was previously published in International Journal of Database Management, Volume 21, Issue 3, edited by Keng Siau, pp. 69-89, copyright 2010 by IGI Publishing (an imprint of IGI Global).

APPENDIX – SURVEY INSTRUMENT

Item	Construct Scale item wording
	Flow: (7-point Likert scale) The following instructions were presented before the Flow items: The word "flow" is used to describe a state of mind that is sometimes experienced by people who are deeply involved in an activity. One example of flow is the case where a computer gamer is deeply involved in a game and achieves a state of mind where nothing else matters but the game. In other words, he or she is completely and totally immersed in it. Some people report this state of mind when engaging in various activities such as watching movies, reading novels, browsing the Web, or working. Activities that lead to flow completely captivate a person for some period of time. When one is in flow, time may seem to stand still, and nothing else seems to matter. Flow may not last for a long time on any particular occasion, but it may come and go over time. Flow has been described as an intrinsically enjoyable experience. Please answer the following questions regarding your experience on the virtual tour:
F1	When carrying out the virtual tour, I experienced flow at some point.
F2	I felt I was in flow during some parts of the virtual tour.
F3	I did not experience any flow during any part of the virtual tour. (Reverse coded.)
F4	I experienced flow during the virtual tour.
	Intention to Visit: (7-point Likert scale) Assuming that this hospital is available in your area...
INT1	...it is likely that I will visit this hospital.
INT2	...I would consider this hospital the next time I need a hospital service.
INT3	...I would recommend this hospital if a friend calls me to get my advice in his/her search for a hospital.
	Brand Equity: (7-point Likert scale)
BE1	Even if another hospital offers the same quality of services as this hospital, I would prefer to use the services of this hospital.
BE2	If there is another hospital as good as this hospital, I prefer to go to this hospital.
BE3	It makes sense to use the services of this hospital instead of services of any other hospitals even if they are the same.
	Balance of Skills and Challenges: (7-point Likert scale)
BSC1	I felt I was competent enough to meet the demands of the task.
BSC2	My skills allowed me to meet the challenge posed by the task.

Chapter 12
Cost and Service Capability Considerations on the Intention to Adopt Application Service Provision Services

Yurong Yao
Suffolk University, USA

Denis M. Lee
Suffolk University, USA

Yang W. Lee
Northeastern University, USA

ABSTRACT

The Application Service Provision (ASP) model offers a new form of IS/IT resource management option for which the vendor remotely provides the usage of applications over a network. Currently, the ASP industry appears to be more vendor-driven. But without a good understanding of how the ASP offerings might appeal to prospective customers, the industry might not survive. This study investigates empirically the intention to adopt an ASP service from the customers' perspective, using survey data collected from a national sample of IS/IT executives. Based on the Transaction Cost Theory (Williamson, 1979, 1985) and service capability, a causal model is developed to examine the effects of perceived cost savings and service capability, as well as their antecedent factors, on the intention to adopt an ASP service. The results show a dominant effect of cost savings consideration on ASP adoption intention.

INTRODUCTION

Dramatically reduced network costs due to the rapid growth of the commercial networks, and the increasing bandwidths together with advances in the security of internet based transactions have led

DOI: 10.4018/978-1-61350-471-0.ch012

to the emergence of application services providers (ASPs) (Susaria et al., 2003). An ASP may be defined broadly as a company that provides software applications to multiple customers over a wide area network in return for payments (e.g., Ma et al., 2005; Smith & Kumar, 2004; Choudhary, 2007). This new concept combines the provision of software and services into a "whole product"

(Feller, Finnegan & Hayes, 2008). The hosting services could include complex packaged enterprise systems (e.g., ERP and CRM) as well as general applications, such as accounting, payroll processing, technical support, and industry specific functions, such as lending systems, course management systems for education and training purpose (Seltsikas & Currie, 2002).

Proponents of the ASP business model for providing software application services on a rental or usage basis have argued that it can offer a number of advantages over the traditional ways of purchasing or leasing software. Its one-to-many hosting model lends itself to certain economies of scale by providing standard applications to multiple clients (Choudhary, 2007). The quick, off-the-shelf IT services require shorter period of time to install and implement new software applications (Mears, 2001). It reduces the need for in-house IT staff for both installation and maintenance, which is especially important for businesses with inadequate internal organizational resources, or organizations with high IT turnover rates (Vizard, 2000; Gewald & Dibbern, 2009). Finally, the ASP model allows for easy growth and scalability. It affords a more flexible approach to meet IT service needs without the uncertainties of committing to a large upfront investment (Jayatilaka et al., 2003).

This ASP online hosting model offers a new IT resource option in which service vendors remotely provide the usage of applications over a network. If successful, it can shift in fundamental ways the strategic allocation of IT resource management for user organizations. Since the emergence of the business concept, the industry seemed to be poised for explosive growth, with an estimated large number of IT firms offering ASP-type services including such industry leaders as IBM, Oracle and SAP (Seltsikas & Currie, 2002). Yet, at the same time, a number of researchers have found that the industry overall has a lack luster record in signing up customers (e.g., Caufield, 2000; Susarla et al., 2003; Ma et al., 2005). In a

study of managers/owners from small and medium enterprises (SMEs), Seltisikas and Currie (2002) found that only 6% indicated that they use the services of an ASP. The factors contributed to this low utilization may include narrow domains of service, lack of successful experiences and risk-avoidance propensity among IT managers.

As pointed out by Ma et al. (2005), the ASP industry appears to be vendor-driven, but without a good understanding of how the ASP offerings might appeal to the customers, the industry might not survive. Researchers have also found a general lack of studies on the user's reception of ASP services adoption (Dibbern et al., 2004). Most available studies have mainly concentrated on exploring the ASP business model using descriptive case studies (e.g. Seltsikas & Currie, 2002; Levina & Ross, 2003). The limited number of empirical studies have examined users' past experience, satisfaction of ASP services (e.g. Ma et al., 2005; Susarla et al., 2003), benefits and localization of service vendors (e.g. Arora & Forman, 2007), and trust relationship with vendors (e.g. Vatanasombut et al., 2008). Only one study seems to be available that has explored the ASP adoption decision among a small focused group of managers (Jayatilaka et al., 2003).

Although the use of the term ASP may be declining in the popular press, emerging forms of online application and service hosting, enabled by new computing and telecommunication technologies and concepts such as cloud computing, enterprise computing in the cloud, cloudy infrastructure, Software as a Service (SaaS), Platform as a Service (PaaS) and Infrastructure as a Service (IaaS), are clearly expanding and evolving (Carr, 2008; Erickson & Siau, 2008). Some advocates even argue that this trend will lead to the next technological revolution (e.g., Hayes, 2008; Choudhary, 2007). Li, Huang, Yen and Chang (2007) also argued that many companies also have struggled to make the transition from the current legacy systems to the web services architecture in order to gain the benefits of network enabled applications. In the context of our present research, we argue that ASP or online hosting can provide a growing and important option for a company to operate and maintain information technology. It is therefore valuable to understand a client's decision to adopt an ASP (Dibbern et al., 2004).

The purpose of this study is to empirically examine the intention to adopt an ASP service from the customers' perspective. In particular, it examines two dominant factors that previous studies have argued to be the most important in determining ASP adoption – cost savings and service capability (e.g., Ma et al., 2005; Susarla et al., 2003; Gewald & Dibbern, 2009), as well as the antecedents of these two factors. A better understanding of how these different factors might relate to the intention of ASP adoption can offer more insight into how to find a better match between clients' requirements and ASPs' service offerings and capabilities. Knowing how to better align vendors' offerings with customers' needs is critical for the future growth of this industry.

THEORETICAL FRAMEWORK AND RESEARCH HYPOTHESES

Traditional Outsourcing Model and ASP Business Model

Broadly speaking, the ASP business model is under the umbrella of IS outsourcing (Smith & Kumar, 2004). However, besides similarities, there are important areas of differences between the traditional outsourcing model and the ASP business model.

The basic purposes of adopting either the traditional outsourcing model or the ASP business model are essentially the same; i.e. to reduce cost, to compensate internal capability deficiencies, to focus on core business, or to leverage external intelligence. In both cases, customers obtain their services/products from an outside supplier. By relying on an external vendor, the customer will lose a certain amount of control on the process and become more dependent on the supplier for certain functional capabilities.

At the same time, the ASP business model differs from IS outsourcing in several significant ways (Yao & Murphy, 2005; Ma et al., 2005):

- The traditional outsourcing vendor typically provides software or products on a case by case basis; whereas the ASP vendor generally provides a standardized application service to multiple customers in order to gain the economies of scale advantage.
- The traditional outsourcing vendor tends to offer many different types of applications, IT infrastructure management and software development; whereas the ASP vendor tends to focus only on online applications.
- In traditional outsourcing, some software or hardware are owned by the clients; whereas an ASP vendor is responsible for all hardware and software maintenance and updates, and data storage at the hosting site.
- The traditional outsourcing vendors tend to be large companies; whereas the ASP vendors have emerged in two major forms: small, start-up companies (e.g. SalesForce.com, Blackboard) and new business developments within existing, large companies (e.g. SAP and Oracle).
- The traditional outsourcing tends to involve long term contracts (e.g. 10 years) while the ASP service contracts are typically much shorter (e.g., 2 or 3 years).

The above comparisons point to some important differences in the structure, offerings, and terms of the services offered by the traditional outsourcing model and the ASP model. These differences could affect the motivation of clients in the adoption decisions. However, while there is an extensive body of research literatures on traditional outsourcing adoption, very few studies have focused specifically on ASP service adoption (Dibbern et al., 2004). In order to understand the growth potential and limitations of this potentially important IT resource management option, it is critically important to have a better understanding of the decision factors from the perspective of the potential ASP adopters. The present study is designed to fill this gap by exploring empirically the economic and service capabilities considerations that could play the most important roles in the intention to adopt ASP.

Adoption of Information Systems in Organization

Before we examine the role of economic and service factors in adoption decision, it might be helpful to take a look at representative literatures associated with IS adoption decision. The studies on the adoption of information systems tend to be diverse and they find their roots in economics, psychology and sociology (e.g., Davis, 1989; Taylor & Todd, 1995b; Venkatesh & Davis, 2000). The different perspectives in the various streams include the theory of reasoned action (e.g. Davis, 1989), the technology acceptance model (e.g. Venkatesh & Davis, 2000), the motivational model (e.g. Vallerand, 1997), the theory of planned behavior (e.g. Taylor & Todd, 1995), and the social cognitive theory (e.g. Compeau & Higgins, 1995). After reviewing and comparing the different theories and their associated constructs, Venkatesh, Morris, Davis and Davis (2003) proposed a unified model which incorporates the major constructs, including performance expectation, effort expectation, social influences and facilitating conditions. They studied how these factors might impact users' acceptance of new systems. More recent studies have also examined the impact of other factors on the adoption of information systems, such as privacy concerns, consumer's habits, and avoidance to the technology threats (e.g., Angst & Agarwal, 2009). Researchers have also started to investigate the continual usage of information

systems and post-adoption behaviors. For example, Kim (2009) proposed a time-based process model to examine the impact of four mechanisms (i.e., reason-oriented actions, sequential updating, feedback and habits) on the user's post adoption behaviors. Based on the status quo bias theory, Kim and Kankanhalli (2009) empirically analyzed the reasons for end user's resistance to the adoption of information technology.

Most of these studies on IT adoption and the associated theories/models focus on the individual acceptance of information technology, rather than the organizational system/service adoption decisions. Very few studies have examined the system adoption decisions at the organizational level. Kwon and Zmud (1987) identified five categories of factors that might influence the adoption and diffusion of information systems, including individual factors, organizational structural factors, technology factors, task factors, and environmental factors. They showed that the adoptions of new technologies in organizations should take other factors into consideration besides the individual differences. Bajaj (2000) interviewed senior IS managers and developed a list of important factors that might impact their organization's adoption on network-based IS architecture. Software quality was listed as the most important concern for IS architecture adoption. Cost of the architecture was also identified as one of the four major factors. Zhu, Kraemer, Gurbaxani and Xu (2006) found that the switching cost consideration plays a big role in the firm's network migration decision from EDI to open-standard architecture. Kauffman and Mohtadi (2004) also found that small size companies tend to adopt less costly EDI products to reduce uncertainty. Additionally, Khoumbati, Themistocleous and Irani (2006) analyzed the hospitals' adoption decision of enterprise integration systems. Their study focused on the benefits, barriers, enhanced patients satisfaction, cost and IT infrastructures. In all these studies, economic considerations and the quality of adopted systems or services are always considered as the critical determinants for the organizational adoption of information systems or technologies.

Our purpose here is not to criticize or summarize the previous literatures in IS adoption decision or implementation processes. In this study, we focus mainly on the organization's adoption decision of hosting services, but not the whole implementation life cycle. In our case, we investigate the ASP hosting adoption particularly from the economic and service perspectives.

Economic Considerations: Transaction Cost Theory

Transaction cost theory (TCT) is concerned with the coordination and regulation of an organization's transactions with another from an economic perspective (Lacity & Hirschheim, 1993). TCT, developed originally by Williamson (1979, 1985), identifies two types of costs: production costs and transaction costs. Production costs, such as labor, raw material, and machine abrasion, are *internal* costs incurred when an organization produces the goods in-house. Transaction costs refer to the time, efforts and cost involved with *external* material exchange or service process, such as those associated with vendor search, negotiation, assessment, and contract enforcement.

In the ASP business model, production costs reflect all the costs the client has to expend for developing, building, delivering and maintaining the application internally. Transaction costs are associated with external service delivery which occurs when the client starts to search for an ASP vendor, then negotiates the contract and finally utilizes the services and monitors the service vendor. The prospective ASP adopter compares the internal production costs versus the external transaction costs to evaluate the desirability of outside service adoption.

The transaction cost theory thus provides a framework to evaluate internal production versus external outsourcing alternatives (Cheon et al., 1995) and it has been used quite extensively in IS

outsourcing studies (e.g., Ang & Straub, 1998; Miranda & Kim, 2006; Tiwana & Bush, 2007). Since cost advantage associated with the ASP business model is continually ranked by CIOs as one of the top reasons for its adoption (e.g., Jayatilaka et al., 2003; Gewald & Dibbern, 2009), transaction cost theory plays a central role in helping to analyze the production costs and transaction costs in the adoption of hosted application services. Economic return on investment has been found to be cited by senior IS managers as one of the most important factors on the adoption decisions (Ven & Verelst, 2008). In addition, asset specificity and functional complexity are two important factors impacting transaction cost (Tiwana & Bush, 2007). Due to the features of ASP business model, other transaction cost factors (e.g. frequency of negotiation, technical uncertainty) may be less important here.

Service Capability Considerations

Cost consideration alone is insufficient to ensure the satisfied usage of information systems (Olson, 2007). Since the essence of an ASP's business is to provide services, the evaluation of the ASP vendor's service capability is thus also a major component of the assessment process for the adoption decision (Han et al., 2008; Kim et al., 2002).

Based on the resource-based theory, service capability refers to the service provider's capability to manage various tangible and intangible resources for providing good service performance (Bharadwaj, 2000). The ASP service capability considerations might include the vendor's understanding of the customer's business needs, functional features, operational requirements, as well as the maintenance and technical support. The vendors' service capability is important in determining its service-oriented performance. It has been suggested that low service capability of current ASP vendors might explain why many ASP vendors struggle to survive (Olson, 2007).

Fundamentally different from physical goods, service is often intangible and it can only be judged by customers' attitudes (Parasuraman et al., 1985). When there is no prior experience associated with service providers, a perceived service capability represents the customer's assessments of the capability of an ASP under consideration. Surprisingly, the impact of the service capability of the ASP on the adoption decision has rarely been studied in prior research (Han et al., 2008). Rai and Sambamurthy (2006) also called for more research attention on the web-enabled IT services (now emerging under new terms such as cloud computing and SaaS), including service design, online business process enabling and infrastructure development for service support. Service providers need to have the capabilities to design the business services with high business intelligence, encapsulate the services with new technology and shape the way the services are accessed. Thus, in this study, we fill in this gap and examine the impact of services capability on the ASP adoption intention.

Research Framework

Based on the above discussions, we argue that cost savings and service capability considerations are two essential factors for the ASP adoption decision.

Cost savings refer to the cost advantage a company anticipates from outsourcing an application to an external vendor instead of developing and maintaining it internally (Tiwana & Bush, 2007). Conceptually, cost savings are based on the differential cost accounting concept (e.g. Hongren et al., 2008) that measures the net cost differences between the costs incurred using internal production versus external outsourcing.

Positive cost savings result when the external hosting costs are lower than internal production costs. To assess the potential cost savings, the company might first estimate the initial set-up investments, subscription fees as well as contract negotiation costs. In addition, costs over the entire hosting life cycle should be included, such as those incurred for vendor searching, conflict resolution,

performance monitoring, and contract renewal negotiations (Lacity & Willcocks, 2001). Second, the internal production costs must also be evaluated. These costs would include the required internal development, software and hardware acquisitions, operations, maintenance and updates. Finally, the cost savings are the differences between these two sets of cost estimates. In practice, the assessment of cost savings might be more complex than the differential cost accounting framework using the simple prescribed net present value calculations. Nonetheless, the differential cost estimates are involved in the economic evaluation of the two alternatives.

Many information systems, particularly packaged enterprise systems are notoriously known for high costs associated with software license purchase, hardware upgrades, system configurations, customizations, end-user training and ongoing maintenance (Dibbern et al., 2002). In some cases, when there are no existing systems satisfying such needs, companies have to self-develop the systems. Many companies lack the capacity to handle such work internally, thus outside consulting services are often required (Gewald & Dibbern, 2009). Challenges can also emerge as the new system might require hiring additional qualified IT professionals (Olson, 2007). Hence, production costs can be very high if the company chooses to develop, implement and manage the applications internally.

Conversely, lower costs and predictable monthly fees (Jayatilaka et al., 2003) are the principal advantages of the ASP business model. With the economies of scale advantage and expertise on system configuration and maintenance, an ASP vendor can provide relatively standard solutions to a client company at a much lower cost (Smith & Kumar, 2004). The perceived cost savings advantage is thus an important consideration in a potential client's decision to adopt an ASP service. Therefore, we argue:

Hypothesis 1: Higher perceived cost savings associated with ASP adoption will lead to a higher degree of ASP adoption intention.

Service is generally defined as "the application of specialized competences (knowledge and skills) through deeds, processes, and performances for the benefit of another entity or the entity itself" (Vargo & Lusch, 2004, p. 2). In order to provide good services, a service provider should have the capability to obtain the specialized competences and deploy them effectively in setting up the applications.

The service provider's service capability thus includes not just the knowledge in technology and processes, but also the competence to successfully apply them in order to achieve the expected results for the client. How to obtain and integrate the specialized knowledge with physical infrastructure in order to provide good performance is thus a central consideration in determining a service provider's service capabilities (Rai et al., 2006). Building upon a resource-based theory of the firm, Grant (1991) argues that an organization's capability is the ability to acquire, assemble and distribute the combined resources. These resources can be classified into three categories: tangible resources, intangible resources and personnel-based resources. Bharadwaj (2000) further applies this classification to take into account different types of IT associated resources. These include: 1) tangible technology resources such as various IT infrastructure and components; 2) intangible IT-enabled resources such as knowledge assets, synergy and customer orientation; and 3) human IT resources which comprise of technical and managerial IT skills and knowledge.

In this study, we define *service capability* as the ability to acquire and integrate IT associated resources to develop and deliver value-added applications to customers. More specifically, we argue that service capability consists of business-oriented service capability and technical-oriented service capability. The business-oriented service capability refers to the ability to provide applicable system functions and system configurations to meet customers' requirements, including application features, and assurance of performance (Han et al., 2008). Business service capabilities include the management of the intangible resources (e.g. business know-how, customer orientation) and the business part of human-resource related knowledge and skills (e.g. employees' knowledge about business process and industry domain application) (Bharadwaj, 2000). The business knowledge is a critical part of organizational competences. Vendors need to have the capability to integrate the business domain knowledge with the design and development of systems and applications in order to deliver a system that can meet the client's needs.

The technology-oriented service capability refers to the ability to achieve prompt response to a customer's requests, maintain robust network connection and system operation, provide 24/7 technical support and timely version upgrades, and ensure the security of data transfer and storage (Zaheer & Venkatraman, 1995). The service provider needs to obtain the tangible IT resources (e.g. data storage and exchange infrastructure, network connections, etc.) and the technical knowledge and skills to manage the infrastructure and deliver the applications. The service provider's capability to build a solid IT infrastructure can ensure prompt response and timely data exchange (Rai et al., 2006). The service provider staff's technical knowledge can also allow them to fully utilize the technology to develop effective applications.

Bharadwaj (2000) argues that a firm's IT associated capability is directly associated with profits and costs. This is particularly true for an IT service provider, whose capabilities can be considered to be its strategic and critical competitive advantage in attracting clients (Lee et al., 1995). Han et al. (2008) found that a vendor's high service capability can effectively increase the interactions with its client, and this can improve the relationships with the client and boost the client's confidence in using the external service. Rai et al. (2006) also point out that a company's capability to integrate different resources and business process can positively impact its performance by building close customer relationship and maintaining efficient operations. Thus, we argue that a high level of service capability along all these facets is expected to lead to a high intention to adopt services.

Hypothesis 2: Higher perceived service capability will lead to a higher degree of ASP adoption intention.

In addition to the individual main effects of cost savings and service capability on the application hosting adoption, a complementary relationship might exist between cost savings and service capability. A complementary relationship here means the ASP adoption intention can be enhanced when a decision factor leads to higher intention in the presence of another decision factor than what might be accounted for by each factor contributing independently (Zhu et al., 2005).

Ma et al. (2005) pointed out that high cost advantages alone cannot ensure the success of application hosting. Customers do not want to suffer the loss of service quality for price. At the same time, they will require higher service capability to keep their operations running smoothly (Han et al., 2008). Similarly, high service capability may not be the only consideration when a customer assesses a potential ASP vendor. High quality but at a high cost is also unlikely to be accepted or justified for external application hosting (Magal, 1991). The complementary combination of high service capability of ASP vendor and high cost advantages resulted from the hosting services arrangements could better boost a client's service adoption intention. Hence we argue that:

Hypothesis 3: A complementary relationship exists between cost savings and service capability on ASP adoption intention.

The transaction cost theory suggests high asset specificity tends to increase transaction costs of the outsourcing arrangement (Williamson, 1985). In the ASP business model, *asset specificity* refers to the uniqueness of applications that clients require from an external hosting vendor. Asset specificity can impact the transaction cost in several ways. First, the customer must spend more time and efforts to seek and evaluate qualified hosting vendors that can deliver their applications with high asset specificity requirements. Thus customer's search cost is high. Second, applications high in asset specificity will require significant investments in hardware and/or software along with system customization. In addition, customers with unique business procedures tied to the data processing will require a higher level of system configuration or modification (Dibbern et al., 2002). In these situations the flexibility associated with the hosting model may be nullified by the clients' special customization requirements. The hosting vendor might find it difficult to realize the economies of scale by hosting the unique processes that cannot be shared by other customers (Grover et al., 1996). Therefore, when the level of customization increases, the hosting vendor may require extended contract terms or set higher prices to compensate for this increased liability. Third, during the service delivery process, customers have to spend extra efforts to communicate and monitor the services as problems are more likely to appear in unique application hosting compared with standard application hosting. Customers' monitoring cost might thus increase. Fourth, in some cases, the vendor might not be able to deliver the service at the promised prices. When the customer wants to move the outsourced applications back in-house, it may cost more to rebuild the internal capability. Therefore, the switching cost is high for applications with high asset specificity.

In contrast, although unique internal business applications can lead to high internal production costs, those costs might still be less than what might cost the outside vendor. System and process customization will generally cost less if they are handled internally rather than externally, since a company typically knows its own unique application requirements better than an ASP vendor could. Therefore, business applications high in asset specificity would be more cost effective to be kept internally (Grover et al., 1994). This leads us to the following hypothesis:

Hypothesis 4: Higher asset specificity will lead to lower perceived cost savings associated with ASP adoption.

Asset specificity might also have an effect on service capability, although this relationship does not appear to have been investigated in prior research. Grover et al. (1996) pointed out that the effect of service capability on outsourcing success tends to vary according to the different types of IS functions. Achieving high service capability on asset-intensive functions that are sensitive to the specific requirements of the organization, such as software development outsourcing, can be challenging. Similarly, it is difficult for an ASP vendor to provide quality services for a client's unique applications. In order to provide a unique application, the hosting vendor needs to acquire specific business knowledge for effective system configuration and application customization (Olson, 2007). Moreover, high customization with difficult to solicit user requirements is more likely to result in poor implementation (Somers & Nelson, 2001), which in turn affects the vendor's capability to provide quality supporting services. Modified codes in customized systems can also cause trouble with standard system upgrades. In some cases, the purchase of additional hardware might also be necessary. These changes will introduce significant uncertainties because they will increase the chance for unexpected problems, further taxing the vendor's business and technology capabilities.

Finally, the unique application requirements might also demand IT staff with specific knowledge. The hosting vendors might have very few people with such knowledge or capabilities and they might not always be on duty when needed. Unique requirements associated with high asset specificity can thus negatively impact the ASP vendor's capabilities to maintain high quality service. Hence, we argue that:

Hypothesis 5: Higher asset specificity will lead to the lower level of perceived service capability of ASP vendor to deliver quality service.

In addition to asset specificity, functional complexity might also be an antecedent factor for cost savings consideration (Tiwana & Bush, 2007). *Functional complexity* refers to the extent of complexity in software, hardware and knowledge requirements in order to provide the outsourced system functions. Complexity might lie in the diversity of business functions in the organization, including the scope of functions, level of authority and multiple operating sites (Ang & Cummings, 1997). Some business applications are not very unique; however, they are often complicated as they might be used by a large number of end users at many different locations and/or they might involve the coordination of various business areas. In order to provide such complicated functions in-house, the company has to invest heavily in IT infrastructure while hiring and retaining skilled IT professionals. Additionally, end-user training and daily application support are costly.

When these complicated functions are outsourced to an ASP vendor, the production costs can be significantly reduced, while the transaction cost may be quite reasonable. Functional complexity may not require the hosting vendor to increase investment in IT infrastructure significantly (Tiwana & McLean, 2005). The hosting vendor usually has large-scale data servers. By using a one-to-many service model, it can leverage the technical capacities to provide the common functions at a lower cost than what the individual customers might have to incur otherwise. The hosting vendor also possesses specialized expertise in these applications or systems, so it is able to manage them more efficiently and effectively than the individual customers (Aubert et al., 2004). Moreover, since the typical interface required for the end-users to access these ASP applications is through the familiar Web, it can reduce the end user training time and costs (Woodie, 2004). Thus, we argue that:

Hypothesis 6: Higher functional complexity will lead to higher perceived cost savings associated with ASP adoption.

Functional complexity can also affect service capability requirements for the ASP vendors. When a customer has complex functionality requirements for an ASP; such as a system with a broad scope of application requirements and /or service delivery to multiple sites, these requirements will increase the difficulty in providing quality services (Tiwana & Bush, 2007). The application hosting for a client organization with thousands of users is quite different in terms of the requirements for accessibility and reliability of service than the hosting requirements for another with only one or two hundred users (Magal, 1991). These complex requirements will increase the probability of problems occurring (Ang &

Cummings, 1997). For the customers with more complex requirements, the ASP vendor is expected to deal with more service requests and the trouble shooting process can be more challenging. The ASP vendor must assign specific, qualified technical support staff to become familiar with the systems of these particular clients. But these few people might not always be available for service on demand. Hence, we argue:

Hypothesis 7: Higher functional complexity will lead to the lower level of perceived service capability of ASP vendors to deliver quality services.

The overall research model is summarized in a causal model, as shown in Figure 1.

RESEARCH METHODOLOGY

Data Collection

We collected the data from a national sample of information system (IS) executives at randomly-selected companies or organizations in the Untied States across different industries. The name and mailing addresses of 1000 IS executives were selected randomly from a private list maintained

Figure 1. Research model of ASP adopt intention

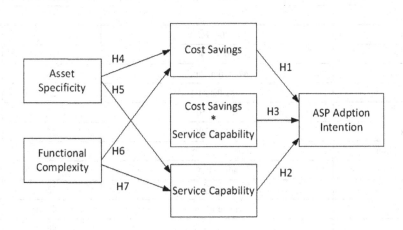

by a consulting firm. All the people selected for the survey were upper level management decision makers. Since ASP outsourcing is generally a major IT investment decision with important organizational implications, we assumed that upper level IS executives will play a key role in the overall decision making process.

Due to inaccuracies in the mailing list, 218 of the surveys were returned as undeliverable, so the final number of delivered surveys was 782. A five-step data collection process as recommended by Dillman (2000) was followed for the survey management, including pre-notice, survey distribution, two rounds of reminders, and a thank-you note to encourage the participation. 93 surveys were returned, which resulted in a net response rate of 12%. The final completed and useful surveys used for our data analysis were 80. Table 1 provides a profile of the respondent companies in this study.

An extrapolation method was adopted to predict non-response bias (Churchill, 1991). No significant demographic differences were found between early and late respondents at the alpha level of 0.05. In addition, no significant differences were found between respondents and non respondents in terms of demographic distribution by size and industry.

Measurement Development

Measurement items for the constructs in the questionnaire were mostly adopted from previously literature, with a few wording modified under the specific context of ASP hosting.

A pre-test of the survey was conducted using five practitioners and six academic professors who have expertise on either the ASP domain or questionnaire development to check for face validity. Based on their comments and suggestions, a few wordings were modified. Then a pilot test was conducted among 40 IT managers to further validate the measurements. An exploratory factor analysis was used on the small data set to check for reliability and discriminant validity, as well as to solicit additional comments. Through this iterative process of reviews and revisions, we established confidence in the content validity and face validity of this survey instrument.

The measure for the dependent variable, hosting adoption intention, was adapted from system adoption intention measure by Davis (1989). It measures the likelihood that the company will adopt an ASP, such as how soon the company will adopt an ASP, will it outsource applications from different business areas to an ASP. The measure for asset specificity was adapted from Ang and

Table 1. Profile of respondent companies

	Category	Number	%
	Less than 20	12	15
No. of	20-99	15	18.75
Employees	100-500	15	18.75
	More than 500	38	47.5
	Less than 10	22	27.50
	10.1 --- 50	13	16.25
Gross	50.1 --- 500	22	27.5
Revenue($ million)	more than 500.1	19	23.75
	not report	4	5
	Service	38	48
Industry	Manufacture	42	52
Total		**80**	**100**

Cummings' (1997) study, which measures the uniqueness of applications by examining the special requirements for an external vendor. Measure for functional complexity was also adapted from the Ang and Cummings' (1997) research, which measures the complexity of a client's applications by comparing them with those of its primary competitors which typically have similar size, product lines and applications. The measure for service capability was developed based on the previous research work of Bharadwaj (2000). To make the questionnaire more relevant for our survey participants of prospective ASP adopters who might not have prior experience with such services, we measure the perceived service capability of an existing ASP vendor in the market. The subjects were asked to refer to the service vendor who is most likely to provide the company's outsourced applications. The measure for cost savings was developed from the research work by Jayatilaka et al. (2003), which includes the cost advantages associated with the IT investments of infrastructure set-up, application modification, and function expansion. A 7-point Likert type scale was used for all the measures. In order to minimize item biases and achieve high indicator stability (Schneeweiss, 1993), each construct included at least four indicators.

Several previous research studies have suggested that company size might be an important factor affecting the IT outsourcing decisions; i.e. small companies tend to receive more relative resource management benefits from IT outsourcing arrangements (e.g. Ang & Straub, 1998; Ma, et al., 2005). Therefore, in this study we include company size as a control variable in our analysis. In addition, we also controlled for the type of industry in this study.

DATA ANALYSIS AND RESULTS

The Partial Least Square (PLS) method was used to analyze the data and test the hypotheses (Chin,

1998). A two-step model approach was used: 1) the measurement model was to test the reliability and discriminant validity of the measures and, 2) the structural model was used to test the research hypotheses (Anderson, 1991).

Measurement Model

The results of the measurement model analysis are presented in Table 2.

In the measurement model, all the loadings for reflective items were larger than the recommended value of 0.7. Composite reliability for each construct was larger than 0.85, exceeding the recommended threshold value of 0.7 (Chin, 1998). Convergent validity and reliability were thus verified. The discriminant validity was assessed by comparing the correlations between constructs to the squared roots of their average extracted value (AVE). As shown in Table 3, the squared root of each construct's AVE is larger than its correlations with other constructs. The results of the exploratory factor analysis also confirm that the item loadings are higher on the constructs that they are supposed to measure than the other constructs, thus confirming the discriminant validity of the measures.

Common method bias was also assessed in the PLS analysis. Following Liang et al.'s (2007) suggestions, we formed a method variable and tested the path relationship between this variable and all the other indicators. The results show that all the indicators have insignificant correlations with the method variable at the $p<0.01$ level, while they maintain significant loading with the designed constructs. In addition, an exploratory factor analysis was also conducted to test common method variance (Malhotra et al., 2006). No single factor can explain up to 50% of the total variance. These results show that common method bias is unlikely to be a serious issue in this study.

Table 2. Measurement model

Construct	Variable	Loading	Composite Reliability
	ASS1	0.88	
Asset Specificity	ASS2	0.86	0.92
	ASS3	0.86	
	ASS4	0.85	
	FUN1	0.81	
Functional Complexity	FUN2	0.89	0.91
	FUN3	0.81	
	FUN4	0.88	
	COS1	0.76	
	COS2	0.8	
	COS3	0.78	
Cost Savings	COS4	0.85	0.95
	COS5	0.92	
	COS6	0.92	
	COS7	0.91	
	QUA1	0.67	
	QUA2	0.66	
Service Capability	QUA3	0.94	
	QUA4	0.83	0.91
	QUA5	0.79	
	QUA6	0.76	
	APPTOTAL	0.92	
Adoption Intention	ADPGEN	0.96	0.97
	ADOPMOST	0.96	
	ADPTIME	0.95	

Table 3. Discriminant analysis based on correlation matrix and AVE

	Mean	AVE	Asset Specificity	Functional Complexity	Cost Savings	Service Capability	Adoption Intention
Asset Specificity	3.27	0.75	**0.86**				
Functional Complexity	4.75	0.71	0.01	**0.84**			
Cost Savings	5.01	0.72	-0.49	0.26	**0.85**		
Service Capability	4.90	0.61	-0.16	0.04	0.40	**0.78**	
Adoption Intention	3.77	0.89	-0.35	0.15	0.68	0.62	**0.95**

Note: The diagonal elements are the square root of the AVE for each construct.

Structural Model

The hypothesized paths were further tested in the structural model. A resampling method was also used to test the precision of the estimates in PLS (Marcoulides & Saunders, 2006). A bootstrap procedure was followed and we compared the path coefficients between the original sample and estimated samples. The changes of path coefficients were smaller than 0.01. It further confirms the stability of the measurements.

The results of the analysis are shown in Figure 2. In the structural model, the interaction construct of cost savings and service capability was specified by using the product variables of cost savings items and service capability items, as recommended by Chin (1998). Since the direction of the paths is pre-specified in the model, we used a one-tailed t-test to test significance.

As hypothesized, both perceived cost savings and service capability are found to have significant effects on adoption intention of ASP; thus, H1 and H2 are supported. However, the interaction effect of these two factors on adoption intention is not significant at the 0.01 level, and the contri-

bution of this path to adoption intention is quite low (i.e., 0.12). Therefore, H3 is rejected.

The results also show that both asset specificity and functional complexity are significant antecedent factors that affect cost savings; thus supporting H4 and H6. But both factors have little impacts on the consideration for service capability. H5 and H7 are thus rejected.

In this model, the overall R square of this model is 0.65, which means that this model can explain about 65% of the variances of ASP adoption intention. Since some paths are not significant, we also run the trimmed model by removing all these insignificant paths. All the other paths remain significant and the R square has improved by 1%.

To have a clearer picture of how cost savings and service capability affect the ASP adoption intention, we classified the respondents according to the cost savings considerations and service capability considerations into low, medium and high groups. A two-way analysis of the mean adoption intention for the four groups of high versus low cost savings and service capability is conducted, as shown in Figure 3. The graph shows that cost savings clearly have much more impact on the adoption intention than service capability. When

Figure 2. Structural model of ASP adoption intention

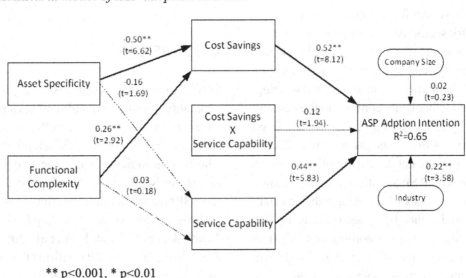

** p<0.001, * p<0.01

Figure 3. Two-way analysis of adoption intention by high vs. low cost savings and service capability

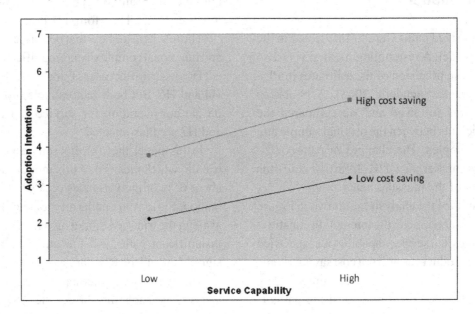

Average Adoption Intention	Low Service Capability	High Service Capability
Low Cost Savings	2.10 (n=17)	3.17 (n=8)
High Cost Savings	3.78 (n=6)	5.24 (n=18)

the cost savings are low, no matter how high the service capability a hosting vendor can reach, the hosting adoption intention is still lower than the adoption intention under the condition that cost savings are high.

Finally, it is also found that the control variable, industry sector, has a significant impact on ASP adoption intention; i.e., companies in the service industry tend to have a higher intention to adopt ASP than those in the manufacturing sector. On the other hand, contrary to the general perception by researchers and practitioners (e.g. Ang & Straub, 1998; Seltsikas & Currie, 2002), company size does not have a significant *linear* relationship with ASP adoption intention. However, further analysis of the data indicates that size, measured either by gross revenue or the number of employees, has a non-linear, U-shaped relationship with adoption intention. As shown in Table 4 and Figure 4, both small companies

(with gross revenues of less than $50M or fewer than 100 employees) and large companies (with gross revenue of more than $500M or more than 500 employees) have higher average intentions to adopt ASP than the medium-sized companies.

DISCUSSION

By combining transaction cost theory and service capability, our study expands the previous research by exploring the impact of both cost saving and service capability on the ASP adoption intention. The results indicate that these two factors are significantly related to the adoption intention of the ASP business model. This finding is consistent with the previous studies (e.g. Ang & Straub, 1998, Jayatilaka et al., 2004, Han et al., 2008, Gewald & Dibbern, 2009) and it confirms the importance of both cost savings and service capability as

Table 4. One-way analysis of ASP adoption intention by organizational size

	Group 1	Group 2	Group 3	Group 4	F Statistic	Significance
Gross Revenue	<$10 M (n=22)	$10.1-50M (n=13)	$50.1- 500M (n=22)	$500.1 - >1000 M (n=19)		
Adoption Intention	4.74	3.46	2.74	3.98	6.45	.001
No. of Employees	< 20 (n=12)	20 – 99 (n=15)	100 – 500 (n=15)	>500 (n=38)		
Adoption Intention	4.89	4.47	2.82	3.51	5.33	.002

Figure 4. ASP adoption intention by organizational size

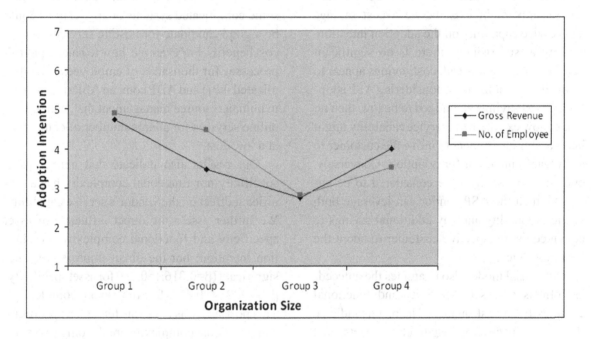

independent contributing factors to the adoption intention. Among the previous IS outsourcing studies from the economic perspective, Ang and Straub (1998) focused on cost considerations and discovered that production cost advantages have a positive impact on IS outsourcing while the additional transaction cost has a negative impact. Jayatilaka et al. (2004) found that cost advantages are ranked as a top reason for the ASP adoption. Gewald and Dibbern (2009) also found that production cost advantages are considered to be a

critical benefit for business process outsourcing. Building upon these studies, our research takes both production costs and transaction costs into account and confirms that cost savings play an important and decisive role in ASP adoption decision. The previous studies, however, did not include the effect of service capability as a determinant factor, even though a study by Han et al. (2008) found that the vendor's IT technical and managerial capabilities can significantly influence the success of IS outsourcing. In addition, previous research has ignored the vendor's service capability in ASP adoption decision. Based on the resource-based theory, service capability, i.e., the capability to manage various tangible and intangible resources for providing good service performance, is important in determining a vendor's service-oriented performance (Bharadwaj, 2000; Oslon, 2007). By including both sets of factors, cost savings and service capability into one model, our study expands the previous studies and provides a more comprehensive framework to analyze the ASP adoption decision.

We also investigated whether a complementary relationship might exist between cost savings and service capability on the adoption intention. Somewhat surprisingly, there is no significant interaction effect. Instead, cost savings appear to be the dominant factor in considering ASP adoption. If cost savings are judged to be low, then no matter how excellent the service capability might be, it is still insufficient to move the customer to a favorable intention for adoption. Conversely, once the cost savings are considered to be adequate, then the ASP vendor can leverage both service capability and any additional savings to convince the prospective customer to adopt the hosting service.

Our causal model also examines the antecedent effects of asset specificity and functional complexity on cost savings. The results indicate that asset specificity negatively impacts cost savings while functional complexity positively affects cost savings. Consistent with previous general research findings on IS/IT outsourcing (Ang & Straub, 1998; Grover et al., 1996), unique applications, special technical requirements, or unusual knowledge acquisition will lower cost advantages associated with ASP adoption. Clients who have unique business processes and require special system configurations should thus retain the system in house (Grover et al., 1998). In addition, the significant positive impact of functional complexity on cost savings implies that when the requirement is not unique, ASP vendors are able

to leverage their technical and labor resources to complement the complexity of functions and systems at a reasonable cost. This result is similar to a research finding on software development outsourcing projects that complicated functions have a higher chance of being outsourced (Tiwana & Bush, 2007). Our finding confirms its economic advantage for the ASP industry. Clients can outsource complicated applications to ASP vendors to gain cost advantages, as long as these functional requirements are not strategically exclusive. This finding can help ASP vendors to identify its business opportunities. It implies that some complicated systems or applications could be a good candidate for hosting services to gain cost benefits. For example, how to handle payroll processes for thousands of employees is a complicated issue and ADP.com, an ASP specializing in human resource management that, can deliver online services for a large number of companies at a low cost.

Our results also indicate that neither asset specificity nor functional complexity has a significant effect on the vendor's service capability. We further assess the direct influence of asset specificity and functional complexity on adoption intention; but the direct impacts were not significant (β=0.016, t=0.250 for asset specificity; β=-0.022, t=0.419 for functional complexity). This post-analysis confirms that asset specificity and functional complexity are the only two antecedents of economic benefit, as predicted by the Transaction Cost Theory.

Overall, the results support the effectiveness of our proposed ASP adoption model. Developed mainly on the basis of economic and service capability considerations, this model can successfully explain 65% variance of ASP adoption intention. It indicates that this model provides a simple but useful framework to understand the determinants associated with application hosting adoption decisions.

Finally, this empirical study also explores how the ASP adoption intention might vary across industry type and company size. Somewhat different from the previous findings (e.g. Ang and Straub, 1998), our data show that small companies (less than 100 employees or less than $50 million annual revenue) or large companies (more than 500 employees or more than $500 million annual revenue) are more likely to adopt ASP model than medium sized companies. Small companies generally lack the internal capabilities to provide all the necessary systems and applications (Smith & Kumar, 2004) while large companies tend to take more advantage of the cost benefits and flexibility of ASP model by shifting the burden of maintaining complex, but non-core systems to external vendors. In addition, service-oriented companies, perhaps less likely to make internal investments in IS/IT, tend to have a higher intention to adopt online hosting services than manufacturing companies. The above findings provide useful guides for ASP vendors to proactively identify prospective customers; i.e., small or large companies in service industries such as banking, healthcare, retailing, publishing, and education could be good candidates for adopting hosting services. However, the relatively low intention of ASP adoption of companies across all industries implies that vendors will have to make more efforts to persuade the customers about the ASP's cost advantages and high service capability.

CONTRIBUTIONS

The rapid growth of the Internet and commercial networks have provided an opportunity for the emergence of the ASP business model as a new resource option for the management of IS/IT services by organizations. However, in spite of its great potential, the growth of the industry seemed to be stymied by a lack of understanding about user's needs (Susaria et al., 2003; Vatanasombut et al., 2008). This empirical study investigates the intention to adopt ASP from the customers' perspective. Our proposed framework, based on the Transaction Cost Theory and service capabil-

ity, provides a simple yet useful causal model that appears to effectively capture the key factors that influence the ASP adoption intention. Our results indicate that cost savings consideration plays the dominant role in influencing the adoption intention, while service capability consideration is only secondary. The results also identify the specific organizational situations that are more conducive to obtaining the economic cost advantages of ASP outsourcing.

The results of our study contribute to both research and practice. For researchers, our study contributes to theory development by combing both transaction cost theory and service capability into a more comprehensive yet simple model. Our results confirm the general validity of economic assessments in considering IS/IT resource management options such as outsourcing considerations and the usefulness of the Transaction Cost Theory as a basis of the theoretical framework. This study goes beyond the previous economic perspective and explores the role of vendor's service capability which has long been ignored in the ASP adoption intention. The results also illustrate the cognitive limitation of IS/IT executives in their assessment of outsourcing options. Although IS/IT managers have always stressed the critical importance of service capability in outsourcing decisions, our results suggest that in practice such factors might play a less important role. Thus, building upon the previous research, this study makes a contribution to the academic literature by enhancing the theoretical understanding on the ASP hosting service adoption intentions from different perspectives and investigating empirically the cognitive limitations of IT managers.

For practitioners, our research suggests that ASP vendors need to better understand the factors that influence the prospective customers' needs and priorities and come up with offerings that can better match their needs. Our findings have also identified specific situations where ASP vendors can better target their customers to exploit the relative economic advantages. It is hoped that these findings would help promote the development of this emerging IS hosting service industry.

Building upon new computing and telecommunication concepts such as cloud computing, grid computing, virtualization, web native applications, the offering of online hosting of services and applications is rapidly growing at the present time, with new terms such as "infrastructure as a service" (IsaS), "platform as a service" (PaaS), "software as a service" (SaaS), or Internet based clouding computing services such as "enterprise computing in the cloud" and "cloudy infrastructure" replacing the older term "ASP". The growing importance of this technological trend may be witnessed by the enormous amount of investments that firms such as Google, Microsoft, Amazon, IBM, Oracle, SAP have invested in developing the technologies in these areas and in building their massive data centers (e.g., Carr, 2008). In addition, some large companies are recognizing that users are placing an inordinate amount of emphasis in cost savings in their adoption of software applications. For example, Microsoft is now stressing cost-saving advantage by emphasizing "virtualization" to sell its financial services in the current difficult economic environment (Heires, 2009), and Google has introduced the free "Google Doc" to lure individual users with a strategic view to develop other innovative commercial applications in the future. Similarly, other firms such as SAS and Salesforce.com are growing their businesses with Internet based hosting of enterprise computing services ; i.e."enterprise computing in the cloud", and Amazon.com has expanded its business model by offering "cloudy infrastructure" e-commerce support services for small businesses (Hayes, 2008) In many ways, the emergence of these new online hosting services is just a part of an important, long term pattern of rapid growths in distributed computing and database management, virtual networks and the Internet. However, the continual growth of online services, as illustrated in our study, also faces hurdles such as the limitations or biases in human decision making. At the same time, the adoption of these new online services will also lead to new challenges in the management of distributed database and applications management (Carr, 2008). The results of our current study have provided some initial guidance and suggestions to both managers and vendors to explore for beneficial areas of application adoption.

CONCLUSION

The purpose of this study is to examine the impact of cost savings and service capability on the ASP adoption intention. Building upon the previous research, our study has combined both transaction cost theory and service capability perspectives into one single model. The empirical results confirm the importance of cost savings in the adoption decisions. Vendor's service capability also greatly impacts the ASP adoption intention, although it is less important than cost savings. It is also found that complicated but non- unique applications are more likely to be the potential hosting services, as vendors can better provide cost savings to customers by achieving economy-of-scale. Our study also identifies the potential target customer segments for ASP vendors. Large companies or small companies are more likely to use hosting services compared with medium size companies. The empirical findings enhance our theoretical understanding of the factors affecting customers' ASP adoption intention and provide some valuable suggestions for practitioners in the selection of beneficial applications.

Although this research has expanded our understand of theory and practice on the adoption decision for this new IS/IT sourcing option that might affect the future growth of the ASP adoption in all industries, our present study is nonetheless a small one with some important limitations. Our sample, though national in nature, is limited because of the difficulty of obtaining responses from IS/IT executives in research studies of this type.

The small sample size does restrict the number of factors that we can include in our research model. Other contingency factors, such as, IT governance, management philosophy and IT culture, power and political process within the organization, may also influence the adoption decision. In addition, we have only focused our investigation on the intention to adopt, which is only a prerequisite to the actual adoption decision, while the investigation of the entire adoption, implementation, routinization, and assessment of actual benefits and costs must await further study. Intensive, longitudinal case studies may be a good methodology for this type of more detailed investigation. The organizational impact of IT may vary significantly depending on the usage (Kang, 2007). Thus, it is also important to study the implementation, usage and consequences of hosting services to the companies after their adoption. These limitations notwithstanding, it is hoped that this study has opened some new grounds for more research in this important and growing area of online hosting services for IS outsourcing.

REFERENCES

Anderson, J. C., & Gerbing, D. W. (1988). Structural equation modeling in practice: a review and recommended two step approach. *Psychological Bulletin*, *103*(3), 411–423. doi:10.1037/0033-2909.103.3.411

Ang, S., & Cummings, L. L. (1997). Strategic response to institutional influences on information systems outsourcing. *Organization Science*, *8*(3), 235–256. doi:10.1287/orsc.8.3.235

Ang, S., & Straub, D. (1998). Production and transaction economies and information systems outsourcing: A study of the US banking industry. *Management Information Systems Quarterly*, *22*(4), 535–552. doi:10.2307/249554

Angst, C. M., & Agarwal, R. (2009). Adoption of electronic health records in the presence of privacy concerns: the elaboration likelihood model and individual persuasion. *Management Information Systems Quarterly*, *33*(2), 339–370.

Arora, A., & Forman, C. (2007). Proximity and information technology outsourcing: how local are IT services markets? *Journal of Management Information Systems*, *24*(2), 73–102. doi:10.2753/MIS0742-1222240204

Aubert, B. A., Rivard, S., & Patry, M. (2004). A transaction cost model of IT outsourcing. *Information & Management*, *41*(7), 921–932. doi:10.1016/j.im.2003.09.001

Bajaj, A. (2000). A study of senior information systems managers' decision models in adopting new computing architectures. *Journal of the Association for Information Systems*, *1*(1), Article 4.

Bharadwaj, A. S. (2000). A resource-based perspective on information technology capability and firm performance: An empirical investigation. *Management Information Systems Quarterly*, *24*(1), 169. doi:10.2307/3250983

Carr, N. (2008). *The big switch: rewiring the world, from Edison to Google*. New York: W. W. Norton & Company.

Caufield, B. (2000). Cover your ASP. *eCompany Now, 2*(1), 138-139.

Cheon, M., Grover, V., & Teng, J. T. C. (1995). Theoretical perspectives on the outsourcing of information systems. *Journal of Information Technology*, *10*(4), 209–220. doi:10.1057/jit.1995.25

Chin, W. W. (1998). The partial least squares approach to structural equation modeling . In Marcoulides, G. A. (Ed.), *Modern Methods of Business Research* (pp. 195–336). Mahwah, NJ: Lawrence Erlbaum Associates.

Choudhary, V. (2007). Comparison of software quality under perpetual licensing and software as a service. *Journal of Management Information Systems, 24*(2), 141–165. doi:10.2753/MIS0742-1222240206

Churchill, G. A. (1991). *Marketing research: methodological foundations* (5th ed.). Chicago: The Dryden Press.

Compeau, D. R., & Higgins, C. A. (1995). Application of social cognitive theory to training for computer skills. *Information Systems Research, 6*(2), 118–143. doi:10.1287/isre.6.2.118

Davis, F. D. (1989). Perceived usefulness, perceived ease of use and user acceptance of information technology . *Management Information Systems Quarterly, 13*(3), 319–340. doi:10.2307/249008

Dibbern, J., & Brehm, A. H. (2002). Rethinking ERP-outsourcing decisions for leveraging technological and preserving business knowledge. In *Proceedings of the 35th Annual Hawaii International Conference on System Sciences*.

Dibbern, J., Goles, T., Hirschheim, R., & Jayatilaka, B. (2004). Information systems outsourcing: A survey and analysis of the literature. *The Data Base for Advances in Information Systems, 35*(4), 6–102.

Dillman, D. A. (2000). *Mail and internet surveys: the tailored design method* (2nd ed.). New York: John Wiley & Sons.

Erickson, J., & Siau, K. (2008). Web services, service-oriented computing, and service-oriented architecture: separating hype from reality. *Journal of Database Management, 19*(3), 42–55.

Feller, J., Finnegan, P., & Hayes, J. (2008). Delivering the 'whole product': business model impacts and agility challenges in a network of open source firms. *Journal of Database Management, 19*(2), 95–109.

Gewald, H., & Dibbern, J. (2009). Risks and benefits of business process outsourcing: a study of transaction services in the German banking industry. *Information & Management, 46*(4), 249–257. doi:10.1016/j.im.2009.03.002

Grover, V., Cheon, M. J., & Teng, J. T. C. (1996). The effects of service quality and partnership on the outsourcing of information system functions. *Journal of Management Information Systems, 12*(4), 89–116.

Grover, V., Teng, J. T. C., & Cheon, M. J. (1998). Towards a theoretically-based contingency model of information systems outsourcing. In Willcocks, L. P., & Lacity, M. (Eds.), *Strategic source of information systems: perspective and practices*. New York: Wiley.

Han, H. S., Lee, J. N., & Seo, Y. W. (2008). Analyzing the impact of a firm's capability on outsourcing success: A process perspective. *Information & Management, 45*(1), 31–42.

Hayes, B. (2008). Cloud computing. *Communications of the ACM, 51*(7), 9–11. doi:10.1145/1364782.1364786

Herires, K. (2009, April 13). Reaching out to financial firms, Microsoft is stressing cost-saving. *Security Industry News*, 19-20

Horngren, C. T., Ittner, C., Foster, G., Rajan, M. V., & Datar, S. M. (2008). *Cost Accounting: A Managerial Emphasis* (13th ed.). Upper Saddle River, NJ: Prentice Hall.

Jayatilaka, B., Schwarz, A., & Hirschheim, R. (2003). Determinants of ASP choice: an integrated perspective. *European Journal of Information Systems, 12*(3), 210–224. doi:10.1057/palgrave.ejis.3000466

Kang, D. (2007). Categorizing post-deployment IT changes: an empirical investigation. *Journal of Database Management, 18*(2), 1–24.

Kauffman, R., & Mohtadi, H. (2004). Proprietary and open systems adoption in E-Procurement: A risk-augmented transaction cost perspective. *Journal of Management Information Systems, 21*(1), 137–166.

Khoumbati, K., Themistocleous, M., & Irani, Z. (2006). Evaluating the adoption of enterprise application integration in health-care organizations. *Journal of Management Information Systems, 22*(4), 69–108. doi:10.2753/MIS0742-1222220404

Kim, H. W., & Kankanhalli, A. (2009). Investigating user resistance to information systems implementation: a status quo bias perspective. *Management Information Systems Quarterly, 33*(3), 567–582.

Kim, J., Lee, J., Han, K., & Lee, M. (2002). Businesses as buildings: metrics for the architectural quality of Internet businesses. *Information Systems Research, 13*(3), 239–254. doi:10.1287/isre.13.3.239.79

Kim, S. S. (2009). The integrative framework of technology use: an extension and test. *Management Information Systems Quarterly, 33*(3), 513–537.

Kwon, T. H., & Zmud, R. W. (1987). Unifying the fragmented models of information systems implementations . In Boland, R., & Hirschheim, R. (Eds.), *Critical Issues in Information Systems Research* (pp. 227–252). Chichester, UK: John Wiley & Sons, Ltd.

Lacity, M., & Hirschheim, R. (1993). *Information systems out-sourcing myths, metaphors, and realities*. New York: John Wiley & Sons, Ltd.

Lacity, M., & Willcocks, L. P. (2001). *Global information technology outsourcing: in search of business advantage*. New York: John Wiley & Sons, Ltd.

Lee, D. M. S., Trauth, E. M., & Farwell, D. (1995). Critical skills and knowledge requirements of IT professionals: a joint academic/industry investigation. *Management Information Systems Quarterly, 19*(3), 313–340. doi:10.2307/249598

Levina, N., & Ross, J. W. (2003). From the vendor's perspective: exploring the value proposition in information technology outsourcing. *Management Information Systems Quarterly, 27*(3), 331–364.

Li, S. S., Huang, S. M., Yen, D. C., & Chang, C. C. (2007). Migrating legacy information systems to Web services architecture. *Journal of Database Management, 18*(4), 1–25.

Liang, H., Saraf, N., Hu, Q., & Xue, Y. (2007). Assimilation of enterprise systems: The effect of institutional pressures and the mediating role of top management. *Management Information Systems Quarterly, 31*(1), 59–87.

Liang, H., & Xue, Y. (2009). Avoidance of information technology threats: A theoretical perspectives. *Management Information Systems Quarterly, 33*(1), 71–90.

Ma, Q., Pearson, J. M., & Tadisina, S. (2005). An exploratory study into factors of service quality for Application Service Providers. *Information & Management, 42*(8), 1067–1080. doi:10.1016/j.im.2004.11.007

Magal, S. R. (1991). A model for evaluating information center success. *Journal of Management Information Systems, 8*(1), 91–106.

Malhotra, N., Kim, S., & Patil, A. (2006). Common method variance in IS research: A comparison of alternative approaches and a reanalysis of past research. *Management Science, 52*(12), 1865–1883. doi:10.1287/mnsc.1060.0597

Marcoulides, G. A., & Saunders, C. (2006). PLS: A silver bullet? *Management Information Systems Quarterly, 30*(2), i–vi.

Mears, J. (2001). Net provider sold on ASP model. *New World (New Orleans, La.)*, *18*(14), 29–30.

Miranda, S. M., & Kim, Y. M. (2006). Professional versus political contexts: institutional mitigation and the transaction cost heuristic in information systems outsourcing. *Management Information Systems Quarterly*, *30*(3), 725–753.

Olson, D. L. (2007). Evaluation of ERP outsourcing. *Computers & Operations Research*, *34*(12), 3715–3724. doi:10.1016/j.cor.2006.01.010

Parasuraman, A., Zeithaml, V. A., & Berry, L. L. (1985). A conceptual model of Service quality and its implications for future research. *Journal of Marketing*, *49*(4), 41–50. doi:10.2307/1251430

Rai, A., Patnayakuni, R., & Seth, N. (2006). Firm performance impacts of digitally enabled supply chain integration capabilities. *Management Information Systems Quarterly*, *30*(2), 225–246.

Rai, A., & Sambamurthy, V. (2006). Editorial notes-the growth of interest in services management: opportunities for information systems scholars. *Information Systems Research*, *17*(4), 327–331. doi:10.1287/isre.1060.0108

Schneeweiss, H. (1993). Consistency at large in models with latent variables. In Haagen, K., Bartholomew, D. J., & Deistler, M. (Eds.), *Statistical modeling and latent variables*. Amsterdam, The Netherlands: Elsevier.

Seltsikas, P., & Currie, W. L. (2002). Evaluating the application service provider (ASP) business model: the challenger of integration. In *Proceedings of the 35th Hawaii International Conference on System Science*.

Smith, M. A., & Kumar, R. L. (2004). A theory of application service provider (ASP) use from a client perspective. *Information & Management*, *41*(8), 977–1002. doi:10.1016/j.im.2003.08.019

Somers, T. M., & Nelson, K. (2001). The impact of critical success factors across the stages of enterprise resource planning implementation. In *Proceedings of the 34th Hawaii International Conference on System Sciences*.

Susarla, A., Barua, A., & Whinston, A. B. (2003). Understanding the service component of application service provision: An empirical analysis of satisfaction with ASP Services. *Management Information Systems Quarterly*, *27*(1), 91–123.

Taylor, S., & Todd, P. A. (1995). Understanding information technology usage: A test of competing models. *Information Systems Research*, *6*(4), 144–176. doi:10.1287/isre.6.2.144

Tiwana, A., & Bush, A. A. (2007). A comparison of transaction cost, agency, and knowledge-based predictors of IT outsourcing decisions: a U.S.–Japan cross-cultural field study. *Journal of Management Information Systems*, *24*(1), 259–300. doi:10.2753/MIS0742-1222240108

Tiwana, A., & McLean, E. R. (2005). Expertise integration and creativity in information systems development. *Journal of Management Information Systems*, *22*(1), 13–43.

Vallerand, R. J. (1997). Toward a hierarchical model of intrinsic and extrinsic motivation. In Zanna, M. (Ed.), *Advances in Experimental Social Psychology* (pp. 271–360). New York: Academic Press.

Vargo, S. L., & Lusch, R. F. (2004). Evolving to a new dominant logic for marketing. *Journal of Marketing*, *68*(1), 1–17. doi:10.1509/jmkg.68.1.1.24036

Vatanasombut, B., Igbaria, M., Stylianou, A. C., & Rodgers, W. (2008). Information systems continuance intention of web-based applications customers: the case of online banking. *Information & Management*, *45*(1), 419–428. doi:10.1016/j.im.2008.03.005

Ven, K., & Verelst, J. (2008). The impact of ideology on the organizational adoption of open source software. *Journal of Database Management, 19*(2), 58–73.

Venkatesh, V., & Davis, F. D. A. (2000). Theoretical extension of the technology acceptance model: four longitudinal field studies. *Management Science, 45*(2), 186–204. doi:10.1287/mnsc.46.2.186.11926

Venkatesh, V., Morris, M. G., Davis, G. B., & Davis, F. D. (2003). User acceptance of information technology: toward a unified view. *Management Information Systems Quarterly, 27*(3), 425–478.

Vizard, M. (2000). EDS looks to extend reach with ASP model. *InfoWorld, 22*(46), 16.

Williamson, O. E. (1979). Transaction cost economics: the governance of contractual relations. *The Journal of Law & Economics, 22*(2), 233–261. doi:10.1086/466942

Williamson, O. E. (1985). *The Economic Institutions of Capitalism*. New York: Free Press.

Woodie, A. (2004). PeopleSoft gives world ERP suite a web interface. *IT Jungle, 4*(2). Retrieved from http://www.itjungle.com/fhs/ fhs032304-story01.html

Yao, Y., & Murphy, L. (2005). A state transition approach to application service provider client-vendor relationship development. *The Data Base for Advances in Information Systems, 36*(3), 8–25.

Zaheer, A., & Venkatraman, N. V. (1995). Relational governance as an interorganizational strategy: an empirical test of the role of trust in economic exchange. *Strategic Management Journal, 16*(5), 373–392. doi:10.1002/smj.4250160504

Zhu, K., Kraemer, K., Xu, S., & Dedrick, J. (2004). Information technology payoff in E-business environments: An international perspective on value creation of e-business in the financial services industry. *Journal of Management Information Systems, 21*(1), 7–54.

Zhu, K., Kraemer, K. L., Gurbaxani, V., & Xu, X. S. (2006). Migration to open-standard interorganizational systems: network effects, switching costs and path dependency. *Management Information Systems Quarterly, 30*(5), 515–539.

APPENDIX SURVEY QUESTIONS

Construct	Variable	Questions
	ASS1	require service vendor make a substantial investment in equipment
Asset	ASS2	require service vendor make great efforts to customize software
Specificity	ASS3	require service vendor specialized technical knowledge
	ASS4	require service vendor possess specialized business knowledge
	FUN1	Compared to competitors, our company used more hardware platforms and multiple systems configurations
Functional	FUN2	Compared to competitors, our company's software portfolio was more sophisticated/complex .
Complexity	FUN3	Compared to competitors, our data processing operations were more complex
	FUN4	Compared to competitors, we needed more specialized IS functions
	COS1	reduce software costs
	COS2	reduce costs of hiring new information systems personnel
	COS3	reduce costs of training new and/or existing information systems personnel
Cost	COS4	reduce costs of modifying existing applications
Savings	COS5	It is cheaper to monitor our hosting vendor than to manage our own data processing facilities
	COS6	It is cheaper to extend an application with our ASP than with traditional software vendors
	COS7	It will require a minimal amount of time and effort to negotiate a contact (e.g. conditions, prices, etc.) with our hosting vendor
	CAP1	perfectly understand business objectives
	CAP2	clearly comprehend their roles and responsibilities in supplying our objectives
Service	CAP3	provide exact functions for business operations
Capability	CAP4	provide clear criteria for its initial application recommendations
	CAP5	assure security for data exchange and storage
	CAP6	ensure network connection for service delivery
	ADPTOTAL	likely to adopt hosting on different applications
Adoption	ADPGEN	likely to use hosting vendor for applications
Intention	ADPMOST	likely to use hosting vendor for most applications
	ADPTIME	likely to use hosting vendor in one or two year .

* Most items are measured by 1-7 Likert scale: 1- strongly disagree, 7: strongly agree

This work was previously published in International Journal of Database Management, Volume 21, Issue 3, edited by Keng Siau, pp. 90-112, copyright 2010 by IGI Publishing (an imprint of IGI Global).

Chapter 13

Co-creation and Collaboration in a Virtual World:
A 3D Visualization Design Project in Second Life

Keng Siau
University of Nebraska-Lincoln, USA

Fiona Fui-Hoon Nah
University of Nebraska-Lincoln, USA

Brian E. Mennecke
Iowa State University, USA

Shu Z. Schiller
Wright State University, USA

ABSTRACT

One of the most successful and useful implementations of 3D virtual worlds is in the area of education and training. This paper discusses the use of virtual worlds in education and describes an innovative 3D visualization design project using one of the most popular virtual worlds, Second Life. This ongoing project is a partnership between IBM and three universities in the United States: the University of Nebraska-Lincoln, Iowa State University, and Wright State University. More than 400 MBA students have participated in this project by completing a creative design project that involves co-creation and collaboration in Second Life. The MBA students from the three universities worked in pairs to create designs to represent concepts related to IBM Power Systems, a family of IBM servers. The paper discusses observations and reflections on the 3D visualization design project. The paper concludes with a discussion of future research directions in applying virtual worlds in education.

DOI: 10.4018/978-1-61350-471-0.ch013

1. INTRODUCTION

With the advent of low cost networks, high speed computing infrastructures, and easy to use social media platforms, a growing number of educators and scholars have begun to attend to the opportunities presented by new media platforms for delivering high quality learning experiences (Erickson & Siau, 2003). 3D virtual world environments, which support a higher level of interactivity and richness for collaboration and communication than traditional media, have the potential to create engaging and meaningful experiences for learners (Eschenbrenner et al., 2008). Guru and Siau (2008) note that the possibilities surrounding these platforms are endless as the technology continues to advance and evolve. Similarly, Zhao et al. (2010) observe that the various types of virtual world platforms are now having major influences on businesses, communities, and society at large.

Most 3D virtual world environments offer various affordances for learning and education that make them attractive as platforms for supporting educational experiences (Dickey, 2005a; Park et al., 2008). These unique affordances enable pedagogical activities related to co-creation and collaboration that often extend well beyond those available to collaborators working with traditional technologies and media. In virtual worlds, users interact and form relationships with one another through their virtual representations called avatars. This embodied representation enables richer forms of interaction compared to traditional media such as chat rooms or web conferencing (Mennecke et al., forthcoming). Interactivity is a critical component of teaching and learning because enhanced interaction can increase the effectiveness of learning (Siau et al., 2006). Unfortunately, the lack of interactivity has been identified as one of the major issues facing many educational pedagogies and techniques (Siau et al., 2006). In this light, Dickey (2005a) points out that creating interactive learning environments is one of the prominent trends in the development of effective pedagogies. Furthermore, at a theoretical level, the focus on interactive learning is supported by an increasing paradigm shift towards constructivism in education, which emphasizes approaches such as learner-centered teaching (Schiller, 2009). This paradigm is premised on the notion that knowledge is constructed by learners and learners need to take an active role in the learning process in order to develop a rich understanding of the concepts and skills associated with their learning experience.

One of the unique features of many virtual worlds is the object affordance (Dickey, 2005a; Dickey, 2005b; Park et al., 2008; Chen et al., 2010). Objects can be created, manipulated, and positioned by users, thereby enabling the users to engage in truly creative endeavors (Osborne & Schiller, 2010). Such freedom in creation supports active learning because it allows users to learn not by simply 'watching', but by 'doing' and creating ideas and concepts in the virtual worlds that may closely resemble their real world counterparts. Additionally, users are able to collaboratively design and co-create objects in the 3D virtual world environment in ways that may not be feasible in the real world. This capability for collaboration is important because it fits with the requirements associated with constructivist learning that is increasingly emphasized in pedagogy (Barab et al., 2000). While it is not appropriate for all learning tasks, collaborative learning is increasing in importance because of its demonstrable effectiveness (Gokhale, 1995; Slavin, 1980, 1983; Unalan, 2008). Further, Nah et al. (2010) demonstrate that with the right balance of skills and challenges in a 3D virtual world, a user's flow experience or engagement increases. As one's flow experience increases, engagement in learning and outcomes of learning also increase (Shin, 2006; Skadberg & Kimmel, 2004).

In this paper, we focus on co-creation and collaboration in virtual worlds' learning activities designed to achieve educational objectives. The paper aims to provide actionable suggestions and findings that academics, instructors, and educational institutions can use in creating a more effective and efficient learning environment in virtual worlds. The paper also reports on a specific 3D visualization design project that was conducted in Second Life and describes our reflections on the use of this environment for learning. The 3D visualization design project is a co-creation and collaboration project that involves students from three universities: the University of Nebraska-Lincoln, Iowa State University, and Wright State University.

The remainder of the paper is organized as follows: In the next section, we review the literature on learning theories as well as provide examples on co-creation and collaboration in virtual worlds. We then describe and discuss a 3D visualization project carried out in collaboration with IBM. Observations and general findings from the 3D visualization project are reported in the paper. The paper concludes with a discussion on potential future research directions.

2. LITERATURE REVIEW

While virtual worlds have been used for a variety of purposes for more than a decade, their applications in education are still limited (Eschenbrenner et al., 2008). In this section, we review learning theories and research works related to co-creation and collaborative learning in virtual worlds.

2.1 Learning Theories and Relationships with Co-Creation and Collaboration

Learning theories can be grouped into three categories: (i) behaviorism; (ii) cognitivism; (iii) constructivism (Ertmer & Newby, 1993; Leidner & Jarvenpaa, 1995; Sheng et al., 2010). Recently, the focus of learning has shifted from the behaviorism and cognitivism models to the constructivism model. The behaviorism model, based on the stimulus and response theory, sug-

gests that learning takes place through reinforcement of behaviors that are triggered by specific environmental stimuli. Hence, the behaviorism model views the learner as a "black box" where the process of learning that takes place in the learner is unknown but is driven by deterministic processes. The cognitivism model, on the other hand, views learning as the active processing of new ideas or concepts and the transfer of these ideas or concepts to a meaningful form in one's knowledge structure. Hence, the learner is an active entity that can influence the learning outcome by active processing and encoding of knowledge into long-term memory. The constructivism model, which focuses on the active construction of knowledge by the learner, has recently garnered a significant following and stands as one of the prominent theories of learning (Steffe & Gale, 1995). One of the widely adopted constructivist learning theories in educational practices is the learner-centered teaching theory. Learner-centered teaching emphasizes students' intrinsic motivation to learn and the development of students' abilities to acquire appropriate techniques in problem solving, thus transforming learners from passive receivers of knowledge to active participants in learning and co-constructors of knowledge (Weimer, 2002; VanderMeer & Dutta, 2009). The learner-centered constructivism model, when properly applied, can maximize student learning (Tobin & Tippins, 1993). Learner-centered teaching methodologies have been further refined by IS educators into a systematic approach in instructional development to achieve successful learning outcomes. Empirical results from prior studies have demonstrated the effectiveness of learner-centered teaching in business and information systems education (Schiller, 2009; Wagner et al., 2008).

Collaborative approaches to learning and co-creation are based on the constructivist learning model. In this context, learning takes place through knowledge discovery and interaction during the process of co-creation of a concept, design, or product. Learners engage not only in knowledge discovery during the process but also through reflective thinking. Instruction is provided to support and engage learners in the learning process, and reflections are used to enhance the learning outcomes. Further, learners create their understanding of concepts through their comprehension and interpretation of information from diverse sources including the social construction of knowledge through interaction with other learners. Co-creation provides not only a conducive collaborative approach for learners to interact and gain knowledge from their peers, but also empowers the users (Fuller et al., 2010).

In the next section, we will present examples of how co-creation and collaboration have been applied in virtual worlds.

2.2 Learning through Co-Creation and Collaboration in Virtual Worlds

Visualization has been shown to enhance student learning (McGrath & Brown, 2005) and is a powerful feature of 3D virtual worlds (Ives & Junglas, 2008). Businesses have used visualization to communicate, discuss, and enhance designs and developments, and to obtain consumer feedback (Ives & Junglas, 2008) whereas educational institutions have used visualization to enhance learning in education (Eschenbrenner et al., 2008). Following the constructivist approach, we can incorporate co-creation and collaboration with visualization in virtual worlds to engage students and further enhance their learning.

There is a general consensus in the education literature that interaction, dialogue, and collaboration are essential for productive learning (Minocha & Roberts, 2008). Minocha and Roberts (2008) suggest that 3D virtual worlds provide a platform where pedagogy can be enhanced through socialization, synchronous communication, and collaboration. Citing Vygotsky (1978), Minocha and Roberts argue that knowledge construction is achieved by "the interaction that takes place within oneself through reflective thinking and by

the interaction that occurs in communications and collaboration with other people" (p. 184).

Various applications of co-creation and collaboration have taken place in 3D virtual worlds such as multidisciplinary collaborative design as an alternative to CAD systems (Gu & Tsai, 2010; Rosenman et al., 2007), new product development by consumers (Fuller, 2010), and team problem solving in a virtual world environment that simulates the real world (Attasiriluk et al., 2009; Rousso et al., 1999).

In the following section, we report on a co-creation and collaboration 3D visualization design project in Second Life. The project is a partnership between IBM and three universities.

3. A 3D VISUALIZATION DESIGN PROJECT IN SECOND LIFE

Researchers from the University of Nebraska-Lincoln, Iowa State University, and Wright State University embarked on an innovative academic project using Second Life. An objective of the project is to educate the MBA students at these three universities, many of whom are working professionals, about concepts, applications, and products related to IBM's Power Systems, a family of IBM servers. Guided by the constructivist learning approach, students collaborated on a creative visualization design project in Second Life to represent concepts related to IBM Power Systems by creating a visualization of these concepts to inform and educate business managers and executives. The 3D virtual world environment was used to facilitate the creative thought processes and critical thinking involved in the co-creation and design processes as well as to promote a deeper understanding of the features and functions related to IBM Power Systems.

As of fall of 2010, more than four hundred MBA students have participated in the collaborative design visualization project in Second Life. The MBA students worked in dyadic teams to create visualization designs in Second Life that represent concepts related to the technology, applications, and/or products of IBM Power Systems. Some of these concepts include AIX, Linux, blade center, Websphere, virtualization, capacity on demand, on demand business, high availability, dynamic computing, green computing, smarter planet, and disaster recovery.

The design project has four stages. In the first stage, participants were guided through orientation activities to familiarize them with the Second Life environment. In addition, we provided training on skills related to building basic prims (i.e., primitive building objects), teleportation and movement, managing inventory objects, and communication in Second Life.

In the second stage, participants were introduced to concepts in IBM Power Systems through display boards in Second Life. The display boards were supplemented with web links to more detailed information on IBM products or applications. Each team conducted their own research on these concepts and the team was free to choose any one of the concepts for their design.

In the third stage, each team with two MBA students co-created their design in Second Life to represent and showcase their chosen concept on IBM Power Systems. The visualization design

was to be completed on a virtual platform sized 10*10 meters in Second Life. Each participant collaborated with his/her partner using his/her own personalized avatar during the period of the design process. In general, depending on the class duration, the students would have 3-4 weeks to complete the project. Each participant received inventory folders containing pre-built objects, which included a diverse set of items such as computer equipment, pieces of furniture, decorations, and other miscellaneous items. Participants were free to use any given item, build their own items, or obtain items from other sources in Second Life. They could also upload images and other contents for use in their designs. Team members were instructed to log into Second Life and work on the project synchronously during the design phase.

In the final stage, upon completion of the design, each team was required to build a note card box and place it by the side of their design. The note card box included a script to display information describing their design. Each participant also submitted a reflection paper that explained the rationale underlying his/her team's design and the collaboration experience. The 400-plus MBA students have designed over 200 concepts in this 3D visualization project. Figures 1 and 2 depict some of the designs.

Figure 1. A Female Avatar Working on a Design

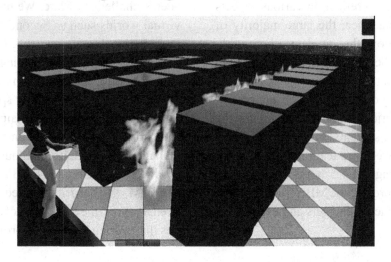

Figure 2. Avatars Working on their Platforms in Second Life

4. OBSERVATIONS AND FINDINGS

The Second Life project is innovative and novel in a number of ways. First, the interactive nature of Second Life promotes the constructivist learning approach, which is an approach to learning that has been shown to be highly effective in the education literature. Students reported that the interactive nature of the environment helped them to attend more intensely to the concepts associated with the design activity, and to actively participate in the learning and design activities when collaborating with a partner.

Second, the project is highly engaging and fun. We asked students to reflect on various aspects of the design experience; the large majority of the comments show that students thoroughly enjoyed creating their designs in Second Life and collaborating with their partners.

Third, working on a hands-on design project for an extended period of time helps to ingrain the IT concepts in the students' minds and to foster relationships between the team members. After spending an average of 4-5 hours a week for a few weeks on the project, the MBA students, most of whom are business managers and executives,

would have gained a deep insight, understanding, and appreciation of IBM Power Systems.

Fourth, the Second Life project generated interest among female MBA students. Second Life is a very sophisticated environment but the impressive interface, the appealing visualizations, and the social content associated with the environment make it an aesthetic environment for users. We found the co-creation and collaborative opportunities afforded by the environment to be inviting for women to learn about IT and their applications. Attracting female students to enroll in technical courses and disciplines such as information systems and computer science has been a challenge of late. We have observed that virtual worlds such as Second Life are effective in engaging female students to learn about IT concepts and in increasing their interests in careers related to information systems and technology.

Fifth, the project is partly sponsored by IBM Power Systems. One of the aims of the Second Life project is to educate and inform business managers and executives about IT concepts and products that are related to IBM Power Systems. For IBM, the benefits derived from the project stretch beyond the boundaries of the three universities that participated in this project. Specifically, more than 400 MBA students in three states – Nebraska, Iowa, and Ohio – have developed an increased awareness of the features associated with IBM Power Systems. Being current and/or future executives in organizations, their increased understanding of IBM Power Systems means that they will likely consider IBM Power Systems in their future IT procurement and investment decisions. The constructivist design experience of concepts in IBM Power Systems will have an important and long lasting influence on their knowledge and appreciation of these systems.

5. REFLECTIONS

Virtual worlds can provide unique educational experiences, with its potential only at the cusp of being explored. The project illustrates that 3D virtual worlds such as Second Life may be a good medium for distance education and learning. The students from the three universities participating in this project were geographically dispersed and they were able to collaborate online and co-create their designs in Second Life. From our observations and the students' feedback, the interactive nature of Second Life is one of its greatest strengths. The ability of Second Life to support co-creation and collaboration enables the instructors to design pedagogical tasks that are creative, innovative, and fun. Some of these pedagogical activities were not possible with traditional teaching methods and media (e.g., one team built an interactive kiosk with ornate sculptures and other objects that would be nearly impossible to replicate in other collaborative environments).

Despite their unique capabilities and strengths in supporting of active learning, virtual worlds, such as Second Life, present a variety of challenges when used as a platform for education. These challenges can be summarized into (i) technical and (ii) behavioral issues.

5.1 Technical Issues

To run Second Life smoothly, the application requires a high-bandwidth Internet connection (i.e., cable or DSL at a minimum) and a computer with an acceptable graphic card. While "modern" computers generally meet the minimum specifications to enable their use for client applications, not all students have ready access to newer computers. Technological barriers related to bandwidth and older machines can be alleviated by offering students other alternatives for accessing Second Life (e.g., university computer labs).

One major constraint in Second Life is that each island has a maximum of 15000 prims (i.e., primitive objects). For our design project, students generate complex and ornate designs that need a substantial number of prims. We found that the number of prims used and remaining for use needed to be constantly monitored and that we needed to actively manage the prim status. Therefore, educators need to be aware of the need to actively manage technical features of the project during its execution when using Second Life for a design project such as this. One solution we developed was to split the project activities onto multiple Second Life islands to distribute the load and reduce these constraints.

Another limitation in Second Life is the number of avatars that each island can support at any time. While technically the upper limit stated by Linden Lab is 300 avatars per island, in practice only about 40-60 avatars could visit an island without significant system lag and communication problems occurring. Because of this limitation, small classes would be more appropriate for Second Life.

Although the 3D graphical environment has been effective in delivering experiences that create perceptions of social presence and a realistic sense of place, the Second Life virtual environment still falls short in creating a realistic simulation of true and real-time facial expressions and non-verbal cues. In other words, while some aspects of "body language" can be expressed (e.g., moving about or interacting with objects), the default settings for avatars do not convey richer and detailed forms of body language. Scripts can be purchased that create talking facial gestures, but these need to be acquired and activated and would likely not be appropriate for most educational applications.

5.2 Human-Factor Issues

Attention should also be paid to social and behavioral issues that can create challenges when using Second Life for educational applications. Because social virtual worlds allow users to "hide" behind their avatars, identity and trust issues may generate problems for educators and researchers (Galanxhi-Janaqi & Nah, 2005). An avatar's real identity may, in some circumstances, be difficult to verify, which can create concerns for educational applications. The fact that users can easily switch identities (e.g., switching gender, species, or general appearance) can cause difficulties in classroom discussions (e.g., keeping track of students' real names), problems with untoward behavior (e.g., uninhibited students may be disruptive), and concerns about attendance or participation (e.g., substitutions). This can also be an issue as students interact with each other in the virtual environment in classroom activities or research sessions as well as when students explore the environment on their own. As a result, some students may feel disconnected from other students, which might reduce their sense of trust with other students. Under the identity "cover" offered by their virtual representation, people may feel comfortable engaging in sexually explicit behaviors, displaying inappropriate content, disturbing others, and otherwise behaving badly (e.g., griefing, harassment, and sharing or executing malicious scripts). Fortunately, instructors are able to keep the island accessible only through invitation to authorized personnel and avatars, which can be used as a deterrent. Additionally, our experience is that most graduate students ap-

proach the experience professionally and refrain from negative behaviors. Plus, students quickly move past the mask and learn about their partners as "real" people. Once students develop these friendships, the trust they generally develop is supportive of constructive behaviors towards each other and other students in their classes. Nevertheless, "bad" things can happen in Second Life, particularly if an island is left open for visitors, so managing negative behaviors is something that needs to be considered in the use of Second Life for education.

Most students have to meet the challenges of the deep learning curves associated with using Second Life. The majority of the participants in our projects were not familiar with Second Life prior to the class. As a result, many experienced difficulties when they first started using the environment. It is important that sufficient guidance and assistance be made available to students. Effective and clear information and instructions should be provided and enough time should be allowed for the participants to finish the project in the virtual environment. Depending on the complexity and scale of the task and the skills of the participants, collaborative activities can sometimes take much more time to be completed than expected. Given these issues, we generally recommend that educators actively monitor their students' use of the Second Life environment, and actively communicate supportive and encouraging messages to students to address questions, and support students in their exploration of the virtual environment.

6. FUTURE RESEARCH DIRECTIONS

In this paper, we have highlighted several opportunities and constraints in using Second Life. Of course, our observations are premised on our own anecdotal experiences with using Second Life for several educational and research activities. Given this, these opportunities and constraints represent areas where additional research is called for. While the spectrum of potential research topics associated with the use of Second Life is vast, we will briefly discuss a few of these areas that are most pertinent for IS researchers using Second Life for education and, by extension, for research.

One of the most important topics for research in Second Life is associated with the fit of the environment for educational activities. As is the case with any software product, the use of a technology like Second Life will be more successful for students and educators if the technology fits the task (See Goodhue & Thompson, 1995). The fact is that many educational activities can be better completed in other venues. In debriefing students who have completed our courses, a consistent theme has emerged. Specifically, students note that Second Life is relevant and useful for some classroom activities but less so or, perhaps, not at all for other types of activities. For example, we used the Second Life environment to bring together students from two institutions to work together on an interactive design project. Most students reported that this was an effective use of Second Life because it fostered rich activity based interactions that allowed students to communicate with their partners in ways that would have been difficult with other media.

On the other hand, we have received mixed feedback regarding attitudes about using Second Life for conducting lectures. Students have noted that when lectures are performed online, it is better if there is some reason to do so in Second Life. For example, we have brought guest speakers who are content experts to our classes using Second Life. In some cases, these speakers took our students on tours or showed them tools or applications within the environment (e.g., touring a NASA platform or walking inside of a blood vessel simulation). Students recognized that these Second Life-centric sessions were best performed in Second Life rather than via some other medium. In addition, we have received feedback suggesting that several educational activities might be

better undertaken using other media. Second Life does not seem to be useful to engage in activities like short meetings, as a means of coordinating or managing team activities (e.g., scheduling or "pinging" other team members for availability), or for working on tasks that feed into "real-world" projects (e.g., working on composing a paper or performing a financial analysis). Other tools such as instant messaging or shared workspaces like SharePoint were offered as preferred tools for many of these tasks. Therefore, a possible venue for future research will be on understanding where and how Second Life and other virtual worlds will be useful in education.

A second focus for research should look at issues related to the adoption and management of the Second Life platform. As a software product, Second Life is within the domain of expertise for IS researchers and much research examining the adoption or diffusion of software within organizations could and should be brought to bear on understanding whether, why, and how virtual worlds can be successfully adopted by educators and researchers (see Davis, 1989; Venkatesh et al., 2003). What factors impede its adoption? What impact do institutional constraints or resources play in influencing faculty decision making about using Second Life? How does Second Life align with educational institutional strategies and how does this influence the decision making process? Finally, what role do the characteristics of the Second Life adopter, such as a faculty member, have in the success or failure of Second Life initiatives? These are but a few of the many types of questions related to adoption and diffusion that could be applied to understand Second Life use in education.

A third stream of research relates to leadership, teamwork, and team composition. Teams lead by the right leader and staffed with the right people are more likely to be effective and efficient (Crowston & Scozzi, 2008, Long & Siau, 2007; Siau et al., 2010b, 2010c). Second Life may be a possible medium for leadership and teamwork training but these are simply hypotheses or conjectures at present. Are there differences between leadership in the real world and leadership in virtual worlds? If so, what are the additional dimensions of leadership that a leader needs to possess to be effective in the virtual environment? How about teamwork characteristics and team composition? What are the necessary skill sets that a team should possess when completing a task in a virtual world and how does this compare to the skills needed in other virtual team contexts?

Another venue for research is on knowledge acquisition, knowledge transfer, knowledge diffusion, and knowledge management in Second Life. The ability to effectively manage distributed knowledge is becoming an essential core competence of today's organizations, including educational institutions (see King, 2006: Cai, 2006: Kwan & Cheung, 2006: Kwahk et al., 2007). Nevertheless, Siau et al. (2010a) emphasize that knowledge management sharing in virtual communities is an important area that remains largely understudied. What are the efficient ways to foster knowledge acquisition, transfer, and diffusion in virtual worlds? How to effectively manage knowledge in virtual worlds? Currently, most faculty members that use Second Life for teaching or research are storing the knowledge outside Second Life. What kind of features and functions should be provided in Second Life to effect management of knowledge?

Numerous research topics could be examined to better understand whether and how Second Life can be used as a platform for education. Those that we discussed above represent some of the more pertinent areas for IS researchers. Scholars in areas like law, sociology, cognitive psychology, and numerous other disciplines have already begun to study questions related to legal, social, psychological, and interpersonal behavioral issues as they apply to Second Life and other virtual world environments. It is time for IS researchers to examine the issues relevant to IS in the adoption and use of virtual worlds.

REFERENCES

Attasiriluk, S., Nakaone, A., Hantanong, W., Prada, R., Kanongchaiyos, P., & Prendinger, H. (2009). Co-presence, collaboration, and control in environmental studies: A Second-Life based approach. *Virtual Reality (Waltham Cross)*, *13*(3), 195–204. doi:10.1007/s10055-009-0130-5

Barab, S. A., Hay, K. E., Squire, K., Barnett, M., Schmidt, R., & Karrigan, K. (2000). Virtual solar system project: Learning through a technology-rich, inquiry-based, participatory learning environment. *Journal of Science Education and Technology*, *9*(1), 7–25. doi:10.1023/A:1009416822783

Cai, J. (2006). Knowledge management within collaboration processes: A perspective modeling and analyzing methodology. *Journal of Database Management*, *17*(1), 33–48.

Chen, K., Chen, J., & Ross, W. (2010). Antecedents of online game dependency: The implications of multimedia realism and uses and gratifications theory. *Journal of Database Management*, *21*(2), 69–99.

Crowston, K., & Barbar, S. (2008). Bug fixing practices within free/libre open source software development teams. *Journal of Database Management*, *19*(2), 1–30.

Davis, F. D. (1989). Perceived usefulness, perceived ease of use, and user acceptance of information technology. *Management Information Systems Quarterly*, *13*(3), 319–340. doi:10.2307/249008

Dickey, M. D. (2005a). Brave new (interactive) worlds: A review of the design affordances and constraints of two 3D virtual worlds as interactive learning environments. *Interactive Learning Environments*, *13*(1-2), 121–137. doi:10.1080/10494820500173714

Dickey, M. D. (2005b). Three-dimensional virtual worlds and distance learning: Two case studies of Active Worlds as a medium for distance education. *British Journal of Educational Technology, 36*(3), 439–451. doi:10.1111/j.1467-8535.2005.00477.x

Erickson, J., & Siau, K. (2003). e-ducation. *Communications of the ACM, 46*(9), 134–140. doi:10.1145/903893.903928

Ertmer, P. A., & Newby, T. J. (1993). Behaviorism, cognitivism, constructivism: comparing critical features from an instructional design perspective. *Performance Improvement Quarterly, 6*(4), 50–72. doi:10.1111/j.1937-8327.1993.tb00605.x

Eschenbrenner, B., Nah, F., & Siau, K. (2008). 3-D virtual worlds in education: Applications, benefits, issues, and opportunities. *Journal of Database Management, 19*(4), 91–110.

Fuller, J. (2010). Refining virtual co-creation from a consumer perspective. *California Management Review, 52*(2), 98–122.

Fuller, J., Hans, M., Kurt, M., & Gregor, J. (2010). Consumer empowerment through Internet-based co-creation. *Journal of Management Information Systems, 26*(3), 71–102. doi:10.2753/MIS0742-1222260303

Galanxhi-Janaqi, H., & Nah, F. (2007). Deception in cyberspace: A comparison of text-only vs. avatar-supported medium. *International Journal of Human-Computer Studies, 65*(9), 770–783. doi:10.1016/j.ijhcs.2007.04.005

Gokhale, A. (1995). Collaborative learning enhances critical thinking. *Journal of Technology Education, 7*(1), 22–30.

Goodhue, D., & Thompson, R. (1995). Task-technology fit and individual performance. *Management Information Systems Quarterly, 19*(2), 213–236. doi:10.2307/249689

Gu, N., & Tsai, J. J.-H. (2010). Interactive graphical representation for collaborative 3D virtual worlds. *Computer-Aided Civil and Infrastructure Engineering, 25*(1), 55–68. doi:10.1111/j.1467-8667.2009.00613.x

Guru, A., & Siau, K. (2008). Developing the IBM i virtual community: iSociety. *Journal of Database Management, 19*(4), i–xiii.

Ives, B., & Junglas, I. (2008). APC forum: Business implications of virtual worlds and serious gaming. *MIS Quarterly Executive, 7*(3), 151–156.

King, W. R. (2006). The critical role of information processing in creating an effective knowledge organization. *Journal of Database Management, 17*(1), 1–15.

Kwahk, K. Y., Kim, H. W., & Chan, H. C. (2007). A knowledge integration approach for organizational decision support. *Journal of Database Management, 18*(2), 41–61.

Kwan, M. M., & Cheung, P. K. (2006). The knowledge transfer process: From field studies to technology development. *Journal of Database Management, 17*(1), 16–32.

Leidner, D. E., & Jarvenpaa, S. L. (1995). The use of information technology to enhance management school education: A theoretical view. *Management Information Systems Quarterly, 19*(3), 265–291. doi:10.2307/249596

Long, Y., & Siau, K. (2007). Social network structures in open source software development teams. *Journal of Database Management, 18*(2), 25–40.

McGrath, M. B., & Brown, J. R. (2005). Visual learning for science and engineering. *IEEE Computer Graphics and Applications, 25*(5), 56–63. doi:10.1109/MCG.2005.117

Mennecke, B. E., Triplett, J., Hassall, L. M., Jordan, Z., & Heer, R. (forthcoming). An examination of the development of embodied social presence during team interaction and collaboration in virtual worlds. *Decision Sciences*.

Minocha, S., & Roberts, D. (2008). Laying the groundwork for socialisation and knowledge construction within 3D virtual worlds. *ALT-J Research in Learning Technology, 16*(3), 181–196.

Nah, F., Eschenbrenner, B., DeWester, D., & Park, S. (2010). Impact of flow and brand equity in 3D virtual worlds. *Journal of Database Management, 21*(3), 69–89.

Osborne, E., & Schiller, S. (2009). Order and creativity in virtual worlds. *Journal of Virtual Worlds Research, 2*(3), 2–16.

Park, S., Nah, F., DeWester, D., Eschenbrenner, B., & Jeon, S. (2008). Virtual world affordances: Enhancing brand value. *Journal of Virtual Worlds Research, 1*(2), 1–18.

Rosenman, M. A., Smith, G., Maher, M. L., Ding, L., & Marchant, D. (2007). Multidisciplinary collaborative design in virtual environments. *Automation in Construction, 16*(1), 37–44. doi:10.1016/j.autcon.2005.10.007

Rousso, M., Johnson, A., Moher, T., Leigh, J., Vasilakis, C., & Barnes, C. (1999). Learning and building together in an immersive virtual world. *Presence (Cambridge, Mass.), 8*(3), 247–263. doi:10.1162/105474699566215

Schiller, S. (2009). Practicing learner-centered teaching: Pedagogical design and assessment of a Second Life project. *Journal of Information Systems Education, 20*(3), 369–381.

Sheng, H., Siau, K., & Nah, F. (2010). Understanding the values of mobile technology in education: A value-focused thinking approach. *The Data Base for Advances in Information Systems, 41*(2), 25–44.

Shin, N. (2006). Online learner's 'flow' experience: An empirical study. *British Journal of Educational Technology, 37*(5), 705–720. doi:10.1111/j.1467-8535.2006.00641.x

Siau, K., Erickson, J., & Nah, F. (2010a). Effect of national culture on knowledge sharing in online virtual communities. *IEEE Transactions on Professional Communication, 53*(3), 278–292. doi:10.1109/TPC.2010.2052842

Siau, K., Long, Y., & Ling, M. (2010b). Toward a unified model of information systems success. *Journal of Database Management, 21*(1), 80–101.

Siau, K., Sheng, H., & Nah, F. (2006). Use of a classroom response system to enhance classroom interactivity. *IEEE Transactions on Education, 49*(3), 398–403. doi:10.1109/TE.2006.879802

Siau, K., Tan, X., & Sheng, H. (2010c). Important characteristics of software development team members: an empirical investigation using repertory grid. *Information Systems Journal, 20*(6), 563–580. doi:10.1111/j.1365-2575.2007.00254.x

Skadberg, Y. X., & Kimmel, J. R. (2004). Visitors' flow experience while browsing a Web site: Its measurement, contributing factors and consequences. *Computers in Human Behavior, 20*(3), 403–422. doi:10.1016/S0747-5632(03)00050-5

Slavin, R. E. (1980). Cooperative learning. *Review of Educational Research, 50*(2), 315–342.

Slavin, R. E. (1983). When does cooperative learning increase student achievement? *Psychological Bulletin, 94*(3), 429–445. doi:10.1037/0033-2909.94.3.429

Steffe, L. P., & Gale, J. (1995). *Constructivism in education*. Mahwah, NJ: Lawrence Erlbaum Associates.

Tobin, K., & Tippins, D. (1993). Constructivism as a referent for teaching and learning . In Tobin, K. (Ed.), *The practice of constructivism in education* (pp. 3–21). Hillsdale, NJ: Lawrence-Erlbaum.

Unalan, H. T. (2009). The effectiveness of collaborative learning applications in art education. *Journal of International Social Research, 1*(5), 868–879.

VanderMeer, D., & Dutta, K. (2009). Applying learner-centered design principles to UML sequence diagrams. *Journal of Database Management, 20*(1), 25–47.

Venkatesh, V., Morris, M. G., Davis, G. B., & Davis, F. D. (2003). User acceptance of information technology: Toward a unified view. *Management Information Systems Quarterly, 27*(3), 425–478.

Vygotsky, L. S. (1978). *Mind in society: The development of higher psychological processes.* Cambridge, MA: Harvard University Press.

Wagner, T., Longenecker, J., Landry, J., Lusk, C., & Saulnier, B. (2008). A methodology to assist faculty in developing successful approaches for achieving learner centered information systems curriculum outcomes: Team based methods. *Journal of Information Systems Education, 19*(2), 181–195.

Weimer, M. (2002). *Learner-centered teaching: Five key changes to practice.* San Francisco, CA: Jossey-Bass.

Zhao, Y., Wang, W., & Zhu, Y. (2010). Antecedents of the closeness of human-avatar relationships in a virtual world. *Journal of Database Management, 21*(2), 41–68.

This work was previously published in International Journal of Database Management, Volume 21, Issue 4, edited by Keng Siau, pp. 1-13, copyright 2010 by IGI Publishing (an imprint of IGI Global).

Chapter 14
Transforming Activity–Centric Business Process Models into Information–Centric Models for SOA Solutions

Rong Liu
IBM T.J. Watson Research Center, USA

Frederick Y. Wu
IBM T.J. Watson Research Center, USA

Santhosh Kumaran
IBM T.J. Watson Research Center, USA

ABSTRACT

Much of the prior work in business process modeling is activity-centric. Recently, an information-centric approach has emerged, where a business process is modeled as the interacting lifecycles of business entities. The benefits of this approach are documented in a number of case studies. In this paper, the authors formalize the information-centric approach and derive the relationships between the two approaches. The authors formally define the notion of a business entity, provide an algorithm to transform an activity-centric model into an information-centric process model, and demonstrate the equivalence between these two models. Further, they show the value of transforming from the activity-centric paradigm to the information-centric paradigm in business process componentization and Service-Oriented Architecture design and also provide an empirical evaluation.

INTRODUCTION

A primary motivation for business process modeling is to define requirements for information technology (IT) systems that support the business operations of an enterprise. To create process models, subject matter experts record the activities that are performed, their sequencing, and their data inputs and outputs. The implementation of these models in IT solutions has generally followed one of two arduous paths:

DOI: 10.4018/978-1-61350-471-0.ch014

1. Business process models are simply documentation of requirements. From these documents, IT solutions are manually designed and implemented by writing custom code, or by customizing and integrating legacy applications and packaged software; or
2. Business process models are automatically converted into workflow definitions which are deployed on workflow engines and augmented with custom code (WfMC, 1995).

The first approach leads to the well-known business-IT gap, characterized by IT solutions that implement misinterpreted requirements, are overdue and over budget, provide inadequate support to operations, and are unresponsive to business changes.

The second approach faces difficulties as well. The workflow approach does not scale well to large, complex business processes. Implementation and maintenance become increasingly difficult and performance degrades. The primary reason for this is that the workflow approach does not lend itself well to componentization (Alonso et al., 1997). Service-Oriented Architecture (SOA) (Arsanjani et al., 2008; Zimmerman et al., 2004) can help to address the complexity and flexibility issues of business processes, and the value of aligning business processes with SOA is well addressed (Arsanjani et al., 2008; Zimmerman et al., 2004). However, this approach suffers from the lack of systematic methods to identify services and service components at the right level of granularity, and to orchestrate services into business processes (Zimmerman et al., 2004). The ad-hoc definitions of services and service components often leave an enterprise with a large, difficult-to-maintain portfolio of inconsistent services.

In response to this situation, a paradigm which models business processes as interacting lifecycles of *business entities* has been proposed. Appropriately, this approach is called *information-centric process modeling*. Business entities that are used to describe business processes in

this manner have had various names, including *adaptive documents* (ADoc) (Kumaran et al., 2003), *adaptive business objects* (ABO) (Nandi et al., 2005), and *business artifacts* (Nigam & Caswell, 2003). In this paper, we will refer to them as business entities. Information-centric modeling first identifies the business entities, or records essential to achieving an operational goal, such as a customer order, and then represents business processes in terms of the lifecycles of the identified business entities, which manage progress towards the goal (Nigam & Caswell, 2003; Bhattacharya, Caswell, Kumaran, Nigam, & Wu, 2007). Information-centric modeling, as exemplified by Model-Driven Business Transformation (Kumaran, 2004), reduces the business-IT gap by enabling the direct generation of business process applications from information-centric process models. Information-centric modeling improves modularity and reduces complexity by decomposing a business process into interacting business entities, each being a module with an information model and a behavior model.

Although this new paradigm has been successfully tested through customer engagements, several issues remain. First, the concept of business entities is informal and lacks theoretical underpinnings. Second, the key step of discovering business entities requires subject matter experts and skilled consultants. Third, there is a lack of understanding of the relationship between this new paradigm and the traditional *activity-centric process modeling* used in workflow management systems (WfMC, 1995). Finally, although a business entity can be intuitively mapped to a service component, the detailed SOA design and reusability of service components need to be explored.

Kumaran et al. (2008) presented an algorithm to transform activity-centric process models into information-centric models. In this paper, we extend this previous effort to formally demonstrate the duality between these two paradigms. We also establish the sufficient conditions under which this transformation is possible. More importantly, we show the value of this transformation in achieving process componentization, reusable SOA design, and accelerated IT solution development.

The remainder of the paper is organized as follows. The concepts related to information-centric process models introduced in Kumaran et al. are reviewed (2008). The following section describes the transformation algorithms, provides a formal proof of the equivalence between activity-centric and information-centric models, and discusses modeling principles that ensure the correctness of transformed information-centric models. We then describe how process components and service interfaces can be derived from information-centric models. We briefly summarize the value of information-centric modeling and report a recent pilot project with a banking client. We also provide a comparison with related work and conclude with a brief description of future work.

DISCOVERING BUSINESS ENTITIES FROM ACTIVITY-CENTRIC PROCESS MODELS

The core of information-centric process modeling is the concept of business entities. In this section, we provide formal definitions of several key notions, including *information entity, process scope, domination, business entity, and activity-centric and information-centric process models*. Then we use an example to illustrate how business entities can be discovered from activity-centric process models.

Activity-Centric Process Models

An *activity* is a logical description of a piece of work that consists of human and/or automated operations and is often realized in conjunction with information processing (van der Aalst & van Hee, 2002; WfMC, 1995). A *business process* (or simply *process*) links activities by transforming inputs into outputs to achieve an operational goal,

for example, to complete an insurance claim (van der Aalst & van Hee, 2002). The data used by activities, including input and output data, form the information domain of the process scope. The atomic elements that make up the information domain are called *information entities* (or *entities* for simplicity).

To define information entities, we assume there exist the following four sets: A of attributes (names), T of primitive types, E of information entities, and U of values, $U = T \cup E$.

Definition 1 (Information Entities or simply Entities): An information entity $e \in E$ is a tuple (S, V, f), where $S \subseteq A$ is an attribute set, $V \subseteq U$ is a value set, and $f: S \rightarrow V$ is a mapping.

In other words, an information entity is self-describing, as it contains metadata that describes its data content. Also, an information entity can be nested within another. An information entity can be an input or output of an activity. An *input information entity* represents information required for an activity to be executed. An *output information entity* is information created or modified during activity execution.

Figure 1 shows a business process for handling a claim. In this process, a claim information entity is created when a loss event is reported. This claim is validated and analyzed, which could lead to one of three outcomes: rejection of the claim, acceptance of the claim, or postponement of a decision pending additional information. If the claim is accepted, the benefit in this claim is determined and then a payment is issued. If the claim is pended, arrival of additional information leads to another round of processing. For simple notation, we use A1, A2,..., A13 to denote the activities in the process, and the same activities in all alternative process representations that will be introduced. For instance, in Figure 1, Loss Event is an input entity of activity A1 (Notify Claim), which produces Claim as an output entity. The execution sequence of these activities is described

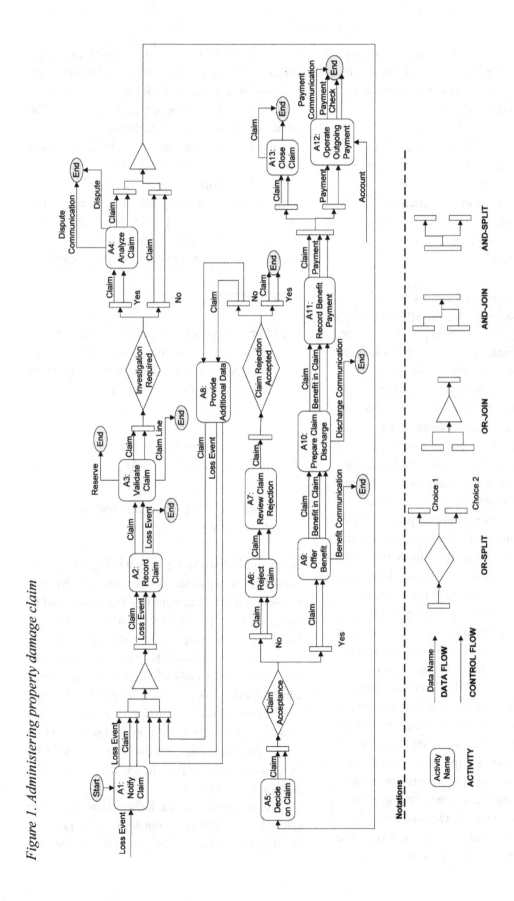

Figure 1. Administering property damage claim

by connectors including data flows, control flows and control nodes (Or-Split, Or-Join, And-Split, and And-Join). We call Figure 1 an activity-centric process model, as defined below.

Definition 2 (Activity-Centric Process Models): An activity-centric process model consists of activities, connectors as control flows describing the execution sequences of these activities, and optional data flow connectors with information entities as inputs or outputs of the activities.

Figure 1 is an activity-centric model with detailed data flows. However, in a typical activity-centric process model, for example, a workflow model, the specification of information entities is not required. A workflow model consists of activities and their execution order, and resources that perform those activities (van der Aalst & van Hee, 2002). The lack of information entity specification likely leads to incomplete understanding of business processes among stakeholders, e.g., process owners, business analysts and system developers. For example, the major concern of a process owner is the end-to-end processing of cases (van der Aalst et al., 2005), such as claims and orders, which are exactly information entities. For a business analyst, it is critical to sort out the execution order of activities in a process, but again, the execution order is primarily determined by resource constraints and information flows. For example, in Figure 1, activity A2 (Record Claim) follows A1 (Notify Claim) because the outputs of A1 are the inputs to A2. Without data flows, it may be difficult for system analysts to reason the execution order and optimize the model. Similarly, because of the lack of information entity specification, during process implementation, system developers need to incorporate custom code to manipulate information, instead of taking a more efficient model-driven approach (Kumaran, 2004).

However, when information entities are brought into process modeling, a major concern is complexity. Often, a process involves a large number of information entities. Capturing all of them in a process model certainly leads to increased model complexity, and therefore, the model correctness may deteriorate.

Given these pros and cons, the information centric approach rethinks the way to represent information entities in process models. Instead of simply bringing every information entity into a process model, this approach first discovers the structure of information entities based on their domination relationships as described below.

Domination

Definition 3 (Process Scopes): A *process scope* *s* is a group of business processes, together providing a well defined end-to-end function to map input I to output O, i.e.

$$s : I \rightarrow O, \quad s = \{p_1, \ p_2, \ ..., \ p_n\},$$
$$I = \{e_{I1}, \ e_{I2}, \ ..., \ e_{Ix}\}, \quad O = \{e_{O1}, \ e_{O2}, \ ..., \ e_{Oy}\}$$

, where each p is a process and each e is an information entity.

For example, the process shown in Figure 1 can be considered as a process scope providing an end-to-end claim management function. The input to this process scope is a loss event and the outputs are a set of information entities including a closed claim, outgoing payments, and communication documents to claimants. Multiple related processes can be grouped as a process scope also. For example, Figure 1 can be combined with an acquiring customer process to form a process scope. In this scope, the acquiring customer process produces customer insurance policies, which are used in administering claims.

Within a process scope, information entities are created or modified through activities to produce the desired outputs as defined in the end-to-end

Box 1.

Proof: Let $I(x)$ be the set of activities where x is an input

$O(x)$ be the set of activities where x is an output, for $x = e_1, e_2,$ or e_3

By $e_1 \mapsto e_2$, $I(e_1) \supseteq I(e_2)$, $O(e_1) \supseteq O(e_2)$, $I(e_1) \cup O(e_1) \supset I(e_2) \cup O(e_2)$

By $e_2 \mapsto e_3$, $I(e_2) \supseteq I(e_3)$, $O(e_2) \supseteq O(e_3)$, $I(e_2) \cup O(e_2) \supset I(e_3) \cup O(e_3)$

Therefore, $I(e_1) \supseteq I(e_3)$, $O(e_1) \supseteq O(e_3)$, $I(e_1) \cup O(e_1) \supset I(e_3) \cup O(e_3)$,

i.e. $e_1 \mapsto e_3$

---

function. From an information-centric point of view, information entities influence activities in the sense that the execution of an activity is predicated on the availability of the right information entities in the right state (van der Aalst et al., 2005). For a set of activities, there is a corresponding set of information entities that influence the execution of these activities. But there are differences in the degree to which a specific information entity influences the activity execution. For example, considering the process shown in Figure 1, obviously, Claim information entity influences most activities in the process. On the other hand, the influence of Claim Line is limited to only a subset of activities that are also influenced by Claim. Therefore, we say Claim dominates Claim Line, as formally defined below.

Definition 4 (Domination): Information entity e_1 dominates information entity e_2 in a process scope s, denoted as $e_1 \mapsto e_2$, *iff*:

1. $\forall a \in s$, if $e_2 \in \bullet a$, then $e_1 \in \bullet a$
2. $\forall a \in s$, if $e_2 \in a\bullet$, then $e_1 \in a \bullet$
3. $\exists a \in s$, s.t. $e_1 \in \bullet a \cup a\bullet$, but $e_2 \notin \bullet a \cup a \bullet$, where $\bullet a$ ($a\bullet$) denotes the input (output) information entities of activity a.

In other words, e_1 dominates e_2, iff (1) for every activity where e_2 is an input (output), e_1 is also an input (output), and (2) e_1 is an input or an output of at least one activity where e_2 is neither an input nor an output.

Lemma 1: Domination is transitive, i.e.

if $e_1 \mapsto e_2$, $e_2 \mapsto e_3$ then $e_1 \mapsto e_3$.

See Box 1.

Definition 5 (Dominant Entity, Dominated Entity, Inclusive Domination, Referential Domination): A *dominant entity* is one that is not dominated by any other entity in a process scope. A *dominated entity* is an entity dominated by at least one entity. If a dominated entity is required only as an input in a process scope, this domination is called *referential domination*. With *inclusive domination*, a dominated entity is an output of at least one activity.

We apply the rules in Definition 4 for every pair of information entities in Figure 1 to determine the domination relationship between them, and display the result in Figure 2. Figure 2 is referred to as an *entity domination graph*. As shown in this figure, Loss Event does not have any dominated entities, but Claim and Payment entities have several dominated entities. Payment referentially dominates Account, as Account is a read-only entity in this process. Note that transitive reduction has been applied to Figure 2. For example, Claim dominates Benefit Communication, but in Figure 2, there is no need to have a directed

Figure 2. Information entity domination graph

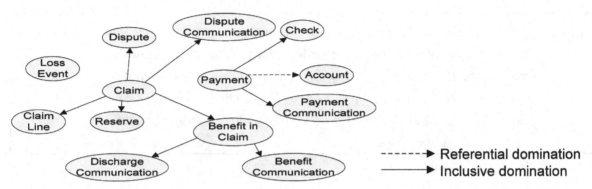

line from Claim to Benefit Communication. This relationship can be derived by Lemma 1.

The domination concept reveals the deep structure of the information domain of a process scope. This structure is represented as entity domination graphs in the form of *directed acyclic graphs* (DAG) (Cormen et al., 2001), with the dominant entities at the source nodes of the DAGs serving as the driving force for the process flows. The dominated entities form the non-source nodes of the DAGs play a subsidiary role in the execution of activities. Usually, the inclusively dominated entities are created during the processing of the dominant entity and their existence depends on the dominant entity. But the dominated entities do play an important role in the lifecycle of the dominant entity. For example, in the insurance claim process, Claim Line is created during the processing of Claim, and a validated Claim is expected to have Claim Lines. A concept closely related to inclusive domination is existence dependency, proposed by Snoeck and Dedene (1999). An information entity, say e_1, is existence dependent on another entity, say e_2, if e_1's life is embedded into the life of e_2. If we consider that an entity's life is composed of activities within a process scope, then inclusive domination is equivalent to existence dependency.

An intuitive explanation of the domination concept can be derived from the Pareto principle which states that, for many events, 80% of the effects come from 20% of the causes. When applied to business process analysis, we observe that a number of information entities serve as key drivers of the flow of most activities. For example, we have observed that among 320 information entities used in IBM Insurance Application Architecture (IBM, 2004), a comprehensive library with over 200 reference process models, only 90 qualify as dominant entities. We can also view domination as a special association rule mining (Agrawal, 1993) for discovering antecedent and consequent information entities and establishing associations between them.

Business Entities

Definition 6 (Business Entities): A business entity is a dominant information entity along with its dominated entities in the context of a process scope. A business entity has an associated data model and an associated behavior model. The data model describes the data dependencies between the dominant entity and the dominated entities as the dominant entity logically containing the dominated entities. The behavior of the business entity consists of activities acting on the dominant entity.

Therefore, by Definition 6, we discover three business entities for the process shown in Figure 1: CLAIM, LOSS EVENT, and PAYMENT. We show the dominant entity name in uppercase to denote a business entity.

From a domination graph, a data model for business entities can be derived using data modeling techniques, for example, containment data modeling (Whitehead 2002). Each dominant entity can be treated as a "container," each inclusively dominated entity is a "contained member," and each referentially dominated entity becomes a "referenced member." Figure 3 shows the data model generated from the entity domination graph of Figure 2. In this data model, each root container is a dominant entity. The CLAIM business entity contains Benefit in Claim, which, in turn, contains Discharge Communication and Benefit Communication. LOSS EVENT business entity does not contain any entity, but it may have attributes and child items. In this paper, for simplicity, we omit the detailed attributes of each entity. In addition, there may be data relationships between business entities. For example, in Figure 1, because Payment is created by Loss Event through activity A11 (Record Benefit Payment), Payment likely has a reference to Claim.

However, Definition 4 does not exclude the situation where an information entity is dominated by multiple dominants. In this situation, extra analysis is needed to determine the boundary of business entities. In principle, we want to have non-overlapping business entities so that they can be designed as decoupled service components, as we will discuss shortly.

The behavior model of a business entity consists of activities that act on the dominant entity. Next, we present business entity behavior models.

INFORMATION-CENTRIC PROCESS MODELS

Definition 7 (Information-Centric Process Models): An information-centric process model of a process scope is a set of connected business entities. Two business entities are connected if their behavior models share at least one activity.

As shown in Figure 2, the information-centric model for the insurance process contains three business entities. The behavior models of these business entities are linked through some shared activities, for example, activity A1 (Notify Claim) in Figure 1. We can represent information-centric

Figure 3. Data model of administering property damage claim

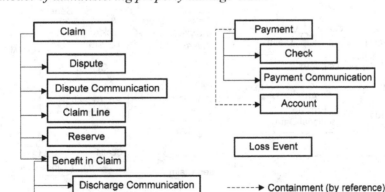

process models in two forms: *business operation models* (Liu et al. 2007), and *state machines*.

Business Operation Model

A business operation model can be generated from an activity-centric model as follows.

Algorithm 1: Transforming Activity-Centric Models into Business Operation Models
1. Discover business entities by Definition 4;
2. For each business entity, find activities where the dominant entity is either an input or an output;
3. Connect these activities by connectors associated with the business entity to preserve the sequence between the activities as in the original activity-centric model.

Figure 4 shows the business operation model transformed from the claim process. It is easy to verify that each activity in this figure acts on one or more dominant entities and the sequence of these activities remains unchanged as in Figure 1.

However, compared with Figure 1, this business operation model has several unique features as described below.

First, only business entities, not information entities, are shown in the data flows. Second, repositories may be used in the situations where: (a) a business entity is at the end of processing, (b) a business entity is read-only by some activities, or (c) a business entity does not trigger the execution of an activity, but is retrieved by the activity when needed. In general, *a repository is an abstraction of a state of a business entity*. For example, repository Pending Claim in Figure 4 indicates that CLAIM is in a Pending state. The repositories are added manually to make the behavior of business entities more comprehensible. Finally, control nodes are omitted in business operation models without causing any ambiguities. For example, it is clear that activity A3 (Validate Claim) is actually embedded with an Or-Split node, as there are two output ports of the CLAIM and each business entity instance can only take one port when leaving A3. Similarly, if an activity has multiple input ports of the same business entity, it indicates an implicit Or-Join. Also, it is straightforward that an activity with multiple

Figure 4. Business operation model – administering property damage claim

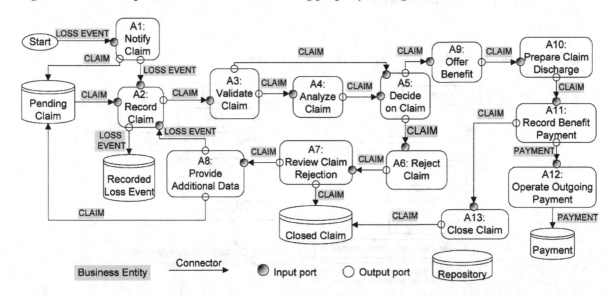

input (output) ports of different business entities indicates an And-Join (And-Split).

With business operation models, IT solutions can be generated automatically using Model Driven Business Transformation Toolkit (Kumaran et al., 2003). This toolkit requires business operation models (e.g. Figure 4) as an input. Typically, it needs effort and special skills to discover business entities and create business operational models manually. Our transformation algorithm provides a fast path to transform business operation models from existing activity-centric models, accelerating IT solution development. Also, this direct transformation from process models to IT solutions reduces the gap between business and IT.

State Machine Representation

Another intuitive representation of a business entity behavior model is a state machine. The state machine can be constructed using Algorithm 2.

Algorithm 2: Transforming Activity-Centric Models into State Machines
  1. Discover business entities by Definition 4;
  2. For each business entity, find activities where the dominant entity is an output;
  3. For each of these activities, create a business entity state for each of the outputs associated with the dominant entity; and
  4. Connect the activity to the states and connect each of the states to the next activity touched by the dominant entity to construct a state machine preserving the sequence between activities as in the original activity-centric business process model.

Figure 5 shows the information-centric process model consisting of three connected state machines, each representing the behavior of one business entity. The state machine of CLAIM describes the lifecycle of the CLAIM business entity and how it interacts with the other business entities, as indicated by the dotted line in Figure 5. For example, during CLAIM's state transition Pending to Recorded, the LOSS EVENT business entity also changes its state from Notified to the final state Recorded. Similarly, activity A11 (Record Benefit Payment) changes the state of the CLAIM business entity from Discharged to Benefit Payment Prepared, while creating a new instance of PAYMENT business entity. Therefore, the business processes are equivalent to the process of business entities walking through their lifecycles, from their initial states to final states. As exemplified by Figure 5, the names of business entity states can be assigned based on the results produced by activities.

An information-centric model of a process scope may contain multiple business entities. The lifecycles of these entities are linked through an instance creation pattern or a synchronization pattern (Liu et al., 2007). In the creation pattern, an existing business entity instance creates a new instance of another business entity as part of an activity. For example, in Figure 5, when activity A1 (Notify Claim) is performed on LOSS EVENT, it creates a new instance of the CLAIM entity (i.e., the state of Claim is changed from Start to Pending). In the synchronization pattern, two existing business entities exchange information as part of performing an activity. An example of this pattern is activity A2 (Record Claim), which results in state changes of both LOSS EVENT and CLAIM.

The state machine representation (denoted as *SM*) of an information-centric model can also be viewed as the dual graph of the corresponding business operation model (*BOM*): each state node in *SM* corresponds to a connector (or a repository with its incoming and outgoing connectors) between two activities in *BOM*, and each state transition in *SM* corresponds to an activity in *BOM*. Therefore, we can also generate *SM* from *BOM*.

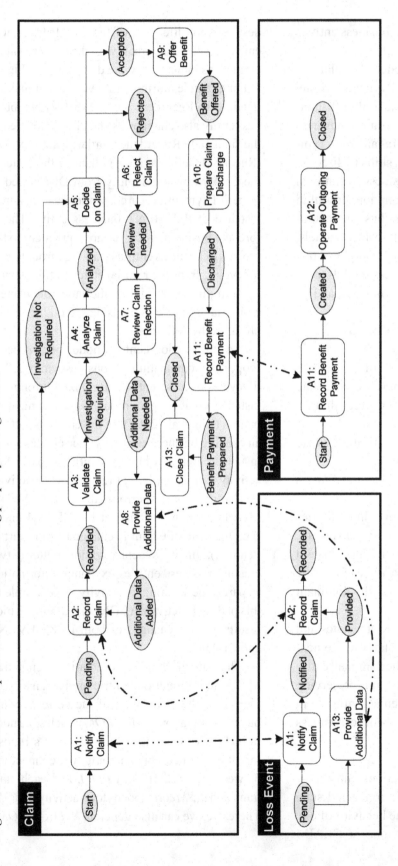

Figure 5. State machine representation – administering property damage claim

The business entity behavior models provide a new perspective to reason about activities. Ideally, an activity should produce some meaningful change to a business entity, resulting in the attainment of a new milestone in the business entity's lifecycle, which should be monitored and tracked for performance management. If an activity does not bring such changes, that activity can either be removed or combined with others. Therefore, business entities actually provide guidelines for determining the right granularity of activities. For example, in Figure 5, activity A9 (Offer Benefit) is likely to notify a claimant without providing any actual changes to the CLAIM business entity. This activity may be merged with A10 (Prepare Claim Discharge).

Compared with the original model in Figure 1, the information-centric model shown in Figure 5 provides better understandability because the introduced business entities highlight the focus of the process. Obviously, the process mainly deals with CLAIM, tracking its behavior through its end-to-end lifecycle from creation to closure. More importantly, the information-centric model is actually modularized into three business entities. Each business entity can be viewed as a module with its own information model and behavior model. The interactions between modules are also identified. The advantages of modularization, including enhanced understandability, localization of changes, and reuse of modules, are well documented (Baldwin and Clark 2000; Reijers and Mendling 2008). In Figure 5, each streamlined state machine has fewer activity nodes than the original process model. Empirical evidence shows that model size and average connector degree significantly affect the understandability of process models (Mendling et al., 2007). Changes to the process may be localized to a particular business entity without a ripple effect. Also, a business entity may be reused across different lines of business. For example, LOSS EVENT and PAYMENT may be used by medical insurance, auto insurance, and other types of insurance.

Conditions for Transformation and Implications for Process Model Quality

The transformation from activity-centric paradigm to information-centric paradigm is generic and can be applied to any activity-centric process model that meets two conditions: (1) each activity has input and output information entities, and (2) the data flows regarding each information entity (instance) are connected such that (i) each input of an activity is connected from either an output of another activity or an external information source, and (ii) each output of an activity is connected to either an input of another activity or an end node indicating no further processing. The first condition is required by Definition 4. Incomplete input and output information entities in the original activity-centric model may result in a poor-quality information-centric process model, characterized by a large number of business entities. The second condition ensures that the generated business entity behavior models are valid. Obviously, with disconnected data flows, the behavior models may be broken into pieces.

In fact, these two conditions are not only specialized for our transformation algorithms, but are required to promote high-quality process models, whether activity-centric or information-centric. For example, for activity A3 (Validate Claim) shown in Figure 1, without input and output information entities, it may be difficult to understand what this activity accomplishes. Similarly, disconnected data flows cause problems in determining proper process execution order.

These two conditions impose no constraints on the format and content of an information entity. However, with respect to the quality of information-centric models, information entities should exhibit the following properties, and hence, they are *normalized*.

- *Non-overlapping*: Information entities partition data in the information domain of a process scope into disjoint sets.
- *Decoupled*: An entity is decoupled from others in the sense that its evolution through activities is not completely identical to that of any other information entity. Any pair of entities should not always be used by the same set of activities. If so, these two entities should be merged into one. In other words, the granularity of information entities is determined by activities.

If the original set of information entities does not possess these properties, the resulting business entities may have degraded modularity as their behavior models could be connected at many shared activities. Therefore, it may be necessary to normalize the information entities by clearly defining their data schema and removing data overlap and coupling between them.

Again, normalized business entities are not only the requirements of successful transformation from activity-centric models into information-centric models, but also general design rules of information entities in process models. For example, overlapping information entities make it difficult to detect concurrency problems in traditional models. Also, the non-overlapping condition is emphasized by traditional entity-relationship data modeling, where each entity can be uniquely identified and exist independently, and is related to other entities by relationships (Chen, 1976). The decoupled condition concerns the granularity of information entities. A process model with a large number of information entities leads to increased complexity and degraded understandability. The decoupled condition prevents information entities in process models from being too granular.

Equivalence between Activity-Centric and Information-Centric Models

Next, we show the equivalence between an activity-centric process model and its corresponding information-centric model based on the notion of bisimulation games (Kiepuszewski et al., 2000). In the context of workflows, two models are considered to be equivalent, if one model can simulate every move (i.e., starting and finishing activities) of the other and vice versa. Similarly, we define the equivalence between information-centric and activity-centric models as follows.

Definition 8 (Model Equivalency): Let $M1$ be an activity-centric process model and $M2$ is the corresponding information-centric process model. $M1$ and $M2$ are equivalent if $M1$ can simulate the activity execution of $M2$ and vice versa.

A workflow model is well-behaved if it can neither lead to deadlock nor result in multiple active instances of the same activity (Kiepuszewski et al., 2000). Figure 6 shows an example workflow model that is not well-behaved. Without considering the data flows, this model can have two active instances of activity $A4$ as an And-Split node is followed by an Or-Join. However, the data flows in this model indicate another problem. Since both activities $A2$ and $A3$ require information entity e_1 as an input, they compete for e_1 after the And-Split node. A possible situation is that when $A3$ reads e_1 which is being changed by $A2$, the content of e_1 retrieved by $A3$ has not been persisted, lead-

Figure 6. Incorrect activity-centric model

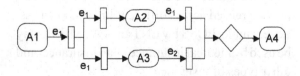

ing to unpredictable execution result of *A3*. If an activity-centric model is not well-behaved, its counterpart information-centric model is unpredictable in terms of its correctness. However, a well-behaved activity-centric model always has its equivalent information-centric model.

Theorem 1: A well-behaved activity-centric model and its corresponding information-centric model are equivalent.

Proof sketch: Assume *M1* is the activity-centric model and *M2* is the corresponding information-centric model in the form of a business operation model. An activity can be executed when all its input information entities have arrived. Let the input of *A* in *M1* be $I_1 = (e_1, e_2, ..., e_m)$, where e_i is an information entity for $1 \leq i \leq m$, and the input of *A* in *M2* be $I_2 = (B_1, B_2, ..., B_n)$, where B_j is a business entity, for $1 \leq j \leq n$. By Definition 6 and Algorithm 1, for every e_i, there exists B_j such that $e_i \in B_j$, and for every B_j, there exists e_i such that $e_i \in B_j$ for $1 \leq i \leq m$ and $1 \leq j \leq n$. Obviously, $I_1 \subset I_2$. Therefore, when entities in I_2 have arrived to trigger *A* in *M2*, all entities in I_1 must be available to initiate the same activity in *M1*.

Next, we show that the *M2* can imitate every move of *M1*. We need to prove that the arrival of entities in I_1 indicates that all entities in I_2 are also available. Taking any entity $e_1 \in I_1$, let *d* be the dominant entity dominating e_1. By Definition 4 and Algorithm 1, $d \in I_1$ and $d \in I_2$. Let e_2 be any information entity dominated by *d* but $e_2 \notin I_1$. Now we can show that when *A* in *M1* is initiated, e_2 is available, i.e., e_2 may be read by other activities, but is not being updated by any activity as an output entity. Otherwise, assuming e_2 is being updated by some activity (say *A'*) when *A* is initiated, then by Definition 4, *d* is also an output of *A'*. Thus, *A* and *A'* compete for *d*, and one of them may not be executed properly — a contradiction to that *M1* is well-behaved. Therefore, when all entities in I_1 arrive for triggering activity *A* in *M1*, the same

activity can also be triggered in *M2*, because all entities in I_2 are available.

We have given the proof that *M1* is equivalent to *M2*, the corresponding business operation model. The state machine representation (say *M3*) of the information-centric model is a dual graph of *M2*. *M2* and *M3* are equivalent. Therefore, *M1* and *M3* are also equivalent.

PROCESS COMPONENTIZATION AND SERVICE DESIGN

The advantages of a modular design in building complex systems are well known (Baldwin & Clark, 2000), but the challenge lies in identifying the right modules. Moreover, with increasing industrialization of services, companies tend to decompose their business processes for selective outsourcing, selective automation, or restructuring to create decoupled composite business services which may be flexibly integrated to support end-to-end business processes (Karmarkar, 2004). A critical issue is how to decompose business processes and design reusable services at the right granularity level. Information-centric modeling provides a solution to these challenges.

Intuitively, we can view each business entity as a *process component*. With the state machine representation, each component implements the behavior of a business entity as a state machine and manages the information entities associated with that business entity. Moreover, the service design for each business entity can be derived following the service oriented architecture (SOA) approach (Arsanjani et al., 2008). Although there is little agreement on a standard definition of SOA (Erickson & Siau, 2008), in this research, we view SOA as a way of defining and structuring services and service components by business needs and emphasize the reusability and flexibility of the defined services. Therefore, the key to SOA is how to design reusable services and organize these services logically into service

Figure 7. Service design of business entities

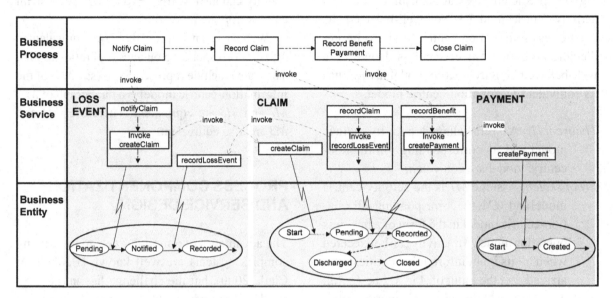

components in support of business processes. The information-centric modeling approach provides a model-driven, systematic solution to such an SOA design.

As shown in Figure 7, this service design can be derived as follows. First, we can declare that each state transition of a business entity is associated with an offered service by default. Each service has the business entity as an input, and when invoked successfully, it changes the business entity state. For example, the offered service associated with the state transition Start to Pending in CLAIM is *createClaim*. Second, if a state transition of a business entity is involved in an interaction with other business entities, we first determine if this business entity controls the interaction. If so, the service associated with this state transition is implemented as a service flow (e.g., BPEL (2003)) which invokes other services involved in the interaction. For example, in Figure 5, there is an interaction involved with the transition Start to Pending (say, T1) in CLAIM, and the transition Pending to Notified (say, T2) in LOSS EVENT. This interaction is controlled by LOSS EVENT because when a loss event is reported to a customer agent, the agent takes the

initiative to record loss event details and create a claim. Therefore, as shown in Figure 7, we associate an atomic service *createClaim* with T1, but a composite service *notifyClaim* with T2. This composite service invokes *createClaim*. Another example is the *recordBenefit* service in CLAIM, which invokes the *createPayment* service offered by PAYMENT.

Therefore, each business entity has offered and consumed services. The offered services may be used internally or exposed for external invocations. For example, in Figure 7, *createClaim* is a service offered by CLAIM, and this service is consumed by LOSS EVENT. Accordingly, the service design of a business entity can be viewed as a three-layer structure as shown in Figure 7. The bottom layer contains business entities which are formally defined with associated data models and behavior models. The middle layer is composed of business services offered by each business entity. The top layer can be viewed as business processes orchestrating business services. For the claim process, each activity can be mapped closely to a service provided by business entities.

Thus, each business entity is equivalent to a service component and can be assembled with other service components to create flexible business process applications in Service Component Architecture (SCA, 2007). The components in this architecture are decoupled and can evolve independently as long as the functionalities required by other components can be faithfully provided as offered services. For example, the CLAIM component can be extended to add new functionality such as handling claim disputes. This extension has no impact on the other components. Also, with well-defined boundaries and service interfaces, business entities can be used to construct new processes to promote reusability. For example, the LOSS EVENT and PAYMENT components can be used for other types of claim processes such as auto claim.

Moreover, since services describe the state changes of business entity lifecycles, these service definitions tend to be stable as long as the business entity lifecycles are unchanged. Interestingly, the lifecycle model of a business entity rarely changes across business scenarios. For example, although the lifecycle of CLAIM in Figure 5 is derived from the Administering Property Damage Claim process, this lifecycle can be adapted for other types of claims, for example, medical expense claims, with few changes. Also, industries often standardize the lifecycle models of key business objects and encourage companies to adopt the standard lifecycles to facilitate interoperability (Ryndina et al., 2007). Therefore, the service definitions likely can be used across business scenarios or even companies. However, the detailed implementation of each service can vary by business scenario or company. For example, composite service "recordBenefit" (see Figure 7) may be implemented as a BPEL flow. In this flow, service "createPayment" may be provided by legacy systems or outsourcing partners. The implementation can be customized case by case. Therefore, the changes can be localized to service implementation, a micro-level design compared with service definitions that are considered at a macro level. In general, the business service

layer in Figure 7 can be configured to implement business requirements as captured in business processes, while the business entity layer can remain relatively stable in spite of changes in business processes. We will evaluate the reusability of this SOA design through a real engagement shortly.

Different from the service design of business entities, traditionally, a business process is implemented as a BPEL (2002) flow. Zimmermann et al. (2005) described a BPEL solution design for an order management scenario. One difficulty of this approach is that changes in the process or information may affect the entire BPEL flow, making it difficult to reuse the process solution design across business scenarios. Also, the process application generated from BPEL is incomplete because of the lack of a data model. An appropriate data model matching with the BPEL messages needs to be added manually to make the application complete. In addition, as process complexity increases, the resulting BPEL flows become extremely large and hard to maintain. These difficulties are discussed in detail by Zimmermann et al. (2005).

Also, Object Oriented Analysis and Design (OOAD) (Booch, 2007) is often used to define SOA, but OOAD is concerned with micro-level abstractions such as classes, which reside at the low level of the abstraction of business services that cannot be closely mapped to business processes (Zimmerman et al., 2004). Instead, in our service design, the services defined concerns the behavior of business entities, not fine-grained information entities. These meaningful services are directly mapped to activities in business processes. Next, we describe a pilot engagement to validate this design.

APPLICATIONS OF INFORMATION-CENTRIC MODELS

Information-centric modeling has been practiced for almost a decade. The resulting models are often referred as business operation models (e.g.

Figure 4). Bhattacharya et al. (2007) summarized the value of information-centric modeling proven by business engagements as reduced complexity, capability of clearly articulating business value propositions, ability to facilitate the analysis and reconciliation of business changes, and rapid IT realizations.

Recently, we applied information-centric modeling and our transformation algorithms to create dynamic product bundling processes for an Asian bank. The focus of this engagement was to test the service design of business entities and the reusability of service components. The process scope in this engagement included (1) a campaign process for promoting product bundles targeted at customer segments, and (2) an arrangement negotiation process for selling bundled products to targeted customers with negotiable terms and conditions. To accelerate the renovation, we used reference models from IBM Information Framework (IFW) (Evernden 1996), a comprehensive set of activity-centric process models representing best practices of the financial service industry. We selected appropriate reference process models and customized them to match our business scenarios. Later, we applied our transformation algorithm and discovered four business entities: CAMPAIGN, CUSTOMER, PRODUCT and ARRANGEMENT. Each business entity was designed as a service component and successfully deployed. The complete details of this engagement, including industry challenges and business scenarios, solution design, and lessons learned, can be found in Liu et al. (2009).

This engagement not only tested our approach but also provided us an opportunity to evaluate the reusability of information-centric models. We would hope that a service component could be used as-is across business scenarios. In reality, 100% reusability is always difficult, if not impossible, to achieve, after considering necessary variations. A more realistic expectation is that only moderate changes are needed and these changes can be isolated to some portions of the process module.

In our approach, a business process is decomposed into business entities and each business entity is further divided into macro level process steps that are captured in the lifecycle model and micro level flows that are defined as composite services. In general, these macro level process steps seldom change. For example, the ARRANGEMENT lifecycle remains the same across various banking business scenarios. Micro level process steps can vary by business scenarios. For example, the arrangement activation in online banking can be quite different from that in retail branch banking. We can localize this difference to micro level process steps, i.e., atomic services or composite services associated with state transitions. Thus, changes can be minimized and the reusability of process components is improved. In addition, changes to information entities can be isolated to specific business entities.

The reusability of our service design was tested by another business engagement. The service design developed for the dynamic product bundling scenario was adapted to support an account opening process for another bank in the United States. This adaptation required little change to business entity lifecycles but major customization on composite services because of variations in business operations and legacy applications.

RELATED WORK

Having given a complete introduction to information-centric modeling and the duality between information-centric and activity-centric models, next we compare our approach with related work in the areas of business process modeling, object-oriented modeling and methodologies, component engineering, and SOA. Our information-centric approach provides a new addition to these areas.

Business process modeling has gained a strong foothold in information system disciplines. Workflow technologies have played a dominant role in this area, and traditionally, most workflow models, for example, Petri net models (van der Aalst & van Hee, 2002), ActivityFlow (Liu et al., 2004), and Event-driven Process Chains (EPC) (Sheer, 1997), are activity-centric. Issues related to activity-centric process models have been well documented in the literature (van der Aalst et al., 2005; Agrawal et al., 1997) and also discussed previously in this paper. Recently, process modeling focused on the data aspect has become an area of growing interest. A case-handling process (van der Aalst et al., 2005) is driven by the presence of data objects instead of control flows. A case is similar to the business entity concept in many respects. Document-driven workflow systems (Wang & Kumar, 2005) are designed based on data dependencies without the need for explicit control flows. In general, these data-driven approaches detail each data object managed and updated in business activities, leading to increased modeling complexity.

Information-centric modeling (which has also called business artifact-centric modeling), as a new data-driven approach, addresses the complexity issue by capturing the deep structures of data objects and grouping data objects into a few business entities (or business artifacts). Nigam and Caswell (2003) introduced the concept of business artifacts and information-centric processing of artifact lifecycles. Kumaran et al. (2003) developed adaptive business documents as the programming model for information-centric business processes and this model later evolved into adaptive business objects (Nandi & Kumaran, 2005). Bhattacharya et al. (2005) described a successful business engagement which applies business artifact techniques to industrialize discovery processes in pharmaceutical research. Liu et al. (2007) formulated nine commonly used patterns in business operation models and developed a computational model based on Petri Nets. Bhattacharya, Gerede, et al. (2007) provided a formal model for artifact-centric business processes with complexity results concerning static analysis of the semantics of such processes. While previous work

on information-centric process modeling mainly focuses on completing this modeling framework from theoretical development to practical engagements, our work bridges the gap between activity-centric and information-centric models and shows the duality between them. In reality, companies often document their processes as activity-centric models. Industry practitioners in business process management can start with these models and use the duality to derive information-centric models to directly harvest the value of information-centric modeling that was summarized by Bhattacharya, Caswell, et al. (2007).

Object-oriented analysis and design (Booch, 2007) is another area related to information centric modeling. OOAD is considered an information system implementation approach, while workflows are used as a conceptual business modeling approach. To develop business process applications based on OOAD, often a transformation is needed to bridge these two approaches. For example, Josten and Purao (2002) provided a mapping between workflow models and object-oriented programming languages based on ontological models. Our information-centric modeling was motivated by OOAD. However, it differs from OOAD in that OOAD is concerned with granular data objects and models a system as a group of interacting objects, while an information-centric model consists of interacting business entities. A typical application, for example, a claim management system, can contain hundreds of data objects. It is always challenging to manage such a large group of data objects and capture their interactions. In addition, the implementation model of business entities can be directly derived from information-centric process models without the need for any extra mapping (Kumaran et al., 2003). Existence dependency (Snoeck & Dedene, 1998) is another object-oriented conceptual modeling technique. This technique is similar to information-centric modeling in that they both identify the structural relationships between data objects. However, this technique, like most OOAD approaches, focuses on the behavior of individual data objects. The information-centric modeling approach, on the other hand, groups them into a few business entities, and then decomposes business processes into interacting business entity lifecycles. The resulting modularity increases process comprehensibility for business stakeholders and simplifies solution implementation.

Another thread of related work is the use of state machines to model object lifecycles. Industries often define data objects and standardize their lifecycles as state machines to facilitate interoperability between industry partners and enforce legal regulations (Ryndina et al., 2007; Küster et al., 2007). Instead of assuming predefined business objects, our approach discovers business entities from process models and then defines their lifecycles as an alternative representation of process models. In addition, event-driven process modeling, for example, Event-driven Process Chains (EPC) (Sheer, 1997), also describes object lifecycles glued by events, such as "material in stock". Our approach in this sense is also event-driven, as each state change of a business entity can be conceptually viewed as an event. However, EPC is still an activity-centric approach as an EPC model focuses on functions and their execution orders.

Some other notable studies that are related to our work are in the areas of component reengineering and process modularization. Component-Based Development (CBD) is a prominent methodology in information system implementation and development. Herzum and Sims (2000) define a business component as an entity that realizes a business concept. A component is reusable and self-contained, and provides services through well-defined interfaces (Huang et al., 2006). From this point of view, a business entity is a well-defined component. The key to CBD is to define components. Dahanayake et al. (2003) pointed out that current CBD methodologies handle components mainly at implementation and deployment phases, not throughout the whole system development life-

cycle. For example, Huang et al. (2006) provided an approach to reengineering a legacy system to component-based systems by transforming data objects into components. The transformed components may be very granular and very specific to the legacy system. Dahanayake et al. (2003) suggested that a component be a technology-independent concept capturing business processes and requirements at a higher level, and be seamlessly transformed into implementation and development phases. Our information-centric modeling provides exactly such a way to define components. Business entities can be derived from traditional activity-centric process models. Each business entity is naturally a component characterized by a self-contained data model, a behavior model, and interfaces for interacting with other components. Therefore, our approach actually modularizes business processes into components. Basu and Blanning (2003) provided another modularization approach based on metagraphs, where data flows between activities can be captured as metapaths. Achieving process modularization is to find independent sub-metagraphs. A practical limitation of this approach is that some data objects (typically, dominant data objects, e.g., Claim in Figure 1) can be both an input and an output of some activities to form many cycles, and therefore, independent sub-metagraphs may not be found.

Finally, the advent of SOA represents an opportunity to design cutting-edge information systems. The real challenges in SOA lie in how to construct service abstractions systematically to align with business processes and also to support reusability and flexibility (Zimmerman et al., 2004). Approaches to structured design of SOA solutions are still lacking in both industry practice and academic research (Arsanjani et al., 2008, Zimmerman et al., 2004). Information-Centric modeling naturally leads to a structured SOA. In this design, services manipulate the behavior or information content of business entity, are closely mapped to activities in business processes, and can be understood by business users. Thus, these services are not defined at granular data objects and are likely to be composite services defined from the point view of business users. Each service definition is reusable but its implementation can be easily adapted for different business scenarios through micro-level service composition. Li et al. (2007) provides an approach to migrating legacy systems to SOA. In this approach, services are defined based on external entities interacting with other elements in EPC models. But it is possible that a large trunk of a process is identified as a single service if there are no external entities in this trunk, leading to inconsistent service granularity. Also the discovered services may be proprietary to the legacy systems and their reusability may be limited. SOMA (Arsanjani et al., 2008) is a software development lifecycle method for designing and building SOA-based solutions. This method provides prescriptive tasks and normative guidance for designing services. Our approach provides a systematic way to identify and specify services and service components aligned with SOMA guidelines.

CONCLUSION AND FUTURE WORK

In this paper, we have presented an approach to discovering business entities from activity-centric process models and transforming such models into information-centric business process models, and illustrated this approach with a comprehensive example. We have also formally demonstrated the duality between these two types of models. In practice, we found that clients often have their processes documented as activity-centric models. The transformation reuses the activity-centric models, greatly accelerates the development of information-centric models, and provides an opportunity to harvest the proven value of information-centric models immediately. Our engagement practice has demonstrated that information-centric modeling is advantageous in addressing the gap between business and IT (Bhattacharya et al., 2008).

In addition, the information-centric modeling approach leads to not only componentized business processes but also systematic service design, a significant advantage over activity-centric modeling. We have provided an intuitive way to design each business entity as a service component with well-defined interfaces following the principles of SOA. To implement business processes in SOA, the key is to identify services and service components at the right level of granularity, but systematic methods for doing so in an automatic or a semi-automatic manner are lacking (Zimmerman et al., 2004). Our approach fills this gap by providing an algorithm to componentize business processes into service components and design services that can be closely mapped to processes. Our recent pilot engagement also demonstrated the effectiveness and reusability of this SOA design.

When an information-centric model is derived from an activity-centric model, certainly the quality of the information-centric model and the subsequent SOA design is determined by that of the activity-centric model. Thus, when an activity-centric model only focuses on control flows between activities and has incomplete information specification, we do not suggest applying the transformation algorithm directly to the model without completing the information perspective. The conditions for applying the transformation algorithm have been discussed previously.

We are currently developing a tool based on this approach and applying this approach to renovating business processes for the financial industry. Another research direction is to relax the concept of domination so that business entities can be discovered from models with incomplete or incorrect specifications of input or output information entities.

ACKNOWLEDGMENT

The authors thank Kumar Bhaskaran, David Cohn, Anil Nigam, John Vergo and other colleagues for their helpful discussions and comments.

REFERENCES

Agrawal, R., Imielinski, T., & Swami, A. (1993). ng Association Rules Between Sets of Items in Large Database. In *Proceedings of ACM-SIGMOD 93* (pp. 207-216).

Alonso, G., Agrawal, D., El Abbadi, A., & Mohan, C. (1997). Functionalities and Limitations of Current Workflow Management Systems. *IEEE Expert, 12*(5).

Arsanjani, A., Ghosh, S., Allam, A., Abdollah, T., Ganapathy, S., & Holley, K. (2008). SOMA: A method for developing service-oriented solutions. *IBM Systems Journal, 47*(3), 377–396. doi:10.1147/sj.473.0377

Baldwin, C. Y., & Clark, K. B. (2000). Design Rules: *Vol. 1. The Power of Modularity*. Cambridge, MA: MIT Press.

Basu, A., & Blanning, R. W. (2003). Synthesis and Decomposition of Processes in Organizations. *Information Systems Research, 14*(4), 337–355. doi:10.1287/isre.14.4.337.24901

Bhattacharya, K., Caswell, N., Kumaran, S., Nigam, A., & Wu, F. (2007). Artifact-centric Operational Modeling: Lessons learned from engagements. *IBM Systems Journal, 46*(4). doi:10.1147/sj.464.0703

Bhattacharya, K., Gerede, C., Richard, H., Liu, R., & Su, J. (2007). Towards Formal Analysis of Artifact-Centric Business Process Models. In *Proceedings of Business Process Management (BPM 2007)* (LNCS 4714, pp. 288-304).

Bhattacharya, K., Guttman, R., Lyman, K., Heath, F. F. III, Kumaran, S., & Nandi, P. (2005). A model-driven approach to industrializing discovery processes in pharmaceutical research. *IBM Systems Journal, 44*(1), 145–162. doi:10.1147/sj.441.0145

Booch, G. (2007). *Object-oriented Analysis and Design with Applications* (3rd ed.). Reading, MA: Addison-Wesley.

BPEL. (2003). *Business Process Execution Language for Web Services, version 1.1*. BEA, IBM, Microsoft, SAP and Siebel Systems.

Chen, P. (1976). The entity-relationship model—toward a unified view of data. *ACM Transactions on Database Systems, 1*(1), 9–36. doi:10.1145/320434.320440

Cormen, T. H., Leiserson, C. E., Rivest, R. L., & Stein, C. (2001). *Introduction to algorithms* (2nd ed.). Cambridge, MA: MIT Press.

Dahanayake, A., Sol, H., & Stojanovic, Z. (2003). Methodology Evaluation Framework for Component-Based System Development. *Journal of Database Management, 14*(1), 1–26.

Erickson, J., & Siau, K. (2008). Web Services, Service-Oriented Computing, and Service-Oriented Architecture: Separating Hype from Reality. *Journal of Database Management, 19*(3), 42–54.

Evernden, R. (1996). The Information Frame-Work. *IBM Systems Journal, 35*(1), 37–68. doi:10.1147/sj.351.0037

Hammer, M. (2004). Deep change: How operational innovation can transform your company. *Harvard Business Review*, 84–93.

Herzum, P., & Sims, O. (2000). *Business Component Factory: A comprehensive Overview of Component-based Development for the Enterprise*. New York: Wiley.

Huang, S., Hung, S., Yen, D., Li, S., & Wu, C. (2006). Enterprise Application System Reengineering: A Business Component Approach. *Journal of Database Management, 17*(3), 66–91.

IBM. (2004). *IBM Insurance Application Architecture, version 7.1*. Retrieved from http://www-03.ibm.com/industries/financialservices/doc/content/solution/278918103.html

Joosten, S., & Purao, S. (2002). A rigorous Approach for Mapping Workflows to Object-Oriented IS Models. *Journal of Database Management, 13*(4), 1–19.

Karmarkar, U. (2004). Will You Survive the Services Revolution? *Harvard Business Review, 82*(6), 100–107.

Kiepuszewski, B., Hofstede, A. H. M., & Bussler, C. (2000). On Structured Workflow Modeling. In *Proceedings of CAiSE'2000* (LNCS 1797).

Kumaran, S. (2004). *Model Driven Enterprise*. Paper presented at the Global Integration Summit 2004, Banff, Canada.

Kumaran, S., Liu, R., & Wu, F. Y. (2008). On the Duality of Information-Centric and Activity-Centric Models of Business Processes. In *Proceedings of the 20th International Conference on Advanced Information Systems Engineering (CAiSE '08)* (LNCS 5074, pp. 32-47).

Kumaran, S., Nandi, P., Heath, T., Bhaskaran, K., & Das, R. (2003). ADoc-oriented programming. In *Proceedings of the Symposium on Applications and the Internet (SAINT)* (pp. 334-343).

Küster, J. M., Ryndina, K., & Gall, H. (2007). Generation of Business Process Models for Object Life Cycle Compliance. In *Proceedings of the 5th International Conference on Business Process Management (BPM 2007)* (LNCS 4714, pp. 165-181).

Li, S., Huang, S., Yen, D. C., & Chang, C. (2007). Migrating Legacy Information Systems to Web Service Architecture. *Journal of Database Management, 18*(4), 1–25.

Liu, L., Pu, C., & Ruiz, D. D. (2004). A systematic Approach to Flexible Specification, Composition, and Restructuring of Workflow Activities. *Journal of Database Management, 15*(1), 1–40.

Liu, R., Bhattacharya, K., & Wu, F. Y. (2007). *Modeling Business Contexture and Behavior Using Business Artifacts.* Paper presented at the 19th International Conference on Advanced Information Systems Engineering (CAiSE'07).

Liu, R., Wu, F. Y., Patnaik, Y., & Kumaran, S. (2009). *Business Entities: An SOA Approach to Progressive Core Banking Renovation.* Paper presented at the IEEE International Conference on Services Computing (SCC 2009).

Mendling, J., Reijers, H. A., & Cardoso, J. (2007). What Makes Process Models Understandable? In *Proceedings of the 5th International Conference on Business Process Management (BPM 2007)* (LNCS 4714, pp. 48-63).

Nandi, P., & Kumaran, S. (2005). Adaptive business objects – a new component model for business integration. In *Proceedings of the International Conference on Enterprise Information Systems* (pp. 179-188).

Nigam, A., & Caswell, N. S. (2003). Business artifacts: An approach to operational specification. *IBM Systems Journal, 42*(3), 428–445. doi:10.1147/sj.423.0428

Reijers, H. A., & Mendling, J. (2008). Modularity in Process Models: Review and Effects. In M. Dumas, M. Reichert, & M.-C. Shan (Eds.), *Proceedings of the 6th International Conference Business Process Management (BPM 2008)* (LNCS 5240, pp. 20-35).

Ryndina, K., Küster, J. M., & Gall, H. (2007). Consistency of Business Process Models and Object Life Cycles. In *Proceedings of the 1st Workshop Quality in Modeling* (LNCS 4364, pp. 80-90).

SCA. (2007). *Service Component Architecture, Version 1.0*. Retrieved from http://www.osoa.org/display/ Main/Service+Component+Architecture+Home

Scheer, A. W. (1997). *Business Process Engineering: Reference Models for Industrial Enterprises* (2nd ed.). New York: Springer.

Snoeck, M., & Dedene, G. (1998). Existence Dependency: The key to semantic integrity between structural and behavioural aspects of object types. *IEEE Transactions on Software Engineering, 24*(4), 233–251. doi:10.1109/32.677182

van der Aalst, W. M. P., & van Hee, K. M. (2002). *Workflow Management: Models, Methods, and Systems*. Cambridge, MA: MIT Press.

van der Aalst, W. M. P., Weske, M., & Grunbauer, D. (2005). Case handling: a new paradigm for business process support. *Data & Knowledge Engineering, 53*, 129–162. doi:10.1016/j.datak.2004.07.003

Wang, J., & Kumar, A. (2005). A Framework for Document-Driven Workflow Systems. In *Proceedings of Business Process Management, 2005*, 285–301. doi:10.1007/11538394_19

WfMC. (1995). *The Workflow Reference Model, Issue 1.1, Document Number TC00-1003*. Winchester, UK: Work-flow Management Coalition.

Whitehead, E. J. (2002). Uniform comparison of data models using containment modeling, In *Proceedings of the thirteenth ACM conference on Hypertext and hypermedia* (pp. 182-191).

Zimmerman, O., Krogdahl, P., & Gee, C. (2004). *Elements of Service-Oriented Analysis and Design*. Retrieved from http://www.ibm.com/developerworks/ library/ws-soad1/

Zimmermann, O., Doubrovski, V., Grundler, J., & Hogg, K. (2005). Service-oriented architecture and business process choreography in an order management scenario: rationale, concepts, lessons learned. In *Proceedings of the 20th SIGPLAN Conference on Object-Oriented Programming, Systems, Languages, and Applications* (pp. 301-312).

This work was previously published in International Journal of Database Management, Volume 21, Issue 4, edited by Keng Siau, pp. 14-34, copyright 2010 by IGI Publishing (an imprint of IGI Global).

Chapter 15
An Integrated Query Relaxation Approach Adopting Data Abstraction and Fuzzy Relation

Soon-Young Huh
Korea Advanced Institute of Science and Technology, Korea

Kae-Hyun Moon
Samsung Electronics Co., Korea

Jinsoo Park
Seoul National University, Korea

ABSTRACT

This paper proposes a cooperative query answering approach that relaxes query conditions to provide approximate answers by utilizing similarity relationships between data values. The proposed fuzzy abstraction hierarchy (FAH) represents a similarity relationship based on the integrated notion of data abstraction and fuzzy relations. Based on FAH, the authors develop query relaxation operators like query generalization, approximation, and specialization of a value. Compared with existing approaches, FAH supports more effective information retrieval by processing various kinds of cooperative queries through elaborate relaxation control and providing ranked query results according to fitness scores. Moreover, FAH reduces maintenance cost by decreasing the number of similarity relationships to be managed.

1. INTRODUCTION

Query processing based on conventional database systems often fails to provide the information users really want if the user does not provide a precise query statement. Database systems may return null responses when the exact answers to queries do not exist. Conversely, the non-empty responses implying a qualified data set to queries may not satisfy the user who wants not only exact answers but also additional approximate answers. Furthermore, the schema and semantics of databases are often too complex for ordinary users to understand in their entirety to compose intended queries.

DOI: 10.4018/978-1-61350-471-0.ch015

If a query processing system understands the schema and semantics of the database, it will be able to return informative responses beyond a query's requested answer set and greatly help the user obtain relevant answers in various decision support application systems. To support such intelligent query processing, a number of cooperative query answering approaches have been introduced, which provide a human-oriented interface to a database system by facilitating the relaxation of query conditions to produce approximate answers. Typically, cooperative query answering analyzes the intent of a query and transforms the query into a new query of greater scope by relaxing the original query conditions (Liu & Chu, 1993; Chu, Yang, Chiang, Minock, Chow, & Larson, 1996; Chu, Yang, & Chow, 1996; Chu & Chen, 1994; Liu & Chu, 2007; Cuppens & Demolombe, 1989; Cuzzocrea, 2005, 2007; De Sean & Furtado, 1998; Godfrey, 1997; Huh & Lee, 2001; Huh & Moon, 2000; Hung, Wermter, & Smith, 2004; Marshall, Chen & Madhusudan, 2005; Mao & Chu, 2007; Motro, 1988, 1990; Minker, 1998; Shin, Huh, Park, & Lee, 2008).

The cooperative query answering approach can be adopted as a key concept in various decision support application systems requiring intelligent and cooperative database access methods. A typical example application is a human resource management system shown in the prototype system in the paper. Specifically, in a knowledge-oriented consulting company having thousands of consultant resources spread globally, approximate query relaxation system will provide very effective consultant search capabilities, identifying appropriate candidate consultants having adequate domain knowledge and project engagement experiences for a project under consideration. To find an appropriate candidate for a marketing related project, a project manager might start by using vague search criteria such as major and career: "Find a marketing professional whose major is management or other similar field, and who has at least four years experience engaged in market-

ing project." Without intelligent assistance, the manager is likely to obtain either a null result to the query or an excess of answers that might not be sorted in any usable way. Additional examples benefiting from the cooperative querying can be found in a wide spectrum of applications ranging from geographic information systems to medical diagnostic systems where queries can be specified graphically or literally and incrementally on digital maps or symptom records, which greatly improves the querying capabilities. In the GIS, a pilot can ask an abstract query, "Find an appropriately-sized nearby airport where a Boeing 777 can land." The approximate query is translated to a distance range based on the position of the airport, and Boeing 777 is translated into the required runway conditions at the airport. The cooperative query processing systems will return relevant associative airport information such as runway condition and distance closeness with ranks. Also, in medical diagnostic systems, search conditions can be expanded for finding information on a rare illness.

To provide a wider range of approximate answers by relaxing search conditions, cooperative query answering requires a human expert's knowledge of the underlying database semantics (e.g., similarity strength between data values). A variety of knowledge representation frameworks have been researched, including the abstraction hierarchy (Cai, Cercone, & Han, 1993; Liu & Chu, 2005; Chu, Yang, Chiang, et al., 1996; Chu, Yang, & Chow, 1996; Liu & Chu, 2007; Huh & Lee, 2001; Huh & Moon, 2000; Shin et al., 2008), the semantic distance (Motro, 1988, 1990), and the logic model (De Sean & Furtado, 1998; Godfrey, 1997). However, each framework is limited for effective cooperative query answering with respect to the following requirements:

- *Diversity.* The knowledge representation framework should support users with varying levels of expertise in information retrieval. The novice user tends to write queries in simplistic forms because she does not have a good understanding of the semantics of the database schema and detailed schema knowledge, and thus often gets very limited results. If the user could express the requests in a simple but conceptual level and consequently obtain vague but richer results, the user would have a better understanding of the database contents and effectively reach the final results. Furthermore, by facilitating reduction of the query scope of conceptual queries, the user may pose queries at a more concrete level and end up with satisfactory results after a session of interactive query relaxation control. Thus, the ability to process diverse cooperative queries is necessary for handling the various requests of diverse users.

- *Measurability*. The framework should provide an appropriate measure to help users determine the priority of each approximate answer (e.g., fitness score) in the query result set. To this end, a measure of similarity relationship between data values is required. A Jaccard's score is a good candidate as the similarity measure. With such a measure, users can obtain ranked result sets which they can use to perform elaborate and flexible query relaxation control through user interaction.

- *Creation/Maintenance*. The framework should help the expert effectively create and maintain semantic knowledge. Although new data values are continuously added to the underlying database, the expert acts to preserve the measure criteria that has been used for assessing the similarity relationship among data values. Simultaneously, the maintenance cost should be kept low even when the number of data values increases enormously as the database expands.

To overcome these limitations, this paper proposes a new knowledge representation framework called fuzzy abstraction hierarchy (FAH) which integrates the abstraction hierarchy and the semantic distance approach. Based on FAH, we develop query relaxation operators including generalization, specialization, and approximation of data values. This paper is organized as follows. The second section reviews prior related approaches. The third section introduces FAH. In the fourth section, we develop basic query relaxation operations for cooperative query answering and introduce a prototype system to demonstrate a way of implementing the query interface. The conclusion is presented in the fifth section.

2. OVERVIEW OF RELATED APPROACHES

Query relaxation is performed by associating the values in the query condition to other related values on the basis of predefined semantic relationships between data values. Thus, an appropriate knowledge representation framework is needed for human experts to extract and manage the semantic relationships between data values. Among previous approaches, the semantic distance and abstraction hierarchy approaches are commonly used to represent semantic knowledge from the underlying database.

2.1 Semantic Distance Approach

The semantic distance approach introduces the notion of distance (i.e., scalar values) to measure the strength of similarity between scalar data values. Generally, there exist two kinds of data values in databases: quantitative and qualitative. For quantitative data values, the distances can be derived by computation based on numerical operators, for instance, the absolute value of the difference (Motro, 1988, 1990). For qualitative data values, the approach determines the distance based on the *semantic distance* between two values. Even though qualitative data values may not have an explicit numerical semantic relationship, the expert administrator may establish the semantic distance between the values in numerical terms that can be stored in a table. The distances are differently assigned by different domain experts; hence, the approach needs to be adaptable to the individual views and priorities of the experts (Motro, 1988).

This approach has the advantage of ease and efficiency in developing query relaxation algorithms because numerical distances between data values are easy to compute. The distances can also be used as a measure to determine the rank of each answer, which helps users find useful information related to the retrieved answers. However, this approach is limited due to the difficulty of transforming quantitative and qualitative data values into a uniform numerical measure. In addition, it is difficult to assess the similarity distance between qualitative data values objectively and consistently because there are no supplementary criteria apart from the expert's subjective criteria. In other words, the similarity distances are totally determined by the expert's subjective criteria only. Semantic distances need to be established for every value pair; thus, the number of value pairs that should be managed quickly becomes unmanageable with real world application systems. As a result, the maintenance cost increases and the consistency of the distance measure is jeopardized.

2.2 The Abstraction Hierarchy Approach

The abstraction hierarchy approach adopts the abstract representation of data values and replaces the values by the abstract concepts to which they belong. The abstract representations form a data abstraction hierarchy where similar values are clustered by the abstract concepts and the individual abstract concepts are related to one another by a certain abstraction function or by abstraction similarities. Thus, this approach is specifically

advantageous when the data values are qualitative and categorical.

To relax a query condition, this approach exploits query *abstraction/refinement* methods that rely on the value abstraction hierarchy. A query abstraction is accomplished by replacing data values from the query with more abstract values from the hierarchy. The resulting query is thus considered more general with a relaxed condition than the original. The general query is then refined into a set of specific queries to be evaluated against the underlying database.

The knowledge abstraction hierarchy (KAH) (Huh & Lee, 2001; Huh & Moon, 2000; Shin et al., 2008) extended previous abstraction hierarchy approaches by capturing not only value abstraction but also domain abstraction knowledge from underlying databases. KAH can support more effective query processing by increasing the diversity of admitted queries and by accommodating dynamic abstraction knowledge maintenance.

In KAH, three semantic relationships exist between data values (i.e., parent, child, and siblings viewed in terms of a tree structure): abstraction, specification, and approximation. A *specific value* (i.e., child) in a lower *abstraction level* is abstracted (generalized) into an *abstract value* (i.e., parent) in a higher abstraction level and the abstract value can be abstracted further into a more abstract value. The highest abstraction level is the *depth* of the hierarchy. The abstract value is called *n-level abstract value* of the specific value, where *n* is the difference in the abstraction levels of the values. Among the values existing in the same abstraction level, *n-level siblings* are defined to be composed of values whose nearest same abstract value is *n*-level abstract value.

Figure 1 shows an example of the KAH of college major. Management is the 1-level abstract value of Finance, and Business is the 2-level abstract value of Finance. Conversely, Finance is the 1-level specific value of Management and the 2-level specific value of Business. Finance, Accounting, and Marketing are 1-level siblings

Figure 1. Example of college majors as a KAH

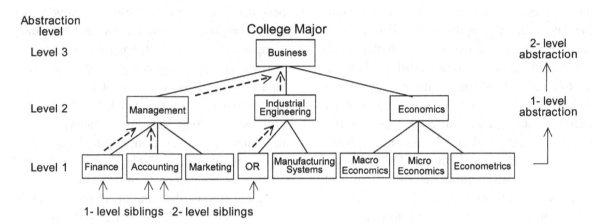

because their nearest same abstract value is 1-level abstract value Management. Accounting and OR are 2-level siblings. In KAH, the approximate values of a value and their similarity distance are described as follows:

- *Monotonously Increasing Range of Approximate Values.* The *n-level approximate values* of a value are restricted to the values ranging from its 1-level siblings to *n*-level siblings that have the same *n*-level abstract value where $n \geq 1$.
- *Uniform Similarity Strength.* The similarity distances between the approximate values are uniform.

The range of approximate values depends on the abstraction level and can be controlled by adjusting the abstraction level. For example, in Figure 1 the approximation of Finance returns {Accounting, Marketing} within the 1-level abstraction because they have the same 1-level abstract value, Management, but it can be extended to {Accounting, Marketing, OR, Manufacturing Systems, Macro Economics, Micro Economics, Econometrics} within the 2-level abstraction. In other words, Manufacturing Systems and OR are not approximate values of Finance within the 1-level abstraction, but they become approximate

values of Finance within the 2-level abstraction as a result of the range's extension by increasing the abstraction level.

Like other data abstraction approaches (Liu & Chu, 2005; Chu, Yang, Chiang, et al., 1996; Liu & Chu, 2007), KAH does not define the measure of the semantic relationship between the values in a hierarchy. Thus, the approximate values have uniform similarity distances with one another because the data abstraction approaches cannot discriminate the similarity distance between the values (*the uniform similarity strength property*). Although the range of approximate values can expand as the abstraction level increases, the similarity distances between the values in the range are always uniform. For example, when approximate values of Finance are requested within the 1-level abstraction, every 1-level sibling should be returned including Marketing and Accounting. In the same way, {Finance, Accounting, OR, Manufacturing Systems, Marketing, Macro Economics, Micro Economics, Econometrics} are uniformly approximate with one another within the 2-level abstraction.

Due to the uniform similarity strength property, the data abstraction approach cannot provide query results ranked by the similarity distances (i.e., fitness scores) from the target value in the query condition. Users themselves should

363

determine the importance of each answer in the query result without any assistance. Likewise, the data abstraction approach has limitations in flexible query relaxation control, which requires the discrimination of similarity distance between approximate values. Specifically, the uniformness property may produce too many query results in each relaxation step because the approximation of a value cannot selectively return its approximate values according to the similarity strength. Recently the abstraction hierarchy approach extends its application into XML data (Chu & Chen, 1994) as well as free-text form database (Liu & Chu, 2005).

2.3 Rule-Based Approach

The rule-based approach (Cuppens & Demolombe, 1989; Hemerly, Casanova, & Furtado, 1994) adopts first-order logic as its formal framework and delineates semantic information about data objects and data integrity constraints using first-order formulas over a set of (base, built-in, derived) predicates. In this approach, the entire database is understood as a set of base predicates, and a database query consists of a predicate rule whereby searching information is specified with free variables. The query is answered through conflict resolution and inference mechanisms, and query relaxation is carried out by coordinating the integrity constraints. The weaknesses of this approach include a lack of systematic organization for guiding the query relaxation process and a less intuitive query answering process.

2.4 Fuzzy Database Approach

The fuzzy database approach (Bosc, Kraft, & Petry, 2005) supports various kinds of fuzziness derived from the data itself and linguistic queries. It assumes that data objects in each domain can be assigned a degree of similarity between 0 and 1. In addition, the knowledge base can store various kinds of imprecise information such as mixed hair

color (i.e., 0.6 brown and 0.4 black) and a certain person's residence (i.e., Boston or New York). Users compose approximate queries using fuzzy comparators such as much-greater-than. Relations are extended to accept fuzzy values or to allow values that are sets of domain objects.

A comparison between FAH and other approaches adopting semantic distance, abstraction hierarchy, fuzzy database, and production rule is summarized in Table 1, where individual approaches are compared in terms of knowledge representation method and query processing diversity. Compared with the semantic distance, abstraction hierarchy, and fuzzy database approaches that can handle the approximate or conceptual queries, FAH aims at handling the approximate and conceptual queries as well as providing fitness scores of answers. More precisely, the strengths of FAH lie at least in three aspects. FAH can perform the more elaborate query relaxation control (i.e., approximate and conceptual queries) through adjusting either threshold similarity strengths or abstraction levels. It also provides the ranked query results, allowing interactive calibration of search criteria until the satisfactory query results are obtained. Finally, FAH facilitates more efficient maintenance and search of the similarity relations. Conclusively, it attempts to integrate the semantic distance and abstraction hierarchy approaches and can thus mutually supplement them by embracing their individual advantages.

Weaknesses of FAH also exist. Assigning the similarity metric to data items still has the subjectivity weakness since a certain expert user is involved in the assigning process. Thus, the similarity strengths can be contextual and vary depending on the user. We assume the similarity strength metric used in a FAH has been discussed sufficiently and commonly agreed by the user's whole community to remedy the subjectivity.

Table 1. Comparison between FAH and other approaches

\ Characteristics Approach	Knowledge Representation Methods		Cooperative Query Processing Diversity			Limitations Compared with FAH
	What to Represent as Semantic Knowledge	How to Represent Semantic Knowledge	Available Types of Cooperative Queries	Availability of Fitness Scores	How to Control Query Relaxation	
Semantic Distance (Motro, 1988, 1990)	− Similarity strength for every value pair	− Numerical distance	− Approximate Query	Yes	− Threshold value for similarity strength	− Similarity strength evaluation depends only upon expert's subjective criteria − High maintenance cost due to exponentially growing number of value pairs
Abstraction Hierarchy (Cai et al., 1993; Liu & Chu, 2005; Chu, Yang, Chiang, et al., 1996; Chu, Yang, & Chow, 1996; Liu & Chu, 2007; Huh & Lee, 2001; Huh & Moon, 2000)	− Generalization/ specialization relationships between data values	− Data abstraction	− Approximate Query − Conceptual Query	No	− Adjusting abstraction levels	− Absence of a quantitative similarity measure
Fuzzy Database (Bosc et al., 2005; Marshall et al., 2006)	− Attribute-level fuzziness − Tuple-level fuzziness − Linguistic fuzziness	− Fuzzy values − Set-valued attribute values	− Approximate Query	Yes	− Threshold value for membership degree	− Un-normalized database relations
Logic (Cuppens & Demolombe, 1989; Hemerly et al., 1994)	− Fact − Rule − Integrity constraints	− First-order formula	− Intentional Query	No	− Conflict resolution and integrity constraints coordination	− Lack of systematic organization for guiding the query relaxation process − Less intuitive query answering process
FAH	− Similarity strength between two data values − Generalization/ specialization relationships between data values	− Data abstraction − Fuzzy relation	− Approximate Query − Conceptual Query	Yes	− Threshold value for similarity strength − Abstraction level	− Blending of semantic distance and abstraction hierarchy models − Embracing the advantages of the two models

3. THE FUZZY ABSTRACTION HIERARCHY

In this section, we propose a new knowledge representation framework, FAH, which can remedy the limitations of existing approaches by integrating the KAH and semantic distance approaches. To integrate these two approaches, we adapt the discriminated similarity strength of semantic distance approach into KAH (Motro, 1988, 1990).

3.1 The Concept of Similarity Strength in FAH

To adapt the discriminated similarity strength into FAH, the following two propositions which modify the uniform similarity strength property of KAH are needed.

Proposition 1: Discriminated Similarity Strength.
The similarity strength between approximate values can be different from one another and be represented by numerical values.

Proposition 2: Monotonously Decreasing Strength.
The similarity strength between $(n+1)$-level siblings is smaller than those between n-level siblings, where $n \geq 1$.

Proposition 1 states that the numerically represented similarity strengths (denoted by μ) between the values within a range of n-level approximate values need not be equal. For example, in Figure 2 Finance is shown to be more approximate with Accounting than with Marketing, even though all three are 1-level siblings. Proposition 1 meets the *measurability requirement* needed to provide query results ranked by strength (e.g., fitness scores). Additionally, more elaborate value approximation can be executed for query relaxation according to the discriminated similarity strength. Cooperative query answering can select only the values that have similarity strengths greater than

a certain threshold value. Thus, query relaxation can be controlled more elaborately as compared to previous data abstraction approaches where only the abstraction level could be controlled.

Proposition 2 describes the monotonousness property of decreasing similarity strength with respect to the abstraction level. The similarity strength between n-level siblings monotonously decreases as the abstraction level n increases. For example, although Finance, Accounting, and OR are approximate values in the 2-level abstraction range, the similarity strength between Finance and OR (i.e., 2-level siblings) must be smaller than that between Finance and Accounting (i.e., 1-level siblings). This proposition, related to the data abstraction level, can be utilized as a supplementary criterion for measuring the similarity strengths and can remedy the shortcomings of semantic distance approaches (i.e., a lack of supplementary criteria). Specifically, in measuring the similarity distance, data abstraction can be used for grouping more similar values. As a result, larger similarity strengths between data values that can be grouped into siblings within a lower abstraction level can be measured. The only problem is that the administrator must assign the similarity strengths to satisfy Proposition 2 in case a large number of values exist at an abstraction level in the hierarchy. This will be discussed later in the paper.

Figure 2. Fuzzy abstraction hierarchy

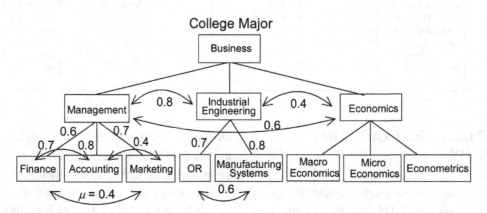

To implement the discriminated similarity strength, FAH adopts the notion of fuzzy relation instead of similarity distance of the semantic distance approach. Fuzzy relations that have been used for determining the strength of the relationship between two objects in fuzzy sets reduce the cost of constructing and maintaining a consistent structure of similarity strengths by providing the theoretical basis and fuzzy operators for deriving similarity strengths.

Ordinarily, when two objects, a and b, have a certain relationship, they can be represented as an ordered pair (a, b). The collection of all ordered pairs that have the same relationship is called relation R. For instance, if $A=\{a\}$ and $B=\{b\}$ are collections of objects denoted generically by a and b, then a subset of $A \times B$, called a relation from A to B, is a collection of ordered pairs (a, b). For a relation R, one often writes $(a, b) \in R$ or $R \subseteq A \times B$ to mean that a and b have the relation R.

In the fuzzy theory, a fuzzy set is a class of objects with a continuum of grades of membership. Such a set is characterized by a membership function that assigns each object a *grade of membership* ranging between 0 and 1. The membership function can be applied to relation R, which results in the fuzzy relation and can be interpreted as the strength of the relationship. Thus, this paper adopts the fuzzy relation as a similarity strength between the values as follows: The membership function on R, μ_R: $V \times V \rightarrow [0, 1]$, where V is the set of values in FAH and R is the similarity relation between the values. We will refer to the number μ_R as the *similarity strength* between data values.

For example, the similarity strength between Finance and Accounting in Figure 2 can be expressed as μ_R(Finance, Accounting) = 0.7, which indicates that the strength of the similarity relation between Finance and Accounting is 0.7. Finance has a stronger similarity strength with Accounting than with Marketing because μ_R(Finance, Accounting) is greater than μ_R(Finance, Marketing). Proposition 2 can be rewritten with the member-

ship function as follows: $\mu_R(v_1, v_2) > \mu_R(v_1, v_3)$, if v_1 and v_2 are i-level siblings and v_1 and v_3 are j-level siblings where $i < j$.

As mentioned in the end of the Section 2, the proposed FAH approach has weakness in assigning the similarity metric to data items since the similarity strengths can vary depending on the user and application. Specifically, Accounting and Finance may be similar for an academic researcher. They may be very different for professional practitioners. In this paper, we assume there is a similarity strength metric that is commonly agreed in the user's community.

3.2 Implementation of Discriminated Similarity Strength

After an FAH instance is constructed on the basis of data abstraction, the administrator assigns a numerical similarity strength between data values by analyzing the semantic relationships. If every pair of values in the hierarchy is considered to determine their strengths, then the number of pairs to be measured increases enormously as the underlying database expands. In measuring the strength, a great number of pairs may cause difficulty in satisfying Proposition 2.

Thus, the administrator needs a method to decrease the number of pairs for explicit consideration, while at the same time he should be able to obtain the similarity strength for every pair of values. The fuzzy relation approach that we adopt in lieu of the semantic distance approach provides the theoretical basis for this. In the hierarchy, the similarity strengths for some pairs are measured explicitly, and a *fuzzy operator* that performs the composition of the fuzzy relations between data values can derive the similarity strengths for the other pairs. We will develop a method and an operator from the structural features of the FAH that is constructed on the basis of the data abstraction.

Proposition 3: Influence of Parents upon Similarity Strength. The similarity strength between

Figure 3. Discriminative similarity strength in FAH

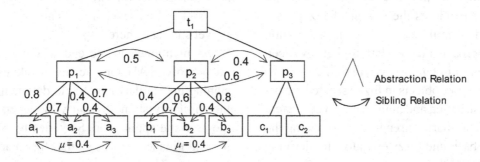

1-level siblings influences the similarity strength between their child values.

Proposition 3 states that the similarity strength between 1-level siblings can also be applied to measure the similarity strength between their child values. On the basis of this proposition, the administrator does not need to measure the similarity strength between the n-level siblings explicitly, where $n \geq 2$. She just needs to measure the *primitive strength*. The primitive refers to (1) the strength between 1-level siblings (i.e., *sibling strength*) and (2) the strength between parent and child (i.e., *abstraction strength*), as shown in Figure 3. Thus, we can define the similarity relation in FAH as definition 1.

Definition 1: Similarity Relation in FAH. The membership function on similarity relation R, μ_R: V × V → (0, 1), where R={(v_1, v_2) | v_1 and v_2 are 1-level siblings or have a 1-level abstraction relationship} and V is the set of values in FAH.

Definition 1 means that the similarity relation in FAH is composed of the pairs of values that have a 1-level sibling relationship or a 1-level abstraction relationship. The similarity strengths between n-level siblings can be derived from their (n-1)-level abstract values that have explicit strength through the composition of fuzzy relation. For example, the similarity strength between a_1

and b_1 can be derived through the *composition* of $\mu_R(a_1, p_1)$, $\mu_R(p_1, p_2)$, and $\mu_R(p_2, b_1)$. Generally, the *composition* or, more specifically, the *max-min composition* of two relations R and S is denoted by R•S, and is defined by the following membership function:

$$\mu_{R \bullet S}(x, z) = \text{Max}_y [\text{Min}(\mu_R(x, y), \mu_S(y, z))], \tag{1}$$

where $(x, y) \in R$, $(y, z) \in S$. The relations R and S can be represented as fuzzy relation matrices M_R and M_S, and the composite relation R•S is obtained by the composition of M_R and M_S. For example, in Figure 3, let AD, DD, and DB be fuzzy relations, AD $\subseteq$ A × D, DD $\subseteq$ D × D, DB $\subseteq$ D × B, where A={a_1, a_2, a_3}, B={b_1, b_2, b_3}, and D={p_1, p_2, p_3}. These relations can be represented as fuzzy relation matrices, M_{AP}, M_{PP}, and M_{PB}, respectively in Figure 4. Note that $\mu_{AD}(a_i, p_2)$ and $\mu_{AD}(a_i, p_3)$ are 0 because a_i has strengths only with its 1-level abstract value p_i; $\mu_{DD}(p_i, p_i) = 1$ in M_{PP}.

From the definitions of the composition, it follows at once that, for any fuzzy relations R⊆X×Y, S⊆Y×Z, and T⊆Z×W, we have R•(S•T) = (R•S)•T (i.e., *associative property*). Thus, in Figure 4, the similarity strength between 2-level siblings, a_1 and b_1, becomes

$$\mu(a_1, b_1) = \text{Max}_{p_i p_j} [\text{Min}(\mu(a_1, p_i), \mu(p_i, p_j), \mu(p_j, b_1))], \tag{2}$$

Figure 4. Composition of similarity relation

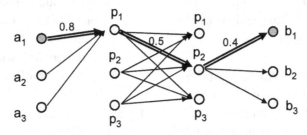

(a) Feasible Relation Path of (a$_1$, b$_1$)

$$M_{AP} = \begin{array}{c|ccc} AP & p_1 & p_2 & p_3 \\ \hline a_1 & 0.8 & 0 & 0 \\ a_2 & 0.4 & 0 & 0 \\ a_3 & 0.7 & 0 & 0 \end{array}
\quad M_{PP} = \begin{array}{c|ccc} PP & p_1 & p_2 & p_3 \\ \hline p_1 & 1 & 0.5 & 0.6 \\ p_2 & 0.5 & 1 & 0.4 \\ p_3 & 0.6 & 0.4 & 1 \end{array}
\quad M_{PB} = \begin{array}{c|ccc} PB & b_1 & b_2 & b_3 \\ \hline p_1 & 0 & 0 & 0 \\ p_2 & 0.4 & 0.6 & 0.8 \\ p_3 & 0 & 0 & 0 \end{array}$$

Composition (= M$_{AP}$•M$_{PP}$)

$$M_{APP} = \begin{array}{c|ccc} AP & p_1 & p_2 & p_3 \\ \hline a_1 & 0.8 & 0.5 & 0.6 \\ a_2 & 0.4 & 0.4 & 0.4 \\ a_3 & 0.7 & 0.5 & 0.6 \end{array}$$

Composition (= M$_{AP}$•M$_{PB}$)

$$M_{AB} = \begin{array}{c|ccc} AB & b_1 & b_2 & b_3 \\ \hline a_1 & 0.4 & 0.5 & 0.5 \\ a_2 & 0.4 & 0.4 & 0.4 \\ a_3 & 0.4 & 0.5 & 0.5 \end{array}$$

(b) Composition of Similarity Strength Using Fuzzy Relation Matrices

where p_i and p_j are 1-level abstract values of a_i and b_j, respectively, or 1-level siblings of the abstract values. In (2), note that (because the abstraction strengths concern only the values having the 1-level abstraction relationship,) the Min operator always includes 0 as $\mu(a_i, p_i)$ or $\mu(p_j, b_j)$, except for the case of $(\mu(a_i, p_i), \mu(p_1, p_2), \mu(p_2, b_j))$, where p_1, and p_2 are 1-level abstract values of a_i and b_j, respectively. We call $(a_i - p_1 - p_2 - b_j)$ a *feasible relation path* of (a_i, b_j), which does not contain zero similarity strength between adjacent values in itself. The feasible path of a_i and b_j is unique in a FAH and consists of 1-level abstract values of a_i and b_j. Thus, (2) becomes

$$\mu(a_i, b_j) = \text{Min}(\mu(a_i, p_1), \mu(p_1, p_2), \mu(p_2, b_j)), \tag{3}$$

where a_i, p_1, p_2, b_j consist the feasible relation path of (a_i, b_j).

Using this composition operator, we can derive the similarity strength of pairs that do not have explicit strength, which is called *derived strength*. However, the operator cannot resolve the problem of satisfying Proposition 2. Thus, we define extended similarity strength by introducing the abstraction level as follows:

Definition 2: Extended Similarity Strength Adopting Abstraction Level. The extended similarity strength between n-level siblings is $\lambda = (D-n)+\mu$, where D is the depth of the hierarchy and μ is the sibling strength ($n=1$) or derived strength ($n \geq 2$).

The similarity strength between n-level siblings is wholly defined to be composed of the derived similarity strength and the abstraction level. For example, the 2-level siblings Finance and OR have the similarity strength λ_R(Finance, OR) = $(3-2)+0.6$ because they are 2-level siblings and their derived strength is μ_R(Finance, OR)=0.6.

The extended notion of similarity strength satisfies Proposition 2. According to Definition 2, the similarity strength between n-level siblings is always smaller than that between $(n$-1)-level siblings, where $n \geq 2$. Conclusively, the administrator assesses only the primitive strength (i.e., sibling strength and abstraction strength), while it is possible to derive the similarity strength for every pair of values with the extended similarity strength without violating Proposition 2.

The existing semantic distance approaches should manage the numerical distances for every pair of data values; however, there will be potential maintenance problems because the number of pairs that need to be considered exponentially increases as the number of data values increase. Compared with the existing semantic distance approaches, the FAH considerably reduces the number of pairs to be managed by classifying similar data values using data abstraction.

Theorem 1:Reduction in the Number of Pairs of Values. The number of pairs in the semantic distance approach is always greater than that in the FAH approach.

Proof:

Let c and d be the *average* number of children of each value and the depth of the hierarchy in our FAH approach, respectively. Then, the number of pairs in the FAH approach and the semantic distance approach can be calculated as follows:

○ FAH

E[number of pairs] = E[number of 1-level sibling groups]
× (E[number of pairs in each sibling group]
+ E[number of abstraction strength in each sibling group])
$= (1 + c + c^2 + \cdots + c^{d-2}) \times (_cC_2 + c)$
$= [(1-c^{d-1})/(1-c)] \times (c(c-1)/2 + c)$
$= (c-c^d)(1+c)/2(1-c).$

○ Semantic approach

E[number of values in a hierarchy] $= 1 + c + c^2 + \cdots + c^{d-1} = (1-c^d)/(1-c).$

E[number of pairs] $= {}_{(1-c^d)/(1-c)}C_2 = (1-c^d)(c-c^d)/2(1-c)^2$

Thus, the ratio of the semantic distance approach to FAH is

$$\frac{(1-c^d)(c-c^d)/2(1-c)^2}{(c-c^d)(1+c)/2(1-c)} = \frac{(c^d-1)}{(c^2-1)} > 1,$$

because $c>1$ and $d>1$.

The ratio between the two approaches increases enormously as the depth of hierarchy and the average number of children of a value increase, as shown in Table 2. For example, if the depth of the hierarchy is 3 and each value has 3 children on average, then the semantic distance approach should maintain 3.25 times as many as pairs in the FAH approach (see Table 2).

Table 2. The ratio of pairs to be assessed of existing semantic distance approach to FAH

Depth of Hierarchy (d)	2	3	3	4	4	5	5
Average Number of Children (c)	3	3	4	3	4	3	4
Ratio $(c^d-1)/(c_2-1)$	1	3.25	4.2	10	17	30.25	68.2

4. QUERY PROCESSING BASED ON THE FAH

To facilitate cooperative query answering, semantics involved in the FAH are incorporated into a semantic knowledge base. A sample semantic knowledge base accommodating the FAH instance in Figure 2 is described in Appendix A. In this section, we discuss query relaxation operators based on the FAH and classify cooperative queries.

4.1 Query Relaxation Operators

In order to facilitate query relaxation, a core part of cooperative query answering, the semantic knowledge base needs the following operations:

generalization, specialization, and approximation for a value. As shown in Figure 5, a 1-level generalization (specialization) returns a 1-level abstract value (specific values) and an abstraction strength by moving up (down) the FAH from a given value in a query condition. The 1-level *GetSiblings*() of a value returns its 1-level siblings and strength measures, which are above the given similarity strength. The detailed definitions with accompanying SQL statements are presented in Appendix A.

To control the query relaxation's range flexibly, we increase or decrease the abstraction level by using *n*-level generalization (i.e., *Generalize(v, n)*) and specialization (i.e., *Specialize(v, n)*) operations shown in Table 3. These operations are

Figure 5. Basic operations for query relaxation

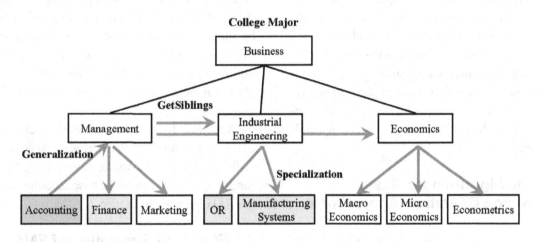

Table 3. The n-level operators for query transformation

Functions	Description
Generalize(v, n)	It returns *n*-level abstract values of a given value *v* and the composite strength between the abstract value and the value *v* by repeating the 1-level generalization *n* times. If the *n*=0, then it returns *v* itself. Define $G(v, n)$ as the set of returned abstract values.
GetSiblings(v, μ)	It returns 1-level abstract values of a given value v and their associated strength which are greater than *μ* (horizontal generalization). Define $GS(v, b)$ as the set of returned values.
Specialize(v, n)	It returns a set of *n*-level specific values of given value *v* and the composite strength between the specific values and the value *v* by repeating the 1-level specialization *n* times. If *n* = 0, then it returns *v* itself. Define $S(v, n)$ as the set of returned values.
Approximate(v, n, μ)	It returns a set of *n*-level siblings of value *v* and the derived strength above the given strength *μ*. It executes $(n-1)$-level generalization, 1-level getting siblings in the *n*-level, and $(n-1)$-level specialization. If the *n*=0, then it returns *v* itself.

Table 4. Four steps of query transformation

Query Transformation	
Approximate(v_q, n, μ) For $k = 1$ to n	**[Step1]** *Generalize*(v, n) Input: v_q, $k-1$ Output: $G(v_q, k-1)$
	[Step2] *GetSiblings*(v, μ) Input: $G(v_q, k-1)$, μ Output: $GS(G(v_q, k-1), \mu)$
	[Step3] *Specialize*(v, n) Input: $GS(G(v_q, k-1), \mu)$, $k-1$ Output: $S(GS(G(v_q, k-1), \mu), k-1)$
	[Step4] Calculate extended similarity strength

initiated by the n-level approximation (i.e., *Approximate*(v, n, μ)) operation, specifically when user expects the 1-level approximate answers to be restrictive (not enough) and thus asks a far broader scope of candidates at once, namely, a set of *n*-level siblings of value *v* with the similarity strength above μ. In principle, an *n*-level abstract value and specific values can be obtained after recursively repeating the 1-level operations *n* times. To obtain *n*-level siblings that have derived similarity strengths greater than the given strength μ, the query relaxation invokes *Approximate*(v, n, μ) for ($n-1$)-level generalization, 1-level *Get-Siblings*() at the *n*-level, and ($n-1$)-level specialization.

4.2 The Algorithm for Query Relaxation Operation, Approximate

The algorithm of our query relaxation, *Approximate*(v, n, μ), is implemented as follows. The four steps are processed by *n* loops from the current value, *v*, to its *n*-level abstract value.

In each loop in Step 1, for a given value *v*, we move up along the hierarchy to find the set of abstract values of value *v* with the designated abstraction level *k*, and thus obtain $G(v, k-1)$. In Step 2, for the set of the abstract values, $G(v, k-1)$, we go horizontally to find their siblings having a strength greater than μ and thus obtain $GS(G(v, k-1), \mu)$. As we have obtained all sibling abstract

values, in Step 3, we come down to the level of the given value *v* to find the *k*-level specific values of the sibling abstract values, $GS(G(v, k-1), \mu)$, and select only qualified specific values having a strength greater than μ, and thus obtain $S(GS(G(v_q, k-1), \mu), k-1)$. Finally, in Step 4, we calculate the extended similarity strength for all the approximate data values and ran all of them by their strengths. Table 4 shows the four steps of the *Approximate*(v, n, μ) with their input and output arguments, and Table 5 shows the detailed algorithm of how each step is implemented in the execution process.

Appendix B shows the exemplary execution of the Approximation, *Approximate*(Accounting, 2, 0.7), with a given value, Accounting, for the sample semantic knowledge base accommodating the FAH instance in Figure 2.

4.3 Efficiency Simulation of FAH

Efficiency of FAH can be explored in terms of three perspectives: creation and maintenance costs of the similarity relations, and the search cost. First, in terms of the creation of the similarity relations, the semantic distance approach needs to preset similarity values for all the pair of leaf nodes, which requires $O(n^2)$ computing time where *n* denotes the number of leaf nodes. In contrast, FAH needs two types of similarity values including the one among the pairs of sibling relations

Table 5. Algorithm for Approximate(v, n, μ)

```
If n > 0
  For k = 1 to n
     call Generalize(v, k−1)
         G(v, k−1) = {(x, y) | x is the k−1 level abstract(vertical) nodes of v in the hierarchy and y is the minimum strength between v
and x}
     call GetSiblings(G(v, k−1), μ)
         GS(G(v, k−1), μ) = {(u, v) | u is the 1-level abstract(horizontal) nodes of x where (x, y) ∈ G(v, k−1) and y ≥ μ; y is the mini-
mum strength between x and u, and v is the minimum derived strength between x and u (i.e., v = min(y, v)}
     call Specialize(GS(G(v, k−1), μ), k−1)
         S(GS(G(v, k−1), μ), k−1) = {(p, q) | p is the k−1 level specific (vertical) nodes of u where (u, v) ∈ GS(G(v, k−1), μ); v is the
minimum strength between x and u, and q is the minimum derived strength between x and p (i.e., q = min(v and p)}
     Calculate the extended similarity distance between v and each element in S(GS(G(v, k−1), μ), k−1) by calculating the minimum
value among the values of strength (i.e., λ(v, p) = (D−k) + μ)
     Approximate = Approximate ∪ {(p, b) | (p, q) ∈ S(GS(G(v, k−1), μ), k−1) and b is the extended similarity distance, λ(v, p), which is
calculated at the above step}
  End for
Else If n = 0
  Approximate = {(v, 0)}
End If
Return Approximate
```

(i.e., between sibling nodes sharing a same parent node) and the other between abstraction relations (i.e., abstract parent nodes and their own children nodes). In such case, the former similarity requires $O(\text{sum of } n_i^2)$ computing time where n_i denotes the number of fan-out, i.e., the number of the local leaf nodes, of i-th abstract parent (where $n_i \ll n$) and the latter similarity requires $O(n)$ computing time, which in total is still quite smaller than that of semantic distance approach, i.e., $O(\text{sum of } n_i^2) + O(n) \ll O(n^2)$. Figure 6(a) shows the creation cost simulation for a sample data set containing 1000 leaf nodes with the fan-out number 5.

Second, the maintenance of the similarity relations arises if a specific leaf node is newly added or relocated to a different place in a FAH, and the similarity between the node and the rest of the leaf nodes needs to be updated accordingly. The FAH approach is still more efficient since the required updates in the member function are minimized by localizing the scope only to the corresponding pairs. More precisely, if the new leaf node is added to the leaf nodes of i-th abstract parent, the required updates are localized only to the n_i sibling leaf nodes (for the sibling relations) and to its parent abstract node (for the abstraction

relation), which requires the $O(n_i + 1)$ computing time in total. Contrastingly, in the semantic distance approach, the total number of updates requires $O(n)$ since the similarity between the new node and the existing leaf nodes is to be assigned by n times. Figure 6(b) shows the maintenance cost simulation for the sample data set.

Third, the search operation in FAH is supported by a cooperative query transformation, namely, the k-level operation for query transformation, which performs a series of member functions such as 1-level *Generalize*() by k times, 1-level *GetSiblings*() once, and 1-level *Specialize*() by k times. Notice that the k designates an approximation level ranging from 0 to the maximum depth, where the maximum depth is $\log_{ni} N$ where n_i is the fan-out number of i-th abstract parent ($n_i \ll N$). The FAH search operation is more efficient since *Generalize*() and *GetSiblings*() perform the pruning process by removing unnecessary intermediate abstract nodes in advance so that the search process can skip the leaf nodes of the removed abstract nodes, and thus, can minimize the number of pairs to be considered. The search computing time varies depending on the approximation level, k. If $k = 1$, the computing

Figure 6. Efficiency simulation of FAH

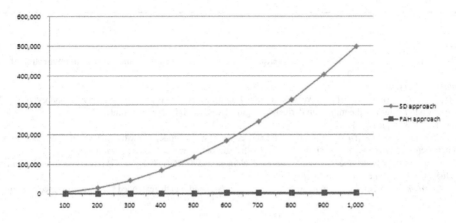

(a) Creation cost simulation (sample data set containing
1000 leaf nodes with the fan-out number 5)

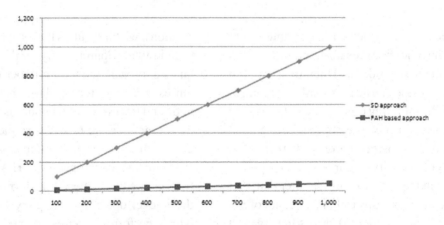

(b) Maintenance cost simulation

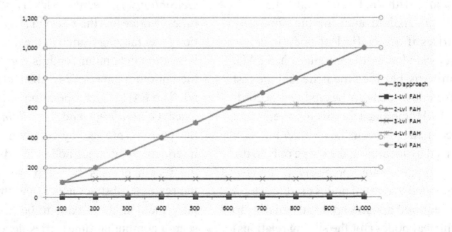

(c) Search cost simulation

search time is $O(1 + n_i \times c)$, and if $k = 2$, the computing time is $O(2 + (n_i)^2 \times c)$ while if $k = \log_{ni} N$, the maximum depth, the computing time is $O(\log_{ni} N + N) = O(N)$. Contrastingly, the search operation in the semantic distance approach for the top-ranked results requires $O(N)$ computing time since it needs to get all the similarity values of the leaf nodes for sorting. As a whole, though the member functions used in FAH require a few additional steps, the increased computing time is not so significant when proper approximate level is asked due to the pruning process and thus FAH cooperative query answering search outperforms the semantic distance approach. Simulation result for the sample data is shown in Figure 6(c).

4.4 Classification of Cooperative Queries

In cooperation with the underlying database, the FAH performs a query relaxation that can be invoked in various ways depending on the user's need and knowledge of FAH. Specifically, FAH supports two kinds of relaxation methods: *approximately equal search* and *conceptually equal search* (see Figure 7). The queries posed to an underlying database are classified according to these relaxation methods of the FAH.

In FAH, parent and child are considered to be *conceptually equal* because they exist in different *conceptual* levels but have an IS-A relationship based on value abstraction. On the other hand, sibling values are *approximately equal* because they are neighborhood values existing in the same conceptual level. To illustrate the query relaxation methods, suppose there is a selection condition in SQL statements WHERE A = V composed of a *target attribute* A and a *target value* V.

First, an approximately equal search provides not only the target value itself but also its approximately equal values although the search condition specifies the target value only. In other words, this search provides neighborhood information other than the exact answers that can be obtained by the conventional query processing. As explained earlier, users can flexibly control the range of approximately equal values—the extent of the relaxation—by adjusting the similarity strength until they are satisfied.

Second, a conceptually equal search is used when users write a search condition with a conceptual target value (i.e., higher-level abstract value). The queries are posed at a higher conceptual level based on the user's context without detailed database schema knowledge. These queries are specifically useful when users are less accustomed

Figure 7. Two kinds of equality for relaxing search conditions

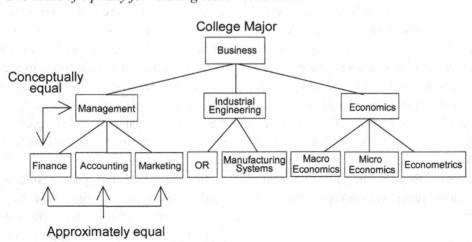

to the details of leaf node data values (i.e., in Figure 7, Finance, Accounting, Marketing, Decision Sciences, Organizational Behavior, International Business, and Strategy) than those of abstract values (i.e., Management), or when institutional users simply prefer to use abstract names than to write detailed multiple approximate queries, conceptual queries can be conveniently adopted. In a conceptually equal search, the target attribute and the target value exist in different abstraction levels. More precisely, it searches for the specific values of the conceptual target value, which we regard as "conceptually equal" with the target value. If proper query transformation is not applied to the conceptual queries, it compares the values existing in different abstraction levels to check if the query condition is satisfied. Thus, the conceptually equal search is rejected in a conventional query processing that provides only exact answers. Note that semantic distance approaches do not support conceptual queries because they cannot represent the abstraction relationship between data values in multiple conceptual levels.

The two query relaxation methods can be extended in the join operation where a target attribute is joined with a range of neighboring values of another join attribute. Accordingly, depending on the kinds of operations and relaxation methods, four types of cooperative queries can be implemented: approximate selection, approximate join, conceptual selection, and conceptual join. Depending on the user's need and knowledge about the FAH, the four types of queries serve different aspects of cooperative query answering and can be selectively combined in a single query, thus enabling more sophisticated queries. Compared with other existing approaches, FAH and KAH (Huh & Lee, 2001; Huh & Moon, 2000) increase the diversity of admitted cooperative queries including the relaxation of the join operation (i.e., approximate join and conceptual join) that facilitates multiple relations to be approximately joined at once.

4.5 Implementation of Query Relaxation Control through User Interaction

Query relaxation control in a real database application can be implemented in various ways. However, for intuitive interaction, it should not impose on novice users the burden of knowing the database semantics. For example, users need not worry about the degree of query relaxation, which is composed of abstraction levels and similarity strengths.

In terms of the degree of query relaxation, the system can guide an *incremental* or *direct* query relaxation process to a desired range of approximate answers through the user interaction, which eventually contributes to flexible and effective query relaxation control. In the incremental process, the user gradually increases the relaxation degree from the range of exact answers until he is satisfied with the relaxed query results. In between query processing, the user decides whether or not he will continue query relaxation after examining the current answers and the answers to be provided in the next relaxation step.

On the other hand, in the direct process, the user may roughly specify the relaxation degree (e.g., the number of query results) as a starting point for query relaxation and then provide interactive feedback to the system until she is satisfied with the query results. If she is not satisfied, the user can proceed with incremental or direct relaxation.

Figure 8 shows a prototype of the query interface that can cooperate with users through the user interaction. In Figure 8(a), a user can easily pose a cooperative query by choosing Finance as a target value out of the possible major values in the underlying database and designating 10 to be the number of results as a substitute for the query relaxation degree.

In Figure 8(b), the query results are sorted (ranked) by fitness scores to the target value, which can provide the user with effective information retrieval and decision support. In each stage

Figure 8. The query processing in a prototype test example

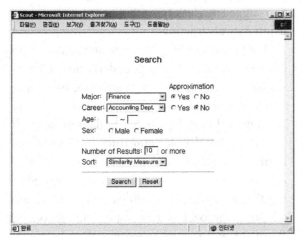

(a) A Request for Query Relaxation

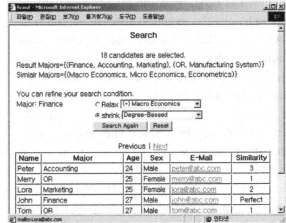

(b) The First Result Set by Query Relaxation

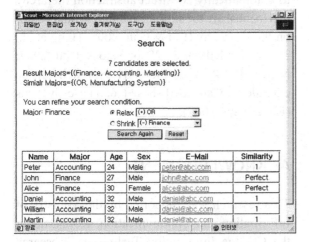

(c) The Second Result Set by Query Shrink

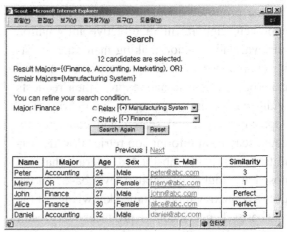

(d) The Third Result Set by Query Relaxation

of query relaxation, the user can determine whether to relax or shrink the query condition after examining the currently relaxed values and the values to be relaxed in the next step. To determine the range of the next query result, the user may specify a value explicitly to be included or excluded in the query result set, or rely on FAH's query processing control based on the similarity strength.

In Figure 8(b), the user decides to shrink the query with FAH's relaxation control because an excessive amount of results is provided. FAH excludes OR and Manufacturing System, which

have the smallest similarity strength from the result set. In Figure 8(c), the query is relaxed again by including a similar value OR. Finally, the user obtains 12 answers composed of Finance, Accounting, Marketing, and OR.

5. CONCLUSION

This paper proposed an integrated cooperative query answering approach that can relax search conditions to provide approximate neighborhood answers in addition to exact answers. For this purpose, we developed a knowledge representation framework, FAH, by combining the abstraction hierarchy and the semantic distance approaches. FAH is a multilevel knowledge representation framework that extracts abstract values from an underlying database and puts them into abstraction hierarchies. Additionally, it adopts fuzzy relations to represent the discriminated similarity strength between data values. Thus, the similarity measure between values in FAH is represented by the integrated notion of data abstraction and fuzzy relations. As a result, FAH acquires richer semantic knowledge of an underlying database and embraces the advantages of existing data abstraction and semantic distance approaches.

The proposed cooperative query answering approach supports more effective information retrieval and decision making than other existing approaches. First, it supports users of diverse expertise levels who may express their requests with diverse kinds of cooperative queries (i.e., approximately equal search and conceptually equal search) in information retrieval. FAH permits conceptually abstracted queries that are posed at a higher conceptual level based on the user's context without detailed knowledge of the database schema. Second, it produces query result sets ranked according to the similarity strength to assist users in determining the priority (i.e., fitness score) of each answer in the result set. Thus, users can preset numeric search criteria, obtain approximated query results that are filtered within the search threshold, and interactively calibrate search criteria for better query results. In addition, by using similarity strengths, it can guide a more elaborate and flexible query relaxation control through user interaction.

Furthermore, FAH facilitates the effective creation and maintenance of semantic knowledge by human experts, which is one of the major shortcomings of the semantic distance approach. Experts can retain consistency by assigning similarity strengths with respect to the target value (i.e., abstraction relationship between data values). FAH considerably reduces maintenance costs by decreasing the number of similarity strengths to be assigned by classifying the approximate values using data abstraction.

For future research, the automatic construction of FAH instances from large underlying databases should be studied. In a large database or even in a data warehouse, the automatic analysis of the semantic relationships between data values will help the administrator construct FAH instances easily. In addition, the validation of similarity relationships by users can be used for updating the semantic relationships. For this, we are adopting approaches using an online dictionary, WordNet, and a vector space model, respectively to automatically construct abstraction hierarchy and to measure the similarities among data values on the hierarchy (Liu & Chu, 2005; Hung et al., 2004; Marshall et al., 2006; Mao & Chu, 2007; Motro, 1988). Also, the FAH approach can be extended to an XML-based database systems (Liu & Chu, 2007).

ACKNOWLEDGMENT

This research was supported by the Ministry of Information and Communication, Korea, under the College Information Technology Research Center Support Program, grant number IITA-2005-C1090-0502-0016.

REFERENCES

Bosc, P., Kraft, D., & Petry, F. (2005). Fuzzy sets in database and information systems: Status and opportunities. *Fuzzy Sets and Systems*, *156*(3), 418–426. doi:10.1016/j.fss.2005.05.039

Cai, Y., Cercone, N., & Han, J. (1993). Attribute-Oriented Induction in Relational Databases. In *Knowledge Discovery in Databases*. Menlo Park, CA: AAAI Press, Chu, W., & Chen, Q. (1994). A Structured Approach for Cooperative Query Answering. *IEEE Transactions on Knowledge and Data Engineering*, *6*(5), 738–749.

Chu, W., Yang, H., Chiang, K., Minock, M., Chow, G., & Larson, C. (1996). CoBase: A Scalable and Extensible Cooperative Information System. *International Journal of Intelligence Information Systems, 6*(1), 223–260. doi:10.1007/BF00122129

Chu, W., Yang, H., & Chow, G. (1996). *A Cooperative Database System (CoBase) for Query Relaxation*. Paper presented at the Third International Conference on Artificial Intelligence Planning Systems, Edinburgh, UK.

Cuppens, F., & Demolombe, R. (1989). Cooperative Answering: A Methodologies to Provide Intelligent Access to Databases. In *Proceedings of the Second International Conference on Expert Database Systems* (pp. 621-643).

Cuzzocrea, A. (2005). Providing probabilistically-bounded approximate answers to non-holistic aggregate range queries in OLAP. In *Proceedings of the 8th ACM International Workshop on Data Warehousing and OLAP* (pp. 97-106).

Cuzzocrea, A. (2007). Approximate range-sum query answering on data cubes with probabilistic guarantees. *Journal of Intelligent Information Systems Archive, 28*(2), 161–197. doi:10.1007/s10844-006-0007-y

De Sean, G. J., & Furtado, A. Z. (1998). Towards a Cooperative Question-Answering Model. In *Proceedings of Flexible Query Answering Systems* (LNCS 1495, pp. 354-365).

Godfrey, P. (1997). Minimization in Cooperative Response to Failing Database Queries. *International Journal of Cooperative Information Systems, 6*(2), 95–149. doi:10.1142/S0218843097000070

Hemerly, A., Casanova, M., & Furtado, A. (1994). Exploiting User Models to Avoid Misconstruals . In *Nonstandard Queries and Nonstandard Answers* (pp. 73–98). Oxford, UK: Oxford Science Publications.

Huh, S., & Lee, J. W. (2001). Providing Approximate Answers Using a Knowledge Abstraction Database. *Journal of Database Management, 12*(2), 14–24.

Huh, S., & Moon, K. H. (2000). A Data Abstraction Approach for Query Relaxation. *Information and Software Technology, 42*(6), 407–418. doi:10.1016/S0950-5849(99)00100-7

Hung, C., Wermter, S., & Smith, P. (2004). Hybrid Neural Document Clustering Using Guided Self-Organization and WordNet. *IEEE Intelligent Systems, 19*(2), 68–77. doi:10.1109/MIS.2004.1274914

Liu, S., & Chu, W. (2007). CoXML: A Cooperative XML Query Answering System. In *APWeb/WAIM 2007* (LNCS 4505, pp. 614-621).

Liu, Z. L., & Chu, W. W. (2005). *Knowledge-Based Query Expansion to Support Scenario-Specific Retrieval of Medical Free Text*. Paper presented at ACM SAC.

Mao, W., & Chu, W. (2007). The phrase-based vector space model for automatic retrieval of free-text medical documents. *Data & Knowledge Engineering, 61*(1), 76–92. doi:10.1016/j.datak.2006.02.008

Marshall, B., Chen, H., & Madhusudan, T. (2006). Matching knowledge elements in concept maps using a similarity flooding algorithm. *Decision Support Systems, 42*(3), 1290–1306. doi:10.1016/j.dss.2005.10.009

Minker, J. (1998). An Overview of Cooperative Answering in Databases. In *Proceedings of Flexible Query Answering Systems* (LNCS 1495, pp. 614-621).

Motro, A. (1988). VAGUE: A User Interface to Relational Databases that Permits Vague Queries. *ACM Transactions on Office Information Systems, 6*(3), 187–214. doi:10.1145/45945.48027

Motro, A. (1990). FLEX: A Tolerent and Cooperative User Interface to Databases. *IEEE Transactions on Knowledge and Data Engineering, 2*(2), 231–246. doi:10.1109/69.54722

Shin, M., Huh, S., Park, D., & Lee, W. (2008). Relaxing Queries with Hierarchical Quantified Data Abstraction. *Journal of Database Management, 19*(4), 47–61.

Varelas, G., Voutsakis, E., Raftopoulou, P., Petrakis, E., & Milios, E. (2005). Semantic similarity methods in wordNet and their application to information retrieval on the web. In *Proceedings of the 7th Annual ACM International Workshop on Web Information and Data Management* (pp. 10-16).

APPENDIX A

This appendix presents a sample semantic knowledge base accommodating the FAH instance in Figure 2. The semantic knowledge base comprises four relations: DOMAIN_ABSTRACTION, VALUE_ABSTRACTION, SIMILARITY_STRENGTH, and ATTRIBUTE_MAPPING. Figure A-1 illustrates two FAH instances, including College Major in Figure 2 and another Career Development Education instance. In the presence of multiple perspectives on a single underlying database, multiple FAH instances are required. In the following ATTRIBUTE_MAPPING relation, the relations and their associated attributes in the underlying database are artificially enumerated for explanatory purposes.

DOMAIN_ABSTRACTION captures the semantics of the domain abstraction hierarchy. A domain can exist in only one FAH instance and has one-to-one mapping correspondence with its super-domain; hence, the Domain attribute becomes the key attribute. VALUE_ABSTRACTION captures the semantics of the value abstraction hierarchy. A value (e.g., Accounting) is not uniquely identified by its name only because the value can exist in multiple hierarchies (i.e., multiple domains). This is called *domain-dependency*. Thus, both the Value and Domain attributes are the composite key of the relation. In terms of abstraction relationships, each tuple of the relations represents only the 1-level abstraction relationship. On the basis of such a relationship, an abstract value in any level can be transitively retrieved.

SIMILARITY_STRENGTH maintains the sibling similarity strength between 1-level siblings in the value abstraction hierarchies. As explained earlier, when compared to the semantic approach, the number of tuples to be maintained is enormously decreased. Finally, ATTRIBUTE_MAPPING maintains the domain information of attributes in the underlying database and helps to analyze the intent of a query. Specifically, it constructs a semantic knowledge base on top of the underlying database by connecting abstraction information to the attributes of the relations. The query relaxation operators are defined as shown in Table A-1.

APPENDIX B

Assume that we execute *Approximate*(Accounting, 2, 0.7) for the FAH in Figure 2. The Approximation operation goes through the steps as shown below.

First, since $n = 2 > 0$, it executes the steps inside the for loop twice, and goes

(1) $k = 1$ (in the 1st-loop, considering only siblings of Accounting)
[Step 1] call *Generalize*(Accounting, 0) // find siblings in the same level as Accounting without moving up along FAH (without any generalization)
G(Accounting, 0) = {(Accounting, 1)} // by definition, G(Acc, 0) returns (Accounting, 1) without any generalization
[Step 2] call *GetSiblings*(G(Accounting, 0), 0.7), i.e., call *GetSiblings*({(Accounting, 1)}, 0.7)
GS({(Accounting, 1)}, 0.7) = {(Accounting, 1), (Finance, 0.7)}. Note that the node (Marketing, 0.4) is dropped since its similarity strength is below 0.7.

Figure 9. The constructor relations of the semantic knowledge base

DOMAIN_ABSTRACTION

Domain	Super_Domain	Hierarchy	Abstraction_Level
MAJOR_NAME	MAJOR_AREA	College Major	1
MAJOR_AREA	MAJOR_GROUP	College Major	2
MAJOR_GROUP		College Major	3
COURSE_NAME	COURSE_AREA	Career Development Education	1
COURSE_AREA	COURSE_GROUP	Career Development Education	2
COURSE_GROUP		Career Development Education	3

VALUE_ABSTRACTION

Value	Domain	Abstract_Value	Abstraction_Strength
Finance	MAJOR_NAME	Management	0.6
Accounting	MAJOR_NAME	Management	0.8
Marketing	MAJOR_NAME	Management	0.7
Macro Economics	MAJOR_NAME	Economics	0.9
Micro Economics	MAJOR_NAME	Economics	0.9
Econometrics	MAJOR_NAME	Economics	0.8
OR	MAJOR_NAME	Industrial Engineering	0.7
Manufacturing Systems	MAJOR_NAME	Industrial Engineering	0.8
Management	MAJOR_AREA	Business	0.9
Economics	MAJOR_AREA	Business	0.8
Industrial Engineering	MAJOR_AREA	Business	0.7
Business	MAJOR_GROUP		
Cost Accounting	COURSE_NAME	Accounting	0.9
Financial Accounting	COURSE_NAME	Accounting	0.9
Accounting	COURSE_AREA	Practical Course	0.7
Practical Course	COURSE_GROUP		

SIMILARITY_STRENGTH

Value1	Value2	Sibling_Strength
Finance	Accounting	0.7
Finance	Marketing	0.4
Accounting	Marketing	0.4
Macro Economics	Micro Economics	0.3
Macro Economics	Econometrics	0.6
Micro Economics	Econometrics	0.6
OR	Manufacturing Systems	0.6
Management	Economics	0.6
Management	Industrial Engineering	0.8
Economics	Industrial Engineering	0.4
Cost Accounting	Financial Accounting	0.8

ATTRIBUTE_MAPPING

Relation	Attribute	Domain
EMPLOYEE	Major	MAJOR_NAME
EDUCATION	Recieved_Course_Area	COURSE_AREA

Table A-1. Query relaxation operators

Processes	Operators	SQL Statements Implementing the Operators
1-level generalization	*Generalize*(v, D, n)	SELECT Abstract_Value, Abstraction_Strength FROM VALUE_ABSTRACTION WHERE Value = v and Domain=D
1-level specialization	*Specialize*(v, D, n)	SELECT V.Value, V.Abstraction_Strength FROM VALUE_ABSTRACTION V, DOMAIN_ABSTRACTION D WHERE D.Super_Domain= D And D.Domain=V.Domain And V.Abstract_Value = v
1-level GetSiblings	*GetSiblings*(v, μ)	(SELECT Value1, Sibling_Strength FROM SIMILARITY_STRENGTH WHERE Value2=v and Sibling_Strength$\geq\mu$) UNION (SELECT Value2, Sibling_Strength FROM SIMILARITY_STRENGTH WHERE Value1=v and Sibling_Strength$\geq\mu$)

[Step 3] call *Specialize*(*GS*({(Accounting, 1)}, 0.7), i.e., call *Specialize*({(Accounting, 1), (Finance, 0.7)}, 0)

S({(Accounting, 1), (Finance, 0.7)}, 0) = {(Accounting, 1), (Finance, 0.7)}. This is to say that there exist two nodes, Accounting and Finance, as the 1st-loop approximation of Accounting. Now, we want to rank the two by their similarity strengths in the following step.

[Step 4] Calculate the extended similarity strength between "Accounting" and each element in {(Accounting, 1), (Finance, 0.7)} as shown below.
λ(Accounting, Accounting) = (3–1) + 1 = 3
λ(Accounting, Finance) = (3–1) + 0.7 = 2.7

Consequently, approximation nodes at the 1st-loop along with their similarity strengths are,

Approximation = {(Accounting, 3), (Finance, 2.7)}
(2) k = 2 (in the 2nd-loop, considering siblings of Management as the abstract value of Accounting)
[Step 1] call *Generalize*(Accounting, 1)
G(Accounting, 1) = {(Management, 0.8)}
[Step 2] call *GetSiblings*({(Management, 0.8)}, 0.7)

GS({(Management, 0.8)}, 0.7) = {(Industrial Engineering, 0.8)}. Note that the node (Economics, 0.6) is dropped since its similarity strength is below 0.7.

[Step 3] call *Specialize*({(Industrial Engineering, 0.8)}, 1)

$S(\{(\text{Industrial Engineering, } 0.8)\}, 1) = \{(\text{OR, } 0.7), (\text{Manufacturing Systems, } 0.8)\}$ This is to say that the two nodes, OR and Manufacturing Systems, are added to the 2nd-loop approximation of Accounting and now we want to rank the two by their similarity strengths together with Accounting and Finance which are obtained in the 1st-loop.

[Step 4] Calculate the extended similarity between v and each element in $\{(\text{OR, } 0.7), (\text{Manufacturing Systems, } 0.8)\}$ as shown below.

$\lambda(\text{Accounting, OR}) = (3-2) + 0.7 = 1.7$

$\lambda(\text{Accounting, Manufacturing Systems}) = (3-2) + 0.8 = 1.8$

Approximation = $\{(\text{Accounting, } 3), (\text{Finance, } 2.7)\} \cup \{(\text{Manufacturing Systems, } 1.8), (\text{OR, } 1.7)\}$

Return Approximation

Finally, we can get the outputs, (Accounting, 3), (Finance, 2.7), (Manufacturing Systems, 1.8), (OR, 1.7), as the result of executing *Approximate*(Accounting, 2, 0.7).

This work was previously published in International Journal of Database Management, Volume 21, Issue 4, edited by Keng Siau, pp. 35-59, copyright 2010 by IGI Publishing (an imprint of IGI Global)

Chapter 16
Accelerating Web Service Workflow Execution via Intelligent Allocation of Services to Servers

Konstantinos Stamkopoulos
University of Ioannina, Greece

Evaggelia Pitoura
University of Ioannina, Greece

Panos Vassiliadis
University of Ioannina, Greece

Apostolos Zarras
University of Ioannina, Greece

ABSTRACT

The appropriate deployment of web service operations at the service provider site plays a critical role in the efficient provision of services to clients. In this paper, the authors assume that a service provider has several servers over which web service operations can be deployed. Given a workflow of web services and the topology of the servers, the most efficient mapping of operations to servers must then be discovered. Efficiency is measured in terms of two cost functions that concern the execution time of the workflow and the fairness of the load distribution among the servers. The authors study different topologies for the workflow structure and the server connectivity and propose a suite of greedy algorithms for each combination.

DOI: 10.4018/978-1-61350-471-0.ch016

INTRODUCTION

A web service is typically defined in the literature –for example, see Alonso, Casati, Kuno and Machiraju (2004)—as an interface that describes a collection of operations provided through the internet and accessed through standard XML messages. The appropriate deployment of web service operations at a service provider site plays a critical role in the efficient provision of services to clients. To effectively provide solutions to users' tasks, web services are *composed* in *workflows* (see Chen, Zhou, & Zhang, 2006) that combine intermediate service results towards achieving a more complex goal. Such workflows are typically specified in appropriate languages such as BPEL (see Andrews, et al., 2003).

Motivating Example

Assume an electronic system that assigns rendez-vous for patients that need to consult doctors. A workflow that arranges a meeting depending on the availability of a doctor is depicted in Figure 1. Once the meeting has been conducted, the system registers any prescribed medicines and communicates via operations with social security agencies to register the assignment of medicines to patients. The detailed description of these operations is not necessary for the purpose of the

paper; still it is important to note that there are *operational services* that receive requests (in the form of XML messages) to which they react (by sending XML messages) and *decision operations* that regulate which operations are to be invoked depending on the state of the workflow.

The whole workflow is supported by web service operations, deployed by the ministry of health and social security. The ministry has 5 servers that can host any of the 15 operations of the workflow and *the problem is to decide which of the possible 5^{15} configurations of the deployment of operations to servers (a) provides the fastest closing of each patient case and (b) loads each server in a fair way, so that whenever additional workflows are deployed, or a server fails, a reasonable load scale-up is still possible.*

Background and Problem Statement

In the problem we are dealing with in this paper, *we assume that a service provider has several servers over which web service operations can be deployed. Then, given a workflow and the topology of the servers, the most efficient deployment of the operations must be discovered.* Different topologies refer to the possibility of different networking infrastructure for the servers; this might include particularities relating to the characteristics of the machinery data center,

Figure 1. Exemplary workflow

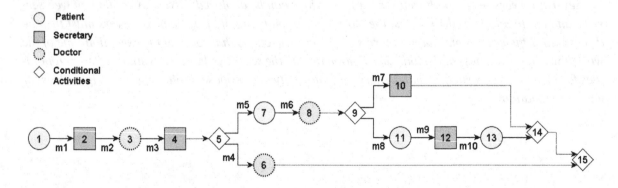

its geographical distribution, etc. The workflows of the organization that we need to deploy might be of arbitrary complexity; ranging from simple linear workflows to graphs of large complexity.

Unfortunately, so far, related work has not equipped us with efforts towards the solution of the problem. There are several works in the area of design, composition and security of web services as well as works on the fine tuning of web service workflows. Concerning the later, there are several works that deal with the regulation of the parameters of a previously obtained server configuration in order to achieve Quality of Service characteristics (see for example, Gillmann, Weikum and Wonner (2002)). However, none of the related research efforts covers the problem of the placement of web services to servers, once the operations and the topology of the servers are given. In other words, we provide the initial step for the administrator or engineer who wants to fine tune the architecture of his system: before fine-tuning for quality of service an initial, high quality allocation of operations to servers must be given; if such an allocation is unsatisfactory, then the approaches of the related work can be used.

Contributions

In our approach, efficiency is measured in terms of two cost functions that concern the execution time of the workflow and the fairness of the load distribution among the servers. The latter means that all servers spend the same amount of time for processing the workflow. This results in a double optimization problem with antagonistic individual measures. We study different topologies for both the workflow and the network of servers and propose algorithms for each case. The contribution of this work lies in (a) the definition of a model which describes the problem, and (b) the proposed algorithms for its solution. Moreover, we have thoroughly experimented and assessed all the proposed algorithms.

This paper is organized as follows: First, we discuss related work. We then start with a formal definition of the problem and introduce algorithms for the deployment of web service operations at the appropriate servers. We also present experimental results, summarize our findings, and discuss issues of future research.

RELATED WORK

Service-Oriented computing has been a very active field of research over the past few years (for general reading around the context of Service Oriented Architectures (SOA) see Erickson & Siau, 2008; Papazoglou & van den Heuvel, 2007; Papazoglou, Traverso, Dustdar, & Leymann, 2007).

The approach proposed in this paper, focuses at the deployment stage of the Web services development lifecycle. Concerning the development of Web services, Yu, Liu, Bouguettaya, and Medjahed (2008) proposed a comparison framework for relevant approaches. The proposed framework consists of a number of key properties involved in facilitating the development of Web services and shall be used hereafter towards orienting the proposed approach with respect to these features and comparing it with other related approaches. Briefly, the key properties identified by Yu et al. (2008) are *interoperability*, *security and privacy*, *quality of Web services* and *management*.

Interoperability, refers to the ability of Web services to collaborate towards achieving a particular goal. As pointed out by Medjahed, Benatallah, Bouguettaya, Ngu, and Elmagarmid, (2003), the basic means for achieving this property are standards and ontologies (e.g. Ding, Fensel, & Klein, 2002), from a specification point-of-view, and mediation, from a technical point of view (e.g. Gravano & Papakonstantinou, 1998). Our approach does not specifically contribute in achieving interoperability. Nevertheless, we rely on the assumption that the composite services that serve as input to the proposed algorithms are able to interoperate as they conform to widely accepted standards such as WSDL, SOAP and BPEL.

As discussed by Geer (2003), security in the field of Web services management is mainly focused in managing the trade-off between high interoperability and low security risks. Privacy, on the other hand relates to careful reasoning about the data that can be released via Web services (Rezgui, Bouguettaya, & Eltoweissy, 2003). The algorithms proposed by our approach do not embed means for dealing with security and privacy. Despite their importance, these issues are orthogonal to the issue of scheduling the deployment of Web services, which is our main concern. Nevertheless, we assume that the use of the proposed algorithms shall be employed in well controlled environments consisting of secure servers. Moreover, we assume that the design and implementation of the composite services that serve as input to the proposed algorithms shall account for privacy issues.

The field of quality of Web services relates to the problem of selecting a Web service out of a set of available competing services with respect to particular quality characteristics (Vinoski, 2002). Quality management is very important for the interaction of the users with web services. As Burstein et al. (2005) mention: "QoS metrics can affect how services are advertised, can be the topic of negotiation processes, and must be monitored during enactment; thus, when clients' procedures or workflows involve multiple services, the underlying discovery, coordination, and execution systems must be able to monitor QoS measures and control the services accordingly". Various quality characteristics of interest that can be used to characterize Web services can be found in the literature (e.g., Maximilien & Singh, 2004; Conti, Kumar, Das & Shirazi, 2002; Zeng, Benatallah, Ngu, Dumas, Kalagnanam, & Chang, 2004) and a very useful taxonomy of them has been proposed by Yu et al. (2008). The proposed taxonomy distinguishes between runtime quality characteristics such as execution time, availability,

reliability, integrity and business quality characteristics such as financial costs, reputation and conformance to standards. In our approach we consider the overall quality of a composite service that should be deployed over a set of available servers. The quality characteristic of interest to us is the composite service execution time. Our approach is complimentary to approaches related to service selection out of a set of competing services. In particular, the proposed algorithms for scheduling the deployment of composite Web services are employed right after the selection of the constituent services that are going to be used in a composite service. The quality characteristics of the constituent services as well as the quality characteristics of the underlying available infrastructure (i.e. servers and network) are the main input parameters of the cost model used by the proposed algorithms.

Our approach is most closely related to the management of Web services. Nevertheless, as Yu et al. (2008) discuss, this issue is also quite broad and encompasses many different dimensions including control management, change management and optimization.

Control management mainly refers to the coordination of Web services towards providing certain dependability guarantees such as the ones achieved through atomicity, isolation and further other transactional properties (for a discussion of the related issues and protocols see Papazoglou, 2003; Papazoglou & Kratz, 2007). This issue is orthogonal to our approach that deals with the deployment of composite Web services. We assume that any required coordination logic is already embedded in the Web services workflows that serve as input to the proposed algorithms.

Change management deals with the maintenance and configuration management of Web service workflows. Related approaches deal with changes in Web service workflows triggered either by evolving business requirements or by the evolving quality characteristics of the participating services.

Our work falls in the category of optimization where the general objective is to tune a Web service composition towards achieving a number of desired quality characteristics. Into this context, Cardoso, Sheth, Miller, Arnold, and Kochut (2004) provide a model that characterizes the quality of a composite service based on response time, cost and reliability. The workflows considered include AND and OR decision nodes. The authors discuss METEOR, a system that traces the behavior of the workflow over time and warns users whenever the QoS dangerously reaches the thresholds originally set by the users. Gillmann, Weikum, and Wonner (2002) present tuning techniques for a workflow management system. The goal of the paper is the optimal tuning of the parameters of an environment where composite workflows are to be executed over a network of servers, in a way that quality of service concerning response time, availability and throughput is guaranteed. There is a huge number of configurable parameters, several architectural options for the involved servers (workflow servers, application servers, communication servers), and most importantly, service replicas. A Markov model is used for the determination of the quality of a workflow and a heuristic algorithm for the overall tuning of the system. Zeng et al. (2004) propose a method that, given a desired quality of service for a composite web service, the most appropriate elementary web services are chosen out of a set of candidate services with similar functionality. Appropriateness is decided on the grounds of execution cost, duration, reliability, availability and reputation. Finally, Salellariou and Zhao (2004) propose a method for the reconfiguration of a system whenever the observed quality of service is not satisfactory. A scheduling algorithm involving the starting and ending timepoints for a workflow is employed. The paper proposes the reallocation of tasks through this scheduling algorithm only whenever changes in the monitored system measures are significant. All these works investigate the problem of dynamically tuning workflows to

achieve desired quality characteristics; still none of them deals with the deployment stage of the composite services lifecycle, which must take place beforehand. Composite service deployment is taken for granted, with extensions involving service replicas by Gillmann et al. (2002) or communities of similar operations by Zeng et al. (2003). Hence, our approach is complementary to the aforementioned approaches. More specifically, it does not aim at providing specific quality guarantees during the execution of composite services. On the contrary, it aims at providing a starting point to such approaches with tuneable configurations concerning the load characteristics of deployed services.

A final point in the related literature concerns approaches outside the context of service-oriented computing from which we were generally inspired such as replication, workflow management, and load balancing. In particular, Leff, Wolf, and Yu (1993) and Laoutaris, Telelis, Zissimopoulos, and Stavrakakis (2005) deal with the problem of object replication and provide interesting insights on the dimensions of the problem and the gain functions. Constantinescu, Binder, and Faltings (2005) and Srivastava, Widom, Mhnagala, and Motwani (2005) assume the continuous execution of a workflow: the former deals with the deployment of triggers to allow for the efficient execution of the workflow, whereas the second deals with the order of activity execution to achieve the optimal throughput. Concerning load balancing to ensuring quality properties for clients in the context of the web where unpredicted loads can occur, see Cherkasova and Peter Phaal (2002) as well as Cherkasova and Gupta (2004) for interesting facts and scheduling tactics. Moreover, large transaction processing systems distribute transaction processing to a number of servers, in order to increase the availability and efficiency of the overall system. Transaction Processing monitors (TP-monitors) regulate the assignment of requests and load balancing is one of the several criteria they employ. The main techniques used involve simple algorithms (since the employed algorithm must be simple, fast and lightweight) such as round-robin or randomized methods. A more elaborate technique is a workload-aware method, where the TP-monitor tracks the individual load of each server and assigns a new transaction to the server with the smallest load. An excellent source of reference for the topic is Lewis, Bernstein, and Kifer (2001).

PROBLEM FORMULATION

In this section, we formally define the problem under consideration. The objective is to provide algorithms that take as input a workflow of web service operations along with a topology of servers and compute an appropriate mapping of operations to servers. In the rest of our deliberations, we will employ the terminology of WSDL. We will also use the terms composite web service, *orchestration*, and *workflow* of web service operations interchangeably.

Formal Definition of the Problem

Assume a finite set of web service operations $O=$ $\{O_1, O_2, ..., O_M\}$ and a finite set of servers $S= \{S_1, S_2, ..., S_N\}$. The term "operation" refers to WSDL operations (i.e., modules that may receive an input XML message and produce a result in the form of an output XML message). A transition (o_p, o_n) is a message sent by the web service operation o_p to the operation o_n, i.e., o_p invokes operation o_n through the submission of an XML message. We call operations o_p and o_n *neighboring operations*. A workflow is a directed graph of operations $W(O, E)$, where $E=\{(o_p, o_n) \mid o_p, o_n \in O, \exists$ a transition from o_p to $o_n\}$. Intuitively, a workflow is a graph, with operations being the nodes of the graph and XML messages being modeled as the edges of the graph. A network of servers is an undirected graph $N(S, L)$, where $L=\{(s_i, s_j) \mid s_i, s_j \in S, \exists$ connection between servers s_i and $s_j\}$. The deployment of an operation o to a server s is denoted by $o \rightarrow s$.

The operations of O can be distinguished into decision and operational ones. This follows the classification proposed by Leymann and Roller (2004), where a workflow comprises a control flow and a data flow subgraph. The operational nodes are the ones performing specific tasks for the workflow, whereas the decision nodes control the flow of execution. Following the fundamental distinction of Leymann and Roller (2004) for control nodes to *forks* (control nodes with multiple outputs, acting as routers for the execution flow) and *joins* (control nodes acting as rendezvous points that synchronize multiple parallel execution flows), we consider three types of decision operations/nodes, namely *AND, OR, and XOR*, as forks. We also assume three complementary types, denoted */AND, /OR* and */XOR* respectively, to allow the definition of *well-formed workflows*. A workflow is well-formed if for every decision node a, there exists a complement node $/a$, and all paths stemming from a also pass from $/a$. Intuitively, decision nodes and their compliments act as parentheses. The reasons for this requirement are hidden in the semantics of the graph. Assuming a decision node (like 1), the semantics are as follows: (a) *AND* nodes involve the execution of all their outgoing paths with a rendezvous barrier at */AND*, (b) *OR* nodes do the same, but it suffices that one of the paths successfully reaches */OR* and (c) *XOR* nodes involve a probabilistically weighted pick of a path to be executed. In BPEL, AND nodes may correspond to plain flow activities, OR nodes may correspond to flow activities with conditional attributes and XOR nodes may correspond to switch or pick activities.

Assume a cost model $Cost(W)$ that computes the cost of successfully completing the workflow W. More details on the alternative costs that can be used are provided in the sequel. In the broadest possible variant of the problem, we can also assume a set of user constraints C, concerning for example an upper bound on the completion

Figure 2. Examined configurations

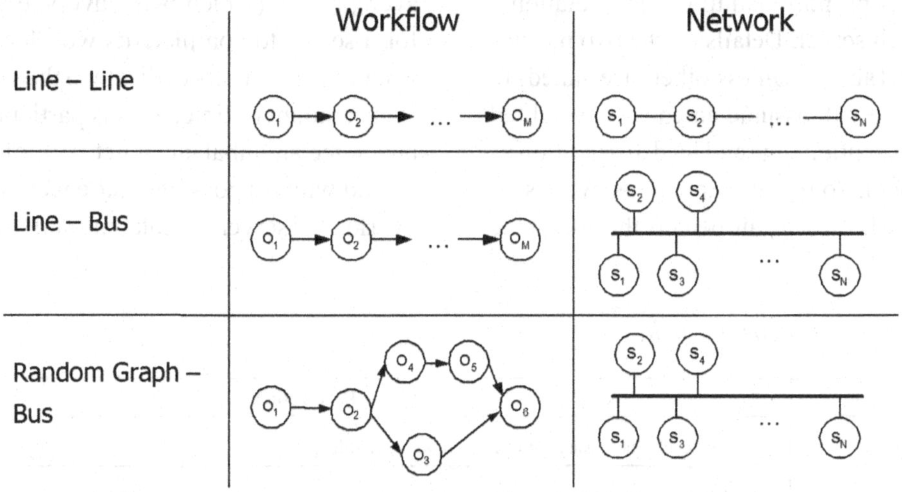

time of a workflow or on the distribution of load among the servers.

The desideratum is a mapping of the operationsOof a workflowWto the set of serversS, such that the operational cost is minimized (and the constraintsCare met). Formally, this optimum assignment of operations to servers is modeled as a finite set $M = \{r_1, r_2, ..., r_M \mid \forall\ i=1,2,...,M:$ r_i a rule of the form $o \rightarrow s,\ o \in O$ and $s \in S\}$ with the minimal $Cost(W)$ that respects C. Obviously, more than one mapping can be derived; we are interested in the one with the lowest possible cost. Depending on the algorithm employed this can be the overall optimal value (e.g., in the case of an exhaustive algorithm), or a local optimum (e.g., in the case of a greedy algorithm).

PROPOSED ALGORITHMS

In this section, we present our proposed algorithms for determining an appropriate deployment of web service operations to servers.

We have experimented with different types of workflow and server topologies. We have considered random graph topologies as well as the special, simple case of linear workflows. The

latter, being the most simple case, has served both the purpose of providing initial foresights for our experimental configuration and as an intuitive aid in the explanation of more complex cases. The network of servers forms either a linear topology (mainly for initial experimental reasons) or a bus topology. In Figure 2, we depict the combinations that were eventually considered as valid cases. In all our deliberations, we assume N servers and M operations.

Exhaustive Algorithm, Metrics and Notation

The exhaustive algorithm considers all possible mappings and outputs the one having the minimum cost. Due to the exponential search space of the exhaustive algorithm (for N servers and M operations, we have N^M configurations), we proceed with a set of heuristic solutions.

Regarding cost, we focus mainly on two cost metrics: *execution time* of the workflow and *load distribution*. Concerning the execution time of the workflow, the obvious desideratum is its minimization. Concerning the fairness of the distribution of load to servers, we want to guide our algorithms to fair solutions where the amount of work (i.e., the sum of computational cycles due to the assigned operations) is proportional to the computational power of each server. Details on the two metrics are given in Table 1. Unless otherwise stated, in the sequel, we will assume an equally weighted sum of the execution time and load distribution as our cost model. To use the same units, we assess fairness in the form of a time penalty that measures the deviation of the load of each server from the average load (which is the average time needed for a server to complete its workload). In a fair situation, all servers dedicate to the workflow the same amount of time. This is particularly important since an unbalanced network of servers has to deal with (a) possible bottlenecks due to some overloaded server in peak time and (b) difficulties

Table 1. Notation and cost formulae

Symbol	Description
$C(op)$	The cycles necessary for operation op to complete
$P(s)$	Computational power of server s (Hz)
$Server(op)$	The server where operation op is deployed
$T_{prop}(s_i, s_j)$	Propagation time of the link between servers s_i and s_j.
$Path(s_i, s_j)$	The path followed by a message from s_i to server s_j.
$T_{trans}(op_i, op_j)$	Transmittance time needed for the communication of operations op_i and op_j. $$T_{trans}(op_i, op_j) = \sum_a \frac{\mathrm{MsgSize}(op_i, op_j)}{\mathrm{Line\_Speed}(s_a, s_b)}, (s_a, s_b) \in Path(Server(op_i), Server(op_j))$$
$T_{proc}(op)$	Processing time of a deployed operation op. $$T_{proc}(op) = \frac{C(op)}{P(Server\ (op))}$$
$MsgSize(op_i, op_j)$	Message size sent from operation op_i to operation op_j, assuming $(op_i, op_j) \in E$.
$Line\_Speed(s_i, s_j)$	Line speed (bps) between servers s_i and s_j.
$Load(s)$	Total load of server s, as the sum of the processing time of operations deployed to it. $$Load(s) = \sum_j T_{proc}(O_j)$$
$T_{comm}(op_i, op_j)$	Assuming $(op_i, op_j) \in E$, the communication time between operations op_i and op_j, $T_{comm}(op_i, op_j) = $ $$\sum_a T_{prop}(s_a, s_b) + T_{trans}(op_i, op_j), (s_a, s_b) \in Path(Server(op_i), Server(op_j))$$
$Time\_Penalty$	A translation of "fairness" to the time that a server needs to conclude its work, as opposed to the avg. such time among all servers $$Time\_Penalty = \sum_{i=1}^{N-1} \sum_{j=i+1}^{N} \frac{|Load(s_i) - Load(s_j)|}{(1/2) \times N \times (N-1)}$$
$T_{execute}$	Execution time of workflow W. $$T_{execute} = \sum_{j=1}^{M} T_{proc}(O_j) + T_{comm}^{(total)}$$

in managing any other tasks, such as operation migration in cases of failures.

Clearly, the two metrics are antagonistic to each other. Take the case of a linear workflow (where each operation waits its preceding one to complete before it starts) where all operations are assigned to the most powerful server. Then, although the completion time is optimized (since no server communication costs are involved), the fairness of load distribution is destroyed. Inverse situations can also be encountered.

We have experimented with the exhaustive algorithm in small configurations to identify the properties that characterize the solutions that are close to the optimal one. These properties can be summarized as follows:

1. *Analogy between load and computational power of a server.* This clearly affects the fairness of load distribution.
2. *Minimization of the size of messages exchanged between servers.* The desideratum here is to distribute the operations to servers in such a way that neighboring operations are preferably assigned to the same server. By doing so, the fraction of messages sent over each communication line is expected to be reduced. At the same time, there is an antagonistic concern of not overloading any-one server too much; in fact, the desideratum is to preserve the aforementioned analogy between load and computational power of a server. Similarly to the minimization of the size of messages among servers, the *minimization of the number of messages exchanged between servers* is also desirable.

Algorithms for a Line: Line Configuration

The case where both the workflow and the server topology are lines is the simplest possible one. Still, it is briefly mentioned here because of the simple observations and heuristics that can be applied to it.

The *Line-Line* algorithm receives a workflow of web service operations $W(O, E)$, and a server configuration $N(S, L)$ as its input. The algorithm operates in two discrete phases. In the first phase, the algorithm tries to produce a load distribution as fair as possible, while attempting to minimize the number of exchanged messages. In the second phase, the algorithm tries to move operations to neighboring servers to avoid sending large messages over low capacity links. For N servers and M operations, the complexity of the first phase is $O(M)$ and the complexity of the second one is $O(N)$. The algorithm is depicted in Figure 4.

First, the algorithm computes the ideal load per server (Line 7). The ideal load is computed as the fraction of the total workload that corresponds to the server given the percentage of the computational power the server can contribute to the overall computational power. Then, it starts assigning the operations of W to the servers of N starting from the first operation/server on the left. When a server comes as close as possible to its ideal load (test in lines 11-12), the algorithm considers the next server. The algorithm makes also some provision for the case when the operations are less than the number of servers (Lines 20-28). The first phase ends, when all operations have been allocated. The second phase of the *Line-Line* algorithm is based on the idea of a *critical bridge*, which is a link between two servers of the network with (a) a small capacity and a large message load (in bytes), plus (b) a small-sized message concerning an adjacent operation. Figure 3 depicts such a case. Whenever a critical bridge is detected, the algorithm deploys the receiver of the large message to the server of the sender of the message (or vice-versa). This is achieved through the call of function *Fix Bad Bridges* (Line 30) which is detailed in Figure 5.

The algorithm *Line-Line* (Figure 4) comes with variants. The first variation simply avoids the second phase of the algorithm. A second variation

Figure 3. Critical bridge

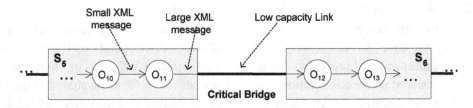

Figure 4. Algorithm line line

Input: A workflow **W**(O, E) (in line topology), where O = (O_1, O_2, ..., O_M) a set of operations, E = {(O_i, O_{i+1}) | ∀ i = 1,..., M-1} the set of transitions among operations and **N**(S, L) a server network (in line topology), where S = {S_1, S_2, ..., S_N} a set of servers and L = {(S_i, S_{i+1}) | ∀ i = 1, ..., N-1} the network connections among servers (M>N).
Output: A mapping **M** of O to S.
Begin

```
1    Operations_List = (O₁, O₂, ..., Oₘ)
2    Servers_List = (S₁, S₂, ..., Sₙ)
                    M
3    Sum_Cycles =  ∑ C(Oᵢ)
                   i=1

                     N
4    Sum_Capacity = ∑ P(Sⱼ)
                    j=1

5    M = ∅
6    s = Servers_List.pop
7    Ideal_Cycles = Sum_Cycles × P(s) / Sum_Capacity
8    Current_Cycles = 0
9    while Operations_List is not empty do
10        o = Operation_List.pop
11        if SizeOf(Operation_List) ≥ SizeOf(Servers_List) then
12            if Current_Cycles + C(o) < Ideal_Cycles + 0.2×Ideal_Cycles or
13            Current_Cycles = 0 or s is Sₙ then
14                Current_Cycles = Current_Cycles + C(o)
15            else
16                s = Servers_List.pop
17                Ideal_Cycles = Sum_Cycles × P(s) / Sum_Capacity
18                Current_Cycles = C(o)
19            end if
20        M = M ∪ {o→s}
21        else
22            s = Servers_List.pop
23            M = M ∪ {o→s}
24            while Operation_List is not empty do
25                o = Operation_List.pop
26                s = Servers_List.pop
27                M = M ∪ {o→s}
28            end while
29        end if
30    end while
31    Fix_Bad_Bridges (W, N, M);
32    return M
```

End

Side annotations:

> *The ideal load per server is computed*

> *Phase A: original mapping of operations to servers.* **While** *unassigned operations exist and operations are more than the servers, pick next*

> **If** *server far from ideal load, assign operation*

> **else,** *pick next*

> *If less operations than servers, simple assignment*

> *Phase B: if critical bridges exist, reallocate operations*

Figure 5. Function fix bad bridges

Function Fix Bad Bridges

Input: The workflow **W**, the network **N** of algorithm Line-Line, and a starting mapping **M**.

Output: A possibly updated mapping **M**. The function checks whether critical bridges exist and moves a deployed operation to the next/previous server (left or right depending on where the expensive message is)

Begin

    1   *Sort the speeds of the lines of* N *at ongoing order in list* L_1.

    2   *Sort the sizes of messages that are sending between servers (from last operation at server* i *to first operation at server* i+1*) at ongoing order in list* L_2.

    3   *for* i=1 *to* N-1 *do*

    4   *if* Is_Critical_Bridge(S, M, i, L_1, L_2, shift_direction) = True *then*

    5   *if* shift_direction = right *then*

    6   **M** = **M** + {LastOperationAt(S_i)→S_{i+1}} − {LastOperationAt(S_i)→S_i}

    7   *else*

    8   **M** = **M** + {FirstOperationAt(S_{i+1})→S_i} − {FirstOperationAt(S_{i+1})→S_{i+1}}

    9   *end if*

    10   *end if*

    11   *end for*

End

Figure 6. Function Is critical bridge

Function Is Critical Bridge

Input: The workflow **W**, the network **N** of algorithm Line-Line, a mapping **M**, an integer "i" representing the bridge to be checked and the sorted lists L_1 and L_2 with the network connections and the message sizes for each bridge, respectively.

Output: the function returns True if the bridge among S_i και S_{i+1} is critical; otherwise it returns False. The shift_direction variable stores the direction of the move that must take place, in the former case.

Begin

    1   *if* Line_Speed(S_i, S_{i+1}) ≤ Top20 of L_1 *and*

        MsgSize(LastOperationAt(S_i), FirstOperationAt(S_{i+1})) ≥ Bottom20 of L_2 *then*

    2   *if* MsgSize(PenultOperationAt(S_i), LastOperationAt(S_i)) ≤ Top20 of L_2 *then*

    3   shift_direction = right

    4   return True

    5   *end if*

    6   *if* MsgSize(FirstOperationAt(S_{i+1}), SecondOperationAt(S_{i+1})) ≤ Top20 of L_2 *then*

    7   shift_direction = left

    8   *return* True

    9   *end if*

    10   *end if*

    11 *return* False

End

---

considers the assignment of operations to servers both from left-to-right and from right-to-left and maintains the better of the two. The combination of these variants produces four alternatives for the computation of the best configuration with the obvious complexities.

Algorithms for a Line: Bus configuration

In this subsection, we move to a more realistic case, where all servers are connected to each other through a network bus. The workflow is

Figure 7. Algorithm fair load

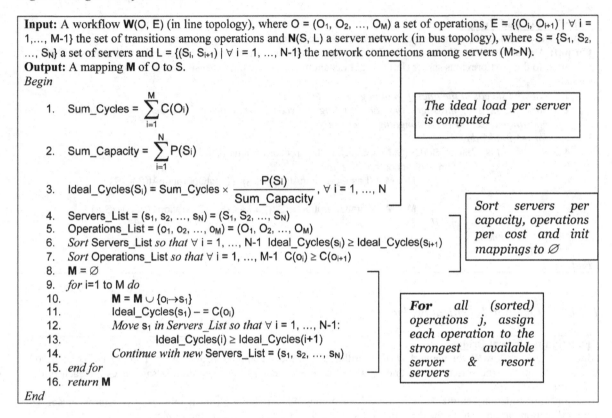

Input: A workflow **W**(O, E) (in line topology), where O = (O₁, O₂, ..., Oₘ) a set of operations, E = {(Oᵢ, Oᵢ₊₁) | ∀ i = 1,..., M-1} the set of transitions among operations and **N**(S, L) a server network (in bus topology), where S = {S₁, S₂, ..., Sₙ} a set of servers and L = {(Sᵢ, Sᵢ₊₁) | ∀ i = 1, ..., N-1} the network connections among servers (M>N).
Output: A mapping **M** of O to S.
Begin

1. $Sum\_Cycles = \sum_{i=1}^{M} C(O_i)$

2. $Sum\_Capacity = \sum_{i=1}^{N} P(S_i)$

3. $Ideal\_Cycles(S_i) = Sum\_Cycles \times \dfrac{P(S_i)}{Sum\_Capacity}, \forall i = 1, ..., N$

> *The ideal load per server is computed*

4. Servers_List = (s₁, s₂, ..., sₙ) = (S₁, S₂, ..., Sₙ)
5. Operations_List = (o₁, o₂, ..., oₘ) = (O₁, O₂, ..., Oₘ)
6. *Sort* Servers_List *so that* ∀ i = 1, ..., N-1 Ideal_Cycles(sᵢ) ≥ Ideal_Cycles(sᵢ₊₁)
7. *Sort* Operations_List *so that* ∀ i = 1, ..., M-1 C(oᵢ) ≥ C(oᵢ₊₁)
8. **M** = ∅

> *Sort servers per capacity, operations per cost and init mappings to ∅*

9. *for* i=1 to M *do*
10.   **M** = **M** ∪ {oᵢ↦s₁}
11.   Ideal_Cycles(s₁) − = C(oᵢ)
12.   *Move* s₁ *in Servers_List so that* ∀ i = 1, ..., N-1:
13.   Ideal_Cycles(i) ≥ Ideal_Cycles(i+1)
14.   *Continue with new* Servers_List = (s₁, s₂, ..., sₙ)
15. *end for*
16. *return* **M**

> ***For** all (sorted) operations j, assign each operation to the strongest available server & resort servers*

End

still a simple line. We can produce several greedy variants of a simple algorithm, which are subsequently listed.

Fair Load: The simplest of all the involved variants is tuned to obtain the best possible load distribution. *Fair Load* (Figure 7) starts by computing the ideal number of cycles that should be assigned to a server based on its capacity. Then, it sorts servers by their capacity and operations by their execution cost. The algorithm processes the sorted list of operations, each time, assigning the next heaviest operation to the most appropriate server. The most appropriate server is the server that needs the most cycles to complete its ideal number of cycles, at the time of the assignment. *Fair Load* is a variant of

the worst-fit algorithm for the bin packing problem.

Fair Load – Tie Resolver for Cycles: *Fair Load* does not take execution time into consideration. A simple extension involves resolving any ties that may come up during the selection process among operations with the same number of cycles. The algorithm *Fair Load – Tie Resolver for Cycles*, (or, $FLTR_1$ for brevity), depicted in Figure 8, operates as *Fair Load* with respect to its basic principle (Figure 8). The difference lies in the fact that whenever we need one among a number of operations with the same cost, we no longer pick one at random. Instead, we employ a gain function, *Gain_Of_Opera-*

Figure 8. Algorithm fair load – tie resolver for cycles

Input: a workflow of web service operations $W(O, E)$, with $O = (O_1, O_2,..., O_M)$ and a server configuration $N(S, L)$, with $S = \{S_1, S_2, ..., S_N\}$ and L all the combinations of server pairs with the same network costs (bus)

Output: a mapping **M** of O to S

Begin

1. $Sum\_Cycles = \sum_{i=1}^{M} C(O_i)$, $Sum\_Capacity = \sum_{i=1}^{N} P(S_i)$ ⎤ *The ideal load per server is computed*

2. $Ideal\_Cycles(S_i) = Sum\_Cycles \times \dfrac{P(S_i)}{Sum\_Capacity}$, $i = 1, ..., N$ ⎦

3. $Servers\_List = (s_1, s_2, ..., s_N) = (S_1, S_2, ..., S_N)$ ⎤ *Sort servers per capacity, operations per cost and init mappings randomly*
4. $Operations\_List = (o_1, o_2, ..., o_M) = (O_1, O_2, ..., O_M)$
5. Sort Servers_List *so that* $\forall\ i = 1, ..., N\text{-}1$ $Ideal\_Cycles(s_i) \geq Ideal\_Cycles(s_{i+1})$
6. Sort Operations_List *so that* $\forall\ i = 1, ..., M\text{-}1$ $C(o_i) \geq C(o_{i+1})$ ⎦
7. *Initialize* **M** *to a random* Mapping
8. *while* Operations_List *is not empty do*
9. $gain_1 = Gain\_Of\_Operation\_At\_Server(o_1, s_1, M)$
10. $i=2$
11.   *while* $C(o_1) = C(o_i)$ *and* $i \leq M$ do{ ⎤ ***While*** *there are operations o_i equally* costly *with current (o_1) that give less cost if placed at current server (s_1), assign o_i at s_1*
12. $gain_2 = Gain\_Of\_Operation\_At\_Server(o_i, s_1, M)$
13.   *if* $gain_2 > gain_1$ {
14. $swap(o_1, o_i)$
15. $gain_1 = gain_2$ }
16. $i++$
17.   } //end inner while ⎦
18. $M = M - \{o_1 \rightarrow Server(o_1)\}$
19. $M = M \cup \{o_1 \rightarrow s_1\}$ ⎤ *When done with tie-breaking, same as before: move to next operation, resort servers, move to next server*
20.   *Delete* o_1 *from* Operations_List
21. $Ideal\_Cycles(s_1) - = C(o_1)$
22.   *Move* s_1 *in* Servers_List *so that* $\forall\ i = 1, ..., N\text{-}1$:
23. $Ideal\_Cycles(i) \geq Ideal\_Cycles(i+1)$
24.   *Continue with new* Servers_List $= (s_1, s_2,..., s_N)$ ⎦
25. } //end outer while
26. *return* **M**

End

tion_At_Server that returns the communication savings (i.e., how many bytes will not be put on the bus), if the next operation is deployed to a certain server (Figure 9). The best such assignment among all candidate operations and servers is picked. The algorithm uses two lists, *Servers_List* και *Operations_List*, with pointers to the respective sets. The algorithm also needs to initialize the mapping *M* to a random configuration, or else, the first calls of function *Gain_Of_Operation_At_Server* would not return any gain at all.

Fair Load – Tie Resolver for Cycles and Servers: The algorithm *Fair Load – Tie Resolver for Cycles* can be extended to also handle ties among servers. The algorithm *Fair Load – Tie Resolver for Cycles and Servers*, (or, *FLTR$_2$* for brevity), depicted in Figure 10, simply customizes appropriately the previous gain function to also consider the case in which there is a tie among the servers to be chosen next, with respect to their distance from their ideal load.

Figure 9. Function gain of operation at server

```
Function Gain_Of _Operation_At_Server    //message size that we avoid putting in the network
Begin
    1.   gain = 0
    2.   if Oᵢ ∈ (O₂, O₃, ..., O_M) and {O_{i-1}→S_j} ∈ M then
    3.         gain += MsgSize(O_{i-1}, O_i)
    4.   if Oᵢ ∈ (O₁, O₂,..., O_{M-1}) and {O_{i+1}→S_j} ∈ M then
    5.         gain += MsgSize(O_i, O_{i+1})
    6.   return gain
End
```

Figure 10. Algorithm fair load – tie resolver for cycles and servers

Input: A workflow $W(O, E)$ (in line topology), where $O = (O_1, O_2, ..., O_M)$ a set of operations, $E = \{(O_i, O_{i+1}) \mid \forall\ i = 1,..., M\text{-}1\}$ the set of transitions among operations and $N(S, L)$ a server network (in bus topology), where $S = \{S_1, S_2, ..., S_N\}$ a set of servers and $L = \{(S_i, S_{i+1}) \mid \forall\ i = 1, ..., N\text{-}1\}$ the network connections among servers ($M > N$).

Output: A mapping M of O to S.

Begin

1. Sum_Cycles = $\sum_{i=1}^{M} C(O_i)$

2. Sum_Capacity = $\sum_{i=1}^{N} P(S_i)$ · *The ideal load per server is computed*

3. Ideal_Cycles(S_i) = Sum_Cycles × $\dfrac{P(S_i)}{\text{Sum\_Capacity}}$, $\forall\ i = 1, ..., N$

4.   Servers_List = ($s_1, s_2, ..., s_N$) = ($S_1, S_2, ..., S_N$)
5.   Operations_List = ($o_1, o_2, ..., o_M$) = ($O_1, O_2, ..., O_M$)
6.   Not_Assigned_Operations = M
7.   *Initialize M to a random Mapping*

> *Sort servers per capacity, operations per cost and init mappings randomly*

8.   *while* Not_Assigned_Operations ≠ 0 *do*
9.   *Sort* Servers_List *so that* $\forall\ i = 1, ..., N\text{-}1$ Ideal_Cycles(s_i) ≥ Ideal_Cycles(s_{i+1})
10.   *Sort* Operations_List *so that* $\forall\ i = 1, ..., $ Not_Assigned_Operations-1 C(o_i) ≥ C(o_{i+1})
11.   best_gain = 0
12.   *for each operation* o_i *in* Operations_List *where* C(o_i) = C(o_1) *do*
13.   *for each server* s_j *in* Servers_List *where* Ideal_Cycles(s_j)=Ideal_Cycles(s_1) *do*
14.   gain = Gain_Of_Put_Operation_At_Server(o_i, s_j, M)
15.   *if* gain > best_gain *then*
16.   best_gain = gain
17.   bestO = o_i
18.   bestS = s_j
19.   *end if*
20.   *end for*
21.   *end for*
22.   M = M − {bestO→Server(bestO)}
23.   M = M ∪ {bestO→bestS}
24.   Not_Assigned_Operations − −
25.   Ideal_Cycles(bestS) − = C(bestO)
26.   *Delete* bestO *from* Operation_List
27. *end while*
28. *return* M

End

> **For all** *unassigned operations (current= o_1) Sort servers per capacity left, operations as before. If there are combinations of servers and operations with a* **tie** *to the current pair of $o1$, $s1$, then find the best pair (bestO, bestS) and assign them the mapping for this round*

> *When done with tie-breaking, move to next operation & housekeeingp*

Summarizing, both *Tie Resolver* algorithms handle practically the same configurations with *Fair Load*, with the only difference that special attention is paid to situations where ties occur, with the overall goal to reduce the communication cost. However, it is still possible to send large messages over the network. The following extension tries to alleviate this problem.

Fair Load–Merge Messages' Ends: Algorithm *Fair Load–Merge Messages' Ends* (or, *FLMME* for brevity), depicted in Figure 11, extends $FLTR_2$ by adding an extra test during the deployment decision. If the assignment of an operation to a server results in a large message, the assignment is cancelled and the operation is assigned to the sender of the message, thus alleviating the need to send the message (see function *There Is Constraint* in Figure 12). A message is considered large whenever the time needed to transfer it is larger than the execution time of the costliest group of operations over the server with the most available cycles at the time the decision is made.

Heavy Operations – Large Messages: Algorithm *Heavy Operations–Large Messages* (Figure 13) operates like *Fair Load*, with the fundamental difference that operations are not treated separately, but as groups. Two operations are clustered in the same group if they exchange a large message. As in the previous case, a message is considered large whenever the time needed to transfer it is larger than the execution time of the costliest group of operations over the server with the most available cycles at the time the decision is made. Recall that, in the bus topology, the communication cost between every pair of servers is considered the same. Activities that have been grouped together are always assigned to the same server.

Initially, each operation constitutes a group by itself. The algorithm employs three lists, one for the available cycles of each server, one for the size of each message and one for the cycles of each group. In the beginning of each step, these

lists are sorted. In each step, the algorithm decides whether (a) to assign the most expensive group of operations to the server with the most available cycles, or (b) to avoid the exchange of a large message over the network. The decision is taken on the basis of the existence of a large message on the top of the list of the messages. If such a message exists, then option (b) is followed. In this case, either (b1) both message ends are placed at the same server, or (b2) the two groups are merged. Option (b1) is followed, if one of the two operations that communicate through the large message is already placed at a server. Otherwise, the groups to which the communicating operations belong are merged. Note that messages must be removed from the list whenever both their ends are placed at the same server.

The complexities of the algorithms are $O(M \times logM + N \times logN + MN)$ for *Fair Load*, and $O(M \times (M \times logM + N \times logN + MN))$ for the rest of the algorithms. In the algorithm *Heavy Operations–Large Messages*, instead of the last operand of the sum (i.e., *MN*) the cost to be added is *1*.

3.4 Algorithms for a Random Graph – Bus configuration

In this third family of algorithms, we consider the case where the servers are still connected through a bus but the workflow is a random graph. All algorithms are practically the same with the category *Line-Bus*, with simple modifications that take the structure of the workflow into account. The algorithms must take into consideration that an operation can receive more than one message and that decision nodes possibly imply the execution of a subset of the workflow. Remember that decision nodes (*AND, OR, XOR*) start subgraphs of the workflow that are executed in parallel for *AND, OR* nodes. For *XOR* nodes, one of the alternatives is chosen. At the same time, the */AND, /OR, /XOR* nodes act as rendezvous points (and thus, they need to wait for at least two messages in the case of */AND, /OR* flows).

Figure 11. Algorithm fair load – merge messages' ends

Input: A workflow **W**(O, E) (in line topology), where O = (O₁, O₂, ..., Oₘ) a set of operations, E = {(Oᵢ, Oᵢ₊₁) | ∀ i = 1,..., M-1} the set of transitions among operations and **N**(S, L) a server network (in bus topology), where S = {S₁, S₂, ..., Sₙ} a set of servers and L = {(Sᵢ, Sᵢ₊₁) | ∀ i = 1, ..., N-1} the network connections among servers (M>N).
Output: A mapping **M** of O to S.
Begin

1. $Sum\_Cycles = \sum_{i=1}^{M} C(O_i)$ *The ideal load per server is computed*

2. $Sum\_Capacity = \sum_{i=1}^{N} P(S_i)$

3. $Ideal\_Cycles(S_i) = Sum\_Cycles \times \dfrac{P(S_i)}{Sum\_Capacity}, \forall i = 1, ..., N$

4.   Servers_List = (s₁, s₂, ..., sₙ) = (S₁, S₂, ..., Sₙ)   *Sort servers per capacity, operations per cost and init mappings randomly*
5.   Operations_List = (o₁, o₂, ..., oₘ) = (O₁, O₂, ..., Oₘ)
6.   Messages_List = (m₁, m₂, ..., mₘ₋₁) = ((O₁, O₂), (O₂, O₃), ..., (Oₘ₋₁, Oₘ))
7.   Sort Messages_List *so that* ∀ i = 1, ..., M-2 MsgSize(mᵢ) ≥ MsgSize(mᵢ₊₁)
8.   Not_Assigned_Operations = M
9.   *Initialize* **M** *to a random Mapping*
10.   *while* Not_Assigned_Operations ≠ 0 *do*
11.   *Sort* Servers_List *so that* ∀ i = 1, ..., N-1 Ideal_Cycles(sᵢ) ≥ Ideal_Cycles(sᵢ₊₁)
12.   *Sort* Operations_List *so that* ∀ i = 1, ..., Not_Assigned_Operations-1 C(oᵢ) ≥ C(oᵢ₊₁)
13.   best_gain = 0;
14.   *for each* operation oᵢ in Operations_List *where* C(oᵢ) = C(o₁) *do*
15.   *for each* server sⱼ in Servers_List *where* Ideal_Cycles(sⱼ)=Ideal_Cycles(s₁) *do*
16.   gain = Gain_Of_Put_Operation_At_Server(oᵢ, sⱼ, **M**)
17.   if gain > best_gain then   ***While*** *there are operations oᵢ* __equally__ __costly__ *with current (o₁) that give less cost if placed at current server (s₁), assign oᵢ at s₁ and keep the winner pair (operation at server) at (bestO, bests)*
18.   best_gain = gain
19.   bestO = oᵢ
20.   bestS = sⱼ
21.   *end if*
22.   *end for*
23.   *end for*
24.   **M** = **M** − {bestO→Server(bestO)}
25.   *if* There_Is_Constraint (bestO, bestS, **M**, MsgSize(m₍ₘ₋₁₎ₓ₀.₁), constraints_flag) *then*
26.   *if* constraints_flag = left_message *then*
27.   **M** = **M** ∪ {bestO→ServerOf(LeftOperationOf(bestO)}
28.   Ideal_Cycles(ServerOf(LeftOperationOf(bestO) − = C(bestO)
29.   *else*   ***If*** *this assignment produces large msg's in the network, move the operation* __left__ *or* __right__ *(according to the result of ThereISConstraint)* ***Else*** *just do the assignment In any case, finally, do housekeeping*
30.   **M** = **M** ∪ {bestO→ServerOf(RightOperationOf(bestO)}
31.   Ideal_Cycles(ServerOf(RightOperationOf(bestO) − = C(bestO)
32.   *end if*
33.   *else*
34.   **M** = **M** ∪ {bestO→bestS}
35.   Ideal_Cycles(bestS) − = C(bestO)
36.   *end if*
37.   Not_Assigned_Operations − −
38.   Delete bestO from Operation_List
39.   *end while*
40.   *return* **M**
End

The extension to the algorithms is quite simple: all the algorithms of this family (with the exception of algorithm *Fair Load* that remains exactly the same) assign an execution probability to each operation (and thus, each message) due to the existence of XOR decision nodes. The determination of this probability is based on monitoring initial executions of the workflow or simple prediction mechanisms. Thus, the execution cost is a practically a weighted cost, amortized for a large number of workflow executions (as opposed to a single execution as in the case of linear workflows).

EXPERIMENTS

In this section, we present experimental results for the assessment of the proposed algorithms. First,

Figure 12. Function there is constraint

```
Function There Is Constraint
Input: An operation Oᵢ∈O, a server Sⱼ∈S, a threshold big_message_size that determines whether a message is large
or not and a mapping M⊆O×S.
Output: True if there is a constraint in assigning Oᵢ to Sⱼ; otherwise False. In the former case, a flag constraints_flag
takes one of the values left_message or right_message to signify which of the two messages (Oᵢ₋₁, Oᵢ) and (Oᵢ, Oᵢ₊₁)
triggers the constraint. If both messages trigger a constraint violation, the one furthest from the threshold value is
highlighted.
Begin
    1.   if  Oᵢ = O₁  then
    2.          if  MsgSize(O₁, O₂) ≥ big_message_size  then
    3.                  constraints_flag = right_message
    4.                  return True
    5.          end if
    6.   else if  Oᵢ = O_M  then
    7.          if  MsgSize(O_{M-1}, O_M) ≥ big_message_size  then
    8.                  constraints_flag = left_message
    9.                  return True
    10.         end if
    11.  else if  Oᵢ ∈ (O₂, O₃,..., O_{M-1})  then
    12.         if  MsgSize(Oᵢ₋₁, Oᵢ) ≥ big_message_size  then
    13.                 constraints_flag = left_message
    14.         end if
    15.         if  MsgSize(Oᵢ, Oᵢ₊₁) ≥ big_message_size  then
    16.                 if constraints_flag = left_message  and  MsgSize(Oᵢ₋₁,Oᵢ) ≥ MsgSize(Oᵢ,Oᵢ₊₁)
    17.                         constraints_flag = left_message
    18.                         return True
    19.                 else
    20.                         constraints_flag = right_message
    21.                         return True
    22.                 end if
    23.         end if
    24.  end if
    25.  return False
End
```

we present an experiment for the validation of the cost model. Then, we discuss experiments for each of the three workflow-network configurations explored in the previous sections, and finally, we summarize our experimental findings.

Cost Model Validation

To validate our cost model we performed an experiment that relied on the reference example discussed previously. More specifically, we implemented the workflow schema of Figure1 using a widely-used infrastructure that supports the development of web services. Then, we ex-

ecuted this implementation in a configuration of three servers S1, S2, S3, and compared the mean execution time of the workflow (calculated over 100 executions of the workflow) with the execution time that is estimated based on the proposed cost model.

To implement the web service operations that constitute the examined workflow we used AXIS v1.1. The web service operations that concern the patient, the secretary and the doctor were deployed, respectively, on a P-IV 3.4 GHz, a P-IV 1.6 GHz and a P-IV 2.13 GHz server. The application server that we used in all three servers

Figure 13. Algorithm heavy operations - large messages

Input: A workflow **W**(O, E) (in line topology), where O = (O$_1$, O$_2$, ..., O$_M$) a set of operations, E = {(O$_i$, O$_{i+1}$) | $\forall$ i = 1,..., M-1} the set of transitions among operations and N(S, L) a server network (in bus topology), where S = {S$_1$, S$_2$, ..., S$_N$} a set of servers and L = {(S$_i$, S$_{i+1}$) | $\forall$ i = 1, ..., N-1} the network connections among servers (M>N).
Output: A mapping **M** of O to S.
Begin

1.　　Sum_Cycles = $\sum_{i=1}^{M} C(O_i)$

2.　　Sum_Capacity = $\sum_{i=1}^{N} P(S_i)$　　　　　　　　　*The ideal load per server is computed*

3.　　Ideal_Cycles(S$_i$) = Sum_Cycles $\times \dfrac{P(S_i)}{Sum\_Capacity}$, $\forall$ i = 1, ..., N

4.　　Servers_List = (s$_1$, s$_2$, ..., s$_N$) = (S$_1$, S$_2$, ..., S$_N$)　　　*Initially, each operation is a separate group*
5.　　Group_Of_Oper_List = (g$_1$, g$_2$, ..., g$_M$) = (O$_1$, O$_2$, ..., O$_M$)
6.　　Messages_List = (m$_1$, m$_2$, ..., m$_{M-1}$) = ((O$_1$, O$_2$), (O$_2$, O$_3$), ..., (O$_{M-1}$, O$_M$))
7.　　Not_Assigned_Operations = M
8.　　*while* Not_Assigned_Operations $\neq$ 0 *do*
9.　　　　*Sort* Servers_List *so that* $\forall$ i=1...N-1 Ideal_Cycles(s$_i$) $\geq$ Ideal_Cycles(s$_{i+1}$)
10.　　　*Sort* Group_Of_Oper_List *so that* $\forall$ i=1...number of groups-1 C(g$_i$) $\geq$ C(g$_{i+1}$)
11.　　　*Sort* Messages_List *so that*
12.　　　　　$\forall$ i = 1, ..., size of Messages_List-1 MsgSize(m$_i$)$\geq$MsgSize(m$_{i+1}$)
13.　　　*if* Tproc(g$_1$) *at server* s$_1$ > Time of sending m$_1$ via bus *then*
14.　　　　　*for each* o$_i \in$g$_1$ *do*
15.　　　　　　　**M** = **M** $\cup$ {o$_i \rightarrow$s$_1$}
16.　　　　　　　Not_Assigned_Operations − −
17.　　　　　　　Ideal_Cycles(s$_1$) − = C(o$_i$)
18.　　　　　*end for*
19.　　　　　*Delete* g$_1$ *from* Group_Of_Oper_List
20.　　　*else*
21.　　　　　*if* source(m$_1$) *is not assigned and* target(m$_1$) *is assigned then*
22.　　　　　　　**M** = **M** $\cup$ {source(m$_1$)$\rightarrow$ServerOf (target(m$_1$))}
23.　　　　　　　Not_Assigned_Operations − −
24.　　　　　　　Ideal_Cycles(ServerOf (target(m$_1$))) − = C(source(m$_1$))
25.　　　　　　　*Delete* source(m$_1$) *from its group in* Group_Of_Oper_List
26.　　　　　*else if* source(m$_1$) *is assigned and* target(m$_1$) *is not assigned then*
27.　　　　　　　**M** = **M** $\cup$ {target(m$_1$)$\rightarrow$ServerOf (source(m$_1$))}
28.　　　　　　　Not_Assigned_Operations − −
29.　　　　　　　Ideal_Cycles(ServerOf (source(m$_1$))) − = C(target(m$_1$))
30.　　　　　　　*Delete* target(m$_1$) *from its group in* Group_Of_Oper_List
31.　　　　　*else* // both source(m$_1$) and target(m$_1$) are not assigned
32.　　　　　　　g$_{new}$ = Merge (group(source(m$_1$)), group(target(m$_1$)))
33.　　　　　　　*Insert* g$_{new}$ *in* Group_Of_Oper_List
34.　　　　　*end if*
35.　　　*end if*
36.　　　*for* i=1 to size of Messages_List *do*
37.　　　　　*if* source(m$_i$) *and* target(m$_i$) *are assigned*
38.　　　　　　　*Delete* m$_i$ *from* Messages_Lists
39.　　*end while*
40.　　*return* **M**
End

The ideal load per server is computed

Initially, each operation is a separate group

While *there are operations unassigned:*
sort servers by remaining capacity, groups by cost and messages by size
if *cost of assigning costliest operation at server is larger than sending larger msg, assign all the group of this operation to the server*

else *pick largest msg m1 and check the ends of its edge; if one of the two ends is unassigned, assigned the other in the same server;* **else** *both ends groups' are merged*

Side-effect of a groups assignment is that some msg will not travel in the network, so it must be removed from the msg list

was Apache Tomcat 4.1. The three servers were connected through a typical 100 Mbps Ethernet.

Concerning the cost model, we measured the cycles required for each web service operation by executing the workflow on a single server (i.e., the P-IV 1.6 GHz). In this context, we measured the time required by each operation to perform its computations, along with the time required

Table 2. Cost Model Parameters for our motivating example

Symbol	Description									
C(op) - The cycles necessary for operation *op* to complete										
C(1)	C(2)	C(3)	C(4)	C(6)	C(7)	C(8)	C(10)	C(11)	C(12)	C(13)
24992000	39632000	39632000	54272000	24992000	39632000	54272000	24992000	39632000	24992000	24992000
P(s) - Computational power of server *s* (Hz)										
P(S1)				P(S2)				P(S3)		
$3.4 * 10^6$				$1.6 * 10^6$				$2.13 * 10^6$		
Server(op) - The server where operation *op* is deployed										
Server(1)	Server(2)	Server(3)	Server(4)	Server(6)	Server(7)	Server(8)	Server(10)	Server(11)	Server(12)	Server(13)
S1	S2	S3	S2	S3	S1	S3	S2	S1	S2	S1

MsgSize(op$_i$, op$_j$) - Message size sent from operation *op$_i$* to operation *op$_j$*, assuming *(op$_i$,op$_j$)* $\in E$ **(Mbits)**	*Line speed (Mbps) between servers s$_i$ and s$_j$*	T_{comm}(op$_i$, op$_j$) - Communication time needed for the communication of operations op$_i$ and op$_j$ (msec)
0.00666	100	0,0666

for preparing its invocations to the web service operations with which it communicates (e.g., for the web service operation 3, we measured the time required for its internal computation and the time required for preparing the invocation of web service operation 4). The sum of the aforementioned execution times was transformed into computational cycles based on the server's computational power. It should be further noted that in the calculation of the estimated execution time of the examined workflow we assumed that the decision operations (operations 5 and 9 of the reference example) do not require any computational cycles. The parameters used in our cost model are given in more detail in Table 2.

The mean execution time that was experimentally measured for the examined workflow was 187 msec. The estimated execution time that was calculated with respect to the parameters of Table 2 was 192 msec, i.e., the cost model overestimated the execution time with the acceptably small error of 2%.

Experimental Methodology

We have varied several parameters of the workflow-network configurations used. We use the results of Head et al. (2005) and Ng, Chen, and Greenfield (2004) to determine appropriate values for our experiments. In Ng et al. (2004), three types of SOAP messages are used: simple messages of 873 bytes (0.00666 Mbits), medium messages of 7581 bytes (0.057838 Mbits), and complex messages of 21392 bytes (0.163208 Mbits). We assume 4, 10, and 20 ms as the time needed for the execution of a web service operation (this includes the serialization, network time, deserialization and server execution time). Assuming a value of 37% for the parsing of a message, this results in 2.5, 6.3 and 12.7 M cycles for simple, medium and complex messages, respectively (over a 1.6 MHz CPU). Based on the previous in our experiments we assume simple, medium and heavy web service operations, requiring respectively, 10, 20 and 30 M cycles.

In each experiment we considered a specific workflow of web service operations deployed over a specific network of servers. The operations' cost,

Table 3. Experimental configuration

$MsgSize(O_i, O_{i+1})$	0.006660 *Mbits* with probability *25%* 0.057838 *Mbits* with probability *50%* 0.163208 *Mbits* with probability *25%*
Line_Speed(S_i, S_{i+1}) (for Line topologies)	10 *Mbps* with probability *25%* 100 *Mbps* with probability *50%* 1000 *Mbps* with probability *25%*
$C(O_i)$	10 *M* cycles with probability *25%* 20 *M* cycles with probability *50%* 30 *M* cycles with probability *25%*
$P(S_i)$	1 *GHz* with probability *25%* 2 *GHz* with probability *50%* 3 *GHz* with probability *25%*

the associated messages, the computational power of the servers and the network characteristics were randomly selected based on the probabilities given in Table 3.

In all the graphical representations, the horizontal axis of each diagram depicts the execution time and the vertical axis the time penalty. The closer a solution to point (0, 0), the better. Assuming different weights for the two measures, different distance measures could also be considered. The average point of the search space of solutions is also depicted as a measure of how a "random" choice of deployment would possibly be. In small configurations this involves all the solutions of the search space; in large configurations a sample of 32,000 solutions).

Experiments for a Line: Line Configuration

The experiments performed for this configuration involve all four variants of the proposed algorithm. Specifically, we have experimented with (a) single dimension (left-to-right) *Line-Line* algorithm with the application of *Fix_Bad_Bridges* (denoted as *1d with Fix*), (b) single dimension (left-to-right) *Line-Line* algorithm without the application of *Fix_Bad_Bridges* (denoted as *1d no Fix*), (c) double dimension (left-to-right and right to left) *Line-Line* algorithm with the application of *Fix_Bad_Bridges* (denoted as *2d with Fix*), and

(d) double dimension (left-to-right and right to left) *Line-Line* algorithm without the application of *Fix_Bad_Bridges* (denoted as *2d no Fix*).

Figure 14 presents four experiments for larger configurations (each reported in the figure). Due to the vastness of the search space, the reported average concerns 32,000 randomly sampled solutions. The different variants of the algorithm do not show significant differences, while presenting satisfactory solutions with respect to both the time penalty and the execution time. Observe how far from the optimal solution the average solution is placed (upper right part of each figure). Similar behaviour was obtained in experiments for smaller configurations of workflows with 8 operations over network topologies of 3 servers.

Experiments for a Line: Bus Configuration

We have conducted all classes of experiments with all the proposed algorithms participating for the configuration of linear workflows executed over a network bus. In Figure 15, we depict comparative results of the employed algorithms by computing the average solution of 50 experiments. We test workflows of 19 operations over network topologies of (a) 5, (b) 10, and (c) 15 servers connected through a bus whose line speed takes one out of the following values: 1, 10, 100 Mbps. Both *Tie Resolver* algorithms provide some improvements

Figure 14. Results for the Line-Line Algorithm in various configurations

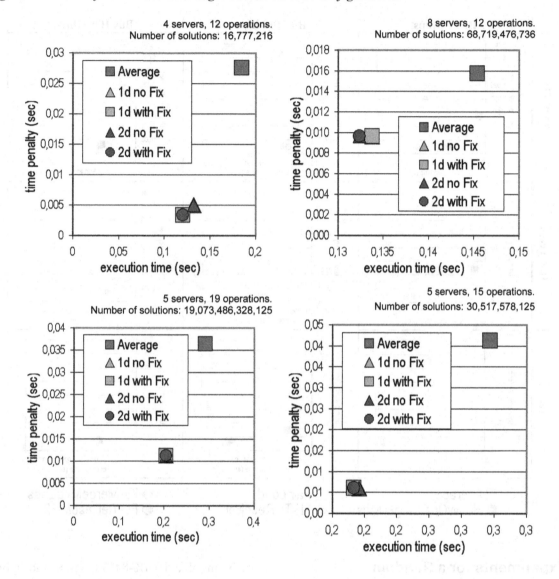

in both dimensions, whereas the *FL- Merge Message's Ends* improves the execution time to a certain extent by deteriorating the load balance. The *HeavyOps-LargeMsgs* algorithm produces quite acceptable execution times, esp. for small bus capacities and practically seems to be the more stable solution compared to all the others. It is interesting that the behavior of the *HeavyOps-LargeMsgs* algorithm remains quite stable even when the fraction of operations to servers (denoted as *K*) increases.

In terms of the quality of the solution, *HeavyOps-LargeMsgs* produces (2.9%, 12%) deviations for execution time/time penalty for 1Mbps bus, and (29%,0.3%) for 100 Mbps bus.

As an overall result, we can safely argue that *FL-Tie Resolver2* seems to provide quite fair solutions, whereas the *HeavyOps-LargeMsgs* algorithm is slightly worse in this category, but provides consistently good execution times in all configurations.

Figure 15. Line – Bus algorithms with 19 operations in the workflow

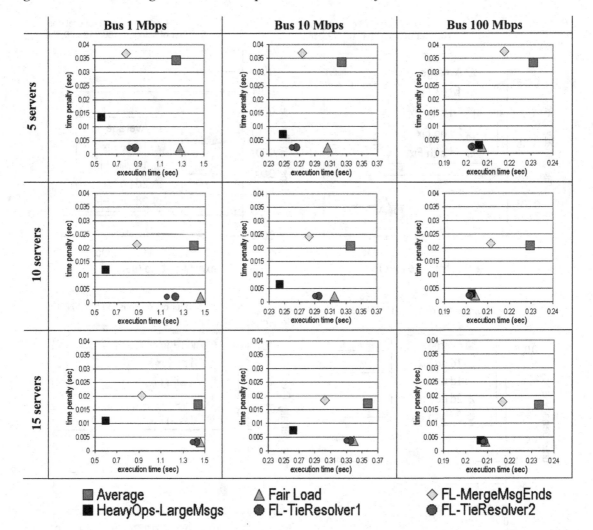

Experiments for a Random Graph: Bus Configuration

In the case of workflows with random graph structures, we have discerned three cases: (a) bushy, (b) lengthy and (c) hybrid graphs. Bushy graphs have a high percentage of decision nodes (and are therefore shorter in length, but with a higher fan-out). Lengthy graphs have a small percentage of decision nodes and involve lengthy paths. Hybrid graphs are somewhere in the middle. Specifically, bushy graphs involve a 50%-50% balance of decision/operational nodes, lengthy graphs involve a 16%-84% balance and hybrid graphs a 35%-65% one.

In Figure 16 we see four experiments for bushy workflows of 19 operations over topologies of (a) 5 or (b) 10 servers connected through a bus whose line speed takes one out of the following values: 1, 100 Mbps. The difference is in the number of servers and the speed of the bus. Algorithm *Fair Load–Merge Messages' Ends* seems to perform better than the rest, especially when the speed of the bus is slow.

In Figure 17 we see the respective experiment for lengthy workflows. It is interesting to see that

Figure 16. Graph – bus algorithms for bushy workflows

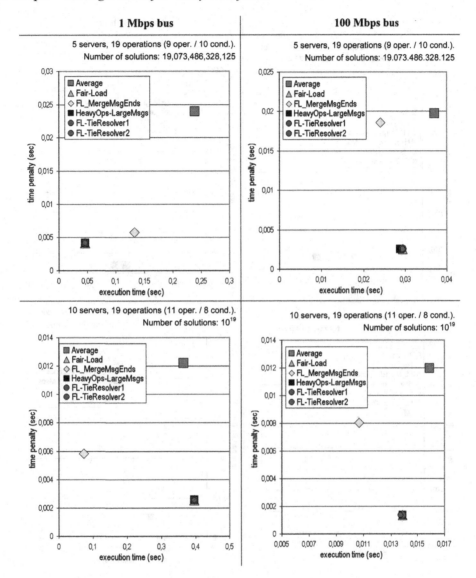

in contrary with the previous experiment, *Fair Load–Merge Messages' Ends* can give very bad solutions. The most reliable algorithm for this category seems to be *HeavyOps-LargeMsgs*. It is also interesting that *Fair Load* can be better than its tie-resolver improvements.

In Figure 18, we depict the average values of 50 experiments for workflows of 19 operations over 10 servers. As one can see, the results are not very different from the ones for the previous topology. For almost all configurations, the *HeavyOps-LargeMsgs* algorithm appears to be a clear winner: it is consistently the best choice in terms of execution time and it also appears to be the quite close to the best solutions in terms of fairness. *FL-Merge Message's Ends* appears to be quite close in terms of execution time (in fact, in individual experiments it has occasionally out-

Figure 17. Graph – bus algorithms for lengthy workflows

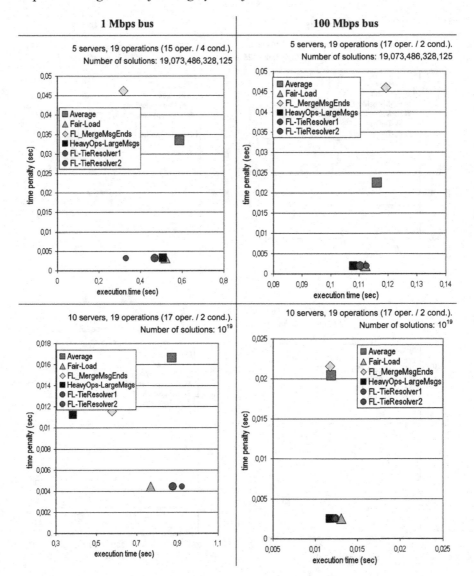

performed *HeavyOps-LargeMsgs*), still it is quite unstable with respect to its fairness.

In terms of the quality of the solution, *HeavyOps-LargeMsgs* produces (29%, 1.8%) deviations for execution time/time penalty for the 1Mbps bus, and (0%, 0%) for the 100 Mbps bus.

Summary of Experimental Findings

In summary, our experimental findings are as follows:

1. In the *Line-Line* configurations, all algorithms behave well and give a solution quite close to the optimal one. The variant of double direction Line-Line algorithm ap-

Figure 18. Graph – bus algorithms organized per graph structure

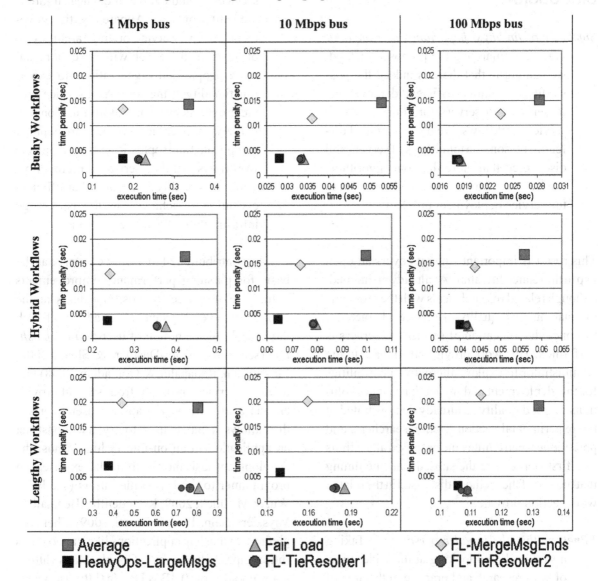

pears to perform slightly better, whereas the fixing of bad bridges appears to work only when the messages are really heavy for the network connections involved.

2. In the *Line-Bus* configurations, the algorithm *Fair Load–Tie Resolver₂* is the most appropriate for fair solutions, whereas the algorithm *Fair Load–Merge Messages' Ends* and *Heavy Operations–Large Messages* are

the most appropriate whenever execution time is more important.

3. In the case of *Graph-Bus* configurations, the same observations still hold. In the case of bushy workflows, the algorithm *Fair Load– Merge Messages' Ends* is better than *Heavy Operations–Large Messages*, especially with respect to the execution time.

DISCUSSION

Summary of findings, importance and implications: Summarizing the proposed method, we can argue that there is indeed the possibility of finding efficient deployments of services to servers for composite web service workflows. We have examined different, reasonable topologies of servers and discovered that more than one algorithms can be applied to provide good solutions to the service deployment problem.

This result is important since it covers an open gap in the related literature. As already mentioned, although related research deals with the problems of guaranteeing quality-of-service characteristics once the allocation of services to servers is performed. This work provides the means to the administrator to explore alternative possibilities for this deployment and in fact, it produces solutions of good quality as already demonstrated at the experimental section. Both researcher s and practitioners can employ the proposed algorithms as a first step before the subsequent fine tuning that the rest of the methods discussed in the related work section provide.

Fitness within the broader perspective: Taking a step back and looking at the wider view of both research and practice in the area of software systems engineering, the software challenge of the near future is dealing with the dramatically increasing complexity and scale of the systems that we build (Northrop et al., 2006). Software systems that rely on Internet technologies in particular must cope with various constantly growing dimensions of scale including load, heterogeneity, broad distribution, cardinality of services that are available and should be coordinated. Therefore, from this boarder perspective the most important factor that affects the way web

services should evolve in the near future is the matter of scale. Apparently, the movement towards a service-oriented architecture of software at the web will drive more and more people and organizations to export functionality at the web. As a service provider exports more and more functionality via services over the web, the more popular, complicated and sophisticated the composite workflows that the users construct will be. Thus, it is highly important that efficient execution is achieved in the back-stage infrastructure of a service provider.

The contribution of this work can serve as the basis for pursuing performance improvements in the case of service compositions that span the borders of several systems. The advent of Web 2.0 brought us the notion of user-defined *mashups* (see Benslimane, Dustdar, & Sheth, 2008; Maximilien, Ranabahu, & Gomadam, 2008) that integrate services possibly from several providers via a user-friendly graphical user interface that allows a naïve user to try and construct an application in an on-line fashion. Thus, the development task moves from the experienced programmer to the less skilled users (see Firat, Wu, & Madnick, 2009; Kongdenfha, Benatallah, Vayssière, Saint-Paul, & Casati, 2009). There is a plethora of mashup applications like Yahoo Pipes (http://pipes.yahoo.com/), Google Maps (http://maps.google.com/), IBM Damia (http://services.alphaworks.ibm.com/damia/), and Microsoft Popfly (http://www.popfly.com/). The on-line nature of such applications makes the optimization of the execution of a workflow more and more important. Fast algorithms that deduce memory allocation, execution and choice of services in an on-line fashion, appropriate for end-users are highly important. This paper can provide a useful basis for subsequent research in this direction.

Limitations and possibilities for further research: A clear limitation of the existing method is the fact that related research has not matured with respect to the cost models for web service execution. Currently, we do not have the experimental findings (also due to the youth of this technology) to be able to predict with accuracy the behavior of a web service. Therefore the designer needs to perform micro-benchmarks to assess the cost of the operations. Moreover, phenomena of load bursts are very common in the internet; this is where the fine-tuning fits. Still, some considerations for burst-handling have not been covered and could be explored as part of future work. Again, before that, we need some good experimental evidence of how bursts happen over the internet – to the best of our knowledge no such data sets exist.

Further Extensions: Other extensions for this work involve the case of multiple workflows (instead of just a single one) and the detailed study of the proposed algorithms whenever user-defined constraints are given. For instance, apart from the overall execution time, the response time of individual operations can also be considered as part of the cost model.

CONCLUSION

In this paper, we have dealt with the problem of discovering the best possible deployment of the operations of a certain workflow given its structure and a topology of servers. To the best of our knowledge, this is the first attempt towards the issue. Thus, our approach fits nicely with existing efforts that are concerned with the fine-tuning of the workflow to obtain desired levels of quality of service as it provides the necessary first step of service deployment, before the fine-tuning can start. We have measured efficiency in terms of two cost functions that concern the execution time of the workflow and the fairness of the load on the servers. We have studied different topologies for the workflow structure and the server connectivity and proposed greedy algorithms for each combination. Our experiments indicate that algorithm *HeavyOps-LargeMsgs* is a good choice for all the considered configurations.

ACKNOWLEDGMENT

We would like the anonymous reviewers of this paper, as well as the reviewers of the first version of this paper (accepted in SEIW 2007) for their constructive comments. This research was co-funded by the European Union in the framework of the program "Pythagoras II" of the "Operational Program for Education and Initial Vocational Training" of the 3rd Community Support Framework of the Hellenic Ministry of Education, funded by 25% from national sources and by 75% from the European Social Fund (ESF).

REFERENCES

Alonso, G., Casati, F., Kuno, H., & Machiraju, V. (2004). *Web Services concepts, architecture and applications*. New York: Springer.

Andrews, T., Curbera, F., Dholakia, H., Golang, Y., Klein, J., Leymann, F., et al. (2003). *Business process execution language for Web services version 1.1*. Retrieved from http://www.ibm.com/developerworks/ library/ws-bpel/

Benslimane, D., Dustdar, S., & Sheth, A. (2008). Services Mashups: The New Generation of Web Applications. *IEEE Internet Computing, 12*(5), 13–15. doi:10.1109/MIC.2008.110

Burstein, M., Bussler, C., Finin, T., Huhns, M., Paolucci, M., & Sheth, A. (2005). A semantic Web services architecture. *IEEE Internet Computing, 9*, 52–61. doi:10.1109/MIC.2005.96

Cardoso, J., Sheth, A., Miller, J., Arnold, J., & Kochut, K. (2004). Quality of service for workflows and Web service processes. *Journal of Web Semantics*, *1*(3), 281–308. doi:10.1016/j.websem.2004.03.001

Chen, Y., Zhou, L., & Zhang, D. (2006). Ontology-supported Web service composition: An approach to service-oriented knowledge management in corporate services. *Journal of Database Management*, *17*(1), 67–84.

Cherkasova, L., & Gupta, M. (2004). Analysis of enterprise media server workloads: access patterns, locality, content evolution, and rates of change. *ACM/IEEE Transactions on Networking*, *12*(5), 781-794.

Cherkasova, L., & Phaal, P. (2002). Session-based admission control: A mechanism for peak load management of commercial web sites. *IEEE Transactions on Computers*, *51*(6), 669–685. doi:10.1109/TC.2002.1009151

Constantinescu, I., Binder, W., & Faltings, B. (2005). Optimally distributing interactions between composed semantic Web services. In A. Gomez-Perez & J. Euzenat (Eds.), *Proceedings of the 2nd European Semantic Web Conference* (pp. 32-46).

Conti, M., Kumar, M., Das, S. K., & Shirazi, B. A. (2002). Quality of service issues in internet Web services. *IEEE Transactions on Computers*, *51*(6), 593–594. doi:10.1109/TC.2002.1009145

Ding, Y., Fensel, D., & Klein, A. B. O. (2002). The semantic Web: yet another hip? *Data & Knowledge Engineering*, *41*(3), 205–227. doi:10.1016/S0169-023X(02)00041-1

Erickson, J., & Siau, K. (2008). Web Services, service-oriented computing, and service-oriented architecture: separating hype from reality. *Journal of Database Management*, *19*(3), 42–54.

Firat, A., Wu, L., & Madnick, S. (2009). General Strategy for Querying Web Sources in a Data Federation Environment. *Journal of Database Management*, *20*(2), 1–18.

Geer, D. (2003). Taking steps to secure web services. *IEEE Computer*, *36*(10), 14–16.

Gillmann, M., Weikum, G., & Wonner, W. (2002). Workflow management with service quality guarantees. In D. DeWitt (Ed.), *ACM SIGMOD International Conference on Management of Data* (pp. 228-239).

Gravano, L., & Papakonstantinou, Y. (1998). Mediating and meta searching on the internet. *A Quarterly Bulletin of the Computer Society of the IEEE Technical Committee on Data Engineering*, *21*(2), 28–36.

Head, M., Govindaraju, M., Slominski, A., Liu, P., Abu-Ghazaleh, N., van Engelen, R., et al. (2005). A benchmark suite for SOAP-based communication in Grid Web services. In W. Kramer (Ed.), *ACM/IEEE Conference on High Performance Networking and Computing* (pp. 19-20).

Kongdenfha, W., Benatallah, B., Vayssière, V., Saint-Paul, R., & Casati, F. (2009). Rapid development of spreadsheet-based web mashups. In *Proceedings of the 18th International Conference on the World Wide Web* (pp. 851-860).

Laoutaris, N., Telelis, O., Zissimopoulos, V., & Stavrakakis, I. (2006). Distributed selfish replication. *IEEE Transactions on Parallel and Distributed Systems*, *17*(12), 1401–1413. doi:10.1109/TPDS.2006.171

Leff, A., Wolf, J. L., & Yu, P. S. (1993). Replication algorithms in a remote caching architecture. *IEEE Transactions on Parallel and Distributed Systems*, *4*(11), 1185–1204. doi:10.1109/71.250099

Lewis, P. M., Bernstein, A. J., & Kifer, M. (2001). *Databases and transaction processing: An application-oriented approach*. Reading, MA: Addison-Wesley.

Leymann, F., & Roller, D. (2000). *Production workflow: concepts and techniques.* Upper Saddle River, NJ: Prentice Hall.

Maximilien, E. M., Ranabahu, A., & Gomadam, K. (2008). An Online Platform for Web APIs and Service Mashups. *IEEE Internet Computing, 12*(5), 32–43. doi:10.1109/MIC.2008.92

Maximilien, E. M., & Singh, M. P. (2004). A framework and ontology for dynamic web services selection. *IEEE Internet Computing, 8*(5), 84–93. doi:10.1109/MIC.2004.27

Northrop, L., Feiler, P., Gabriel, R. P., Goodenough, J., Linger, R., & Longstaff, T. (2006). *Ultra Large Scale Systems. The Software Challenge of the Future. Software Engineering Institute.* Pittsburgh, PA: Carnegie Mellon.

Papazoglou, M. (2003). Web services and business transactions. *World Wide Web (Bussum), 6*(1), 49–91. doi:10.1023/A:1022308532661

Papazoglou, M., & Kratz, B. (2007). Web services technology in support of business transactions. *Service Oriented Computing and Applications, 1*(1), 51–63. doi:10.1007/s11761-007-0002-3

Papazoglou, M., Traverso, P., Dustdar, S., & Leymann, F. (2007). Service-oriented computing: State of the art and research directions. *IEEE Computer, 40*(11), 64–71.

Papazoglou, M., & van den Heuvel, W. J. (2007). Service oriented architectures: Approaches, technologies and research issues. *Very Large Database Journal, 16*(3), 389–415. doi:10.1007/s00778-007-0044-3

Rezgui, A., Bouguettaya, A., & Eltoweissy, M. Y. (2003). Privacy on the Web: facts, challenges, and solutions. *IEEE Security and Privacy, 1*(6), 40–49. doi:10.1109/MSECP.2003.1253567

Salellariou, R., & Zhao, H. (2004). A low-cost rescheduling policy for efficient mapping of workflows on Grid systems. *Science Progress, 12*(4), 253–262.

SOAP. (2003). *Simple Object Access Protocol version 1.2.* Retrieved from http://www.w3.org/TR/ soap12-part0

Srivastava, U., Widom, J., Munagala, K., & Motwani, R. (2005). *Query optimization over Web services.* Retrieved from http://dbpubs.stanford.edu:8090/ pub/2005-30

Vinoski, S. (2002). Web services interaction models, part 1: current practice. *IEEE Internet Computing, 6*(3), 89–91. doi:10.1109/MIC.2002.1003137

WSDL. (2003). *Web services description language version 2.0.* Retrieved from http://www.w3.org/TR/wsdl20

Yu, Q., Liu, X., Bouguettaya, A., & Medjahed, B. (2008). Deploying and managing Web services: issues, solutions, and directions. *Very Large Database Journal, 17,* 537–572. doi:10.1007/s00778-006-0020-3

Zeng, L., Benatallah, B., Ngu, A., Dumas, M., Kalagnanam, J., & Chang, H. (2004). Qos-aware middleware for web services composition. *IEEE Transactions on Software Engineering, 30*(5), 311–327. doi:10.1109/TSE.2004.11

APPENDIX A: BACKGROUND TERMINOLOGY AND STANDARDS

SOAP: The Simple Object Access Protocol (SOAP) is the means that facilitates web service communication and the basis for the development of practically all other protocols in the area. SOAP specifies a message format for the communication with Web services along with the bindings to HTTP and SMTP protocols for the delivery of messages. The communication in SOAP is one-way and asynchronous. The messages are XML documents, consisting of *envelopes* comprising a *header*, with meta-information for the processing of the message and a *body* with the actual contents of the message.

WSDL: The Web Services Description Language (WSDL) is a specification language for the generation of XML documents that (a) *describe* and (b) *automate the deployment* of web services. In practice, WSDL documents play the role of IDL's in conventional middleware: they provide a description of the available interfaces of a web service and at the same time, they can serve as an input to the appropriate compiler to generate client stubs and server skeletons.

WSDL descriptions are decomposed into two parts, or *perspectives*. In the *logical perspective*, α WSDL document specifies the interface of a web service. In the case of web services, the traditional middleware interface is replaced by a set of *messages* that the web service generates or receives. In practice, there are four modes that a service can use to interact with other programs: *one-way* (simply receives messages), *request-response* (sends a request message and waits for an answer), *solicit-response* (receives a message and responds appropriately) and *notification* (sends a message). A fault message can be sent, in some of these cases, whenever an error is encountered. This kind of modus operandi in WSDL is regulated by *operations*. In fact, operations are the counterpart of "interface" in traditional middleware. Operations are grouped by *port types*. Intuitively, a port type is a collection of operations, offered by the same organization, towards semantically similar functionalities. Port types are the coarser granule of logical organization in the WSDL specification. At the other end of the spectrum, the finest granule in the logical perspective involves message *parts*. Each message is an XML document organized in parts. Each part is assumed to be a typed granule of information; still, complex parts can be defined, too.

The logical perspective of WSDL documents is accompanied by the *physical* perspective, responsible for the description of the communication protocols and the ports where functionality is exposed. A *binding* specifies how a certain operation will communicate with the rest of the world; this is typically done via the HTTP or the SMTP (e-mail, that is) protocols. Technicalities of the message that is transported are also hidden behind the *style* of the binding. At the same time, a *port* (or *end-point*) offers a URI for a certain binding. Naturally, more than one bindings can be offered for the same operation and consequently, more than one ports. A *WSDL service* is a collection of ports, i.e., a set of URI's where functionality of the organization is exported. It is interesting that, in the WSDL specification, a service is an object in the physical perspective: the logical definitions are part of the specification but embodied in the overall service.

WSDL acts both as a service *description* language and a service *definition* language. As a description language, the WSDL documentation is a form of contract that describes the set of messages that the services guarantees to receive (input messages) and deliver (output messages). As a definition language,

WSDL is employed as the means to generate the actual code that is exported in order to invoke the service. This follows a traditional IDL approach, where the development and invocation of an application are guided through an IDL definition both at the server and at the client (through the well-known stub/skeleton mechanism).

BPEL: The Business Process Execution Language (BPEL) is employed in order to specify abstract compositions of web services as well as their concrete coordination. The basic entity in the component model of BPEL is the *activity*. Activities can be classified as *basic* (simple, that is) and *structured* (composite). The orchestration of web service scenarios involves the possibility of combining services through *sequence*, *switch* (conditional routing), *pick* (non-deterministic choice), *while* and *flow* (parallel) activities. Data management is handled through a blackboard approach, where a set of "global" variable names handles the flow of data among activities. The selection of services involves the introduction of partner link types, i.e., roles that exchange messages and partner links, which are specific services materializing these roles. Exceptions are managed in a try-catch approach.

APPENDIX B: DETAILED INFORMATION ON DEVIATIONS FOR THE DERIVED SOLUTIONS

Table 6 depicts detailed results for the deviation from the optimal values for a large-size configuration.

Table 4. Line-Bus configuration. All solutions for 100 experiments with 8 operations, 3 servers

	1 Mbps Bus		100 Mbps Bus	
	$T_{execute}$	Time Penalty	$T_{execute}$	Time Penalty
Fair Load	70%	0.2%	44%	1%
FL-Tie Resolver$_1$	52%	0.2%	40%	1%
FL-Tie Resolver$_2$	48%	0.2%	37%	1%
FL-MergeMsgEnds	37%	34%	39%	32%
HeavyOps-LargeMsgs	17%	19%	42%	2%

Table 5. Line-Bus configuration. Sampling of 32,000 solutions for 50 experiments with 19 operations, 5 servers

	1 Mbps Bus		100 Mbps Bus	
	$T_{execute}$	Time Penalty	$T_{execute}$	Time Penalty
Fair Load	75%	0.08%	31%	0%
FL-Tie Resolver$_1$	32%	0.08%	26%	0%
FL-Tie Resolver$_2$	24%	0.08%	25%	0%
FL-MergeMsgEnds	26%	34%	32%	36%
HeavyOps-LargeMsgs	2.9%	12%	29%	0.3%

Table 6. Graph-Bus configuration. Sampling of 32,000 solutions for 50 experiments with 19 operations (65% operational, 35% conditional), 5 servers

	1 Mbps bus		100 Mbps bus	
	$T_{execute}$	Time Penalty	$T_{execute}$	Time Penalty
Fair Load	63%	0%	1.7%	0%
FL-Tie Resolver1	56%	0%	1.7%	0%
FL-Tie Resolver2	53%	0%	0.9%	0%
FL-MergeMsgEnds	34%	32%	4.5%	30%
HeavyOps-LargeMsgs	29%	1.8%	0%	0%

Chapter 17
Matching Attributes across Overlapping Heterogeneous Data Sources Using Mutual Information

Huimin Zhao
University of Wisconsin-Milwaukee, USA

ABSTRACT

Identifying matching attributes across heterogeneous data sources is a critical and time-consuming step in integrating the data sources. In this paper, the author proposes a method for matching the most frequently encountered types of attributes across overlapping heterogeneous data sources. The author uses mutual information as a unified measure of dependence on various types of attributes. An example is used to demonstrate the utility of the proposed method, which is useful in developing practical attribute matching tools.

INTRODUCTION

As we are continually building more databases, there is accordingly a growing need for integrating these databases. The need arises due to independent development of local data islands within an organization, business mergers and acquisitions,

and collaboration across business partners. Studying distributed and heterogeneous computing environments has become an important research topic for MIS researchers (March et al., 2000).

Identifying matching attributes across heterogeneous data sources is a critical and time-consuming step in integrating the data sources (Clifton et al., 1997), either physically (e.g., by consolidating local data sources into a central data

DOI: 10.4018/978-1-61350-471-0.ch017

warehouse) or logically (e.g., by constructing a federated mediating system). Despite over two decades of extensive research, schema matching still seems to largely involve ad hoc solutions (Gal, 2006). More effective techniques that can provide analysts with automated support are still in high demand. Schema matching remains an active research area, exemplified by abundant recent publications (e.g., Bonifati et al., 2008; Bozovic & Vassalos, 2008; Kang & Naughton, 2008; Rull et al., 2008; Saleem et al., 2008; Zhao & Ram, 2008).

Recently, Zhao and Soofi (2006) proposed a method that uses mutual information to explore correspondences between free-text character attributes in heterogeneous databases. This method computes a degree of similarity between two attributes and uses mutual information to measure the dependence between attribute matching and record matching. In this paper, we further extend this method and propose a comprehensive method for matching most frequently encountered types of attributes across heterogeneous data sources that share some overlapping records. We use mutual information as a unified measure of dependence on various types of attributes. We also simplify the analysis of free-text character attributes by transformations, eliminating the need for additional attribute matching functions.

The rest of the paper is organized as follows. We first present an example of heterogeneous databases. We then review some related work in the field. We then describe the proposed approach and its application in the chosen example. Finally, we conclude the paper with contributions, limitations, and potential future research directions.

ONLINE BOOKSTORE EXAMPLE

We will use an example of heterogeneous databases for illustrative purposes. In this case, there are two book catalogs extracted from the Web sites of two leading online bookstores. The catalogs

have several corresponding attributes. However, most of the attribute names are not displayed on the Web sites. We manually extracted 737 and 722 records from the Web sites of the two stores, respectively. Tables 1 and 2 show some sample entries of the two catalogs. The attribute names were manually assigned to facilitate discussion, but are not used by the attribute matching method proposed in this paper and have no effect on its result. There is a common key, the ISBN, across the two catalogs. There are 702 matching records, according to the ISBN, in the two sample tables we extracted. Note that the attribute referred to as "Author" may contain multiple authors for a book. This is what we can directly observe at the Web sites of the bookstores. We do not attempt to speculate upon the actual schemas of the back-end databases hidden in the "deep Web" (He & Chang, 2006; Su et al., 2006; Wang et al., 2004). We analyze the fields displayed at the Web sites as they are.

There are various discrepancies across the two catalogs. There are spelling errors in some attributes (e.g., "Developers" vs. "Developer's" in a book title). Some author names may be shorter in one catalog than in the other (e.g., "Oracle Corp" vs. "Oracle Corporation"). The subtitle of a book may appear in one catalog but not in the other (e.g., "HTML 4 for the World Wide Web: Visual QuickStart Guide"). Some of the edition numbers are missing. Cover is coded differently (e.g., "H" vs. "Hardcover", "P" vs. "Paperback"). Publisher may be named differently (e.g., "Osborne McGraw-Hill" vs. "McGraw-Hill Professional Book Group"). Publishing date has different formats in the two catalogs. The supplemental information is described differently (e.g., "Bk&Cd Rom" vs. "BK+CD"). Prices are recorded in number of dollars in catalog 1 and number of cents in catalog 2. The sales rank and rating are conducted independently by the two bookstores and are different in general. The task is to determine the corresponding attributes based on this sample of matching records.

Table 1. Sample entries of book catalog 1

ISBN	Author	Title	Edition	Cover
0071341161	Simon St. Laurent, Ethan Cerami	Building XML Applications		Paperback
0072119772	Thomas A. Powell	HTML: The Complete Reference	2	Paperback
0072122455	Sumit Sarin	Oracle DBA Tips and Techniques	1	Paperback
0130123811	Guy Harrison	Oracle SQL High-Performance Tuning	2	Paperback
0201354934	Elizabeth Castro	HTML 4 for the World Wide Web	4	Paperback
047139288X	Oracle Corp	Oracle 8I		Hardcover
0130106208	Albert Lulushi, Michael Stowe	Oracle Developer's Resource Library	1	Paperback

Publisher	Pubdate	Supplement	Listprice	Ourprice	Pages	Salesrank	Rating
McGraw-Hill Professional Publishing	May-1999	Bk&Cd Rom	49.99	39.99	551	21526	3.5
Osborne McGraw-Hill	Feb-1999			39.99	1130	8771	4.5
Osborne McGraw-Hill	Apr-2000		49.99	39.99	737	33259	4
Prentice Hall PTR/Sun Microsystems Press	Dec-2000			49.99	656	13542	4.5
Peachpit Press	Jan-2000		19.99	15.99	384	238	4.5
John Wiley & Sons	Jun-2000	Cd-Rom		15.65		734684	4
Prentice Hall	Dec-1998	Bk&Cd Rom		119.99		287454	4

Table 2. Sample entries of book catalog 2

ISBN	Author	Title	Edition	Cover
0071341161	Simon St Laurent, Ethan Cerami	Building XML Applications	1	P
0072119772	Thomas A. Powell	HTML: The Complete Reference	2	P
0072122455	Sumit Sarin	Oracle8 DBA		P
0130123811	Guy Harrison	Oracle SQL High-Performance Tuning	2	P
0201354934	Elizabeth Castro	HTML 4 for the World Wide Web: Visual QuickStart Guide	4	P
047139288X	Oracle Corporation	Oracle 8i		H
0130106208	Albert Lulushi, Michael Stowe	Oracle Developers Resource Library	1	P

Publisher	Pubdate	Supplement	Listprice	Ourprice	Pages	Salesrank	Rating
McGraw-Hill Professional Book Group	6/1999	BK+CD	4999	3999	551	198667	
McGraw-Hill Professional Book Group	3/1999		3999	3199	1130	61422	4.5
McGraw-Hill Professional Book Group	1/2000	BK+CD	4999	3999	740	33771	
Prentice Hall	12/2000		4999	3999	656	5167	
Peachpit Press	11/1999		1999	1799	384	162	4.5
Wiley, John & Sons, Incorporated	6/2000	CD		1565		508107	
Prentice Hall	12/1998			119.99		558348	

RELATED WORK

Enormous research effort has been devoted to attribute matching (more generally, schema matching) in the past two decades or so. Many approaches have been proposed in the literature. Some of the approaches will be discussed in this section. There have also been several surveys of this literature (e.g., Rahm & Bernstein, 2001; Do et al., 2003; Doan & Halevy, 2005; Shvaiko & Euzenat, 2005). Driven by the development of the emerging semantic Web, there is a renewed interest in schema matching, with applications in matching ontologies (Choi et al., 2006; Hu et al., 2008; Su & Gulla, 2006; Pirrò & Talia, 2008) and interfaces of Web databases hidden in the "deep Web" (He & Chang, 2006; Su et al., 2006; Wang et al., 2004).

Some approaches determine the degree of similarity between attributes mainly based on meta-data without investigating the actual stored data at the instance level (Zhao & Ram, 2004). Linguistic techniques have been used to measure the similarity between attribute names (Bright et al., 1994; Johannesson, 1997). Heuristic formulae have been designed to compute the degree of similarity between attributes based on attribute names and schematic specifications (Palopoli et al., 2000). Information retrieval techniques have been used to measure the degree of similarity between text documents describing attributes or textual values ((Benkley et al., 1995; Cohen, 2000; Pirrò & Talia, 2008). Clustering and classification techniques have also been used to group similar schema elements based on meta-data (Li & Clifton, 2000; Zhao & Ram, 2004). Xu and Embley (2006) combined multiple types of meta-data, including terminological relationships, data-value characteristics, and domain-specific patterns. Giunchiglia et al. (2007) used natural language processing techniques, along with the WordNet lexicon, to analyze the meanings of schema elements. The success of such conceptual analysis approaches relies on the availability of complete and unambiguous descriptions of the schema elements.

Some approaches also investigate the actual stored data at the instance level. Some researchers have proposed the use of correlation and regression analysis for exploring correspondences between numerical attributes in different databases when some matching records are available (Fan et al., 2001; Fan et al., 2002; Lu et al., 1997). Chua et al. (2003) used a variety of correlation measures to match different types of attributes. Bilke and Naumann (2005) used a similarity measure named SoftTFIDF, which is a variation of the well-known TFIDF measure developed in the information retrieval field (Baeza-Yates & Ribeiro-Neto, 1999).

More recently, mutual information has been used to measure the dependence between record matching and a degree of similarity between two free-text character attributes from heterogeneous databases (Zhao & Soofi, 2006). A high level of dependence indicates a potential corresponding attribute pair. Mutual information has also been used in other manners. Kang and Naughton (2003, 2008) used mutual information to measure the attribute dependencies within each database and then identified potential corresponding attributes based on similarity of the entropy or/and dependency patterns across the databases. Such dependency graphs cannot distinguish between corresponding and non-corresponding attributes when the attributes have similar entropies and dependency patterns (Zhao & Soofi, 2006). Wang et al. (2004) used mutual information in a particular scenario, intra-site schema matching, where global schema, interface schema, and result schema about the same Web database need to be matched. This method essentially treats attributes with similar value sets as candidate corresponding ones and does not account for value coding and other transformations.

Some approaches also make use of external evidence beyond the meta-data and data of the data sources to be matched. For example, Madhavan et al. (2005) proposed a method that leverages previous matching experiences in the domain in matching new schemas.

While most studies have focused on one-to-one attribute matching, some have investigated complex matching between sets of attributes. Identifying complex matches is much more complex, as the number of attribute subsets that need to be evaluated is exponential and the number of possible functions for combining attributes is unbounded. An exhaustive search for candidate complex matches is infeasible. Dhamanka et al. (2004) used domain knowledge and a set of searchers specializing on particular types of complex matches to reduce the search space. Wu et al. (2004) proposed some heuristics for identifying one-to-many mappings. He and Chang (2006) proposed a framework named DCM, which uses co-occurrence patterns in query interfaces to identify likely related attribute groups. They further investigated an ensemble of multiple matchers, which vote on the final recommendations. Su et al. (2006) proposed another framework named HSM, which improves upon DCM with more reliable measurement and a more efficient algorithm.

It has been recognized that most techniques have their strengths and weaknesses and no single technique has been found to be a champion for all situations (Domshlak et al., 2007). Many composite matching systems combining multiple components have recently been developed to take advantage of the merits of multiple techniques. Nottelmanna and Straccia (2007) combined multiple probabilistic matchers through a weighted summation of the matching probability estimates made by individual matchers. Do and Rahm (2007) proposed a tool named COMA++, which provides a collection of individual matchers and a flexible infrastructure for combining the matchers. Quick-Mig (Drum et al., 2007) is a further development of COMA++. Lee et al. (2007) proposed a system named eTuner for automatically selecting the right components and tuning the "knobs" (e.g., thresholds, formula coefficients) in a composite matching system. Domshlak et al. (2007) proposed

a general framework and several algorithms for composing an ensemble of individual matchers. Bozovic and Vassalos (2008) proposed a two-phase approach, where presumably "strong" matchers are first combined (via voting) to produce strong matches and "weak" matchers are then combined (again via voting) to provide additional evidence for attributes left unmatched.

Despite the abundance of simple or complex matching techniques, totally automating the attribute matching process is an unrealistic expectation, as the meta-data and data do not completely and unambiguously convey the semantics of different databases (Gal, 2006). Reviewing and validating the candidate matches is a necessary follow-up step. Tools can help but cannot totally replace human analysts (Zhao & Ram, 2004). Bernstein et al. (2006) developed a tool that allows the user to easily navigate through match candidates and incrementally match large schemas, avoiding overwhelming the user. Bonifati et al. (2008) proposed a structural analysis technique for mapping verification. Rull et al. (2008) proposed an approach for validating whether candidate mappings have several desirable properties. In a large-scale scenario where a large number of schemas need to be matched, however, human intervention may be infeasible and performance may be an even more critical criterion than quality. Saleem et al. (2008) proposed a holistic approach that can automatically and efficiently match many schemas in such scenarios.

Another problem closely related to attribute matching is record matching, i.e., identifying semantically corresponding records across data sources (Chua et al., 2003; Bilke & Naumann, 2005; Zhao & Ram, 2008). Zhao and Ram (2007) proposed an iterative procedure for detecting both attribute correspondences and record correspondences.

Table 3. Major built-in data types of oracle 10g and Microsoft SQL server 2008

Category	Oracle 10g	Microsoft SQL Server 2008
Numerical	INTEGER, BIT, BIGINT, SMALLINT, TINYINT, DECIMAL, NUMERIC, NUMBER, DOUBLE PRECISION, FLOAT, REAL	INT, BIT, BIGINT, SMALLINT, TINYINT, DECIMAL, NUMERIC, SMALLMONEY, MONEY, FLOAT, REAL
Temporal	DATE, TIME, TIMESTAMP	DATE, TIME, DATETIME, DATETIME2, SMALLDATETIME, DATETIMEOFFSET
Character	CHAR, LONG, VARCHAR, VARCHAR2, LONG VARCHAR, CLOB	CHAR, VARCHAR, TEXT, NCHAR, NVARCHAR, NTEXT, XML
Binary	BINARY, VARBINARY, LONG VARBINARY, RAW, LONG RAW, BLOB	BINARY, VARBINARY, IMAGE

ATTRIBUTE MATCHING USING MUTUAL INFORMATION

Our objective is to develop a method for matching most frequently encountered types of attributes across heterogeneous data sources. Table 3 shows major built-in data types supported by two database management system (DBMS) products, Oracle 10g and Microsoft SQL Server 2008, as examples. These data types can be categorized into several groups. Numerical types are used to store integer or real numbers. The differences between the types are mainly in their ranges and precisions. Temporal types, such as DATE and TIME, may be converted into numerical types. For example, a date value—regardless of its presentation format—may be converted into the number of days since a particular chosen reference date. Character data types are used to store character strings. The differences between the types are mainly in whether they allow variable-length strings and the maximum length of strings. Binary data types can be used to store any data whose interpretation is beyond the responsibility of the DBMS. Some examples are formatted documents (e.g., Microsoft Word, Adobe PDF, etc.) and multimedia objects (e.g., images, audio/video clips, etc.). We evaluate different types of attributes under several categories.

To identify potential matching attributes, we first evaluate the dependence among the attributes. Two attributes that are highly mutually dependent are likely to be matching attributes. There are various measures of dependence among random variables. The best known is perhaps the Pearson product-moment correlation coefficient, which has indeed been applied in matching numerical attributes across databases (Fan et al., 2001; Fan et al., 2002; Lu et al., 1997). It is a parametric statistic and indicates the strength and direction of a linear relationship between two variables. It is well known that the correlation analysis does not apply when some or all of the attributes under consideration are character type and performs best when the numerical variables are normally distributed. There are also non-parametric correlation measures, such as Spearman's ρ, Kendall's τ, and Goodman and Kruskal's λ, some of which have also been applied in attribute matching (Chua et al., 2003). Spearman's ρ and Kendall's τ are applicable to variables that are at least ordinal. Goodman and Kruskal's λ is applicable to nominal variables. Mutual information is a more general measure of dependence. It is defined for both discrete (including nominal) and continuous variables and is invariant under any one-to-one transformations, linear or nonlinear. We, therefore, use mutual information as a unified measure of dependence in attribute matching. While we focus on attribute matching across two databases, multiple databases may be compared in a pairwise fashion using the same method.

CATEGORY I ATTRIBUTES: CATEGORICAL

If an attribute has only a few distinct values, regardless of its data type, we can consider it as a potential categorical (or discrete) attribute. We classify an attribute as a discrete variable, if *frequency* $< \tau_1$, where *frequency* is defined as the ratio of the number of non-missing values of the attribute to the number of distinct values. It reflects the number of times an attribute value appears on average. τ_1 is a chosen threshold. Note that the condition can be equivalently specified in terms of the maximum percentage of non-missing values that are distinct. For example, Cover and Edition in the book catalogs can be considered categorical.

Assuming that a sample of matching record pairs has been identified from the databases, the mutual dependence between two categorical attributes X and Y can be measured based on this sample using the mutual information, which is defined as

$$M(X, Y) = \sum_{y}\sum_{x} p(x,y) \log \frac{p(x, y)}{p(x)p(y)}, \qquad (1)$$

where $p(x, y)$ is the joint distribution of X and Y, $p(x)$ and $p(y)$ are the marginal distributions of X and Y, respectively (Shannon, 1948).

Mutual information is closely related to Shannon entropy (Shannon, 1948). The entropy of a categorical or discrete random variable X is defined as

$$H(X) = -\sum_{x} p(x) \log p(x). \qquad (2)$$

The discrete entropy is nonnegative. It measures the amount of uncertainty in the variable. It equals zero if there is no uncertainty (i.e., the distribution of the variable totally concentrates at a single value) and is maximal if the variable

is uniformly distributed. Mutual information between two variables then measures the amount of uncertainty in one variable that is reduced when given the knowledge of the other variable.

$$M(X, Y) = H(X) - H(X|Y) = H(Y) - H(Y|X) = H(X) + H(Y) - H(X, Y). \qquad (3)$$

$M(X, Y) \geq 0$ and the equality holds if and only if X and Y are independent random variables (otherwise, X and Y are not totally independent). $M(X,Y) \leq H(X)$ and $M(X,Y) \leq H(Y)$; the equality holds if and only if there is a one-to-one mapping between X and Y. Based on these properties, various mutual information indices have been constructed. Such indices give $M(X,Y)$ in terms of a fraction of an entropy or a fraction of a function of the entropies (e.g., minimum, maximum, sum, product of $H(X)$, $H(Y)$), as suited for the application context (Soofi & Retzer, 2002). We use the following mutual information index:

$$I(X, Y) = \frac{M(X,Y)}{\sqrt{H(X)H(Y)}}. \qquad (4)$$

This index ranges from zero to one: $I(X, Y) = 0$ if and only if the two variables are independent and $I(X, Y) = 1$ if and only if the two variables are functionally related in some form; otherwise, there is some degree of dependence between the two variables.

The previous correlation analysis approach (Fan et al., 2001; Fan et al., 2002; Lu et al., 1997) does not apply to non-numerical attributes. Mutual information can measure the dependence between non-numerical attributes and is invariant under any one-to-one transformations, such as the different coding schemes on Cover in the two catalogs.

CATEGORY II ATTRIBUTES: NUMERICAL

We can consider a numerical attribute as a potential continuous variable or a discretized version of a continuous variable. For example, Listprice, Ourprice, and pages in the book catalogs are numerical. Note that temporal data types may be converted into numerical types. For example, Pubdate in the book catalogs can be converted into the number of months since a particular reference month.

For two continuous variables, the mutual information is defined by (1) where $p(x)$, $p(y)$, and $p(x, y)$ are density functions and the summations become integrals. Mutual information is also defined when one of the two variables is continuous and the other variable is categorical or discrete. For this case, one of the summations in (1) is replaced with an integral.

For a continuous random variable, the entropy is defined by (2) where $p(x)$ is the density and the summation is replaced with an integral. However, the entropy of a continuous distribution can be negative. For this and some other technical reasons, the mutual information index for two continuous random variables X and Y is computed by the following exponential transformation:

$$I(X, Y) = 1 - e^{-2M(X,Y)}. \tag{5}$$

This index also ranges from zero to one: $I(X, Y)$ = 0 if and only if the two variables are independent, and $I(X, Y) = 1$ if and only if the two variables are functionally related, linearly or nonlinearly.

For the discrete case, computation of all information quantities is simple. When the probability distributions, $p(x, y)$, $p(x)$, and $p(y)$, are known, the information quantities are at hand. When the probability distributions are not known, they can be easily estimated by the sample proportions.

For the continuous case, the information quantities can be computed when the density functions are known. An easy case for computing mutual information occurs when two random variables

X and Y have a bivariate normal distribution and correlation coefficient $\rho(X, Y)$. Then

$$M(X, Y) = -.5 \log[1-\rho^2(X, Y)], \tag{6}$$

$$I(X, Y) = \rho^2(X, Y). \tag{7}$$

Thus, for the bivariate normal case, the mutual information is a function of the correlation and the mutual information index is the same as the squared correlation.

Computing mutual information is also easy when the variables X and Y are not normally distributed, but some transformations to normality are possible. An important property of mutual information is its invariance under one-to-one transformations of the variables. That is, if $V=V(X)$ and $W=W(Y)$ are one-to-one functions, then $M(X,Y)$, $M(V,Y)$, $M(X,W)$, and $M(V,W)$ are all equivalent. For example, when X and Y are not bivariate normal variables, but $V = \sqrt{X}$ and $W = \log Y$ are normally distributed, the invariance property implies that:

$$M(X, Y) = M(V, W) = -.5 \log[1-\rho^2(V, W)], \tag{8}$$

$$I(X, Y) = \rho^2(V,W). \tag{9}$$

However, the correlation coefficient is not invariant under nonlinear transformations, that is, $\rho(V,W) \neq \rho(X,Y)$. The relationship between two corresponding attributes from different data sources can be nonlinear. Hence, the correlation coefficient may not be useful, but the mutual information is an appropriate dependence measure.

In general, the mutual information must be estimated if one or both of the variables are continuous and transformations to normality cannot be found. For example, the histogram entropy estimate of Hall and Morton (1993) leads to formula (1) where one or both variables have several categories, respectively.

CATEGORY III ATTRIBUTES: NON-CATEGORICAL, NON-NUMERICAL

For other non-numerical attributes that have many distinct values, directly using the mutual information between two such attributes may not be appropriate, as the mutual information will be similar no matter whether the attributes match or not. We classify an attribute as a non-categorical, non-numerical attribute if the attribute is not numerical (or can be converted into a numerical type) and *frequency* $> \tau_2$, where τ_2 is a chosen threshold. For example, Title and Author in the book catalogs are neither numerical nor categorical.

For such attributes, we can use the approach proposed by Zhao and Soofi (2006). We sample both matching and non-matching record pairs from the databases, compute a similarity measure (referred to as attribute matching function) between two attributes, and measure the mutual information between record matching and this attribute matching function. A high level of dependence indicates potential attribute correspondence.

Such attributes may belong to several data types. Different attribute matching functions need to be designed to compare different types of attributes. For example, string similarity measures (Stephen, 1994) may be used to compare relatively short strings. Text document similarity measures developed in the information retrieval field may be used to compare long texts (Baeza-Yates & Ribeiro-Neto, 1999). Content similarity measures for multimedia objects may be used to compare large multimedia objects.

Another potentially cheaper alternative to Zhao and Soofi (2006) is to find a transformation that transforms such Category III attributes into Category I or Category II attributes. Then, the mutual information between the transformed attributes can be used to identify potential correspondences, eliminating the need for additional attribute matching functions. In general, such transformations may take a portion or a descriptive property of the original attribute. They should be discriminative,

leading to high dependence among corresponding attributes and low dependence among unrelated attributes. Promising candidates for particular application scenarios may rise from experiments and practical experiences. An example for Category III to Category II transformation is the length of a string. An example for Category III to Category I transformation is a substring function that takes the first several characters of a string.

When there are several possible transformations, as in the case of substrings with different lengths, to find the best transformation, we define the following goodness measure

$$Contrast = Average(\frac{\max_{i.}}{\min_{i.}}, \frac{\max_{.j}}{\min_{.j}}), \qquad (10)$$

where $\max_{i.}$ and $\min_{i.}$ denote the maximum and minimum of $I(i, j)$ for all j, respectively; $\max_{.j}$ and $\min_{.j}$ denote the maximum and minimum of $I(i, j)$ for all i, respectively. This measure reflects the dispersion of the mutual information measures. The larger the dispersion, the further matching and non-matching attribute pairs are separated. The transformation that results in the largest *Contrast* is then chosen.

OVERLAPPING AMONG THE CATEGORIES

As the above classification of attributes is not precise, it is necessary to evaluate some attributes, which are not classified into a particular category with sufficient certainty, under multiple categories. In other words, we may set $\tau_1 > \tau_2$ to avoid missing matching attributes due to wrong classifications of attributes. A non-numerical attribute with a *frequency* between τ_1 and τ_2 is evaluated under both categories I and III. Using conservative criteria (large τ_1 and small τ_2) increases the number of

Table 4. Summary characteristics of the attributes of the two catalogs

Attribute	Catalog 1			Catalog 2			Category		
	Number of Values			Number of Values			I	II	III
	Distinct	Not Null	Frequency	Distinct	Not Null	Frequency			
ISBN	737	737	1	722	722	1			
Author	616	720	1.2	623	718	1.2			√
Title	706	737	1	687	722	1.1			√
Edition	10	240	24	9	245	27.2	√	√	
Cover	16	711	44.4	16	717	44.8	√		
Publisher	204	707	3.5	202	708	3.5	√		√
Pubdate	119	711	6	126	719	5.7	√	√	
Supplement	47	218	4.6	49	207	4.2	√		√
Listprice	69	421	6.1	64	368	5.8	√	√	
Ourprice	190	704	3.7	167	631	3.8	√	√	
Pages	330	564	1.7	371	658	1.8		√	
Salesrank	688	688	1	540	540	1		√	
Rating	10	567	56.7	10	174	17.4	√	√	

attribute pairs to be evaluated but helps to avoid losing attribute correspondences due to incorrect classification. If high dependence is found between two attributes under both categories, it provides more confidence that the two attributes are potential corresponding ones. If the correspondence is not identified under one category, it may still be identified under another category. For attributes considered under multiple categories, if the matching results are conflicting, all results may be presented to the analyst for evaluation and confirmation. On the other hand, using aggressive criteria can reduce the number of attribute pairs that need to be evaluated, with increased risk of losing attribute correspondences due to incorrect categorization.

In addition, numerical attributes with high repeating frequency are evaluated both as potential discrete variables and as potential continuous variables (i.e., under both categories I and II). In the most conservative case, every attribute may be evaluated under every applicable category to avoid missing correspondences due to type differences across data sources (e.g., a phone number

is stored as a character string in one database and as a number in another database; a categorical attribute, such as gender, is coded using numbers and appears to be numerical in some database).

APPLICATION TO THE BOOKSTORE EXAMPLE

We have applied the proposed method in matching the attributes across the two bookstore catalogs. We first categorized the attributes into the three categories discussed above. Table 4 summarizes the characteristics of the attributes. We used relatively conservative criteria: $\tau_1 = 15$, $\tau_2 = 2$. That is, an attribute is considered a potential categorical one if its values appear at least twice on average and a potential non-categorical one if its values appear less than 15 times on average. For example, we evaluated Publisher under both category I and category III, although it has many distinct values and may not be considered a real Category I attribute. All numerical attributes are considered potential continuous variables or potential discretized versions of continuous variables. Category I attributes include Edition, Cover, Publisher, Pubdate, Supplement, Listprice, Ourprice, and Rating. Category II attributes include Edition, Pubdate, Listprice, Ourprice, Pages, Salesrank, and Rating. Pubdate is converted into the number of months since January 1990 when evaluated under Category II. Category III attributes include Author, Title, Publisher, and Supplement.

Some attributes are evaluated in multiple categories to avoid losing potential attribute correspondences due to errors in the categorization. Edition, Pubdate, Listprice, Ourprice, and Rating are evaluated under both category I and category II. Publisher and Supplement are evaluated under both category I and category III. Note that the categorization of the attributes may not be accurate and only provides a basis for the detection of possible correspondences. An attribute is evaluated under a particular category as long as it is suspected to be a potential member of that category. For example, Pubdate, Listprice, and Ourprice are evaluated under category I, although they are not strictly categorical.

We computed the mutual information both with and without using missing values in the attributes. When missing values are not considered, the records that have a missing value in any of the two attributes under investigation are removed in the computation. When missing values are considered, they are treated as a special value. The attribute matching function for Category III attributes returns special values if one or both of the parameters are missing. The mutual information between two numerical attributes is estimated using the histogram entropy method (Hall & Morton, 1993) with ten categories.

For Category III attributes, we used three methods, as described in the previous section. First, we used the earlier method proposed by Zhao and Soofi (2006), which evaluates the mutual information between record matching and an attribute matching function for comparing two attributes. Following Zhao and Soofi (2006), we

Figure 1. Contrast under various n values without using missing attribute values

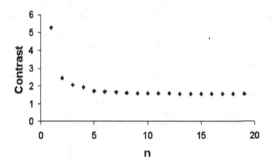

used the edit distance function (Stephen, 1994) as a measure of string similarity and generated a balanced sample (with 702 matching record pairs and 702 non-matching record pairs). Two records with different ISBN values were deemed non-matching. We repeated the estimation 200 times, randomly selecting 702 non-matching record pairs each time, and used the averages as the final estimates to get more reliable results.

Second, we transformed the Category III attributes into Category II attributes by taking the length of each string. Third, we transformed the Category III attributes into Category I attributes using the substring function, extracting the first n characters of a string. Such transformations simplify the process by eliminating the need for non-matching record pairs and string similarity functions. Figure 1 shows the *Contrast* values under various n values for the substring transformation. It turned out that $n = 1$ is the best choice in this case.

Tables 5 to 9 summarize the results. Note that the mutual information index matrices reported in the tables are not symmetric, as the columns and rows represent two sets of attributes from different databases. For example, in Table 5, without considering missing values, the mutual information index between Listprice of catalog 1 and Ourprice of catalog 2 is 0.89, while that be-

Table 5. Mutual information between potential categorical attributes

Catalog 1	Catalog 2							
	Edition	Cover	Publisher	Pubdate	Supplement	Listprice	Ourprice	Rating
Without Missing Values								
Edition	**0.77**	0.07	0.19	0.19	0.36	0.19	0.23	0.12
Cover	0.11	**0.41**	0.28	0.17	0.29	0.18	0.26	0.06
Publisher	0.21	0.32	**0.91**	0.56	0.55	0.52	0.63	0.28
Pubdate	0.25	0.19	0.55	**0.74**	0.54	0.46	0.55	0.30
Supplement	0.35	0.29	0.55	0.56	**0.91**	0.53	0.59	0.26
Listprice	0.21	0.18	0.53	0.45	0.51	**0.96**	**0.89**	0.27
Ourprice	0.23	0.32	0.65	0.55	0.59	**0.90**	0.88	**0.31**
Rating	0.06	0.05	0.22	0.18	**0.25**	0.18	0.22	0.21
With Missing Values								
Edition	**0.37**	0.05	0.17	0.12	0.09	0.12	0.17	0.03
Cover	0.06	**0.37**	0.28	0.20	0.14	0.13	0.24	0.04
Publisher	0.17	0.31	**0.89**	0.56	0.28	0.38	0.60	**0.17**
Pubdate	0.15	0.19	0.54	**0.72**	0.25	0.31	0.51	0.14
Supplement	0.12	0.14	0.30	0.28	**0.53**	0.20	0.30	0.08
Listprice	0.11	0.14	0.43	0.34	0.22	**0.64**	0.67	0.13
Ourprice	0.17	0.31	0.64	0.55	0.30	0.58	**0.80**	0.16
Rating	0.05	0.06	**0.26**	0.21	0.12	0.17	0.24	0.10

(Note: For each attribute in one catalog, the highest mutual information measure (between this attribute and another attribute in the other catalog) is highlighted in bold font. A highlighted measure that is not on the diagonal indicates an error.)

Table 6. Mutual information between potential numerical attributes

Catalog 1	Catalog 2						
	Edition	Pubdate	Listprice	Ourprice	Pages	Salesrank	Rating
Without Missing Values							
Edition	**0.77**	0.02	0.09	0.05	0.06	0.06	0.17
Pubdate	0.05	**0.58**	0.05	0.00	0.04	0.06	0.00
Listprice	0.07	0.03	**0.69**	0.24	0.22	0.05	0.19
Ourprice	0.04	0.01	0.25	**0.80**	0.05	0.01	0.05
Pages	0.07	0.02	0.21	0.08	**0.49**	0.07	0.19
Salesrank	0.04	0.08	0.09	0.04	0.07	**0.19**	0.08
Rating	0.05	0.04	0.07	0.02	0.01	0.04	**0.24**
With Missing Values							
Edition	**0.36**	0.03	0.06	0.05	0.03	0.05	0.03
Pubdate	0.03	**0.41**	0.05	0.05	0.04	0.07	0.03
Listprice	0.03	0.07	**0.43**	0.17	0.18	0.16	0.06
Ourprice	0.02	0.03	0.10	**0.29**	0.06	0.03	0.03
Pages	0.04	0.08	0.18	0.11	**0.40**	0.11	0.07
Salesrank	0.05	0.11	0.12	0.13	0.10	**0.21**	0.04
Rating	0.03	0.05	0.09	0.05	0.04	0.09	**0.09**

Table 7. Mutual information between record matching and similarity of potential non-categorical, non-numerical attributes

Catalog 1	Catalog 2			
	Author	Title	Publisher	Supplement
	Without Missing Values			
Author	**0.47**	0.00	0.01	0.00
Title	0.00	**0.49**	0.00	0.01
Publisher	0.01	0.00	**0.24**	0.01
Supplement	0.00	0.01	0.00	**0.27**
	With Missing Values			
Author	**0.46**	0.00	0.01	0.00
Title	0.00	**0.49**	0.00	0.00
Publisher	0.01	0.00	**0.22**	0.00
Supplement	0.00	0.00	0.00	**0.09**

Table 8. Mutual information between the lengths of potential non-categorical, non-numerical attributes

Catalog 1	Catalog 2			
	Author	Publisher	Title	Supplement
	Without Missing Values			
Author	**0.33**	0.03	0.03	0.03
Publisher	0.03	**0.23**	0.04	0.10
Title	0.02	0.03	**0.30**	0.03
Supplement	0.03	0.07	0.04	**0.66**
	With Missing Values			
Author	**0.32**	0.04	0.03	0.02
Publisher	0.04	**0.22**	0.04	0.04
Title	0.02	0.03	**0.30**	0.02
Supplement	0.02	0.04	0.02	**0.32**

Table 9. Mutual information between substrings (length = 1) of potential non-categorical, non-numerical attributes

Catalog 1	Catalog 2			
	Author	Publisher	Title	Supplement
	Without Missing Values			
Author	**0.86**	0.15	0.14	0.23
Publisher	0.17	**0.75**	0.22	0.24
Title	0.14	0.20	**0.89**	0.17
Supplement	0.18	0.26	0.16	**0.70**
	With Missing Values			
Author	**0.84**	0.16	0.15	0.09
Publisher	0.16	**0.71**	0.21	0.10
Title	0.15	0.20	**0.89**	0.08
Supplement	0.07	0.10	0.06	**0.35**

tween Ourprice of catalog 1 and Listprice of catalog 2 is 0.90.

Table 5 shows that most of the corresponding categorical attributes, except Ourprice and Rating, can be identified; the mutual information between two corresponding attributes is higher than that between non-corresponding ones (Mann-Whitney test shows the difference is statistically significant at the 0.01 level, with or without missing values). The problem with Ourprice is mainly due to its high dependence on Listprice. While the mutual information between the two Ourprice attributes is indeed relatively high, the mutual information between Ourprice and Listprice is also high. However, when missing values are considered, the mutual information between Ourprice and Listprice is substantially lowered, better revealing the correspondence between the two Ourprice attributes. This is because Ourprice has many more missing values than Listprice has; Ourprice was deliberately left blank if it was considered identical to Listprice. This shows that under special situations like this, where there are systematic missing values, considering the missing values may be beneficial. Other than for Ourprice, discarding missing values results in better estimations than otherwise. This shows that random missing values tend to mask the dependence between attributes in general. The mutual information between the two Rating attributes is relatively low. The main reason is that the two catalogs conducted their ratings independently and resulted in very different outcomes. In addition, catalog 2 has collected much fewer ratings from reviewers.

Table 6 shows that all of the corresponding numerical attributes can be identified; the mutual information between two corresponding attributes is higher than that between non-corresponding ones (Mann-Whitney test shows the difference is statistically significant at the 0.01 level, with or without missing values). Discarding missing values results in better estimations than otherwise for all of the numerical attributes. Note that the

correspondence between the Ourprice attributes is better revealed with missing values under category I and without missing values under category II. This shows the usefulness of conducting evaluation both with and without missing values.

Table 7 shows that all of the corresponding non-categorical, non-numerical attributes can be identified; the mutual information between record matching and attribute similarity for corresponding attributes is higher than that for non-corresponding attributes (Mann-Whitney test shows the difference is statistically significant at the 0.01 level, with or without missing values). Record matching is a binary indicator of whether a record pair in the sample is a matching or non-matching one. The similarity between two attribute values is measured using the edit distance. Entry (i, j) in Table 7 is the mutual information between the record matching indicator and the similarity between attribute i in catalog 1 and attribute j in catalog 2.

Table 8 shows that all of the corresponding non-categorical, non-numerical attributes can be identified after taking the length of each string value; the mutual information between the lengths of two corresponding attributes is higher than that between non-corresponding ones (Mann-Whitney test shows the difference is statistically significant at the 0.01 level, with or without missing values).

Table 9 shows that all of the corresponding non-categorical, non-numerical attributes can also be identified after taking a substring ($n = 1$) of each string value; the mutual information between the substrings of two corresponding attributes is higher than that between non-corresponding ones (Mann-Whitney test shows the difference is statistically significant at the 0.01 level, with or without missing values). For all three methods, discarding missing values results in better estimations than otherwise for these attributes.

Some of the corresponding attributes are identified under multiple categories, boosting the confidence in the results. Edition and Listprice are revealed under both categories I and II. While

Ourprice and Rating are not clearly identified under category I, they are better revealed under category II. Publisher and Supplement are clearly revealed under both categories I and III. This shows the usefulness of evaluating some attributes under multiple categories.

The results show that mutual information can be used as a unified dependence measure to adequately identify correspondences between attributes of all three categories. For free-text character attributes, some simple transformations, such as length and substring, may achieve results comparable to those by the more involved approach of Zhao and Soofi (2006), which requires the preparation of a sample consisting of not only matching record pairs but also non-matching record pairs, as well as a similarity function for comparing attribute values. Since the method tries to measure the dependence, rather than value correspondence, between attributes, some value discrepancies across databases can be handled. For example, author names may be recorded in different ways in the two catalogs. If first name and last name are recorded in different orders, the substring transformation becomes useless but the length transformation is less affected. If one catalog records first initial and last name while the other records the complete first name and last name, the lengths of the author names in the two catalogs will be different but still correlated to certain degree, and the substring transformation (of length one) is even less affected. However, the proposed method is certainly not a panacea and may fail to handle some other types of discrepancies across databases.

FURTHER ANALYSIS

We further analyzed the relationship between the performance and the number of sample matching record pairs used. Performance is measured using accuracy, which is defined as the percentage of attributes whose corresponding attributes can be correctly identified. When using Zhao and Soofi's method for Category III attributes, we used an equal number of matching and non-matching record pairs. We randomly generated 500 samples for each selected sample size. Figure 2 shows the result, where each point is an average over 500 runs.

The result shows that several hundred matching record pairs are needed to get relatively reliable performance in this case. The accuracy for Category I attributes does not seem to converge to 100%, due to the large dependency between Listprice and Ourprice. The problem is less pronounced when Listprice and Ourprice are evaluated as potential Category II attributes.

CONTRIBUTIONS, LIMITATIONS, AND FUTURE RESEARCH DIRECTIONS

This paper proposed a method for attribute matching across overlapping heterogeneous data sources and reported on an empirical evaluation. The method extends a previous method by Zhao and Soofi (2006). The evaluation results demonstrate the utility of the proposed method. The method can be applied to evaluate most frequently encountered types of attributes, including categorical attributes, numerical attributes, and other non-categorical, non-numerical attributes, such as strings. It has, therefore, expanded applicability over and above the previous correlation analysis approach (Fan et al., 2001; Fan et al., 2002, Lu et al., 1997) and the recent information theoretic approach for free-text character attributes (Zhao & Soofi, 2006). The correlation analysis approach cannot deal with non-numerical attributes, such as Author, Title, Cover, Publisher, and Supplement in the book catalog example. It is also not appropriate for evaluating non-linear dependence between numerical attributes.

This paper makes contributions to both research and practice. It advocates the application

Figure 2. Accuracy versus the number of sample matching record pairs

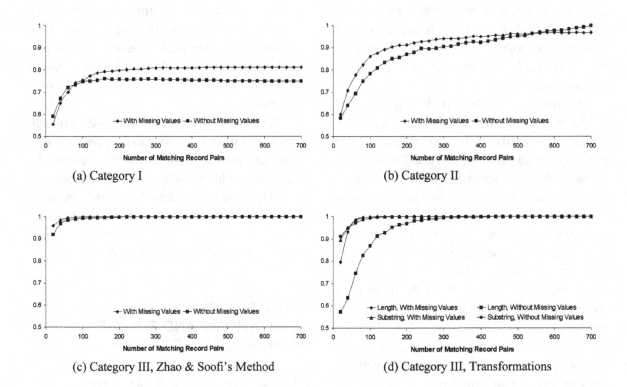

(a) Category I

(b) Category II

(c) Category III, Zhao & Soofi's Method

(d) Category III, Transformations

of information theoretic constructs in solving the attribute matching problem. The proposed method may be found useful in developing practical tools that can be used in data integration and data warehousing practices.

The paper inevitably has its limitations, some of which may be addressed in future research. The proposed method is applicable to data sources that contain some overlapping records. It is not suited for disjoint data sources, for example, two employee databases resulted from the merge of two companies that do not share any employee. Even if there are overlapping records in the data sources, identifying such overlapping records can be difficult. In the book catalogs used in the evaluation, there is a common key, ISBN, across the catalogs, making it easy to identify matching records. However, in a general case where such a common key does not exist, record matching can

itself be a difficult task (Zhao & Ram, 2008). In such cases, it may be necessary to deal with the two problems (record matching and attribute matching) together in an iterative and incremental manner (Bilke & Naumann, 2005; Chua et al., 2003; Zhao & Ram, 2007). Attribute matching methods that are mainly based on meta-data analysis can be used first to identify some matching attributes. Record matching techniques are then applied based on the initial matching attributes. The identified matching records can then be analyzed using attribute matching methods that perform instance data analysis. Any improved understanding of one level (attribute or record) can prompt a reanalysis of the other level.

Like other methods, the proposed method has its strengths, as demonstrated in the evaluation, but also weaknesses. It focuses on instance data analysis and does not evaluate meta-data. It may be inferior to methods that perform meta-data analysis if the semantics of the schemas are well captured in meta-data but the instance data are extremely dirty. It may be used as a component in a composite matching system (Bozovic & Vassalos, 2008; Do & Rahm, 2007; Domshlak et al., 2007; Drum et al., 2007; Lee et al., 2007; Nottelmanna & Straccia, 2007), but it cannot solve the entire matching problem alone. Further research is still needed to understand how the proposed method performs, in comparison with other existing methods, under various situations.

We have used a simple case to illustrate the application of the proposed method. Industry-strength application scenarios can be much "messier," due to a variety of "dirty data" problems and discrepancies across data sources. For example, instead of being defined as temporal types, date/time attributes may be stored as strings using varying formats. Even temporal data types may have different "anchors" and different minimum granularities in different systems. While appearing to be promising, the proposed method still needs to be applied to industry-strength data scrubbing, cleansing, and integration scenarios in different domains in the future to validate its real utility. In the evaluation, we used two simple transformations, which only apply to strings. For other complex data types, such as formatted documents and multimedia objects, appropriate transformations characterizing the original complex objects need to be designed and experimented in the future. While our preliminary analysis shows that several hundred matching record pairs are needed to get relatively reliable performance in this case, more comprehensive experiments are still needed to understand the effects of various factors, such as data value range, database size, data quality, and extent of discrepancy across databases.

In this paper, we have focused on one-to-one attribute matching. The method needs to be extended to deal with complex many-to-many matching. For some cases where sets of categorical or numerical attributes are functionally related, *multiple mutual information* (Zhao & Soofi, 2006) can be used to measure the dependency between sets of attributes. More generally, however, non-categorical, non-numerical attributes may be combined in many different ways. Possible functions for combining attributes need to be tried on subsets of attributes. Mutual information can then be used to measure the dependence between such functions. The search space then becomes very large and even infinite, such that heuristics, such as those proposed by Dhamanka et al. (2004), Wu et. al. (2004), He and Chang (2006), and Su et al. (2006), need to be used to make the search feasible.

Even for simple one-to-one matches, the proposed method can only suggest likely candidates, which then need to be evaluated by human experts based on domain knowledge. Mutually dependent attributes (e.g., Listprice and Ourprice in the book catalogs) may represent related, but not corresponding, concepts. Tools that help analysts review and validate the candidate matches are also highly desired (Bernstein et al., 2006; Bonifati et al., 2008; Rull et al., 2008).

Finally, we used a simple method for estimating the mutual information between two continuous variables (Category II) or between a continuous variable and a discrete variable (Category III) in our evaluation. This simple method resulted in satisfactory results. There are more accurate, but more computationally involved, estimation methods (e.g. Beirlant et al., 1997; Darbellay, 1999), which may be evaluated in the future.

ACKNOWLEDGMENT

The author is grateful to Prof. Ehsan S. Soofi and the anonymous reviewers for their many valuable suggestions.

REFERENCES

Baeza-Yates, R., & Ribeiro-Neto, B. (1999). *Modern Information Retrieval*. Reading, MA: Addison-Wesley.

Beirlant, J., Dudewicz, E. J., Gyorfi, L., & van der Meulen, E. C. (1997). Non-parametric entropy estimation: an overview. *International Journal of Mathematical and Statistical Sciences*, *6*(1), 17–39.

Benkley, S. S., Fandozzi, J. F., Housman, E. M., & Woodhouse, G. M. (1995). *Data Element Tool-based Analysis (DELTA) (Tech. Rep. MTR 95B0000147)*. Bedford, MA: The MITRE Corporation.

Bernstein, P. A., Melnik, S., & Churchill, J. E. (2006). Incremental schema matching. In *Proceedings of the 32nd International Conference on Very Large Data Bases* (pp. 1167-1170).

Bilke, A., & Naumann, F. (2005). Schema Matching Using Duplicates. In *Proceedings of the 21st International Conference on Data Engineering* (pp. 69-80).

Bonifati, A., Mecca, G., Pappalardo, A., Raunich, S., & Summa, G. (2008). Schema mapping verification: the spicy way. In *Proceedings of the 11th International Conference on Extending Database Technology: Advances in Database Technology* (pp. 85-96).

Bozovic, N., & Vassalos, V. (2008). Two-phase schema matching in real world relational databases. In *Proceedings of the ICDE Workshop on Information Integration Methods* (pp. 290-296).

Bright, M. W., Hurson, A. R., & Pakzad, S. H. (1994). Automated resolution of semantic heterogeneity in multidatabases. *ACM Transactions on Database Systems*, *19*(2), 212–253. doi:10.1145/176567.176569

Choi, N., Song, I.-Y., & Han, H. (2006). A survey on ontology mapping. *SIGMOD Record*, *35*(3), 34–41. doi:10.1145/1168092.1168097

Chua, C. E. H., Chiang, R. H. L., & Lim, E.-P. (2003). Instance-based attribute identification in database integration. *The VLDB Journal*, *12*(3), 228–243. doi:10.1007/s00778-003-0088-y

Clifton, C., Housman, E., & Rosenthal, A. (1997). Experience with a combined approach to attribute-matching across heterogeneous databases. In *Proceedings of the IFIP Working Conference on Data Semantics (DS-7)* (pp. 429-451).

Cohen, W. W. (2000). Data integration using similarity joins and a word-based information representation language. *ACM Transactions on Information Systems*, *18*(3), 288–321. doi:10.1145/352595.352598

Darbellay, G. A. (1999). An estimator of the mutual information based on a criterion for independence. *Computational Statistics & Data Analysis*, *32*(1), 1–17. doi:10.1016/S0167-9473(99)00020-1

Dhamanka, R., Lee, Y., Doan, A., Halevy, A., & Domingos, P. (2004). iMAP: discovering complex semantic matches between database schemas. In *Proceedings of the 2004 ACM SIGMOD International Conference on Management of Data* (pp. 383-394).

Do, H.-H., Melnik, S., & Rahm, E. (2003). Comparison of schema matching evaluations. In *Proceedings of the 2nd International Workshop on Web Databases* (pp. 221-237).

Do, H.-H., & Rahm, E. (2007). Matching large schemas: approaches and evaluation. *Information Systems*, *32*(6), 857–885. doi:10.1016/j.is.2006.09.002

Doan, A., & Halevy, A. (2005). Semantic-integration research in the database community: A Brief Survey. *AI Magazine*, *26*(1), 83–94.

Domshlak, C., Gal, A., & Roitman, H. (2007). Rank aggregation for automatic schema matching. *IEEE Transactions on Knowledge and Data Engineering, 19*(4), 538–553. doi:10.1109/TKDE.2007.1010

Drum, C., Schmitt, M., Do, H.-H., & Rahm, E. (2007). QuickMig - automatic schema matching for data migration projects. In *Proceedings of the 16th Conference on Information and Knowledge Management (CIKM2007)* (pp. 107-116).

Fan, W., Lu, H., Madnick, S. E., & Cheung, D. W. (2001). Discovering and reconciling value conflicts for numerical data integration. *Information Systems, 26*(8), 635–656. doi:10.1016/S0306-4379(01)00043-6

Fan, W., Lu, H., Madnick, S. E., & Cheung, D. W. (2002). DIRECT: a system for mining data value conversion rules from disparate sources. *Decision Support Systems, 34*(1), 19–39. doi:10.1016/S0167-9236(02)00006-4

Gal, A. (2006). Why is schema matching tough and what can we do about it? *SIGMOD Record, 35*(4), 2–5. doi:10.1145/1228268.1228269

Giunchiglia, F., Yatskevich, M., & Shvaiko, P. (2007). Semantic Matching: Algorithms and Implementation. *Journal on Data Semantics, 9*, 1–38.

Hall, P., & Morton, S. C. (1993). On the estimation of entropy. *Annals of Institute of Mathematical Statistics, 45*(1), 69–88. doi:10.1007/BF00773669

He, B., & Chang, K. C.-C. (2006). Automatic complex schema matching across web query interfaces: a correlation mining approach. *ACM Transactions on Database Systems, 31*(1), 346–395. doi:10.1145/1132863.1132872

Hu, W., Qu, Y., & Cheng, G. (2008). Matching large ontologies: A divide-and-conquer approach. *Data & Knowledge Engineering, 67*(1), 140–160. doi:10.1016/j.datak.2008.06.003

Johannesson, P. (1997). Supporting schema integration by linguistic instruments. *Data & Knowledge Engineering, 21*(2), 165–182. doi:10.1016/S0169-023X(96)00031-6

Kang, J., & Naughton, J. F. (2003). On schema matching with opaque column names and data values. In *Proceedings of the 2003 ACM SIGMOD International Conference on Management of Data* (pp. 205-216).

Kang, J., & Naughton, J. F. (2008). Schema matching using interattribute dependencies. *IEEE Transactions on Knowledge and Data Engineering, 20*(10), 1393–1407. doi:10.1109/TKDE.2008.100

Lee, Y., Sayyadian, M., Doan, A., & Rosenthal, A. S. (2007). eTuner: tuning schema matching software using synthetic scenarios. *The VLDB Journal, 16*(1), 97–122. doi:10.1007/s00778-006-0024-z

Li, W. S., & Clifton, C. (2000). SEMINT: a tool for identifying attribute correspondences in heterogeneous databases using neural networks. *Data & Knowledge Engineering, 33*(1), 49–84. doi:10.1016/S0169-023X(99)00044-0

Lu, H., Fan, W., Goh, C. H., Madnick, S. E., & Cheng, D. W. (1997). Discovering and reconciling semantic conflicts: a data mining perspective. In *Proceedings of the IFIP Working Conference on Data Semantics (DS-7)* (pp. 410-427).

Madhavan, J., Bernstein, P., Doan, A., & Halevy, A. (2005). Corpus-based schema matching. In *Proceedings of the 18th International Conference on Data Engineering* (pp. 57-68).

March, S. T., Hevner, A., & Ram, S. (2000). Research commentary: an agenda for information technology research in heterogeneous and distributed environments. *Information Systems Research, 11*(4), 327–341. doi:10.1287/isre.11.4.327.11873

Nottelmanna, H., & Straccia, U. (2007). Information retrieval and machine learning for probabilistic schema matching. *Information Processing & Management, 43*(3), 552–576. doi:10.1016/j.ipm.2006.10.014

Palopoli, L., Pontieri, L., Terracina, G., & Ursino, D. (2000). Intensional and extensional integration and abstraction of heterogeneous databases. *Data & Knowledge Engineering, 35*(3), 201–237. doi:10.1016/S0169-023X(00)00028-8

Pirrò, G., & Talia, D. (2008). LOM: a linguistic ontology matcher based on information retrieval. *Journal of Information Science, 34*(6), 845–860. doi:10.1177/0165551508091014

Rahm, E., & Bernstein, P. A. (2001). A survey of approaches to automatic schema matching. *The VLDB Journal, 10*(4), 334–350. doi:10.1007/s007780100057

Rull, G., Farré, C., Teniente, E., & Urpí, T. (2008). Validation of mappings between schemas. *Data & Knowledge Engineering, 66*(3), 414–437. doi:10.1016/j.datak.2008.04.009

Saleem, K., Bellahsene, Z., & Hunt, E. (2008). PORSCHE: Performance ORiented SCHEma mediation. *Information Systems, 33*(7-8), 637–657. doi:10.1016/j.is.2008.01.010

Shannon, C. E. (1948). A mathematical theory of communication. *The Bell System Technical Journal, 27*, 379–423.

Shvaiko, P., & Euzenat, J. (2005). A survey of schema-based matching approaches. *Journal of Data Semantics, 4*, 146–171.

Soofi, E. S., & Retzer, J. J. (2002). Information indices: unification and applications. *Journal of Econometrics, 107*(1-2), 17–40. doi:10.1016/S0304-4076(01)00111-7

Stephen, G. A. (1994). *String Searching Algorithms*. Singapore: World Scientific Publishing Company.

Su, W., Wang, J., & Lochovsky, F. (2006). Holistic schema matching for web query interface. In *Proceedings of the International Conference on Extending Database Technology (EDBT)* (pp. 77-94).

Su, X., & Gulla, J. A. (2006). An information retrieval approach to ontology mapping . *Data & Knowledge Engineering, 58*(1), 47–69. doi:10.1016/j.datak.2005.05.012

Wang, J., Wen, J., Lockovsky, F., & Ma, W. (2004). Instance-based schema matching for web databases by domain-specific query probing. In *Proceedings of the 30th International Conference on Very Large Data Bases* (pp. 408-419).

Wu, W., Yu, C., Doan, A., & Meng, W. (2004). An interactive clustering-based approach to integrating source query interfaces on the deep web. In *Proceedings of the 2004 ACM SIGMOD International Conference on Management of Data* (pp. 95-106).

Xu, L., & Embley, D. W. (2006). A composite approach to automating direct and indirect schema mappings. *Information Systems, 31*(8), 697–732. doi:10.1016/j.is.2005.01.003

Zhao, H., & Ram, S. (2004). Clustering schema elements for semantic integration of heterogeneous data sources. *Journal of Database Management, 15*(4), 88–106.

Zhao, H., & Ram, S. (2007). Combining schema and instance information for integrating heterogeneous data sources. *Data & Knowledge Engineering, 61*(2), 281–303. doi:10.1016/j.datak.2006.06.004

Zhao, H., & Ram, S. (2008). Entity matching across heterogeneous data sources: an approach based on constrained cascade generalization. *Data & Knowledge Engineering, 66*(3), 368–381. doi:10.1016/j.datak.2008.04.007

Zhao, H., & Soofi, E. S. (2006). Exploring attribute correspondences across heterogeneous databases by mutual information. *Journal of Management Information Systems, 22*(4), 305–336. doi:10.2753/MIS0742-1222220411

Chapter 18
Disclosure Control of Confidential Data by Applying Pac Learning Theory

Ling He
Saginaw Valley State University, USA

Haldun Aytug
University of Florida, USA

Gary J. Koehler
University of Florida, USA

ABSTRACT

This paper examines privacy protection in a statistical database from the perspective of an intruder using learning theory to discover private information. With the rapid development of information technology, massive data collection is relatively easier and cheaper than ever before. The challenge is how to provide database users with reliable and useful data while protecting the privacy of the confidential information. This paper discusses how to prevent disclosing the identity of unique records in a statistical database. The authors' research extends previous work and shows how much protection is necessary to prevent an adversary from discovering confidential data with high probability at small error.

INTRODUCTION

Statistical organizations, such as the U.S. Census Bureau, collect large amounts of data every year and make it available to the public as statistical databases (SDBs). These organizations have the legal and ethical obligations to maintain the accuracy, integrity and privacy of the information contained in their databases. In order to protect the identity of unique records in SDBs, only limited aggregate queries, such as Sum, Count and Mean, are allowed.

Statistical Disclosure Control (SDC) methods are designed to protect confidential information in a database (minimizing the disclosure risk) while providing the SDB users with reliable and useful data (minimizing the information loss). The goal of disclosure control is to prevent users

DOI: 10.4018/978-1-61350-471-0.ch018

from inferring confidential data on the basis of those successive statistical queries. It is also our research focus.

In contrast to the traditional SDC methods we approach the database security problem from a different perspective: we assume that an adversary regards the true confidential data in the database as an unknown target concept and tries to discover it within a limited number of queries using learning methods.

Probably Approximately Correct (PAC) learning theory is a framework for analyzing machine learning (ML) algorithms (Valiant, 1984). This paradigm focuses on learning algorithms that discover a target concept from examples which are randomly drawn from an unknown but fixed distribution. Given accuracy and confidence parameters, the PAC model bounds the error that the discovered concept may make.

We take as the database administrator's security problem that of determining how to make the adversarial learning task difficult while still providing useful information to legitimate users. That is, we look at the trade-offs between the confidence an adversary can achieve in discovering confidential data, the number of queries he or she must run and the resulting accuracy. We provide a bound that describes the trade-off between the number of queries, accuracy and confidence using PAC learning theory.

Research on privacy of statistical databases has emphasized developing methods to protect privacy without worrying about how much protection is enough. Our results quantify "how much protection one buys when using additive data/ query perturbation."

TRADITIONAL APPROACHES FOR DISCLOSURE CONTROL METHODS

A *compromise* of a database occurs when confidential information is disclosed exactly, partially or inferentially in such a way that the user can link the data to an entity. *Inferential disclosure* or *statistical inference* (Más, 2000) refer to the situation that an unauthorized user can infer the confidential data with a high probability by running sequential queries and the probability exceeds a predetermined threshold of disclosure. For example, assume a hospital database has a binary filed called HIV-Status. A user can issue several SUM (HIV-Status) queries against this database. Individually, these queries may not pose a threat, however, when combined the adversary might infer the HIV-Status of a patient (for a full example see Garfinkel, Gopal, & Goes, 2002). This is known as an inference problem, which falls within our research focus.

Adam and Wortmann (1989) classify SDC methods for SDBs into four categories: Conceptual, Query Restriction, Data Perturbation, and Output Perturbation. Perturbations are achieved by applying either an additive or multiplicative technique. An additive technique (Muralidhar, Parsa, & Sarathy, 1999) adds noise to the confidential data. Multiplicative data perturbation (Muralidhar, Batra, & Kirs, 1995) protects the sensitive information by multiplying the original data with a random variable, with mean 1 and a pre-specified variance.

Data shuffling, a perturbation technique, proposed and further studied by Muralidhar and Sarathy (2006) and Muralidhar, Sarathy, and Dandekar (2006) offers a high level of data utility while reducing the disclosure risk by shuffling data among observations. Data shuffling maintains all advantages of perturbation methods and provides a better performance than other data protection methods.

Muralidhar and Sarathy (2008) recently proposed a methodology for generating sufficiency-based non-synthetic perturbed data, which provides the masked data with the same mean vector and covariance matrix as those of the original data, and further prevents the information loss.

Nunez, Garfinkel, and Gopal (2007) developed a hybrid method that combines both data perturbation and query restriction to provide stochastic protection. The hybrid approach answers some queries exactly while answering others inexactly. It handles linear and nonlinear queries on both numerical and categorical data, and maintains the statistical properties of data as in the standard perturbation method. So the upsides of data perturbation and query restriction are maintained in this new method which also provides best possible information to a database user. Canfora and Cavallo (2009) proposed a new Bayesian model, which presents a probabilistic approach to deal with on-line max and min query auditing, a type of query restriction method. In the model, probabilistic inferences on user knowledge can be drawn from released data, then a decision is made on whether or not to further answer the query.

Our study focuses on additive noise perturbation methods, which are usually employed to protect confidential numerical data. Notation for terms used in the paper is summarized in Figure 1.

PAC Learning:

n number of records/attributes

ℓ training sample size/number of queries.

C set of all concepts.

H hypothesis space.

$\bar{X}$ instance space.

$\bar{Y}$ classes (binary in this paper).

$f\left(\overline{x}\right)$ is the target concept to be learned.

$$f : \bar{X} \rightarrow \bar{Y} .$$

S training set/sample set. $S = \left(\left(\overline{x}_1, \overline{y}_1\right), \dots, \left(\overline{x}_\ell, \overline{y}_\ell\right)\right)$

D fixed but unknown sample distribution.

$\underset{D}{err}\left(h\right)$ the error of hypothesis h.

$$\underset{D}{err}\left(h\right) = \Pr_D \left\{\left(\overline{x}, f\left(\overline{x}\right)\right) : h\left(\overline{x}\right) \neq f\left(\overline{x}\right)\right\}$$

ε error level.

δ $1 - \delta$ is the PAC confidence level.

Dinur and Nissim:

e perturbation.

$q \subseteq \left\{1, \cdots, n\right\}$ a query.

$A\left(q\right)$ perturbed sum of query q.

$\tilde{a}_q$ observed value of $A\left(q\right)$.

$d_i \in \left\{0, 1\right\}$ i^{th} value of protected database column.

K $K = \left\{0, \frac{1}{k}, \frac{2}{k}, \dots, \frac{k-1}{k}, 1\right\}$

c LP solutions. $c \in H_2 = \left[0, 1\right]^n$,

c' c rounded. $c' \in H_0 = \left\{0, 1\right\}^n$.

h_0 $h_0 : H_i \rightarrow H_0$ $\left(i = 1, \ 2\right)$.

$\overline{c} \in K^n = H_1$ c rounded to nearest vector in K.

h_1 $h_1 : H_2 \rightarrow H_1$.

X, U

$$X = \left\{x \in K^n \mid \Pr_i \left[\left\|x_i - d_i\right| \geq 1/3\right] > \varepsilon n\right\}$$

is the set of all vectors which are likely far away from the true vector d.

$\xi, \xi\left(\varepsilon\right)$ lower bound of the disqualifying lemma.

$\kappa\left(\varepsilon\right)$ $\kappa\left(\varepsilon\right) = 1 - \xi\left(\varepsilon\right)$.

$dist\left(c, d\right)$ Hamming distance between c and d.

$\gamma\left(S\right)$ represents an LP mapping from a sample S to an output vector.

$E\left[\ \right]$ expectation.

A THEORETICAL BASIS

Dinur and Nissim (2003) concluded that a minimum perturbation magnitude of $\Omega\left(\sqrt{n}\right)$ is required for each query, q, in order to maintain even weak privacy of a database that has n records. Otherwise, an adversary could reconstruct the statistical database using $\ell = n\left(\lg n\right)^2$ (lg is the base 2 logarithm) queries with high probability. The SDB can be protected from disclosure if the perturbation value is bounded by $e > o\left(\sqrt{n}\right)$, however, such data may not be useful because of the large perturbation. Since Dinur and Nissim

Figure 1. Summary of notation

PAC Learning:

n	number of records/attributes
ℓ	training sample size/number of queries.
C	set of all concepts.
H	hypothesis space.
$\bar{X}$	instance space.
$\bar{Y}$	classes (binary in this paper).

$f(\bar{x})$ is the target concept to be learned. $f : \bar{X} \to \bar{Y}$.

S	training set/sample set. $S = ((\bar{x}_1, \bar{y}_1), ..., (\bar{x}_\ell, \bar{y}_\ell))$.
D	fixed but unknown sample distribution.
$err_D(h)$	the error of hypothesis h. $err_D(h) = \Pr_D\{(\bar{x}, f(\bar{x})): h(\bar{x}) \neq f(\bar{x})\}$
ε	error level.
δ	$1 - \delta$ is the PAC confidence level.

Dinur and Nissim:

e	perturbation.
$q \subseteq \{1, \cdots, n\}$	a query.
$A(q)$	perturbed sum of query q.
$\tilde{a}_q$	observed value of $A(q)$.
$d_i \in \{0,1\}$	i^{th} value of protected database column.
K	$K = \left\{0, \frac{1}{k}, \frac{2}{k}, ..., \frac{k-1}{k}, 1\right\}$
c	LP solutions. $c \in H_2 = [0,1]^n$,
c'	c rounded. $c' \in H_0 = \{0,1\}^n$.
h_0	$h_0 : H_i \to H_0 \quad (i = 1, 2)$.
$\bar{c} \in K^n = H_1$	c rounded to nearest vector in K.
h_1	$h_1 : H_2 \to H_1$.
X, U	$X = \left\{x \in K^n \mid \Pr_i\left[\|x_i - d_i\| \geq 1/3\right] > \varepsilon n\right\}$ is the set of all vectors which are likely

far away from the true vector d.

$\xi, \xi(\varepsilon)$	lower bound of the disqualifying lemma.
$\kappa(\varepsilon)$	$\kappa(\varepsilon) = 1 - \xi(\varepsilon)$.
$dist(c,d)$	Hamming distance between c and d.
$\gamma(S)$	represents an LP mapping from a sample S to an output vector.
$E[\ ]$	expectation.

make no assumptions beyond assuming the additive error is fixed, their results are valid both for data perturbation and output perturbation methods using fixed additive error.

Dinur and Nissim modeled a single confidential field in the database as an n-bit binary string, where n is the number of records, $(d_1, ..., d_n) \in \{0,1\}^n$. The true answer for a SUM query q, $q \subseteq \{1, \cdots, n\}$, is computed as $\sum_{i \in q} d_i$

. The perturbed answer for a query q is $A(q)$ obtained by adding a perturbation $\left|A(q) - \sum_{i \in q} d_i\right| \leq e$, where $e > o(\sqrt{n})$ is the bound for the perturbation of each query.

The authors gave a Linear Programming (LP) algorithm (see Figure 2) to generate a candidate confidential vector that an adversary would use to compromise the database.

Figure 2. LP algorithm (Adapted from Dinur & Nissim, 2003)

[Query Phase]

Let $l = n(\lg n)^2$. For $1 \leq j \leq \ell$ choose uniformly at random

$q_j \subseteq \{1, \cdots, n\}$, and set $\tilde{a}_{q_j} \leftarrow A(q_j)$.

[Weeding Phase]

Using any linear objective, solve the linear program having constraints:

$\tilde{a}_{q_j} - e \leq \sum_{i \in q_j} c_i \leq \tilde{a}_{q_j} + e \qquad \text{for } 1 \leq j \leq \ell$

$0 \leq c_i \leq 1 \qquad\qquad \text{for } 1 \leq i \leq n$

[Rounding Phase]

Let $c_i' = 1$ if $c_i > \frac{1}{2}$ and $c_i' = 0$ otherwise. Output c'.

The LP algorithm outputs c. The n-bit binary vector c' is obtained by rounding c. A third vector $\bar{c}$ is obtained by rounding c to the nearest integer multiple of $\frac{1}{k}$, where k represents a precision parameter (they chose $k = n$), and $K = \left\{0, \frac{1}{k}, \frac{2}{k}, ..., \frac{k-1}{k}, 1\right\}$. Hence $\bar{c} \in K^n$. They proved that $\left|\sum_{i \in q_j} (\bar{c}_i - d_i)\right| \leq 2e + 1$.

Dinur and Nissim (2003) showed that vectors that are far away from the true confidential vector d are weeded out by the algorithm by proving a Disqualifying Lemma where ℓ random queries $q_1, ..., q_\ell$ would weed out all vectors

$$x \in X = \left\{x \in K^n \mid \Pr_i\left[\|x_i - d_i\| \geq 1/3\right] > \varepsilon n\right\}$$

. $\qquad\qquad\qquad\qquad\qquad\qquad\qquad (1)$

X denotes the set of all vectors which are likely far away from the true vector d. Consequently, c' must be close to d.

The Disqualifying Lemma specifically states that

$$\Pr_{q \subseteq_R [n]}\left[\left|\sum_{i \in q} (x_i - d_i)\right| \geq 2e + 1\right] > \xi. \qquad (2)$$

It guarantees that if x is far away from d then at least one of the ℓ queries $q_1, \cdots, q_\ell$ would disqualify x with high probability.

One missing piece is the relationship between inequalities (1) and (2) that relates ε to ξ. The proof of the disqualifying lemma establishes this link and it is possible to think of ξ as a function of ε, $\xi(\varepsilon)$. We discuss this further in the next section.

If ℓ queries $q_1, \cdots, q_\ell$ are chosen independently and randomly, then for each $x \in X$, the probability that all ℓ queries do not disqualify x is $(1 - \xi)^\ell$. A conclusion derived from the Disqualifying Lemma is

$$1 - \Pr_{q_1, \cdots q_\ell \subseteq_R [n]}\left[\forall x \in X \; \exists i, \; q_i \text{ disqualifies } x\right] \leq (n+1)^n (1-\xi)^\ell \leq neg(n)$$

Thus, the probability that none of the ℓ queries can disqualify $x \in X$ is bounded by a very small number $neg(n) > 0$. Therefore, the Disqualifying Lemma guarantees ruling out all disqualifying vectors $x \in X$ with high probability

$(1 - neg(n))$ and guarantees that the hamming distance, dist(), between the final candidate vector c' and true vector d is small, that is, $dist(c', d) \leq \varepsilon n$. The number of queries that are required to weed out disqualified vectors is computed from the Disqualifying Lemma. That is,

$$\ell = n(\lg n)^2.$$

PROPOSED PAC APPROACH FOR FIXED-DATA PERTURBATION

A PAC learning method learns from examples of the target concept *(or target function)* f which is a function that maps data from the input space $\bar{X}$ ($\bar{x} \in \bar{X} \subseteq \Re^n$) to the output space $\bar{Y}$ ($\bar{y} \in \bar{Y}$), where n is the number of attributes of an instance[1]. If $\bar{y}$ is binary, $f(\bar{x})$ classifies all *instances* $\bar{x} \in \bar{X}$ into two classes (e.g., $\bar{X} \subseteq \Re^n \xrightarrow{f} \bar{Y} \subseteq \{0,1\}$). For boolean classification, which is relevant to our problem, f is in the *concept space* $C = 2^{\bar{X}}$ of all possible boolean functions (i.e., $\bar{X} \subseteq \{0,1\}^n$). Suppose a sample S includes ℓ pairs of training examples, $S = ((\bar{x}_1, \bar{y}_1), ..., (\bar{x}_\ell, \bar{y}_\ell))$. Each $\bar{x}_i$ is an instance, and $\bar{y}_i$ is $\bar{x}_i$'s true classification label.

The learning algorithm inputs the training sample and outputs an hypothesis $h(\bar{x})$ from the set of all hypotheses which best approximates $f(\bar{x})$. An *hypothesis space* H is a set of all hypotheses under consideration. It is usually assumed that H satisfies $H \subseteq C$.

The PAC learning model (Vapnik, 1998) quantifies the worst-case risk associated with learning a function. Suppose a sample S of size ℓ is generated independently and identically from an unknown but fixed probability distribution D over the instance space $\bar{X}$. The learning task is to choose a specific boolean function in polynomial time.

The error of $h \in H$ with respect to $f \in C$, is the probability that h and f disagree on the classification of an instance $\bar{x} \in \bar{X}$ drawn from D. This is denoted by $err_D(h) = \Pr_D \{(\bar{x}, f(\bar{x})) : h(\bar{x}) \neq f(\bar{x})\}$.

The PAC model utilizes an accuracy parameter ε and a confidence parameter δ to measure the quality of an hypothesis h. A PAC model strives to bound the probability that an hypothesis h gives large error by δ as in $\Pr_D^\ell \{S : err_D(h_s) > \varepsilon\} < \delta$ where h_s is the output of the learning algorithm based on S.

An hypothesis h that classifies S correctly is called a *consistent hypothesis*. The following inequality bounds the probability that a consistent hypothesis will have error greater than ε:

$$\Pr_D^\ell \{S : h \text{ consistent and } err_D(h) > \varepsilon\}$$
$$\leq |H|(1-\varepsilon)^\ell \leq |H| e^{-\varepsilon \ell}.$$

The idea behind the PAC bound is to bound this unlucky scenario (i.e., h, though consistent with S, happens to have error greater than ε) by δ.

Figure 3 demonstrates the dual connection between the methodologies employed in PAC learning theory and the database protection approach in Dinur and Nissim (2003). It indicates that both approaches determine a training sample size ℓ which is necessary to accomplish the desired goal. The probability that a query disqualifies the $x \in X$ with probability greater than $\xi(\varepsilon)$ is bounded by the union bound of X, high probability $\xi(\varepsilon)$, and further bounded by a small probability $neg(n)$. These three parameters correspond to the cardinality of the hypothesis space $|H|$, the accuracy parameter ε, and the confidence level δ in the PAC learning theory. They are

Figure 3. Illustration of the connection between the PAC learning and data perturbation

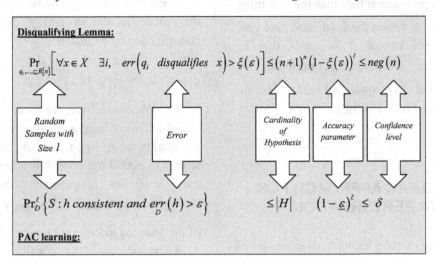

shown in Figure 3 as matched terms even though different notation and terminologies are adopted.

From the perspective of learning theory, we regard the true confidential field as the target concept that an adversary seeks to discover within a limited number of queries in the presence of random perturbation. Building on Dinur and Nissim's definition we provide the following definition of a *Non-Private Database*: a database is non-private if a computationally-bound adversary can expose $1 - \varepsilon$ fraction of the confidential data for $\varepsilon > 0$ with probability $1 - \delta$, where $\delta > 0$.

Consider a statistical database with one confidential field which is a binary string of size n, denoted as $(d_1, ..., d_n)' \in \{0,1\}^n$. For example, in a hospital database "HIV" status may be the confidential vector of interest. An hypothesis space H_0 contains n-bit binary vectors, each of which is an hypothesis $h \in H_0 = \{0,1\}^n$. The true confidential field is regarded as the target concept $d \in H_0$. The online database receives a SUM query q sent by the user and responds with a perturbed answer $A(q)$ of the true answer

$a_q = \sum_{i \in q} d_i$. A perturbation is bounded by $e \geq |a_q - A(q)|$.

We take ℓ samples consisting of queries and their perturbed responses $S = ((q_1, A(q_1)), \cdots, (q_\ell, A(q_\ell)))$. Paralleling Dinur and Nissim, we have the related counterparts:

a. the learning algorithm is a linear program;

b. $H_2 = [0,1]^n$ corresponds to the LP solution space;

c. $H_1 = K^n$ corresponds to rounding to grid values;

Note that $H_0 \subseteq H_1 \subseteq H_2$ where all containments are strict when $n > 1$.

Let $h_1 : H_2 \to H_1$ by rounding each component in H_2 to the nearest integer multiple of $1/n$ (midpoints rounded down). Further, let $h_0 : H_i \to H_0$ $(i = 1, 2)$ by rounding each component in H_i to the nearest of 0 and 1 (0.5 rounds down). Note that $h_1(c) = c + g$, where

$$|g_i| < \frac{1}{n} \qquad i = 1, \cdots, n.$$

The LP finds $c \in H_2$, from which one can output $h_0(c)$. We represent this algorithm by $c \leftarrow \gamma(S)$.

Let $c \in H_0$, then the hamming distance between c and d is

$$dist(c,d) = \left| \{ i : c_i \neq d_i \} \right| = \sum_{i=1}^{n} |c_i - d_i|.$$

Let $x \in H_2$. $\Pr_i \left[|x_i - d_i| \geq 1/3 \right] > \varepsilon$ means the probability of choosing $i \in \{ 1, \cdots, n \}$ randomly such that $|x_i - d_i| \geq 1/3$. That is, for this x there are εn expected number of bits with $|x_i - d_i| \geq 1/3$. Denote this by $E_i \left[|x_i - d_i| \geq 1/3 \right] > \varepsilon n$ where $\varepsilon > 0$. We wish to show how to choose a sample size ℓ so that $dist \left(h_0(\gamma(S)), d \right) \leq \varepsilon n$.

Lemma:

If $x \in K^n$ and $E_i \left[|x_i - d_i| \geq 1/3 \right] \leq \varepsilon n$, then $dist \left(h_0(x), d \right) \leq \varepsilon n$.

Proof:

First note that if $|x_i - d_i| \leq 1/3$ then $\left| h_0(x)_i - d_i \right| \leq 1/2 - 1/3 < 1/3$. Thus since no more than εn i's, on average, have $|x_i - d_i| \geq 1/3$, then no more than εn number, on average, of $h_0(x)$ can have $\left| h_0(x)_i - d_i \right| \geq 1/3$. The number $1/3$ in $|x_i - d_i| \leq 1/3$ guarantees that x_i round to the same number as d_i. Q.E.D.

Let

$$U = \left\{ x \in K^n \mid \Pr_i \left[|x_i - d_i| \geq 1/3 \right] > \varepsilon n \right\} .$$

From the point of view of the intruder, we want our sample of queries to disqualify all points of U with high probability, $(1 - \delta)$, where $\delta \in (0,1)$. For a sample of size ℓ, generated independently and identically according to an unknown but fixed distribution D, the probability that an hypothesis c is far away from the true target d is measured by the risk functional

$$err_D(c) = 1 - \Pr_D \left(q \subseteq \{ 1, \cdots, n \} : \left| \sum_{i \in q} (c_i - d_i) \right| \leq 1 + 2e \right) =$$

$$\Pr_D \left(q \subseteq \{ 1, \cdots, n \} : \left| \sum_{i \in q} (c_i - d_i) \right| > 1 + 2e \right)$$

where $c \in H_1$.

As stated earlier, the solution c from the LP can be rounded either to a binary vector $h_0(c)$ or a vector $h_1(c) \in K^n$. The probability that the distance between the true vector d and the rounded vector $h_1(c)$ is greater than $1/3$ is bounded by ε. Based on this condition, for any random query, the difference between the answers from these two vectors is bounded by a function of the perturbation, $2e + 1$. So, we can see that e and ε are related and they describe the error from different perspectives. Then we use ξ to bound the risk functional as $err_D(c) > \xi(\varepsilon)$. We intend to bound $\Pr_D^\ell \left(S : err_D \left(h_1(\gamma(S)) \right) > \xi(\varepsilon) \right)$ using $\delta > 0$.

Provided $e = o(\sqrt{n})$, the Disqualifying Lemma proved $\xi(\varepsilon) > 0$. Then, for $\kappa(\varepsilon) = 1 - \xi(\varepsilon)$,

$$\Pr_D^\ell \left(S : err_D \left(h_1(\gamma(S)) \right) > \xi(\varepsilon) \right) \leq (n+1)^n \left(1 - \xi(\varepsilon) \right)^\ell = (n+1)^n \kappa^\ell(\varepsilon) \quad (3)$$

where $(n+1)^n = |K| \geq |X|$ is the union bound over X, and therefore the worst-case scenario is bounded. Thus, (see Appendix A)

Table 1. bounds on the sample size with different values of n.

n	$\ell \geq \dfrac{\lg(\delta) - n\lg(n+1)}{\lg(1-\xi(\varepsilon))}$	2^n
10	626,058	1,024
50	4,632,231	1.1259E+15
100	10,780,799	1.2677E+30
500	72,210,390	3.2734E+150
1000	160,415,387	1.0715E+301
5000	988,473,927	---

$$\kappa(\varepsilon) \leq \min\left(1 - \left(1 - 2e^{-T^2/8}\right), 1 - \frac{\alpha}{3\beta}\right)$$

with $T \geq \sqrt{\dfrac{\varepsilon}{500}}$. Using this, in Appendix A, we derive the following expression:

$$\xi(\varepsilon) = x\frac{2-x}{(1-x)^2} \text{ where } x = e^{-\beta/2} \text{ with } \beta$$

chosen large enough.

If we bound the probability in (3) with the confidence parameter $\delta > 0$ and take the logarithm on both sides, we get

$$\lg\left[(n+1)^n\left(1-\xi(\varepsilon)\right)^\ell\right] \leq \lg\delta.$$

Hence $\ell \geq \dfrac{\lg(\delta) - n\lg(n+1)}{\lg(1-\xi(\varepsilon))}$ and ℓ is

bounded from below by three parameters δ, ε and n.

Table 1 shows the PAC bounds for $\delta = 0.05$ and $\varepsilon = 0.1$ for different values of n. The second column is our bound on the number of queries required to compromise a database. The last column is the number of all possible queries one can run on a binary field in a database of size n. As n increases the gap between the two columns in-creases demonstrating the utility of the algorithm in Figure 2 and the associated bound.

Given n, we derive the necessary number of queries an intruder needs to generate to discover $1 - \varepsilon$ fraction of the records with probability $1 - \delta$. Dinur and Nissim state that with probability $1 - neg(n)$ using $\ell = n(\lg n)^2$ queries an intruder can discover $1 - \varepsilon$ fraction of the database. Their formula does not state what ε is or what *neg(n)* is. We quantify the relationship between ε and *neg(n)*.

CONCLUSION

The major contribution of this paper is that we approach the database privacy problem from the perspective of learning theory, where we regard an adversary of the database as a learner who tries to discover the confidential information within a certain number of queries.

We extended the previous work by Dinur and Nissim (2003). Specifically, we showed how to apply PAC learning theory to develop a new bound for this problem. We determined the minimum number of queries an adversary needs to ask to compromise the database with high probability and small error. This can be used to determine how much protection would be necessary to prevent the disclosure of the confidential information in a statistical database.

Our results show that absolute protection is not possible and that small perturbations leave the data vulnerable to attacks with high probability. Larger perturbations protect the data better forcing the adversary to run substantially more queries to attain worthwhile results. However, an adversary with enough computing power can still link the protected fields to records while the proper users of the database are penalized since larger perturbations affect the accuracy of their analyses. We think these results suggest that additive perturbation may not be sufficiently safe and other methods of data protection should be investigated further.

The basic PAC model is a noise-free model since it assumes that the training set is error-free, meaning that the given training examples are correctly labeled and not corrupted. The PAC algorithm has been extended to account for noisy inputs (Angluin & Laird, 1988). Kearns (1993) initiated another well-studied model in the machine learning area, the Statistical Query model (SQ), which provides a framework for a noise-tolerant learning algorithm. For more details about types of noise, see papers by Kearns and Li (1993) and Goldman and Sloan (1995). Future research can explore extending this line of inquiry to the SDC problem noting that the noise may not be i.i.d.

REFERENCES

Adam, N. R., & Wortmann, J. C. (1989). Security-Control methods for statistical database: a comparative study. *ACM Computing Surveys*, *21*(4), 515–556. doi:10.1145/76894.76895

Angluin, D., & Laird, P. (1988). Learning from noisy examples. *Machine Learning*, *2*(4), 343–370. doi:10.1007/BF00116829

Canfora, G., & Cavallo, B. (2009). A Bayesian model for disclosure control in statistical databases. *Data Knowledge Engineering*. doi:10.1016/j.datak. 2009.06.006

Dinur, I., & Nissim, K. (2003). Revealing information while preserving privacy. In *Proceedings of the Twenty-Second ACM SIGACT-SIGMOD-SIGART Symposium on Principles of Database Systems* (pp. 202-210).

Garfinkel, R., Gopal, R., & Goes, P. (2002). Privacy protection of binary confidential data against deterministic, stochastic, and insider threat. *Management Science*, *48*(6), 749–764. doi:10.1287/mnsc.48.6.749.193

Goldman, S. A., & Sloan, R. (1995). Can PAC learning algorithms tolerate random attribute noise? *Algorithmica*, *14*(1), 70–84. doi:10.1007/BF01300374

Kearns, M. (1993). Efficient noise-tolerant learning from statistical queries. In *Proceedings of the 25th Annual ACM Symposium on Theory of Computing* (pp. 392-401).

Kearns, M., & Li, M. (1993). Learning in the presence of malicious errors. *SIAM Journal on Computing*, *22*(4). doi:10.1137/0222052

Más, M. (2000). *Statistical data protection techniques*. Retrieved from http://www.eustat.es/document/ datos/ct_02_i.pdf

Muralidhar, K., Batra, D., & Kirs, P. J. (1995). Accessibility, security, and accuracy in statistical database: the case for the multiplicative fixed data perturbation approach. *Management Science*, *41*(9), 1549–1564. doi:10.1287/mnsc.41.9.1549

Muralidhar, K., Parsa, R., & Sarathy, R. (1999). A general additive data perturbation method for database security. *Management Science*, *45*(10), 1399–1415. doi:10.1287/mnsc.45.10.1399

Muralidhar, K., & Sarathy, R. (2006). Data shuffling-A new masking approach for numerical data. *Management Science, 52*(5), 658–670. doi:10.1287/mnsc.1050.0503

Muralidhar, K., & Sarathy, R. (2008). Generating Sufficiency-based Non-Synthetic Perturbed Data. *Transactions on Data Privacy, 1*(1), 17–33.

Muralidhar, K., Sarathy, R., & Dandekar, R. (2006). Why swap when you can shuffle? A comparison of the proximity swap and data shuffle for numeric data . In Domingo-Ferrer, J., & Franconi, L. (Eds.), *Privacy in Statistical Databases* (pp. 164–176). Berlin, Heidelberg: Springer. doi:10.1007/11930242_15

Nunez, M., Garfinkel, R., & Gopal, R. (2007). Stochastic protection of confidential information in statistical databases: A hybrid of query restriction and data perturbation. *Operations Research, 55*(5), 890–908. doi:10.1287/opre.1070.0407

Sloan, R. (1995). Four types of noise in data for PAC learning. *Information Processing Letters, 54*, 157–162. doi:10.1016/0020-0190(95)00016-6

Valiant, L. G. (1984). A theory of the learnable. *Communications of the ACM, 17*(11), 1134–1142. doi:10.1145/1968.1972

Vapnik, V. (1998). *Statistical Learning Theory*. New York: John Wiley & Sons.

ENDNOTE

[1] From a learning perspective the number of records in Dinur and Nissim's paper is equivalent to the number of attributes in PAC notation. So we will use n throughout this paper.

APPENDIX A

Recall that the Disqualify Lemma (Dinur & Nissim, 2003) proves

$$\Pr_{q \subseteq_R [n]} \left[\left| \sum_{i \in q} (x_i - d_i) \right| \geq 2e + 1 \right] > \xi \, .$$

In the proof, $\varpi_1, \varpi_2, \cdots, \varpi_n$ are defined as independent random variables such that $\varpi_i = x_i - d_i$ and $\varpi_i = 0$ both with probability $\frac{1}{2}$. Let $\varpi = \sum_{i=1}^{n} \varpi_i$. The authors approached the proof by dividing it into two cases based on the size of the expected value of ϖ, denoted as $E(\varpi)$. Let $T \geq \sqrt{\dfrac{\varepsilon}{500}}$ be a constant to be specified later in the proof. When $E(\varpi) \geq T\sqrt{n}$, the probability satisfies

$$\Pr_{q \subseteq_R [n]} \left[\left| \sum_{i \in q} (x_i - d_i) \right| \geq 2e + 1 \right] \geq 1 - 2e^{-T^2/8} \, .$$

In the second case, $E(\varpi) < T\sqrt{n}$, the probability satisfies

$$\Pr_{q \subseteq_R [n]} \left[\left| \sum_{i \in q} (x_i - d_i) \right| \geq 2e + 1 \right] \geq \frac{\alpha}{3\beta} \, .$$

From the result of the Disqualifying Lemma, we choose $\kappa(\varepsilon)$ to be the minimum of the probabilities from these two cases. So, in the first term, $1 - 2e^{-T^2/8} = 1 - 2e^{-\varepsilon/4000} < 0$, so $1 - \left(1 - 2e^{-T^2/8}\right) > 1$. In the second term, we know $\alpha = \dfrac{\varepsilon}{36}$, so $\dfrac{\alpha}{3\beta} = \dfrac{\varepsilon}{108\beta} \geq 0$ and $1 - \dfrac{\alpha}{3\beta} < 1$. Hence

$$\kappa(\varepsilon) \leq \min\left(\underbrace{1 - \left(1 - 2e^{-T^2/8}\right)}_{(1)}, \; \underbrace{1 - \frac{\alpha}{3\beta}}_{(2)} \right) = 1 - \frac{\alpha}{3\beta}$$

Thus, $\xi(\varepsilon) \geq \dfrac{\alpha}{3\beta}$ where we choose $\xi(\varepsilon) = \dfrac{\alpha}{3\beta}$ for the worst case. Dinur and Nissim choose β large enough so that $\alpha > 3\sum_{k=1}^{\infty} \beta(k+1)e^{-k\beta/2}$ (note the right side is decreasing in β). Simple manipulations show that $\sum_{k=1}^{\infty} e^{-k\beta/2} = \dfrac{e^{-\beta/2}}{1 - e^{-\beta/2}}$. After taking the partial derivative with respects to β for the above formula we obtain

$$-2\frac{\partial}{\partial\beta}\sum_{k=1}^{\infty}e^{-k\beta/2}=\sum_{k=1}^{\infty}ke^{-k\beta/2}=\frac{e^{-\beta/2}}{\left(1-e^{-\beta/2}\right)^{2}}.$$

$$\sum_{k=1}^{\infty}\left(k+1\right)e^{-k\beta/2}=\frac{e^{-\beta/2}}{\left(1-e^{-\beta/2}\right)^{2}}+$$

Thus
$$\frac{e^{-\beta/2}}{1-e^{-\beta/2}}=e^{-\beta/2}\frac{2-e^{-\beta/2}}{\left(1-e^{-\beta/2}\right)^{2}}.$$

We need $\alpha>3\sum_{k=1}^{\infty}\beta\left(k+1\right)e^{-k\beta/2}=3\beta e^{-\beta/2}\frac{2-e^{-\beta/2}}{\left(1-e^{-\beta/2}\right)^{2}}.$

Since $\alpha=\dfrac{\varepsilon}{36}$, we get $\varepsilon>108\beta e^{-\beta/2}\dfrac{2-e^{-\beta/2}}{\left(1-e^{-\beta/2}\right)^{2}}.$

Let $x=e^{-\beta/2}$. Then $\varepsilon>108\beta x\dfrac{2-x}{\left(1-x\right)^{2}}.$

β is decided by ε (ε is a pre-defined parameter). For $0<\varepsilon<1$, numerical calculations show we need $\beta>16.33845$. Since $\kappa\left(\varepsilon\right)\leq1-\dfrac{\alpha}{3\beta}=1-\dfrac{\varepsilon}{108\beta}$, substituting

$\varepsilon>108\beta x\dfrac{2-x}{\left(1-x\right)^{2}}$ gives $\kappa\left(\varepsilon\right)\leq1-x\dfrac{2-x}{\left(1-x\right)^{2}}$ where $\xi\left(\varepsilon\right)=\dfrac{\alpha}{3\beta}=x\dfrac{2-x}{\left(1-x\right)^{2}}.$

This work was previously published in International Journal of Database Management, Volume 21, Issue 4, edited by Keng Siau, pp. 111-123, copyright 2010 by IGI Publishing (an imprint of IGI Global).

Compilation of References

Aaker, D. A. (1991). *Managing brand equity*. New York: Free Press.

Abdel-Hamid, T. K., Sengupta, K., & Swett, C. (1999). The Impact of Goals on Software Project Management: An Experimental Investigation. *MIS Quarterly*, *23*(4), 531–555. doi:10.2307/249488

Abdul Jalil, M., & Azman Mohd Noah, S. (2007). The difficulties of Using Design Patterns among Novices: An Exploratory Study. In M. L. Gavrilova & O. Gervasi (Eds.), *Proceedings of the 2007 International Conference on Computational Science and its Applications – ICCSA 2007* (pp. 97-103). Washington, DC: IEEE Computer Society.

Acharya, S., Alonso, S., Franklin, M. J., & Zdonik, S. B. (1995). Broadcast Disks: Data Management for Asymmetric Communication. In *Proceedings of the ACM SIGMOD Conference* (pp. 199-210).

Acknowledgement

Adam, N. R., & Wortmann, J. C. (1989). Security-Control methods for statistical database: a comparative study. *ACM Computing Surveys*, *21*(4), 515–556. doi:10.1145/76894.76895

Adya, A., Blakeley, J., Melnik, S., & Muralidhar, S. (2007). Anatomy of the ADO.NET Entity Framework. *In Proceedings of ACM SIG Conference on Management of Data*, 877-888.

Agarwal, R., & Karahanna, E. (2000). Time flies when you are having fun: Cognitive absorption and beliefs about information technology usage. *Management Information Systems Quarterly*, *24*(4), 665–694. doi:10.2307/3250951

Agrawal, R., Imielinski, T., & Swami, A. (1993). ng Association Rules Between Sets of Items in Large Database. In *Proceedings of ACM-SIGMOD 93* (pp. 207-216).

Aharoni, E., & Fridlund, A. J. (2007). Social reactions toward people vs. Computers: How mere labels shape interactions. *Computers in Human Behavior*, *23*(5), 2175–2189. doi:10.1016/j.chb.2006.02.019

Ajzen, I. (1991). The theory of planned behavior. *Organizational Behavior and Human Decision Procedures*, *50*(2), 179–211. doi:10.1016/0749-5978(91)90020-T

Ajzen, I., & Fishbein, M. (1973). Attitudinal and normative variables as predictors of specific behaviors. *Journal of Personality and Social Psychology*, *27*(1), 41–57. doi:10.1037/h0034440

Alavi, M., & Leidner, D. E. (2001). Review: Knowledge Management and Knowledge Management Systems: Conceptual Foundations and Research Issues. *MIS Quarterly*, *25*(1), 107–136. doi:10.2307/3250961

Allen, D. G., Mahto, R. V., & Otondo, R. F. (2007). Web-based recruitment: Effects of information, organizational brand, and attitudes toward a Web site on applicant attraction. *The Journal of Applied Psychology*, *92*(6), 1696–1708. doi:10.1037/0021-9010.92.6.1696

Allison, B. Z., & Polich, J. (2008). Workload assessment of computer gaming using a single-stimulus event-related potential paradigm. *Biological Psychology*, *77*(3), 277–283. doi:10.1016/j.biopsycho.2007.10.014

Al-Natour, S., & Benbasat, I. (2009). The adoption and use of IT artifacts: A new interaction-centric model for the study of user-artifact relationships. *Journal of the Association for Information Systems*, *10*(9), 661–685.

Alonso, G., Agrawal, D., El Abbadi, A., & Mohan, C. (1997). Functionalities and Limitations of Current Workflow Management Systems. *IEEE Expert*, *12*(5).

Alonso, G., Casati, F., Kuno, H., & Machiraju, V. (2004). *Web Services concepts, architecture and applications.* New York: Springer.

Alter, S. (1978). Development Patterns for Decision Support Systems. *MIS Quarterly, 2*(3), 33–42. doi:10.2307/249176

Alter, S. (2005). Architecture of Syspernato: A Model-Based Ontology of the IS Field . *Communications of the Association for Information Systems, 15,* 1–40.

Alty, J. L., Knott, R. P., Anderson, B., & Smyth, M. (2000). A framework for engineering metaphor at the user interface. *Interacting with Computers, 13*(2), 301–322. doi:10.1016/S0953-5438(00)00047-3

An, Y., Borgida, A., & Mylopoulos, J. (2005a). Constructing Complex Semantic Mappings between XML Data and Ontologies. In *Proceedings of the International Conference on Semantic Web (ISWC)* (pp. 6-20).

An, Y., Borgida, A., & Mylopoulos, J. (2005b). Inferring Complex Semantic Mappings between Relational Tables and Ontologies from Simple Correspondences. In *Proceedings of International Conference on Ontologies, Databases, and Applications of Semantics (ODBASE)* (pp. 1152-1169).

An, Y., Borgida, A., Miller, R. J., & Mylopoulos, J. (2007). A Semantic Approach to Discovering Schema Mapping Expressions. *In Proceedings of International Conference on Data Engineering (ICDE),* 206-215.

Andersen, J. R. (1983). A spreading activation theory of memory. *Journal of Verbal Learning and Verbal Behavior, 22,* 261–295. doi:10.1016/S0022-5371(83)90201-3

Anderson, J. C., & Gerbing, D. W. (1988). Structural equation modeling in practice: a review and recommended two step approach. *Psychological Bulletin, 103*(3), 411–423. doi:10.1037/0033-2909.103.3.411

Anderson, J. R., & Pirolli, P. L. (1984). Spread of activation. *Journal of Experimental Psychology. Learning, Memory, and Cognition, 10*(4), 791–798. doi:10.1037/0278-7393.10.4.791

Andrews, T., Curbera, F., Dholakia, H., Golang, Y., Klein, J., Leymann, F., et al. (2003). *Business process execution language for Web services version 1.1.* Retrieved from http://www.ibm.com/developerworks/ library/ws-bpel/

Angeles, P. (1981). *Dictionary of Philosophy.* New York: Harper Perennial.

Angluin, D., & Laird, P. (1988). Learning from noisy examples. *Machine Learning, 2*(4), 343–370. doi:10.1007/BF00116829

Ang, S., & Cummings, L. L. (1997). Strategic response to institutional influences on information systems outsourcing. *Organization Science, 8*(3), 235–256. doi:10.1287/orsc.8.3.235

Ang, S., & Straub, D. (1998). Production and transaction economies and information systems outsourcing: A study of the US banking industry. *Management Information Systems Quarterly, 22*(4), 535–552. doi:10.2307/249554

Angst, C. M., & Agarwal, R. (2009). Adoption of electronic health records in the presence of privacy concerns: the elaboration likelihood model and individual persuasion. *Management Information Systems Quarterly, 33*(2), 339–370.

An, Y., Borgida, A., & Mylopoulos, J. (2006). Discovering the Semantics of Relational Tables through Mappings. *Journal on Data Semantics, VII,* 1–32.

Arakji, R. Y., & Lang, K. R. (2007). The virtual cathedral and the virtual bazaar. *The Data Base for Advances in Information Systems, 38*(4), 33–39.

Arens, Y., Knoblock, C. A., & Shen, W. (1996). Query reformulation for dynamic information integration. *Journal of Intelligent Information Systems, 6*(2-3), 99–130. doi:10.1007/BF00122124

Argyris, C., & Schon, D. A. (1978). *Organizational Learning: A Theory of Action Perspective.* Reading, MA: Addison-Wesley.

Arion, A., Bonifati, A., Manolescu, I., & Pugliese, A. (2007). XqueC: A Query-Concious Compressed XML Database. *ACM Transactions on Internet Technology, 7*(2). doi:10.1145/1239971.1239974

Arnold, J. T. (2009). Gaming technology used to orient new hires. *HR Magazine, 54*(1), 36-37. Beard, J. W. (Ed.). (1996). *Impression management and information technology.* Greenwich, CT: Quorum.

Aronson, E., & Carlsmith, J. M. (1962). Performance Expectancy as a Determinant of Actual Performance. *Journal of Abnormal and Social Psychology*, *65*(3), 178–182. doi:10.1037/h0042291

Arora, A., & Forman, C. (2007). Proximity and information technology outsourcing: how local are IT services markets? *Journal of Management Information Systems*, *24*(2), 73–102. doi:10.2753/MIS0742-1222240204

Arsanjani, A., Ghosh, S., Allam, A., Abdollah, T., Ganapathy, S., & Holley, K. (2008). SOMA: A method for developing service-oriented solutions. *IBM Systems Journal*, *47*(3), 377–396. doi:10.1147/sj.473.0377

Ashford, R. (2008, June 16). *About my Second Life avatar gender identity.* Retrieved from http://librarianbydesign. blogspot.com/2008/ 06/about-my-second-life-avatar-identity.html

Ashmore, R. W., & Herman, B. (2006). Managing the risk of employee blogging. *Risk Management*, *53*(4), 40–43.

Attasiriluk, S., Nakaone, A., Hantanong, W., Prada, R., Kanongchaiyos, P., & Prendinger, H. (2009). Co-presence, collaboration, and control in environmental studies: A Second-Life based approach. *Virtual Reality (Waltham Cross)*, *13*(3), 195–204. doi:10.1007/s10055-009-0130-5

Aubert, B. A., Rivard, S., & Patry, M. (2004). A transaction cost model of IT outsourcing. *Information & Management*, *41*(7), 921–932. doi:10.1016/j.im.2003.09.001

Avila-Campillo, I., Green, T. J., Gupta, A., Onizuka, M., Raven, D., & Suciu, D. (2002). *XMLTK: An XML Toolkit for Scalable XML Stream Processing*. Paper presented at PLANX.

Avison, D., & Fitzgerald, G. (2008). *Information Systems Development: Methodologies, Techniques and Tools* (4th ed.). New York: McGraw Hill.

Bacharach, S. (1989). Organizational theories: Some criteria for evaluation. *Academy of Management Review*, *14*(4), 496–515. doi:10.2307/258555

Baddeley, A. (1994). The magical number seven: Still magic after all these years. *Psychological Review*, *101*(2), 353–356. doi:10.1037/0033-295X.101.2.353

Baeza-Yates, R., & Ribeiro-Neto, B. (1999). *Modern Information Retrieval*. Reading, MA: Addison-Wesley.

Bajaj, A. (2000). A study of senior information systems managers' decision models in adopting new computing architectures. *Journal of the Association for Information Systems, 1*(1), Article 4.

Baldwin, C. Y., & Clark, K. B. (2000). Design Rules: *Vol. 1. The Power of Modularity*. Cambridge, MA: MIT Press.

Ballard-Reisch, D. S., & Weigel, D. J. (1999). Communication process in marital commitment: An integrative approach . In Adams, J. M., & Jones, W. H. (Eds.), *Handbook of interpersonal commitment and relationship stability* (pp. 407–424). New York: Kluwer Academic / Plenum Publishers.

Bandura, A. (1969). Social-learning theory of identificatory processes . In Goslin, D. A. (Ed.), *Handbook of socialization theory and research* (pp. 213–262). Chicago: Rand McNally.

Banerjee, J., Kim, W., Kim, H.-J., & Korth, H. F. (1987). Semantics and Implementation of Schema Evolution in Object-Oriented Databases. *SIGMOD Record*, *16*(3), 311–322. doi:10.1145/38714.38748

Barab, S. A., Hay, K. E., Squire, K., Barnett, M., Schmidt, R., & Karrigan, K. (2000). Virtual solar system project: Learning through a technology-rich, inquiry-based, participatory learning environment. *Journal of Science Education and Technology*, *9*(1), 7–25. doi:10.1023/A:1009416822783

Barclay, D., Higgins, C., & Thompson, R. (1995). The partial least square (PLS) approach to casual modeling: Personal computer adoption and use as an illustration. *Technology Studies*, *2*(2), 285–309.

Bariff, M. L., & Lusk, E. J. (1977). Cognitive and personality tests for the design of management information systems. *Management Science*, *23*(8), 820–829. doi:10.1287/mnsc.23.8.820

Barki, H., & Hartwick, J. (1994). User Participation, Conflict, and Conflict Resolution: The Mediating Roles of Influence. *Information Systems Research*, *5*(4), 422–438. doi:10.1287/isre.5.4.422

Barki, H., & Hartwick, J. (2001). Interpersonal Conflict and Management in Information Systems Development. *MIS Quarterly*, *25*(2), 195–228. doi:10.2307/3250929

Barnes, S. (2007). Virtual worlds as a medium for advertising. *The Data Base for Advances in Information Systems, 38*(4), 45–55.

Baron, R. M., & Kenny, D. A. (1986). The moderator-mediator variable distinction in social psychological research: Conceptual, strategic, and statistical considerations. *Journal of Personality and Social Psychology, 51*, 1173–1182. doi:10.1037/0022-3514.51.6.1173

Barton, C., Charles, P., Goyal, D., Raghavachari, M., Fontoura, M., & Josifovski, V. (2003). Streaming Xpath Processing with Forward and Backward Axes. In *Proceedings of the International Conference on Data Engineering* (pp. 455-466).

Basu, A., & Blanning, R. W. (2003). Synthesis and Decomposition of Processes in Organizations. *Information Systems Research, 14*(4), 337–355. doi:10.1287/isre.14.4.337.24901

Batra, D. (2005). Conceptual Data Modeling Patterns: Representation and Validation. *Journal of Database Management, 16*(2), 84–106.

Bauer, C., & King, G. (2006). *Java Persistence with Hibernate.* Greenwich, CT . *Manning Publications., ISBN-10*, 1932394885.

Baumeister, R. F., & Leary, M. R. (1995). The need to belong: Desire for interpersonal attachments as a fundamental human motivation. *Psychological Bulletin, 117*(3), 497–529. doi:10.1037/0033-2909.117.3.497

Bause, F., & Kritzinger, P. S. (1996). *Stochastic Petri Nets, An introduction to the Theory.* Berlin: Verlag-Vieweg.

Bayardo, R. J., Bohrer, W., Brice, R., Cichocki, A., Fowler, G., Helai, A., et al. (1997). InfoSleuth: Agent-based semantic integration of information in open and dynamic environments. In *Proceedings of ACM SIGMOD* (pp. 195-206).

Beirlant, J., Dudewicz, E. J., Gyorfi, L., & van der Meulen, E. C. (1997). Non-parametric entropy estimation: an overview. *International Journal of Mathematical and Statistical Sciences, 6*(1), 17–39.

Benbasat, I., & Taylor, R. N. (1978). The Impact of Cognitive Styles on Information System Design. *MIS Quarterly, 2*(2), 43–54. doi:10.2307/248940

Bendapudi, N., & Berry, L. L. (1997). Customers' motivations for maintaining relationships with service providers. *Journal of Retailing, 73*(1), 15–37. doi:10.1016/S0022-4359(97)90013-0

Benkley, S. S., Fandozzi, J. F., Housman, E. M., & Woodhouse, G. M. (1995). *Data Element Tool-based Analysis (DELTA) (Tech. Rep. MTR 95B0000147).* Bedford, MA: The MITRE Corporation.

Benslimane, D., Dustdar, S., & Sheth, A. (2008). Services Mashups: The New Generation of Web Applications. *IEEE Internet Computing, 12*(5), 13–15. doi:10.1109/MIC.2008.110

Bera, P., Krasnoperova, A., & Wand, Y. (2010). Using Ontology Languages for Conceptual Modeling. *Journal of Database Management, 21*(1), 1–28.

Berners-Lee, T., Hendler, J., & Lassila, O. (2001). The Semantic Web. *Scientific American, May.*

Bernstein, P. A., Melnik, S., & Churchill, J. E. (2006). Incremental schema matching. In *Proceedings of the 32nd International Conference on Very Large Data Bases* (pp. 1167-1170).

Berscheid, E., Snyder, M., & Omoto, A. M. (1989). The relationship closeness inventory: Assessing the closeness of interpersonal relationships. *Journal of Personality and Social Psychology, 57*(5), 792–807. doi:10.1037/0022-3514.57.5.792

Bettman, J. R., & Kakkar, P. (1977). Effects of information presentation format on consumer information acquisition strategies. *The Journal of Consumer Research, 3*(4), 233–240. doi:10.1086/208672

Bettman, J. R., & Park, C. W. (1980). Effects of prior knowledge and experience and phase of the choice process on consumer decision processes: A protocol analysis. *The Journal of Consumer Research, 7*(3), 234–248. doi:10.1086/208812

Bharadwaj, A. S. (2000). A resource-based perspective on information technology capability and firm performance: An empirical investigation. *Management Information Systems Quarterly, 24*(1), 169. doi:10.2307/3250983

Bhattacharya, K., Gerede, C., Richard, H., Liu, R., & Su, J. (2007). Towards Formal Analysis of Artifact-Centric Business Process Models. In *Proceedings of Business Process Management (BPM 2007)* (LNCS 4714, pp. 288-304).

Bhattacharya, K., Caswell, N., Kumaran, S., Nigam, A., & Wu, F. (2007). Artifact-centric Operational Modeling: Lessons learned from engagements. *IBM Systems Journal, 46*(4). doi:10.1147/sj.464.0703

Bhattacharya, K., Guttman, R., Lyman, K., Heath, F. F. III, Kumaran, S., & Nandi, P. (2005). A model-driven approach to industrializing discovery processes in pharmaceutical research. *IBM Systems Journal, 44*(1), 145–162. doi:10.1147/sj.441.0145

Biehal, B., & Chakravarti, D. (1982). Information-presentation format and learning goals as determinants of consumers' memory retrieval and choice processes. *The Journal of Consumer Research, 8*(4), 431–441. doi:10.1086/208883

Bilke, A., & Naumann, F. (2005). Schema Matching Using Duplicates. In *Proceedings of the 21st International Conference on Data Engineering* (pp. 69-80).

Blomqvist, E. (2005). Fully Automatic Construction of Enterprise Ontologies Using Design Patterns: Initial Method and First Experiences. In R. Meersman, Z. Tari, M-S. Hacid, J. Mylopoulous, B. Pernici, O.,Babaoglu, *et al.* (Eds.), *On the Move to Meaningful Internet Systems 2005: CoopIS, DOA, and ODBASE* (LNCS 3761, pp. 1314-1329). Berlin-Heidelberg, Germany: Springer.

Bodart, F., Sim, M., Patel, A., & Weber, R. (2001). Should optional properties be used in conceptual modelling? A theory and three empirical tests. *Information Systems Research, 12*(4), 384–405. doi:10.1287/isre.12.4.384.9702

Boehm, B. (1981). *Software Engineering Economics*. Upper Saddle River, NJ: Prentice-Hall.

Boehm, B. W. (1987). Improving Software Productivity. *Computer*, (September): 43–57. doi:10.1109/MC.1987.1663694

Bollen, K. A., & Stine, R. (1990). Direct and indirect effects: Classical *and bootstrap esti*mates of variability. *Sociological Methodology, 20*, 115–140. doi:10.2307/271084

Bollen, K., & Lennox, R. (1991). Conventional wisdom on measurement: A structural equation perspective. *Psychological Bulletin, 110*(2), 305–313. doi:10.1037/0033-2909.110.2.305

Bonifati, A., Chang, E. Q., Ho, T., Lakshmanan, V. S., & Pottinger, R. (2005). HePToX: Marring XML and Heterogeneity in Your P2P Databases. In *Proceedings of International Conference on Very Large Data Bases (VLDB)* (pp. 1267-1270).

Bonifati, A., Mecca, G., Pappalardo, A., Raunich, S., & Summa, G. (2008). Schema mapping verification: the spicy way. In *Proceedings of the 11th International Conference on Extending Database Technology: Advances in Database Technology* (pp. 85-96).

Booch, G., Rumbaugh, J., & Jacobson, I. (2005). *The Unified Modeling Language User Guide* (2nd ed.). Reading, MA: Addison Wesley.

Booch, G. (2007). *Object-oriented Analysis and Design with Applications* (3rd ed.). Reading, MA: Addison-Wesley.

Bosc, P., Kraft, D., & Petry, F. (2005). Fuzzy sets in database and information systems: Status and opportunities. *Fuzzy Sets and Systems, 156*(3), 418–426. doi:10.1016/j.fss.2005.05.039

Bouguettaya, A., Malik, Z., Rezgui, A., & Korff, L. (2006). A Scalable Middleware for Web Databases. *Journal of Database Management, 17*(4), 20–46.

Bousfield, W. A. (1953). The occurrence of clustering in the recall of randomly arranged associates. *The Journal of General Psychology, 49*(October), 229–240.

Bozovic, N., & Vassalos, V. (2008). Two-phase schema matching in real world relational databases. In *Proceedings of the ICDE Workshop on Information Integration Methods* (pp. 290-296).

BPEL. (2003). *Business Process Execution Language for Web Services, version 1.1*. BEA, IBM, Microsoft, SAP and Siebel Systems.

Bradley, J. H., & Hebert, F. J. (1997). The effect of personality type on team performance. *Journal of Management Development, 16*(5/6), 337–353. doi:10.1108/02621719710174525

Brancheau, J. C., & Wetherbe, J. C. (1987). Key issues in information systems management. *MIS Quarterly, 11*(1), 23–45. doi:10.2307/248822

Brandon, J. (2007, May 2). The top eight corporate sites in Second Life. *Computer World*.

Brien, P. M., & Poulovassilis, A. (2002). Schema Evolution in Heterogeneous Database Architectures, A Schema Transformation Approach. In *Proceedings of Conference on Advanced Information Systems Engineering (CAiSE)* (pp. 484-499).

Bright, M. W., Hurson, A. R., & Pakzad, S. H. (1994). Automated resolution of semantic heterogeneity in multidatabases. *ACM Transactions on Database Systems, 19*(2), 212–253. doi:10.1145/176567.176569

Brown, H. G., Marshall, S. P., & Rodgers, T. L. (2004). International traits, complementarity and trust in virtual collaboration. *Journal of Management Information Systems, 20*(4), 115–137.

Bruckman, A., & Jensen, C. (2002). The mystery of the death of MediaMOO . In Renninger, K. A., & Shumar, W. (Eds.), *Building virtual communities: Learning and change in cyberspace* (pp. 21–33). New York: Cambridge University Press. doi:10.1017/CBO9780511606373.006

Brydon, M., & Vining, A. R. (2008). Adoption, Improvement, and Disruption: Predicting the Impact of Open Source Applications in Enterprise Software Markets. *Journal of Database Management, 19*(2), 73–94.

Brynjolfsson, E., Hu, Y., & Smith, M. D. (2003). Consumer surplus in the digital economy: Estimating the value of increased product variety at online booksellers. *Management Science, 49*(11), 1580–1596. doi:10.1287/mnsc.49.11.1580.20580

Bunge, M. (1977). *Ontology I: The Furniture of the World*. New York: D. Reidel Publishing.

Bunge, M. (1977). Treatise on Basic Philosophy: *Vol. 3. Ontology I: The Furniture of the World*. Boston: Reidel.

Bunge, M. (1979). Treatise on Basic Philosophy: *Vol. 4. Ontology II: A World of Systems*. Boston: Reidel.

Burslem, J. (2007). Future of real estate marketing. *Inman News*. Retrieved May 6, 2008, from http://www.futureofrealestatemarketing.com/ coldwell-banker-tours-a-home-in-cyberspace

Burstein, M., Bussler, C., Finin, T., Huhns, M., Paolucci, M., & Sheth, A. (2005). A semantic Web services architecture. *IEEE Internet Computing, 9*, 52–61. doi:10.1109/MIC.2005.96

Burton-Jones, A., & Meso, A. P. (2006). Conceptualizing systems for understanding: An empirical test of decomposition principles in object-oriented analysis. *Information Systems Research, 17*(1), 38–60. doi:10.1287/isre.1050.0079

Burton-Jones, A., Wand, Y., & Weber, R. (2009). Guidelines for Empirical Evaluations of Conceptual Modeling Grammars . *Journal of AIS, 10*(6), 495–532.

Buschmann, F., & Meunier, R. (1995). A System of Patterns. In J. O. Coplien & D. C. Schmidt (Eds.), *Pattern Language for Program Design* (pp. 325-343). New York: Addison-Wesley.

Buschmann, F., Meunier, R., Rohnert, H., Sommerland, P., & Stal, M. (1996). *Pattern-Oriented Software Architecture: A System of Patterns*. Chichester, UK: John Wiley & Sons.

Cable News Network. (2008, November 14). *Second Life affair ends in divorce*. Retrieved from http://www.cnn.com/2008/ WORLD/europe/11/14/ second.life.divorce/index.html

Cai, J. (2006). Knowledge management within collaboration processes: A perspective modeling and analyzing methodology. *Journal of Database Management, 17*(1), 33–48.

Cai, S., & Xu, Y. (2008). Designing product lists for e-commerce: The effects of sorting on consumer decision making. *International Journal of Human-Computer Interaction, 24*(7), 700–721. doi:10.1080/10447310802335730

Cai, Y., Cercone, N., & Han, J. (1993). Attribute-Oriented Induction in Relational Databases. In *Knowledge Discovery in Databases*. Menlo Park, CA: AAAI Press, Chu, W., & Chen, Q. (1994). A Structured Approach for Cooperative Query Answering. *IEEE Transactions on Knowledge and Data Engineering, 6*(5), 738–749.

Calvanese, D., Giacomo, G. D., Lenzerini, M., Nardi, D., & Rosati, R. (2001). Data integration in data warehouse. *Cooperative Information Systems*, *10*(3), 237–271. doi:10.1142/S0218843001000345

Candan, K. S., Hsiung, W.-P., Chen, S., Tatemura, J., & Agrawal, D. (2006). *AFilter: Adaptable XML Filtering with Prefix-Caching and Suffix-Clustering*. In Paper presented at the VLDB Conference.

Canfora, G., & Cavallo, B. (2009). A Bayesian model for disclosure control in statistical databases. *Data Knowledge Engineering*. doi: 10.1016/j.datak. 2009.06.006

Cardoso, J. (2005). Control-flow complexity measurement of processes and Weyuker's Properties . In *Transactions on Informatika, Systems Sciences and Engineering, Budapest 2005* (*Vol. 8*, pp. 213–218). Berlin: Springer Verlag.

Cardoso, J., Sheth, A., Miller, J., Arnold, J., & Kochut, K. (2004). Quality of service for workflows and Web service processes. *Journal of Web Semantics*, *1*(3), 281–308. doi:10.1016/j.websem.2004.03.001

Carr, N. (2008). *The big switch: rewiring the world, from Edison to Google*. New York: W. W. Norton & Company.

Carroll, J. M. (1997). Human-computer interaction: Psychology as a science of design. *Annual Review of Psychology*, *48*, 61–83. doi:10.1146/annurev.psych.48.1.61

Caufield, B. (2000). Cover your ASP. *eCompany Now*, *2*(1), 138-139.

Ceri, S., & Widom, J. (1991). Deriving Production Rules for Incremental View Maintenance. In *Proceedings of International Conference on Very Large Data Bases (VLDB)* (pp. 277-289).

Chak, K., & Leung, L. (2004). Shyness and Locus of Control as predictors of Internet addiction and Internet use. *Cyberpsychology & Behavior*, *7*(5), 559–570.

Chan, C.-Y., Felber, P., Garofalakis, M., & Rastogi, R. (2002). *Efficient Filtering of XML Documents with XPath Expressions*. Paper presented at the International Conference on Data Engineering.

Chan, M. J. (2007, June 14). *Identity in a virtual world*. Retrieved from http://edition.cnn.com/2007/ TECH/06/07/ virtual_identity/ index.html

Chan, H., Wei, K., & Siau, K. (1993). User-Database Interface: The Effect of Abstraction Levels on Query Performance. *Management Information Systems Quarterly*, *17*(4), 441–464. doi:10.2307/249587

Chan, H., Wei, K., & Siau, K. (1994). An Empirical Study on End Users' Update Performance for Different Abstraction Levels. *International Journal of Human-Computer Studies*, *41*(3), 309–328. doi:10.1006/ijhc.1994.1061

Chan, H., Wei, K., & Siau, K. (1995). The Effect of a Database Feedback System on User Performance. *Behaviour and Information Technology: An International Journal on the Human Aspects of Computing*, *14*(3), 152–162.

Chan, Y. E., Copeland, D. G. D., & Barclay, W. (1997). Business strategy, information systems strategy, and strategic alignment. *Information Systems Research*, *8*(2), 125–150. doi:10.1287/isre.8.2.125

Chaudron, M., van Hee, K., & Somers, L. (2003). Use cases as workflows. In W. M. P. van der Aalst et al. (Eds.): *Business Process Modeling 2003* (LNCS 2678, pp. 88-103).

Cheng, K., & Cairns, P. A. (2005). Behaviour, realism and immersion in games. In *Proceedings of the Conference on Human Factors in Computing Systems* (pp. 1272-1275).

Chen, H. (2006). Flow on the net-detecting Web users' positive affects and their flow states. *Computers in Human Behavior*, *22*(2), 221–233. doi:10.1016/j.chb.2004.07.001

Chen, H., Wigand, R. T., & Nilan, M. (2000). Exploring Web users' optimal flow experiences. *Information Technology & People*, *13*(4), 263–281. doi:10.1108/09593840010359473

Chen, J. V., & Park, Y. (2005). The differences of addiction causes between massive multiplayer online game and multi user domain. *International Review of Information Ethics*, *4*, 53–60.

Chen, K., Chen, I., & Paul, H. (2001). Explaining online behavioral differences: an Internet dependency perspective. *Journal of Computer Information Systems*, *41*(3), 59–63.

Chen, K., Chen, J. V., & Ross, W. H. (2010). Antecedents of online game dependency: The implications of multimedia realism and uses and gratifications theory. *Journal of Database Management*, *21*(2), 69–99.

Chen, K., Tarn, J. M., & Han, B. (2004). Internet dependency: its impact on online behavioral patterns in e-commerce. *Human Systems Management, 23*(1), 49–58.

Chen, M. S., Wu, K. L., & Yu, P. S. (2003). Optimizing Index Allocation for Sequential Data Broadcasting in Wireless Mobile Computing. *IEEE Transactions on Knowledge and Data Engineering, 15*(1), 161–173. doi:10.1109/TKDE.2003.1161588

Chen, P. (1976). The entity-relationship model—toward a unified view of data. *ACM Transactions on Database Systems, 1*(1), 9–36. doi:10.1145/320434.320440

Chen, P. P. S. (1976). The entity-relationship model: Toward a unified view of data. *ACM Transactions on Database Systems, 1*(1), 9–36. doi:10.1145/320434.320440

Chen, Y., Zhou, L., & Zhang, D. (2006). Ontology-supported Web service composition: An approach to service-oriented knowledge management in corporate services. *Journal of Database Management, 17*(1), 67–84.

Cheon, M., Grover, V., & Teng, J. T. C. (1995). Theoretical perspectives on the outsourcing of information systems. *Journal of Information Technology, 10*(4), 209–220. doi:10.1057/jit.1995.25

Cherkasova, L., & Gupta, M. (2004). Analysis of enterprise media server workloads: access patterns, locality, content evolution, and rates of change. *ACM/IEEE Transactions on Networking, 12*(5), 781-794.

Cherkasova, L., & Phaal, P. (2002). Session-based admission control: A mechanism for peak load management of commercial web sites. *IEEE Transactions on Computers, 51*(6), 669–685. doi:10.1109/TC.2002.1009151

Chin, W. W. (1998). The partial least squares approach to structural equation modeling. In Marcoulides, G. A. (Ed.), *Modern methods for business research* (pp. 295–336). Hillsdale, NJ: Lawrence Erlbaum Associates.

Chin, W. W., Marcolin, B. L., & Newsted, P. R. (2003). A partial least squares latent variable modeling approach for measuring interaction effects: Results from a Monte Carlo simulation study and an electronic-mail emotion/adoption study. *Information Systems Research, 14*(2), 189–217. doi:10.1287/isre.14.2.189.16018

Chisholm, R. (1996). *A Realistic Theory of Categories: An Essay on Ontology.* Cambridge, UK: Cambridge University Press.

Choi, D., & Kim, J. (2004). Why people continue to play online games: in search of critical design factors to increase customer loyalty to online contents. *Cyberpsychology & Behavior, 7*(1), 11–24. doi:10.1089/109493104322820066

Choi, N., Song, I.-Y., & Han, H. (2006). A survey on ontology mapping. *SIGMOD Record, 35*(3), 34–41. doi:10.1145/1168092.1168097

Choi, R. H., & Wong, R. K. (2009). Efficient Filtering of Branch Queries for High-Performance XML Data Services. *Journal of Database Management, 20*(2), 58–83.

Chou, C., & Hsiao, M.-C. (2000). Internet addiction, usage, gratification, and pleasure experience: the Taiwan college students' case. *Computers & Education, 35*(1), 65–80. doi:10.1016/S0360-1315(00)00019-1

Choudhary, V. (2007). Comparison of software quality under perpetual licensing and software as a service. *Journal of Management Information Systems, 24*(2), 141–165. doi:10.2753/MIS0742-1222240206

Chou, T. J., & Ting, C. C. (2003). The Role of Flow Experience in Cyber-Game Addiction. *Cyberpsychology & Behavior, 6*(6), 663–675. doi:10.1089/109493103322725469

Chrastowski-Wachtel, P., Benatallah, B., Hamadi, R., O'Dell, M., & Susanto, A. (2003). A top-down Petri net-based approach for dynamic workflow modeling. In W. M. P. van der Aalst et al. (Eds.), *Business Process Modeling* 2003 (LNCS 2678, pp. 336-353).

Chu, W., Yang, H., & Chow, G. (1996). *A Cooperative Database System (CoBase) for Query Relaxation.* Paper presented at the Third International Conference on Artificial Intelligence Planning Systems, Edinburgh, UK.

Chua, C. E. H., Chiang, R. H. L., & Lim, E.-P. (2003). Instance-based attribute identification in database integration. *The VLDB Journal, 12*(3), 228–243. doi:10.1007/s00778-003-0088-y

Chung, Y. D., & Kim, M. H. (2000). An Index Replication Scheme for Wireless Data Broadcasting. *Journal of Systems and Software, 51*(3), 191–199. doi:10.1016/S0164-1212(99)00123-5

Churchill, G. A. (1991). *Marketing research: methodological foundations* (5th ed.). Chicago: The Dryden Press.

Chu, W., Yang, H., Chiang, K., Minock, M., Chow, G., & Larson, C. (1996). CoBase: A Scalable and Extensible Cooperative Information System. *International Journal of Intelligence Information Systems, 6*(1), 223–260. doi:10.1007/BF00122129

Cialdini, R. B., & Goldstein, N. J. (2004). Social influence: Compliance and conformity. *Annual Review of Psychology, 55,* 591–621. doi:10.1146/annurev.psych.55.090902.142015

Cialdini, R. B., & Trost, M. R. (1998). Social influence: Social norms, conformity, and compliance . In Gilbert, D. T., Fiske, S. T., & Lindzey, G. (Eds.), *The handbook of social psychology* (*Vol. 2*, pp. 151–192). New York: Random House.

Clark, J., & Derose, S. (1999). XML Path Language (XPath), Version 1.0. *W3C Recommendation.* Retrieved from http://www.w3c.org/TR/XPath

Claypool, K. T., Jin, J., & Rundensteiner, E. (1998). SERF: Schema Evolution through an Extensible, Re-usable, and Flexible Framework. In *Proceedings of Int. Conf. on Information and Knowledge Management (CIKM)* (pp. 314-321).

Clee, M. A., & Wicklund, R. A. (1980). Consumer behavior and psychological reactance. *The Journal of Consumer Research, 6*(4), 389–405. doi:10.1086/208782

Clifton, C., Housman, E., & Rosenthal, A. (1997). Experience with a combined approach to attribute-matching across heterogeneous databases. In *Proceedings of the IFIP Working Conference on Data Semantics (DS-7)* (pp. 429-451).

Cobb-Walgren, C. J., Ruble, C. A., & Donthu, N. (1995). Brand equity, brand preference, and purchase intent. *Journal of Advertising, 24*(3), 25–40.

Cohen, J. (1988). *Statistical power for the behavioral sciences* (2nd ed.). Hilldale, NJ: Lawrence Erlbaum Associates.

Cohen, W. W. (2000). Data integration using similarity joins and a word-based information representation language. *ACM Transactions on Information Systems, 18*(3), 288–321. doi:10.1145/352595.352598

Colazzo, D., & Sartiani, C. (2005). Mapping Maintenance in XML P2P Databases. In *Database Programming Languages* (LNCS 3774, pp. 74-89).

Collet, C., Huhns, M. N., & Shen, W.-M. (1991). Resource integration using a large knowledge base in Carnot. *IEEE Computer, 24,* 55–62.

Collins, A. M., & Quillian, M. R. (1969). Retrieval time from semantic memory. *Journal of Verbal Learning and Verbal Behavior, 8,* 240–247. doi:10.1016/S0022-5371(69)80069-1

Compeau, D. R., & Higgins, C. A. (1995). Application of social cognitive theory to training for computer skills. *Information Systems Research, 6*(2), 118–143. doi:10.1287/isre.6.2.118

Connolly, T., & Begg, C. (2005). *Database Systems: A Practical Approach to Design, Implementation, and Management* (4th ed.). Harlow, UK: Addison-Wesley.

Constantinescu, I., Binder, W., & Faltings, B. (2005). Optimally distributing interactions between composed semantic Web services. In A. Gomez-Perez & J. Euzenat (Eds.), *Proceedings of the 2nd European Semantic Web Conference* (pp. 32-46).

Conti, M., Kumar, M., Das, S. K., & Shirazi, B. A. (2002). Quality of service issues in internet Web services. *IEEE Transactions on Computers, 51*(6), 593–594. doi:10.1109/TC.2002.1009145

Conway, J. C., & Rubin, A. M. (1991). Psychological Predictors of Television Viewing Motivation . *Communication Research, 18*(4), 443–463. doi:10.1177/009365091018004001

Cooper, R. B. (2000). Information Technology Development Creativity: A Case Study of Attempted Radical Change. *MIS Quarterly, 24*(2), 245–276. doi:10.2307/3250938

Cormen, T. H., Leiserson, C. E., Rivest, R. L., & Stein, C. (2001). *Introduction to algorithms* (2nd ed.). Cambridge, MA: MIT Press.

Corrigan, M. W. (2001). *Social exchange theory, interpersonal communication motives, and volunteerism: Identifying motivation to volunteer and the rewards and costs associated.* Unpublished master's thesis, West Virginia University, Morgantown, WV.

Couger, J. D. (1990). Ensuring Creative Approaches in Information System Design. *Managerial & Decision Economics, 11*(5), 281–295. doi:10.1002/mde.4090110503

Cowan, J., & Tobin, R. (2004). XML Information Set. *W3C Recommendation*. Retrieved from Web: http://www.w3.org/TR/2001/ CR-xml-infoset-20010514/

Crowston, K., & Barbar, S. (2008). Bug fixing practices within free/libre open source software development teams. *Journal of Database Management, 19*(2), 1–30.

Crush, P. (2008). Virtually speaking. *Human Resources,* 38-41. Retrieved from http://www.humanresourcesmagazine.com/ news/search/864791/E-learning-Virtual-worlds---Virtually-speaking/

Csikszentmihalyi, M. (1975). *Beyond boredom and anxiety*. San Francisco: Jossey-Bass.

Csikszentmihalyi, M. (1988). *Optimal Experience: Psychological Studies of Flow in Consciousness*. Cambridge, UK: Cambridge University Press.

Csikszentmihalyi, M. (1990). *Flow: The psychology of optimal experience*. New York: Harper & Row.

Csikszentmihalyi, M. (1993). *The evolving self: A psychology for the third millennium*. New York: HarperCollins.

Csikszentmihalyi, M. (1997). *Finding flow: The psychology of engagement with everyday life*. New York: HarperCollins.

Csikszentmihalyi, M., & Csikszentmihalyi, I. S. (1988). *Optimal experience: Psychological studies of flow in consciousness*. New York: Cambridge University Press.

Csikszentmihalyi, M., & Lefavre, J. (1989). Optimal experience in work and leisure. *Journal of Personality and Social Psychology, 56*(5), 815–822. doi:10.1037/0022-3514.56.5.815

Cuppens, F., & Demolombe, R. (1989). Cooperative Answering: A Methodologies to Provide Intelligent Access to Databases. In *Proceedings of the Second International Conference on Expert Database Systems* (pp. 621-643).

Cutler, N. E., & Danowski, J. A. (1980). Process gratification in aging cohorts. *The Journalism Quarterly, 57,* 269–277.

Cuzzocrea, A. (2005). Providing probabilistically-bounded approximate answers to non-holistic aggregate range queries in OLAP. In *Proceedings of the 8th ACM International Workshop on Data Warehousing and OLAP* (pp. 97-106).

Cuzzocrea, A. (2007). Approximate range-sum query answering on data cubes with probabilistic guarantees. *Journal of Intelligent Information Systems Archive, 28*(2), 161–197. doi:10.1007/s10844-006-0007-y

Daft, R., Lengel, R., & Trevino, L. (1987). Message equivocality, media selection, and manager performance. *MIS Quarterly, 11*(3), 355–366. doi:10.2307/248682

Dahanayake, A., Sol, H., & Stojanovic, Z. (2003). Methodology Evaluation Framework for Component-Based System Development. *Journal of Database Management, 14*(1), 1–26.

Damanpour, F. (1991). Organizational innovation: A meta-analysis of effects of determinants and moderators. *Academy of Management Journal, 34*(3), 555–590. doi:10.2307/256406

Darbellay, G. A. (1999). An estimator of the mutual information based on a criterion for independence. *Computational Statistics & Data Analysis, 32*(1), 1–17. doi:10.1016/S0167-9473(99)00020-1

Data Repository, X. M. L. (2007). Retrieved from the World Wide Web: http://www.cs.washington.edu/ research /xmldatasets

Date, C. J. (2003). *An Introduction to Database Systems* (8th ed.). Reading, MA: Addison-Wesley.

Davies, I., Green, P., Rosemann, M., Indulska, M., & Gallo, S. (2006). How do practitioners use conceptual modeling in practice? *Data & Knowledge Engineering, 58*(3), 358–380. doi:10.1016/j.datak.2005.07.007

Davis, A., Murphy, J., Owens, D., Khazanchi, D., & Zigurs, I. (2009). Avatars, people, and virtual worlds: Foundations for research in metaverses. *Journal of the Association for Information Systems, 10*(2), 90–117.

Davis, F. (1989). Perceived usefulness, perceived ease of use, and user acceptance of Information technology. *MIS Quarterly, 13*(3), 319–340. doi:10.2307/249008

Davis, F. D. (1989). Perceived usefulness, perceived ease of use and user acceptance of information technology. *Management Information Systems Quarterly*, *13*(3), 319–340. doi:10.2307/249008

De Sean, G. J., & Furtado, A. Z. (1998). Towards a Cooperative Question-Answering Model. In *Proceedings of Flexible Query Answering Systems* (LNCS 1495, pp. 354-365).

De Souza, C. S., & Preece, J. (2004). A framework for analyzing and understanding online communities. *Interacting with Computers*, *16*(3), 579–610. doi:10.1016/j.intcom.2003.12.006

DeLone, W. H., & McLean, E. R. (1992). Information systems success: The quest for the dependent variable. *Information Systems Research*, *3*(1), 60–95. doi:10.1287/isre.3.1.60

Demeyer, S., Ducasse, S., Tichelaar, S., & Tichelaar, E. (1999). Why Unified is not Universal - UML Shortcomings for Coping with Round-trip Engineering. *Proceedings UML'99 (The Second International Conference on The Unified Modeling Language), volume 1723 of LNCS, 630-645.*

Denkel, A. (1996). *Object and Property*. Cambridge, UK: Cambridge University Press. doi:10.1017/CBO9780511554575

DeSanctis, G. (1983). Expectancy Theory as an Explanation of Voluntary Use of a Decision-Support System. *Psychological Reports*, *52*(1), 247–260.

Desel, J., & Esparza, J. (1995). Free Choice Petri Nets. In *Cambridge Tracts in Theoretical Computer Science* (*Vol. 40*). Cambridge, UK: Cambridge University Press.

Dhamanka, R., Lee, Y., Doan, A., Halevy, A., & Domingos, P. (2004). iMAP: discovering complex semantic matches between database schemas. In *Proceedings of the 2004 ACM SIGMOD International Conference on Management of Data* (pp. 383-394).

Diamantopoulos, A., & Winklhofer, H. M. (2001). Index construction with formative indicators: An alternative to scale development. *JMR, Journal of Marketing Research*, *38*(2), 269–277. doi:10.1509/jmkr.38.2.269.18845

Diao, Y., Altinel, M., Franklin, M., Zhang, H., & Fischer, P. (2003). Path Sharing and Predicate Evaluation for High-Performance XML Filtering. *ACM Transactions on Database Systems*, *28*(4), 467–516. doi:10.1145/958942.958947

Dibbern, J., & Brehm, A. H. (2002). Rethinking ERP-outsourcing decisions for leveraging technological and preserving business knowledge. In *Proceedings of the 35th Annual Hawaii International Conference on System Sciences*.

Dibbern, J., Goles, T., Hirschheim, R., & Jayatilaka, B. (2004). Information systems outsourcing: A survey and analysis of the literature. *The Data Base for Advances in Information Systems*, *35*(4), 6–102.

Dickey, M. D. (2005). Brave new (interactive) worlds: A review of the design affordances and constraints of two 3D virtual worlds as interactive learning environments. *Interactive Learning Environments*, *13*(1-2), 121–137. doi:10.1080/10494820500173714

Dickey, M. D. (2005b). Three-dimensional virtual worlds and distance learning: Two case studies of Active Worlds as a medium for distance education. *British Journal of Educational Technology*, *36*(3), 439–451. doi:10.1111/j.1467-8535.2005.00477.x

Diehl, K. (2005). When two rights make a wrong: Searching too much in ordered environment. *JMR, Journal of Marketing Research*, *42*(3), 313–322. doi:10.1509/jmkr.2005.42.3.313

Dillman, D. A. (2000). *Mail and internet surveys: the tailored design method* (2nd ed.). New York: John Wiley & Sons.

Dimmick, J., Kline, S., & Stafford, L. (2000). The Gratification Niches of Personal E-mail and the Telephone. *Communication Research*, *27*(2), 227–248. doi:10.1177/009365000027002005

Ding, Y., Fensel, D., & Klein, A. B. O. (2002). The semantic Web: yet another hip? *Data & Knowledge Engineering*, *41*(3), 205–227. doi:10.1016/S0169-023X(02)00041-1

Dinur, I., & Nissim, K. (2003). Revealing information while preserving privacy. In *Proceedings of the Twenty-Second ACM SIGACT-SIGMOD-SIGART Symposium on Principles of Database Systems* (pp. 202-210).

Do, H.-H., Melnik, S., & Rahm, E. (2003). Comparison of schema matching evaluations. In *Proceedings of the 2nd International Workshop on Web Databases* (pp. 221-237).

Doan, A., & Halevy, A. (2005). Semantic-integration research in the database community: A Brief Survey. *AI Magazine, 26*(1), 83–94.

Do, H.-H., & Rahm, E. (2007). Matching large schemas: approaches and evaluation. *Information Systems, 32*(6), 857–885. doi:10.1016/j.is.2006.09.002

Domshlak, C., Gal, A., & Roitman, H. (2007). Rank aggregation for automatic schema matching. *IEEE Transactions on Knowledge and Data Engineering, 19*(4), 538–553. doi:10.1109/TKDE.2007.1010

Dong, J., Alencar, P. S. C., Cowan, D. D., & Yang, S. (2007). Composing pattern-based components and verifying correctness. *Journal of Systems and Software, 80*(11), 1755–1769. doi:10.1016/j.jss.2007.03.005

Dong, J., Yang, S., & Zhang, K. (2007). Visualizing Design Patterns in their Applications and Composition. *IEEE Transactions on Software Engineering, 33*(7), 433–453. doi:10.1109/TSE.2007.1012

Dori, D. (2002). *Object-Process Methodology – A Holistic System Paradigm*. London: Springer.

Dourish, P. (1998). Introduction: The state of play. *Computer Supported Cooperative Work: The Journal of Collaborative Computing, 7*(1/2), 1–7. doi:10.1023/A:1008697019985

Drengner, J., Gaus, H., & Jahn, S. (2008). Does flow influence the brand image in event marketing. *Journal of Advertising Research, 48*(1), 138–147. doi:10.2501/S0021849908080148

Drum, C., Schmitt, M., Do, H.-H., & Rahm, E. (2007). QuickMig - automatic schema matching for data migration projects. In *Proceedings of the 16th Conference on Information and Knowledge Management (CIKM2007)* (pp. 107-116).

Ducheneaut, N., Moore, R., & Nickell, E. (2007). Virtual "Third places": a case study of sociability in massively multiplayer games. *Computer Supported Cooperative Work, 16*, 129–166. doi:10.1007/s10606-007-9041-8

Dufourd, C., Finkel, A., & Schnoebelen, P. (1998). Reset nets between decidability and undecidability. In K. Larsen, S. Skyum, & G. Winskel (Eds.), *Proceedings of the 25th International Colloquium on Automata, Languages and Programming* (LNCS 1443, pp. 103-115).

Durdell, A., & Thomson, K. (1997). Gender and computing: a decade of change? *Computers & Education, 28*(1), 1–9. doi:10.1016/S0360-1315(96)00034-6

Dussart, A., Aubert, B. A., & Patry, M. (2004). An evaluation of inter-organizational workflow modeling formalisms. *Journal of Database Management, 15*(2), 74–104.

DVB Document A081. (2004). *Digital Video Broadcasting (DVB) Transmission System for Handheld Terminals DVB-H.*

Earl, M. J. (1987). Information systems strategy formulation. In R. J. Boland Jr. & R. A. Hirschheim (Eds.), *Critical Issues in Information Systems Research* (pp. 157-178). New York: Wiley.

Eden, A. H. (1999). *Precise Specification of Design Patterns and Tool Support in Their Application*. Unpublished PhD thesis, University of Tel Aviv.

Eden, A. H. (2002). A Visual Formalism for Object-Oriented Architectures. In J. C. Peterson, B. Kraemer, & B. Enders (Eds.), *Proceedings of the 6th World Conference on Integrated Design and Process Technology (IDPT'2002)*. Pasadena, CA: Society for Design and Process Science.

Eighmey, J. (1997). Profiling User Responses to Commercial Web Sites. *Journal of Advertising Research, 37*(3), 59–66.

Ein-Dor, P., & Segev, E. (1978). Organizational Context and the Success of Management Information Systems. *Management Science, 24*(10), 1064–1077. doi:10.1287/mnsc.24.10.1064

Elmasri, R., & Navathe, S. B. (2006). *Fundamentals of Database Systems* (5th ed.). Upper Saddle River, NJ, USA: Addison Wesley.

England, D., & Gray, P. (1998). Temporal aspects of interaction in shared virtual worlds. *Interacting with Computers, 11*(1), 87–105. doi:10.1016/S0953-5438(98)00033-2

Erickson, J., Lyytinen, K., & Siau, K. (2005). Agile Modeling, Agile Software Development, and Extreme Programming: The State of Research. *Journal of Database Management, 16*(4), 88–100.

Erickson, J., & Siau, K. (2003). e-ducation. *Communications of the ACM, 46*(9), 134–140. doi:10.1145/903893.903928

Erickson, J., & Siau, K. (2007). Theoretical and Practical Complexity of Modeling Methods. *Communications of the ACM, 50*(8), 46–51. doi:10.1145/1278201.1278205

Erickson, J., & Siau, K. (2008). Web Services, service-oriented computing, and service-oriented architecture: separating hype from reality. *Journal of Database Management, 19*(3), 42–54.

Ericsson, K., & Simon, H. (1984). *Protocol Analysis: Verbal Reports as Data.* Cambridge, MA: MIT Press.

Ertmer, P. A., & Newby, T. J. (1993). Behaviorism, cognitivism, constructivism: comparing critical features from an instructional design perspective. *Performance Improvement Quarterly, 6*(4), 50–72. doi:10.1111/j.1937-8327.1993.tb00605.x

Eschenbrenner, B., Nah, F. F. H., & Siau, K. (2008). 3-D virtual Worlds in Education: Applications, Benefits, Issues, and Opportunities. *Journal of Database Management, 19*(4), 91–110.

Eschenbrenner, B., Nah, F., & Siau, K. (2008). 3-D virtual worlds in education: Applications, benefits, issues, and opportunities. *Journal of Database Management, 19*(4), 91–110.

Esparza, J., & Silva, M. (1990). Circuits, Handles, Bridges and Nets. In G. Rozenberg (Ed.), *Advances in Petri Nets 1990* (LNCS 483, pp. 210-242).

Etton, P., Martin, A., Sharma, R., & Johnston, K. (2000). A model of Information systems development project performance. *Information Systems Journal, 10*(4), 263–289. doi:10.1046/j.1365-2575.2000.00088.x

Evermann, J. (2008). Theories of Meaning in Schema Matching: A Review. *Journal of Database Management, 19*(3), 55–82.

Evermann, J., & Wand, Y. (2005). Ontology Based Object-Oriented Domain Modelling: Fundamental Concepts. *Requirements Engineering Journal, 10*(2), 146–160. doi:10.1007/s00766-004-0208-2

Evermann, J., & Wand, Y. (2006). Ontological Modelling Rules for UML: An Empirical Assessment. *Journal of Computer Information Systems, 46*(5), 14–19.

Evermann, J., & Wand, Y. (2009). Ontology based object-oriented domain modeling: Representing behavior. *Journal of Database Management, 20*(1), 48–77.

Evernden, R. (1996). The Information FrameWork. *IBM Systems Journal, 35*(1), 37–68. doi:10.1147/sj.351.0037

Falkenberg, E., Hesse, W., Lindgreen, P., & Nilsson, E. (1998). *A framework of information system concepts: The FRISCO report.* International Federation of Information Processing (IFIP).

Fan, H., & Poulovassilis, A. (2004). Schema Evolution in Data Warehousing Environments: a schema transformation-based approach. *In Proceedings of International Conference on Conceptual Modeling (ER)*, 639-653.

Fan, W., Lu, H., Madnick, S. E., & Cheung, D. W. (2001). Discovering and reconciling value conflicts for numerical data integration. *Information Systems, 26*(8), 635–656. doi:10.1016/S0306-4379(01)00043-6

Fan, W., Lu, H., Madnick, S. E., & Cheung, D. W. (2002). DIRECT: a system for mining data value conversion rules from disparate sources. *Decision Support Systems, 34*(1), 19–39. doi:10.1016/S0167-9236(02)00006-4

Felix, R. G., & Harrison, W. L. (1984). Project Management Considerations for Distributed Applications. *MIS Quarterly, 8*(3), 161–170. doi:10.2307/248663

Feller, J., Finnegan, P., & Hayes, J. (2008). Delivering the 'whole product': business model impacts and agility challenges in a network of open source firms. *Journal of Database Management, 19*(2), 95–109.

Ferrandina, F., Ferran, G., Meyer, T., Madec, J., & Zicari, R. (1995). Schema and Database Evolution in the O2 Object Database System. *In PRoceedings of International Conference on Very Large Databases (VLDB)*, 170-181.

Field, A. (2009). *Discovering statistics using SPSS* (3rd ed.). London: SAGE.

Finneran, C. M., & Zhang, P. (2005). Flow in computer-mediated environment: Promises and challenges. *Communications of the Association for Information Systems*, *15*, 82–101.

Firat, A., Wu, L., & Madnick, S. (2009). General Strategy for Querying Web Sources in a Data Federation Environment. *Journal of Database Management*, *20*(2), 1–18.

Floyd, C. (1986). A comparative evaluation of system development methods . In Olle, T. W., Sol, H. G., & Verrijn-Stuart, A. A. (Eds.), *Information System Design Methodologies: Improving the Practice* (pp. 19–54). Amsterdam, The Netherlands: North-Holland.

Fong, J., & Wong, H. K. (2004). XTOPO: An XML-Based Topology for Information Highway on the Internet. *Journal of Database Management*, *15*(3), 18–44.

Fornell, C., & Bookstein, F. L. (1982). Two structural equation models: LISREL and PLS applied to consumer exit-voice theory. *Journal of Marketing*, *19*(4), 440–452. doi:10.2307/3151718

Fornell, C., & Larcker, D. F. (1981). Evaluating structural equation models with unobservable variables and measurement error. *JMR, Journal of Marketing Research*, *18*(1), 39–50. doi:10.2307/3151312

Fornell, C., & Larcker, D. F. (1981). Evaluating structural equation models with unobservable variables and measurement error. *JMR, Journal of Marketing Research*, *18*(1), 39–50. doi:10.2307/3151312

Fortin, D. R., & Dholakia, R. R. (2005). Interactivity and vividness effects on social presence and involvement with a Web-based advertisement. *Journal of Business Research*, *58*(3), 387–396. doi:10.1016/S0148-2963(03)00106-1

France, R. B., Kim, D.-K., Ghosh, S., & Song, E. (2004). A UML-Based Pattern Specification Technique. *IEEE Transactions on Software Engineering*, *30*(3), 193–206. doi:10.1109/TSE.2004.1271174

Fredrickson, B. L. (2001). The role of positive emotions in positive psychology: The broaden-and-build theory of positive emotions. *The American Psychologist*, *56*(3), 218–226. doi:10.1037/0003-066X.56.3.218

Fredrickson, B. L., Tugade, M. M., Waugh, C. E., & Larkin, G. R. (2003). What good for positive emotions in crises? A prospective study of resilience and emotions following the terrorist attacks on the United States on September 11th, 2001. *Journal of Personality and Social Psychology*, *84*(2), 365–376. doi:10.1037/0022-3514.84.2.365

Freedman, J. L., Birsky, J., & Cavoukian, A. (1980). Environmental determinants of behavioral contagion: Density and number . *Basic and Applied Social Psychology*, *1*(2), 155–161. doi:10.1207/s15324834basp0102_4

French, J. R. P., & Raven, B. (2001). The bases of social power . In Asherman, I., Bob, P., & Randall, J. (Eds.), *The negotiation sourcebook* (2nd ed., pp. 61–74). Amherst, MA: Human Resource Development Press.

Fuller, J. (2010). Refining virtual co-creation from a consumer perspective. *California Management Review*, *52*(2), 98–122.

Fuller, J., Hans, M., Kurt, M., & Gregor, J. (2010). Consumer empowerment through Internet-based co-creation. *Journal of Management Information Systems*, *26*(3), 71–102. doi:10.2753/MIS0742-1222260303

Gal, A. (2006). Why is schema matching tough and what can we do about it? *SIGMOD Record*, *35*(4), 2–5. doi:10.1145/1228268.1228269

Galanxhi, H., & Nah, F. F.-H. (2007). Deception in cyberspace: A comparison of text-only vs. Avatar-supported medium. *International Journal of Human-Computer Studies*, *65*(9), 770–783. doi:10.1016/j.ijhcs.2007.04.005

Gallagher, C. A. (1974). Perceptions of the Value of a Management Information System. *Academy of Management Journal*, *17*(1), 46–55. doi:10.2307/254770

Galloway, A. (2004). Social Realism in Gaming. *International Journal of Computer Game Research*, *4*(1). Retrieved from http://www.gamestudies.org/ 0401/ galloway/.

Gamma, E., Helm, R., Johnson, R., & Vlissides, J. (1994). *Design Patterns: Elements of Reusable Object-Oriented Software*. Reading, MA: Addison-Wesley.

Garau, M., Slater, M., Vinayagamoorthy, V., Brogni, A., Steed, A., & Sasse, M. A. (2003). The impact of avatar realism and eye gaze control on perceived quality of communication in a shared immersive virtual environment. In *Proceedings of the SIGCHI conference on Human factors in computing systems,* Ft. Lauderdale, FL (pp. 529-536).

Garfinkel, R., Gopal, R., & Goes, P. (2002). Privacy protection of binary confidential data against deterministic, stochastic, and insider threat. *Management Science, 48*(6), 749–764. doi:10.1287/mnsc.48.6.749.193

Garland, H., & Newport, S. (1991). Effects of absolute and relative sunk costs on the decision to persist with a course of action. *Organizational Behavior and Human Decision Processes, 48*(1), 55–69. doi:10.1016/0749-5978(91)90005-E

Geer, D. (2003). Taking steps to secure web services. *IEEE Computer, 36*(10), 14–16.

Gefen, D., Straub, D. W., & Boudreau, M.-C. (2000). Structural equation modeling and regression: Guidelines for research practice. *Communications of the Association for Information Systems, 4*, 1–77.

Gefen, D., Straub, D., & Boudreau, M. (2000). Structural equation modeling and regression: Guidelines for research practice. *Communications of the Association for Information Systems, 4*(5), 1–77.

Gemino, A. (1998). *Comparing Object Oriented with Structured Analysis Techniques in Conceptual Modeling.* Unpublished doctoral dissertation, University of British Columbia, Vancouver.

Gemino, A. (1999). *Empirical methods for comparing system analysis modelling techniques.* Unpublished doctorial dissertation, University of British Columbia.

Gemino, A., & Wand, Y. (2004). A framework for empirical evaluation of conceptual modelling techniques. *Requirements Engineering, 9*, 248–260. doi:10.1007/s00766-004-0204-6

Gemino, A., & Wand, Y. (2005). Complexity and clarity in conceptual modeling: Comparison of mandatory and optional properties. *Data & Knowledge Engineering, 55*, 301–326. doi:10.1016/j.datak.2004.12.009

Gensch, D. H. (1987). A two-stage disaggregate attribute choice model. *Marketing Science, 6*(3), 223–239. doi:10.1287/mksc.6.3.223

Gewald, H., & Dibbern, J. (2009). Risks and benefits of business process outsourcing: a study of transaction services in the German banking industry. *Information & Management, 46*(4), 249–257. doi:10.1016/j.im.2009.03.002

Ghani, J. A., Supnik, R., & Rooney, P. (1991). The experience of flow in computer-mediated and in face-to-face groups. In *Proceedings of the Twelfth International Conference on Information Systems* (pp. 229-236).

Ghani, J. A. (1995). Flow in human computer interactions: Test of a model . In Carey, J. (Ed.), *Human factors in information systems: Emerging theoretical bases* (pp. 291–311). New York: Ablex Publishing.

Ghani, J. A., & Deshpande, S. P. (1994). Task characteristics and the experience of optimal flow in human-computer interaction. *The Journal of Psychology, 128*(4), 381–391.

Giffin, K. (1967). The contribution of studies of source credibility to a theory of interpersonal trust in the communication process. *Psychological Bulletin, 68*(2), 104–120. doi:10.1037/h0024833

Gillmann, M., Weikum, G., & Wonner, W. (2002). Workflow management with service quality guarantees. In D. DeWitt (Ed.), *ACM SIGMOD International Conference on Management of Data* (pp. 228-239).

Ginzberg, M. J. (1981). Early diagnosis of MIS implementation failure: Promising results and unanswered questions. *Management Science, 27*(4), 459–478. doi:10.1287/mnsc.27.4.459

Giunchiglia, F., Yatskevich, M., & Shvaiko, P. (2007). Semantic Matching: Algorithms and Implementation. *Journal on Data Semantics, 9*, 1–38.

Goasdoue, F., Lattes, V., & Rousset, M. (1999). The Use of Carin Language and Algorithm for Information Integration: The PICSEL Project. *International Journal of Cooperative Information Systems, 9*(4), 383–401. doi:10.1142/S0218843000000181

Godfrey, P. (1997). Minimization in Cooperative Response to Failing Database Queries. *International Journal of Cooperative Information Systems, 6*(2), 95–149. doi:10.1142/S0218843097000070

Goel, L., & Mousavidin, E. (2007). vCRM: Virtual customer relationship management. *The Data Base for Advances in Information Systems, 38*(4), 56–60.

Gokhale, A. (1995). Collaborative learning enhances critical thinking. *Journal of Technology Education, 7*(1), 22–30.

Goldman, S. A., & Sloan, R. (1995). Can PAC learning algorithms tolerate random attribute noise? *Algorithmica, 14*(1), 70–84. doi:10.1007/BF01300374

Golub, A., & Lingley, K. (2008). 'Just like the Qing Empire': Internet addiction, MMOGs, and moral crisis in contemporary China. *Games and Culture: A Journal of Interactive Media, 3*(1), 59-75.

Gomez-Perez, A., Fernandez-Lopez, M., & Corcho, O. (2004). *Ontological Engineering: With examples for the area of knowledge management, e-commerce and the semantic web*. London: Springer-Verlag Limited.

Goodhue, D., & Thompson, R. (1995). Task-technology fit and individual performance. *Management Information Systems Quarterly, 19*(2), 213–236. doi:10.2307/249689

Gou, G., & Chirkova, R. (2007). Efficiently querying large XML data repositories: A survey. *IEEE Transactions on Knowledge and Data Engineering, 19*(10). doi:10.1109/TKDE.2007.1060

Gravano, L., & Papakonstantinou, Y. (1998). Mediating and meta searching on the internet. *A Quarterly Bulletin of the Computer Society of the IEEE Technical Committee on Data Engineering, 21*(2), 28–36.

Green, P., & Rosemann, M. (2000). Integrated Process Modeling: An ontological evaluation. *Information Systems, 25*(2), 73–87. doi:10.1016/S0306-4379(00)00010-7

Green, P., & Rosemann, M. (2004). Applying ontologies to business and systems modelling techniques and perspectives: Lessons learned. *Journal of Database Management, 15*(2), 105–117.

Griffiths, M. (1998). Internet addiction: Does it really exist? In Gackenback, J. (Ed.), *Psychology and the Internet: Intrapersonal, interpersonal and transpersonal implications* (pp. 61–75). New York: Academic Press.

Griffiths, M. D., Davies, M. N. O., & Chappell, D. (2004). Demographic factors and playing variables in online computer gaming. *Cyberpsychology & Behavior, 7*(4), 479–487. doi:10.1089/cpb.2004.7.479

Griffith, T. L., Sawyer, J. E., & Neale, M. A. (2003). Virtualness and Knowledge in Teams: Managing the Love Triangle of Organizations, Individuals, and Information Technology. *MIS Quarterly, 27*(2), 265–287.

Grohol, J. M. (2005). *Internet Addiction Guide*. Retrieved from http://psychcentral.com/ netaddiction/

Grover, V., Cheon, M. J., & Teng, J. T. C. (1996). The effects of service quality and partnership on the outsourcing of information system functions. *Journal of Management Information Systems, 12*(4), 89–116.

Grover, V., Teng, J. T. C., & Cheon, M. J. (1998). Towards a theoretically-based contingency model of information systems outsourcing . In Willcocks, L. P., & Lacity, M. (Eds.), *Strategic source of information systems: perspective and practices*. New York: Wiley.

Gruber, T. (1993). A Translation Approach to Portable Ontology Specification. *Knowledge Acquisition, 5*(2), 199–220. doi:10.1006/knac.1993.1008

Guennec, A. L., Sunye, G., & Jezequel, J.-M. (2000). Precise Modeling of Design Patterns. In A. Evans, S. Kent, & B. Selic (Eds.), *<<UML>> 2000 – The Unified Modeling Language. Advancing the Standard* (LNCS 1939, pp. 482-496). Berlin-Heidelberg, Germany: Springer.

Guinan, P. J., Cooprider, J. G., & Faraj, S. (1998). Enabling software development team performance during requirements definition: A behavioral versus technical approach. *Information Systems Research, 9*(2), 101–125. doi:10.1287/isre.9.2.101

Guizzardi, G., Ferreira, P. L., & van Sinderen, M. (2005). An ontology-based approach for evaluating the domain appropriateness and comprehensibility appropriateness of modeling languages. In *ACM/IEEE 8th International Conference on Model Driven Engineering Languages and Systems,* Montego Bay, Jamaica (LNCS 3713).

Guizzardi, G., Herre, H., & Wagne, G. (2002). *On the General Ontological Foundations of Conceptual Modeling*. In S. Spaccapietra, S. T. March, & Y. Kambayashi (Eds.), *Proceedings of ER 2002* (LNCS 2503, pp. 65-78)

Gu, N., & Tsai, J. J.-H. (2010). Interactive graphical representation for collaborative 3D virtual worlds. *Computer-Aided Civil and Infrastructure Engineering, 25*(1), 55–68. doi:10.1111/j.1467-8667.2009.00613.x

Guo, Y. M., & Poole, M. S. (2009). Antecedents of flow in online shopping: A test of alternative models. *Information Systems Journal, 19*(4), 369–390. doi:10.1111/j.1365-2575.2007.00292.x

Guo, Y. M., & Ro, Y. K. (2008). Capturing flow in the business classroom. *Decision Sciences Journal of Innovative Education, 6*(2), 437–462. doi:10.1111/j.1540-4609.2008.00185.x

Gupta, A. K., & Suciu, D. (2003). *Stream Processing of XPath Queries with Predicates*. Paper presented at the ACM SIGMOD Conference.

Gupta, A., Mumick, I., & Ross, K. (1995). Adapting Materialized Views After Redefinition. *In Proceedings of ACM SIG Conference on Management of Data*, 211-222.

Gupta, S., & Kim, H. (2007). The moderating effect of transaction experience on the decision calculus in on-line repurchase. *International Journal of Electronic Commerce, 12*(1), 127–158. doi:10.2753/JEC1086-4415120105

Guru, A., & Siau, K. (2008). Developing the IBM i virtual community: iSociety. *Journal of Database Management, 19*(4), i–xiii.

Guthrie, A. (1974). Attitudes of User-Managers towards Management Information Systems. *Management Informatics, 3*(5), 221–232.

Haas, L. M., Miller, R. J., Niswonger, B., Roth, M. T., Schwarz, P. M., & Wimmers, E. L. (1999). Transforming Heterogeneous Data with Database Middleware: Beyond Integration. *A Quarterly Bulletin of the Computer Society of the IEEE Technical Committee on Data Engineering, 22*(1), 31–36.

Hackman, J. R. (1987). The design of work teams. In J. W. Lorsch (Ed.), *Handbook of organizational behavior* (pp. 315-342). Englewood Cliffs, NJ: Prentice Hall.

Hahsler, M. (2003). *A Quantitative Study of the Application of Design Patterns in Java* (Working Papers on Information Processing and Information Management No. 01/2003). Wien, Austria: Institute of Information Processing and Information Management.

Hahsler, M. (2004). A Quantitative Study of the Adoption of Design Patterns by Open Source Software Developers. In S. Koch (Ed.), *Free/Open Source Software Development*. Hershey, PA: Idea Group.

Ha, I., Yoon, Y., & Choi, M. (2007). Determinants of adoption of mobile games under mobile broadband wireless access environment. *Information & Management, 44*(3), 276–286. doi:10.1016/j.im.2007.01.001

Hainaut, J.-L. (1998). Database reverse engineering [online]. Available: http://citeseer.ist.psu.edu/article/hainaut98database.html.

Hall, P., & Morton, S. C. (1993). On the estimation of entropy. *Annals of Institute of Mathematical Statistics, 45*(1), 69–88. doi:10.1007/BF00773669

Halpin, T., & Morgan, T. (2008). *Information Modeling and Relational Databases, 2nd edition*. San Fransisco: Morgan Kaufmann.

Halpin, T. A. (2008). *Information Modeling and Relational Databases* (2nd ed.). San Francisco: Morgan Kaufman.

Hammer, M. (2004). Deep change: How operational innovation can transform your company. *Harvard Business Review*, 84–93.

Han, W.-S., Jiang, H., Ho, H., & Li, Q. (2008). StreamTX: Extracting Tuples from Streaming XML Data. In *Proceedings of the VLDB Endowment* (pp. 289-300).

Han, H. S., Lee, J. N., & Seo, Y. W. (2008). Analyzing the impact of a firm's capability on outsourcing success: A process perspective. *Information & Management, 45*(1), 31–42.

Harder, T., Haustein, M., Mathis, C., & Wagner, M. (2007). Node labeling schemes for dynamic XML documents reconsidered. *Data & Knowledge Engineering, 60*(1), 126–149. doi:10.1016/j.datak.2005.11.008

Hardgrave, B. C., & Johnson, R. A. (2003). Toward an Information Systems Development Acceptance Model: The Case of Object-Oriented Systems Development. *IEEE Transactions on Engineering Management, 50*(3), 322–336. doi:10.1109/TEM.2003.817293

Hardgrave, B. C., Wilson, R. L., & Eastman, K. (1999). Toward a Contingency Model for Selecting an Information System Prototyping Strategy. *Journal of Management Information Systems, 16*(2), 113–136.

Haubl, G., & Trifts, V. (2000). Consumer decision making in online shopping environments: The effects of interactive decision aids. *Marketing Science, 19*(1), 4–21. doi:10.1287/mksc.19.1.4.15178

Haustein, M., & Harder, T. (2007). An efficient infrastructure for native transactional XML processing. *Data & Knowledge Engineering, 61*(3), 500–523. doi:10.1016/j.datak.2006.06.015

Hayes, B. (2008). Cloud computing. *Communications of the ACM, 51*(7), 9–11. doi:10.1145/1364782.1364786

Head, M., Govindaraju, M., Slominski, A., Liu, P., Abu-Ghazaleh, N., van Engelen, R., et al. (2005). A benchmark suite for SOAP-based communication in Grid Web services. In W. Kramer (Ed.), *ACM/IEEE Conference on High Performance Networking and Computing* (pp. 19-20).

He, B., & Chang, K. C.-C. (2006). Automatic complex schema matching across web query interfaces: a correlation mining approach. *ACM Transactions on Database Systems, 31*(1), 346–395. doi:10.1145/1132863.1132872

Hecht, D., & Reiner, M. (2007). Field dependency and the sense of object-presence in haptic virtual environments. *Cyberpsychology & Behavior, 10*(2), 243–251. doi:10.1089/cpb.2006.9962

Heckman, F. (1997). Designing organizations for flow experiences. *Journal for Quality and Participation, 20*(2), 24–33.

Helm, R. (2005). Patterns in Practice. In R. E. Johnson & R. P. Gabriel (Eds.), *Proceedings of the 10th Annual Conference on Object-Oriented Programming Systems, Languages, and Applications (OOPSLA'2005)* (pp. 337-341). New York: ACM Publishing.

Hemerly, A., Casanova, M., & Furtado, A. (1994). Exploiting User Models to Avoid Misconstruals. In *Nonstandard Queries and Nonstandard Answers* (pp. 73–98). Oxford, UK: Oxford Science Publications.

Hemp, P. (2006). Avatar-based marketing. *Harvard Business Review, 84*(6), 48–57.

Henderson, J. C., & Sifonis, J. G. (1988). The value of strategic IS planning: understanding consistency, validity, and IS markets. *MIS Quarterly, 12*(2), 187–200. doi:10.2307/248843

Hendrick, S. S. (2004). *Understanding close relationships*. Boston: Allyn & Bacon.

Henriksson, A., & Larsson, H. (2003). *A Definition of Round-trip Engineering*. Linköping, Sweden: Department of Computer and Information Science, Linköpings Universitet.

Henry, R. M., Dickson, G. W., & LaSalle, J. (1973). Human resources for MIS: A report of research. In *Proceedings of the Fifth Annual Conference of the Society for Management Information Systems,* Chicago (pp. 21-34).

Henry, K. B., Arrow, H., & Carini, B. (1999). A Tripartite Model of Group Identification: Theory and Measuremen. *Small Group Research, 30*(5), 555–581. doi:10.1177/104649649903000504

Herires, K. (2009, April 13). Reaching out to financial firms, Microsoft is stressing cost-saving. *Security Industry News*, 19-20

Herzum, P., & Sims, O. (2000). *Business Component Factory: A comprehensive Overview of Component-based Development for the Enterprise*. New York: Wiley.

Hevner, A., March, S., Park, J., & Ram, S. (2004). Design Science Research in Information Systems. *MIS Quarterly, 28*(1), 75–105.

Hirschheim, R., & Klein, H. K. (1989). Four Paradigms of Information Systems Development. *Communications of the ACM, 32*(10), 1199–1216. doi:10.1145/67933.67937

Hirschheim, R., Klein, H., & Lyytinen, K. (1995). *Information Systems Development and Data Modeling: Conceptual Foundations and Philosophical Foundations*. Cambridge, UK: Cambridge University Press.

Hirschheim, R., & Newman, M. (1988). Information Systems and User Resistance: Theory and Practice. *The Computer Journal, 31*(5), 398–408. doi:10.1093/comjnl/31.5.398

Hobson, N. (2006). Is it time you got a Second Life? *Strategic Communication Management, 11*(1). Retrieved September 14, 2008, from http://www.nevillehobson.com/resources/ is-it-time-you-got-a-second-life/

Hoffman, D. L., & Novak, T. P. (1996). Marketing in hypermedia computer-mediated environment. *Journal of Marketing, 60*(3), 50–68. doi:10.2307/1251841

Hoffman, D. L., & Novak, T. P. (2009). Flow Online: Lessons Learned and Future Prospects. *Journal of Interactive Marketing, 23*(1), 23–34. doi:10.1016/j.intmar.2008.10.003

Holzner, B., & Marx, J. (1979). *The Knowledge Application: The Knowledge System in Society*. Boston: Allyn-Bacon.

Holzwarth, M., Janiszewski, C., & Neumann, M. M. (2006). The influence of avatars on online consumer shopping behavior. *Journal of Marketing, 70*(4), 19–36. doi:10.1509/jmkg.70.4.19

Hong, W., Thong, J. Y. L., & Tam, K. Y. (2004a). Designing product listing pages on e-commerce websites: An examination of presentation mode and information format. *International Journal of Human-Computer Studies, 61*(4), 481–503. doi:10.1016/j.ijhcs.2004.01.006

Hong, W., Thong, J. Y. L., & Tam, K. Y. (2004b). The effects of information format and shopping task on consumers' online shopping behavior: A cognitive fit perspective. *Journal of Management Information Systems, 21*(3), 149–184.

Horngren, C. T., Ittner, C., Foster, G., Rajan, M. V., & Datar, S. M. (2008). *Cost Accounting: A Managerial Emphasis* (13th ed.). Upper Saddle River, NJ: Prentice Hall.

Horridge, M., Rector, A., Knublauch, H., Stevens, R., & Wroe, C. (2004). *A Practical Guide to Building OWL Ontologies Using the Protege-OWL Plugin and CO-ODE Tool Edition 1.0*. Retrieved from http://www.co-ode.org/resources/tutorials/ProtegeOWLTutorial.pdf

Hsu, C.-L., & Lu, H.-P. (2004). Why do people play online games? An extended TAM with social influences and flow experience. *Information & Management, 41*(7), 853–868. doi:10.1016/j.im.2003.08.014

Huang, E. (2008). Use and gratification in e-consumers. *Internet Research, 18*(4), 405–426. doi:10.1108/10662240810897817

Huang, M.-H. (2003). Designing website attributes to induce experiential encounters. *Computers in Human Behavior, 19*(4), 425–442. doi:10.1016/S0747-5632(02)00080-8

Huang, S., Hung, S., Yen, D., Li, S., & Wu, C. (2006). Enterprise Application System Reengineering: A Business Component Approach. *Journal of Database Management, 17*(3), 66–91.

Huang, S.-M., Yen, D. C., & Hsueh, H.-Y. (2007). A Space-Efficient Protocol for Consistency of External View Maintenance on Data Warehouse Systems: A Proxy Approach. *Journal of Database Management, 18*(3), 21–47.

Huh, S., & Lee, J. W. (2001). Providing Approximate Answers Using a Knowledge Abstraction Database. *Journal of Database Management, 12*(2), 14–24.

Huh, S., & Moon, K. H. (2000). A Data Abstraction Approach for Query Relaxation. *Information and Software Technology, 42*(6), 407–418. doi:10.1016/S0950-5849(99)00100-7

Hulland, J. (1999). Use of partial least squares (PLS) in strategic management research: A review of four recent studies. *Strategic Management Journal, 20*(2), 195–204. doi:10.1002/(SICI)1097-0266(199902)20:2<195::AID-SMJ13>3.0.CO;2-7

Hung, C., Wermter, S., & Smith, P. (2004). Hybrid Neural Document Clustering Using Guided Self-Organization and WordNet. *IEEE Intelligent Systems, 19*(2), 68–77. doi:10.1109/MIS.2004.1274914

Hu, W., Qu, Y., & Cheng, G. (2008). Matching large ontologies: A divide-and-conquer approach. *Data & Knowledge Engineering, 67*(1), 140–160. doi:10.1016/j.datak.2008.06.003

IBM. (2004). *IBM Insurance Application Architecture, version 7.1*. Retrieved from http://www-03.ibm.com/industries/financialservices/ doc/content/solution/278918103.html

Iivari, J., Hirschheim, R., & Klein, H. K. (1998). A Paradigmatic Analysis Contrasting Information Systems Development Approaches and Methodologies. *Information Systems Research*, *9*(2), 164–193. doi:10.1287/isre.9.2.164

Im, I., Kim, Y., & Han, H.-J. (2008). The effects of perceived risk and technology type on users' acceptance of technologies. *Information & Management*, *45*(1), 1–9.

Imielinski, T., Viswanathan, S., & Badrinath, B. R. (1994). Energy Efficient Indexing on Air. In *Proceedings of the ACM SIGMOD Conference* (pp. 25-36).

Imielinski, T., & Badrinath, B. R. (1993). Data Management for Mobile Computing. *SIGMOD Record*, *22*(1), 34–39. doi:10.1145/156883.156888

Imielinski, T., Viswanathan, S., & Badrinath, B. R. (1997). Data on Air: Organization and Access. *IEEE Transactions on Knowledge and Data Engineering*, *9*(3), 353–372. doi:10.1109/69.599926

Ives, B., & Junglas, I. (2008). APC forum: Business implications of virtual worlds and serious gaming. *MIS Quarterly Executive*, *7*(3), 151–156.

Ives, B., & Olson, M. (1984). User Involvement and MIS Success: A Review of Research. *Management Science*, *30*(5), 586–603. doi:10.1287/mnsc.30.5.586

Jarvenpaa, S. L. (1989). The effect of task demands and graphical format on information processing strategies. *Management Science*, *35*(3), 285–303. doi:10.1287/mnsc.35.3.285

Jarvenpaa, S. L., Knoll, K., & Leidner, D. E. (1998). Is anybody out there? Antecedents of trust in global virtual teams. *Journal of Management Information Systems*, *14*(4), 29–64.

Jayatilaka, B., Schwarz, A., & Hirschheim, R. (2003). Determinants of ASP choice: an integrated perspective. *European Journal of Information Systems*, *12*(3), 210–224. doi:10.1057/palgrave.ejis.3000466

Jennings, N., & Collins, C. (2007). Virtual or virtually u: Educational institutions in Second Life. *International Journal of Social Sciences*, *2*(3), 180–186.

Jensen, K. (1990). Coloured Petri Nets: A High Level Language for System Design and Analysis. In G. Rozenberg (Ed.), *Advances in Petri Nets 1990* (LNCS 483, pp. 342-416).

Jensen, K. (1997). *Coloured Petri Nets. Basic Concepts, Analysis Methods and Practical Use (Vol. 1)*. Berlin: Springer-Verlag.

Jianchun, S., & Dongqing, Y. (2009). Process mining: Algorithm for S-Coverable workflow nets. In *WKDD 2009: Proceedings of the Second International Workshop on Knowledge Discovery and Data Mining* (pp. 239-244). Washington, DC: IEEE Computer Society.

Jiang, Z., & Benbasat, I. (2005). Virtual product experience: Effects of visual and functional control of products on perceived diagnosticity and flow in electronic shopping. *Journal of Management Information Systems*, *21*(3), 111–148.

Jiang, Z., & Benbasat, I. (2007). The effects of presentation formats and task complexity on online consumers' product understanding. *Management Information Systems Quarterly*, *31*(3), 475–500.

Johannesson, P. (1997). Supporting schema integration by linguistic instruments. *Data & Knowledge Engineering*, *21*(2), 165–182. doi:10.1016/S0169-023X(96)00031-6

Joosten, S., & Purao, S. (2002). A rigorous Approach for Mapping Workflows to Object-Oriented IS Models. *Journal of Database Management*, *13*(4), 1–19.

Josifovski, V., Fontoura, M., & Barta, A. (2004). Querying XML Streams. *The VLDB Journal*, *14*(2), 197–210. doi:10.1007/s00778-004-0123-7

Jung, C. G. (1923). *Psychological Types*. London: Rutledge and Kegan Paul.

Jung, C. G. (1968). *Analytical Psychology: Its Theory and Practice*. New York: Vintage Press.

Junglas, I. A., Johnson, N. A., Steel, D. J., Abraham, D. C., & Loughlin, P. M. (2007). Identity formation, learning styles and trust in virtual worlds. *The Data Base for Advances in Information Systems*, *38*(4), 90–96.

Kaiser, K., & Bostrom, R. (1982). Personality Characteristics of MIS Design Project Teams: An Empirical Study and Action-Research Design. *MIS Quarterly, 6*(4), 43–60. doi:10.2307/249066

Kalfoglou, Y., & Scholemmer, M. (2003). Ontology Mapping: The State of the Art. *The Knowledge Engineering Review, 18*(1), 1–31. doi:10.1017/S0269888903000651

Kanade, T., Rander, P., & Narayanan, P. J. (1997). Virtualized reality: Constructing virtual worlds from real scenes. *IEEE MultiMedia, 4*(1), 34–47. doi:10.1109/93.580394

Kandell, J. J. (1998). Internet addiction on campus: The vulnerability of college students. *Cyberpsychology & Behavior, 1*(1), 11–17. doi:10.1089/cpb.1998.1.11

Kang, J., & Naughton, J. F. (2003). On schema matching with opaque column names and data values. In *Proceedings of the 2003 ACM SIGMOD International Conference on Management of Data* (pp. 205-216).

Kang, D. (2007). Categorizing post-deployment IT changes: an empirical investigation. *Journal of Database Management, 18*(2), 1–24.

Kang, J., & Naughton, J. F. (2008). Schema matching using interattribute dependencies. *IEEE Transactions on Knowledge and Data Engineering, 20*(10), 1393–1407. doi:10.1109/TKDE.2008.100

Kappelman, L., & McLean, E. (1991). The Respective Roles of User Participation and User Involvement in Information Systems Implementation Success. *International Conference on Information Systems*, New York (pp. 339-348).

Karahanna, E., Straub, D. W., & Chervany, N. L. (1999). Information Technology Adoption Across Time: Cross-Sectional Comparison of Pre-Adoption and Post-Adoption Beliefs. *MIS Quarterly, 23*(2), 183–213. doi:10.2307/249751

Karmarkar, U. (2004). Will You Survive the Services Revolution? *Harvard Business Review, 82*(6), 100–107.

Katz, E., Blumler, J., & Gurevitch, M. (1974). *The Use of Mass Communication*. Beverly Hills, CA: Sage.

Kauffman, R., & Mohtadi, H. (2004). Proprietary and open systems adoption in E-Procurement: A risk-augmented transaction cost perspective. *Journal of Management Information Systems, 21*(1), 137–166.

Kaushik, R., Shenoy, P., Bohannon, P., & Gudes, E. (2002). Exploiting Local Similarity for Indexing of Paths in Graph-Structured Data. In *Proceedings of International Conference on Data Engineering* (pp. 129-140).

Kazmer, M. M. (2007). Beyond C U L8R: Disengaging from online social worlds . *New Media & Society, 9*(1), 111–138. doi:10.1177/1461444807072215

Kearns, M. (1993). Efficient noise-tolerant learning from statistical queries. In *Proceedings of the 25th Annual ACM Symposium on Theory of Computing* (pp. 392-401).

Kearns, M., & Li, M. (1993). Learning in the presence of malicious errors. *SIAM Journal on Computing, 22*(4). doi:10.1137/0222052

Kedad, Z., & Bouzeghoub, M. (1999). Discovering View Expressions from a Multi-Source Information Systems. *In Proceedings of International Conference on Cooperative Information Systems (CoopIS)*, 57-68.

Kedad, Z., & Xue, X. (2005). Mapping Discovery for XML Data Integration. In *Proceedings of International Conference on Cooperative Information Systems (CoopIS)* (pp. 166-182).

Keeling, K., Mcgoldrick, P., & Beatty, S. (2007). Virtual onscreen assistants: A viable strategy to support online customer relationship building? *Advances in Consumer Research. Association for Consumer Research (U. S.), 34*, 138–144.

Keeney, R. L. (1999). The value of Internet commerce to the customer. *Management Science, 15*(4), 533–542. doi:10.1287/mnsc.45.4.533

Keil, M. (1995). Pulling the Plug: Software Project Management and the Problem of Project Escalation. *MIS Quarterly, 19*(4), 421–447. doi:10.2307/249627

Keil, M., Mann, J., & Rai, A. (2000). Why Software Projects Escalate: An Empirical Analysis and Test of Four Theoretical Models. *MIS Quarterly, 24*(4), 631–664. doi:10.2307/3250950

Keil, M., & Robey, D. (1999). Turning Around Troubled Software Projects: An Exploratory Study of the De-escalation of Commitment to Failing Courses of Action. *Journal of Management Information Systems, 15*(4), 63–87.

Keller, K. L. (1993). Conceptualizing, measuring, and managing customer brand equity. *Journal of Marketing, 57*(1), 1–30. doi:10.2307/1252054

Keller, K. L. (1998). *Strategic brand management: Building, measuring and managing brand equity.* Upper Saddle River, NJ: Prentice Hall.

Kelley, H. H., Berscheid, E., Christensen, A., Harvey, J. H., Huston, T. L., & Levinger, G. (1983). *Close relationships.* New York: W.H. Freeman.

Kelly, R. V. (2004). *Massively Multiplayer Online Role-Playing Games: The people, the addiction, and the playing experience.* Jefferson, NC: McFarland & Company.

Kent, W. (1978). *Data and Reality.* Amsterdam, The Netherlands: North-Holland.

Keppel, G., & Wickens, T. D. (2004). *Design and Analysis: A Researcher's Handbook.* Upper Saddle River, NJ: Pearson Prentice Hall.

Khoumbati, K., Themistocleous, M., & Irani, Z. (2006). Evaluating the adoption of enterprise application integration in health-care organizations. *Journal of Management Information Systems, 22*(4), 69–108. doi:10.2753/MIS0742-1222220404

Kiepuszewski, B., Hofstede, A. H. M., & Bussler, C. (2000). On Structured Workflow Modeling. In *Proceedings of CAiSE'2000* (LNCS 1797).

Kiepuszewski, B., ter Hofstede, A. H. M., & van der Aalst, W. M. P. (2003). Fundamentals of control flow in workflows. *Acta Informatica, 39*(3), 143–209. doi:10.1007/s00236-002-0105-4

Kim, D. J., Ferrin, D. L., & Rao, H. R. (2009). Trust and satisfaction, two stepping stones for successful e-commerce relationships: A longitudinal exploration. *Information Systems Research, 20*(2), 237–257. doi:10.1287/isre.1080.0188

Kim, D. K., France, R. B., & Ghosh, S. (2004). A UML-based language for specifying domain-specific patterns. *Journal of Visual Languages and Computing, 15*(3-4), 265–289. doi:10.1016/j.jvlc.2004.01.004

Kim, E. J., Namkoong, K., Ku, T., & Kim, S. J. (2008). The relationship between online game addiction and aggression, self-control, and narcissistic personality traits. *European Psychiatry, 23*(3), 212–218. doi:10.1016/j.eurpsy.2007.10.010

Kim, H. W., & Kankanhalli, A. (2009). Investigating user resistance to information systems implementation: a status quo bias perspective. *Management Information Systems Quarterly, 33*(3), 567–582.

Kim, J.-H., Kim, M., & Lennon, S. J. (2009). Effects of web site atmospherics on consumer responses: Music and product presentation. *Direct Marketing, 3*(1), 4–19. doi:10.1108/17505930910945705

Kim, J., Lee, J., Han, K., & Lee, M. (2002). Businesses as buildings: metrics for the architectural quality of Internet businesses. *Information Systems Research, 13*(3), 239–254. doi:10.1287/isre.13.3.239.79

Kim, K. H., Park, J. Y., Kim, D. Y., Moon, H. I., & Chun, H. C. (2002). E-lifestyle and motives to use online games. *Irish Marketing Review, 15*(2), 71–77.

Kim, K. K. (1989). User satisfaction: A synthesis of three different perspectives. *The Journal of Information Systems, 4*(1), 1–12.

Kim, M., & Lennon, S. (2008). The effects of visual and verbal information on attitudes and purchase intentions in internet shopping. *Psychology and Marketing, 25*(2), 146–178. doi:10.1002/mar.20204

Kim, S. S. (2009). The integrative framework of technology use: an extension and test. *Management Information Systems Quarterly, 33*(3), 513–537.

Kim, Y. J. (2007). An exploratory study of social factors influencing virtual community members' satisfaction with avatars. *Communications of the Association for Information Systems, 20*, 1–44.

Kim, Y. Y., Oh, S., & Lee, H. (2005). What makes people experience flow? Social characteristics of online games. *International Journal of Advanced Media and Communication, 1*(1), 76–92. doi:10.1504/IJAMC.2005.007724

King, W. R. (2006). The Critical Role of Information Processing in Creating An Effective Knowledge Organization. *Journal of Database Management, 17*(1), 1–15.

King, W. R., & Teo, T. S. H. (1997). Integration between business planning and information systems planning: Validating a stage hypothesis. *Decision Sciences, 28*(2), 279–308. doi:10.1111/j.1540-5915.1997.tb01312.x

Klein, L. R. (2003). Creating virtual product experiences: The role of telepresence. *Journal of Interactive Marketing, 17*(1), 41–55. doi:10.1002/dir.10046

Klimmt, C. (2009). Key dimensions of contemporary video game literacy: Towards a normative model of the competent digital gamer. *Journal for Computer Game Culture, 3*(1), 23–31.

Klyne, G., & Carroll, J. J. (2003). *Resource Description Framework (RDF): Concepts and Abstract Syntax*. Retrieved from http://www.w3.org/ TR/rdf-concepts

Knublauch, H., & Rose, T. (2000). Round-Trip Engineering of Ontologies for Knowledge-based Systems. In *Proceedings of the Twelfth International Conference on Software Engineering and Knowledge Engineering (SEKE)* (pp. 239-247).

Koch, C., Scherzinger, S., & Schmidt, M. (2007). The GCX System: Dynamic Buffer Minimization in Streaming Xquery Evaluation. In *Proceedings of the VLDB Conference* (pp. 1378-1381).

Koch, S., & Neumann, C. (2008). Exploring the Effects of Process Characteristics on Product Quality in Open Source Software Development. *Journal of Database Management, 19*(2), 31–57.

Kongdenfha, W., Benatallah, B., Vayssière, V., Saint-Paul, R., & Casati, F. (2009). Rapid development of spreadsheet-based web mashups. In *Proceedings of the 18th International Conference on the World Wide Web* (pp. 851-860).

Korzaan, M. L. (2003). Going with the flow: Predicting online purchase intentions. *Journal of Computer Information Systems, 43*(4), 25–31.

Koufaris, M. (2002). Applying the technology acceptance model and flow theory to online consumer behavior. *Information Systems Research, 13*(2), 205–223. doi:10.1287/isre.13.2.205.83

Krotoski, A., Cezanne, P., Rymaszewski, M., Rossignol, J., & Au, W. J. (2008). *Second Life: The Official Guide* (2nd ed.). New York: Wiley.

Kücklich, J. (2007, September 24-28). MMOGs and the Future of Literature. In *Situated Play: Proceedings of [Digital Games Research Association] DiGRA 2007 Conference*, Tokyo (pp. 319- 326).

Kumaran, S. (2004). *Model Driven Enterprise*. Paper presented at the Global Integration Summit 2004, Banff, Canada.

Kumaran, S., Liu, R., & Wu, F. Y. (2008). On the Duality of Information-Centric and Activity-Centric Models of Business Processes. In *Proceedings of the 20th International Conference on Advanced Information Systems Engineering (CAiSE '08)* (LNCS 5074, pp. 32-47).

Kumaran, S., Nandi, P., Heath, T., Bhaskaran, K., & Das, R. (2003). A Doc-oriented programming. In *Proceedings of the Symposium on Applications and the Internet (SAINT)* (pp. 334-343).

Kumar, S., Chhugani, J., Kim, C., Kim, D., Nguyen, A., & Dubey, P. (2008). Second Life and the New Generation of Virtual Worlds. *Computer, 41*(9), 46–53. doi:10.1109/MC.2008.398

Kung, C., & Solvberg, A. (1986). Activity modelling and behavior modelling of information systems. In T. W. Olle, H. G. Sol, & A. A. Verrijn-Stuart, A. A. (Eds.), *Information Systems Design Methodologies: Improving the Practice*. Amsterdam, The Netherlands: North-Holland.

Kurdek, L. A. (2000). Attractions and constraints as determinants of relationship commitment: Longitudinal evidence from gay, lesbian, and heterosexual couples. *Personal Relationships, 7*(3), 245–262. doi:10.1111/j.1475-6811.2000.tb00015.x

Küster, J. M., Ryndina, K., & Gall, H. (2007). Generation of Business Process Models for Object Life Cycle Compliance. In *Proceedings of the 5th International Conference on Business Process Management (BPM 2007)* (LNCS 4714, pp. 165-181).

Kwahk, K. Y., Kim, H. W., & Chan, H. C. (2007). A knowledge integration approach for organizational decision support. *Journal of Database Management, 18*(2), 41–61.

Kwan, M. M., & Cheung, P. K. (2006). The knowledge transfer process: From field studies to technology development. *Journal of Database Management, 17*(1), 16–32.

Kwon, T. H., & Zmud, R. W. (1987). Unifying the fragmented models of information systems implementations. In Boland, R., & Hirschheim, R. (Eds.), *Critical Issues in Information Systems Research* (pp. 227–252). Chichester, UK: John Wiley & Sons, Ltd.

Laarni, J., Simola, J., Kojo, I., & Risto, N. (2004). Reading vertical text from a computer screen. *Behaviour & Information Technology, 23*(2), 75–82. doi:10.1080/01449290310001648260

Lacity, M., & Hirschheim, R. (1993). *Information systems out-sourcing myths, metaphors, and realities.* New York: John Wiley & Sons, Ltd.

Lacity, M., & Willcocks, L. P. (2001). *Global information technology outsourcing: in search of business advantage.* New York: John Wiley & Sons, Ltd.

Lafayette, J. (2007). Life's a virtual beach for Pepsi. *Television Week, 26*(17), 29–30.

Lam, W. Y., Ng, W., Wood, P. T., & Levene, M. (2003). *XCQ: XML Compression and Querying System.* Paper presented at the International WWW Conference.

Lam, S. Y., Chau, A. W.-L., & Wong, T. J. (2007). Thumbnails as online product displays: How consumers process them. *Journal of Interactive Marketing, 21*(1), 36–59. doi:10.1002/dir.20073

Lance, C. E., & Vandenberg, R. J. (2008). *Statistical and methodological myths and urban legends: Doctrine, verity, and fable in organizational and social sciences.* London: Taylor & Francis.

Lanthier, R. P., & Windham, R. G. (2004). Internet use and college adjustment: The moderating role of gender. *Computers in Human Behavior, 20*(5), 591–606. doi:10.1016/j.chb.2003.11.003

Laoutaris, N., Telelis, O., Zissimopoulos, V., & Stavrakakis, I. (2006). Distributed selfish replication. *IEEE Transactions on Parallel and Distributed Systems, 17*(12), 1401–1413. doi:10.1109/TPDS.2006.171

Lassen, K. B., & van der Aalst, W. M. P. (2009). Complexity metrics for workflow nets. *Information and Software Technology, 51*, 610–626. doi:10.1016/j.infsof.2008.08.005

Lauder, A., & Kent, S. (1998). Precise Visual Specification of Design Patterns. In E. Jul (Ed.), *ECOOP '98 – Object Oriented Programming* (LNCS 1445, pp. 114-136). Berlin-Heidelberg, Germany: Springer.

Lawrence, M., & Low, G. (1993). Exploring Individual User Satisfaction within User-Led Development. *MIS Quarterly, 17*(2), 195–208. doi:10.2307/249801

Le, B., & Agnew, C. R. (2003). Commitment and its theorized determinants: A meta-analysis of the investment model. *Personal Relationships, 10*(1), 37–57. doi:10.1111/1475-6811.00035

Lederer, A. L., & Mendelow, A. L. (1989). Coordination of information systems plans with business plans. *Journal of Management Information Systems, 6*(2), 5–19.

Lederer, A., & Mendelow, A. (1986). Issues in information systems planning. *Information & Management, 10*(5), 245–254. doi:10.1016/0378-7206(86)90027-3

Lee, A., Nica, A., & Rundensteiner, E. (2002). The EVE Approach: View Synchronization in Dynamic Distributed Environment. *IEEE Transactions on Knowledge and Data Engineering, 14*(5), 931–954. doi:10.1109/TKDE.2002.1033766

Lee, D. M. S., Trauth, E. M., & Farwell, D. (1995). Critical skills and knowledge requirements of IT professionals: a joint academic/industry investigation. *Management Information Systems Quarterly, 19*(3), 313–340. doi:10.2307/249598

Lee, J., & Truex, D. P. (2000). Exploring the impact of formal training in ISD methods on the cognitive structure of novice information systems developers. *Information Systems Journal, 10*(4), 347–367. doi:10.1046/j.1365-2575.2000.00086.x

Lee, M. S., Ko, Y. H., Song, H. S., Kwon, K. H., Lee, H. S., & Nam, M. (2007). Characteristics of Internet use in relation to game genre in Korean adolescents. *Cyberpsychology & Behavior, 10*(2), 278–285. doi:10.1089/cpb.2006.9958

Lee, Y., Sayyadian, M., Doan, A., & Rosenthal, A. S. (2007). eTuner: tuning schema matching software using synthetic scenarios. *The VLDB Journal, 16*(1), 97–122. doi:10.1007/s00778-006-0024-z

Leff, A., Wolf, J. L., & Yu, P. S. (1993). Replication algorithms in a remote caching architecture. *IEEE Transactions on Parallel and Distributed Systems, 4*(11), 1185–1204. doi:10.1109/71.250099

Leggatt, H. (2007, March 29). Second Life citizens want engaging marketing and brands. *BizReport*. Retrieved September 14, 2008, from http://www.bizreport.com/2007/03/ second_life_citizens_want_engaging_marketing_and_brands.html

Lehtinen, O. (1974). A brand choice model: Theoretical framework and empirical results. *Journal of European Research, 2*, 51–68.

Leidner, D. E., & Jarvenpaa, S. L. (1995). The use of information technology to enhance management school education: A theoretical view. *Management Information Systems Quarterly, 19*(3), 265–291. doi:10.2307/249596

Lenzerini, M. (2002). Data Integration: A Theoretical Perspective. In *Proceedings of the ACM Symposium on Principles of Database Systems (PODS)* (pp. 233-246).

Leonard, D., & Sensiper, S. (1998). The Role of Tacit Knowledge in Group Innovation. *California Management Review, 40*(3), 112–132.

Leung, L. (2004). Net-generation attributes and seductive properties of the Internet as predictors of online activities and Internet addiction. *Cyberpsychology & Behavior, 7*(3), 333–348. doi:10.1089/1094931041291303

Levina, N., & Ross, J. W. (2003). From the vendor's perspective: exploring the value proposition in information technology outsourcing. *Management Information Systems Quarterly, 27*(3), 331–364.

Levy, A. Y., Srivastava, D., & Kirk, T. (1996). Data Model and Query Evaluation in Global Information Systems. *Journal of Intelligent Information Systems, 5*(2), 121–143. doi:10.1007/BF00962627

Lewis, J. (2007, April 17). Coke Expands Viral Marketing Efforts Online. *WebProNews*. Retrieved September 14, 2008, from http://www.webpronews.com/topnews/2007/04/17/coke-expands-viral-marketing-efforts-online

Lewis, P. M., Bernstein, A. J., & Kifer, M. (2001). *Databases and transaction processing: An application-oriented approach*. Reading, MA: Addison-Wesley.

Leymann, F., & Roller, D. (2000). *Production workflow: concepts and techniques*. Upper Saddle River, NJ: Prentice Hall.

Liang, H., Saraf, N., Hu, Q., & Xue, Y. (2007). Assimilation of enterprise systems: The effect of institutional pressures and the mediating role of top management. *Management Information Systems Quarterly, 31*(1), 59–87.

Liang, H., & Xue, Y. (2009). Avoidance of information technology threats: A theoretical perspectives. *Management Information Systems Quarterly, 33*(1), 71–90.

Liang, T. P., Lai, H. J., & Ku, Y. C. (2006). Personalized Content Recommendation and User Satisfaction: Theoretical Synthesis and Empirical Findings. *Journal of Management Information Systems, 23*(3), 45. doi:10.2753/MIS0742-1222230303

Lichtash, A. E. (2004). Inappropriate use of e-mail and the Internet in the workplace: The arbitration picture. *Dispute Resolution Journal, 59*(1), 26–36.

Li, D., & Browne, G. J. (2006). The role of need for cognition and mood in online flow experience. *Journal of Computer Information Systems, 46*(3), 11–17.

Liefke, H., & Suciu, D. (2000). XMill: An Efficient Compressor for XML Data. In *Proceedings of the ACM SIGMOD Conference* (pp. 153-164).

Linden Lab. (2010). *What is teen Second Life?* Retrieved from http://teen.secondlife.com/whatis

Linden Research Inc. (2009, December 8). *Economic statistics*. Retrieved from http://secondlife.com/whatis/economy_stats.php

Lindland, O. I., Sindre, G., & Solvberg, A. (1994). Understanding quality in conceptual modeling. *IEEE Software, 11*(2), 42–49. doi:10.1109/52.268955

Li, S. S., Huang, S. M., Yen, D. C., & Chang, C. C. (2007). Migrating legacy information systems to Web services architecture. *Journal of Database Management, 18*(4), 1–25.

Li, S., Huang, S., Yen, D. C., & Chang, C. (2007). Migrating Legacy Information Systems to Web Service Architecture. *Journal of Database Management, 18*(4), 1–25.

Liu, R., Bhattacharya, K., & Wu, F. Y. (2007). *Modeling Business Contexture and Behavior Using Business Artifacts.* Paper presented at the 19th International Conference on Advanced Information Systems Engineering (CAiSE'07).

Liu, R., Wu, F. Y., Patnaik, Y., & Kumaran, S. (2009). *Business Entities: An SOA Approach to Progressive Core Banking Renovation.* Paper presented at the IEEE International Conference on Services Computing (SCC 2009).

Liu, S., & Chu, W. (2007). CoXML: A Cooperative XML Query Answering System. In *APWeb/WAIM 2007* (LNCS 4505, pp. 614-621).

Liu, Z. L., & Chu, W. W. (2005). *Knowledge-Based Query Expansion to Support Scenario-Specific Retrieval of Medical Free Text.* Paper presented at ACM SAC.

Liu, D., Wang, J., Chan, S., Sun, J., & Zhang, L. (2002). Modeling workflow processes with colored Petri nets. *Computers in Industry, 49,* 267–281. doi:10.1016/S0166-3615(02)00099-4

Liu, L., Pu, C., & Ruiz, D. D. (2004). A systematic Approach to Flexible Specification, Composition, and Restructuring of Workflow Activities. *Journal of Database Management, 15*(1), 1–40.

Li, W. S., & Clifton, C. (2000). SEMINT: a tool for identifying attribute correspondences in heterogeneous databases using neural networks. *Data & Knowledge Engineering, 33*(1), 49–84. doi:10.1016/S0169-023X(99)00044-0

Lohse, G. L. (1997). Consumer eye movement patterns on yellow pages advertising. *Journal of Advertising, 26*(1), 62–74.

Lohse, G. L., & Spiller, P. (1998). Electronic shopping. *Communications of the ACM, 41*(7), 81–87. doi:10.1145/278476.278491

Lok, B. C. (2004). Toward the merging of real and virtual spaces. *Communications of the ACM, 47*(8), 48–53. doi:10.1145/1012037.1012061

Lombard, M., & Ditton, T. (1997). At the heart of it all: The concept of presence. *Journal of Computer Mediated Communication, 3*(2). Retrieved September 14, 2008, from http://jcmc.indiana.edu/vol3/ issue2/lombard.html

Long, Y., & Siau, K. (2007). Social Network Structures in Open Source Software Development Teams. *Journal of Database Management, 18*(2), 25–40.

Lo, S. K., Wang, C. C., & Fang, W. (2005). Physical interpersonal relationships and social anxiety among online game players. *Cyberpsychology & Behavior, 8*(1), 15–20. doi:10.1089/cpb.2005.8.15

Lu, H., Fan, W., Goh, C. H., Madnick, S. E., & Cheng, D. W. (1997). Discovering and reconciling semantic conflicts: a data mining perspective. In *Proceedings of the IFIP Working Conference on Data Semantics (DS-7)* (pp. 410-427).

Ludascher, B., Mukhopadhyay, P., & Papakonstantinou, Y. (2002). A Transducer-based XML Query Processor. In *Proceedings of the VLDB Conference* (pp. 227-238)

Luftman, J., Papp, R., & Brier, T. (1999). Enablers and inhibitors of business-IT alignment. *Communication of AIS, 1*(11).

Luna, D., Peracchio, L. A., & de Juan, M. D. (2002). Cross-cultural and cognitive aspects of Web site navigation. *Journal of the Academy of Marketing Science, 30*(4), 397–410. doi:10.1177/009207002236913

Luna, D., Peracchio, L. A., & de Juan, M. D. (2003). Flow in individual Web sites: Model estimation and cross-cultural validation. *Advances in Consumer Research. Association for Consumer Research (U. S.), 30,* 280–281.

Lussier, D. A., & Olshavsky, R. W. (1979). Task complexity and contingent processing in brand choice. *The Journal of Consumer Research, 6*(2), 154–165. doi:10.1086/208758

MacKinnon, D. P., Krull, J. L., & Lockwood, C. M. (2000). Equivalence of the mediation, confounding and suppression effects. *Prevention Science, 1*(4), 173–181. doi:10.1023/A:1026595011371

MacKinnon, D. P., Lockwood, C. M., Hoffman, J. M., West, S. G., & Sheets, V. (2002). A comparison of methods to test mediation and other intervening variable effects. *Psychological Methods, 7*(1), 83–104. doi:10.1037/1082-989X.7.1.83

Madhavan, J., Bernstein, P., Doan, A., & Halevy, A. (2005). Corpus-based schema matching. In *Proceedings of the 18th International Conference on Data Engineering* (pp. 57-68).

Madhavan, J., Bernstein, P., Domingos, P., & Halevy, A. (2002). Representing and reasoning about mappings between domain models. In *Proceedings of Eighteenth National Conference on American Association Artificial Intelligence* (pp. 80-86).

Mafé, C. R., & Blas, S. S. (2006). Explaining Internet dependency: An exploratory study of future purchase intention of Spanish Internet users. *Internet Research, 16*(4), 380–397. doi:10.1108/10662240610690016

Magal, S. R. (1991). A model for evaluating information center success. *Journal of Management Information Systems, 8*(1), 91–106.

Mak, J. K. H., Choy, C. S. T., & Lun, D. P. K. (2004). Precise Modeling of Design Patterns in UML. In A. Finkelstein, J. Estublier, & D. S. Rosenblum (Eds.), *Proceedings of the 26ᵗʰ International Conference on Software Engineering (ICSE'04)* (pp. 252-261). Washington, DC: IEEE Computer Society.

Malhotra, N., Kim, S., & Patil, A. (2006). Common method variance in IS research: A comparison of alternative approaches and a reanalysis of past research. *Management Science, 52*(12), 1865–1883. doi:10.1287/mnsc.1060.0597

Manola, F., & Miller, E. (2004). *RDF Primer*. Retrieved from http://www.w3.org/TR/ rdf-primer/.

Mao, W., & Chu, W. (2007). The phrase-based vector space model for automatic retrieval of free-text medical documents. *Data & Knowledge Engineering, 61*(1), 76–92. doi:10.1016/j.datak.2006.02.008

Mapelsden, D., Hosking, J., & Grundy, J. (2002). Design Pattern Modeling and Instantiation using DPML. In J. Noble & J. Potter (Eds.), *Proceeding of TOOLS Pacific 2002 – Objects for Internet, Mobile and Embedded Applications. Conference in Research and Practice in Information Technology* (Vol. 10, pp. 3-11). Darlinghurst, Australia: ACS.

Ma, Q., Pearson, J. M., & Tadisina, S. (2005). An exploratory study into factors of service quality for Application Service Providers. *Information & Management, 42*(8), 1067–1080. doi:10.1016/j.im.2004.11.007

March, J. G. (1991). Exploration and exploitation in organizational learning. *Organization Science, 2*(1), 71–87. doi:10.1287/orsc.2.1.71

March, S. T., Hevner, A., & Ram, S. (2000). Research commentary: an agenda for information technology research in heterogeneous and distributed environments. *Information Systems Research, 11*(4), 327–341. doi:10.1287/isre.11.4.327.11873

Marcoulides, G. A., & Saunders, C. (2006). PLS: A silver bullet? *Management Information Systems Quarterly, 30*(2), i–vi.

Markus, M. L., & Robey, D. (1988). Information Technology and Organizational Change: Causal Structure in Theory and Research. *Management Science, 34*(5), 583–598. doi:10.1287/mnsc.34.5.583

Marshall, B., Chen, H., & Madhusudan, T. (2006). Matching knowledge elements in concept maps using a similarity flooding algorithm. *Decision Support Systems, 42*(3), 1290–1306. doi:10.1016/j.dss.2005.10.009

Más, M. (2000). *Statistical data protection techniques*. Retrieved from http://www.eustat.es/document/ datos/ct_02_i.pdf

Maximilien, E. M., Ranabahu, A., & Gomadam, K. (2008). An Online Platform for Web APIs and Service Mashups. *IEEE Internet Computing, 12*(5), 32–43. doi:10.1109/MIC.2008.92

Maximilien, E. M., & Singh, M. P. (2004). A framework and ontology for dynamic web services selection. *IEEE Internet Computing, 8*(5), 84–93. doi:10.1109/MIC.2004.27

Mayer, R. (1989). Models for Understanding. *Review of Educational Research, 59*(1), 43–64.

Mayer, R. E., & Gallini, J. K. (1990). When is an illustration worth ten thousand words? *Journal of Educational Psychology, 82*(4), 715–726. doi:10.1037/0022-0663.82.4.715

McCann, R., AlShebli, B., Le, Q., Nguyen, H., Vu, L., & Doan, A. (2005). Maveric: Mapping Maintenance for Data Integration Systems. In *Proceedings of International Conference on Very Large Databases (VLDB)* (pp. 1018-1029).

McConnell, S. (1996). *Rapid Development*. Redmond, WA: Microsoft Press.

McDonald, S. C. (1997). The once and future web; Scenarios for advertisers. *Journal of Advertising Research*, *37*(2), 21–28.

McDowell, W., & Sutherland, J. (2000). Choice versus chance: Using brand equity theory to explore TV audience lead-in effects, a case study. *Journal of Media Economics*, *13*(4), 233–247. doi:10.1207/S15327736ME1304_3

McGee, M. K. (2008). Hospital takes its grand opening to Second Life. *InformationWeek*. Retrieved February 25, 2008, from http://www.informationweek.com/news/internet/ebusiness/showArticle.jhtml? articleID=206801783

McGrath, J. E. (1984). *Groups: Interaction and Performance*. Englewood Cliffs, NJ: Prentice-Hall.

McGrath, M. B., & Brown, J. R. (2005). Visual learning for science and engineering. *IEEE Computer Graphics and Applications*, *25*(5), 56–63. doi:10.1109/MCG.2005.117

McGuinness, D. L., & v. Harmelen, F. (2004). *OWL Web Ontology Language Overview*. Retrieved from http://www.w3c.org/ TR/owl-features

McGuinness, D., Smith, K., & Welty, C. (2004). *OWL Web Ontology Language Guide*. Retrieved from http://www.w3.org/TR/owl-guide/

McKeen, J. D., & Guimaraes, T. (1997). Successful strategies for user participation in systems development. *Journal of Management Information Systems*, *14*(2), 133–150.

McKeen, J. D., Guimaraes, T., & Wetherbe, J. C. (1994). The Relationship Between User Participation and User Satisfaction: An Investigation of Four Contingency Factors. *MIS Quarterly*, , 427–451. doi:10.2307/249523

McKnight, D. H., Choudhury, V., & Kacmar, C. (2002). Developing and validating trust measures for e-commerce: an integrative typology. *Information Systems Research*, *13*(3), 334–359. doi:10.1287/isre.13.3.334.81

Mears, J. (2001). Net provider sold on ASP model. *New World (New Orleans, La.)*, *18*(14), 29–30.

Melnik, S., Garcia-Molina, H., & Rahm, E. (2002). Similarity flooding: a versatile graph matching algorithm and its application to schema matching. In *Proceedings of the International Conference on Data Engineering (ICDE)* (pp. 117-128).

Melone, N. A. (1990). Theoretical Assessment of the User-Satisfaction Construct in Information Systems Research. *Management Science*, *36*(1), 76–91. doi:10.1287/mnsc.36.1.76

Mena, E., Illarramendi, A., Kashyap, V., & Sheth, A. P. (1996). OBSERVER: An approach for query processing in global information systems based on interoperation across pre-existing ontologies. In . *Proceedings of CoopIS*, *96*, 14–25.

Mendling, J. (2007). *Detection and Prediction of Errors in EPC Business Process Models*. Unpublished PhD thesis, Vienna University of Economics and Business Administration.

Mendling, J., Reijers, H. A., & Cardoso, J. (2007). What Makes Process Models Understandable? In *Proceedings of the 5th International Conference on Business Process Management (BPM 2007)* (LNCS 4714, pp. 48-63).

Mendling, J., & Strembeck, M. (2008). Influence Factors of Understanding Business Process Models. *Business Information Systems.* (*LNBIP*, *7*, 142–153.

Mennecke, B. E., Mcneill, D., Ganis, M., Roche, E. M., Bray, D. A., & Konsynski, B. (2008). Second Life and other virtual worlds: A roadmap for research. *Communications of the Association for Information Systems*, *22*, 371–388.

Mennecke, B. E., Triplett, J., Hassall, L. M., Jordan, Z., & Heer, R. (forthcoming). An examination of the development of embodied social presence during team interaction and collaboration in virtual worlds. *Decision Sciences*.

Messinger, P. R., Stroulia, E., Lyons, K., Bone, M., Niu, R., & Smirnov, K. (2009). Virtual worlds—past, present, and future: New directions in social computing. *Decision Support Systems*, *47*(3), 204–228. doi:10.1016/j.dss.2009.02.014

Mikropoulos, T. A., & Strouboulis, V. (2004). Factors that influence presence in educational virtual environments. *Cyberpsychology & Behavior*, *7*(5), 582–591.

Miller, R. J., Haas, L. M., & Hernandez, M. A. (2000). Schema Mapping as Query Discovery. In *Proceedings of the 26th International Conference on Very Large Data Bases* (pp. 77-88).

Miller, G. A. (1956). The magical number seven plus or minus two: Some limits on our capacity for processing information. *Psychological Review*, *63*, 81–97. doi:10.1037/h0043158

Milner, R., Parrow, J., & Walker, D. (1992). A calculus of mobile processes. *Information and Computation*, *100*(100), 1–40. doi:10.1016/0890-5401(92)90008-4

Milo, T., & Zohar, S. (1998). Using Schema Matching to Simplify Heterogeneous Data Translation. In *Proceedings of International Conference on Very Large Data Bases (VLDB)* (pp. 122-133).

Milton, S. (2000). *An Ontological Comparison and Evaluation of Data Modelling Frameworks.* Unpublished doctoral dissertation, University of Tasmania, Hobart.

Milton, S., & Kazmierczak, E. (2004). An Ontology of Data Modelling Languages: A Study Using a Common-Sense Realistic Ontology. *Journal of Database Management*, *15*(2), 19–38.

Min, J.-K., Park, M.-J., & Chung, C.-W. (2003). XPRESS: A Queriable Compression for XML Data. In *Proceedings of the ACM SIGMOD Conference* (pp. 122-133).

Minker, J. (1998). An Overview of Cooperative Answering in Databases. In *Proceedings of Flexible Query Answering Systems* (LNCS 1495, pp. 614-621).

Minocha, S., & Roberts, D. (2008). Laying the groundwork for socialisation and knowledge construction within 3D virtual worlds. *ALT-J Research in Learning Technology*, *16*(3), 181–196.

Miranda, S. M., & Kim, Y. M. (2006). Professional versus political contexts: institutional mitigation and the transaction cost heuristic in information systems outsourcing. *Management Information Systems Quarterly*, *30*(3), 725–753.

Mohania, M., & Dong, G. (1996). Algorithms for adapting materialized views in data warehouses. In *Proceedings of the International Symposium On Cooperative Database Systems for Advanced Applications* (pp. 62-69).

Moody, D. (2002). *Dealing with complexity: A practical method for representing large entity-relationship models.* Unpublished doctoral dissertation, University of Melbourne.

Moody, D. L., & Shanks, G. (1998). Improving the quality of entity-relationship models: An action research programme. *The Australian Computer Journal*, *30*, 129–138.

Moore, G. C., & Benbasat, I. (1991). Development of an instrument to measure the perception of adoption an information technology innovation. *Information Systems Research*, *2*(3), 192–222. doi:10.1287/isre.2.3.192

Morahan-Martin, J., & Schumacher, P. (2000). Incidence and correlates of pathological Internet use. *Computers in Human Behavior*, *16*(1), 13–29. doi:10.1016/S0747-5632(99)00049-7

Mori, M. (1970). The uncanny valley. *Energy*, *7*(4), 33–35.

Moro, M., Bakalov, P., & Tsotras, V. J. (2007). Early Profile Pruning on XML-aware Publish-Subscribe Systems. In *Proceedings of the VLDB Endowment* (pp. 866-877).

Mossholder, K. W., Bennett, N., Kemery, E. R., & Wesolowski, M. A. (1998). Relationships between bases of power and work reactions: The mediational role of procedural justice. *Journal of Management*, *24*(4), 533–552. doi:10.1016/S0149-2063(99)80072-5

Motro, A. (1988). VAGUE: A User Interface to Relational Databases that Permits Vague Queries. *ACM Transactions on Office Information Systems*, *6*(3), 187–214. doi:10.1145/45945.48027

Motro, A. (1990). FLEX: A Tolerent and Cooperative User Interface to Databases. *IEEE Transactions on Knowledge and Data Engineering*, *2*(2), 231–246. doi:10.1109/69.54722

Mulpuru, S., Johnson, C., McGowan, B., & Wright, S. (2008). US eCommerce Forecast: 2008 To 2012: B2C eCommerce expected to top $300B in five years. *Forrester Research*.

Mumick, I. S., Quass, D., & Mumick, B. S. (1997). Maintenance of Data Cubes and Summary Tables in a Warehouse. In *Proceedings of ACM SIG Conference on Management of Data* (pp. 100-111).

Mummalaneni, V. (2005). An empirical investigation of Web site characteristics, consumer emotional states and on-line shopping behaviors. *Journal of Business Research, 58*(4), 526–532. doi:10.1016/S0148-2963(03)00143-7

Muralidhar, K., Batra, D., & Kirs, P. J. (1995). Accessibility, security, and accuracy in statistical database: the case for the multiplicative fixed data perturbation approach. *Management Science, 41*(9), 1549–1564. doi:10.1287/mnsc.41.9.1549

Muralidhar, K., Parsa, R., & Sarathy, R. (1999). A general additive data perturbation method for database security. *Management Science, 45*(10), 1399–1415. doi:10.1287/mnsc.45.10.1399

Muralidhar, K., & Sarathy, R. (2006). Data shuffling-A new masking approach for numerical data. *Management Science, 52*(5), 658–670. doi:10.1287/mnsc.1050.0503

Muralidhar, K., & Sarathy, R. (2008). Generating Sufficiency-based Non-Synthetic Perturbed Data. *Transactions on Data Privacy, 1*(1), 17–33.

Muralidhar, K., Sarathy, R., & Dandekar, R. (2006). Why swap when you can shuffle? A comparison of the proximity swap and data shuffle for numeric data . In Domingo-Ferrer, J., & Franconi, L. (Eds.), *Privacy in Statistical Databases* (pp. 164–176). Berlin, Heidelberg: Springer. doi:10.1007/11930242_15

Mylopoulos, J. (1992). Conceptual modeling and telos. In P. Loucopoulos, & R. Zicari (Eds.), *Conceptual modeling, Databases and CASE: An Integrated View of Information Systems* (pp. 49-68). New York: John Wiley & Sons.

Mylopoulos, J. (1998). Information Modeling in the Time of the Revolution. *Information Systems, 23*, 127–155. doi:10.1016/S0306-4379(98)00005-2

Nah, F. F.-H., Hong, W., Chen, L., & Lee, H.-H. (2010). Information search patterns in e-commerce product comparison services. *Journal of Database Management, 21*(2), 26–40.

Nah, F., & Davis, S. (2002). HCI research issues in electronic commerce. *Journal of Electronic Commerce Research, 3*(3), 98–113.

Nah, F., Eschenbrenner, B., DeWester, D., & Park, S. (2010). Impact of flow and brand equity in 3D virtual worlds. *Journal of Database Management, 21*(3), 69–89.

Nah, F., Siau, K., & Tian, Y. (2005). Knowledge Management Mechanisms of Financial Service Sites. *Communications of the ACM, 48*(6), 117–123. doi:10.1145/1064830.1064836

Nah, F., Siau, K., Tian, Y., & Ling, M. (2002). Knowledge Management Mechanisms in E-Commerce: A Study of Online Retailing and Auction Sites. *Journal of Computer Information Systems, 42*(5), 119–128.

Name Watch, S. L. (2009, December 10). *Site statistics.* [Online]. Retrieved December 10, 2009, http://slname-watch.com/

Nandi, P., & Kumaran, S. (2005). Adaptive business objects – a new component model for business integration. In *Proceedings of the International Conference on Enterprise Information Systems* (pp. 179-188).

Nass, C., & Moon, Y. (2000). Machines and mindlessness: Social responses to computers. *The Journal of Social Issues, 56*(1), 81–103. doi:10.1111/0022-4537.00153

Nauman, J. D., Davis, G. B., & McKeen, J. D. (1980). Determining Information Requirements: A Contingency Method for Selection of a Requirements Assurance Strategy. *Journal of Systems and Software, 1*, 273–281. doi:10.1016/0164-1212(79)90029-3

Nel, D., van Niekerk, R., Berthon, J., & Davies, T. (1999). Going with the flow: Web sites and customer involvement. *Internet Research, 9*(2), 109–116. doi:10.1108/10662249910264873

Nestorov, S., Ullman, J., Weiner, J., & Chawathe, S. (1997). Representative Object: Concise Representations of Semi-structured, Hierarchical Data. In *Proceedings of the International Conference on Data Engineering* (pp. 79-90).

Newman, M., & Sabherwal, R. (1989). A Process Model for the Control of Information System Development Projects. In *Proceedings of ICIS* (pp. 185-197).

Ng, A. C. Y., Phillips, D. R., & Lee, W. K.-M. (2002). Persistence and challenges to filial piety and informal support of older persons in a modern Chinese society a case study in Tuen Mun, Hong Kong. *Journal of Aging Studies, 16*(2), 135–153. doi:10.1016/S0890-4065(02)00040-3

Ng, B., & Wiemer-Hastings, P. (2004). Addiction to massively multiplayer online role-playing games. *Annual Review of Cybertherapy and Telemedicine, 2*, 97–101.

Nidumolu, S. (1995). The Effect of Coordination and Uncertainty on Software Project Performance: Residual Performance Risk as an Intervening Variable. *Information Systems Research, 6*(3), 191–219. doi:10.1287/isre.6.3.191

Nigam, A., & Caswell, N. S. (2003). Business artifacts: An approach to operational specification. *IBM Systems Journal, 42*(3), 428–445. doi:10.1147/sj.423.0428

Nijssen, G. M. (1976). *Modelling in Database Management Systems.* Amsterdam: North Holland.

Nilakanta, S., & Scamell, R. W. (1990). The Effect of Information Sources and Communication Channels on the Diffusion of Innovation in a Data Base Development Environment. *Management Science, 36*(1), 24–40. doi:10.1287/mnsc.36.1.24

Noble, J. (1998). Classifying relationships between Object-Oriented Design Patterns. In *Proceedings of the Australian Software Engineering Conference* (pp. 98-108). Washington, DC: IEEE Computer Society.

Northrop, L., Feiler, P., Gabriel, R. P., Goodenough, J., Linger, R., & Longstaff, T. (2006). *Ultra Large Scale Systems. The Software Challenge of the Future. Software Engineering Institute.* Pittsburgh, PA: Carnegie Mellon.

Nottelmanna, H., & Straccia, U. (2007). Information retrieval and machine learning for probabilistic schema matching. *Information Processing & Management, 43*(3), 552–576. doi:10.1016/j.ipm.2006.10.014

Novak, T. P., Hoffman, D. L., & Duhachek, A. (2003). The influence of goal-directed and experiential activities on online flow experiences. *Journal of Consumer Psychology, 13*(1/2), 3–16.

Novak, T. P., Hoffman, D., & Yung, Y. (2000). Measuring the customer experience in online environments: A structural modeling approach. *Marketing Science, 19*(1), 22–44. doi:10.1287/mksc.19.1.22.15184

Nowak, L., Thach, L., & Olsen, J. E. (2006). Wowing the millennials: Creating brand equity in the wine industry. *Journal of Product and Brand Management, 15*(5), 316–323. doi:10.1108/10610420610685712

Nunez, M., Garfinkel, R., & Gopal, R. (2007). Stochastic protection of confidential information in statistical databases: A hybrid of query restriction and data perturbation. *Operations Research, 55*(5), 890–908. doi:10.1287/opre.1070.0407

Nunnally, J. (1978). *Psychometric theory.* New York: McGraw-Hill.

Object Management Group (OMG). (2006). *Business Process Modeling Notation Specification.* Retrieved from http://[REMOVED HYPERLINK FIELD]www.bpmn.org

Object Management Group. (2002). *UML 2.0 Superstructure FTF convenience document.* Retrieved from http://www.omg.org/docs/ ptc/04-10-02.zip

Object Management Group. (2003). *Meta Object Facility (MOF™) version 1.4.* Retrieved from http://www.omg.org/docs/ formal/02-04-03.pdf

Object Venture Inc. (2002). *Pattern and Component Markup Language.* Retrieved from http://www.object-venture.com/ pcml.html

Odell, P. M., Korgen, K., Schumacher, P., & Delucchi, M. (2000). Internet use among female and male college students. *Cyberpsychology & Behavior, 3*(5), 855–862. doi:10.1089/10949310050191836

Ojanpaa, H., Nasanen, R., & Kojo, I. (2002). Eye movements in the visual search of word lists. *Vision Research, 42*(12), 1499–1512. doi:10.1016/S0042-6989(02)00077-9

O'keefe. D. J. (2002). *Persuasion: Theory and research.* Thousand Oaks, CA: SAGE.

Olle, T. W., Sol, H. G., & Tully, C. J. (Eds.). (1983). *Information System Design Methodologies: A Feature Analysis.* Amsterdam, The Netherlands: North-Holland.

Olson, D. L. (2007). Evaluation of ERP outsourcing. *Computers & Operations Research, 34*(12), 3715–3724. doi:10.1016/j.cor.2006.01.010

Olson, G. M., & Olson, J. S. (2003). Human-computer interaction: Psychological aspects of the human use of computing. *Annual Review of Psychology, 54*, 491–516. doi:10.1146/annurev.psych.54.101601.145044

Olteanu, D. (2007). SPEX: Streamed and Progressive Evaluation of XPath. *IEEE Transactions on Knowledge and Data Engineering, 19*(7), 934–949. doi:10.1109/TKDE.2007.1063

Online Computer Library Center. (2007). *Introduction to the Dewey Decimal Classification*. Retrieved from http://www.oclc.org/dewey/about

Opdahl, A., & Henderson-Sellers, B. (2001). Grounding the OML meta-model in ontology. *Journal of Systems and Software, 57*(2), 119–143. doi:10.1016/S0164-1212(00)00123-0

Opdahl, A., & Henderson-Sellers, B. (2002). Ontological evaluation of the UML using the Bunge-Wand-Weber model. *Software and Systems Modeling, 1*(1), 43–67.

Osborne, E., & Schiller, S. (2009). Order and creativity in virtual worlds. *Journal of Virtual Worlds Research, 2*(3), 2–16.

Oz, E., & Sosik, J. J. (2000). Why information systems projects are abandoned: a leadership and communication theory and exploratory study. *Journal of Computer Information Systems, 41*(1), 66–88.

Pace, S. (2004). A grounded theory of the flow experiences of Web users. *International Journal of Human-Computer Studies, 60*(3), 327–363. doi:10.1016/j.ijhcs.2003.08.005

Painton, S., & Gentry, J. W. (1985). Another look at the impact of information presentation. *The Journal of Consumer Research, 12*(2), 240–244. doi:10.1086/208512

Palopoli, L., Pontieri, L., Terracina, G., & Ursino, D. (2000). Intensional and extensional integration and abstraction of heterogeneous databases. *Data & Knowledge Engineering, 35*(3), 201–237. doi:10.1016/S0169-023X(00)00028-8

Papacharissi, Z., & Rubin, A. M. (2000). Predictors of Internet Use. *Journal of Broadcasting & Electronic Media, 44*(2), 175–196. doi:10.1207/s15506878jobem4402_2

Papazoglou, M. (2003). Web services and business transactions. *World Wide Web (Bussum), 6*(1), 49–91. doi:10.1023/A:1022308532661

Papazoglou, M., & Kratz, B. (2007). Web services technology in support of business transactions. *Service Oriented Computing and Applications, 1*(1), 51–63. doi:10.1007/s11761-007-0002-3

Papazoglou, M., Traverso, P., Dustdar, S., & Leymann, F. (2007). Service-oriented computing: State of the art and research directions. *IEEE Computer, 40*(11), 64–71.

Papazoglou, M., & van den Heuvel, W. J. (2007). Service oriented architectures: Approaches, technologies and research issues. *Very Large Database Journal, 16*(3), 389–415. doi:10.1007/s00778-007-0044-3

Parasuraman, A., Zeithaml, V. A., & Berry, L. L. (1985). A conceptual model of Service quality and its implications for future research. *Journal of Marketing, 49*(4), 41–50. doi:10.2307/1251430

Parasuraman, A., Zeithaml, V. A., & Berry, L. L. (1988). SERVQUAL: A multiple-item scale for measuring consumer perceptions of service quality. *Journal of Retailing, 64*(1), 12–40.

Park, C.-S., Kim, C. S., & Chung, Y. D. (2005). Efficient Stream Organization for Wireless Broadcasting of XML Data. In *Proceedings of the Asian Computing Science Conference* (pp. 223-235).

Park, S. H., Choi, J. H., & Lee, S. (2006). An Effective, Efficient XML Data Broadcasting Method in Mobile Wireless Network. In *Proceedings of the DEXA Conference* (pp. 358-367).

Park, J., Stoel, L., & Lennon, S. J. (2008). Cognitive, affective and conative responses to visual simulation: The effects of rotation in online product presentation. *Journal of Consumer Behaviour, 7*(1), 72–87. doi:10.1002/cb.237

Park, S. R., Nah, F. F.-H., DeWester, D., Eschenbrenner, B., & Jeon, S. (2008). Virtual world affordances: Enhancing brand value. *Journal of Virtual Worlds Research, 1*(2), 1–18.

Park, S., Nah, F., DeWester, D., Eschenbrenner, B., & Jeon, S. (2008). Virtual world affordances: Enhancing brand value. *Journal of Virtual Worlds Research, 1*(2), 1–18.

Parsons, J. (1996). An information model based on classification theory. *Management Science, 42*(10), 1437–1453. doi:10.1287/mnsc.42.10.1437

Parsons, J., & Cole, L. (2005). What do the pictures mean? Guidelines for experimental evaluation of representation fidelity in diagrammatical conceptual modelling techniques. *Data & Knowledge Engineering, 55,* 327–342. doi:10.1016/j.datak.2004.12.008

Parsons, J., & Wand, Y. (1997). Using Objects for Systems Analysis. *Communications of the ACM, 40*(12), 104–110. doi:10.1145/265563.265578

Parsons, J., & Wand, Y. (2000). Emancipating instances from the tyranny of classes in information modelling. *ACM Transactions on Database Systems, 25*(2), 228–268. doi:10.1145/357775.357778

Parsons, J., & Wand, Y. (2008a). Using Cognitive Principles to Guide Classification in Information Systems Modeling. *Management Information Systems Quarterly, 32*(4), 839–868.

Parsons, J., & Wand, Y. (2008b). A question of class. *Nature, 455,* 1040–1041. doi:10.1038/4551040a

Pawlak, C. (2002). Correlates of Internet use and addiction in adolescents. *Dissertation Abstracts International, Section A: Humanities and Social Sciences, 63*(5-A), 1727.

Payne, J. W. (1976). Task complexity and contingent processing in decision making: An information search and protocol analysis. *Organizational Behavior and Human Performance, 16*(2), 366–387. doi:10.1016/0030-5073(76)90022-2

Payne, J. W., Bettman, J. R., & Johnson, E. J. (1993). *The Adaptive Decision Maker.* New York: Cambridge University Press.

Peng, F., & Chawathe, S. S. (2003). XPath Queries on Streaming Data. In *Proceedings of the ACM SIGMOD Conference* (pp. 431-442).

Pentland, B. T. (1995). Information Systems and Organizational Learning: The Social Epistemology of Organizational Knowledge Systems. *Accounting. Management and Information Technologies, 5*(1), 1–21. doi:10.1016/0959-8022(95)90011-X

Petri, C. A. (1962) *Kommunikation mit Automaten.* PhD thesis, Fakult¨at f¨ur Mathematik und Physik, Technische Hochschule Darmstadt, Darmstadt, Germany.

Petter, S., Straub, D., & Rai, A. (2007). Specifying formative constructs in information systems research. *Management Information Systems Quarterly, 31*(4), 623–656.

Phillips, T. (1999, March). The enemy within. *Director (Cincinnati, Ohio), 54,* 89.

Piccoli, G., & Ives, B. (2003). Trust and the unified effects of behavior control in virtual teams. *MIS Quarterly, 27*(3), 365–395.

Pickin, S., & Manjarrés, A. (2002). Describing AI Analysis Patterns with UML. In A. Evans, S. Kent, & B. Selic (Eds.), *<<UML>> 2000 – The Unified Modeling Language. Advancing the Standard* (LNCS 1939, pp. 466-481). Berlin-Heidelberg, Germany: Springer.

Pilke, E. M. (2004). Flow experiences in information technology use. *International Journal of Human-Computer Studies, 61*(3), 347–357. doi:10.1016/j.ijhcs.2004.01.004

Pirrò, G., & Talia, D. (2008). LOM: a linguistic ontology matcher based on information retrieval. *Journal of Information Science, 34*(6), 845–860. doi:10.1177/0165551508091014

Pisan, Y. (2007, December 3-5). My guild, my people: role of guilds in massively multiplayer online games. In *Proceedings of the 4th Australasian conference on Interactive Entertainment,* Melbourne, Australia. Retrieved from http://portal.acm.org/toc.cfm?id= 1367956&type= proceeding&coll=ACM&dl=ACM&CFID=27655947& CFTOKEN=58909698

Pitt, L., Watson, R. T., & Kavan, C. B. (1995). Service quality: a measure of information systems effectiveness. *MIS Quarterly, 19*(2), 173–187. doi:10.2307/249687

Podsakoff, P. M., Mackenzie, S. B., & Podsakoff, N. P. (2003). Common method biases in behavioral research: A critical review of the literature and recommended remedies. *The Journal of Applied Psychology*, *88*(5), 879–903. doi:10.1037/0021-9010.88.5.879

Podsakoff, P. M., & Organ, D. W. (1986). Self-reports in organizational research: Problems and prospects. *Journal of Management*, *12*(4), 531–544. doi:10.1177/014920638601200408

Popa, L., Velegrakis, Y., Miller, R. J., Hernández, M. A., & Fagin, R. (2002). Translating Web Data. In *Proceedings of the International Conference on Very Large Data Bases (VLDB)* (pp. 598-609).

Popper, K. R. (1961). *The Logic of Scientific Discovery*. New York: Science Editions.

Preacher, K. J., & Hayes, A. F. (2008). Asymptotic and resampling strategies for assessing and comparing indirect effects in multiple mediator models. *Behavior Research Methods*, *40*(3), 879–891. doi:10.3758/BRM.40.3.879

Prechelt, L., Unger, B., Philipssen, M., & Tichy, W. (2002). Two Controlled Experiments Assessing the Usefulness of Design Pattern Documentation in Program Maintenance. *IEEE Transactions on Software Engineering*, *28*(6), 595–606. doi:10.1109/TSE.2002.1010061

Preece, J. (2001). Sociability and usability in online communities: Determining and measuring success. *Behaviour & Information Technology*, *20*(5), 347–356. doi:10.1080/01449290110084683

Pressman, R. S. (1997). *Software Engineering: A Practitioner's Approach* (4th ed.). New York: McGraw-Hill.

Protege. (2003). *Protégé User Guide*. Retrieved from http://protege.stanford.edu/doc/ users_guide/index.html

Pu, P., Chen, L., & Kumar, P. (2008). Evaluating product search and recommender systems for e-commerce environments. *Electronic Commerce Research*, *8*(1-2), 1–27. doi:10.1007/s10660-008-9015-z

Purao, S., Storey, V. C., & Han, T. (2003). Improving Analysis Pattern Reuse in Conceptual Design: Augmenting Automated Processes with Supervised Learning. *Information Systems Research*, *14*(3), 244–268. doi:10.1287/isre.14.3.269.16559

Rahm, E., & Bernstein, P. (2006). An On-line Bibliography on Schema Evolution. *SIGMOD Record*, *35*(4), 30–31. doi:10.1145/1228268.1228273

Rahm, E., & Bernstein, P. A. (2001). A Survey of Approaches to Automatic Schema Matching. *The VLDB Journal*, *10*, 334–350. doi:10.1007/s007780100057

Rai, A., Lang, S. S., & Welker, R. B. (2000). Assessing the validity of IS Success Models: An empirical test and theoretical analysis. *Information Systems Research*, *13*(1), 50–69. doi:10.1287/isre.13.1.50.96

Rai, A., Patnayakuni, R., & Seth, N. (2006). Firm performance impacts of digitally enabled supply chain integration capabilities. *Management Information Systems Quarterly*, *30*(2), 225–246.

Rai, A., & Sambamurthy, V. (2006). Editorial notes-the growth of interest in services management: opportunities for information systems scholars. *Information Systems Research*, *17*(4), 327–331. doi:10.1287/isre.1060.0108

Rash, R. H., & Tosi, H. L. (1992). Factors Affecting Software Developers' Performance: An Integrated Approach. *MIS Quarterly*, *16*(3), 395–413. doi:10.2307/249535

Ravichandran, T., & Rai, A. (2000). Total quality management in information systems development: key constructs and relationships. *Journal of Management Information Systems*, *16*(3), 119–155.

Rayner, K. (1998). Eye movements in reading and information processing: 20 years of research. *Psychological Bulletin*, *124*(3), 372–422. doi:10.1037/0033-2909.124.3.372

Rayner, K., & Pollatsek, A. (1989). *The Psychology of Reading*. Englewood Cliffs, NJ: Prentice-Hall.

Recker, J., & Indulska, M. (2007). An Ontology-Based Evaluation of Process Modeling with Petri Nets. *Journal of Interoperability in Business Information Systems*, *2*(1), 45–64.

Reeves, B., & Nass, C. I. (1996). *The media equation: How people treat computers, television, and new media like real people and places*. Stanford, CA: CSLI Publications.

Reich, B. H., & Benbasat, I. (1996). Measuring the Linkage between Business and Information Technology Objectives. *MIS Quarterly*, *20*(1), 55–81. doi:10.2307/249542

Reid, D. (2004). A model of playfulness and flow in virtual reality interactions. *Presence (Cambridge, Mass.)*, *13*(4), 451–462. doi:10.1162/1054746041944777

Reijers, H. A., & Mendling, J. (2008). Modularity in Process Models: Review and Effects. In M. Dumas, M. Reichert, & M.-C. Shan (Eds.), *Proceedings of the 6th International Conference Business Process Management (BPM 2008)* (LNCS 5240, pp. 20-35).

Reinhartz-Berger, I., & Dori, D. (2005). A Reflective Metamodel of Object-Process Methodology: The System Modeling Building Blocks. In P. Green & M. Rosemann (Eds.), *Business Systems Analysis with Ontologies* (pp. 130-173). Hershey, PA: Idea Group.

Reinhartz-Berger, I., & Sturm, A. (2007). Enhancing UML Models: A Domain Analysis Approach. *Journal of Database Management*, *19*(1), 74–94.

Rettie, R. (2001). An exploration of flow during Internet use. *Internet Research*, *11*(2), 103–113. doi:10.1108/10662240110695070

Revest, R. L. (1992). *The MD5 Message Digest Algorithm* (RFC 1321). IETF.

Rezgui, A., Bouguettaya, A., & Eltoweissy, M. Y. (2003). Privacy on the Web: facts, challenges, and solutions. *IEEE Security and Privacy*, *1*(6), 40–49. doi:10.1109/MSECP.2003.1253567

Rice, R. E., Grant, A., Schmitz, J., & Torobin, J. (1990). Individual and Network Influences on the Adoption and Perceived Outcomes of Electronic Messaging. *Social Networks*, *12*(1), 27–55. doi:10.1016/0378-8733(90)90021-Z

Ringle, C. M., Wende, S., & Will, S. (2005). *SmartPLS (Version 2.0 (M3) Beta)*.

Riva, G., Mantovani, F., Capideville, C. S., Preziosa, A., Morganti, F., & Villani, D. (2007). Affective interactions using virtual reality: The link between presence and emotions. *Cyberpsychology & Behavior*, *10*(1), 45–56. doi:10.1089/cpb.2006.9993

Robey, D., Smith, L., & Vijayasarathy, L. (1993). Perceptions of Conflict and Success in Information Systems Development Projects. *Journal of Management Information Systems*, *10*(1), 123–139.

Rosemann, M., Davies, I., & Green, P. (2003). The very model of modern BPM. *Information Age, February/March*, 24-29.

Rosenfeld, P., Giacalone, R. A., & Riordan, C. (2001). *Impression management: Building and enhancing reputations at work*. Florence, KY: Cengage Learning Business Press.

Rosen, L. D., & Weil, M. M. (1995). Adult and teenage use of consumer, business, and entertainment technology: Potholes on the information superhighway? *The Journal of Consumer Affairs*, *29*(1), 55–84.

Rosenman, M. A., Smith, G., Maher, M. L., Ding, L., & Marchant, D. (2007). Multidisciplinary collaborative design in virtual environments. *Automation in Construction*, *16*(1), 37–44. doi:10.1016/j.autcon.2005.10.007

Rousso, M., Johnson, A., Moher, T., Leigh, J., Vasilakis, C., & Barnes, C. (1999). Learning and building together in an immersive virtual world. *Presence (Cambridge, Mass.)*, *8*(3), 247–263. doi:10.1162/105474699566215

Rull, G., Farré, C., Teniente, E., & Urpí, T. (2008). Validation of mappings between schemas. *Data & Knowledge Engineering*, *66*(3), 414–437. doi:10.1016/j.datak.2008.04.009

Rusbult, C. E. (1983). A longitudinal test of the investment model: The development (and deterioration) of satisfaction and commitment in heterosexual involvements. *Journal of Personality and Social Psychology*, *45*(1), 101–117. doi:10.1037/0022-3514.45.1.101

Rusbult, C. E., Martz, J. M., & Agnew, C. R. (1998). The investment model scale: Measuring commitment level, satisfaction level, quality of alternatives, and investment size. *Personal Relationships*, *5*(4), 357–387. doi:10.1111/j.1475-6811.1998.tb00177.x

Rusbult, C. E., Olsen, N., Davis, J. L., & Hannon, P. A. (2001). Commitment and relationship maintenance mechanism . In Harvey, J. H., & Wenzel, A. (Eds.), *Close romantic relationships: Maintenance and enhancement* (pp. 87–114). Mahwah, NJ: Lawrence Erlbaum Associates, Inc.

Rusbult, C. E., Wieselquist, J., Foster, C. A., & Witcher, B. S. (1999). Commitment and trust in close relationships: An interdependence analysis . In Adams, J. M., & Jones, W. H. (Eds.), *Handbook of interpersonal commitment and relationship stability* (pp. 427–449). New York: Kluwer Academic / Plenum Publishers.

Rushinek, A., & Rushinek, S. F. (1986). What Makes Users Happy? *Communications of the ACM, 29*(7), 594–598. doi:10.1145/6138.6140

Russell, N., ter Hofstede, A. H. M., van der Aalst, W. M. P., & Mulyar, N. (2006). *Workflow Control-Flow Patterns: A Revised View* (BPM Center Rep. No. BPM-06-22). BPMcenter.org.

Russo, J., & Dosher, B. (1983). Strategies for multiattribute binary choice. *Journal of Experimental Psychology: Learning and Memory, 9*(4), 676–696. doi:10.1037/0278-7393.9.4.676

Ryndina, K., Küster, J. M., & Gall, H. (2007). Consistency of Business Process Models and Object Life Cycles. In *Proceedings of the 1st Workshop Quality in Modeling* (LNCS 4364, pp. 80-90).

Saarinen, T., & Vepsalainen, A. P. J. (1994). Procurement strategies for information systems. *Journal of Management Information Systems, 11*(2), 187–208.

Sabherwal, R., & Chan, Y. E. (2001). Alignment between business and IS strategies: A study of Prospectors, Analyzers, and Defenders. *Information Systems Research, 12*(1), 11–33. doi:10.1287/isre.12.1.11.9714

Sadiq, W., & Orlowska, M. E. (1997). On Correctness Issues in Conceptual Modeling of Workflows. In *Proceedings of the 5th European Conference on Information Systems*, Cork, Ireland (pp. 943-964).

Sagayama, K., Kanenishi, K., Matsuura, K., Kume, K., Miyoshi, Y., Matsumoto, J., et al. (2008). Application of campus SNS for supporting students and their behavior. In *Proceedings of the 16th International Conference on Computers in Education*, Taipei, Taiwan.

Salaway, G. (1987). An Organizational Learning Approach to Information Systems Development. *MIS Quarterly, 11*(2), 244–260. doi:10.2307/249370

Saleem, K., Bellahsene, Z., & Hunt, E. (2008). PORSCHE: Performance ORiented SCHEma mediation. *Information Systems, 33*(7-8), 637–657. doi:10.1016/j.is.2008.01.010

Salellariou, R., & Zhao, H. (2004). A low-cost rescheduling policy for efficient mapping of workflows on Grid systems. *Science Progress, 12*(4), 253–262.

Salimifard, K., & Wright, M. (2001). Petri net-based modeling of workflow systems: An overview. *European Journal of Operational Research, 134*, 664–676. doi:10.1016/S0377-2217(00)00292-7

Sambamurthy, V., & Zmud, R. W. (1999). Arrangements for IT Governance: A Theory of Multiple Contingencies. *MIS Quarterly, 23*(2), 261–290. doi:10.2307/249754

Sanders, G. L. (1984). MIS/DSS Success Measure. *Systems, Objectives . Solutions, 4*(1), 29–34.

Sattar, P., & Ramaswamy, S. (2004). Internet gaming addiction. *Canadian Journal of Psychiatry, 49*(12), 871–872.

Sauer, C. (1993). *Why information systems fall: A case study approach*. Henley-on-Thames, UK: Alfred Waller.

SAX. (2004). *Simple API for XML*. Retrieved from http://www.saxproject.org/

Sayre, C. (2008, December 1). Imaginary Trends. *Time*, 22.

SCA. (2007). *Service Component Architecture, Version 1.0*. Retrieved from http://www.osoa.org/display/ Main/Service+Component+ Architecture+Home

Schank, R. C. (1982). *Dynamic Memory: A Theory of Learning in People and Computers*. Cambridge, UK: Cambridge University Press.

Scheer, A. (1999). *ARIS: Business Process Frameworks* (2nd ed.). New York: Springer.

Scheer, A. W. (1997). *Business Process Engineering: Reference Models for Industrial Enterprises* (2nd ed.). New York: Springer.

SchemaWeb. (n.d.). *SchemaWeb - RDF schemas directory*. Retrieved September 14, 2007, from http://www.schemaweb.info

Schenk, K. D., Vitalari, N. P., & Davis, K. S. (1998). Differences between novice and expert systems analysts: What do we know and what do we do? *Journal of Management Information Systems*, *15*(1), 9–51.

Scherer, K. (1997). College life on-line: healthy and unhealthy Internet use. *Journal of College Student Development*, *38*(6), 655–665.

Schiller, S. (2009). Practicing learner-centered teaching: Pedagogical design and assessment of a Second Life project. *Journal of Information Systems Education*, *20*(3), 369–381.

Schmidt, D. (1995). Experience Using Design Patterns to Develop Reusable Object-Oriented Communication Software. *Communications of the ACM*, *38*(10), 65–74. doi:10.1145/226239.226255

Schneeweiss, H. (1993). Consistency at large in models with latent variables . In Haagen, K., Bartholomew, D. J., & Deistler, M. (Eds.), *Statistical modeling and latent variables*. Amsterdam, The Netherlands: Elsevier.

Schutz, W. (1966). *The interpersonal underworld*. Palo Alto, CA: Science & Behavior Books.

Scoble, R. (2006, May 5). *Rules and rule breaking in Second Life*. Retrieved from http://scobleizer. com/2006/05/05/ rules-and-rulebreaking-in-second-life/

Scott, D. M. (2007). Marketing a Second Life. *EContent*, *30*(2), 56–56.

Seay, A. F., Jerome, W. J., Lee, K. S., & Kraut, R. E. (2004, April 24-29). *Project massive: A study of online gaming communities*. Paper presented at the Computer-Human Interaction conference, Vienna, Austria.

Seddon, P. A. (1997). Respecification and Extension of the DeLone and McLean Model of IS Success. *Information Systems Research*, *8*(3), 240–253. doi:10.1287/isre.8.3.240

Segars, A., & Grover, V. (1998). Strategic information systems planning success: An investigation of the construct and its measurement. *MIS Quarterly*, *22*(2), 139–163. doi:10.2307/249393

Seiler, R. E., & Boockholdt, J. L. (1983). Creative Development of Computerized Information Systems. *Long Range Planning*, *16*(5), 100–106. doi:10.1016/0024-6301(83)90084-5

Seltsikas, P., & Currie, W. L. (2002). Evaluating the application service provider (ASP) business model: the challenger of integration. In *Proceedings of the 35th Hawaii International Conference on System Science*.

Sendall, S., & Kuster, J. (2004). Taming Model Round-Trip Engineering. In *Proceedings of the Workshop on Best Practices for Model-Driven Software Development*.

Senge, P. M. (1990). The leader's new work: Building learning organizations. *Sloan Management Review*, *32*(1), 7–23.

Senn, J. A. (1987). *Information Systems in Management* (3rd ed.). Belmont, CA: Wadsworth Publishing.

Shalloway, A., & Trott, J. (2001). *Design Patterns Explained: A New Perspective on Object-Oriented Design*. Reading, MA: Addison-Wesley.

Shanks, G., Nuredini, J., Tobin, D., & Weber, R. (2003b). Representing Things and Properties in Conceptual Modeling: Understanding the Impact of Task Type. In *Proceedings of the Twenty-Third International Conference on Information Systems*, Barcelona, Spain (pp. 909-913).

Shanks, G., Tansley, E., Nuredini, J., Tobin, D., & Weber, R. (2008). Representing Part-Whole Relations in Conceptual Modeling: An Empirical Evaluation. *MIS Quarterly*, *32*(3), 553–573.

Shanks, G., Tansley, E., & Weber, R. (2003). Using Ontology to Validate Conceptual Models. *Communications of the ACM*, *46*(10), 85–89. doi:10.1145/944217.944244

Shanks, G., Weber, R., & Nuredini, J. (2004). Evaluating Conceptual Modelling Practices . In Rosemann, M., & Green, P. (Eds.), *Business Systems Analysis with Ontologies* (pp. 28–55). Hershey, PA: Idea Group Publishing.

Shannon, C. E. (1948). A mathematical theory of communication. *The Bell System Technical Journal*, *27*, 379–423.

Sharman, R., Kishore, R., & Ramesh, R. (2004). Computational Ontologies and Information Systems II: Formal specification. *Communications of the Association for Information Systems*, *14*, 184–205.

Sheng, H., Siau, K., & Nah, F. (2010). Understanding the values of mobile technology in education: A value-focused thinking approach. *The Data Base for Advances in Information Systems, 41*(2), 25–44.

Sherry, J. L. (2004). Flow and media enjoyment . *Communication Theory, 14*(4), 328–347. doi:10.1111/j.1468-2885.2004.tb00318.x

Shin, M., Huh, S., Park, D., & Lee, W. (2008). Relaxing Queries with Hierarchical Quantified Data Abstraction. *Journal of Database Management, 19*(4), 47–61.

Shin, N. (2006). Online learner's 'flow' experience: An empirical study. *British Journal of Educational Technology, 37*(5), 705–720. doi:10.1111/j.1467-8535.2006.00641.x

Shiu, H., & Fong, J. (2009). Reverse Engineering from an XML Document into an Extended DTD Graph. *Journal of Database Management, 20*(2), 38–57.

Shrout, P. E., & Bolder, N. (2002). Mediation in experimental and nonexperimental studies: New procedures and recommendations. *Psychological Methods, 7*(4), 422–445. doi:10.1037/1082-989X.7.4.422

Shubik, M. (1979). Computers and Modeling. In M. L. Dertouzos & J. Moses (Eds.), *The Computer Age: A Twenty Year View*. Cambridge, MA: MIT Press.

Shvaiko, P., & Euzenat, J. (2005). A Survey of Schema-Based Matching Approaches. *J. Data Semantics, IV,* 146–171.

Sia, S. K., & Soh, C. (2002). Severity assessment of ERP-organizational misalignment: Honing in on ontological structure and context specificity. In *Proceedings of the Twenty-Third International Conference on Information Systems*, Barcelona, Spain (pp. 723-729).

Siau, K. (1996). Electronic Creativity Techniques for Organizational Innovation. *The Journal of Creative Behavior, 30*(4), 283–293.

Siau, K. (2004). Informational and computational equivalence in comparing conceptual modeling methods . *Journal of Database Management, 15*(1), 73–86.

Siau, K., & Cao, Q. (2001). Unified Modeling Language – A Complexity Analysis. *Journal of Database Management, 12*(1), 26–34.

Siau, K., Erickson, J., & Lee, L. (2005). Theoretical vs. Practical Complexity: The Case of UML. *Journal of Database Management, 16*(3), 40–57.

Siau, K., Erickson, J., & Nah, F. (2010a). Effect of national culture on knowledge sharing in online virtual communities. *IEEE Transactions on Professional Communication, 53*(3), 278–292. doi:10.1109/TPC.2010.2052842

Siau, K., Long, Y., & Ling, M. (2010b). Toward a unified model of information systems success. *Journal of Database Management, 21*(1), 80–101.

Siau, K., & Loo, P. (2006). Identifying Difficulties in Learning UML. *Information Systems Management, 23*(3), 43–51. doi:10.1201/1078.10580530/46108.23.3.20060601/93706.5

Siau, K., & Messersmith, J. (2003). Analyzing ERP Implementation at a Public University Using the Innovation Strategy Model. *International Journal of Human-Computer Interaction, 16*(1), 57–80. doi:10.1207/S15327590IJHC1601_5

Siau, K., Nah, F., & Ling, M. (2007). National Culture and its Effects on Knowledge Communication in Online Virtual Communities. *International Journal of Electronic Business, 5*(5), 518–532. doi:10.1504/IJEB.2007.015450

Siau, K., & Rossi, M. (2007). *Evaluation techniques for systems analysis and design modelling methods – A review and comparative analysis*. Information Systems Journal.

Siau, K., & Rossi, M. (in press). Systems Analysis and Design: Evaluation Techniques for Conceptual and Data Modeling Methods. *Information Systems Journal.*

Siau, K., Sheng, H., & Nah, F. (2006). Use of a classroom response system to enhance classroom interactivity. *IEEE Transactions on Education, 49*(3), 398–403. doi:10.1109/TE.2006.879802

Siau, K., & Shen, Z. (2003). Building Customer Trust in Mobile Commerce. *Communications of the ACM, 46*(4), 91–94. doi:10.1145/641205.641211

Siau, K., & Tan, X. (2005). Evaluation Criteria for Information Systems Development Methodologies. *Communications of the AIS, 16*, 856–872.

Siau, K., & Tan, X. (2006). Cognitive Mapping Techniques for User-Database Interaction. *IEEE Transactions on Professional Communication, 49*(2), 96–108. doi:10.1109/TPC.2006.875074

Siau, K., Tan, X., & Sheng, H. (2010c). Important characteristics of software development team members: an empirical investigation using repertory grid. *Information Systems Journal, 20*(6), 563–580. doi:10.1111/j.1365-2575.2007.00254.x

Siau, K., Wand, Y., & Benbasat, I. (1997). The Relative Importance of Structural Constraints and Surface Semantics in Information Modeling. *Information Systems, 22*(2-3), 155–170. doi:10.1016/S0306-4379(97)00009-4

Siekpe, J. S. (2005). An examination of the multidimensionality of flow construct in a computer-mediated environment. *Journal of Electronic Commerce Research, 6*(1), 31–43.

Sillince, J. A., & Mouakket, S. (1997). Varieties of Political Process during Systems Development. *Information Systems Research, 8*(4), 368–397. doi:10.1287/isre.8.4.368

Silvasti, P., Sippu, S., & Soisalon-Soininen, E. (2009). Schema-Conscious Filtering of XML Documents. In *Proceedings of the International Conference on Extending Database Technology* (pp. 970-981).

Simsion, G., & Witt, G. (2001). *Data Modelling Essentials: Analysis* (2nd ed.). Design and Innovation.

Skadberg, Y. X., & Kimmel, J. R. (2004). Visitors' flow experience while browsing a Web site: Its measurement, contributing factors and consequences. *Computers in Human Behavior, 20*(3), 403–422. doi:10.1016/S0747-5632(03)00050-5

Slater, M., Steed, A., & Chrysanthou, Y. (2001). *Computer Graphics and Virtual Environments: From Realism to Real-Time*. Reading, MA: Addison Wesley.

Slavin, R. E. (1980). Cooperative learning. *Review of Educational Research, 50*(2), 315–342.

Slavin, R. E. (1983). When does cooperative learning increase student achievement? *Psychological Bulletin, 94*(3), 429–445. doi:10.1037/0033-2909.94.3.429

Sloan, R. (1995). Four types of noise in data for PAC learning. *Information Processing Letters, 54*, 157–162. doi:10.1016/0020-0190(95)00016-6

Smith, B. (2001). *Ontology and Information Systems*. Retrieved from http://ontology.buffalo.edu/ontology%28PIC%29.pdf.

Smith, M. A., & Kumar, R. L. (2004). A theory of application service provider (ASP) use from a client perspective. *Information & Management, 41*(8), 977–1002. doi:10.1016/j.im.2003.08.019

Smolander, K., & Rossi, M. (2008). Conflicts, Compromises, and Political Decisions: Methodological Challenges of Enterprise-Wide E-Business Architecture Creation. *Journal of Database Management, 19*(1), 19–40.

Snoeck, M., & Dedene, G. (1998). Existence Dependency: The key to semantic integrity between structural and behavioural aspects of object types. *IEEE Transactions on Software Engineering, 24*(4), 233–251. doi:10.1109/32.677182

SOAP. (2003). *Simple Object Access Protocol version 1.2*. Retrieved from http://www.w3.org/TR/soap12-part0

Social Research Foundation. (2008). *2008 Second Life survey*. New York: Social Research Foundation.

Soffer, P., Wand, Y., & Kaner, M. (2007). Semantic Analysis of Flow Patterns in Business Process Modeling. In *Proceedings of Business Process Management (BPM'07)* (LNCS 4714, pp. 400-407).

Soffer, P. (2005). Structural Equivalence in Model-Based Reuse: Overcoming Differences in Abstract Level. *Journal of Database Management, 16*(3), 21–39.

Soffer, P., & Wand, Y. (2005). On the notion of soft goals in business process modeling. *Business Process Management Journal, 11*(6), 663–679. doi:10.1108/14637150510630837

Soffer, P., & Wand, Y. (2007). Goal-Driven Multi-Process Analysis. *Journal of the Association for Information Systems, 8*(3), 175–203.

Somers, T. M., & Nelson, K. (2001). The impact of critical success factors across the stages of enterprise resource planning implementation. In *Proceedings of the 34th Hawaii International Conference on System Sciences*.

Sommerville, I. (1996). *Software Engineering* (5th ed.). Reading, MA: Addison-Wesley.

Song, I., Larose, R., Eastin, M. S., & Lin, C. A. (2004). Internet gratifications and Internet addiction: On the uses and abuses of new media. *Cyberpsychology & Behavior, 7*(4), 384–394. doi:10.1089/cpb.2004.7.384

Soofi, E. S., & Retzer, J. J. (2002). Information indices: unification and applications. *Journal of Econometrics, 107*(1-2), 17–40. doi:10.1016/S0304-4076(01)00111-7

Soule, L. C., Shell, L. W., & Kleen, B. A. (2003). Exploring Internet addiction: Demographic characteristics and stereotypes of heavy Internet users. *Journal of Computer Information Systems, 44*(1), 64–73.

Sowa, J. (2000). *Knowledge Representation: Logical, Philosophical, and Computational Foundations*. Pacific Grove, CA: Brooks Cole.

Spence, J. W., & Tsai, R. J. (1997). On human cognition and the design of information systems. *Information & Management, 32*(2), 66–74. doi:10.1016/S0378-7206(97)00012-8

Spender, J. C. (1996). Making Knowledge the Basis of a Dynamic Theory of the Firm. *Strategic Management Journal, 17*(2), 45–62.

Srivastava, U., Widom, J., Munagala, K., & Motwani, R. (2005). *Query optimization over Web services*. Retrieved from http://dbpubs.stanford. edu:8090/ pub/2005-30

Stafford, T. F. (2008). Social and usage-process motivations for consumer Internet access. *Journal of Organizational and End User Computing, 20*(3), 1–21.

Stafford, T. F., & Stafford, M. R. (2001). Identifying motivations for the use of commercial Web sites. *Information Resources Management Journal, 14*(1), 22–30.

Stafford, T. F., Stafford, M. R., & Schkade, L. L. (2004). Determining uses and gratifications for the Internet. *Decision Sciences, 35*(2), 259–288. doi:10.1111/j.00117315.2004.02524.x

Stanley, S. M., & Markman, H. J. (1992). Assessing commitment in personal relationships. *Journal of Marriage and the Family, 54*(3), 595–608. doi:10.2307/353245

Stanton, J. M. (2002). Company profile of the frequent internet user. *Communications of the ACM, 45*(1), 55–59. doi:10.1145/502269.502297

Steffe, L. P., & Gale, J. (1995). *Constructivism in education*. Mahwah, NJ: Lawrence Erlbaum Associates.

Stein, E. W., & Vandenbosch, B. (1996). Organizational learning during advanced system development: Opportunities and obstacles. *Journal of Management Information Systems, 13*(2), 115–136.

Steinriede, K. (2007). Virtual world, real awareness: Kraft sees future in Second Life. *Stagnito's New Products Magazine*. Retrieved November 13, 2007, from http://www.allbusiness.com/manufacturing/ food-manufacturing/ 4510733-1.html

Stephen, G. A. (1994). *String Searching Algorithms*. Singapore: World Scientific Publishing Company.

Steuer, J. (1992). Defining virtual reality: Dimensions determining telepresence. *The Journal of Communication, 42*(4), 73–93. doi:10.1111/j.1460-2466.1992.tb00812.x

Stone, C. A., & Sobel, M. E. (1990). The robustness of estimates of total indirect effects. *Psychometrika, 55*(2), 337–352. doi:10.1007/BF02295291

Straub, D., Boudreau, M.-C., & Gefen, D. (2004). Validation guidelines for is positivist research. *Communications of the Association for Information Systems, 13*, 380–427.

Sturm, A., Dori, D., & Shehory, O. (2006). Domain Modeling with Object-Process Methodology. In Y. Manolopoulos, J. Filipe, P. Constantopoulos, & J. Cordeiro (Eds.), *Proceedings of the 8th International Conference on Enterprise Information Systems (ICEIS'2006)* (pp. 144-151). Paphos, Cyprus: ICEIS.

Su, W., Wang, J., & Lochovsky, F. (2006). Holistic schema matching for web query interface. In *Proceedings of the International Conference on Extending Database Technology (EDBT)* (pp. 77-94).

Sundar, S. S. (1994). *Is human-computer interaction social or parasocial?* Paper presented at the Annual Convention of the Association for Education in Journalism and Mass communication, Atlanta, GA.

Sundaresan, N., & Moussa, R. (2001). Algorithm and Programming Models for Efficient Representation of XML for Internet Application. In *Proceedings of the international WWW Conference* (pp. 366-375).

Sundar, S. S., & Nass, C. (2000). Source orientation in human-computer interaction: Programmer, networker, or independent social actor? *Communication Research, 27*(6), 683–703. doi:10.1177/009365000027006001

Suri, R., Kohli, C., & Monroe, K. B. (2007). The effects of perceived scarcity on consumers' processing of price information. *Journal of the Academy of Marketing Science, 35*(1), 89–100. doi:10.1007/s11747-006-0008-y

Susarla, A., Barua, A., & Whinston, A. B. (2003). Understanding the service component of application service provision: An empirical analysis of satisfaction with ASP Services. *Management Information Systems Quarterly, 27*(1), 91–123.

Su, X., & Gulla, J. A. (2006). An information retrieval approach to ontology mapping . *Data & Knowledge Engineering, 58*(1), 47–69. doi:10.1016/j.datak.2005.05.012

Swanson, E. B. (1974). Management Information Systems: Appreciation and Involvement. *Management Science, 21*(2), 178–188. doi:10.1287/mnsc.21.2.178

Systems, O. P. C. A. T. *OPCAT web site*. Retrieved from http://www.opcat.com/

Szajna, B., & Scamell, R. W. (1993). The effects of information system user expectations on their performance and perceptions. *MIS Quarterly, 17*(4), 493–516. doi:10.2307/249589

Tabachnick, B. G., & Fidell, L. S. (2007). *Using Multivariate Statistics* (5th ed.). Boston: Allyn and Bacon.

Taibi, T., & Ngo, D. C. L. (2003). Formal Specification of Design Patterns – A Balanced Approach. *Journal of Object Technology, 2*(4), 127–140.

Tait, P., & Vessey, I. (1988). The Effect of User Involvement on System Success: A Contingency Approach. *MIS Quarterly, 12*(1), 91–108. doi:10.2307/248809

Tarafdar, M., & Zhang, J. (2007/2008). Determinants of reach and loyalty - A study of website performance and implications for website design. *Journal of Computer Information Systems, 48*(2), 16–25.

Tarasewich, P., Pomplun, M., Fillion, S., & Broberg, D. (2005). The enhanced restricted focus viewer. *International Journal of Human-Computer Interaction, 19*(1), 35–54. doi:10.1207/s15327590ijhc1901_4

Taylor, T. L. (2003). *Power gamers just want to have fun?: Instrumental play in a MMOG.* Paper presented at the Digital Games Research Conference (Level Up), Utrecht, the Netherlands.

Taylor, S. A., Hunter, G. L., & Lindberg, D. L. (2007). Understanding (Customer-based) Brand Equity in Financial Services. *Journal of Services Marketing, 21*(4), 241–252. doi:10.1108/08876040710758540

Taylor, S., & Todd, P. A. (1995). Understanding information technology usage: A test of competing models. *Information Systems Research, 6*(4), 144–176. doi:10.1287/isre.6.2.144

Teorey, T. J., Yang, D., & Fry, J. P. (1986). A logical design methodology for relational databases using the extended entity-relationship model. *ACM Computing Surveys, 18*(2), 197–222. doi:10.1145/7474.7475

Terdiman, D. (2007). *The entrepreneur's guide to Second Life: Making money in the metaverse.* Hoboken, NJ: Sybex.

Thatcher, A., Wretschko, G., & Fridjhon, P. (2008). Online flow experiences, problematic Internet use and Internet procrastination. *Computers in Human Behavior, 24*(5), 2236–2254. doi:10.1016/j.chb.2007.10.008

The authors would like to thank the special issue Editor, Shu Schiller, and the anonymous referees for their valuable comments on the earlier versions of the paper. The work described in the paper was partially supported by grants from the Research Grants Council of Hong Kong S.A.R. (Project No. CityU 150207) and from the National Natural Science Foundation of China (NSFC) under grants #70890082 and #70872059.

Thompson, L. L. (1999). *Making the Team.* Upper Saddle River, NJ: Prentice Hall.

Tinker, M. A. (1955). Perceptual and oculomotor efficiency in reading materials in vertical and horizontal arrangements. *The American Journal of Psychology, 68*(3), 444–449. doi:10.2307/1418529

Tiwana, A., & Bush, A. A. (2007). A comparison of transaction cost, agency, and knowledge-based predictors of IT outsourcing decisions: a U.S.–Japan cross-cultural field study. *Journal of Management Information Systems*, *24*(1), 259–300. doi:10.2753/MIS0742-1222240108

Tiwana, A., & McLean, E. R. (2005). Expertise integration and creativity in information systems development. *Journal of Management Information Systems*, *22*(1), 13–43.

Tobin, K., & Tippins, D. (1993). Constructivism as a referent for teaching and learning . In Tobin, K. (Ed.), *The practice of constructivism in education* (pp. 3–21). Hillsdale, NJ: Lawrence-Erlbaum.

Todd, P., & Benbasat, I. (1987). Process tracing methods in decision support systems research: Exploring the black box. *Management Information Systems Quarterly*, *11*(4), 493–512. doi:10.2307/248979

Tolani, P. M., & Haritsa, J. R. (2002). *XGRIND: A Query-Friendly XML Compressor*. Paper presented at the International Conference on Data Engineering.

Torkzadeh, G., & Dhillon, G. (2002). Measuring factors that influence the success of internet commerce. *Information Systems Research*, *13*(2), 187–204. doi:10.1287/isre.13.2.187.87

Transport Protocol Experts Group. (2006). *Traveller Information Services Association*. Retrieved from http://www.tpeg.org/

Trevino, L. K., & Webster, J. (1992). Flow in computer-mediated communication. *Communication Research*, *19*(5), 539–573. doi:10.1177/009365092019005001

Trimmer, K. J., Domino, M. A., & Blanton, J. E. (2002). The Impact of Personality Diversity on Conflict in ISD Teams. *Journal of Computer Information Systems*, *42*(4), 7–14.

Tung, W., Moore, R., & Engelland, B. (2006). Exploring attitudes and purchase intentions in a brand-oriented, highly interactive Web sites setting. *Marketing Management Journal*, *16*(2), 94–106.

Tzelgov, J., & Henik, A. (1991). Suppression situations in psychological research: Definitions, implications, and applications. *Psychological Bulletin*, *109*(3), 524–536. doi:10.1037/0033-2909.109.3.524

Unalan, H. T. (2009). The effectiveness of collaborative learning applications in art education. *Journal of International Social Research*, *1*(5), 868–879.

University of Washington. (2007). *XML Data Repository*. Retrieved from http://www.cs.washington.edu/ research/xmldatasets

Uschold, M., & Gruninger, M. (1996). Ontologies: Principles, Methods and Applications. *The Knowledge Engineering Review*, *11*(2), 93–136. doi:10.1017/S0269888900007797

Valiant, L. G. (1984). A theory of the learnable. *Communications of the ACM*, *17*(11), 1134–1142. doi:10.1145/1968.1972

Vallerand, R. J. (1997). Toward a hierarchical model of intrinsic and extrinsic motivation . In Zanna, M. (Ed.), *Advances in Experimental Social Psychology* (pp. 271–360). New York: Academic Press.

van der Aalst, W. M. P. (2000). Workflow Verification: Finding Control-Flow Errors Using Petri-Net-Based Techniques, In W.M.P. van der Aalst, J. Desel, & A. Oberweis (Eds.), *Business Process Management: Models, Techniques, and Empirical Studies* (LNCS 1806, pp. 161-183).

van der Aalst, W. M. P. (1998). The application of petri nets to workflow management. *The Journal of Circuits . Systems and Computers*, *8*(1), 21–66.

van der Aalst, W. M. P. (1999). Formalization and verification of Event-driven Process Chains. *Information and Software Technology*, *41*(10), 639–650. doi:10.1016/S0950-5849(99)00016-6

van der Aalst, W. M. P. (2003). Challenges in business process management: Verification of business processes using Petri nets. *Bulletin of the EATCS*, *80*, 174–199.

van der Aalst, W. M. P., & ter Hofstede, A. H. M. (2005). YAWL: Yet Another Workflow Language. *Information Systems*, *30*(4), 245–275. doi:10.1016/j.is.2004.02.002

van der Aalst, W. M. P., ter Hofstede, A. H. M., Kiepuszewski, B., & Barros, A. P. (2003). Workflow Patterns. *Distributed and Parallel Databases*, *14*(1), 5–51. doi:10.1023/A:1022883727209 van der Aalst, W. M. P., van Dongen, B. F., Herbst, J., Maruster, L., Schimm, G., & Weijters, A. J. M. M. (2007). Workflow mining: A survey of issues and approaches. *Information Systems, 32*(5), 713–732.

van der Aalst, W. M. P., & van Hee, K. M. (2002). *Workflow Management: Models, Methods, and Systems.* Cambridge, MA: MIT Press.

van der Aalst, W. M. P., & Weijters, A. J. M. M. (2004). Process mining: a research agenda. *Computers in Industry, 53*(3), 231–244. doi:10.1016/j.compind.2003.10.001

van der Aalst, W. M. P., Weske, M., & Grunbauer, D. (2005). Case handling: a new paradigm for business process support. *Data & Knowledge Engineering, 53,* 129–162. doi:10.1016/j.datak.2004.07.003

van Hee, K., Sidorova, N., & Voorhoeve, M. (2008). Soundness and separability of workflow nets in the stepwise refinement approach. In W.M.P. van der Aalst & E. Best (Eds.), *ICATPN 2003* (LNCS 2679, pp. 337-356).

van Hee, K., Oanea, O., Serebrenik, A., Sidorova, N., & Voorhoeve, M. (2008). History-based joins: semantics, soundness and implementation. *Data & Knowledge Engineering, 64,* 24–37. doi:10.1016/j.datak.2007.06.005

Van Vugt, H. C., Konijn, E. A., Hoorn, J. F., Keur, I., & Eliens, A. (2007). Realism is not all! User engagement with task-related interface characters. *Interacting with Computers, 19*(2), 267–280. doi:10.1016/j.intcom.2006.08.005

Vandenbroeck, M., Verschelden, G., & Boonaert, T. (2008). E-learning in a low-status female profession: The role of motivation, anxiety, and social support in the learning divide. *Journal of Computer Assisted Learning, 24*(3), 181–190. doi:10.1111/j.1365-2729.2007.00252.x

Vander Meer, D., & Dutta, K. (2009). Applying Learner-Centered Design Principles to UML Sequence Diagrams. *Journal of Database Management, 20*(1), 25–47.

Vapnik, V. (1998). *Statistical Learning Theory.* New York: John Wiley & Sons.

Varelas, G., Voutsakis, E., Raftopoulou, P., Petrakis, E., & Milios, E. (2005). Semantic similarity methods in wordNet and their application to information retrieval on the web. In *Proceedings of the 7th Annual ACM International Workshop on Web Information and Data Management* (pp. 10-16).

Vargo, S. L., & Lusch, R. F. (2004). Evolving to a new dominant logic for marketing. *Journal of Marketing, 68*(1), 1–17. doi:10.1509/jmkg.68.1.1.24036

Vatanasombut, B., Igbaria, M., Stylianou, A. C., & Rodgers, W. (2008). Information systems continuance intention of web-based applications customers: the case of online banking. *Information & Management, 45*(1), 419–428. doi:10.1016/j.im.2008.03.005

Velegrakis, Y., Miller, R., & Popa, L. (2004). Preserving mapping consistency under schema changes. *The VLDB Journal, 13*(3), 274–293. doi:10.1007/s00778-004-0136-2

Venezia, P. (2007). Virtualization. *InfoWorld, 29*(1), 16–17.

Ven, K., & Verelst, J. (2008). The Impact of Ideology on the Organizational Adoption of Open Source Software. *Journal of Database Management, 19*(2), 58–72.

Venkatesh, V., & Davis, F. D. A. (2000). Theoretical extension of the technology acceptance model: four longitudinal field studies. *Management Science, 45*(2), 186–204. doi:10.1287/mnsc.46.2.186.11926

Venkatesh, V., Morris, M. G., Davis, G. B., & Davis, F. D. (2003). User acceptance of information technology: toward a unified view. *Management Information Systems Quarterly, 27*(3), 425–478.

Vessey, I. (1991). Cognitive fit: A theory-based analysis of the graphs versus tables literature. *Decision Sciences, 22*(2), 219–240. doi:10.1111/j.1540-5915.1991.tb00344.x

Vessey, I., & Galletta, D. (1991). Cognitive Fit: An Empirical Study of Information Acquisition. *Information Systems Research, 2*(1), 63–84. doi:10.1287/isre.2.1.63

Vinoski, S. (2002). Web services interaction models, part 1: current practice. *IEEE Internet Computing, 6*(3), 89–91. doi:10.1109/MIC.2002.1003137

Vitalari, N. P. (1985). Knowledge as a Basis for Expertise in Systems Analysis: An Empirical Study. *MIS Quarterly, 9*(3), 221–240. doi:10.2307/248950

Vizard, M. (2000). EDS looks to extend reach with ASP model. *InfoWorld, 22*(46), 16.

Vygotsky, L. S. (1978). *Mind in society: The development of higher psychological processes.* Cambridge, MA: Harvard University Press.

W3C Recommendation. (2006). *Extensible Markup Language (XML) 1.0* (4th ed.). Retrieved from http://www.w3.org/XML

Wagner, C. (2005). Supporting Knowledge Management in Organizations with Conversational Technologies: Discussion Forums, Weblogs, and Wilds. *Journal of Database Management, 16*(2), 1–8.

Wagner, T., Longenecker, J., Landry, J., Lusk, C., & Saulnier, B. (2008). A methodology to assist faculty in developing successful approaches for achieving learner centered information systems curriculum outcomes: Team based methods. *Journal of Information Systems Education, 19*(2), 181–195.

Wand, Y., & Weber, R. (1990a). Mario Bunge's ontology as a formal foundation for information systems concepts. In P. Weingartner & G. W. D. Dorn (Eds.), *Studies on Mario Bunge's Treatise.* Atlanta, GA: Rodopi.

Wand, Y., & Weber, R. (1997). *Ontological Foundations of Information Systems: Coopers and Lybrand Research Methodology, Vol. 4.* Melbourne, Australia: Coopers and Lybrand Research Methodology.

Wand, Y., Monarchi, D., Parsons, J., & Woo, C. (1995). Theoretical Foundations for Conceptual Modeling in Information Systems Development. *Decision Support Systems, 15*, 285–304. doi:10.1016/0167-9236(94)00043-6

Wand, Y., Storey, V., & Weber, R. (1999). An Ontological Analysis of the Relationship Construct in Conceptual Modeling. *ACM Transactions on Database Systems, 24*(4), 494–528. doi:10.1145/331983.331989

Wand, Y., & Weber, R. (1990b). An Ontological Model of an Information System. *IEEE Transactions on Software Engineering, 16*(11), 1282–1992. doi:10.1109/32.60316

Wand, Y., & Weber, R. (1993). On the ontological expressiveness of information systems analysis and design grammars . *Journal of Information Systems, 3*, 217–237. doi:10.1111/j.1365-2575.1993.tb00127.x

Wand, Y., & Weber, R. (1993). On the ontological expressiveness of information systems analysis and design grammars. *Journal of Information Systems, 3*, 217–237. doi:10.1111/j.1365-2575.1993.tb00127.x

Wand, Y., & Weber, R. (1995). Towards a theory of deep structure of information systems. *Journal of Information Systems, 5*(3), 203–223. doi:10.1111/j.1365-2575.1995.tb00108.x

Wand, Y., & Weber, R. (2002). Information systems and conceptual modelling: A research agenda. *Information Systems Research, 13*, 363–376. doi:10.1287/isre.13.4.363.69

Wand, Y., & Weber, R. (2002). Research Commentary: Information Systems and Conceptual Modeling – a Research Agenda. *Information Systems Research, 13*(4), 363–378. doi:10.1287/isre.13.4.363.69

Wang, J., Wen, J., Lockovsky, F., & Ma, W. (2004). Instance-based schema matching for web databases by domain-specific query probing. In *Proceedings of the 30th International Conference on Very Large Data Bases* (pp. 408-419).

Wang, C.-C., & Wang, C.-H. (2008). Helping others in online games: Prosocial behavior in cyberspace. *Cyberpsychology & Behavior, 11*(3), 344–346. doi:10.1089/cpb.2007.0045

Wang, J., & Kumar, A. (2005). A Framework for Document-Driven Workflow Systems. In . *Proceedings of Business Process Management, 2005*, 285–301. doi:10.1007/11538394_19

Wang, W., & Benbasat, I. (2007). Recommendation Agents for Electronic Commerce: Effects of Explanation Facilities on Trusting Beliefs. *Journal of Management Information Systems, 23*(4), 217–246. doi:10.2753/MIS0742-1222230410

Wang, W., & Benbasat, I. (2008). Attributions of Trust in Decision Support Technologies: A Study of Recommendation Agents for E-Commerce. *Journal of Management Information Systems, 24*(4), 249–273. doi:10.2753/MIS0742-1222240410

Wang, W., & Benbasat, I. (2009). Interactive Decision Aids for Consumer Decision Making in e-Commerce: The Influence of Perceived Strategy Restrictiveness. *Management Information Systems Quarterly, 33*(2), 293–320.

Wan, Y., Menon, S., & Ramaprasad, A. (2007). A classification of product comparison agents. *Communications of the ACM, 50*(8), 65–71. doi:10.1145/1278201.1278208

Warmer, J., & Kleppe, A. (1998). *The Object Constraint Language: Precise Modeling with UML*. Reading, MA: Addison-Wesley.

Waugh, C. E., & Fredrickson, B. L. (2006). Nice to know you: Positive emotions, self-other overlap, and complex understanding in the formation of a new relationship. *The Journal of Positive Psychology*, *1*(2), 93–106. doi:10.1080/17439760500510569

Weathers, D., Sharma, S., & Wood, S. L. (2007). Effects of online communication practices on consumer perceptions of performance uncertainty for search and experience goods. *Journal of Retailing*, *83*(4), 393–401. doi:10.1016/j.jretai.2007.03.009

Weber, R. (1996). Are attributes entities? A study of database designers' memory structures. *Information Systems Research*, *7*, 137–162. doi:10.1287/isre.7.2.137

Weber, R. (1997). *Ontological Foundations of Information Systems*. Melbourne, Australia: Coopers & Lybrand.

Weber, R. (2003). Conceptual Modelling and Ontology: Possibilities and Pitfalls. *Journal of Database Management*, *14*(3), 1–20.

Weber, R., & Zhang, Y. (1996). An Analytic Evaluation of NIAM's grammar for Conceptual Schema Diagrams. *Information Systems*, *6*(2), 147–170. doi:10.1111/j.1365-2575.1996.tb00010.x

Webster, J., Trevino, L. K., & Ryan, L. (1993). The dimensionality and correlates of flow in human-computer interactions. *Computers in Human Behavior*, *9*(4), 411–426. doi:10.1016/0747-5632(93)90032-N

Weimer, M. (2002). *Learner-centered teaching: Five key changes to practice*. San Francisco, CA: Jossey-Bass.

Wendorff, P. (2001). Assessment of design patterns during software reengineering: Lessons learned from a large commercial project. In *Proceedings of the 5th Conference on Software Maintenance and Reengineering* (pp. 77-84). Los Alamitos, CA: IEEE Computer Society Press.

WfMC. (1995). *The Workflow Reference Model, Issue 1.1, Document Number TC00-1003*. Winchester, UK: Work-flow Management Coalition.

White, B. A. (2008). *Second Life: A guide to your virtual world*. Indianapolis, IN: Que Publishing.

Whitehead, E. J. (2002). Uniform comparison of data models using containment modeling, In *Proceedings of the thirteenth ACM conference on Hypertext and hypermedia* (pp. 182-191).

White, K. B., & Leifer, R. (1986). Information Systems Development Success: Perspectives from Project Team Participants. *MIS Quarterly*, *10*(3), 215–223. doi:10.2307/249253

Wiggins, B. C. (2000). *Detecting and deleting with outliers in univariate and multivariate context*. Paper presented at the Annual Meeting of the Mid-South Educational Research Association, Bowling Green, KY.

Williams, D. (2006). Groups and goblins: The social and civic impact of an online game . *Journal of Broadcasting & Electronic Media*, *50*(4), 651–670. doi:10.1207/s15506878jobem5004_5

Williamson, O. E. (1979). Transaction cost economics: the governance of contractual relations. *The Journal of Law & Economics*, *22*(2), 233–261. doi:10.1086/466942

Williamson, O. E. (1985). *The Economic Institutions of Capitalism*. New York: Free Press.

Willoughby, T. (2008). A short-term longitudinal study of Internet and computer game use by adolescent boys and girls: prevalence, frequency of use and psychosocial predictors. *Developmental Psychology*, *44*(1), 195–204. doi:10.1037/0012-1649.44.1.195

Witkin, H. A. (1973). The role of cognitive style in academic performance and in teacher-student relations. *Educational Testing Service Research Bulletin*, 73-101.

Wixom, B. H., & Watson, H. J. (2001). An Empirical Investigation of the Factors Affecting Data Warehouse Success. *MIS Quarterly*, *25*(1), 17–41. doi:10.2307/3250957

Wolfendale, J. (2007). My avatar, my self: Virtual harm and attachment. *Ethics and Information Technology*, *9*(2), 111–119. doi:10.1007/s10676-006-9125-z

Wong, E. Y. C., Chan, A., & Leong, H. (2004). Xstream: A Middleware for Streaming XML Contents over Wireless Environments. *IEEE Transactions on Software Engineering*, *30*(12), 918–935. doi:10.1109/TSE.2004.108

Woodie, A. (2004). PeopleSoft gives world ERP suite a web interface. *IT Jungle, 4*(2). Retrieved from http://www.itjungle.com/fhs/ fhs032304-story01.html

Wood, N. T., Solomon, M. R., & Englis, B. G. (2006). Personalization of the web interface: The impact of web avatars on users' responses to e-commerce sites. *Journal of Website Promotion, 2*(1/2), 53–69.

Wood, W. (2000). Attitude change: Persuasion and social influence. *Annual Review of Psychology, 51,* 539–570. doi:10.1146/annurev.psych.51.1.539

WSDL. (2003). *Web services description language version 2.0.* Retrieved from http://www.w3.org/TR/wsdl20

Wu, W., Yu, C., Doan, A., & Meng, W. (2004). An interactive clustering-based approach to integrating source query interfaces on the deep web. In *Proceedings of the 2004 ACM SIGMOD International Conference on Management of Data* (pp. 95-106).

Wu, J., Li, P., & Rao, S. (2008). Why do they enjoy virtual game worlds? An empirical investigation. *Journal of Electronic Commerce Research, 9*(3), 219–231.

Wu, J., & Liu, D. (2007). The effects of trust and enjoyment on intention to play online games. *Journal of Electronic Commerce Research, 8*(2), 128–140.

Xu, L., & Embley, D. W. (2006). A composite approach to automating direct and indirect schema mappings. *Information Systems, 31*(8), 697–732. doi:10.1016/j.is.2005.01.003

Yacoub, S., & Ammar, H. (2003). *Pattern-oriented analysis and design: Composing patterns to design software systems.* Boston: Addison-Wesley.

Yan, L. L., Miller, R. J., Haas, L., & Fagin, R. (2001). Data-Driven Understanding and Refinement of Schema Mappings. In *Proceedings of the ACM SIGMOD* (pp. 485-496).

Yang, S. C., & Tung, C.-J. (2007). Comparison of Internet addicts and non-addicts in Taiwanese high schools. *Computers in Human Behavior, 23*(1), 79–96. doi:10.1016/j.chb.2004.03.037

Yao, Y., & Murphy, L. (2005). A state transition approach to application service provider client-vendor relationship development. *The Data Base for Advances in Information Systems, 36*(3), 8–25.

Ybarra, M. L., Alexander, M. P. H., & Mitchell, K. J. (2005). Depressive symptomatology, youth Internet use, and online interactions: A national survey. *The Journal of Adolescent Health, 36*(1), 9–18. doi:10.1016/j.jadohealth.2003.10.012

Yee, N. (2006). Motivations for play in online games. *Cyberpsychology & Behavior, 9*(6), 772–775. doi:10.1089/cpb.2006.9.772

Yin, R. K. (1994). *Case Study Reaserch. Design and Methods* (2nd ed.). Thousand Oaks, CA: Sage.

Yoo, B., & Donthu, N. (2001). Developing and validating a multidimensional consumer-based brand equity scale. *Journal of Business Research, 52*(1), 1–14. doi:10.1016/S0148-2963(99)00098-3

Young, K. S. (1996, August, 15). *Internet addiction: The emergence of a new clinical disorder.* Paper presented at the 104th annual meeting of the American Psychological Association, Toronto, Canada. Retrieved from http://www.netaddiction.com/ articles/newdisorder.htm

Young, K. S. (1997). *What Makes the Internet Addictive? Potential Explanations for Pathological Internet Use.* Paper presented at the 105th annual conference of the American Psychological Association. Retrieved from http://www.healthyplace.com/Communities/Addictions/netaddiction/articles/ habitforming.htm

Young, K. S. (1998a). *Caught in the Net: How to recognize the signs of Internet addiction and a winning strategy for recovery.* New York: Wiley.

Young, K. S. (1998b). Internet addiction: The emergence of a new clinical disorder. *Cyberpsychology & Behavior, 1,* 237–244. doi:10.1089/cpb.1998.1.237

Young, K. S. (2007). Cognitive Behavior Therapy with Internet Addicts: Treatment Outcomes and Implications. *Cyberpsychology & Behavior, 10*(5), 671–679. doi:10.1089/cpb.2007.9971

Yu, C., & Popa, L. (2005). Semantic Adaptation of Schema Mappings when Schema Evolve. In *Proceedings of the International Conference on Very Large Data bases (VLDB)* (pp. 1006-1017).

Yukl, G., Kim, H., & Falbe, C. M. (1996). Antecedents of influence outcomes. *The Journal of Applied Psychology*, *81*(3), 309–317. doi:10.1037/0021-9010.81.3.309

Yu, Q., Liu, X., Bouguettaya, A., & Medjahed, B. (2008). Deploying and managing Web services: issues, solutions, and directions. *Very Large Database Journal*, *17*, 537–572. doi:10.1007/s00778-006-0020-3

Zackariasson, P., & Wilson, T. L. (2008). Game on: Competition and competitiveness in the video game industry. *Competition Forum*, *6*(1), 43–52.

Zaheer, A., & Venkatraman, N. V. (1995). Relational governance as an interorganizational strategy: an empirical test of the role of trust in economic exchange. *Strategic Management Journal*, *16*(5), 373–392. doi:10.1002/smj.4250160504

Zeng, L., Benatallah, B., Ngu, A., Dumas, M., Kalagnanam, J., & Chang, H. (2004). Qos-aware middleware for web services composition. *IEEE Transactions on Software Engineering*, *30*(5), 311–327. doi:10.1109/TSE.2004.11

Zhang, H., Kishore, R., & Ramesh, R. (2007). Semantics of the MibML Conceptual Modeling Grammar: An Ontological Analysis Using the Bunge-Wand-Weber Framework. *Journal of Database Management*, *18*(1), 1–19.

Zhang, P., Nah, F., & Benbasat, I. (2005). Human-computer interaction research in management information systems. *Journal of Management Information Systems*, *22*(3), 9–14. doi:10.2753/MIS0742-1222220301

Zhao, H., & Ram, S. (2004). Clustering schema elements for semantic integration of heterogeneous data sources. *Journal of Database Management*, *15*(4), 88–106.

Zhao, H., & Ram, S. (2007). Combining schema and instance information for integrating heterogeneous data sources. *Data & Knowledge Engineering*, *61*(2), 281–303. doi:10.1016/j.datak.2006.06.004

Zhao, H., & Ram, S. (2008). Entity matching across heterogeneous data sources: an approach based on constrained cascade generalization. *Data & Knowledge Engineering*, *66*(3), 368–381. doi:10.1016/j.datak.2008.04.007

Zhao, H., & Soofi, E. S. (2006). Exploring attribute correspondences across heterogeneous databases by mutual information. *Journal of Management Information Systems*, *22*(4), 305–336. doi:10.2753/MIS0742-1222220411

Zhao, L., & Siau, K. (2007). Information Mediation Using Metamodels: An Approach Using XML and Common Warehouse Metamodel. *Journal of Database Management*, *18*(3), 69–82.

Zhao, Y., Wang, W., & Zhu, Y. (2010). Antecedents of the closeness of human-avatar relationships in a virtual world. *Journal of Database Management*, *21*(2), 41–68.

Zhu, K., Kraemer, K. L., Gurbaxani, V., & Xu, X. S. (2006). Migration to open-standard interorganizational systems: network effects, switching costs and path dependency. *Management Information Systems Quarterly*, *30*(5), 515–539.

Zhu, K., Kraemer, K., Xu, S., & Dedrick, J. (2004). Information technology payoff in E-business environments: An international perspective on value creation of e-business in the financial services industry. *Journal of Management Information Systems*, *21*(1), 7–54.

Zimmer, W. (1995). Relationships between Design Patterns. In J. O. Coplien & D. C. Schmidt (Eds.), *Pattern Language for Program Design* (pp. 345-364), New York: Addison-Wesley.

Zimmerman, O., Krogdahl, P., & Gee, C. (2004). *Elements of Service-Oriented Analysis and Design*. Retrieved from http://www.ibm.com/developerworks/library/ws-soad1/

Zimmermann, O., Doubrovski, V., Grundler, J., & Hogg, K. (2005). Service-oriented architecture and business process choreography in an order management scenario: rationale, concepts, lessons learned. In *Proceedings of the 20th SIGPLAN Conference on Object-Oriented Programming, Systems, Languages, and Applications* (pp. 301-312).

Zmud, R. W. (1979). Perceptions of Cognitive Styles: Acquisition, Exhibition and Implications for Information System Design. *Journal of Management*, *5*(1), 7–20. doi:10.1177/014920637900500101

Zuberek, W. M. (1991). Timed Petri nets – definitions, properties and applications. *Microelectronics and Reliability* . *Special Issue on Petri Nets and Related Graph Models*, *31*(4), 627–644.

About the Contributors

Keng Siau is the E. J. Faulkner Chair Professor of Management Information Systems (MIS) and Full Professor of Management at the University of Nebraska-Lincoln (UNL). He is the Director of the UNL-IBM Global Innovation Hub, editor-in-chief of the *Journal of Database Management*, North America Regional editor of the *Requirements Engineering Journal*, and co-editor-in-chief of the Advances in Database Research series. He received his PhD degree from the University of British Columbia (UBC). His master's and bachelor's degrees are in computer and information sciences from the National University of Singapore. Professor Siau has over 250 academic publications. He has published more than 100 refereed journal articles, and these articles have appeared in journals such as *Management Information Systems Quarterly, Journal of the Association for Information Systems, Communications of the ACM, IEEE Computer, Information Systems Journal, Journal of Strategic Information Systems, Information Systems, ACM SIGMIS's Database, IEEE Transactions on Systems, Man, and Cybernetics, IEEE Transactions on Professional Communication, IEEE Transactions on Information Technology in Biomedicine, IEICE Transactions on Information and Systems, Data and Knowledge Engineering, Journal of Information Technology, International Journal of Human-Computer Studies*, and others. He served as the organizing and program chairs of the International Conference on Evaluation of Modeling Methods in Systems Analysis and Design (EMMSAD) (1996 – 2005). He also served on the organizing committees of AMCIS 2005, ER 2006, AMCIS 2007, EuroSIGSAND 2007, EuroSIGSAND 2008, and ICMB 2009. He received the International Federation for Information Processing (IFIP) Outstanding Service Award in 2006, and the IBM Faculty Award in 2006 and 2008.

* * *

Dr. Yuan An received a PhD degree from the University of Toronto in 2007 in Computer Science. He has been an assistant professor in the College of Information Science and Technology at Drexel University since that year. He has research interests in semantic technologies for information integration, information modeling including ontology design, schema/ontology mapping, and the Semantic Web. Dr. An designed and developed the MAPONTO tool for creating semantic mappings between ontologies and database schemas. Dr. An also has 10 years working experience in the Information Technology industry. As a principal developer and team leader, he designed and led the development of various management information systems. Dr. An has a Master's degree in Computer Science from Dalhousie University, Canada. He also earned a Master's degree in Electrical Engineering from Tsinghua University, China, in 1989 and a Bachelor's degree in Electrical Engineering from the same Chinese university in 1987.

Haldun Aytug is an Associate Professor of Information Systems and Operations Management at the Warrington College of Business, University of Florida. He has a B.S. degree in industrial and engineering and a Ph.D. in business. His research interests include machine learning, theory of genetic algorithms, capacity modeling for data networks and scheduling. He is a member of INFORMS and ACM.

Jengchung V. Chen (Ph.D. in CIS, University of Hawaii) is Associate Professor of International Management at National Cheng Kung University, Taiwan. His research interests are information ethics (e.g. trust and privacy), project management, electronic commerce (e.g. online auction and user behavior), and service quality. He has published articles in refereed journals such as: *Information & Management, Decision Support Systems, CyberPsychology & Behavior, Journal of Computer Information Systems, Information & Software Technology, Industrial Management & Data System*, and others. He is currently the President-Elect of the International Chinese Information Systems Association (ICISA) and VP-Publication in the Association for Chinese Management Educators (ACME).

Kuanchin Chen is an Associate Professor of Computer Information Systems at Department of Business Information Systems, Western Michigan University. Dr. Chen's research interests include electronic business, privacy & security, online behavioral issues (e.g., interactivity, dependency, and tracking/protection), Internet frauds, usability, data mining, and human computer interactions. He has published articles in journals and other academic publication outlets, including *Decision Support Systems, IEEE Transactions on Systems, Man, and Cybernetics, Information & Management, Communications of the Association for Information Systems (CAIS), IEEE Transactions on Education, Journal of Computer Information Systems* and many others. He currently serves on the editorial or advisory boards of *Information Resources Management Journal, International Journal of Information Systems and Change Management, Journal of Website Promotion, Communications of the ICISA*, IGI Global (formerly Idea Group), eWeek, and CMP.

Liqiang Chen is an MIS Lecturer in the Department of Management at the University of Nebraska-Lincoln. He received his BSc in Meteorology from Nanjing University of Information Science & Technology in China, and both his MSc in Computer Science and PhD in Management Information Systems from the University of Nebraska-Lincoln. His research interest includes online consumer behaviour and human-computer interaction.

Yon Dohn Chung received his BS degrees in computer science from Korea University, Seoul, Korea, in 1994, and MS and PhD degrees in computer science from KAIST, Deajeon, Korea, in 1996 and 2000, respectively. In 2006, he joined the faculty of the Department of Computer Science and Engineering, Korea University, Seoul, Korea. His research interests include broadcast databases, sensor networks, MANET/VANET, XML databases, mobile computing and database systems. He is a member of the ACM and IEEE computer Society.

David DeWester is a Ph.D. student at University of Nebraska–Lincoln. He received his B.S. in Mathematics from Colorado State University and his M.A. in Mathematics from Central Michigan University, where his thesis was nominated for Best Thesis of the Year. After moving to Nebraska, he received an M.S. in Computer Science, an M.B.A. with specialization in International Business, and an M.A. in Business with a specialization in Management Information Systems. His research interests include human-computer interaction, computer applications in cognitive psychology, statistics, and 3-D virtual worlds. He has several years of work experience in information technology related areas from help desk support to e-commerce consulting.

Dov Dori is information and systems engineering Professor at the Faculty of Industrial Engineering and Management, Technion, Israel Institute of Technology, and Research Affiliate with the Engineering Systems Division at Massachusetts Institute of Technology, where he was Visiting Professor during 1999-2001 and 2008-2009. His research interests include conceptual modeling of complex systems, systems architecture and design, and software and information engineering. Prof. Dori has invented and developed Object-Process Methodology (OPM), presented in his 2002 book. He won the Technion Klein Research Award for OPM, the Hershel Rich Innovation Award for OPCAT, the OPM supporting software, and the Dudi Ben Aharon Research Award for Document Image Understanding. Prof. Dori has authored over 100 journal publications and book chapters. He is Fellow of the International Association for Pattern Recognition and Senior Member of IEEE and ACM.

Brenda Eschenbrenner is completing her Ph.D. in Management Information Systems, with concentrations in accounting, information technology, and human cognition, at the University of Nebraska–Lincoln. She is joining the faculty of University of Nebraska–Kearney in 2010. Her research interests include virtual worlds, human acceptance and use of current and emerging technologies, factors contributing to information system proficiency, and technology applications in education and training. She has over 10 years of work experience including management positions with a former Fortune 500 company and involvement with system implementation efforts.

Ling He is an Assistant Professor of Information Systems at the Cameron School of Business, University of North Carolina Wilmington. Her degrees include B. Economics from University of International Business and Economics, M.S. and Ph.D. (Decision Information Systems) from the University of Florida. Dr He has research interests in database management systems, information security, E-commerce, PAC learning theory, online auction and online review. Her publications have appeared in Decision Support Systems and Journal on Computing.

Weiyin Hong is an Associate Professor in the Department of Management Information Systems at the University of Nevada, Las Vegas. She received her BSc in Management Information Systems from Fudan University, China, and her PhD in Information and Systems Management from the Hong Kong University of Science and Technology. Her research interest includes user acceptance of emerging technologies and human-computer interaction. Her work has appeared in *Information Systems Research, Journal of Management Information Systems, Communications of the ACM, International Journal of Human-Computer Studies,* and *Journal of the American Society for Information Science and Technology.* She is a Past Chair of Association for Information Systems Special Interest Group on Human-Computer Interaction (SIGHCI).

Xiaohua (Tony) Hu is currently an associate professor and the founding director of the data mining and bioinformatics lab at the College of Information Science and Technology at Drexel University. His current research interests are in biomedical literature data mining, bioinformatics, text mining, semantic Web mining and reasoning, rough set theory and application, information extraction, and information retrieval. He has published more than 160 peer-reviewed research papers in various journals, conferences and books such as various IEEE/ACM Transactions. He has received a few prestigious awards including the 2005 National Science Foundation (NSF) Career award, the best paper award at the 2007 International Conference on Artificial Intelligence, the best paper award at the 2004 IEEE Symposium on Computational Intelligence in Bioinformatics and Computational Biology. He serves as the IEEE Computer Society Bioinformatics and Biomedicine Steering Committee Chair, and the IEEE Computational Intelligence Society Granular Computing Technical Committee Chair (2007-2008).

Gary J. Koehler is the John B. Higdon Eminent Scholar of Management Information Systems at the University of Florida. He received his Ph. D. from Purdue University in 1974. He has held academic positions at Northwestern University and Purdue University and between 1979-1987 was a cofounder and CEO of a high-tech company which grew to over 260 employees during that period. His research interests are in areas formed by the intersection of the Operations Research, Artificial Intelligence and Information Systems areas and include such areas as genetic algorithm theory, machine learning, e-commerce, quantum computing and decision support systems.

Santhosh Kumaran works in IBM Software Group as the Senior Manager of Banking Solutions and the CTO of Banking Industry Framework. In this role, he leads a worldwide technical team of architects for the Banking industry with focus on the solution frameworks, serves as a member of Industry Framework Architecture Board, and works with clients worldwide on model driven business transformation. In 2009, he was appointed as a Senior Technical Staff Member (STSM) and a Master Inventor of IBM Corporation. He has published over 50 technical papers, filed over 30 patents, and won numerous awards including the Daniel H. Wagner Prize, and several Outstanding Technical Achievement Awards from IBM. He holds a PhD in Computer Science from Oregon State University.

Denis M. S. Lee is Professor of Information Systems and Operations Management in the Sawyer Business School at Suffolk University, USA. He received his Ph.D. from the Sloan School of Management at MIT. His research interests are related to the management of technology, information systems, and technical professionals. His publications have appeared in *MIS Quarterly, Academy of Management Journal, Management Science, IEEE Transactions on Engineering Management, Engineering Management Journal, and the Journal of Engineering and Technology Management.* He has been the recipient of a number of competitive research grants from the National Science Foundation and industry for over two decades.

Hong-Hee Lee is a Full-time Lecturer at Dankook University in Korea. He received his BA from Kyung Hee University in Korea, and his MA and PhD from the Department of Management at the University of Nebraska-Lincoln. He has worked as Deputy General Manager at Daegu Digital Industry Promotion Agency in Korea. His research areas are ERP, HCI, and SCM.

Yang W. Lee is Associate Professor of Information Operations and Analysis Group, College of Business School at Northeastern University. Her research focuses on information quality, IT-mediated institutional learning, systems integration, and medical errors. Her publications have appeared in *Journal of MIS, Communications of the ACM, Sloan Management Review, Journal of Database Management, IEEE Computer,* and *Information and Management.* She published *Journey to Data Quality* (MIT Press, 2006), *Data Quality* (Kluwer Academic Publishers, 2000), and*Quality Information and Knowledge* (Prentice Hall, 1999). She received her Ph.D. from MIT. She is a founding Editor-in-Chief of *ACM Journal of Data and Information Quality.*

Min Ling received her PhD in management information systems from the University of Nebraska-Lincoln. Her research areas include website personalization, virtual collaboration, and knowledge management. Dr. Ling has published papers in *Journal of Computer Information System* and *International Journal of Electronic Business.*

Rong Liu is a Research Scientist at IBM T. J. Watson Research Center. She received her Ph. D. in Business Administration from The Pennsylvania State University. Her research interest includes business process management, workflow systems, supply chain management, and model-driven business transformation.

Yuan (Yoanna) Long is an assistant professor at Hasan School of Business of Colorado State University-Pueblo. Her current research focuses on virtual collaboration, social network, knowledge management, and open source software development. Dr. Long has published papers in *Journal of Computer Information Systems, Journal of Global Information Management, Industrial Management & Data Systems,* and *Annals of Cases on Information Technology.*

Daniel Moody is a consultant in data management. He has held several academic positions at universities throughout Australia and Europe. His research interests include conceptual modeling, software quality, data warehousing and medical informatics.

Fiona Fui-Hoon Nah is an Associate Professor of Management Information Systems (MIS) at the University of Nebraska–Lincoln. Her research interests include human-computer interaction, 3-D virtual worlds, computer-supported collaborative work, knowledge-based and decision support systems, and mobile and ubiquitous commerce. She has published her research in journals such as *Journal of the Association for Information Systems, Communications of the Association for Information Systems, Communications of the ACM, IEEE Transactions on Education, International Journal of Human-Computer Studies, Journal of Strategic Information Systems, Journal of Information Technology,* among others. Dr. Nah received the University of Nebraska–Lincoln College of Business Administration Distinguished Teaching Award in 2001, the Best Paper Award at the 2003 Pre-ICIS HCI Research in MIS Workshop, the Outstanding Service Award from the Association for Information Systems (AIS) Special Interest Group on Human-Computer Interaction (SIGHCI) in 2005, and the University of Nebraska–Lincoln College of Business Administration Research Award in 2006. She is an Associate Editor of *AIS Transactions on Human-Computer Interaction, International Journal of Human-Computer Studies,* and *Journal of Electronic Commerce Research.* She also serves on the Editorial Board of more than ten other MIS journals. She has served as a guest editor for various special issues including *Journal of Management Information Systems, International Journal of Human-Computer Studies, International Journal of*

Human-Computer Interaction, and *IEEE Transactions on Education*. Dr. Nah is a co-Founder and Past Chair of AIS SIGHCI, and is a featured volunteer for Association for Information Systems (June 2008). She received her Ph.D. in MIS from the University of British Columbia, and her M.S. and B.S. (Honors) in Computer and Information Sciences from the National University of Singapore. She was previously on the faculty of School of Computing, National University of Singapore, and the Krannert School of Management, Purdue University.

Jasmina Nuredini is a consultant in data management. She was previously a research assistant at the University of Melbourne.

Chang-Sup Park received his BS, MS, and PhD degrees in computer science from KAIST, Daejeon, Korea, in 1995, 1997, and 2002, respectively. From 2002 to 2005, he worked for the R&D Center of KT Corporation in Seoul, Korea. In 2005, he joined the faculty of the University of Suwon, Korea. He joined the Department of Computer Science at Dongduk Women's University in 2009, where currently he is an assistant professor. His research interests include wireless information systems, XML data management, semantic Web, and information retrieval. He is a member of the KIISE.

Jun Pyo Park received his BS degree in computer science from Dongguk University, Seoul, Korea, in 2005, and MS degree in computer science from Korea University, Seoul, Korea, in 2009. In 2009, he entered the PhD course of computer science at Korea University, where currently he is PhD candidate. His research interests include XML data management, wireless broadcast system and mobile computing.

So Ra Park is a Ph.D. student at the University of Nebraska–Lincoln. Her research interests are in 3-D virtual worlds, organizational blogging, and Web 2.0.

Evaggelia Pitoura received her B.Sc. from the University of Patras, Greece in 1990 and her M.Sc. and Ph.D. in computer science from Purdue University in 1993 and 1995, respectively. Since June 2005, she is an associate professor at the Department of Computer Science of the University of Ioannina, Greece where she leads the distributed data management group. Her publications include more than 70 articles in international journals and conferences and a book on mobile computing. She has also co-authored two tutorials on mobile computing for IEEE ICDE 2000 and 2003. She is recipient of the best paper award of IEEE ICDE 1999 and two "Recognition of Service Awards" from ACM.

Iris Reinhartz-Berger is a faculty member at the Department of Management Information Systems, Haifa University, Israel. She received her BSc degree in applied mathematics and computer science from the Technion, Israel Institute of Technology in 1994. She obtained a MSc degree in 1999 and a PhD in 2003 in information management engineering from the Technion, Israel Institute of Technology. Her research interests include domain engineering, conceptual modeling, software analysis and design, development processes, and methodologies.

William Ross (PhD, Industrial/Organizational Psychology, University of Illinois) is Professor of Management at the University of Wisconsin – La Crosse. He publishes articles on psychological factors related to the use of – and reactions to – business technology. He writes about specific topics such as procedural design, information privacy, electronic monitoring, trust, and dispute resolution. These articles appear in the following journals: *Journal of Applied Psychology, Advanced Management Journal, Personnel Psychology, Information, Communication, and Society, Academy of Management Review, International Journal of Organizational Analysis, CyberPsychology & Behavior, International Journal of Mobile Communications, Info, Journal of Information Privacy & Security*, and *Labor Law Journal*.

Graeme Shanks is Professor in the Department of Information Systems at the University of Melbourne. His research interests include conceptual modeling, data quality and the impact of business analytics systems on firm performance. He was recently awarded an Australian Professorial Fellowship from the Australian Research Council.

Galia Shlezinger received her BSc degree in 2003 from the Faculty of computer science, Technion, Israel Institute of Technology and her MSc degree in 2008 from the Faculty of Industrial Engineering and Management, Technion, Israel Institute of Technology. The work reported in this paper is part of her master degree. Her research interests include system architecture, system design, and development methodologies.

Il-Yeol Song is a professor of the College of Information Science and Technology at Drexel University. He received the M.S. and Ph.D. degrees from the Department of Computer Science, Louisiana State University, in 1984 and 1988, respectively. His research interests include conceptual modeling, object-oriented analysis & design, data warehousing, and bioinformatics. He has published over 160 peer-reviewed papers. He has won three teaching awards from Drexel University. He is a Co-Editor-in-Chief of Journal of Computing Science and Engineering (JCSE). He is also associate editors for many prestigious journals including *International Journal of E-Business Research* as well as on the Editorial Board of *Data & Knowledge Engineering (DKE)*. Dr. Song is a steering committee member of several conferences including International Conference on Conceptual Modeling. He served as a program/general chair of 18 international conferences/workshops. He is also currently serving as the General co-Chair for International Conference on Information and Knowledge Management 2009.

Konstantinos Stamkopoulos received his Bachelor's degree from the Department of Computer Science of the University of Ioannina, Greece in 2004 and his MSc in Computer Science from the same department in 2006. His research interests include web services, especially in their interaction with databases.

Daniel Tobin is a marketing manager at the University of Melbourne. He was previously a data management consultant and a research assistant at the University of Melbourne.

Panos Vassiliadis received his PhD from the National Technical University of Athens in 2000. He joined the Department of Computer Science of the University of Ioannina in 2002. Currently, Dr. Vassiliadis is also a member of the Distributed Management of Data (DMOD) Laboratory (http://www.dmod.cs.uoi.gr/). His research interests include data warehousing, web services and database design and modeling. Dr. Vassiliadis has published more than 25 papers in refereed journals and international conferences in the above areas.

Weiquan Wang is an assistant professor in the Department of Information Systems at the College of Business, City University of Hong Kong. He obtained his PhD in Management Information Systems from the Sauder School of Business, the University of British Columbia. His research interests include online consumer decision support, human-computer interaction, and e-commerce.

Ron Weber is Dean of the Faculty of Information Technology, Monash University. His primary research interests lie in the ontological foundations of information systems. He is a past president of the Association for Information Systems and a past editor-in-chief of the MIS Quarterly. In 2000, he won the Australian Prime Minister's Award for University Teacher of the Year.

Frederick Y. Wu is Manager, Model-Driven Enterprise Solutions at the IBM T.J. Watson Research Center. He has worked in the area of electronic commerce and business integration for the past fourteen years. Recently he has focused on business operations modeling and transformation using the business entity concept. Dr. Wu holds the S.B., S.M., and Ph.D. degrees from the Massachusetts Institute of Technology.

Yurong Yao is Assistant Professor of Information Systems and Operations Management in the Sawyer business School at Suffolk University. Her research interests are the adoption of information systems, IS outsourcing and electronic government. Her publications have appeared in *European Journal of Information Systems, Communications of the ACM, Database for Advances in Information Systems, Journal of Computer Information System and IEEE IT professionals*. She received her Ph.D. from Louisiana State University.

Apostolos Zarras received his B.Sc. in Computer Science in 1994 from the Computer Science Department, University of Crete. From the same department he received his M.Sc. in Distributed Systems and Computer Architecture. In 1999 he received his Ph.D in Distributed Systems and Software Architecture from the University of Rennes I. From 2004 until now he holds a position at the Department of Computer Science of the University of Ioannina. Apostolos Zarras has published over 20 papers in international conferences, journals and magazines. He is currently a member of the IEEE computer society. His research interests include middleware, model-driven architecture development, quality analysis of software systems and pervasive computing.

Huimin Zhao is an Associate Professor of MIS at the Sheldon B. Lubar School of Business, University of Wisconsin–Milwaukee. He received his BE and ME in automation from Tsinghua University, China (1990 and 1993, respectively), and Ph.D. in MIS from The University of Arizona (2002). His current research interests are in the areas of data mining, data integration, and medical informatics. His research has been published in several journals, including Journal of Management Information Systems, Communications of the ACM, IEEE Transactions on Knowledge and Data Engineering, IEEE Transactions on Systems, Man, and Cybernetics, Information Systems, Data and Knowledge Engineering, Decision Support Systems, and Journal of Database Management. He was a co-chair of the Nineteenth Workshop on Information Technologies and Systems (WITS'09).

Yi Zhao is an M.Phil student in the Department of Information Systems at the College of Business, City University of Hong Kong. He obtained his bachelor's degree in Information Management & Information System from Sun Yat-sen University, China. His research interests include e-commerce, virtual community, and virtual team.

Yan Zhu is currently an Associate Professor in the Department of Management Science and Engineering at the School of Economics and Management, Tsinghua University. He received his PhD in engineering from Tsinghua University. His research interests include management information systems, e-business, virtual enterprises, project management, and intelligent systems and decision-making support systems.

Index